A HISTORY OF WORLD SOCIETIES

A HISTORY OF WORLD SOCIETIES

VOLUME A
FROM ANTIQUITY TO 1500

SIXTH EDITION

JOHN P. McKAY

University of Illinois at Urbana-Champaign

BENNETT D. HILL

Georgetown University

JOHN BUCKLER

University of Illinois at Urbana-Champaign

PATRICIA BUCKLEY EBREY

University of Washington

HOUGHTON MIFFLIN COMPANY
Boston   New York

Publisher: Charles Hartford
Editor-in-Chief: Jean L. Woy
Senior Sponsoring Editor: Nancy Blaine
Development Editor: Julie Dunn
Senior Project Editor: Christina M. Horn
Editorial Assistant: Talia M. Kingsbury
Senior Production/Design Coordinator: Jennifer Meyer Dare
Senior Manufacturing Coordinator: Marie Barnes
Senior Marketing Manager: Sandra McGuire

Text credits appear on page I-34.

Volume A cover image: Bas-relief of the goddess Maat. Painted stone relief, Egypt, Nineteenth Dynasty. Museo Archeologico, Florence, Italy/Scala/Art Resource, NY.

Printed in the U.S.A.

Library of Congress Control Number: 2002117257

ISBN: 0-618-30198-4

2 3 4 5 6 7 8 9-VH-07 06 05 04 03

ABOUT THE AUTHORS

JOHN P. McKAY Born in St. Louis, Missouri, John P. McKay received his B.A. from Wesleyan University (1961) and his Ph.D. from the University of California, Berkeley (1968). He began teaching history at the University of Illinois in 1966 and became a professor there in 1976. John won the Herbert Baxter Adams Prize for his book *Pioneers for Profit: Foreign Entrepreneurship and Russian Industrialization, 1885–1913* (1970). He has translated Jules Michelet's *The People* (1973) and has written *Tramways and Trolleys: The Rise of Urban Mass Transport in Europe* (1976), as well as more than a hundred articles, book chapters, and reviews, which have appeared in numerous publications. His research has been supported by fellowships from the Ford Foundation, the Guggenheim Foundation, the National Endowment for the Humanities, and IREX. Recently, he contributed extensively to C. Stewart and P. Fritzsche, eds., *Imagining the Twentieth Century* (1997).

BENNETT D. HILL A native of Philadelphia, Bennett D. Hill earned advanced degrees from Harvard (A.M., 1958) and Princeton (Ph.D., 1963). He taught history at the University of Illinois at Urbana, where he was department chairman from 1978 to 1981. He has published *English Cistercian Monasteries and Their Patrons in the Twelfth Century* (1968), *Church and State in the Middle Ages* (1970), and articles in *Analecta Cisterciensia, The New Catholic Encyclopaedia, The American Benedictine Review,* and *The Dictionary of the Middle Ages.* His reviews have appeared in *The American Historical Review, Speculum,* and the *Journal of World History.* He is one of the contributing editors to *The Encyclopedia of World History* (2001). He has been a Fellow of the American Council of Learned Societies and served as vice president of the American Catholic Historical Association (1995–1996). A Benedictine monk of St. Anselm's Abbey in Washington, D.C., he is also a Visiting Professor at Georgetown University.

JOHN BUCKLER Born in Louisville, Kentucky, John Buckler received his B.A. (summa cum laude) from the University of Louisville (1967) and his Ph.D. from Harvard University (1973). From 1984 to 1986 he was an Alexander von Humboldt Fellow at the Institut für Alte Geschichte, University of Munich. He has lectured at the Fondation Hardt at the University of Geneva and at the University of Freiburg. He is currently a professor of Greek history at the University of Illinois. In 1980 Harvard University Press published his *Theban Hegemony, 371–362 B.C.* He has also published *Philip II and the Sacred War* (Leiden 1989) and co-edited *BOIOTIKA: Vorträge vom 5. Internationalen Böotien-Kolloquium* (Munich 1989). He has contributed articles to *The American Historical Association's Guide to Historical Literature* (Oxford 1995), *The Oxford Classical Dictionary* (Oxford 1996), and *Encyclopedia of Greece and the Hellenic Tradition* (London 1999).

PATRICIA BUCKLEY EBREY Born in Hasbrouck Heights, New Jersey, Patricia Ebrey received her A.B. from the University of Chicago in 1968 and her M.A. and Ph.D. from Columbia University in 1970 and 1975. Formerly a faculty member at the University of Illinois, she now teaches at the University of Washington. Her books include *The Aristocratic Families of Early Imperial China* (1978), *Family and Property in Sung China* (1984), *Confucianism and Family Rituals in Imperial China* (1991), *The Inner Quarters: Marriage and the Lives of Chinese Women in the Sung Period* (1993), and *The Cambridge Illustrated History of China* (1996), which has been translated into four languages, including Chinese and Korean. *The Inner Quarters* was awarded the Levenson Prize of the Association for Asian Studies. She has also edited or coedited several important works, most notably *Chinese Civilization: A Sourcebook* (1981, 1993).

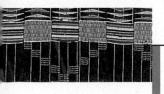

BRIEF CONTENTS

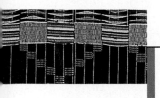

CONTENTS

MAPS

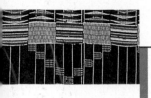

LISTENING TO THE PAST

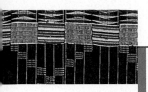

PREFACE

In this age of a global environment and global warming, of a global economy and global banking, of global migration and rapid global travel, of global sports and global popular culture, the study of world history becomes more urgent. Surely, an appreciation of other, and earlier, societies helps us to understand better our own and to cope more effectively in pluralistic cultures worldwide. The large numbers of Turks living in Germany, of Italians, Hungarians, and Slavic peoples living in Australia, of Japanese living in Peru and Argentina, and of Arabs, Mexicans, Chinese, and Filipinos living in the United States—to mention just a few obvious examples—represent diversity on a global scale. The movement of large numbers of peoples from one continent to another goes back thousands of years, at least as far back as the time when Asian peoples migrated across the Bering Strait to North America. Swift air travel and the Internet have accelerated these movements, and they testify to the incredible technological changes the world has experienced in the last half of the twentieth century.

For most peoples, the study of history has traditionally meant the study of their own national, regional, and ethnic pasts. Fully appreciating the great differences among various societies and the complexity of the historical problems surrounding these cultures, we have wondered if the study of local or national history is sufficient for people who will spend most of their lives in the twenty-first century on one small interconnected planet. The authors of this book believe the study of world history in a broad and comparative context is an exciting, important, and highly practical pursuit.

It is our conviction, based on considerable experience in introducing large numbers of students to the broad sweep of civilization, that a book reflecting current trends can excite readers and inspire a renewed interest in history and the human experience. Our strategy has been twofold.

First, we have made social history the core element of our work. We not only incorporate recent research by social historians but also seek to re-create the life of ordinary people in appealing human terms. A strong social element seems especially appropriate in a world history text, for identification with ordinary people of the past allows today's reader to reach an empathetic understanding of different cultures and civilizations. At the same time we have been mindful of the need to give great economic, political, intellectual, and cultural developments the attention they deserve. We want to give individual students and instructors a balanced, integrated perspective so that they can pursue on their own or in the classroom those themes and questions that they find particularly exciting and significant.

Second, we have made every effort to strike an effective global balance. We are acutely aware of the great drama of our times—the passing of the era of Western dominance and the simultaneous rise of Asian and African peoples in world affairs. Increasingly, the whole world interacts, and to understand that interaction and what it means for today's citizens, we must study the whole world's history. Thus we have adopted a comprehensive yet manageable global perspective. We study all geographical areas and the world's main civilizations, conscious of their separate identities and unique contributions. We also stress the links among civilizations, for it is these links that have been transforming multicentered world history into the complex interactive process of different continents, peoples, and cultures that we see today.

CHANGES IN THE SIXTH EDITION

In preparing the Sixth Edition of this book, we have worked hard to keep our book up-to-date and to strengthen our distinctive yet balanced approach.

Organizational Changes

In order to give greater depth to our world focus, major organizational changes again proved essential. In preparing the Fifth Edition of this book, the fortunate addition of a distinguished Asian specialist, Patricia Buckley Ebrey, to our author team enabled us to expand coverage of Asian developments and to concentrate on those historical problems that scholars today consider most current. In revising the text for this Sixth Edition, Professor Ebrey's contributions on Asian civilizations have broadened. Chapters 7 and 12 now cover only East Asia, rather than all of Asia, allowing for greater in-depth treatment. The old Chapter 11 on Asia, 800–1400, has been split into two separate chapters on South and East Asia, now Chapters 11 and 12.

Other broad organizational changes include the combination of the old Chapters 12 and 13 on the Middle Ages into one chapter, now Chapter 13. The old Chapter 27, "Africa and Asia in the Era of Western Industrialization, 1800–1914," has been split into two separate chapters: one on West Asia and Africa, now Chapter 26, and one on Asia, now Chapter 27. In keeping with our general goal of expanding coverage of non-Western parts of the world, we have incorporated material on the "Changing Life of the People in Europe," formerly in Chapter 19, into the revised Chapter 18. And, together with a reduction of European material, the section on the United States in Chapter 31 has been cut back.

"Global Trade" Feature

The Sixth Edition introduces a new feature on trade. In the form of four two-page essays, each focused on a particular commodity, the authors explore world trade in that commodity, the social and economic impact of the commodity, and the cultural influence the commodity has had. Each essay is accompanied by a detailed map showing the trade routes of the commodity. The essays deal with the international trade in pottery in the Greek and Roman worlds (Chapter 6), tea in the medieval and early modern worlds (Chapter 12), slaves in the early modern, modern, and contemporary worlds (Chapter 19), and oil in the modern world (Chapter 33). We believe that careful attention to these essays will enable the student to appreciate the ways in which trade has connected the various parts of the world.

Expanded Ethnic and Geographic Scope

In the Sixth Edition we have added significantly more discussion of groups and regions that are often shortchanged in the general histories of world civilizations. This expanded scope is, we feel, an important improvement. It reflects the renewed awareness within the profession of the enormous diversity of the world's peoples, and of those peoples' efforts (or lack thereof) to understand others' regional, ethnic, and cultural identities. Examples of this enlarged scope include new material on Muslim attitudes toward blacks (Chapter 9) and on the Mongols and other peoples of Central Asia (Chapter 11); a broadened treatment of Europe's frontier regions—Iberia, Ireland, Scotland, eastern Europe, and the Baltic region (Chapter 13); the peoples of the Indian Ocean—of the Malay archipelago and the Philippines (Chapter 16); and a completely fresh discussion of twentieth-century eastern Europe (Chapters 29 and 33). Our broader treatment of Jewish history has been integrated in the text, with stimulating material on anti-Semitism during the Crusades (Chapter 13), during the Spanish Inquisition (Chapter 15), Jewish Enlightenment thought in Germany (Chapter 18), and the unfolding of the Holocaust during the Second World War (Chapter 32). Just as the Fifth Edition developed our treatment of the history of women and gender, so in this Sixth Edition significant issues of gender are explored with respect to Native American peoples (Chapter 14) and Indian Ocean peoples (Chapter 16). Overall, an expanded treatment of non-European societies and cultures has been achieved by reducing detailed coverage of Europe.

Incorporation of Recent Scholarship

As in previous revisions, we have made a strenuous effort to keep our book up-to-date with new and important scholarship. Because the authors are committed to a balanced approach that reflects the true value of history, we have continued to incorporate significant new findings on political, cultural, and intellectual developments in this Sixth Edition. The treatment of Paleolithic and Neolithic civilizations in Chapter 1 has been revised, including a discussion of Stonehenge as an example of Neolithic civilization. Material on the Phoenicians and early Judaism in Chapter 2 has been revised, again, and fresh information on the Greek gods and heroes added in Chapter 5. Recent scholarship on the role of the army in Muslim expansion and on the formative period of Muslim theology and law has been incorporated into Chapter 9, as well as new material on Sufism. Likewise, the treatment of Bantu-speaking people in Africa and of the role of Islam in East Africa has been revised in Chapter 10. The Mongols receive a much more extensive treatment in Chapter 11, which complements discussion of them in the Islamic chapters, 9 and 20. The role of war in Aztec society, along with a detailed analysis of an actual battle, provides a fuller treatment of indigenous peoples of the Americas in Chapter 14, as does a new section on the mound builders of North America.

Moreover, the Sixth Edition gives more attention to the role of spices in the transmission of cultures (Chapter 16) and to the evolution of coffee drinking in the Ottoman world (Chapter 20). New scholarship has been added on the French Revolution in Chapter 22 and on nationalism in Chapter 24. Chapter 27 on Asia in the nineteenth century offers much greater coverage of colonial India and a completely new section on the Philippines. In Chapter 34, the coverage of South Asia and the Muslim world has been split to allow for greater treatment of each. Material on the Middle East—most notably on the Arab-Israeli conflict, Iraq, and Iran—has been considerably expanded. Finally, in addition to a new treatment of Jewish emancipation in the nineteenth century (Chapter 25) and expanded coverage of eastern Europe in several chapters, the last chapter, 36, brings international relations up to the present and includes a new discussion on terrorism.

Revised Full-Color Art and Map Program

Finally, the illustrative component of our work has been carefully revised. We have added many new illustrations to our extensive art program, which includes over three hundred color reproductions, letting great art and important events come alive. Illustrations have been selected to support and complement the text, and, wherever possible, illustrations are contemporaneous with the textual material discussed. Considerable research went into many of the captions in order to make them as informative as possible. We have reflected on the observation that "there are more valid facts and details in works of art than there are in history books," and we would modify it to say that art is "a history book." Artwork remains an integral part of our book; the past can speak in pictures as well as in words. The use of full color serves to clarify the maps and graphs and to enrich the textual material. The maps and map captions have been updated to correlate directly to the text, and several new maps have been added, as in Chapters 3, 8, 9, 11, 12, 14, 19, and 33.

DISTINCTIVE FEATURES

In addition to the new "Global Trade" essays, distinctive features from earlier editions guide the reader in the process of historical understanding. Many of these features also show how historians sift through and evaluate evidence. Our goal is to suggest how historians actually work and think. We want the reader to think critically

and to realize that history is neither a list of cut-and-dried facts nor a senseless jumble of conflicting opinions. To help students and instructors realize this goal, we include a substantial discussion of "what is history" in Chapter 1.

"Individuals in Society" Feature

In each chapter of the Fifth Edition we added a short study of a fascinating man or woman or group of people, which is carefully integrated into the main discussion in the text. This "Individuals in Society" feature grew out of our long-standing focus on people's lives and the varieties of historical experience, and we believe that readers will empathize with these flesh-and-blood human beings as they themselves seek to define their own identities today. The spotlighting of individuals, both famous and obscure, carries forward the greater attention to cultural and intellectual developments that we have used to invigorate our social history, and it reflects changing interests within the historical profession as well as the development of "micro history."

The men and women we have selected represent a wide range of careers and personalities. Several are well-known historical or present-day figures, such as Queen Cratesicleia, the Hellenistic queen who allowed herself to be held as a hostage for Sparta (Chapter 5); Theodora, the Byzantine empress (Chapter 8); Ibn Battuta, the Muslim world-traveler (Chapter 9); Leonardo da Vinci, the great Renaissance artist and polymath (Chapter 15); Olaudah Equiano, the black slave, entrepreneur, and navigator (Chapter 19); Theodor Herzl, the Zionist leader (Chapter 25); Gustav Stresemann, the German foreign minister (Chapter 31); and Kofi Annan, secretary general of the United Nations (Chapter 36). Other individuals and groups, perhaps less well-known, illuminate aspects of their times: Mukhali, a Mongol army officer (Chapter 11); Zheng He, a Muslim admiral in the service of the Chinese emperor (Chapter 16); Madame du Coudray, the pioneering French midwife (Chapter 18); Hurrem, wife of Suleiman the Magnificent (Chapter 20); and Shen Gua, a widely traveled Chinese official who wrote extensively on medicine and mathematics (Chapter 27). Creative artists and intellectuals include the ancient Egyptian scholar-bureaucrat Wen-Amon (Chapter 2); the Chinese poet Tao Qian (Chapter 7); an unknown West African artist from Djenné (Chapter 10); the prolific Japanese artist Hokusai (Chapter 21); and the influential romantic writer Germaine de Staël (Chapter 24).

Revised Primary Source Feature

A two-page excerpt from a primary source concludes each chapter. This important feature, entitled "Listening to the Past," extends and illuminates a major historical issue considered in the chapter, and it has been well received by instructors and students. In the Sixth Edition we have reviewed our selections and made judicious substitutions. For example, in Chapter 5 the Seleucid emperor Antiochus III bestows benefits on the Jews; in Chapter 9 an eleventh-century physician provides a guide for buying slaves; in Chapter 11 a Sanskrit inscription in stone praises the capital city of Delhi in India; in Chapter 15 the Protestant reformer Martin Luther presents his concept of liberty; in Chapter 18 the French philosophe Jean-Jacques Rousseau discusses gendered education; in Chapter 26 the French statesman Jules Ferry defends French imperialism; and in Chapter 31 the English writer George Orwell analyzes British unemployment during the Great Depression. Several primary source readings new to the Fifth Edition, such as the Portuguese Barbosa's description of the Swahili city-states in Chapter 19, the weighing of Shah Jahan in Mughal India in Chapter 20, and the Polish Solidarity activist Adam Michnik's defense of nonviolent resistance in Chapter 33, have proved stimulating for student discussions.

Each primary source opens with a problem-setting introduction and closes with "Questions for Analysis" that invite students to evaluate the evidence as historians would. Drawn from a range of writings addressing a variety of social, cultural, political, and intellectual issues, these sources promote active involvement and critical interpretation. Selected for their interest and importance and carefully fitted into their historical context, these sources do indeed allow the student to "listen to the past" and to observe how history has been shaped by individual men and women, some of them great aristocrats, others ordinary folk.

Improved Chapter Features

Other distinctive features from earlier editions have been reviewed and improved in the Sixth Edition. To help guide the reader toward historical understanding, we pose specific historical questions at the beginning of each chapter. These questions are then answered in the course of the chapter, and each chapter concludes with a concise summary of its findings. All of the questions and summaries have been re-examined and frequently revised in order to maximize the usefulness of this popular feature.

A list of Key Terms concludes each chapter, another new feature of the Sixth Edition. These terms are high-lighted in boldface in the text. The student may use these terms to test his or her understanding of the chapter's material.

In addition to posing chapter-opening questions and presenting more problems in historical interpretation, we have quoted extensively from a wide variety of primary sources in the narrative, demonstrating in our use of these quotations how historians evaluate evidence. Thus primary sources are examined as an integral part of the narrative as well as presented in extended form in the "Listening to the Past" chapter feature. We believe that such an extensive program of both integrated and separate primary source excerpts will help readers learn to interpret and think critically.

Each chapter concludes with carefully selected suggestions for further reading. These suggestions are briefly described to help readers know where to turn to continue thinking and learning about the world. Also, chapter bibliographies have been thoroughly revised and updated to keep them current with the vast amount of new work being done in many fields.

Revised Timelines

New comparative timelines now begin each chapter. These timelines organize historical events into three categories: political/military, social/economic, and intellectual/religious. In addition, the topic-specific timelines appearing in earlier editions have been revised for this edition. Once again we provide a unified timeline in an appendix at the end of the book. Comprehensive and easy to locate, this useful timeline allows students to compare simultaneous political, economic, social, cultural, intellectual, and scientific developments over the centuries.

Flexible Format

World history courses differ widely in chronological structure from one campus to another. To accommodate the various divisions of historical time into intervals that fit a two-quarter, three-quarter, or two-semester period, *A History of World Societies* is published in three versions that embrace the complete work:

- One-volume hardcover edition: *A History of World Societies*
- Two-volume paperback edition: *Volume I: To 1715* (Chapters 1–17); and *Volume II: Since 1500* (Chapters 16–36)
- Three-volume paperback edition: *Volume A: From Antiquity to 1500* (Chapters 1–14); *Volume B: From*

800 to 1815 (Chapters 13–22); and *Volume C: From 1775 to the Present* (Chapters 22–36)

Overlapping chapters in two-volume and three-volume editions facilitate matching the appropriate volume with the opening and closing dates of a specific course.

ANCILLARIES

Our learning and teaching ancillaries enhance the usefulness of the textbook:

- *GeoQuest™ World CD-ROM*
- *@history website*
- *Study Guide*
- *Instructor's Resource Manual*
- *Test Items*
- *HM ClassPrep with HM Testing* (contains PowerPoint maps and other presentation materials)
- *Blackboard™ and WebCT™ course cartridges*
- *Website for instructors and students*
- *Map Transparencies*

A CD-ROM, *GeoQuest™ World,* features thirty interactive maps that illuminate world history events from the days of the Persian Empire to the present. Each map is accompanied by exercises with answers and essay questions. The four different types of interactivity allow students to move at their own pace through each section.

Houghton Mifflin's *@history website* provides the finest text-based materials available for students and instructors. For students, this site offers primary sources, text-specific self-tests, and gateways to relevant history sites. Additional resources are provided for instructors.

The excellent *Study Guide* has been thoroughly revised by Professor James Schmiechen of Central Michigan University. Professor Schmiechen has been a tower of strength ever since he critiqued our initial prospectus, and he has continued to give us many valuable suggestions as well as his warmly appreciated support. His *Study Guide* contains learning objectives, chapter summaries, chapter outlines, review questions, extensive multiple-choice exercises, self-check lists of important concepts and events, and a variety of study aids and suggestions. The Sixth Edition also retains the study-review exercises on the interpretation of visual sources and major political ideas as well as suggested issues for discussion and essay, chronology reviews, and sections on studying effectively. To enable both students and instructors to use the *Study Guide* with the greatest possible flexibility, the guide is available in two volumes, with considerable overlapping of chapters. Instructors and students who use only Volumes A and B of the textbook have all the pertinent study materials in a single volume, *Study Guide,* Volume I (Chapters 1–22). Those who use only Volumes B and C of the textbook also have all the necessary materials in one volume, *Study Guide,* Volume II (Chapters 13–36).

The *Instructor's Resource Manual,* prepared by John Reisbord of Vassar College, contains instructional objectives, annotated chapter outlines, suggestions for lectures and discussion, paper and class activity topics, primary source exercises, map activities, and lists of audio-visual resources. The accompanying *Test Items,* by Professor Matthew Lenoe of Assumption College, offer identification, multiple-choice, map, and essay questions for a total of approximately two thousand test items. These test items are available to adopters in a computerized version, with editing capabilities.

New to this edition is *HM ClassPrep with HM Testing,* the latest comprehensive instructor's resource in computerized testing, which includes electronic versions of the *Instructor's Resource Manual* and *Test Items,* as well as PowerPoint maps, timelines, and chronologies from the text.

Course material is offered in both Blackboard™ and Web CT™ formats.

The text-specific website has been thoroughly revised and expanded for this edition. It now includes web activities, links to web resources, interactive exercises on the "Individuals in Society" and "Global Trade" features, chronological ordering exercises, and the ACE self-testing quiz program.

In addition, a set of full-color *Map Transparencies* of all the maps in the textbook is available on adoption.

ACKNOWLEDGMENTS

It is a pleasure to thank the many instructors who have read and critiqued the manuscript through its development:

Calvin W. Allen, Jr.
University of Memphis

David H. Anthony
University of California, Santa Cruz

Major Peter K. Bacon
United States Military Academy

Eva Semien Baham
Southern University

Richard B. Barnett
University of Virginia

Roger B. Beck
Eastern Illinois University

Major Arnold A. Bennett
United States Military Academy

Paul Brians
Washington State University

James W. Brodman
University of Central Arkansas

Clarence B. Davis
Marian College of Fond du Lac

Charles T. Evans
Northern Virginia Community College

Michael A. Gomez
New York University

Sumit Guha
Brown University

Kenda Mutongi
Williams College

Peter von Sivers
University of Utah

It is also a pleasure to thank our many editors at Houghton Mifflin for their efforts over many years. To Christina Horn, who guided production in the ever-more intensive email age, and to Julie Dunn, our development editor, we express our admiration and special appreciation. And we thank Carole Frohlich for her contributions in photo research and selection.

Many of our colleagues at the University of Illinois and at Georgetown University continued to provide information and stimulation, often without even knowing it. We thank them for it. John McKay wishes to thank and acknowledge Professor Charles Crouch of Georgia Southern University for his valuable contribution to the revision of Chapters 17–19, 23–26, and 29–30 in the Fifth Edition. He also happily acknowledges the fine research assistance provided by Patricia Clark and Bryan Ganaway and thanks them for it. Finally, he also expresses his deep appreciation to Jo Ann McKay for her sharp-eyed editorial support and unfailing encouragement. Bennett Hill wishes to thank Alice Croft for her technical assistance and Donald Franklin for his patience, understanding, and support.

Each of us has benefited from the criticism of his or her coauthors, although each of us assumes responsibility for what he or she has written. John Buckler has written Chapters 1–2 and 5–6; Patricia Buckley Ebrey has contributed Chapters 3, 4, 7, 11, 12, and 27; Bennett Hill has continued the narrative in Chapters 8–10, 13–16, 19–21, and 28; and John McKay has written Chapters 17, 18, 22–26, and 29–36. Finally, we continue to welcome the many comments and suggestions that have come from our readers, for they have helped us greatly in this ongoing endeavor.

J. P. M.   B. D. H.   J. B.   P. B. E.

A HISTORY OF WORLD SOCIETIES

King Menkaure and Queen. The pharaoh and his wife represent all the magnificence, serenity, and grandeur of Egypt. *(Old Kingdom, Dynasty 4, reign of Mycerinus, 2532–2510 B.C.E.; Greywacke; H × W × D: 54¹¹/₁₆ × 22⅜ × 21⁵/₁₆ in. (139 × 57 × 54 cm). Harvard University— Museum of Fine Arts Expedition, 11.1738. Museum of Fine Arts, Boston.)*

1

ORIGIN OF CIVILIZATIONS IN WEST ASIA AND NORTH AFRICA

The civilization and cultures of the modern Western world, like great rivers, have many sources. These sources have flowed from many places and directions. Peoples in western Europe developed numerous communities uniquely their own but also sharing some common features. They mastered such diverse subjects as astronomy, mathematics, geometry, trigonometry, engineering, religious practices, and social organization. Yet the earliest of these peoples did not record their learning and lore in systems of writing. Their lives and customs are consequently largely lost to us.

In the East, however, other early peoples confronted many of the same basic challenges as those in the West. They also made progress, but they took the important step of recording their experiences in writing. The most enduring innovations occurred in the ancient Near East, a region that includes the lands bordering the Mediterranean's eastern shore, the Arabian peninsula, parts of northeastern Africa, and perhaps above all Mesopotamia, the area of modern Iraq. Fundamental to the development of Western civilization and culture was the invention of writing by the Sumerians, which allowed knowledge of the past to be preserved. It also facilitated the spread and accumulation of learning, science, and literature. Ancient Near Eastern civilizations also produced the first written law codes, as well as religious concepts that still permeate daily life. Writing is the primary reason modern people look to the East as the richest sources of their origins.

But how do we know and understand these things? Before embarking on the study of history, it is necessary to ask, "What is it?" Only then can the peoples and events of tens of thousands of years be placed into a coherent whole. Once the nature of history is understood, further questions can be asked and reasonably answered. Specifically for this chapter,

- What were the fundamental Neolithic contributions to the rise of Western civilization?
- What caused Mesopotamian culture to become predominate in most of the ancient Near East?
- How did the Egyptians contribute to this vast story?

- What did the arrival of the Hittites on the frontiers of Mesopotamia and Egypt mean to the more advanced cultures of their new neighbors?

These are the questions we will explore in this chapter.

WHAT IS HISTORY AND WHY?

History is the effort to reconstruct the past to discover what people thought, what they did, and how their beliefs and actions continue to influence human life. In order to appreciate the past fully, we must put it into perspective so that we can understand the factors that have helped to shape us as individuals, the society in which we live, and the nature of other peoples' societies. Why else should we study civilizations as separated from ours through time, distance, and culture as classical Greece, medieval Germany, and modern Russia? Although many of the people involved in these epochs are long dead, what they did has touched everyone alive today.

To answer the questions above, historians examine primary sources, the firsthand accounts of people who lived through the events, people in the best position to know what happened. Historians normally use a variety of evidence in their search for an accurate understanding of the past. Most important are documents written by people who recorded their experiences and analyzed the significance of them. They investigated what happened, who was responsible for it, why it happened, and what it meant. Another written historical source is the chronicle. Writers of chronicles noted events in their chronological order (therefore the name) and sometimes added a brief explanation of the events.

Historians also rely on other, nonliterary evidence. In nearly all periods of early history, people inscribed laws, treaties with other states, and honors to individuals in stone. Governments still engrave similar documents in bronze. Even today, one cannot visit a Civil War battlefield without encountering a plaque giving information about what happened there. In the medieval period scribes produced thousands of documents giving detailed accounts of agricultural life on manors—how they were run, what the local customs were, and how society actually functioned. These scribes, many of them Christian monks, also left a record of religious and political affairs.

With the modern period has come an explosion of information. In addition to the traditional sources of historical knowledge, we have official statistics covering virtually everything from the annual number of deaths in automobile accidents to the daily results of the stock market. Public and private archives preserve a wealth of material that is useful in understanding governments, corporations, and private people. All these materials are the raw resources of historians.

In the face of the evidence, historians must determine what is accurate and what is false or biased. They do so by taking the earliest information first. They compare various versions of particular events or large trends with one another. Some people who have left us with evidence of the past were more intelligent or better informed than others. Therefore, their testimony is preferred and indeed strengthened by other writers who independently reported the same things. When two or more dependable sources record the same thing in the same way, historians conclude that they present an accurate account of events.

Once historians have determined which sources are reliable, they use this information to conclude that they have established a fact or that they are in a position to understand the significance of the information. Understanding the past does not necessarily come easily, which is one of the joys and frustrations of history. Unlike the more exact physical sciences, history cannot reproduce experiments under controlled conditions, because no two historical events are precisely alike. People cannot be put into test tubes, and they are not as predictable as atoms or hydrocarbons. That is hardly surprising, for history is about people, the most complex organisms on this planet.

To complicate matters, for many epochs of history only the broad outlines are known, so interpretation is especially difficult. For example, historians know that the Hittite Empire collapsed at the height of its power, but interpretations of the causes of the catastrophe are still speculative. On the other end of the spectrum, some developments are so vast and complex that historians must master mountains of data before they can even begin to interpret them properly. Events as diverse as the end of the western Roman Empire, the origins of the Industrial Revolution, and the causes of the French Revolution are very complicated because so many people brought so many different forces to bear for so many reasons. In such cases, there is never one simple explanation that will satisfy everyone, which testifies to the complexity of life in developed societies.

Still another matter complicates an accurate understanding of the past. The attempt to understand history is uniquely human. Interpretations of the past sometimes change because people's points of view change in the course of life. The values and attitudes of one generation may not be shared by another. Despite such differences in interpretation, the efforts of historians to examine and

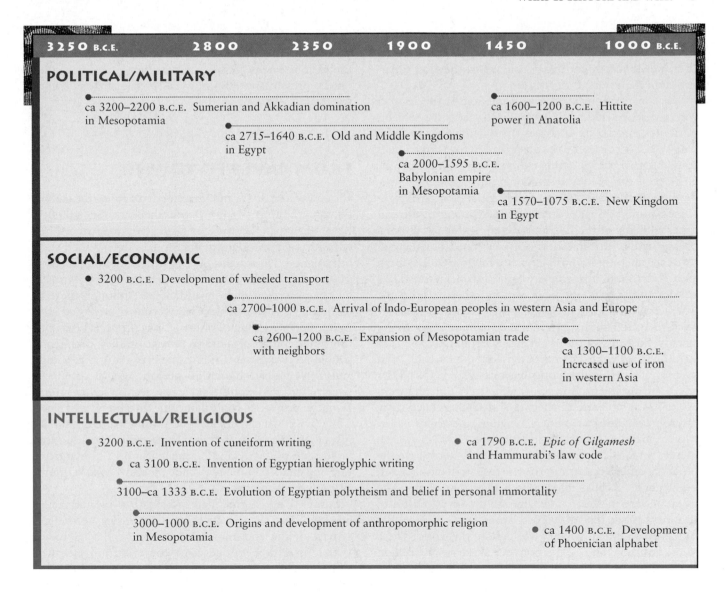

| 3250 B.C.E. | 2800 | 2350 | 1900 | 1450 | 1000 B.C.E. |

POLITICAL/MILITARY

ca 3200–2200 B.C.E. Sumerian and Akkadian domination in Mesopotamia

ca 2715–1640 B.C.E. Old and Middle Kingdoms in Egypt

ca 2000–1595 B.C.E. Babylonian empire in Mesopotamia

ca 1600–1200 B.C.E. Hittite power in Anatolia

ca 1570–1075 B.C.E. New Kingdom in Egypt

SOCIAL/ECONOMIC

3200 B.C.E. Development of wheeled transport

ca 2700–1000 B.C.E. Arrival of Indo-European peoples in western Asia and Europe

ca 2600–1200 B.C.E. Expansion of Mesopotamian trade with neighbors

ca 1300–1100 B.C.E. Increased use of iron in western Asia

INTELLECTUAL/RELIGIOUS

3200 B.C.E. Invention of cuneiform writing

ca 3100 B.C.E. Invention of Egyptian hieroglyphic writing

ca 1790 B.C.E. *Epic of Gilgamesh* and Hammurabi's law code

3100–ca 1333 B.C.E. Evolution of Egyptian polytheism and belief in personal immortality

3000–1000 B.C.E. Origins and development of anthropomorphic religion in Mesopotamia

ca 1400 B.C.E. Development of Phoenician alphabet

understand the past can give them a perspective that is valuable to the present. It is through this process of analysis and interpretation of evidence that historians come to understand not only the past but its relation to life today.

Social history, an important subject of this book, is itself an example of the historian's reappraisal of the meaning of the past. For centuries people took the basic facts, details, and activities of life for granted. Obviously, people lived in certain types of houses, ate certain foods that they either raised or bought, and reared families. These matters seemed so ordinary that few serious historians gave them much thought. Yet within this generation a growing number of scholars have demonstrated that studies of the ways in which people have lived over the years deserve

as much attention as the reigns of monarchs, the careers of great political figures, and the outcomes of big battles.

The topics of history and human societies lead to the question, "What is civilization?" *Civilization* is a word easier to describe than to define. It comes from the Latin adjective *civilis,* which refers to a citizen. Citizens willingly and mutually bind themselves in political, economic, and social organizations in which individuals merge themselves, their energies, and their interests in a larger community.

Civilization, however, goes far beyond politics. It also includes an advanced stage of social development, which entails enlightenment and education. Civilized society is refined, possessing the notion of law to govern the conduct of its members. It includes a code of manners and social conduct that creates an atmosphere of harmony and peace within the community. It creates art and generates science and philosophy to explain the larger world. It creates theology so that people can go beyond superstition in their pursuit of religion.

The spread of civilization is in one sense only another way to describe cultural diffusion. Each society has valuable attributes of its own. It shares them with other societies with which it comes into contact, and in turn contributes something to them. If this concept seems unnecessarily abstract, it can readily be understood by looking at the development of the United States. A land originally occupied by aboriginal peoples saw the coming of the Europeans, many of them from different social and cultural backgrounds. Africans soon came by force, but the culture they encountered was already a mixture of European and American. Their contributions also helped create a culture that could not be found anywhere else in the world. Still later, peoples from Latin America and Asia arrived to assimilate the customs and traditions they found already existing, but they likewise fertilized what they found. They were all from start to last streams that poured their singular contributions into the broader river. The result is an American culture very different from any of its ingredients, a society that has rather successfully incorporated different cultures, religions, and philosophies, while remaining nonetheless distinctive.

Another way to understand this idea is to observe the origins and development of the chief Western civilizations, analyzing similarities and differences among them. The term *Western* in this context means the ideas, customs, and institutions that developed primarily in Europe, the Americas, and their colonies throughout the world. These ideas, customs, and institutions set Western civilization apart from other civilizations, such as the African and Asian, that developed their unique way of life as a result of different demands, challenges, and opportunities, both human and geographical. Yet even the term *Western* has its irony. Some of the roots of this civilization lie in western Asia and northern Africa. Mesopotamia, and to a lesser extent Egypt, created concepts that are basic to Western thought and conduct. The term *Western* in this context means the ideas, customs, and institutions that set Western civilization apart from others. Yet no civilization stands alone. Each influences its neighbors, all the while preserving the essentials that make it distinctive.

At the fundamental level, the similarities of Western civilization are greater than the differences. Almost all people in Europe and the Americas share some values, even though they may live far apart, speak different languages, and have different religions and political and social systems. These values are the bonds that hold a civilization together. By studying these shared cultural values, which stretch through time and across distance, we can see how the various events of the past have left their impression on the present and even how the present may influence the future.

FROM CAVES TO TOWNS

Virtually every day brings startling news about the path of human evolution. We now know that by about 400,000 B.C.E. early peoples were making primitive stone tools, which has led historians to refer to this time as the Paleolithic period. During this period, which lasted until about 7000 B.C.E., people survived as nomadic hunters, usually living in caves or temporary shelters. Although they accomplished striking achievements, they contributed little to our understanding of history. They properly belong to the realm of anthropology, which studies prehistoric peoples. A reasonable dividing line between anthropology and history is the **Neolithic period,** usually dated between 7000 and 3000 B.C.E. The term *Neolithic* stems from the new stone tools that came into use at that time. The ways in which peoples used these tools led to fundamental changes in civilization. With them Neolithic folk built a life primarily and permanently based on agriculture and animal husbandry. They thereby broke with previous nomadic practices.

Sustained agriculture made possible a stable and secure life. Neolithic farmers developed the primary economic activity of the ancient world and one still vital today. With this settled routine came the evolution of towns and eventually of cities. Neolithic farmers usually raised more food than they could consume, so their surpluses permitted larger, healthier populations. Population growth in turn created an even greater reliance on settled farming, as only systematic agriculture could sustain the increased numbers of people. Since surpluses of food could also be bartered for other commodities, the Neolithic era witnessed the beginnings of the large-scale exchange of goods. Neolithic farmers also improved their tools and agricultural techniques. They domesticated bigger, stronger animals to work for them, invented the plow, and developed new mutations of seeds. By 3000 B.C.E. they had invented the wheel. Agricultural surpluses also made possible the division of labor. It freed some people to become craftsmen and artisans, who made tools, pottery vessels, woven baskets, clothing, and jewelry. In short, these advances resulted in a wealthier, more comfortable, and more complex life.

Return of the Iceman   This scene captures the discovery of a Neolithic herdsman who was trapped in the ice about 5,300 years ago. The discovery was made by chance in September 1991. In an ancient accident, he was sealed in ice with all of his tools, thus providing modern scholars with a unique view of the past. The discovery is so important that scientists have not yet done an autopsy on the corpse. *(Paul Hanny/Gamma)*

These developments generally led to the further evolution of towns and a whole new way of life. People not necessarily related to one another created rudimentary governments that transcended the family. These governments, led by a recognized central authority, made decisions that channeled the shared wisdom, physical energy, and resources of the whole population toward a common goal. These societies made their decisions according to custom, the generally accepted norms of traditional conduct. Here was the beginning of law. Towns also meant life in individual houses or groups of them, which led to greater personal independence. Growing wealth and the need for communal cooperation prompted people to erect public buildings and religious monuments. These groups also protected their possessions and themselves by raising walls.

Many scholars consider walled towns the basic feature of Neolithic society. Yet numerous examples prove that some Neolithic towns existed without stone or mud-brick walls. For instance, at Stonehenge in England the natives erected wooden palisades for safety. At Unteruhldingen in Germany the community established its unwalled town just offshore on a lake. They let nature defend them. The most concentrated collection of walled towns is found in Mesopotamia. This fact presents a historical problem. Since generations of archaeologists and historians have concentrated their attention on this region, they have considered it typical. Yet they have failed to appreciate properly circumstances elsewhere. The fundamental points about this period are that these folk created stable communities based on agriculture. They defended their towns in various ways by common consent and effort. This organized communal effort is far more important than the types of defenses they built.

The simplest way to support these conclusions is to examine briefly Stonehenge now and Mesopotamia afterward, each in its own unique context. A mute but engaging glimpse of a particular Neolithic society can readily be seen today in industrial England. Between 4700 and 2000 B.C.E. arose the Stonehenge people, named after the famous stone circle on Salisbury Plain. Though named after a single spot, this culture spread throughout Great Britain, Ireland, and Brittany in France. Circles like Stonehenge sometimes contained the houses of permanent settlers. Some were fortified enclosures, in which the inhabitants established a safe haven for themselves. Both were proto-urban centers. Some of these sites have yielded burial remains. Others were dedicated to religious rituals. They provided magical, not military, protection. They all served diverse social functions, another testimony to Neolithic creativity. Stonehenge and neighboring sites reveal the existence of prosperous, well-organized, and centrally led communities. They also provide evidence for cooperation among similarly constituted societies. None of them individually could have built the circle. By pooling their resources, human and material,

Stonehenge   Seen in regal isolation, Stonehenge sits among the stars and in April 1997 along the path of the comet Hale-Bopp. Long before Druids existed, a Neolithic society laboriously built this circle to mark the passing of the seasons. *(Jim Burgess)*

they raised it. Thus Stonehenge itself testifies to contact and cohesion among stable groups that cooperated toward a common goal. These factors alone prove the widening horizon of these Neolithic peoples.

Stonehenge offers another insight into this Neolithic culture. It indicates an intellectual world that encompassed astronomy, the environment, and religion. The circle is oriented toward the midwinter sunset and the midsummer sunrise. Stonehenge thus marked the clocklike celestial change of the seasons. This silent evidence proves the existence of a society prosperous enough to endure over long periods during which lore about heaven and earth could be preserved and passed along to successive generations. It also demonstrates that these communities considered themselves members of a wider world that they amiably shared with the deities of nature and the broader universe. Even the magnificent Stonehenge, however, cannot lead to history. The Stonehenge people achieved wonders, but they lacked the literacy to spread their legacy to others beyond their own culture. That breakthrough came in Mesopotamia.

MESOPOTAMIAN CIVILIZATION

In the East peoples faced many challenges similar to those of their Western contemporaries. In western Asia this process can easily be seen in Mesopotamia, the Greek name for the land between the Euphrates and Tigris Rivers. There the arid climate confronted the peoples with the hard problem of farming with scant water supplies. In the East farmers learned to irrigate their land and later to drain it to prevent the buildup of salt in the soil. **Irrigation** on a large scale, like building stone circles in the West, demanded organized group effort. That in turn underscored the need for strong central authority to direct it. In the East, as in the West, this corporate spirit led to governments in which individuals participated in the whole community while subordinating some of their particular concerns to its broader interests. These factors made urban life possible in a demanding environment. By about **3000** B.C.E. the Sumerians, whose origins are mysterious, established a number of cities in the south-

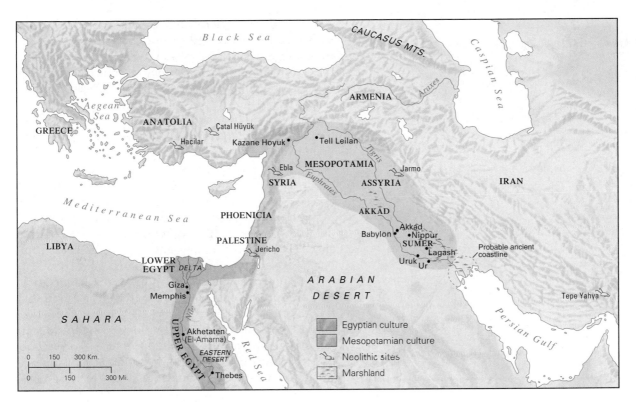

MAP 1.1 Spread of Cultures in the Ancient Near East   This map illustrates the spread of the Mesopotamian and Egyptian cultures through a semicircular stretch of land often called the Fertile Crescent. From this area knowledge and use of agriculture spread throughout the western part of Asia Minor.

ernmost part of Mesopotamia, which became known as Sumer. The Sumerians soon turned the region into what generations have called the "cradle of civilization" (see Map 1.1). Some might argue that this phrase should be honorably retired, for civilization was advancing by various degrees from England to Mesopotamia. No one, however, can deny that the fundamental innovation of the Sumerians was the creation of writing, which helped unify this society culturally and opened it to the broader world that we still share today.

The Invention of Writing and the First Schools

The origins of writing probably go back to the ninth millennium B.C.E., when Near Eastern peoples used clay tokens as counters for record keeping. By the fourth millennium people had realized that drawing pictures of the tokens on clay was simpler than making tokens. This breakthrough in turn suggested that more information could be conveyed by adding pictures of still other ob-

jects. The result was a complex system of pictographs, in which each sign pictured an object. These pictographs were the forerunners of a Sumerian form of writing known as **cuneiform,** from the Latin term for "wedge-shaped," used to describe the strokes of the stylus.

How did this pictographic system work, and how did it evolve into cuneiform writing? At first, if a scribe wanted to indicate a star, he simply drew a picture of it (line A of Figure 1.1) on a wet clay tablet, which became rock-hard when baked. Anyone looking at the picture would know what it meant and would think of the word for star. This complicated and laborious system had serious limitations. It could not represent abstract ideas or combinations of ideas. For instance, how could it depict a slave woman?

The solution appeared when the scribe discovered that signs could be combined to express meaning. To refer to a slave woman the scribe used the sign for woman (line B) and the sign for mountain (line C)—literally, "mountain woman" (line D). Because the Sumerians regularly obtained their slave women from the mountains, this combination of signs was easily understandable.

MEANING	PICTOGRAPH	IDEOGRAM	PHONETIC SIGN
A Star			
B Woman			
C Mountain			
D Slave woman			
E Water In			

FIGURE 1.1 Sumerian Writing   *(Source: Excerpted from S. N. Kramer,* The Sumerians: Their History, Culture and Character, *University of Chicago Press, Chicago, 1963, pp. 302–306. Reprinted by permission.)*

The next step was to simplify the system. Instead of drawing pictures, the scribe made conventionalized signs that were generally understood to represent ideas. Thus the signs became *ideograms:* they symbolized ideas. The sign for star could also be used to indicate heaven, sky, or even god.

The real breakthrough came when the scribe learned to use signs to represent sounds. For instance, the scribe drew two parallel wavy lines to indicate the word *a* or "water" (line E). Besides water, the word *a* in Sumerian also meant "in." The word *in* expresses a relationship that is very difficult to represent pictorially. Instead of trying to invent a sign to mean "in," some clever scribe used the sign for water because the two words sounded alike. This phonetic use of signs made possible the combining of signs to convey abstract ideas.

The Sumerian system of writing was so complicated that only professional scribes mastered it, and even they had to study it for many years. By 2500 B.C.E. scribal schools flourished throughout Sumer. Most students came from wealthy families and were male. Each school had a master, teachers, and monitors. Discipline was strict, and students were caned for sloppy work and mis-

Aerial View of Ur   This photograph gives a good idea of the size and complexity of Ur, one of the most powerful cities in Mesopotamia. In the lower right-hand corner stands the massive ziggurat of Umammu. *(Georg Gerster/ Photo Researchers)*

behavior. One graduate of a scribal school had few fond memories of the joy of learning:

My headmaster read my tablet, said:
"There is something missing," caned me.

. . . .

The fellow in charge of silence said:
"Why did you talk without permission," caned me.
The fellow in charge of the assembly said:
"Why did you stand at ease without permission," caned me.[1]

The Sumerian system of schooling set the educational standards for Mesopotamian culture, and the Akkadians and, later, the Babylonians adopted its practices and techniques. Mesopotamian education always had a practical side because of the economic and administrative importance of scribes. Most scribes took administrative positions in the temple or palace, where they kept records of business transactions, accounts, and inventories. But scribal schools did not limit their curriculum to business affairs. They were also centers of culture and scholarship. Topics of study included mathematics, botany, and linguistics. Advanced students copied and studied the classics of Sumerian literature. Talented students and learned scribes wrote compositions of their own. As a result, many literary, mathematical, and religious texts survive today, giving a full picture of Mesopotamian intellectual and spiritual life.

Mesopotamian Thought and Religion

The Mesopotamians made significant and sophisticated advances in mathematics using a numerical system based on units of sixty, ten, and six. They developed the concept of place value—that the value of a number depends on where it stands in relation to other numbers. The Mesopotamians did not consider mathematics a purely theoretical science. The building of cities, palaces, temples, and canals demanded practical knowledge of geometry and trigonometry.

Mesopotamian medicine was a combination of magic, prescriptions, and surgery. Mesopotamians believed that demons and evil spirits caused sickness and that magic spells could drive them out. Or, they believed, the physician could force the demon out by giving the patient a foul-tasting prescription. As medical knowledge grew, some prescriptions were found to work and thus were true medicines. In this slow but empirical fashion medicine grew from superstition to an early form of rational treatment.

Mesopotamian thought had a profound impact in theology and religion. The Sumerians originated many beliefs, and their successors added to them. The Mesopotamians believed that many gods run the world, but they did not consider all gods and goddesses equal. Some deities had very important jobs, taking care of music, law, sex, and victory, while others had lesser tasks, overseeing leatherworking and basketweaving. The god in charge of metalworking was hardly the equal of the god of wisdom.

Mesopotamian gods lived their lives much as human beings lived theirs. The gods were anthropomorphic, or human in form. Unlike men and women, they were powerful and immortal and could make themselves invisible. Otherwise, Mesopotamian gods and goddesses were very human: they celebrated with food and drink, and they raised families. They enjoyed their own "Garden of Eden," a green and fertile place. They could be irritable, vindictive, and irresponsible.

The Mesopotamians did not worship their deities because the gods were benevolent. Human beings were too insignificant to pass judgment on the conduct of the gods, and the gods were too superior to honor human morals. Rather, the Mesopotamians worshiped the gods because they were mighty. Likewise, it was not the place of men and women to understand the gods. The Sumerian equivalent to the biblical Job once complained to his god:

The man of deceit has conspired against me,
And you, my god, do not thwart him,
You carry off my understanding.[2]

The motives of the gods were not always clear. In times of affliction one could only pray and offer sacrifices to appease them.

The Mesopotamians had many myths to account for the creation of the universe. According to one Sumerian myth (echoed in Genesis, the first book of the Bible), only the primeval sea existed at first. The sea produced heaven and earth, which were united. Heaven and earth gave birth to Enlil, who separated them and made possible the creation of the other gods. Babylonian beliefs were similar. In the beginning was the primeval sea, the goddess Tiamat, who gave birth to the gods. When Tiamat tried to destroy the gods, Marduk, the chief god of the Babylonians, proceeded to kill her and divide her body and thus created the sky and earth. These myths are the earliest known attempts to answer the question, "How did it all begin?" The Mesopotamians obviously thought about these matters, as about the gods, in human terms. They never organized their beliefs into a philosophy, but their myths offered understandable explanations of natural phenomena. The myths were emotionally satisfying, and that was their greatest appeal.

Votive Dog Many Sumerian dedications to their gods were as artistic as this statuette of a dog that dates from 1900 B.C.E. The body of the dog bears a cuneiform inscription that informs the viewer and the goddess Ninisinna of the nature of the donor's prayer. *(Réunion des Musées Nationaux/Art Resource, NY)*

In addition to myths, the Sumerians produced the first epic poem, the *Epic of Gilgamesh,* which evolved as a re-working of at least five earlier myths. An epic poem is a narration of the achievements, labors, and sometimes the failures of heroes that embodies a people's or a nation's conception of its own past. Historians can use epic poems to learn about various aspects of a society, and to that extent epics can be used as historical sources. The Sumerian epic recounts the wanderings of Gilgamesh—the semihistorical king of Uruk—and his companion Enkidu, their fatal meeting with the goddess Ishtar, after which Enkidu dies, and Gilgamesh's subsequent search for eternal life. During his search Gilgamesh learns that life after death is so dreary that he returns to Uruk, where he becomes a good king and ends his life happily. The *Epic of Gilgamesh* is not only an excellent piece of literature but also an intellectual triumph. It shows the Sumerians grappling with such enduring questions as life and death, humankind and deity, and immortality. Despite its great antiquity, it addresses questions of importance to people today. (See the feature "Listening to the Past: A Quest for Immortality" on pages 28–29.)

Sumerian Society

Their harsh environment fostered a grim, even pessimistic, spirit among the Mesopotamians. The Sumerians sought to please and calm the gods, especially the patron deity of the city. Encouraged and directed by the traditional priesthood, which was dedicated to understanding the ways of the gods, the people erected shrines in the center of each city and then built their houses around them. The best way to honor the gods was to make the shrine as grand and as impressive as possible, for gods who had a splendid temple might think twice about sending floods to destroy the city.

Sumerian society was a complex arrangement of freedom and dependence, and its members were divided into four categories: nobles, free clients of the nobility, commoners, and slaves. **Nobles** consisted of the king and his family, the chief priests, and high palace officials. Generally, the king rose to power as a war leader, elected by the citizenry, who established a regular army, trained it, and led it into battle. The might of the king and the frequency of warfare quickly made him the supreme figure in the city, and kingship soon became hereditary. The symbol of royal status was the palace, which rivaled the temple in grandeur.

The king and the lesser nobility held extensive tracts of land that were, like the estates of the temple, worked by slaves and clients. **Clients** were free men and women who were dependent on the nobility. In return for their labor, the clients received small plots of land to work for themselves. Although this arrangement assured the clients of a livelihood, the land they worked remained the possession of the nobility or the temple. Thus not only did the nobility control most—and probably the best—land, they also commanded the obedience of a huge segment of society. They were the dominant force in Mesopotamian society.

Commoners were free citizens. They were independent of the nobility; however, they could not rival the nobility in social status and political power. Commoners belonged to large patriarchal families who owned land in their own right. Commoners could sell their land, if the family approved, but even the king could not legally take their land without their approval. Commoners had a voice in the political affairs of the city and full protection under the law.

Until comparatively recent times, slavery has been a fact of life throughout the history of Western society. Some Sumerian slaves were foreigners and prisoners of war. Some were criminals who had lost their freedom as punishment for their crimes. Still others served as slaves to repay debts. These were more fortunate than the others, because the law required that they be freed after three years. But all slaves were subject to whatever treatment their owners might mete out. They could be beaten and even branded. Yet they were not considered dumb beasts. Slaves engaged in trade and made profits. Indeed, many slaves were able to buy their freedom. They could borrow money and received at least some legal protection.

THE SPREAD OF MESOPOTAMIAN CULTURE

The Sumerians established the basic social, economic, and intellectual patterns of Mesopotamia, but the Semites played a large part in spreading Sumerian culture far beyond the boundaries of Mesopotamia. The interaction of the Sumerians and Semites, in fact, gives one of the very first glimpses of a phenomenon that can still be seen today. History provides abundant evidence of peoples of different origins coming together, usually on the borders of an established culture. The result was usually cultural change, outweighing any hostility, for each side learned from the other. The outcome in these instances was the evolution of a new culture that consisted of two or more old parts. Although the older culture almost invariably looked on the newcomers as inferior, the new just as invariably contributed something valuable to the old. So it was in 2331 B.C.E. The Semitic chieftain Sargon conquered Sumer and created a new empire. The symbol of his triumph was a new capital, the city of Akkad. Sargon, the first "world conqueror," led his armies to the Mediterranean Sea. Although his empire lasted only a few generations, it spread Mesopotamian culture throughout the Fertile Crescent, the belt of rich farmland that extends from Mesopotamia in the east up through Syria in the north and down to Egypt in the west (see Map 1.1).

The question to answer is why Mesopotamian culture had such an immediate and wide appeal. In the first place it was successful and enjoyed the prestige of its success. Newcomers wanted to find a respectable place in this old and venerated culture. It also provided an easy means of communication among people on a broad scale. The Eblaites (a Semitic people) could efficiently deal with the Mesopotamians and others who embraced this culture in ways that all could understand. Culture ignores borders. Despite local variations, so much common ground existed that similar political and economic institutions, exchange of ideas and religious beliefs, methods of writing, and a shared etiquette served as links among all who embraced Mesopotamian culture.

The Triumph of Babylon

Although the empire of Sargon was extensive, it was short-lived. The Akkadians, too, failed to solve the problems posed by Mesopotamia's geography and population pattern. It was left to the Babylonians to unite Mesopotamia politically and culturally. The Babylonians were Amorites, a Semitic people who had migrated from Arabia and settled on the site of Babylon along the middle Euphrates, where that river runs close to the Tigris. Babylon enjoyed an excellent geographical position and was ideally suited to be the capital of Mesopotamia. It dominated trade on the Tigris and Euphrates Rivers: all commerce to and from Sumer and Akkad had to pass by its walls. It also looked beyond Mesopotamia. Babylonian merchants followed the Tigris north to Assyria and Anatolia. The Euphrates led merchants to Syria, Palestine, and the Mediterranean. The city grew great because of its commercial importance and soundly based power.

Babylon was also fortunate to have a farseeing and able king, Hammurabi (r. 1792–1750 B.C.E.). Hammurabi set out to do three things: make Babylon secure, unify Mesopotamia, and win for the Babylonians a place in Mesopotamian civilization. The first two he accomplished by conquering Assyria in the north and Sumer and Akkad in the south. Then he turned to his third goal.

Politically, Hammurabi joined in his kingship the Semitic concept of the tribal chieftain and the Sumerian idea of urban kingship. Culturally, he encouraged the spread of myths that explained how Marduk, the god of Babylon, had been elected king of the gods by the other Mesopotamian deities. Hammurabi's success in making Marduk the god of all Mesopotamians made Babylon the

Life Under Hammurabi

One of Hammurabi's most memorable accomplishments was the proclamation of a **law code** that offers a wealth of information about daily life in Mesopotamia. Hammurabi's was not the first law code in Mesopotamia; indeed, the earliest goes back to about 2100 B.C.E. Like earlier lawgivers, Hammurabi proclaimed that he issued his laws on divine authority "to establish law and justice in the language of the land, thereby promoting the welfare of the people." Hammurabi's code inflicted such penalties as mutilation, whipping, and burning. Despite its severity, a spirit of justice and a sense of responsibility pervade the code. Hammurabi genuinely felt that his duty was to govern the Mesopotamians as righteously as possible. He tried to regulate the relations of his people so that they could live together in harmony.

The practical impact of Hammurabi's code is much debated. There is much disagreement about whether it recorded laws already established, promulgated new laws, or simply proclaimed what was just and proper. It is also unknown whether Hammurabi's proclamation, like others before it, was legally binding on the courts. At the very least, Hammurabi pronounced to the world what principles of justice he encouraged, while giving everyone visible evidence of his intentions as ruler of Babylonia.

The Code of Hammurabi has two striking characteristics. First, the law differed according to the social status of the offender. Aristocrats were not punished as harshly as commoners, nor commoners as harshly as slaves. Second, the code demanded that the punishment fit the crime. It called for "an eye for an eye, and a tooth for a tooth," at least among equals. However, an aristocrat who destroyed the eye of a commoner or slave could pay a fine instead of losing his own eye. Otherwise, as long as criminal and victim shared the same social status, the victim could demand exact vengeance.

Hammurabi's code began with legal procedure. There were no public prosecutors or district attorneys, so individuals brought their own complaints before the court. Each side had to produce written documents or witnesses to support its case. In cases of murder, the accuser had to prove the defendant guilty; any accuser who failed to do so was put to death. This strict law was designed to prevent people from lodging groundless charges. The Mesopotamians were very worried about witchcraft and sorcery. Anyone accused of witchcraft, even if the charges were not proved, underwent an ordeal by water. The gods themselves would decide the case. The defendant was thrown into the Euphrates, which was considered the instrument of the gods. A defendant who sank was

Law Code of Hammurabi   Hammurabi ordered his code to be inscribed on a stone pillar and set up in public. At the top of the pillar Hammurabi is depicted receiving the scepter of authority from the god Shamash. *(Hirmer Verlag München)*

religious center of Mesopotamia. Through Hammurabi's genius the Babylonians made their own contribution to Mesopotamian culture—a culture vibrant enough to maintain its identity while assimilating new influences. Hammurabi's conquests and the activity of Babylonian merchants spread this enriched culture north to Anatolia and west to Syria and Palestine.

guilty; a defendant who floated was innocent. Another procedural regulation covered the conduct of judges. Once a judge had rendered a verdict, he could not change it. Any judge who did so was fined heavily and deposed. In short, the code tried to guarantee a fair trial and a just verdict.

Consumer protection is not a modern idea; it goes back to Hammurabi's day. Merchants and businessmen had to guarantee the quality of their goods and services. A boat builder who did sloppy work had to repair the boat at his own expense. A boatman who lost the owner's boat or sank someone else's boat replaced it and its cargo. House builders guaranteed their work with their lives. Careless work could result in the collapse of a house and the death of its inhabitants. If that happened, the builder was put to death. A merchant who tried to increase the interest rate on a loan forfeited the entire amount. Hammurabi's laws tried to ensure that consumers got what they paid for and paid a just price.

Because farming was essential to Mesopotamian life, Hammurabi's code dealt extensively with agriculture. Tenant farming was widespread, and tenants rented land on a yearly basis. Instead of money they paid a portion of their crops as rent. Unless the land was carefully cultivated, it quickly reverted to wasteland. Therefore, tenants faced severe penalties for neglecting the land or not working it at all. Since irrigation was essential to grow crops, tenants had to keep the canals and ditches in good repair. Otherwise the land would be subject to floods and farmers would face crippling losses. Anyone whose neglect of the canals resulted in damaged crops had to bear all the expense of the lost crops. Those tenants who could not pay the costs were forced into slavery.

Hammurabi gave careful attention to marriage and the family. As elsewhere in the Near East, marriage had aspects of a business agreement. The prospective groom and the father of the future bride arranged everything. The man offered the father a bridal gift, usually money. If the man and his bridal gift were acceptable, the father provided his daughter with a dowry. After marriage the dowry belonged to the woman (although the husband normally administered it) and was a means of protecting her rights and status. Once the two men agreed on financial matters, they drew up a contract; no marriage was considered legal without one. Either party could break off the marriage, but not without paying a stiff penalty. Fathers often contracted marriages while their children were still young. The girl either continued to live in her father's house until she reached maturity or went to live in the house of her father-in-law. During this time she was legally considered a wife. Once she and her husband came of age, they set up their own house.

The wife was expected to be rigorously faithful. The penalty for adultery was death. According to Hammurabi's code: "If the wife of a man has been caught while lying with another man, they shall bind them and throw them into the water."[3] The husband had the power to spare his wife by obtaining a pardon for her from the king. He could, however, accuse his wife of adultery even if he had not caught her in the act. In such a case she could try to clear herself before the city council that investigated the charge. If she was found innocent, she could take her dowry and leave her husband. If a woman decided to take the direct approach and kill her husband, she was impaled.

The husband had virtually absolute power over his household. He could even sell his wife and children into slavery to pay debts. Sons did not lightly oppose their fathers, and any son who struck his father could have his hand cut off. A father was free to adopt children and include them in his will. Artisans sometimes adopted children to teach them the family trade. Although the father's power was great, he could not disinherit a son without just cause. Cases of disinheritance became matters for the city to decide, and the code ordered the courts to forgive a son for his first offense. Only if a son wronged his father a second time could he be disinherited.

Law codes, preoccupied as they are with the problems of society, provide a bleak view of things. Other Mesopotamian documents give a happier glimpse of life. Although Hammurabi's code dealt with marriage in a hard-fisted fashion, a Mesopotamian poem tells of two people meeting secretly in the city. Their parting is delightfully romantic:

Come now, set me free, I must go home,
Kuli-Enlil . . . set me free, I must go home.
What can I say to deceive my mother?[4]

Countless wills and testaments show that husbands habitually left their estates to their wives, who in turn willed the property to their children. All this suggests happy family life. Hammurabi's code restricted married women from commercial pursuits, but financial documents prove that many women engaged in business without hindrance. Some carried on the family business, while others became wealthy landowners in their own right. Mesopotamians found their lives lightened by holidays and religious festivals. Traveling merchants brought news of the outside world and swapped marvelous tales. Despite their pessimism, the Mesopotamians enjoyed a vibrant and creative culture, a culture that left its mark on the entire Near East.

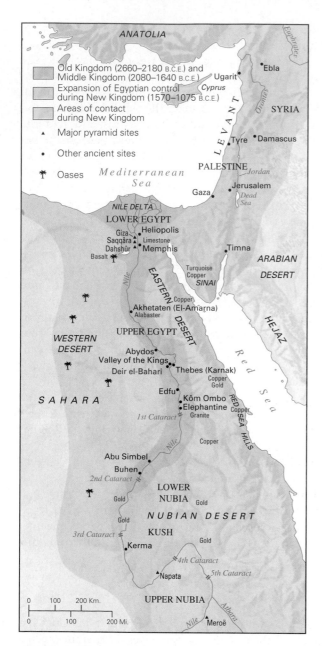

MAP 1.2 Ancient Egypt Geography and natural resources provided Egypt with centuries of peace and abundance.

EGYPT, THE LAND OF THE PHARAOHS (3100–1200 B.C.E.)

The Greek historian and traveler Herodotus in the fifth century B.C.E. called Egypt the "gift of the Nile." No other single geographical factor had such a fundamental and profound impact on the shaping of Egyptian life, so-

ciety, and history as the Nile (see Map 1.2). Unlike the rivers of Mesopotamia, it rarely brought death and destruction by devastating entire cities. The river was primarily a creative force. The Egyptians never feared the relatively tame Nile in the way the Mesopotamians feared the Tigris. Instead, they sang its praises:

Hail to thee, O Nile, that issues from the earth and comes to keep Egypt alive! . . .
He that waters the meadows which Re [Ra] created,
He that makes to drink the desert . . .
He who makes barley and brings emmer [wheat] into being . . .
He who brings grass into being for the cattle . . .
He who makes every beloved tree to grow . . .
O Nile, verdant art thou, who makest man and cattle to live.[5]

In the mind of the Egyptians, the Nile was the supreme fertilizer and renewer of the land. Each September the Nile floods its valley, transforming it into a huge area of marsh or lagoon. By the end of November the water retreats, leaving behind a thin covering of fertile mud ready to be planted with crops.

The annual flood made the growing of abundant crops almost effortless, especially in southern Egypt. Herodotus, used to the rigors of Greek agriculture, was amazed by the ease with which the Egyptians raised crops:

For indeed without trouble they obtain crops from the land more easily than all other men. . . . They do not labor to dig furrows with the plough or hoe or do the work which other men do to raise grain. But when the river by itself inundates the fields and the water recedes, then each man, having sown his field, sends pigs into it. When the pigs trample down the seed, he waits for the harvest. Then when the pigs thresh the grain, he gets his crop.[6]

The extraordinary fertility of the Nile Valley made it easy to produce an annual agricultural surplus, which in turn sustained a growing and prosperous population. The Nile also unified Egypt. The river was the region's principal highway, promoting easy communication throughout the valley.

Egypt was fortunate in that it was nearly self-sufficient. Besides the fertility of its soil, Egypt possessed enormous quantities of stone, which served as the raw material of architecture and sculpture. Abundant clay was available for pottery, as was gold for jewelry and ornaments. The raw materials that Egypt lacked were close at hand. The Egyptians could obtain copper from Sinai and timber from Lebanon. They had little cause to look to the outside world for their essential needs, a fact that helps to explain the insular quality of Egyptian life.

The God-King of Egypt

Geographical unity quickly gave rise to political unification of the country under the authority of a king whom the Egyptians called "pharaoh." The precise details of this process have been lost. The Egyptians themselves told of a great king, Menes, who united Upper and Lower Egypt into a single kingdom around 3100 B.C.E. Thereafter the Egyptians divided their history into dynasties, or families of kings. For modern historical purposes, however, it is more useful to divide Egyptian history into periods (see page 18). The political unification of Egypt ushered in the period known as the Old Kingdom (2660–2180 B.C.E.), an era remarkable for prosperity, artistic flowering, and the evolution of religious beliefs.

In religion, the Egyptians developed complex, often contradictory, ideas of their gods. They were polytheistic in that they worshiped many gods, some mightier than others. Their beliefs were all rooted in the environment and human ecology. The most powerful of these gods was Amon, a primeval sky-god, and Ra, the sun-god. Amon created the entire cosmos by his thoughts. He caused the Nile to make its annual inundations and the northern wind to blow. He brought life to the land and its people, and he sustained both. The Egyptians cherished Amon because he championed fairness and honesty, especially for the common people. The Egyptians called him the "vizier of the humble" and the "voice of the poor." He was also a magician and physician who cured ills, protected people from natural dangers, and protected travelers. The Egyptians considered Ra the creator of life. He commanded the sky, earth, and underworld. This giver of life could also take it without warning. Ra was associated with the falcon-god Horus, the "lord of the sky," who served as the symbol of divine kingship. Horus united Egypt and bestowed divinity on the pharaoh. The obvious similarities between Amon and Ra eventually led the Egyptians to combine them into one god, **Amon-Ra.** Yet the Egyptians never fashioned a

Ra and Horus The god Ra appears on the left in a form associated with Horus, the falcon-god. The red circle over Ra's head identifies him as the sun-god. In this scene Ra also assumes characteristics of Osiris, god of the underworld. He stands in judgment of the dead woman on the right. She meets the god with respect but without fear, as he will guide her safely to a celestial heaven. (*Egyptian Museum, Cairo*)

PERIODS OF EGYPTIAN HISTORY

PERIOD	DATES	SIGNIFICANT EVENTS
Archaic	3100–2660 B.C.E.	Unification of Egypt
Old Kingdom	2715–2180 B.C.E.	Construction of the pyramids
First Intermediate	2180–2080 B.C.E.	Political chaos
Middle Kingdom	2080–1640 B.C.E.	Recovery and political stability
Second Intermediate	1640–1570 B.C.E.	Hyksos "invasion"
New Kingdom	1570–1075 B.C.E.	Creation of an Egyptian empire Akhenaten's religious policy

formal theology to resolve these differences. Instead they worshiped these gods as different aspects of the same celestial phenomena.

The Egyptians likewise developed views of an afterlife that reflected the world around them. The dry air of Egypt preserves much that would decay in other climates. Thus there was a sense of permanence about Egypt: the past was never far from the present. The dependable rhythm of the seasons also shaped the fate of the dead. According to the Egyptians, Osiris, a fertility god associated with the Nile, died each year, and each year his wife, Isis, brought him back to life. Osiris eventually became king of the dead, and he weighed human beings' hearts to determine whether they had lived justly enough to deserve everlasting life. Osiris's care of the dead was shared by Anubis, the jackal-headed god who annually helped Isis to resuscitate Osiris. Anubis was the god of mummification, so essential to Egyptian funerary rites. The Egyptians preserved these ideas in the **Book of the Dead,** which explained that after death the soul left the body to become part of the divine. It entered gladly through the gate of heaven and remained in the presence of Aton (a sun-god) and the stars. Thus the Egyptians did not draw a firm boundary between the human and the divine, and life did not end with death.

The focal point of religious and political life in the Old Kingdom was the **pharaoh,** who commanded the wealth, resources, and people of all Egypt. The pharaoh's power was such that the Egyptians considered him to be Horus in human form. The link between the pharaoh and Horus was doubly important. In Egyptian religion Horus was the son of Osiris, which meant that the pharaoh, a living god on earth, became one with Osiris after death. The

Anubis and the Underworld In this scene from a coffin, Anubis embalms a body. The jars containing the corpse's internal organs are lined up beneath the bier. The heads on the jars represent the sons of Horus, who like their father tended the dead. The remains will all be buried together for eternity. *(Egyptian Museum, Cairo)*

pharaoh was not simply the mediator between the gods and the Egyptian people. Above all, he was the power that achieved the integration between gods and human beings, between nature and society, that ensured peace

Pyramids of Giza   Giza was the burial place of the pharaohs of the Old Kingdom and of their aristocracy, whose smaller rectangular tombs surround the two foremost pyramids. The small pyramid probably belonged to a pharaoh's wife. *(© John Ross)*

and prosperity for the land of the Nile. The pharaoh was thus a guarantee to his people, a pledge that the gods of Egypt (strikingly unlike those of Mesopotamia) cared for their people.

The king's surroundings had to be worthy of a god. Only a magnificent palace was suitable for his home; in fact, the very word *pharaoh* means "great house." Only later, in the Eighteenth Dynasty (see page 21), did it come to mean "king." Just as the pharaoh occupied a great house in life, so he reposed in a great **pyramid** after death. The massive tomb contained all the things needed by the pharaoh in his afterlife. The walls of the burial chamber were inscribed with religious texts and spells relating to the king's journeys after death. Contrary to common belief, no curses for violation of the pyramid have been found. The pyramid also symbolized the king's power and his connection with the sun-god. After burial the entrance was blocked and concealed to ensure the pharaoh's undisturbed peace. To this day the great pyramids at Giza near Cairo bear silent but magnificent testimony to the god-kings of Egypt.

The Pharaoh's People

Because the common folk stood at the bottom of the social and economic scale, they were always at the mercy of grasping officials. The arrival of the tax collector was never a happy occasion. One Egyptian scribe described the worst that could happen:

And now the scribe lands on the river-bank and is about to register the harvest-tax. The janitors carry staves and the Nubians rods of palm, and they say, Hand over the corn, though there is none. The cultivator is beaten all over, he is bound and thrown into a well, soused and dipped head downwards. His wife has been bound in his presence and his children are in fetters.[7]

That was an extreme situation. Nonetheless, taxes might amount to 20 percent of the harvest, and tax collection could be brutal.

The regularity of the climate meant that the agricultural year was also routine and dependable. For the Egyptian peasants who formed the bulk of the population, the

Hippopotamus Hunt   This wall painting depicts the success of two men in a small boat who have killed a hippopotamus, seen in the lower right-hand corner. Behind the hippopotamus swims a crocodile hoping for a snack. *(Egyptian Museum SMPK, Berlin/Bildarchiv Preussischer Kulturbesitz)*

agricultural year normally began in July, when the mud of the Nile covered the land. The waters receded four months later, and then the land was plowed and sowed. This was a particularly busy time, for the crop had to be planted before the land dried. The next period, from mid-March to July, saw the harvesting of crops. Farmers also nurtured a large variety of fruit trees, vegetables, and vines. They tended cattle and poultry, and when time permitted, they hunted and fished in the marshlands of the Nile. People could routinely depend on these aspects of life. This very regularity gave a sense of calm and order to Egypt that was not found in Mesopotamia or later in Greece.

Egyptian society seems to have been a curious mixture of freedom and constraint. Slavery did not become widespread until the New Kingdom (1570–1200 B.C.E.). There was neither a caste system nor a color bar, and humble people could rise to the highest positions if they possessed talent. On the other hand, most ordinary folk were probably little more than serfs who could not easily leave the land of their own free will. Peasants were also subject to forced labor, including work on the pyramids and canals. Young men were drafted into the pharaoh's army, which served both as a fighting force and as a labor corps.

The vision of thousands of people straining to build the pyramids and countless artists adorning the pharaoh's tomb brings to the modern mind a distasteful picture of oriental despotism. Indeed, the Egyptian view of life and society is alien to those raised on the Western concepts of individual freedom and human rights. To ancient Egyptians the pharaoh embodied justice and order—harmony among human beings, nature, and the divine. If the pharaoh was weak or allowed anyone to challenge his unique position, he opened the way to chaos. Twice in Egyptian history the pharaoh failed to maintain rigid centralization. During those two eras, known as the First and Second Intermediate Periods, Egypt was exposed to civil war and invasion. Yet the monarchy survived, and in each period a strong pharaoh arose to crush the rebels or expel the invaders and restore order.

The Hyksos in Egypt (1640–1570 B.C.E.)

While Egyptian civilization flourished behind its bulwark of sand and sea, momentous changes were taking place in the ancient Near East, changes that would leave their mark even on rich, insular Egypt. These changes involved enormous and remarkable movements, especially of peoples who spoke Semitic tongues.

The original home of the Semites was perhaps the Arabian peninsula. Some tribes moved into northern

Mesopotamia, others into Syria and Palestine, and still others into Egypt. Shortly after 1800 B.C.E. people whom the Egyptians called **Hyksos,** which means "Rulers of the Uplands," began to settle in the Nile Delta. The movements of the Hyksos were part of a larger pattern of migration of peoples during this period. The history of Mesopotamia records many such wanderings of people in search of better homes for themselves. Such nomads normally settled in and accommodated themselves with the native cultures. The process was mutual, for each group had something to give and to learn from the other.

So it was in Egypt, but Egyptian tradition, as later recorded by the priest Manetho in the third century B.C.E., depicted the coming of the Hyksos as a brutal invasion:

In the reign of Toutimaios—I do not know why—the wind of god blew against us. Unexpectedly from the regions of the east men of obscure race, looking forward confidently to victory, invaded our land, and without a battle easily seized it all by sheer force. Having subdued those in authority in the land, they then barbarously burned our cities and razed to the ground the temples of the gods. They fell upon all the natives in an entirely hateful fashion, slaughtering them and leading both their children and wives into slavery. At last they made one of their people king, whose name was Salitis. This man resided at Memphis, leaving in Upper and Lower Egypt tax collectors and garrisons in strategic places.[8]

The Hyksos created a capital city at Avaris, located in the northeastern Nile Delta, but they probably exerted direct rule no farther south.

Although the Egyptians portrayed the Hyksos as a conquering horde, they were probably no more than nomads looking for good land. Their entry into the delta was probably gradual and generally peaceful. The Hyksos brought with them the method of making bronze and casting it into tools and weapons that became standard in Egypt. They thereby brought Egypt fully into the **Bronze Age** culture of the Mediterranean world, a culture in which the production and use of bronze implements became basic to society. Bronze tools made farming more efficient than ever before because they were sharper and more durable than the copper tools they replaced. The Hyksos' use of bronze armor and weapons as well as horse-drawn chariots and the composite bow, made of laminated wood and horn and far more powerful than the simple wooden bow, revolutionized Egyptian warfare. However much the Egyptians learned from the Hyksos, Egyptian culture eventually absorbed the newcomers. The Hyksos came to worship Egyptian gods and modeled their monarchy on the pharaonic system.

The New Kingdom: Revival and Empire (1570–1075 B.C.E.)

Politically, Egypt was only in eclipse. The Egyptian sun shone again when a remarkable line of kings, the pharaohs of the Eighteenth Dynasty, arose to challenge the Hyksos. These pharaohs pushed the Hyksos out of the delta, subdued Nubia in the south, and conquered Palestine and parts of Syria in the northeast. In this way, Egyptian warrior-pharaohs inaugurated the New Kingdom—a period in Egyptian history characterized by enormous wealth and conscious imperialism. During this period, probably for the first time, widespread slavery became a feature of Egyptian life. The pharaoh's armies returned home leading hordes of slaves, who constituted a new labor force for imperial building projects.

The kings of the Eighteenth Dynasty created the first Egyptian empire. They ruled Palestine and Syria through their officers and incorporated into the kingdom of Egypt the neighboring region of Nubia. Egyptian religion and customs flourished in Nubia, making a huge impact on African culture there and in neighboring areas. The warrior-kings celebrated their success with monuments on a scale unparalleled since the pharaohs of the Old Kingdom had built the pyramids. Even today the colossal granite statues of these pharaohs and the rich tomb objects of Tutankhamon ("King Tut") testify to the might and splendor of the New Kingdom.

One of the most extraordinary of this unusual line of kings was Akhenaten (r. 1367–1350 B.C.E.), a pharaoh more concerned with religion than with conquest. Nefertiti, his wife and queen, encouraged his religious bent. (See the feature "Individuals in Society: Nefertiti, the 'Great Wife.'") The precise nature of Akhenaten's religious beliefs remains debatable. The problem began during his own lifetime. His religion was often unpopular among the people and the traditional priesthood, and its practice declined in the later years of his reign. After his death, it was condemned and denounced; consequently, not much is known about it. Most historians, however, agree that Akhenaten and Nefertiti were monotheists; that is, they believed that the sun-god Aton, whom they worshiped, was universal, the only god. They considered all other Egyptian gods and goddesses frauds and disregarded their worship. Yet their belief suffered from an obvious flaw. The pharaoh himself was considered the son of god, and monotheism obviously cannot have two gods. What Akhenaten meant by **monotheism** is that only Aton among the traditional Egyptian deities was god.

Akhenaten's monotheism, imposed from above, failed to find a place among the people. The prime reason for

Tutankhamon as Pharaoh   This painted casket depicts the pharaoh as the defender of the kingdom repulsing its invaders. Tutankhamon rides into battle under the signs of the sun-disk and the vulture-goddess, indicating that he and Egypt enjoy the protection of the gods. *(Egyptian Museum, Cairo)*

Akhenaten's failure is that his god had no connection with the past of the Egyptian people, who trusted the old gods and felt comfortable praying to them. Average Egyptians were no doubt distressed and disheartened when their familiar gods were outlawed, for those gods were the heavenly powers that had made Egypt powerful and unique. The fanaticism and persecution that accompanied the new monotheism were in complete defiance of the Egyptian tradition of tolerant **polytheism,** or worship of several gods. Thus, when Akhenaten died, his religion died with him.

THE HITTITES

About the time the Hyksos entered the Nile Delta, the Hittites, who had long been settled in Anatolia (modern Turkey), became a major power in that region and began to expand eastward (see Map 1.3). The Hittites were an Indo-European people. The term **Indo-European** refers to a large family of languages that includes English, most of the languages of modern Europe, Greek, Latin, Persian, and Sanskrit, the sacred tongue of ancient India. During the eighteenth and nineteenth centuries European scholars learned that peoples who spoke related languages had spread as far west as Ireland and as far east as Central Asia. Archaeologists were able to date the migrations roughly and put them into their historical context.

The rise of the Hittites to prominence in Anatolia is reasonably clear. During the nineteenth century B.C.E. the native kingdoms in the area engaged in suicidal warfare that left most of Anatolia's once-flourishing towns in ashes and rubble. In this climate of exhaustion the Hittite king Hattusilis I built a hill citadel at Hattusas, the modern Boghazköy, from which he led his Hittites against neighboring kingdoms. Hattusilis's grandson and successor,

INDIVIDUALS IN SOCIETY

NEFERTITI, THE "GREAT WIFE"

Nefertiti, queen of Egypt. (Staatliche Muzeen zu Berlin/ Bildarchiv Preussischer Kultur- besitz. Photo: Margarete Busing)

The Egyptians always named the pharaoh's wife the "great wife," somewhat in the way that Americans refer to the president's wife as the "first lady." The great wife legitimized her husband's exercise of power through religious beliefs. The Egyptians believed that she was divinely born and that Amon took the human form of her husband, impregnated her, oversaw the development of the child in her womb, and ensured a healthy delivery. Thus the child was the offspring of both the god and the pharaoh. The great wife could not legally be pharaoh, for only a male could exercise that power. Yet only she could make legitimate a man's right to power. The Egyptians literally and formally considered hers the throne of power, although her power was passive rather than active. Egyptian artists usually depicted the great wife with as much care and dignity as they did the pharaoh. They stylized her body as that of the ideal woman, and her portrait was more idealized than realistic.

So stood things until Nefertiti, who was an exceptional great wife. Unlike her predecessors, she was not content to play a passive role in Egyptian life. Like her husband, Akhenaten, she passionately embraced the worship of Aton. She used her position to support her husband's zeal to spread the god's worship. Together they built a new palace at Akhetaten, the present Amarna, away from the old centers of power. There they developed and promulgated the cult of Aton to the exclusion of the traditional deities. Nearly the only literary survival of their religious belief is the "Hymn to Aton," which declares Aton to be the only god. It also mentions Nefertiti as "the great royal consort whom he !Akhenaten! loves, the mistress of the Two Lands !Upper and Lower Egypt!"

Yet something mysterious and unexplained later occurred at the royal court. Akhenaten stripped Nefertiti of her crown name, which was the equivalent of divorce, and exiled her to a palace in the northernmost part of Amarna. It is quite possible, but beyond proof, that Akhenaten wanted a reconciliation with the old gods and their priests. The cult of Aton was so unpopular among the Egyptians that many considered it sacrilegious. Unwilling to alienate the Egyptian people and their religious leaders any longer, Akhenaten may have dropped or at least softened his insistence on Aton's divine position. Nefertiti in that case may have held true to her religious faith and been punished accordingly. At the death of Akhenaten his memory

and that of Nefertiti were cursed, and their palace at Amarna was abandoned. This abandonment (and the fact that Amarna was recovered only in the twentieth century) accounts for the little that is now known of the royal couple. Nonetheless, no queen before Nefertiti had played such an active part in Egyptian religious life.

Nefertiti likewise played a novel role in Egyptian art. In funerary and temple art she is usually depicted with Akhenaten and their daughters. This practice went against the tradition of presenting the royal couple as austere and aloof. Instead, Nefertiti and Akhenaten were portrayed as an ordinary family. Their daughters often appear playing on their parents' laps or with one another. Even Nefertiti's own appearance in Egyptian art was a departure from tradition. As the illustration here shows, the famous bust of her is a realistic, not an idealized, portrait. The face is one of grace, beauty, and dignity. It is the portrait of an individual, not a type.

Nefertiti's bust has its own story. When Akhenaten's successor abandoned the palace at Amarna, the site was ignored, except as a source for building materials. Nefertiti's bust remained in the sculptor's workroom, which eventually caved in. There it lay, undamaged, for more than three thousand years. On December 6, 1912, a German archaeological team discovered it intact and sent it to Germany. After World War II, the bust was moved to its current home outside Berlin, where Nefertiti can still be admired today.

QUESTIONS FOR ANALYSIS

1. Did Nefertiti's individualism have any effect on Egyptian society?
2. Did she have a more profound and philosophical concept of divinity, or were her beliefs purely personal?

23

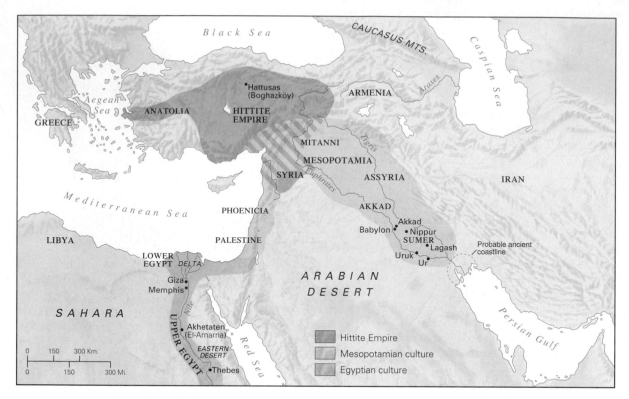

MAP 1.3 Balance of Power in the Near East This map shows the regions controlled by the Hittites and Egyptians at the height of their power. The striped area represents the part of Mesopotamia conquered by the Hittites during their expansion eastward.

Mursilis I (r. ca 1595 B.C.E.), extended the Hittite conquests as far as Babylon. Upon his return home, the victorious Mursilis was assassinated by members of his own family, an act that plunged the kingdom into confusion and opened the door to foreign invasion. Mursilis's career is representative of the success and weakness of the Hittites. They were extremely vulnerable to attack by vigilant and tenacious enemies. Yet once they were united behind a strong king, the Hittites were a power to be reckoned with.

Hittite Solar Disk This cult standard represents Hittite concepts of fertility and prosperity. The circle surrounding the animals is the sun, beneath which stands a stag flanked by two bulls. Stylized bull's horns spread from the base of the disk. The symbol is also one of might and protection from outside harm. *(Museum of Anatolian Civilizations, Ankara)*

The Hittites, like the Egyptians of the New Kingdom, produced an energetic and able line of kings who built a powerful empire. Perhaps their major contribution was the introduction of iron into war and agriculture in the form of weapons and tools. Around 1300 B.C.E. the Hittites stopped the Egyptian army of Rameses II at the Battle of Kadesh in Syria. Having fought each other to a standstill, the Hittites and Egyptians first made peace, then an alliance. Alliance was followed by friendship, and friendship by active cooperation. The two greatest powers of the early Near East tried to make war between them impossible.

They next included the Babylonians in their diplomacy. All three empires developed an official etiquette in which they treated one another as "brothers." They made alliances for offensive and defensive protection, and swore to uphold one another's authority. These contacts facilitated the exchange of ideas throughout the Near East. Furthermore, the Hittites passed much knowledge and lore from the Near East to the newly arrived Greeks in Europe. The details of Hittite contact with the Greeks are unknown, but enough literary themes and physical objects exist to prove the connection.

THE FALL OF EMPIRES AND THE SURVIVAL OF CULTURES (CA 1200 B.C.E.)

The height of Hittite and Egyptian power came to a tumultuous end, but the achievements of these peoples lasted long after their governments had been overthrown or diminished in power. New political alignments appeared, but to some degree they all adopted and adapted the examples of their predecessors. They likewise embraced the cultures of those whom they had replaced on the political map.

Political Chaos

Like the Hittite kings, Rameses II (r. ca 1290–1224 B.C.E.) used the peace after the Battle of Kadesh to promote the prosperity of his own kingdom. Free from the expense and waste of warfare, he concentrated the income from the natural wealth and the foreign trade of Egypt on internal affairs. In many ways, he was the last great pharaoh of Egypt.

This stable and generally peaceful situation endured until the late thirteenth century B.C.E., when both the Hittite and the Egyptian empires were destroyed by in-

vaders. The most famous of these marauders, called the **Sea Peoples** by the Egyptians, remain one of the puzzles of ancient history. Despite much new work, modern archaeology is still unable to identify the Sea Peoples satisfactorily. The reason for this uncertainty is that the Sea Peoples were a collection of peoples who went their own, individual ways after their attacks on the Hittites and Egyptians. It is known, however, that their incursions were part of a larger movement of peoples. Although there is serious doubt about whether the Sea Peoples alone overthrew the Hittites, they did deal both the Hittites and the Egyptians a hard blow, making the Hittites vulnerable to overland invasion from the north and driving the Egyptians back to the Nile Delta. The Hittites fell under the external blows, but the Egyptians, shaken and battered, retreated to the delta and held on.

Cultural Endurance and Dissemination

The Egyptians and Mesopotamians established basic social, economic, and cultural patterns in the ancient Near East. Moreover, they spread them far beyond their homelands. Egypt exerted vast influence in Palestine and Syria, while Mesopotamia was influential in southern Anatolia (modern Turkey). Yet it is a mistake to think that these older civilizations moved into a cultural vacuum.

In Palestine and southern Syria the Egyptians found Semitic peoples living in small walled towns. Municipal life was quite advanced, with towns that included urban centers and small outlying hamlets. Although these societies were primarily based on agriculture, there is ample evidence of international trade. In short, both Palestine and Syria possessed an extensive political, social, and religious organization even before the arrival of the Egyptians. Contact had begun as early as the Bronze Age, when the Egyptians had moved along the eastern Mediterranean coast. The contact immediately led to trade. The Egyptians exploited the turquoise and copper trade in the area, and exported local pottery and other goods. Sometimes the Egyptians traded peacefully, but at other times they resorted to military invasion.

Farther north the Egyptians made maritime contact with the Phoenicians, most clearly seen from the excavations at Byblos. The two peoples exchanged not only goods but also technological knowledge. The Egyptians learned many shipbuilding techniques, their own boats being better designed for the Nile than the open sea. The Phoenicians in turn adopted aspects of Egyptian technology. Yet the cultural exchange between the two peoples was by far more important. The Phoenicians honored some Egyptian gods and adopted Egyptian artistic motifs. They learned the Egyptian script and became acquainted with some Egyptian myths. At the same time some deities of Byblos made their appearance in Egypt. Despite armed conflict, trade, not warfare, generally characterized relations in the area.

The situation in northern Syria was similar to that in southern Syria and Palestine. Cities were common, normally ruled by royal families. The families usually shared power and dealt jointly with foreign affairs. They often left the internal administration of the cities to local elders. The cities were primarily mercantile centers but also rich in agricultural produce, timber, and metal deposits. The need for record keeping soon led to the development of writing. These northern Semites adopted Sumerian writing in order to understand their neighbors to the east, but they also adapted it to write their own northern Semitic language. Their texts provide a wealth of information about the life of northern Syria. In the process, northern Syrians gained a solid knowledge of Mesopotamian literature, mathematics, and culture. Both local and Sumerian deities were honored. Despite Mesopotamian influence, northern Syria maintained its native traditions. The cultural exchange was a mixture of adoption, adaptation, contrast, and finally balance, as the two cultures came to understand each other.

Southern Anatolia presented a somewhat similar picture. Human settlement there consisted of trading colonies and small agricultural communities. Thousands of cuneiform tablets testify to commercial and cultural exchanges with Mesopotamia. In Anatolia kingship and temple were closely allied, but the government was not a **theocracy** (rule by a priestly order). A city assembly worked together with the king, and provincial cities were administered by a prince. The political and social organization was one of a firmly established native culture that gladly received foreign ideas while keeping its own identity.

A pattern emerged in Palestine, Syria, and Anatolia. In these areas native cultures established themselves during the prehistoric period. Upon coming into contact with the Egyptian and Mesopotamian civilizations, they adopted many aspects of these cultures, adapting them to their own traditional customs. Yet they also contributed to the advance of Egyptian and Mesopotamian cultures by introducing new technologies and religious ideas. The result was the emergence of a huge group of communities stretching from Egypt in the south to Anatolia in the north and from the Levant in the west to Mesopotamia in the east. Each enjoyed its own individual character, while at the same time sharing many common features with its neighbors.

SUMMARY

For thousands of years Paleolithic peoples roamed this planet seeking game. Only in the Neolithic era—with the invention of new stone tools, a reliance on sustained agriculture, and the domestication of animals—did people begin to live in permanent locations. These villages evolved into towns, where people began to create new social bonds and political organizations. The result was economic prosperity.

The earliest area where these developments led to genuine urban societies is Mesopotamia. Here the Sumerians and then other Mesopotamians developed writing, which enabled their culture to be passed on to others. The wealth of the Mesopotamians made it possible for them to devote time to history, astronomy, urban planning, medicine, and other arts and sciences. Mesopotamian culture was so rich and advanced that neighboring peoples eagerly adopted it, thereby spreading it through much of the Near East.

Nor were the Mesopotamians alone in advancing the civilization of the day. In Egypt another strong culture developed, one that made an impact in Africa, the Near East, and, later, in Greece. The Egyptians too enjoyed such prosperity that they developed writing of their own, mathematical skills, and religious beliefs that influenced the lives of their neighbors. Into this world came the Hittites, an Indo-European people who were culturally less advanced than the Mesopotamians and Egyptians. The Hittites learned from their neighbors and rivals, but they also introduced their own sophisticated political system for administering their empire, a system that in some ways influenced both their contemporaries and later peoples.

KEY TERMS

Neolithic period	monotheism
irrigation	polytheism
cuneiform	Indo-European
nobles	Sea Peoples
clients	theocracy
law code	
Amon-Ra	
Book of the Dead	
pharaoh	
pyramid	
Hyksos	
Bronze Age	

NOTES

1. Quoted in S. N. Kramer, *The Sumerians* (Chicago: University of Chicago Press, 1963), p. 238. John Buckler is the translator of all uncited quotations from a foreign language in Chapter 1.
2. J. B. Pritchard, ed., *Ancient Near Eastern Texts,* 3d ed. (Princeton, N.J.: Princeton University Press, 1969), p. 590. Hereafter called ANET.
3. Ibid., p. 171.
4. Kramer, p. 251.
5. ANET, p. 372.
6. Herodotus, *The Histories* 2.14.
7. Quoted in A. H. Gardiner, "Ramesside Texts Relating to the Taxation and Transport of Corn," *Journal of Egyptian Archaeology* 27 (1941): 19–20.
8. Manetho, *History of Egypt,* frag. 42.75–77.

SUGGESTED READING

Some very illuminating general studies of Near Eastern developments have been published. A broad-ranging work, A. Kuhrt, *The Ancient Near East,* 2 vols. (1995), covers the region from the earliest time to Alexander's conquest, as does C. Snell, *Life in the Ancient Near East, 3100–332 B.C.E.,* which also covers social history. Most welcome is D. Schmandt-Besserat's two-volume work on the origins of writing, *Before Writing,* vol. 1 (1992), which explores the origins of writing, and vol. 2 (1992), which provides actual evidence on the topic. G. Visicato, *The Power of Writing* (2000), studies the practical importance of early Mesopotamian scribes. For the Stonehenge people A. Burl, the leading expert on the topic, provides *The Stonehenge People* (1987) and *Great Stone Circles* (1999), which examine the people and their monuments.

D. T. Potts, *Mesopotamian Civilization* (1996), presents a view of Mesopotamians from their material remains but is not purely architectural. H. W. F. Saggs, *The Babylonians* (2000), treats all the eras of Mesopotamian history. G. Stein and M. S. Rothman, *Chiefdoms and Early States in the Near East* (1994), provides a clear view of the political evolution of the region. An ambitious work is M. Hudson and B. Levine, *Privatization in the Ancient Near East and the Classical World* (1996), which treats the concept of private prop-

erty. A very ambitious and thoughtful book, G. Algaze, *The Uruk World System* (1993), examines how the early Mesopotamians expanded their civilization.

K. Mysliwiec, *The Twilight of Ancient Egypt* (2000), provides a history of Egypt in the first millennium B.C.E. D. P. Silverman, *Ancient Egypt* (1997), also gives a good general account of the region. S. Donadoni, ed., *The Egyptians* (1997), treats various aspects of Egyptian history and life. A. G. McDowell, *Village Life in Ancient Egypt* (1999), is a readable study of the basic social and economic factors of the entire period. D. Meeks and C. Favard-Meeks, *Daily Life of the Egyptian Gods* (1996), with a learned and original point of view, discusses how the Egyptian gods are sometimes treated in literature as an ethnic group not so very different from human beings. A. R. David, *Pyramid Builders of Ancient Egypt,* 2d ed. (1996), studies the lives of the people who actually labored to build the pyramids for their pharaohs. A. Blackman, *Gods, Priests and Men* (1993), is a series of studies in the religion of pharaonic Egypt. Z. Hawass, *Silent Images: Women in Pharaonic Egypt* (2000), blends text and pictures to draw a history of ancient Egyptian women. W. L. Moran, *The Amarna Letters* (1992), is a translation of the Egyptian documents so important to the understanding of the events of the New Kingdom. E. D. Oren, *The Hyksos* (1997), concentrates on the archaeological evidence for them.

The coming of the Indo-Europeans receives the attention of M. R. Dexter and K. Jones-Bley, eds., *The Kurgan Culture and the Indo-Europeanization of Europe* (1997), a controversial work that explores the homeland of the Indo-Europeans and the nature of their movements. Less challenging but perhaps more useful is A. Harding, *European Societies in the Bronze Age* (2000), a comprehensive survey of developments in Europe. Often and unfortunately neglected, the Hittites have received relatively little new attention. Dated but solid is O. R. Gurney, *The Hittites,* 2d ed. (1954), a fine introduction by an eminent scholar. Good also is J. G. Mac-Queen, *The Hittites and Their Contemporaries in Asia Minor,* 2d ed. (1986). The Sea Peoples have been studied by T. and M. Dothan, *People of the Sea* (1992), who concentrate their work on the Philistines.

A truly excellent study of ancient religions, from Sumer to the late Roman Empire, is M. Eliade, ed., *Religions of Antiquity* (1989), which treats concisely but amply all of the religions mentioned in Chapters 1, 2, 5, and 6.

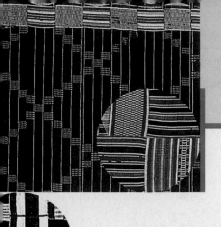

A QUEST FOR IMMORTALITY

The human desire to escape the grip of death, to achieve immortality, is one of the oldest wishes of all peoples. The Sumerian *Epic of Gilgamesh is the earliest recorded treatment of this topic. The oldest elements of the epic go back at least to the third millennium* B.C.E. *According to tradition, Gilgamesh was a king of Uruk whom the Sumerians, Babylonians, and Assyrians considered a hero-king and a god. In the story Gilgamesh and his friend Enkidu set out to attain immortality and join the ranks of the gods. They attempt to do so by performing wondrous feats against fearsome agents of the gods, who are determined to thwart them.*

During their quest Enkidu dies. Gilgamesh, more determined than ever to become immortal, begins seeking anyone who might tell him how to do so. His journey involves the effort not only to escape from death but also to reach an understanding of the meaning of life.

The passage begins with Enkidu speaking of a dream that foretells his own death.

Listen, my friend [Gilgamesh], this is the dream I dreamed last night. The heavens roared, and earth rumbled back an answer; between them I stood before an awful being, the sombre-faced man-bird; he had directed on me his purpose. His was a vampire face, his foot was a lion's foot, his hand was an eagle's talon. He fell on me and his claws were in my hair, he held me fast and I smothered; then he transformed me so that my arms became wings covered with feathers. He turned his stare towards me, and he led me away to the palace of Irkalla, the Queen of Darkness [the goddess of the underworld; in other words, an agent of death], to the house from which none who enters ever returns, down the road from which there is no coming back.

At this point Enkidu dies, whereupon Gilgamesh sets off on his quest for the secret of immortality. During his travels he meets with Siduri, the wise and good-natured goddess of wine, who gives him the following advice.

Gilgamesh, where are you hurrying to? You will never find that life for which you are looking. When the gods created man they allotted to him death, but life they retained in their own keeping. As for you, Gilgamesh, fill your belly with good things; day and night, night and day, dance and be merry, feast and rejoice. Let your clothes be fresh, bathe yourself in water, cherish the little child that holds your hand, and make your wife happy in your embrace; for this too is the lot of man.

Ignoring Siduri's advice, Gilgamesh continues his journey, until he finds Utnapishtim. Meeting Utnapishtim is especially important because, like Gilgamesh, he was once a mortal, but the gods so favored him that they put him in an eternal paradise. Gilgamesh puts to Utnapishtim the question that is the reason for his quest.

Oh, father Utnapishtim, you who have entered the assembly of the gods, I wish to question you concerning the living and the dead, how shall I find the life for which I am searching?

Utnapishtim said, "There is no permanence. Do we build a house to stand forever, do we seal a contract to hold for all time? Do brothers divide an inheritance to keep forever, does the flood-time of rivers endure? . . . What is there between the master and the servant when both have fulfilled their doom? When the Anunnaki [the gods of the underworld], the judges, come together, and Mammetun [the goddess of fate] the mother of destinies, together they decree the fates of men. Life and death they allot but the day of death they do not disclose.

Then Gilgamesh said to Utnapishtim the Faraway, "I look at you now, Utnapishtim, and your appearance is no different from mine; there is nothing strange in your features. I thought I should find you like a hero prepared for battle, but you lie here taking your ease on your back. Tell me truly, how was it that you came to enter the company of the gods and to possess everlasting life?" Utnapishtim said to Gilgamesh, "I shall reveal to you a mystery, I shall tell you a secret of the gods."

Utnapishtim then tells Gilgamesh of a time when the great god Enlil had become angered with the Sumerians and encouraged the other gods to wipe out humanity. The god Ea, however, warned Utnapishtim about the gods' decision to send a great flood to destroy the Sumerians. He commanded Utnapishtim to build a boat big enough to hold his family, various artisans, and all animals in order to survive the flood that was to come. Although Enlil was infuriated by the Sumerians' survival, Ea rebuked him. Then Enlil relented and blessed Utnapishtim with eternal paradise. After telling the story, Utnapishtim foretells Gilgamesh's fate.

Utnapishtim said, ". . . The destiny was fulfilled which the father of the gods, Enlil of the mountain, had decreed for Gilgamesh: In nether-earth the darkness will show him a light: of mankind, all that are known, none will leave a monument for generations to compare with his. The heroes, the wise men, like the new moon have their waxing and waning. Men will say, Who has ever ruled with might and power like his? As in the dark month, the month of shadows, so without him there is no light. O Gilgamesh, this was the meaning of your dream [of immortality]. You were given the kingship, such was your destiny, everlasting life was not your destiny. Because of this do not be sad at heart, do not be grieved or oppressed; he [Enlil] has given you power to bind and to loose, to be the darkness and the light of mankind. He has given unexampled supremacy over the people, victory in battle from which no

Gilgamesh, from decorative panel of a lyre unearthed at Ur. *(The University Museum, University of Pennsylvania, neg. T4-108)*

fugitive returns, in forays and assaults from which there is no going back. But do not abuse this power, deal justly with your servants in the palace, deal justly before the face of the Sun."

QUESTIONS FOR ANALYSIS

1. What does the *Epic of Gilgamesh* reveal about Sumerian attitudes toward the gods and human beings?

2. At the end of his quest, did Gilgamesh achieve immortality? If so, what was the nature of that immortality?

3. What does the epic tell us about Sumerian views of the nature of human life? Where do human beings fit into the cosmic world?

Source: The Epic of Gilgamesh, translated by N. K. Sanders. Penguin Classics 1960, Second revised edition, 1972, pp. 91–119. Copyright © N. K. Sanders, 1960, 1964, 1972. Reproduced by permission of Penguin Books Ltd.

Reconstruction of the "Ishtar Gate," Babylon, early sixth century B.C.E. Located in the Berlin Museum. *(Staatliche Museen zu Berlin/Bildarchiv Preussicher Kulturbesitz)*

CHAPTER

2

SMALL KINGDOMS AND MIGHTY EMPIRES IN THE NEAR EAST

CHAPTER OUTLINE

- Recovery and Diffusion

- A Shattered Egypt and a Rising Phoenicia

- The Children of Israel

- Assyria, the Military Monarchy

- The Empire of the Persian Kings

The migratory invasions that brought down the Hittites and stunned the Egyptians in the late thirteenth century B.C.E. ushered in an era of confusion and weakness. Although much was lost in the chaos, the old cultures of the ancient Near East survived to nurture new societies. In the absence of powerful empires, the Phoenicians, Hebrews, and many other peoples carved out small independent kingdoms, until the Near East was a patchwork of them. During this period Hebrew culture and religion evolved under the influence of urbanism, kings, and prophets.

In the ninth century B.C.E. this jumble of small states gave way to an empire that for the first time embraced the entire Near East. Yet the very ferocity of the Assyrian Empire led to its downfall only two hundred years later. In 550 B.C.E. the Persians and Medes, who had migrated into Iran, created a "world empire" stretching from Anatolia in the west to the Indus Valley in the east. For over two hundred years the Persians gave the ancient Near East peace and stability.

- How did Egypt, its political greatness behind it, pass on its cultural heritage to its African neighbors?
- How did the Hebrew state evolve, and what was daily life like in Hebrew society?
- What forces helped to shape Hebrew religious thought, still powerfully influential in today's world?
- What enabled the Assyrians to overrun their neighbors, and how did their cruelty finally cause their undoing?
- Last, how did Iranian nomads create the Persian Empire?

This chapter will look at these questions.

RECOVERY AND DIFFUSION

If the fall of empires was a time of massive political disruption, it also ushered in a period of cultural diffusion, an expansion of what had already blossomed in the broad region. Even though empires expired, many small kingdoms survived, along with a largely shared culture. These small states and local societies had

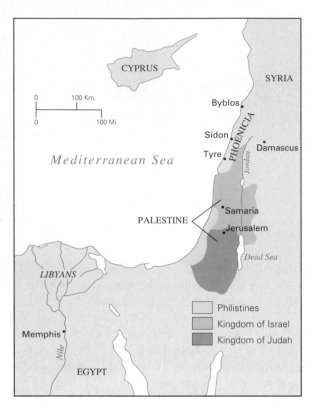

MAP 2.1 Small Kingdoms of the Near East   This map illustrates the political fragmentation of the Near East after the great wave of invasions that occurred during the thirteenth century B.C.E.

learned much from the great powers, but they nonetheless retained their own lore and native traditions, which they passed on to their neighbors, thus diffusing a Near Eastern culture that was slowly becoming common in nature. The best-known examples can be found along the coast of the eastern Mediterranean, where various peoples—some of them newcomers—created homes and petty kingdoms in Phoenicia and Palestine. After the Sea Peoples raided Egypt, a branch of them, known in the Bible as Philistines, settled along the coast of Palestine (see Map 2.1). Establishing themselves in five cities somewhat inland from the sea, the Philistines set about farming and raising flocks.

A SHATTERED EGYPT AND A RISING PHOENICIA

The invasions of the Sea Peoples brought the great days of Egyptian power to an end. The long wars against invaders weakened and impoverished Egypt, causing polit-

ical upheaval and economic chaos. One scribe left behind a somber portrait of Egypt stunned and leaderless:

The land of Egypt was abandoned and every man was a law to himself. During many years there was no leader who could speak for others. Central government lapsed, small officials and headmen took over the whole land. Any man, great or small, might kill his neighbor. In the distress and vacuum that followed . . . men banded together to plunder one another. They treated the gods no better than men, and cut off the temple revenues.[1]

No longer able to dream of foreign conquests, Egypt looked to its own security from foreign invasion. Egyptians suffered a four-hundred-year period of political fragmentation, a new dark age known to Egyptian specialists as the Third Intermediate Period (eleventh to seventh centuries B.C.E.). (See the feature "Individuals in Society: Wen-Amon" on page 35.)

The decline of Egypt was especially sharp in foreign affairs. Whereas the pharaohs of the Eighteenth Dynasty had held sway as far abroad as Syria, their weak successors found it unsafe to venture far from home. In the wake of the Sea Peoples, numerous small kingdoms sprang up in the Near East, each fiercely protective of its own independence. To them Egypt was a memory. Disrupted at home and powerless abroad, Egypt fell prey to invasion by its African neighbors. From 950 to 730 B.C.E. northern Egypt was ruled by Libyan pharaohs, who had come from North Africa. The Libyans built cities, and for the first time a sturdy urban life grew up in the Nile Delta. Although the Libyans changed the face of the delta, they genuinely admired Egyptian culture and eagerly adopted Egypt's religion and way of life.

In southern Egypt, meanwhile, the pharaoh's decline opened the way to the energetic Nubians, who extended their authority northward throughout the Nile Valley. Since the imperial days of the Eighteenth Dynasty (see pages 21–22), the Nubians, too, had adopted many features of Egyptian culture. Now Nubian kings and aristocrats embraced Egyptian culture wholesale. Thus the Nubians and the Libyans repeated an old Near Eastern phenomenon: new peoples conquered old centers of political and military power but were assimilated into the older culture.

The reunification of Egypt occurred late and unexpectedly. With Egypt distracted and disorganized by foreign invasions, an independent African state, the kingdom of Kush, grew up in the region of modern Sudan with its capital at Nepata. Like the Libyans, the Kushites worshiped Egyptian gods and used Egyptian hieroglyphs. In the eighth century B.C.E. their king, Piankhy, swept through the entire Nile Valley from Nepata in the south to the delta in the north. United once again, Egypt enjoyed a brief

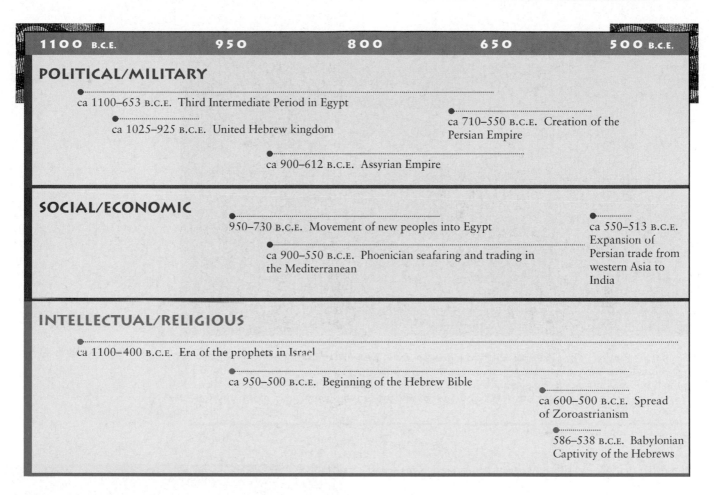

1100 B.C.E.	950	800	650	500 B.C.E.

POLITICAL/MILITARY

ca 1100–653 B.C.E. Third Intermediate Period in Egypt

ca 1025–925 B.C.E. United Hebrew kingdom

ca 710–550 B.C.E. Creation of the Persian Empire

ca 900–612 B.C.E. Assyrian Empire

SOCIAL/ECONOMIC

950–730 B.C.E. Movement of new peoples into Egypt

ca 550–513 B.C.E. Expansion of Persian trade from western Asia to India

ca 900–550 B.C.E. Phoenician seafaring and trading in the Mediterranean

INTELLECTUAL/RELIGIOUS

ca 1100–400 B.C.E. Era of the prophets in Israel

ca 950–500 B.C.E. Beginning of the Hebrew Bible

ca 600–500 B.C.E. Spread of Zoroastrianism

586–538 B.C.E. Babylonian Captivity of the Hebrews

period of peace during which the Egyptians continued to assimilate their conquerors. Nonetheless, reunification of the realm did not lead to a new Egyptian empire.

Yet Egypt's legacy to its African neighbors remained vibrant and rich. By trading and exploring southward along the coast of the Red Sea, the Egyptians introduced their goods and ideas as far south as the land of Punt, probably a region on the Somali coast. Egypt was the primary civilizing force in Nubia, which became another version of the pharaoh's realm, complete with royal pyramids and

Life Goes On   Although the Egyptians suffered political defeat, much of their society continued without interruption. Here a farmer and two oxen still plow their field as usual. In many instances, a change of rule did not greatly affect the lives of ordinary people. *(Archaeological site, Luxor/ Erich Lessing/Art Resource, NY)*

Nubian Pyramids   The Nubians adopted many aspects of Egyptian culture and customs. The pyramids shown here are not as magnificent as their Egyptian predecessors, but they served the same purpose of honoring the dead king. Their core was constructed of bricks, which were then covered with stone blocks. At the doors of the pyramids stood monumental gates to the interiors of the tombs. *(Michael Yamashita)*

Egyptian deities. Egyptian religion penetrated as far south as Ethiopia.

One of the sturdy peoples who rose to prominence were the Phoenicians, a Semitic-speaking people who had long inhabited several cities along the coast of modern Lebanon. They had lived under the shadow of the Hittites and Egyptians, but in this period the Phoenicians enjoyed full independence. Unlike the Philistine newcomers, who turned from seafaring to farming, the Phoenicians took to the sea and became outstanding merchants and explorers. They played a predominate role in international trade, manufacturing many goods. The most valued products were purple and blue textiles, from which originated their Greek name, Phoenicians, meaning **"Purple People."** They also worked metals, which they shipped processed or as ore. They imported rare goods and materials from Persia in the East and from their neighbors to the south. Their exported wares went to Egypt, as far west as North Africa and Spain, and even into the Atlantic. The variety and quality of their exports generally made them welcome visitors. Although their goal was trade, not colonization, they nevertheless founded Carthage in 813 B.C.E., a city that would one day struggle with Rome for domination of the western

Phoenician Maritime Trade   In this Assyrian relief dating from the eighth century B.C.E., Phoenician ships tow hewn logs for building purposes to a foreign port. Phoenician ships like these not only plied the eastern Aegean but also ventured into the western Mediterranean. *(Louvre/Erich Lessing/Art Resource, NY)*

INDIVIDUALS IN SOCIETY

WEN-AMON

Pillars of the great temple of Amon at Karnak, New Kingdom. (Marc Bernheim/Woodfin Camp & Associates)

Surprising as it may sound, the life of a bureaucrat is not always easy. Wen-Amon, an official of the temple of Amon-Ra at Karnak in Egypt, learned that on an authorized mission to Phoenicia. He left his own narrative of his travels, which date to sometime in the eleventh century B.C.E. Egypt, the shattered kingdom, could no longer exert the authority that it had enjoyed under the pharaohs of the New Kingdom. Despite this political disruption, Egyptian officials continued to expect the traditional respect of the people whom they called "Asiatics." These Asiatics, however, had begun to doubt the power of Egypt and expressed their independence by openly opposing its authority.

Wen-Amon personally experienced this changed atmosphere when he was sent to Byblos in Phoenicia to obtain lumber for Amon-Ra's ceremonial barge. Wen-Amon's detailed account of his experiences comes in the form of an official report to the chief priest of the temple.

Entrusted with ample funds in silver to pay for the lumber, Wen-Amon set out on his voyage. He docked at Dor, in modern Israel, which was independent of the pharaoh, but the local prince received him graciously. While his ship was at anchor, one of Wen-Amon's own sailors vanished with the silver. Wen-Amon immediately reported the robbery to the prince and demanded that he investigate the theft. Wen-Amon pointed out that the silver belonged to Amon-Ra and the great men of Egypt. The prince flatly told Wen-Amon that he did not care whether Wen-Amon and the others were important men. He pointed out that an Egyptian, one of Wen-Amon's own men, had stolen the silver. It was not the prince's problem. No earlier Asian prince would have dared speak to a high Egyptian official in such terms.

Although rebuffed, Wen-Amon found a ship from Byblos and robbed it of an equivalent amount of silver. When he left Dor and entered the harbor of Byblos, the prince there, who had learned of the theft, ordered him to leave. For twenty-nine days there was an impasse. Each day that Wen-Amon remained, the prince told him to get out, but respect both for the great days of Egypt and for Amon-Ra kept the prince from laying hands on Wen-Amon. Finally, the prince sent for Wen-Amon and asked for his papers. A heated argument ensued, with the prince shouting, "I am not your servant. I am not the servant of him who sent you either." Then he asked Wen-Amon what silly voyage he was making. By this time the Egyptian was greatly annoyed, and he reminded the prince of the greatness of Amon-Ra. He flatly stated that unless the prince honored the great god, he and his land would have neither health nor prosperity. When the two calmed down, the prince agreed to send the timber to Egypt.

After the timber was loaded aboard his ship, Wen-Amon saw eleven enemy ships entering the harbor. They anchored, and those in charge reported to the prince of Byblos that they had come for the Egyptians. He refused to hand them over, saying that he would never arrest a messenger of Amon-Ra. He agreed, however, to send Wen-Amon away first and allow the enemy ships to pursue the Egyptians. Stormy seas blew the Egyptian ship into Hittite territory. When Wen-Amon landed there, Queen Heteb granted him protection and asylum.

The papyrus breaks off at this point, but it is obvious that Wen-Amon weathered his various storms to return safely to Egypt. The document illustrates the presumption of power by Wen-Amon and his bluster at the lack of respect shown him. It also shows how Egypt's neighbors no longer feared Egyptian power. Finally, it illustrates the impact of Egyptian culture and religion on the peoples living along the coast of the Levant. Although Egyptian political power was in eclipse, its cultural legacy endured.

QUESTIONS FOR ANALYSIS

1. What do Wen-Amon's experiences tell us about political conditions in the eastern Mediterranean?
2. Since Wen-Amon could no longer depend upon the majesty of Egypt for respect, how did he fulfill his duty?

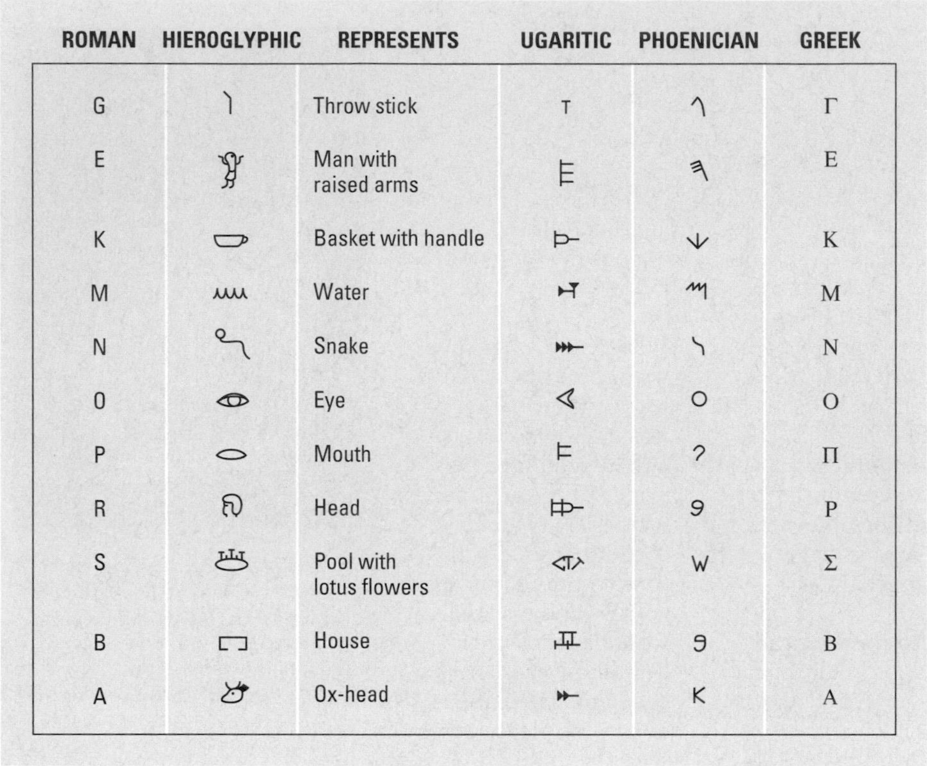

ROMAN	HIEROGLYPHIC	REPRESENTS	UGARITIC	PHOENICIAN	GREEK
G		Throw stick			Γ
E		Man with raised arms			E
K		Basket with handle			K
M		Water			M
N		Snake			N
O		Eye			O
P		Mouth			Π
R		Head			P
S		Pool with lotus flowers			Σ
B		House			B
A		Ox-head			A

FIGURE 2.1 Origins of the Alphabet   List of Roman, hieroglyphic, Ugaritic, Phoenician, and Greek sign forms. *(Source: A. B. Knapp,* The History and Culture of Ancient Western Asia and Egypt, *Dorsey Press, Chicago, 1988, p. 191. Reprinted by permission of Wadsworth, a division of Thomson Learning.)*

Mediterranean. Their voyages naturally brought them into contact with the Greeks, to whom they introduced the older cultures of the Near East. Indeed, their enduring significance lay in their spreading the experiences of the East throughout the western Mediterranean.

Phoenician culture was urban, based on the prosperous commercial centers of Tyre, Sidon, and Byblos. The Phoenicians' overwhelming cultural achievement was the development of an alphabet (see Figure 2.1): they, unlike other literate peoples, used one letter to designate one sound, a system that vastly simplified writing and reading. The Greeks modified this alphabet and then used it to write their own language.

THE CHILDREN OF ISRAEL

The fall of the Hittite Empire and Egypt's collapse created a vacuum of power in the western Near East that allowed for the rise of numerous small states. South of Phoenicia arose a small kingdom, the land of the ancient Jews or Hebrews. It is difficult to say precisely who the Hebrews were and what brought them to this area, because virtually the only source for much of their history is

the Bible, which is essentially a religious document. Even though it contains much historical material, it also contains many Hebrew myths and legends. Moreover, it was compiled at different times, with the earliest parts dating to between about 950 and 800 B.C.E.

Earlier Mesopotamian and Egyptian sources refer to people called the **Hapiru,** which seems to mean homeless, independent **nomads.** These nomads led roaming lives, always in search of pasturage for their flocks. According to Hebrew tradition, the followers of Abraham migrated from Mesopotamia, but Egyptian documents record Hapiru already in Syria and Palestine in the second millennium B.C.E. The Hebrews were probably a part of them. Together with other seminomadic peoples, they probably migrated into the Nile Delta seeking good land. According to the Bible the Egyptians enslaved them. One group, however, under the leadership of Moses, perhaps a semimythical figure, left Egypt in what the Hebrews remembered as the Exodus. From Egypt they wandered in the Sinai Peninsula, until they settled in Palestine in the thirteenth century B.C.E.

In Palestine the Hebrews encountered the Philistines; the Amorites, relatives of Hammurabi's Babylonians; and the Semitic-speaking Canaanites. Despite numerous wars, contact between the Hebrews and their new neighbors was not always hostile. The Hebrews freely mingled with the Canaanites, and some went so far as to worship **Baal,** an ancient Semitic fertility god represented as a golden calf. Archaeological research supports the biblical account of these developments. In 1990 an expedition sponsored by Harvard University discovered a statue of a golden calf in its excavations of Ashkelon in modern Israel. Despite the anger expressed in the Bible over Hebrew worship of Baal, there is nothing surprising about the phenomenon. Once again, newcomers adapted themselves to the culture of an older, well-established people.

The greatest danger to the Hebrews came from the Philistines, whose superior technology and military organization at first made them invincible. In Saul (ca 1000 B.C.E.), a farmer of the tribe of Benjamin, the Hebrews found a champion and a spirited leader. In the biblical account Saul carried the war to the Philistines, often without success. Yet in the meantime he established a monarchy over the twelve Hebrew tribes.

Saul's work was carried on by David of Bethlehem, who in his youth had followed Saul into battle against the Philistines. Through courage and cunning, David pushed back the Philistines and waged war against his other neighbors. To give his kingdom a capital, he captured the city of Jerusalem, which he enlarged, fortified, and made the religious and political center of his realm. David's military successes won the Hebrews unprecedented security, and his forty-year reign was a period of vitality and political consolidation. His work in consolidating the monarchy and enlarging the kingdom paved the way for his son Solomon.

Solomon (ca 965–925 B.C.E.) applied his energies to creating a nation out of a collection of tribes ruled by a king. He divided the kingdom into twelve territorial districts cutting across the old tribal borders. To bring his kingdom up to the level of its more sophisticated neighbors, he set about a building program to make Israel a respectable Near Eastern state. Work was begun on a magnificent temple in Jerusalem and on cities, palaces, fortresses, and roads. Solomon dedicated the temple in grand style and made it the home of the Ark of the Covenant, the cherished chest that contained the holiest of Hebrew religious articles. The temple in Jerusalem was intended to be the religious heart of the kingdom and the symbol of Hebrew unity. Solomon turned a rude kingdom into a state with broad commercial horizons and greater knowledge of the outside world. At his death, the Hebrews broke into two political halves (see Map 2.1). The northern part of the kingdom of David and Solomon became Israel, with its capital at Samaria. The southern

half was Judah, and Jerusalem remained its center. With political division went a religious rift: Israel, the northern kingdom, established rival sanctuaries for gods other than Yahweh. The Hebrew nation was divided, but at least it was divided into two far more sophisticated political units than before the time of Solomon. Nonetheless, war soon broke out between them, as recorded in the Bible. Unexpected and independent evidence of this warfare came to light in August 1993, when an Israeli archaeologist found an inscription that refers to the "House of David," the royal line of Israel. The stone celebrates an Israelite victory from the early ninth century B.C.E. This discovery is the first mention of King David's royal family outside

The Golden Calf   According to the Hebrew Bible, Moses descended from Mount Sinai, where he had received the Ten Commandments, to find the Hebrews worshiping a golden calf, which was against Yahweh's laws. In July 1990 an American archaeological team found this model of a gilded calf inside a pot. The figurine, which dates to about 1550 B.C.E., is strong evidence for the existence of the cult represented by the calf in Palestine. *(Courtesy of the Leon Levy Expedition to Ashkelon. Photo: Carl Andrews)*

Megiddo This aerial view shows the substantial fortress of Megiddo, in modern Israel, which was a stronghold on the frontiers of Syria and Egypt. Standing atop a small plateau, it was heavily fortified and commanded a fertile plain. It also stood astride the major road between Egypt and the north, making it strategically valuable. It was the scene of a major battle in which the Egyptians routed a Canaanite army. *(Rolf Michael Kneller)*

the Bible and helps to confirm the biblical account of the fighting between the two kingdoms.

Eventually, the northern kingdom of Israel was wiped out by the Assyrians, but the southern kingdom of Judah survived numerous calamities until the Babylonians crushed it in 587 B.C.E. The survivors were sent into exile in Babylonia, a period commonly known as the **Babylonian Captivity.** In 538 B.C.E. the Persians, under their king, Cyrus the Great, permitted some forty thousand exiles to return to Jerusalem. During and especially after the Babylonian Captivity, the exiles redefined their beliefs and practices, and thus established what they believed was the law of Yahweh. Those who lived by these precepts can be called *Jews*.

The Evolution of Jewish Religion

Hand in hand with their political evolution from fierce nomads to urban dwellers, the Hebrews were evolving spiritual ideas that still permeate Western society. Their chief literary product, the Hebrew Bible, has fundamentally influenced both Christianity and Islam and still exerts a compelling force on the modern world.

Fundamental to an understanding of Jewish religion is the concept of the **Covenant,** a formal agreement between Yahweh and the Hebrew people. According to the Bible, the god **Yahweh,** who in medieval Latin became "Jehovah," appeared to Moses on Mount Sinai. There Yahweh made a covenant with the Hebrews that was in fact a contract: if the Hebrews worshiped Yahweh as their only god, he would consider them his chosen people and protect them from their enemies. The Hebrews believed that Yahweh had led them out of bondage in Egypt and had helped them to conquer their new land, the Promised Land. In return, the Hebrews worshiped Yahweh alone and obeyed his Ten Commandments, an ethical code of conduct revealed to them by Moses.

At first Yahweh was probably viewed as no more than the god of the Hebrews, who sometimes faced competition from Baal and other gods in Palestine. Enlil, Marduk, Amon-Ra, and the others sufficed for foreigners. In time, however, the Hebrews came to regard Yahweh as the only god. This was the beginning of true monotheism.

Unlike Akhenaten's monotheism, Hebrew monotheism became the religion of a whole people, deeply felt and cherished. Some might fall away from Yahweh's worship, and various holy men had to exhort the Hebrews to honor the Covenant, but on the whole the people clung to Yahweh. Yet the Hebrews did not consider it their duty to spread the belief in the one god, as later Christians did. As the chosen people, their chief duty was to maintain the worship of Yahweh as he demanded. That worship was embodied in the Ten Commandments, which forbade the Hebrews to steal, murder, lie, or commit adultery. The Covenant was a constant force in Hebrew life (see the feature "Listening to the Past: The Covenant Between Yahweh and the Hebrews" on pages 50–51), and the Old Testament records one occasion when the entire nation formally reaffirmed it:

And the king [of the Jews] stood by a pillar, and made a covenant before the lord, to walk after the lord, and to keep his commandments and his testimonies and his statutes with all their heart and all their soul, to perform the words of this covenant that were written in this book [Deuteronomy]. And all the people stood to the covenant.[2]

From the Ten Commandments evolved Hebrew law, a code of law and custom originating with Moses and built on by priests and prophets. The earliest part of this code, the **Torah** or Mosaic law, was often as harsh as Hammurabi's code, which had a powerful impact on it. Later tradition, largely the work of prophets who lived from the eleventh to the fifth centuries B.C.E., was more humanitarian. The work of the prophet Jeremiah (ca 626 B.C.E.) exemplifies this gentler spirit. According to Jeremiah, Yahweh demanded righteousness from his people and protection for the weak and helpless.

The uniqueness of this phenomenon can be seen by comparing the essence of Hebrew monotheism with the religious outlook of the Mesopotamians. Whereas the Mesopotamians considered their gods capricious, the Hebrews knew what Yahweh expected. The Hebrews believed that their god would protect them and make them prosper if they obeyed his commandments. The Mesopotamians thought human beings insignificant compared to the gods, so insignificant that the gods might even be indifferent to them. The Hebrews, too, considered themselves puny in comparison to Yahweh. Yet they were Yahweh's chosen people, whom he had promised never to abandon. Finally, though the Mesopotamians believed that the gods generally preferred good to evil, their religion did not demand ethical conduct. The Hebrews could please their god only by living up to high moral standards as well as worshiping him.

Daily Life in Israel

The nomadic Hebrews first entered modern Palestine as tribes, numerous families who thought of themselves as all related to one another. At first, good farmland, pastureland, and water spots were held in common by the tribe. Common use of land was—and still is—characteristic of nomadic peoples. Typically each family or group of families in the tribe drew lots every year to determine who worked which fields. But as formerly nomadic peoples turned increasingly to settled agriculture, communal use of land gave way to family ownership. In this respect the experience of the ancient Hebrews seems typical of that of many early peoples. Slowly the shift from nomad to farmer affected far more than just how people fed themselves. Family relationships reflected evolving circumstances. With the transition to settled agriculture, the tribe gradually became less important than the extended family. With the advent of village life and finally full-blown urban life, the extended family in turn gave way to the nuclear family.

For women, however, the evolution of Jewish society led to less freedom of action, especially in religious life. At first women served as priestesses in festivals and religious cults. Some were considered prophetesses of Yahweh, although they never conducted his official rituals. In the course of time, however, the worship of Yahweh became more male-oriented and male-dominated. Increasingly, he also became the god of holiness, and to worship him people must be pure in mind and body. Women were seen as ritually impure because of menstruation and childbirth. Because of these "impurities," women now played a much reduced role in religion. Even when they did participate in religious rites, they were segregated from the men. For the most part, women were largely confined to the home and the care of the family.

Marriage was one of the most important and joyous events in Hebrew family life. The typical marriage in ancient Israel was monogamous, and a virtuous wife was revered and honored.

As in most other societies, in ancient Israel the early education of children was in the mother's hands. She taught her children right from wrong and gave them their first instruction in the moral values of society. As boys grew older, they received education from their fathers in religion and the history of their people. Many children were taught to read and write, and the head of each family was probably able to write. Fathers also taught sons the family craft or trade. Boys soon learned that inattention could be painful, for Jewish custom advised fathers to be strict: "He that spareth his rod hateth his son: but he that loveth him chasteneth him betimes."[3]

The land was precious to the family, not simply because it provided a living, but also because it was a link to the past. Ironically, the success of the first Hebrew kings endangered the future of many family farms. With peace, more settled conditions, and increasing prosperity, some Jews began to amass larger holdings by buying out poor and struggling farmers. Far from discouraging this development, the kings created their own huge estates. In many cases slaves, both Jewish and foreign, worked these large farms and estates shoulder to shoulder with paid free men. In still later times, rich landowners rented plots of land to poor, free families; the landowners provided the renters with seed and livestock and normally took half the yield as rent. Although many Bible prophets denounced the destruction of the family farm, the trend continued toward large estates that were worked by slaves and hired free men.

The development of urban life among the Jews created new economic opportunities, especially in crafts and trades. People specialized in certain occupations, such as milling flour, baking bread, making pottery, weaving, and carpentry. All these crafts were family trades. Sons worked with their father, daughters with their mother. If the business prospered, the family might be assisted by a few paid workers or slaves. The practitioners of a craft usually lived in a particular section of town, a custom still prevalent in the Middle East today. Commerce and trade developed later than crafts. Trade with neighboring countries was handled by foreigners, usually Phoenicians. Jews dealt mainly in local trade, and in most instances craftsmen and farmers sold directly to their customers.

These social and economic developments also left their mark on daily life by prompting the compilation of two significant works, the Torah and the Talmud. The Torah is basically the Mosaic law, or the first five books of the Bible. The Talmud is a later work composed during the period between the Roman destruction of the second temple in 70 C.E. to the Arab conquest of 636 C.E. The **Talmud** records civil and ceremonial law and Jewish legend. The dietary rules of the Jews provide an excellent example of both the relationship between the Torah and the Talmud and their effect on ordinary life and culture. According to the Torah, people were not to eat meat that they found in the field. This very sensible prohibition protected them from eating dangerous food. Yet if meat from the countryside could not be eaten, some rules were needed for meat in the city. The solution found in the Talmud was a set of regulations for the proper way to conduct ritual slaughter. Together these two works regulated and codified Jewish dietary customs.

ASSYRIA, THE MILITARY MONARCHY

Small kingdoms like those of the Phoenicians and the Hebrews could exist only in the absence of a major power. The beginning of the ninth century B.C.E. saw the rise of such a power: the Assyrians of northern Mesopotamia, whose chief capital was at Nineveh on the Tigris River. The Assyrians were a Semitic-speaking people heavily influenced, like so many other peoples of the Near East, by the Mesopotamian culture of Babylon to the south. They were also one of the most warlike peoples in history, largely because throughout their history they were threatened by neighboring folk. Living in an open, exposed land, the Assyrians experienced frequent and devastating attacks by the wild, war-loving tribes to their north and east and by the Babylonians to the south. The constant threat to survival experienced by the Assyrians promoted political cohesion and military might. Yet they were also a mercantile people who had long pursued commerce with both the Babylonians in the south and other peoples in the north.

The Power of Assyria

For over two hundred years the Assyrians labored to dominate the Near East. In 859 B.C.E. the new Assyrian king, Shalmaneser, unleashed the first of a long series of attacks on the peoples of Syria and Palestine. Year after relentless year, Assyrian armies hammered at the peoples of the West. These ominous events inaugurated two turbulent centuries marked by Assyrian military campaigns, constant efforts by Syria and the two Jewish kingdoms to maintain or recover their independence, and eventual Assyrian conquest

Surrender of the Jews   The Jewish king Jahu finally surrendered to the Assyrians. Here his envoy kneels before the Assyrian king Shalmaneser III in total defeat. Although the Assyrian king treated Jahu well, his people were led off into slavery. *(British Museum/ Michael Holford)*

of Babylonia and northern Egypt. In addition, periodic political instability occurred in Assyria itself, which prompted stirrings of freedom throughout the Near East.

Under the Assyrian kings Tiglath-pileser III (774–727 B.C.E.) and Sargon II (r. 721–705 B.C.E.), both mighty warriors, the Near East trembled as never before under the blows of Assyrian armies. The Assyrians stepped up their attacks on Anatolia, Syria, and Palestine. The kingdom of Israel and many other states fell; others, like the

kingdom of Judah, became subservient to the warriors from the Tigris. In 717 to 716 B.C.E., Sargon led his army in a sweeping attack along the Philistine coast, where he defeated the pharaoh. Sargon also lashed out at Assyria's traditional enemies to the north and then turned south against a renewed threat in Babylonia. By means of almost constant warfare, Tiglath-pileser III and Sargon carved out an Assyrian empire that stretched from east and north of the Tigris River to central Egypt (see Map 2.2). Revolt

Siege of a City   Art here serves to glorify horror. The Assyrian king Tiglath-pileser III launches an assault on a fortified city. The impaled bodies shown at center demonstrate the cruelty of Assyrian warfare. Also noticeable are the various weapons and means of attack used against the city. *(Courtesy of the Trustees of the British Museum)*

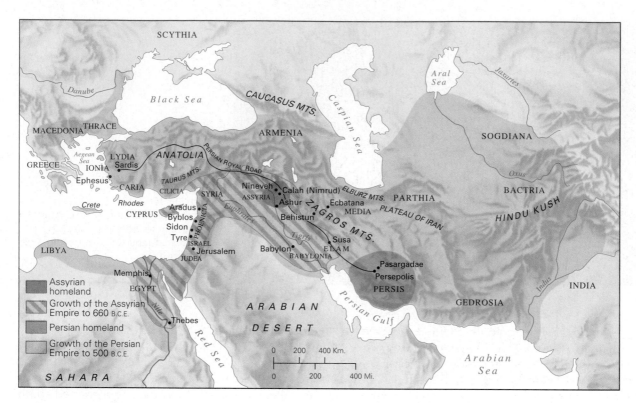

MAP 2.2 The Assyrian and Persian Empires   The Assyrian Empire at its height (ca 650 B.C.E.) included almost all of the old centers of power in the ancient Near East. By 513 B.C.E., however, the Persian Empire not only included more of that area but also extended as far east as western India. With the rise of the Medes and Persians, the balance of power in the Near East shifted east of Mesopotamia for the first time.

against the Assyrians inevitably promised the rebels bloody battles and cruel sieges.

Though atrocity and terrorism struck unspeakable fear into Assyria's subjects, Assyria's success was actually due to sophisticated, farsighted, and effective military organization. By Sargon's time the Assyrians had invented the mightiest military machine the ancient Near East had ever seen. The mainstay of the Assyrian army was the infantryman armed with spear and sword and protected by helmet and armor. The Assyrian army also featured archers, some on foot, others on horseback, still others in chariots—the latter ready to wield lances once they had expended their supply of arrows. Some infantry archers wore heavy armor. These soldiers served as a primitive field artillery, whose job was to sweep the enemy's walls of defenders so that others could storm the defenses. Slingers also served as artillery in pitched battles. For mobility on the battlefield, the Assyrians organized a corps of chariots.

Assyrian military genius was remarkable for the development of a wide variety of siege machinery and tech-

niques, including excavation to undermine city walls and battering rams to knock down walls and gates. Never before in the Near East had anyone applied such technical knowledge to warfare. The Assyrians even invented the concept of a corps of engineers, who bridged rivers with pontoons or provided soldiers with inflatable skins for swimming. And the Assyrians knew how to coordinate their efforts, both in open battle and in siege warfare. King Sennacherib's account of his siege of Jerusalem in 701 B.C.E. is a vivid portrait of the Assyrian war machine:

As to Hezekiah, the Jew, he did not submit to my yoke, I laid siege to 46 of his strong cities, walled forts and to the countless small villages in their vicinity, and conquered them by means of well-stamped earth-ramps, and battering rams brought thus near to the walls combined with the attack by foot soldiers, using mines, breaches as well as sapper work. . . . Himself I made prisoner in Jerusalem, his royal residence, like a bird in a cage. I surrounded him with earthwork in order to molest those who were leaving his city's gate.[4]

Assyrian Rule and Culture

Not only did the Assyrians know how to win battles, but they also knew how to use their victories. As early as the reign of Tiglath-pileser III, the Assyrian kings began to organize their conquered territories into an empire. The lands closest to Assyria became provinces governed by Assyrian officials. Kingdoms beyond the provinces were not annexed but became dependent states that followed Assyria's lead. The Assyrian king chose their rulers either by regulating the succession of native kings or by supporting native kings who appealed to him. Against more distant states the Assyrian kings waged frequent war in order to conquer them outright or make the dependent states secure.

In the seventh century B.C.E. Assyrian power seemed firmly established. Yet the downfall of Assyria was swift and complete. Babylon finally won its independence in 626 B.C.E. and joined forces with a newly aggressive people, the Medes, an Indo-European-speaking folk from Iran. Together the Babylonians and the Medes destroyed the Assyrian Empire in 612 B.C.E., paving the way for the rise of the Persians. The Hebrew prophet Nahum spoke for many when he asked: "Nineveh is laid waste: who will bemoan her?"[5] Their cities destroyed and their power shattered, the Assyrians disappeared from history, remembered only as a cruel people of the Old Testament who oppressed the Hebrews. Two hundred years later, when the Greek adventurer and historian Xenophon passed by the ruins of Nineveh, he marveled at the extent of the former city but knew nothing of the Assyrians. The glory of their empire was forgotten.

Yet modern archaeology has brought the Assyrians out of obscurity. In 1839 the intrepid English archaeologist and traveler A. H. Layard began the most noteworthy excavations of Nineveh, then a mound of debris beside the Tigris. His findings electrified the world. Layard's workers unearthed masterpieces, including monumental sculpted figures—huge winged bulls, human-headed lions, and sphinxes—as well as brilliantly sculpted friezes. Equally valuable were the numerous Assyrian cuneiform documents, which ranged from royal accounts of mighty military campaigns to simple letters by common people.

Among the most renowned of Layard's finds were the Assyrian palace reliefs, whose number was increased by the discoveries of twentieth-century archaeologists. Assyrian kings delighted in scenes of war, which their artists depicted in graphic detail. By the time of Ashurbanipal (r. 668–633 B.C.E.), Assyrian artists had hit on the idea of portraying a series of episodes—in fact, a visual narrative of

Royal Lion Hunt This relief from the palace of Ashurbanipal at Nineveh, which shows the king fighting a lion, is a typical representation of the energy and artistic brilliance of Assyrian sculptors. The lion hunt, portrayed in a series of episodes, was a favorite theme of Assyrian palace reliefs. *(Courtesy of the Trustees of the British Museum)*

events that had actually taken place. Scene followed scene in a continuous frieze, so that the viewer could follow the progress of a military campaign from the time the army marched out until the enemy was conquered.

Assyrian art fared better than Assyrian military power. The techniques of Assyrian artists influenced the Persians, who adapted them to gentler scenes. In fact, many Assyrian innovations, military and political as well as artistic, were taken over wholesale by the Persians. Although the memory of Assyria was hateful throughout the Near East, the fruits of Assyrian organizational genius helped enable the Persians to bring peace and stability to the same regions where Assyrian armies had spread terror.

THE EMPIRE OF THE PERSIAN KINGS

Like the Hittites before them, the Iranians were Indo-Europeans from central Europe and southern Russia. They migrated into the land to which they have given their name, the area between the Caspian Sea and the Persian Gulf. Like the Hittites, they then fell under the spell of the more sophisticated cultures of their Mesopotamian neighbors. Yet the Iranians went on to create one of the greatest empires of antiquity, one that encompassed scores of peoples and cultures. The Persians, the most important of the Iranian peoples, had a farsighted conception of empire. Though as conquerors they willingly used force to accomplish their ends, they normally preferred to depend on diplomacy to rule. They usually respected their subjects and allowed them to practice their native customs and religions. Thus the Persians gave the Near East both political unity and cultural diversity. Never before had Near Eastern people viewed empire in such intelligent and humane terms.

The Land of Mountains and Plateau

Persia—the modern country of Iran—is a stark land of towering mountains and flaming deserts, with a broad central plateau in the heart of the country (see Map 2.2). Iran stretches from the Caspian Sea in the north to the Persian Gulf in the south. Between the Tigris-Euphrates Valley in the west and the Indus Valley in the east rises an immense plateau, surrounded on all sides by lofty mountains that cut off the interior from the sea.

At the center of the plateau lies an enormous depression—a forbidding region devoid of water and vegetation, so glowing hot in summer that it is virtually impossible to

cross. This depression forms two distinct grim and burning salt deserts, perhaps the most desolate spots on earth.

Iran's geographical position and topography explain its traditional role as the highway between East and West. Throughout history wild, nomadic peoples migrating from the broad steppes of Russia and Central Asia have streamed into Iran. The very harshness of the geography urged them to continue in search of new and more hospitable lands. Confronting the uncrossable salt deserts, most have turned either eastward or westward, moving on until they reached the advanced and wealthy urban centers of Mesopotamia and India. When cities emerged along the natural lines of East-West communication, Iran became the area where nomads met urban dwellers, a meeting ground of unique significance for the civilizations of both East and West.

The Coming of the Medes and Persians

The Iranians entered this land around 1000 B.C.E. They were part of the vast movement of Indo-European-speaking peoples whose wanderings led them into Europe, the Near East, and India in many successive waves (see page 22). These Iranians were nomads who migrated with their flocks and herds. Like their kinsmen the Aryans, who moved into India, they were also horse breeders, and the horse gave them a decisive military advantage over the prehistoric peoples of Iran. The Iranians rode into battle in horse-drawn chariots or on horseback and easily swept the natives before them. Yet, because the influx of Iranians went on for centuries, there continued to be constant cultural interchange between conquering newcomers and conquered natives.

The Iranians initially created a patchwork of tiny kingdoms, of which Siyalk was one. The chieftain or petty king was basically a warlord who depended on fellow warriors for aid and support. This band of noble warriors formed the fighting strength of the army. The king owned estates that supported him and his nobles; for additional income the king levied taxes, which were paid in kind and not in cash. He also demanded labor services from the peasants. Below the king and his warrior nobles were free people who held land and others who owned nothing. Artisans produced the various goods needed to keep society running. At the bottom of the social scale were slaves—probably both natives and newcomers—to whom fell the drudgery of hard labor and household service to king and nobles.

Gradually two groups of Iranians began coalescing into larger units. The Persians had settled in Persia, the modern region of Fars, in southern Iran. Their kinsmen the Medes occupied Media in the north, with their capital at

Ecbatana, the modern Hamadan. The Medes were exposed to attack by nomads from the north, but their greatest threat was the frequent raids of the Assyrian army. Even though distracted by grave pressures from their neighbors, the Medes united under one king around 710 B.C.E. and extended their control over the Persians in the south. In 612 B.C.E. the Medes were strong enough to join the Babylonians in overthrowing the Assyrian Empire. With the rise of the Medes, the balance of power in the Near East shifted for the first time east of Mesopotamia.

The Creation of the Persian Empire

In 550 B.C.E. Cyrus the Great (r. 559–530 B.C.E.), king of the Persians and one of the most remarkable statesmen of antiquity, threw off the yoke of the Medes by conquering them and turning their country into his first *satrapy,* or province. In the space of a single lifetime, Cyrus created one of the greatest empires of antiquity. Two characteristics lift Cyrus above the common level of warrior-kings. First, he thought of Iran, not just Persia and Media, as a state. His concept has survived a long, complex, and often turbulent history to play its part in the contemporary world.

Second, Cyrus held an enlightened view of empire. Many of the civilizations and cultures that fell to his armies were, he realized, far older, more advanced, and more sophisticated than his. Free of the narrow-minded snobbery of the Egyptians, the religious exclusiveness of the Hebrews, and the calculated cruelty of the Assyrians, Cyrus gave Near Eastern peoples and their cultures his respect, toleration, and protection. Conquered peoples continued to enjoy their institutions, religions, languages, and ways of life under the Persians. The Persian Empire, which Cyrus created, became a political organization sheltering many different civilizations. To rule such a vast area and so many diverse peoples demanded talent, intelligence, sensitivity, and a cosmopolitan view of the world. These qualities Cyrus and many of his successors possessed in abundance. Though the Persians were sometimes harsh, especially with those who rebelled against them, they were for the most part enlightened rulers. Consequently, the Persians gave the ancient Near East over two hundred years of peace, prosperity, and security.

Cyrus showed his magnanimity at the outset of his career. Once the Medes had fallen to him, Cyrus united them with his Persians. Persepolis became a Persian seat of power. Medes were honored with important military and political posts and thenceforth helped the Persians to rule the expanding empire. Cyrus's conquest of the Medes resulted not in slavery and slaughter but in the union of Iranian peoples.

With Iran united, Cyrus looked at the broader world. He set out to achieve two goals. First, he wanted to win control of the west and thus of the terminal ports of the great trade routes that crossed Iran and Anatolia. Second, Cyrus strove to secure eastern Iran from the pressure of nomadic invaders. In 550 B.C.E. neither goal was easy to accomplish. To the northwest was the young

Tomb of Cyrus   For all of his greatness Cyrus retained a sense of perspective. His tomb, though monumental in size, is rather simple and unostentatious. Greek writers reported that it bore the following epitaph: "O man, I am Cyrus the son of Cambyses. I established the Persian Empire and was king of Asia. Do not begrudge me my memorial." *(The Oriental Institute, University of Chicago)*

kingdom of Lydia in Anatolia, whose king Croesus was proverbial for his wealth. To the west was Babylonia, enjoying a new period of power now that the Assyrian Empire had been crushed. To the southwest was Egypt, still weak but sheltered behind its bulwark of sand and sea. To the east ranged tough, mobile nomads, capable of massive and destructive incursions deep into Iranian territory.

Cyrus turned first to Croesus's Lydian kingdom, which fell to him around 546 B.C.E. He established a garrison at Sardis, the capital of Lydia, and ordered his generals to subdue the Greek cities along the coast of Anatolia. Cyrus had thus gained the important ports that looked out to the Mediterranean world. In addition, for the first time the Persians came into direct contact with the Greeks, a people with whom their later history was to be intimately connected.

From Lydia, Cyrus next marched to the far eastern corners of Iran. In a brilliant campaign he conquered the regions of Parthia and Bactria. All of Iran was now Persian, from Mesopotamia in the west to the western slopes of the Hindu Kush in the east. In 540 B.C.E. Cyrus moved against Babylonia, now isolated from outside help. When Persian soldiers marched quietly into Babylon the next year, the Babylonians welcomed Cyrus as a liberator. Cyrus won the hearts of the Babylonians with humane treatment, toleration of their religion, and support of their efforts to refurbish their capital.

Cyrus was equally generous toward the Jews. He allowed them to return to Palestine, from which they had been deported by the Babylonians. He protected them, gave them back the sacred items they used in worship, and rebuilt the temple of Yahweh in Jerusalem. The Old Testament sings the praises of Cyrus, whom the Jews considered the shepherd of Yahweh, the lord's anointed. Rarely have conquered peoples shown such gratitude to their conquerors. Cyrus's benevolent policy created a Persian Empire in which the cultures and religions of its members were respected and honored. Seldom have conquerors been as wise, sensitive, and farsighted as Cyrus and his Persians.

Thus Spake Zarathustra

Iranian religion was originally simple and primitive. **Ahuramazda,** the chief god, was the creator and benefactor of all living creatures. Yet, unlike Yahweh, he was not a lone god. The Iranians were polytheistic. Mithra, the sun-god, whose cult would later spread throughout the Roman Empire, saw to justice and redemption. Other Iranian deities personified the natural elements: moon, earth, water, and wind. As in ancient India, fire was a particularly important god. The sacred fire consumed the blood sacrifices that the early Iranians offered to all of their deities.

Early Iranian religion was close to nature and unencumbered by ponderous theological beliefs. A priestly class, the **Magi,** developed among the Medes to officiate at sacrifices, chant prayers to the gods, and tend the sacred flame. In time the Iranians built fire temples for these sacrifices. As late as the nineteenth century, fire was still worshiped in Baku, a major city on the Russian-Iranian border.

Around 600 B.C.E. the religious thinking of Zarathustra—Zoroaster, as he is better known—breathed new meaning into Iranian religion. So little is known of Zoroaster that even the date of his birth is unknown, but it cannot be earlier than around 1100 B.C.E. The most reliable information about Zoroaster comes from the *Zend Avesta,* a collection of hymns and poems, the earliest part of which treats Zoroaster and primitive Persian religion. Zoroaster preached a novel concept of divinity and human life. Life, he taught, is a constant battleground for two opposing forces, good and evil. Ahuramazda embodied good and truth but was opposed by Ahriman, a hateful spirit who stood for evil and falsehood. Ahuramazda and Ahriman were locked together in a cosmic battle for the human race, a battle that stretched over thousands of years.

Zoroaster emphasized the individual's responsibility to choose between good and evil. He taught that people possessed the free will to decide between Ahuramazda and Ahriman and that they must rely on their own conscience to guide them through life. Their decisions were crucial, Zoroaster warned, for there would be a time of reckoning. He promised that Ahuramazda would eventually triumph over evil and lies, and that at death each person would stand before the tribunal of good. Ahuramazda, like the Egyptian god Osiris, would judge whether the dead had lived righteously and on that basis would weigh their lives in the balance. In short, Zoroaster taught the concept of a Last Judgment at which Ahuramazda would decide each person's eternal fate.

In Zoroaster's thought the Last Judgment was linked to the notion of a divine kingdom after death for those who had lived according to good and truth. Liars and the wicked, denied this blessed immortality, would be condemned to eternal pain, darkness, and punishment. Thus Zoroaster preached a Last Judgment that led to a heaven or a hell.

Though tradition has it that Zoroaster's teachings originally met with opposition and coldness, his thought converted Darius (r. 521–486 B.C.E.), one of the most energetic men ever to sit on the Persian throne. The Persian royal family adopted **Zoroastrianism** but did not try

The Impact of Zoroastrianism   The Persian kings embraced Zoroastrianism as the religion of the realm. This rock carving at Behistun records the bond. King Darius I is seen trampling on one rebel with others behind him. Above is the sign of Ahuramazda, the god of truth and guardian of the Persian king. *(Robert Harding Picture Library)*

to impose it on others. Under the protection of the Persian kings, Zoroastrianism swept through Iran, winning converts and sinking roots that sustained healthy growth for centuries. Zoroastrianism survived the fall of the Persian Empire to influence liberal Judaism, Christianity, and early Islam, largely because of its belief in an afterlife that satisfied the longings of most people. Good behavior in the world, even though unrecognized at the time, would be amply rewarded in the hereafter. Evil, no matter how powerful in life, would be punished after death. Zoroastrianism presented the ideal of a fair god who would honor the good with a happy life in heaven. It had a profound impact on Manichaeism, a religion that was to pose a significant challenge to Christianity and to spread through the Byzantine Empire. In some form or another Zoroastrian concepts still pervade the major religions of the West and every part of the world touched by Islam. A handful of the faithful still follow the teachings of Zoroaster, whose vision of divinity and human life has long outlived him.

Persia's World Empire

Cyrus's successors rounded out the Persian conquest of the ancient Near East. In 525 B.C.E. Cyrus's son Cambyses (r. 530–522 B.C.E.) subdued Egypt. Darius (r. 521–486 B.C.E.) and his son Xerxes (r. 486–464 B.C.E.) invaded

Greece but were forced to retreat (see page 116); the Persians never won a permanent foothold in Europe. Yet Darius carried Persian arms into India. Around 513 B.C.E. western India became the Persian satrapy of Hindush, which included the valley of the Indus River. Thus within thirty-seven years (550–513 B.C.E.) the Persians transformed themselves from a subject people to the rulers of an empire that included Anatolia, Egypt, Mesopotamia, Iran, and western India. They had created a **world empire** encompassing all of the oldest and most honored kingdoms and peoples of the ancient Near East. Never before had the Near East been united in one such vast political organization (see Map 2.2).

The Persians knew how to use the peace they had won on the battlefield. Unlike the Assyrians, they did not resort to royal terrorism to keep order. Like the Assyrians, however, they employed a number of bureaucratic techniques to bind the empire together. The sheer size of the empire made it impossible for one man to rule it effectively. Consequently, the Persians divided the empire into some twenty huge satrapies measuring hundreds of square miles apiece, many of them kingdoms in themselves. Each satrapy had a governor, usually drawn from the Median and Persian nobility and often a relative of the king; the governor, or **satrap,** was directly responsible to the king. Others were local dynasts subject to the Persian king. An army officer, also responsible to the

The Royal Palace at Persepolis   King Darius began and King Xerxes finished building a grand palace worthy of the glory of the Persian Empire. Pictured here is the monumental audience hall, where the king dealt with ministers of state and foreign envoys. *(George Holton/Photo Researchers)*

king, commanded the military forces stationed in the satrapy. Still another official collected the taxes. Moreover, the king sent out royal inspectors to watch the satraps and other officials, a method of surveillance later used by the medieval king Charlemagne.

Effective rule of the empire demanded good communications. To meet this need the Persians established a network of roads. The main highway, known as the **Royal Road,** spanned some 1,677 miles from the Greek city of Ephesus on the coast of Asia Minor to Susa in western Iran. The distance was broken into 111 post stations, each equipped with fresh horses for the king's messengers. Other roads branched out to link all parts of the empire from the coast of Asia Minor to the valley of the Indus River. This system of communications enabled the Persian king to keep in intimate touch with his subjects and officials. He was able to rule efficiently, keep his ministers in line, and protect the rights of the peoples under his control.

SUMMARY

During the centuries following the Sea Peoples' invasions, Egypt was overrun by its African neighbors, but its long and rich traditions and culture, its firmly established religion, and its administrative techniques became the heritage of these conquerors. The defeat of Egypt also led to conditions that allowed the Hebrews to create their own state. A series of strong leaders fighting hard wars won the Hebrews independence and security. In this atmosphere Hebrew religion evolved and flourished, thanks to priests, prophets, and common piety among the people. Daily life involved the transition from nomad to farmer, and people's lives revolved around the religious and agricultural year.

In the eighth century B.C.E. the Hebrews and others in the ancient Near East fell to the onslaught of Assyria, a powerful Mesopotamian kingdom. The Assyrians combined administrative skills, economic acumen, and wealth with military organization to create an aggressive military state. Yet the Assyrians' military ruthlessness and cruelty raised powerful enemies against them. The most important of these enemies were the Iranians, who created the Persian Empire. The Persians had migrated into Iran, settled the land, and entered the cultural orbit of the Near East. The result was rapid progress in culture, economic prosperity, and increase in population, which enabled them to create the largest empire yet seen in the Near East. Unlike the Assyrians, however, they ruled mildly and gave the Near East a long period of peace.

KEY TERMS

"Purple People"	Talmud
Hapiru	Ahuramazda
nomads	Magi
Baal	Zoroastrianism
Babylonian Captivity	world empire
Covenant	satrap
Yahweh	Royal Road
Torah	

NOTES

1. James H. Breasted, *Ancient Records of Egypt,* vol. 4 (Chicago: University of Chicago Press, 1907), para. 398.
2. 2 Kings 23:3.
3. Proverbs 13:24.
4. J. B. Pritchard, ed., *Ancient Near Eastern Texts,* 3d ed. (Princeton, N.J.: Princeton University Press, 1969), p. 288.
5. Nahum 3:7.

SUGGESTED READING

Although late Egyptian history is still largely a specialist's field, K. A. Kitchen, *The Third Intermediate Period in Egypt* (1973), is a sturdy synthesis of the period from 1100 to 650 B.C.E. D. B. Redford, *Egypt, Canaan, and Israel in Ancient Times* (1992), is an excellent study of relations among the three states. D. O'Connor, *Ancient Nubia* (1994), which is well illustrated, gives the freshest treatment of that region and points to its importance in African developments.

R. G. Morkot, *The Black Pharaohs* (2000), examines the growth of the Kushite kingdom and its rule over pharaonic Egypt in the eighth century B.C.E. G. Herm, *The Phoenicians* (1975), treats Phoenician seafaring and commercial enterprises, as does the more recent G. E. Markoe, *The Phoenicians* (2000), a fresh investigation of these sailors at home and abroad in the western Mediterranean. Similarly, M. Gil, *A History of Palestine* (1997), provides the most recent treatment of that region.

The Jews have been one of the best-studied people in the ancient world, so the reader can easily find many good treatments of Jewish history and society. A rewarding approach is J. Bartlett, ed., *Archaeology and Biblical Interpretation* (1997). More general is W. R. F. Browning, ed., *Oxford Dictionary of the Bible* (1996), which is very rich in a variety of topics. Similar is R. S. Zwi Werblowsky and G. Wigoder, eds., *The Oxford Dictionary of the Jewish Religion* (1997). For the Jews in Egypt, two good studies have appeared: J. K. Hoffmeier, *Israel in Egypt* (1997), which discusses the evidence for the authenticity of the tradition concerning the Exodus; and J. Assmann, *Moses the Egyptian* (1997), which is a study in monotheism. B. N. Porter, ed., *One God or Many?* (2000), explores the concept of monotheism in Assyrian and Jewish religion. A broader interpretation of Jewish religious developments can be found in S. Niditch, *Ancient Israelite Religion* (1997). G. Alon, *The Jews in Their Land* (1989), covers the Talmudic age. H. Shanks, ed., *The Rise of Ancient Israel* (1991), is a collection of papers that treat numerous aspects of the period. R. Tappy, *The Archaeology of Israelite Samaria* (1993), studies the archaeological remains of the period. S. Niditch, *War in the Hebrew Bible* (1992), addresses the ethics of violence in the Bible. H. W. Attridge, ed., *Of Scribes and Scrolls* (1990), gives a fascinating study of the Hebrew Bible and of Christian origins. Turning to politics, M. Smith, *Palestinian Parties and Politics That Shaped the Old Testament,* 2d ed. (1987), takes a practical look at events. W. D. Davis et al., *The Cambridge History of Judaism,* vol. 1 (1984), begins an important synthesis with work on Judaism in the Persian period. R. Hachlili, *Ancient Jewish Art and Archaeology in the Land of Israel* (1988), attempts to trace the development and meaning of Jewish art in its archaeological context.

The Assyrians, despite their achievements, have not attracted the scholarly attention that other Near Eastern peoples have. Even though woefully outdated, A. T. Olmstead, *History of Assyria* (1928), has the merit of being soundly based in the original sources. H. W. F. Saggs, *Everyday Life in Babylonia and Assyria,* rev. ed. (1987), offers a general and well-illustrated survey of Mesopotamian history from 3000 to 300 B.C.E. M. T. Larsen, *The Conquest of Assyria* (1996), gives a fascinating account of the modern discovery of the Assyrians. Those who appreciate the vitality of Assyrian art should start with the masterful work of R. D. Barnett and W. Forman, *Assyrian Palace Reliefs,* 2d ed. (1970), an exemplary combination of fine photographs and learned, but not difficult, discussion.

A comprehensive survey of Persian history is given by one of the leading scholars in the field, R. N. Frye, *History of Ancient Iran* (1984). I. Gershevitch, ed., *The Cambridge History of Iran,* vol. 2 (1985), provides the reader with a full account of ancient Persian history, but many of the chapters are out-of-date. E. Herzfeld, *Iran in the Ancient East* (1987), puts Persian history in a broad context. Most welcome is M. A. Dandamaev, *A Political History of the Achaemenid Empire* (1989), which discusses in depth the history of the Persians and the organization of their empire. Finally, M. Boyce, a leading scholar in the field, provides a sound and readable treatment of the essence of Zoroastrianism in her *Zoroastrianism* (1979).

THE COVENANT BETWEEN YAHWEH AND THE HEBREWS

These passages from the Hebrew Bible address two themes important to Hebraic thinking. The first is the meaning of kingship; the second is the nature of the Covenant between the Hebrews and the Lord, Yahweh. The selection also raises the difficult question of how much of the Hebrew Bible can be accepted historically. As we discussed in this chapter, the Hebrew Bible is not a document that we may accept as literal truth, but it does tell us a great deal about the people who created it. From the following passages we may discern what the Hebrews thought about their own past and religion.

The background of the excerpt is a political crisis that has some archaeological support. The war with the Philistines put a huge strain on Hebrew society. The passage below describes one such incident when Nahash, the king of the Ammonites, threatens to destroy the Hebrews. A new and effective political and military leadership was needed to meet the situation. The elders of the tribes had previously chosen judges to lead the community only in times of crisis. The Hebrews, however, demanded that a kingship be established, even though Yahweh was their king. They turned to Samuel, the last of the judges, who anointed Saul as the first Hebrew king. In this excerpt Samuel reviews the political, military, and religious situation confronting the Hebrews, reminding them of their obligation to honor the Covenant and expressing hesitation in naming a king.

Then Nahash the Ammonite came up and encamped against Jabeshgilead: and all the men of Jabesh said unto Nahash, Make a covenant with us, and we will serve thee. And Nahash the Ammonite answered them, On this condition will I make a covenant with you, that I may thrust out all your right eyes, and lay it for a reproach upon all Israel. And the elders of Jabesh said unto him, Give us

seven days' respite, that we may send messengers unto all the coasts of Israel: and then, if there be no man to save us, we will come out to thee.

Then came the messengers to Gibeah of Saul, and told the tidings in the ears of the people: and all the people lifted up their voices, and wept. And, behold, Saul came after the herd out of the field; and Saul said, What aileth the people that they weep? And they told him the tidings of the men of Jabesh. And the Spirit of God came upon Saul when he heard those tidings, and his anger was kindled greatly. And he took a yoke of oxen, and hewed them in pieces, and sent them throughout all the coasts of Israel by the hands of messengers, saying, Whosoever cometh not forth after Saul and after Samuel, so shall it be done unto his oxen. And the fear of the Lord fell on the people, and they came out with one consent. And when he numbered them in Bezek, the children of Israel were three hundred thousand, and the men of Judah thirty thousand. And they said unto the messengers that came, Thus shall ye say unto the men of Jabeshgilead, To morrow, by that time the sun be hot, ye shall have help. And the messengers came and shewed it to the men of Jabesh; and they were glad. Therefore the men of Jabesh said, To morrow we will come out unto you, and ye shall do with us all that seemeth good unto you. And it was so on the morrow, that Saul put the people in three companies; and they came into the midst of the host in the morning watch, and slew the Ammonites until the heat of the day: and it came to pass, that they which remained were scattered, so that two of them were not left together.

And the people said unto Samuel, Who is he that said, Shall Saul reign over us? bring the men, that we may put them to death. And Saul said, There shall not a man be put to death this day: for to day the Lord hath wrought salvation in Israel. Then said Samuel to the people, Come, and let us go to Gilgal, and renew the kingdom there. And

Ark of the Covenant, depicted in a relief from Capernaum Synagogue, second century C.E. *(Ancient Art & Architecture Collection)*

all the people went to Gilgal; and there they made Saul king before the Lord in Gilgal; and there they sacrificed sacrifices of peace offerings before the Lord; and there Saul and all the men of Israel rejoiced greatly.

And Samuel said unto all Israel, Behold, I have hearkened unto your voice in all that you said to me, and have made a king over you. And now, behold, the king walks before you; and I am old and gray-headed; and behold, my sons are with you: and I have walked before you from my childhood until this day. Behold, here I am: witness against me before the Lord, and before his anointed: whose ox have I taken? or whose ass have I taken? or whom have I defrauded? whom have I oppressed? or of whose hand have I received any bribe to blind my eyes with it? and I will restore it to you.

And they said, You have not defrauded us, nor oppressed us, neither have you taken anything from any man's hand. And he said to them, the Lord is witness against you, and his anointed is witness this day, that you have not found anything in my hand. And they answered, he is witness. And Samuel said unto the people, It is the Lord that advanced Moses and Aaron, and that brought your fathers up out of the land of Egypt. Now therefore stand still, that I may reason with you before the Lord of all the righteous acts of the Lord, which he did to you and your fathers.

At this point Samuel reminds the Hebrews of their Covenant with Yahweh. He lists the times when they had broken that Covenant, the times when they had served other gods. He also reminds them of Yahweh's punishment for their backsliding. He tells them frankly that they are wrong to demand a king to rule over them, for Yahweh was their lord, god, and king. Nonetheless, Samuel gives way to their demands.

Now therefore behold the king whom you have chosen, and whom you have desired! and behold, the Lord has set a king over you. If you will fear the Lord, and serve him, and obey his voice, and not rebel against the commandment of the Lord, then shall both you and also the king who reigns over you continue following the Lord your God: But if you will not obey the voice of the Lord, but rebel against the commandment of the Lord, then shall the hand of the Lord be against you, as it was against your fathers. Now therefore stand and see this great thing, which the Lord will do before your eyes. Is it not wheat harvest today? I will call to the Lord, and he shall send thunder and rain; that you may perceive and see that your wickedness is great, which you have done in the sight of the Lord, in asking you a king. So Samuel called to the Lord; and the Lord sent thunder and rain that day: and all the people greatly feared the Lord and Samuel. And all the people said to Samuel, pray for your servants to the Lord your God, so that we will not die: for we have added to all of our sins this evil, to ask us for a king. And Samuel said to the people, Fear not: you have done all this wickedness; yet turn not aside from following the Lord, but serve the Lord with all your heart; And do not turn aside; for then should you go after vain things, which cannot profit nor deliver; for they are vain. For the Lord will not forsake his people for his great name's sake: because it pleases the Lord to make you his people. Moreover, as for me, God forbid that I should sin against the Lord in ceasing to pray for you: but I will teach you the good and the right way: Only fear the Lord, and serve him in truth with all your heart: for consider how great things he has done for you. But if you shall still act wickedly, you will be consumed, both you and your king.

QUESTIONS FOR ANALYSIS

1. How did Samuel explain his anointment of a king?

2. What was Samuel's attitude toward kingship?

3. What were the duties of the Hebrews toward Yahweh?

4. Might those duties conflict with those toward the secular king? If so, in what ways, and how might the Hebrews avoid the conflict?

Source: 1 Samuel 11:1–15, 12:1–7, 13–25. Abridged and adapted from *The Holy Bible,* King James Version.

The North Gate is one of four ornately carved gates guarding the Buddhist memorial shrine at Sanchi, Madhya Pradesh. Satavahana, second century B.C.E. *(Jean-Louis Nou)*

3

THE FOUNDATION OF INDIAN SOCIETY, TO 300 C.E.

During the centuries when the peoples of ancient Mesopotamia and Egypt were developing urban civilizations, people in India were wrestling with the same challenges—making the land yield food, improving agricultural techniques, building cities and urban cultures, grappling with the political administration of large tracts of land, and asking basic questions about human life and the cosmos.

Like the civilizations of the Middle East, the earliest Indian civilization centered on a great river, the Indus. From about 2800 to 1800 B.C.E., this Indus, or Harappan, culture thrived, and numerous cities were built over a huge area. A very different Indian society emerged after the decline of this civilization. It was dominated by the Aryans, warriors who spoke an early version of Sanskrit. The Indian caste system and the Hindu religion, key features of Indian society into modern times, had their origins in early Aryan society. The earliest Indian literature consists of the epics and religious texts of these Aryan tribes.

By the middle of the first millennium B.C.E., the Aryans had set up numerous small kingdoms throughout north India. This was the great age of Indian religious creativity, when Buddhism and Jainism were founded and the early Brahmanic religion of the Aryans developed into Hinduism. Alexander the Great invaded north India in 326 B.C.E., and after his army withdrew, the first major Indian empire was created by the Mauryan dynasty (ca 322–ca 180 B.C.E.), which unified most of north India. This dynasty reached its peak under the great king Ashoka (r. ca 269–232 B.C.E.), who actively promoted Buddhism both within his realm and beyond it. Not long afterward, however, the dynasty broke up, and for several centuries India was politically divided.

- What does archaeology tell us about the earliest civilization in India?
- What kind of social and political organization developed in India?
- What intellectual and religious values did this society generate?
- How were developments in India linked to developments outside it?
- Which features of ancient Indian culture and society shaped later developments most profoundly?

These questions are the central concerns of this chapter.

THE LAND AND ITS FIRST SETTLERS (CA 3000–1500 B.C.E.)

The subcontinent of India, a landmass as large as western Europe, juts southward into the warm waters of the Indian Ocean. Today this region is divided into the separate countries of Pakistan, Nepal, India, Bangladesh, and Sri Lanka, but these divisions are recent, and for premodern times the entire subcontinent will be called India here.

In India, as elsewhere, the possibilities for both agriculture and communication have always been strongly shaped by geography (see Map 3.1). Some regions are among the wettest on earth; others are arid deserts and scrubland. The lower reaches of the Himalaya Mountains in the northeast are covered by some of India's densest forests, sustained by heavy rainfall. Immediately to the south, the land drops away to the fertile valleys of the Indus and Ganges Rivers. These lowland plains, which stretch all the way across the subcontinent, over time were tamed for agriculture, and India's great empires were centered there. To the west of them are the great deserts of Rajasthan and southeastern Pakistan, historically important in part because their flat terrain enabled invaders to sweep into India from the northwest. South of the great river valleys rise the jungle-clad Vindhya Mountains and the dry, hilly Deccan Plateau. In this part of India, only along the coasts do the hills give way to narrow plains where crop agriculture flourished. Throughout much of antiquity, the Indian Ocean served to keep out invaders on India's south coast while fostering maritime trade both with the Near East and with China and Southeast Asia. Thus India's geography ensured that it would never be an isolated civilization and channeled contact in certain directions.

MAP 3.1 India from ca 2500 B.C.E. to 300 C.E.   The earliest civilization in India developed in the Indus River valley in the west of the subcontinent. The Ganges River valley was the heart of the later Mauryan Empire. Although India is protected from the cold by mountains in the north, mountain passes in the northwest allowed both migration and invasion.

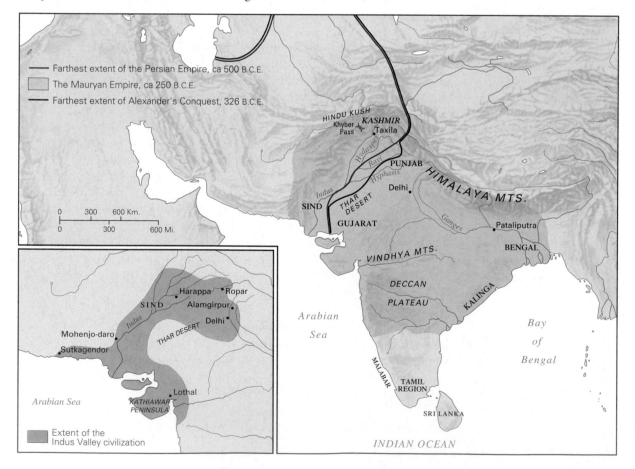

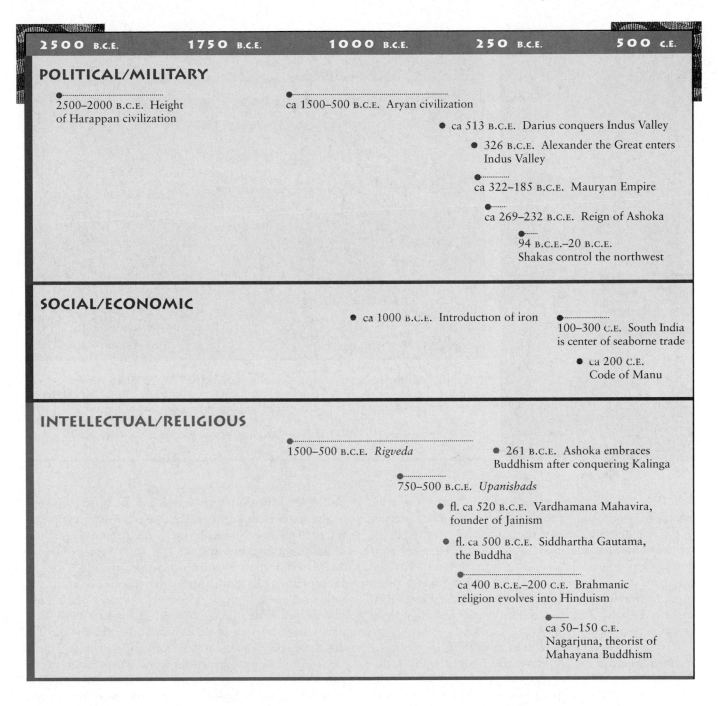

2500 B.C.E.	1750 B.C.E.	1000 B.C.E.	250 B.C.E.	500 C.E.

POLITICAL/MILITARY

2500–2000 B.C.E. Height of Harappan civilization

ca 1500–500 B.C.E. Aryan civilization

ca 513 B.C.E. Darius conquers Indus Valley

326 B.C.E. Alexander the Great enters Indus Valley

ca 322–185 B.C.E. Mauryan Empire

ca 269–232 B.C.E. Reign of Ashoka

94 B.C.E.–20 B.C.E. Shakas control the northwest

SOCIAL/ECONOMIC

ca 1000 B.C.E. Introduction of iron

100–300 C.E. South India is center of seaborne trade

ca 200 C.E. Code of Manu

INTELLECTUAL/RELIGIOUS

1500–500 B.C.E. *Rigveda*

261 B.C.E. Ashoka embraces Buddhism after conquering Kalinga

750–500 B.C.E. *Upanishads*

fl. ca 520 B.C.E. Vardhamana Mahavira, founder of Jainism

fl. ca 500 B.C.E. Siddhartha Gautama, the Buddha

ca 400 B.C.E.–200 C.E. Brahmanic religion evolves into Hinduism

ca 50–150 C.E. Nagarjuna, theorist of Mahayana Buddhism

India's climate is shaped by the ocean and mountains. The Himalayas shield the subcontinent from the northern cold. Most areas are warm all year, with temperatures over 100°F common. Average temperatures range from 79°F in the north to 85°F in the south. The mountains also hold in the monsoon rains that sweep northward from the Indian Ocean each summer. The monsoons and the melting snows of the Himalayas provide India with most of its water. In some areas the resulting moisture has created vast tracts of jungle and swamp. The Ganges, for example, was in ancient times a particularly forbidding region, and only gradually did settlers move there from the tamer west and clear it for agriculture. India's climate has shaped not only its agriculture but also its religions. Given the heat and regular rainfall characteristic of the Indian heartland, it is not surprising that both fire and water came to play central roles in Indian religions. Moreover, the extreme ascetic practices of many Indian

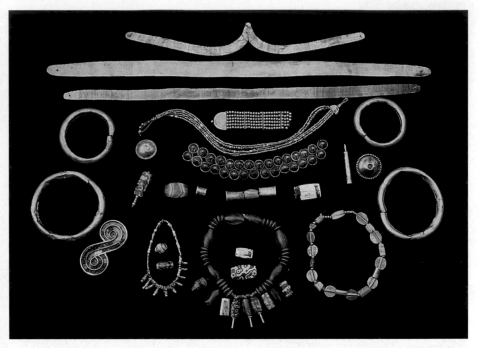

Harappan Artifacts   Small objects like seals and jewelry found at Harappan sites provide glimpses of early Indian religious imagination and daily life. The molded tablet shown on the left depicts a female deity battling two tigers. She stands above an elephant. The jewelry found at these sites, such as those pieces shown on the right, makes much use of gold and precious stones. *(J. M. Kenoyer/Courtesy Department of Archaeology and Museums, Government of Pakistan)*

religious sects would be possible only in a land where the people did not require much protection from the elements.

Neolithic settlement of the Indian subcontinent occurred somewhat later than in the Middle East, but agriculture was well established by about 7000 B.C.E. Wheat and barley were the early crops, probably having spread in their domesticated form from the Middle East. Farmers also domesticated cattle, sheep, and goats and learned to make pottery.

The story of the first civilization in India is one of the most dramatic in the ancient world. From the Bible, Europeans knew about ancient Egypt and Ur, but no one knew about the ancient cities of the Indus Valley until 1921, when archaeologists found astonishing evidence of a thriving and sophisticated Bronze Age urban culture dating to about 2500 B.C.E. at Mohenjo-daro in what is now Pakistan. This city had obviously been planned and built before being settled; it had straight streets, uniform houses, and underground sewers. To some the advanced culture of this site suggested that a powerful state had moved into the area or sent colonists there, but it is also possible that early stages of the development of this civi-

lization have not yet been discovered. Because of the rise of the water table at the major sites, it has been impossible to excavate to lower levels to investigate the earliest stages of the civilization.

This civilization is known today as the Indus or the **Harappan** civilization, from the modern names of the river and a major city, respectively. Archaeologists have discovered some three hundred Harappan cities and many more towns and villages in both Pakistan and India, making it possible to see both the vast regional extent of the Harappan civilization and its evolution over a period of nearly a millennium. It was a literate civilization, like those of Egypt and Mesopotamia, but no one has been able to decipher the more than four hundred symbols inscribed on stone seals and copper tablets. Its most flourishing period was 2500 to 2000 B.C.E.

The Indus civilization extended over nearly 500,000 square miles in the Indus Valley, making it more than twice as large as the territories of the ancient Egyptian and Sumerian civilizations. Numerous sites are still being excavated, but it is already clear that the Harappan civilization was marked by a striking uniformity. Through-

Mohenjo-daro
Mohenjo-daro was a planned city, built of fired mud brick. Its streets were straight, and covered drain-pipes were installed to carry away waste. From sites like this, we know that the early Indian political elite had the power and technical expert-ise to organize large, coor-dinated building projects. (*Josephine Powell*)

out the region, for instance, even in small villages, bricks were made to standard proportions of 4:2:1. Standard-ized weights have been found at all sites as well as at ports along the Arabian Sea. Figurines of pregnant women, be-lieved to represent fertility goddesses, have been found throughout the area, suggesting common religious ideas and practices. Yet compared to archaeological sites in Egypt and Sumer, relatively few graves have been found at Harappan sites. Thus the luxury goods of the rich and powerful have not been preserved to the extent that they have been in other early civilizations. Bronze objects have been found throughout the Harrapan region, but they are usually utilitarian tools rather than the highly decorated vessels and jewelry found in Egyptian and Sumerian tombs.

Like Mesopotamian cities, Harappan cities were cen-ters for crafts and trade surrounded by extensive farm-land. Fine ceramics were made on the potter's wheel and decorated with geometric designs. Cotton was used to make cloth (the earliest anywhere) and was so abundant

that goods were wrapped in it for shipment. Trade was extensive. As early as the reign of Sargon of Akkad in the third millennium B.C.E., trade between India and Meso-potamia carried goods and ideas between the two cul-tures, probably by way of the Persian Gulf. The port of Lothal had a stone dock seven hundred feet long, next to which were massive granaries and beadmaking factories. Hundreds of seals were found there, some of Persian Gulf origin, indicating that Lothal was a major port of exit and entry.

The best-known cities of the Harappan civilization are Mohenjo-daro, in southern Pakistan, and Harappa, some four hundred miles to the north in the Punjab region of Pakistan. Both cities were huge, more than three miles in circumference, and housed populations estimated at thirty-five thousand to forty thousand. Three other cities of similar size have been identified but have not yet been excavated.

Built of fired mud brick, Mohenjo-daro and Harappa were both defended by great citadels that towered forty

Figurine from Mohenjo-daro   This small stone figure, about seven inches tall, is thought to depict a priest-king. The man's beard is carefully trimmed and his upper lip shaved. The headband and armband have circular ornaments, probably once filled with colored paste. His robe with its trefoil designs was probably also filled with colors to suggest the fabric more vividly. *(National Museum, Karachi)*

to fifty feet above the surrounding plain and may have had walls surrounding them, though only small sections survive. Both cities were logically planned from the outset, not the outcomes of villages that grew and sprawled haphazardly. In both, blocks of houses were laid out on a grid plan, centuries before the Greeks or Chinese used this method of urban design. Streets were straight and varied from nine to thirty-four feet in width. The houses were substantial—many two stories tall, some perhaps three—and their brick exteriors were unadorned. The focal point of the houses was a central courtyard onto which the rooms opened, much like many houses today in both rural and urban India.

Perhaps the most surprising aspect of the elaborate planning of these cities is their complex system of drainage, well preserved at Mohenjo-daro. Each house had a bathroom with a drain connected to brick-lined drains located under the major streets. Openings allowed the refuse to be collected, probably to be used as fertilizer on nearby fields. No other ancient city had such an advanced sanitation system.

Both cities also contained numerous large structures, which excavators think were public buildings. One of the most important was the large ventilated storehouse for the community's grain. Moreover, a set of tenement buildings next to a series of round work areas near the granary at Harappa suggests that the central government dominated the storage and processing of the city's cereal crops. Near the citadel at Mohenjo-daro were a marketplace or place of assembly, a palace, and a huge bath featuring a pool some thirty-nine feet long by twenty-three feet wide and eight feet deep. The bath resembles the later Roman baths in that it is an intricate structure with spacious dressing rooms for the bathers. Because the Great Bath at Mohenjo-daro resembles the ritual purification pools of later Indian society, some scholars have speculated that power was in the hands of a priest-king and that the Great Bath played a role in the religious rituals of the city.

The prosperity of the Indus civilization depended on constant and intensive cultivation of the rich river valley. Although rainfall seems to have been greater then than in recent times, the Indus, like the Nile, flowed through a relatively dry region, made fertile by annual floods and irrigation. And as in Egypt, agriculture was aided by a long growing season of high temperatures and near constant sunshine. Besides growing wheat, barley, vegetables, and cotton, the Indus people domesticated cattle, water buffalo, fowl, and possibly pigs and asses. Their efforts led to agricultural surpluses that they traded with Mesopotamia. They also traded with peoples to the south for gold and to the north for lapis lazuli.

Because the written language of the Harappan people has not been deciphered, their political, intellectual, and religious life is largely unknown. There clearly was a political structure with the authority to organize city planning and facilitate trade, but we do not even know whether there were hereditary kings. There are clear connections between Harappan civilization and Sumerian, but just as clear differences. For instance, the Harappan script was incised on clay tablets and seals, as it was at Sumer, but the script has no connection to Sumerian cuneiform, and the artistic style of the seals also is distinct. There are many signs of continuity with later Indian civilization, ranging from the sorts of pottery ovens used to some of the images of gods. A three-headed figure surrounded by animals that was found at Mohenjo-daro closely resembles later depictions of Shiva, a major

Hindu god. There are also many female figurines and other signs of fertility cults. Because of evidence like this, some scholars think that the people of Harappa may have been the ancestors of the Dravidian-speaking peoples of modern south India. Analysis of skeletons, however, indicates that the population of the Indus Valley in ancient times was very similar to the modern population of the same region.

The decline of Harappan civilization, which began soon after 2000 B.C.E., cannot be attributed to the arrival of powerful invaders, as was once thought. Rather the decline was internally generated. The port of Lothal was abandoned by about 1900 B.C.E., and other major centers came to house only a fraction of their earlier populations. Scholars have offered many explanations for the mystery of the abandonment of these cities. Perhaps an earthquake led to a shift in the course of the river, or perhaps rainfall and snowmelt decreased and the rivers dried up. Perhaps the long-term practice of irrigation led to the buildup of salts and alkalines in the soil until they reached levels toxic to plants. Perhaps long-distance commerce collapsed, leading to an economic depression. Perhaps the population fell prey to diseases, such as malaria, that led people to flee the cities. Even though the Harappan population apparently lived on after scattering to villages, they were not able to retain key features of the high culture of the Indus civilization. For the next thousand years, there were no large cities, no kiln-fired bricks, and no written language in India.

THE ARYANS AND THE VEDIC AGE (CA 1500–500 B.C.E.)

After the decline of the Indus Valley civilization, a people who called themselves **Aryans** became dominant in north India. They were speakers of an early form of Sanskrit, which was an Indo-European language closely related to ancient Persian and more distantly related to Latin, Greek, Celtic, and their modern descendants, such as English. The Sanskrit *nava,* "ship," is related to the English word *naval; deva,* "god," to *divine; raja,* "ruler," to *regal;* and so on. The word *Aryan* itself comes from *Arya,* "noble" or "pure" in Sanskrit, and has the same root as Iran and Eire.

Until relatively recently, the dominant theory was that the Aryans came into India from outside, perhaps as a part of the same movements of people that led to the Hittites occupying parts of Anatolia, the Achaeans entering Greece, and the Kassites conquering Sumer—all in the period from about 1900 to 1750 B.C.E. (see Chapter 1). Some

scholars, however, have proposed that the Indo-European languages spread to this area much earlier; to them it is possible that the Harappan people were speakers of an early Indo-European language. If that was the case, the Aryans would just be one of the groups descended from this early population.

Modern politics complicates analysis of the appearance of the Aryans and their role in India's history. It was Europeans in the eighteenth and nineteenth century who developed the concept of Indo-European languages, and they did it in an age both highly conscious of race and in the habit of identifying races with languages. The racist potential of the concept was fully exploited by the Nazis, with their glorification of the Aryans as a superior race. But even in less politicized contexts, the notion of a group of people who entered India from outside and made themselves its rulers is troubling to many. Does it mean that the non-Aryans are the true Indians? Or, to the contrary, does it add legitimacy to those who in later times conquered India from outside? Does it justify or undermine the caste system? One of the difficulties faced by scholars who wish to take a dispassionate view of these issues is that the evidence for the earlier Harappan culture is entirely archaeological and the evidence for the Aryans is almost entirely based on linguistic analysis of modern languages and orally transmitted texts of uncertain date.

The central source for the early Aryans is the *Rigveda,* the earliest of the Vedas, a collection of hymns, ritual texts, and philosophical treatises composed between 1500 and 500 B.C.E. in Sanskrit. Like Homer's epics in Greece, these texts were transmitted orally and are in verse. Since writing was not used in the early Vedic period, events in early Indian history can be dated only approximately.

The *Rigveda* portrays the Aryans as warrior tribes who glorified military skill and heroism; loved to drink, hunt, race, and dance; and counted their wealth in cattle. They looked down on the short, dark-skinned indigenous people, whom they did their best to subjugate. The Aryans did not sweep across India in a quick campaign, nor were they a disciplined army led by one conqueror. Rather they were a collection of tribes who frequently fought with each other and only over the course of several centuries came to dominate north India.

Those the Aryans fought often lived in fortified towns and put up a strong defense against them. The key to the Aryans' success probably lay in their superior military technology: they had fast two-wheeled chariots, horses, and bronze swords and spears. Their epics, however, present the struggle in religious terms: their chiefs were godlike heroes, their opponents irreligious savages who did not perform the proper sacrifices. In time, however, the Aryans clearly absorbed much from those they conquered.

At the head of each Aryan tribe was a chief, or **raja,** who led his followers in battle and ruled them in peacetime. The warriors in the tribe elected the chief for his military skills. Next in importance to the chief was the priest, entrusted with sacrifices to the gods and the knowledge of sacred rituals. In time, as Aryan society put increasing emphasis on proper performance of the religious rituals, priests evolved into a distinct class possessing precise knowledge of the complex rituals and of the invocations and formulas that accompanied them, rather like the priest classes in ancient Egypt, Mesopotamia, and Persia. The warrior nobility rode into battle in chariots and

perhaps on horseback; they met at assemblies to reach decisions and advise the raja. The common tribesmen tended herds and in time worked the land. To the conquered non-Aryans fell the drudgery of menial tasks. It is difficult to define precisely their social status. Though probably not slaves, they were certainly subordinate to the Aryans and worked for them in return for protection.

Over the course of several centuries, the Aryans pushed farther east into the valley of the Ganges River, at that time a land of thick jungle populated by aboriginal forest peoples. The jungle was as stubborn an enemy as its inhabitants. The tremendous challenge of clearing it was made somewhat easier by the introduction of iron around 1000 B.C.E. Iron made it possible to produce strong axes and knives relatively cheaply. During this time the Aryans and those they displaced or conquered undoubtedly borrowed cultural elements from each other. Rice, for instance, was grown in the Ganges Valley, apparently introduced from Southeast Asia, where it had been cultivated since at least 5000 B.C.E. Rice, in time, became a central element of the Indian diet.

The Aryans did not gain dominance over the entire Indian subcontinent. South of the Vindhya range, people speaking Dravidian languages maintained their control. In the great Aryan epics the *Ramayana* and *Mahabharata,* the people of the south and Sri Lanka are spoken of as dark-skinned savages and demons who resisted the Aryans' conquests. Still, in time these epics became part of the common cultural heritage of all of India.

Early Indian Society, 1000–500 B.C.E.

As Aryan rulers came to dominate large settled populations, the style of political organization changed from tribal chieftainship to territorial kingship. In other words, the ruler controlled an area whose people might change, not a nomadic tribe who might move as a group. Moreover, kings no longer needed to be elected by the tribe; it was enough to be invested by priests and to perform the splendid royal ceremonies they designed. The priests, or **Brahmans,** supported the growth of royal power in return for royal confirmation of their own religious rights, power, and status. The Brahmans also served as advisers to the kings. In the face of this royal-priestly alliance, the old tribal assemblies of warriors withered away. By the time Persian armies reached the Indus around 513 B.C.E., there were sixteen major kingdoms in north India.

Early Aryan society had distinguished among the warrior elite, the priests, ordinary tribesmen, and conquered subjects. These distinctions gradually evolved into the **caste system.** Society was conceived in terms of four

Bronze Sword   A striking example of the quality of Aryan arms is this bronze sword, with its rib in the middle of the blade for strength. Native Indians lacked comparable weapons. *(Courtesy of the Trustees of the British Museum)*

hierarchical strata that do not eat with each other or marry each other. These strata (called **varna**) are *Brahman* (priests), *Kshatriya* (warriors and officials), *Vaishya* (merchants and artisans), and *Shudra* (peasants and laborers). The lowest level probably evolved out of the efforts of the numerically outnumbered Aryans to maintain their dominance over their subjects and not be absorbed by them. The three upper varnas probably accounted for no more than 30 percent of the population. Social and religious attitudes entered into these distinctions as well. Aryans considered the work of artisans impure. They left all such work to the local people, who were probably superior to them in these arts anyway. Trade, by contrast, was not viewed as demeaning, and Aryans would practice it. Brahmanic texts of the period refer to trade as equal in value to farming, serving the king, or serving as a priest.

In the *Rigveda,* the caste system is attributed to the gods:

When they divided the [primeval] Man into how many parts did they divide him?
What was his mouth, what were his arms, what were his thighs and his feet called?
The Brahman was his mouth, of his arms was made the warrior.
His thighs became the Vaishya, of his feet the Shudra was born.[1]

Those without places in this tidy social division—that is, those who entered it later than the others or who had lost their caste status through violations of ritual—were **outcastes.** That simply meant that they belonged to no caste. In time, some of these people became "untouchables," because they were "impure." They were scorned because they earned their living by performing such "polluting" jobs as slaughtering animals and dressing skins.

Slavery was also a feature of early Indian social life, as it was in Egypt, Mesopotamia, and elsewhere in antiquity. Slaves were often people captured in battle, but these captives could be ransomed by their families. Later, slavery was less connected with warfare and became more of an economic and social institution. As in ancient Mesopotamia, a free man might sell himself and his family into slavery because he could not pay his debts. And, as in Hammurabi's Mesopotamia, he could, if clever, hard-working, or fortunate, buy his and his family's way out of slavery. At birth, slave children automatically became the slaves of their parents' masters. Indian slaves could be bought, used as collateral, or even given away.

Slaves in India performed tasks similar to those of slaves in other societies. Like Joseph in ancient Egypt, a man might serve as a royal counselor, having more actual authority than many a free man. Otherwise slaves served in their masters' fields, mines, or houses. Whatever their economic function, socially they were members of their masters' households, and Indian masters were required to perform the customary duties necessary for the welfare of the soul of a deceased slave. Indian law forbade a master from abandoning his slaves in their old age; it also recommended manumission of slaves as an act of piety. Nonetheless, in Indian literature there is ample evidence of the abuse of slaves, for in India as in other societies— both ancient and modern—laws and social injunctions were not always obeyed.

Women's lives in early India varied according to their social status, much as men's did. Like most nomadic tribes, the Aryans were patrilineal and patriarchal (tracing descent through males and placing power over family members in the senior men of the family). Thus women in Aryan society probably had more subordinate roles than did women among the local Dravidian population, many of whom were matrilineal. But even in Aryan society, women were treated somewhat more favorably than in later Indian society. They were not yet given in child-marriage, and widows had the right to remarry. In the epics such as the *Ramayana,* women are often portrayed as forceful personalities, able to achieve their goals both by feminine ploys of cajoling men and by more direct action. (See the feature "Listening to the Past: Rama and Sita" on pages 76–77.)

Brahmanism

The gods of the Aryans shared some features with the gods of other early Indo-European societies such as the Persians and Greeks. Some of them were great brawling figures, such as Agni, the god of fire; Indra, wielder of the thunderbolt and god of war, who each year slew a dragon to release the monsoon rains; and Rudra, the divine archer who spread disaster and disease by firing his arrows at people. Others were shadowy figures, such as Dyaus, the father of the gods, related to the Greek Zeus and the Roman Jupiter. Varuna, the god of order in the universe, was a hard god, quick to punish those who sinned and thus upset the balance of nature. Ushas, the goddess of dawn, was a refreshingly gentle deity who welcomed the birds, gave delight to human beings, and warded off evil spirits.

The core of the Aryans' religion was its focus on sacrifice. By giving valued things to the gods, people strengthened them and established relationships with them. As in ancient Persia, the fire-god Agni was a particularly important god. Agni had three forms: fire, lightning, and the sun. In his capacity as the sacrificial fire of the priests, he served as a liaison between human beings and the gods, carrying to the gods the offerings made by the Brahman priests. The fire sacrifice was the most elaborate of the sacrifices, but all the Aryan gods enjoyed having offerings made to them. Gradually, under the priestly monopoly of the Brahmans, correct sacrifice and proper ritual became so important that most Brahmans believed that a properly performed ritual would force a god to grant a worshiper's wish.

The *Upanishads* record speculations about the mystical meaning of sacrificial rites and about cosmological questions of man's relationship to the universe. They document a gradual shift from the mythical world-view of the early Vedic age to a deeply philosophical one. Associated with this shift was a movement toward *asceticism*—severe self-discipline and self-denial. In search of wisdom, some men retreated to the forests. These ascetics concluded that disciplined meditation on the ritual sacrifice could produce the same results as the physical ritual itself. Thus they reinterpreted ritual sacrifices as symbolic gestures with mystical meanings.

These Brahmanic thinkers also developed ideas about the nature of the cosmos. Ancient Indian cosmology focused not on a creator who made the universe out of nothing, but rather on endlessly repeating cycles. Key ideas were **samsara,** the transmigration of souls by a continual process of rebirth, and **karma,** the tally of good and bad deeds that determined the status of an individual's next life. Good deeds led to better future lives, evil deeds to worse future lives—even to reincarnation as an animal. Thus gradually arose the concept of a wheel of life that included human beings, animals, and even gods. Reward and punishment worked automatically; there was no all-knowing god who judged people and could be petitioned to forgive a sin, and each individual was responsible for his or her own destiny in a just and impartial world.

To most people, especially those on the low end of the economic and social scale, these concepts were attractive. All existence, no matter how harsh and bitter, could lead to better things. By living righteously and doing good deeds, people could improve their lot in the next life. Yet there was another side to these ideas: the wheel of life could be seen as a treadmill, giving rise to a yearning for release from the relentless cycle of birth and death. One solution offered in the *Upanishads* was **moksha,** or release from the wheel of life. Brahmanic mystics claimed that life in the world was actually an illusion, and the only way to escape it and the wheel of life was to realize that the ultimate reality was unchanging.

This unchanging, ultimate reality was called **brahman.** The multitude of things in the world were all fleeting; the only true reality was brahman. Even the individual soul or self, *atman,* is ultimately the same substance as the universal brahman, in the same way that each spark is in substance the same as a large fire. Equating the individual self with the ultimate reality suggested that the apparent duality in the world is in some sense unreal. At the same time it conveyed that all people had in themselves an eternal truth, which corresponded to an identical but greater all-encompassing reality. The profound and subtle teaching of the connections between brahman and atman was summed up in the *Upanishads* in one sentence: "Thou art That." The *Chandogya Upanishad* tells the story of a father explaining this sentence to his son:

"Believe me, my son, an invisible and subtle essence is the Spirit of the whole universe. That is Reality. That is Atman. THOU ART THAT."

"Explain more to me, father," said Svetaketu.

"So be it, my son.

"Place this salt in water and come to me tomorrow morning."

Svetaketu did as he was commanded, and in the morning his father said to him: "Bring me the salt you put into the water last night."

Svetaketu looked into the water, but could not find it, for it had dissolved.

His father then said: "Taste the water from this side. How is it?"

"It is salt."

"Taste it from the middle. How is it?"

"It is salt."

"Taste it from that side. How is it?"

"It is salt."

"Look for the salt again and come again to me."

The son did so, saying: "I cannot see the salt. I only see water."

His father then said: "In the same way, O my son, you cannot see the Spirit. But in truth he is here.

"An invisible and subtle essence is the Spirit of the whole universe. That is Reality. That is Truth. THOU ART THAT."[2]

The *Upanishads* gave the Brahmans a high status to which the poor and lowly could aspire in a future life. Consequently, the Brahmans greeted the concepts presented in these works and those who taught them with tolerance and understanding and made a place for them in traditional religious practice. The rulers of Indian society also encouraged the new trends, since the doctrines of samsara and karma encouraged the poor and oppressed to labor peacefully and dutifully. In other words, although the new doctrines were intellectually revolutionary, in social and political terms they supported the existing power structure.

INDIA'S GREAT RELIGIONS

By the sixth and fifth centuries B.C.E., cities had reappeared in India, and merchants and trade were thriving. Bricks were again baked in kilns and used to build ramparts around cities. The center of population had shifted to the Ganges Valley. One particular kingdom, Magadha, had become much more powerful than any of the other states in the Ganges plain, defeating its enemies by using war elephants and catapults for hurling stones. Written language had by this point reappeared.

This was a period of intellectual ferment throughout Eurasia—the period of the early Greek philosophers, the Hebrew prophets, Zoroaster in Persia, Confucius and the early Daoists in China. In India it led to numerous sects that rejected various elements of Brahmanic teachings. (See the feature "Individuals in Society: Gosala.") The two most important in world-historical terms were Jainism and Buddhism. Their founders were contemporaries, both living in east India in minor states of the Ganges plain. Hinduism emerged in response to these new religions but at the same time was the most direct descendant of the old Brahmanic religion.

Jainism

The key figure of Jainism, Vardhamana Mahavira (fl. ca 520 B.C.E.), was the son of the chief of a petty state. Like many ascetics of the period, he left home to become a holy man (a wandering mendicant ascetic), and for twelve years, from ages thirty to forty-two, he wandered through the Ganges Valley until he found enlightenment and became a "completed soul." Mahavira taught his doctrines for about thirty years, founding a disciplined order of monks and gaining the support of many lay followers, male and female.

Mahavira accepted the doctrines of karma and rebirth but developed these ideas in new directions. He argued that human beings, animals, plants, and even inanimate objects and natural phenomena all have living souls enmeshed in matter, accumulated through the workings of karma. Even a rock has a soul locked inside it, enchained by matter but capable of suffering if someone kicks it. Unlike the earlier concept of atman, which referred to immaterial and infinite souls, the souls conceived by the Jains have finite dimensions. They float or sink depending on the amount of matter with which they are enmeshed. The ascetic, who willingly undertakes suffering, can dissipate some of the karma accumulated and make progress toward liberation. If a soul at last escapes from all the matter weighing it down, it becomes lighter than ordinary objects and floats to the top of the universe, where it remains forever in inactive bliss.

Jain Ascetic The most extreme of Jain ascetics not only endured the elements without the help of clothes but were also generally indifferent to bodily comfort. The Jain saint depicted in this eighth-century cave temple has maintained his yogic posture for so long that vines have grown up around him. *(Courtesy, Robert Fisher)*

Mahavira's followers pursued salvation by living lives of asceticism and avoiding evil thoughts and actions. The Jains considered all life sacred and tried to live without destroying other life. Some early Jains went to the extreme of starving themselves to death, since it is impossible to eat without destroying at least plants, but most took the less extreme step of distinguishing between different levels of life. The most sacred life forms were human beings, followed by animals, plants, and inanimate objects. A Jain who wished to avoid violence to life became a vegetarian and took pains not to kill any creature, even tiny insects in the air and soil. Farming was impossible for Jains, who tended instead to take up trade. Among the most conservative, priests practiced nudity, for clinging to clothes, even a loincloth, was a form of attachment. Lay Jains could pursue Jain teachings by practicing nonviolence and purity through more moderate means of self-control. They wore clothes but did not eat meat. The Jains' radical nonviolence was motivated by a desire to escape the karmic consequences of causing harm to a life. In other words, violence had to be avoided above all because it harms the person who commits it.

For the first century after Mahavira's death, the Jains were a comparatively small and unimportant sect. Jainism began to flourish under the Mauryan dynasty (ca 322–ca 180 B.C.E.; see pages 70–72), and Jain tradition claims the Mauryan Empire's founder, Chandragupta, as a major patron. About 300 B.C.E. the Jain scriptures were recorded, and the religion split into two sects, one maintaining the tradition of total nudity, the other choosing to wear white robes, on the grounds that clothes were an insignificant external sign, unrelated to true liberation. Over the next few centuries, Jain monks were particularly important in spreading northern culture into the Deccan and Tamil regions of south India.

Although Jainism never took hold as widely as Hinduism and Buddhism, it has been an influential strand in Indian thought and has several million adherents in India today. Fasting and nonviolence as spiritual practices in India owe much to Jain teachings. Mahatma Gandhi was influenced by these ideas through his mother, and Dr. Martin Luther King, Jr., was influenced by Gandhi.

Siddhartha Gautama and Buddhism

Siddhartha Gautama (fl. ca 500 B.C.E.), also called Shakyamuni ("sage of the Shakya tribe"), is best known as the Buddha ("enlightened one"). He was a contemporary of Mahavira and came from the same social class (that is, warrior, not Brahman). He was born the son of a chief of one of the tribes in the Himalayan foothills in what is now Nepal. At age twenty-nine, unsatisfied with his life of comfort and troubled by the suffering he saw around him, he left home to become a wandering ascetic. He traveled south to the kingdom of Magadha, where he studied with yoga masters, but later took up extreme asceticism. According to tradition, he reached enlightenment while meditating under a bo tree at Bodh Gaya, gaining perfect insight into the processes of the universe. After several weeks of meditation, he preached his first sermon, urging a "middle way" between asceticism and worldly life. For the next forty-five years, the Buddha traveled through the Ganges Valley, propounding his ideas, refuting his adversaries, making converts, and attracting followers. These followers can be called monks, members of a religious community much like others of the time in India, including the Jains. To reach as wide an audience as possible, the Buddha preached in the local language, Magadhi, rather than Sanskrit, which was already becoming a priestly language. Probably because he refused to recognize the divine authority of the Vedas and dismissed sacrifices, he attracted followers mostly from among merchants, artisans, and farmers, rather than Brahmans.

In his first sermon, the Buddha outlined his main message, summed up in the **Four Noble Truths** and the **Eightfold Path.** The truths are as follows: (1) pain and suffering, frustration and anxiety, are ugly but inescapable parts of human life; (2) suffering and anxiety are caused by human desires and attachments; (3) people can understand these weaknesses and triumph over them; and (4) this triumph is made possible by following a simple code of conduct, the Eightfold Path. The basic insight of Buddhism is thus psychological. The deepest human longings can never be satisfied, and even those things that seem to give pleasure cause anxiety because we are afraid of losing them. Attachment to people and things causes sorrow at their loss.

The Buddha offered an optimistic message, however, because everyone can set out on the Eightfold Path toward liberation. All they have to do is take steps such as recognizing the universality of suffering, deciding to free themselves from it, and choosing "right conduct," "right speech," "right livelihood," and "right endeavor." For instance, they should abstain from taking life. The seventh step is "right awareness," constant contemplation of one's deeds and words, giving full thought to their importance and whether they lead to enlightenment. "Right contemplation," the last step, entails deep meditation on the impermanence of everything in the world. Those who achieve liberation are freed from the cycle of birth and death and enter the state called **nirvana,** a kind of blissful nothingness and freedom from reincarnation.

GOSALA

Texts that survive from early India are rich in religious and philosophical speculation and tales of gods and heroes, but not in history of the sort written by the early Chinese and Greeks. Because Indian writers and thinkers of antiquity found little interest in recording the actions of rulers or accounting for the rise and decline of different states, few people's lives are known in any detail.

Religious literature, however, does sometimes include details of the lives of followers and adversaries. The life of Gosala, for instance, is known primarily from early Buddhist and Jain scriptures. He was a contemporary of both Mahavira, the founder of the Jains, and Gautama, the Buddha, and both saw him as one of their most pernicious rivals.

According to the Jain account, Gosala was born in the north Indian kingdom of Magadha, the son of a professional mendicant. The name Gosala, which means "cowshed," alluded to the fact that he was born in a cowshed where his parents had taken refuge during the rainy season. The Buddhist account adds that he became a naked wandering ascetic when he fled from his enraged master after breaking an oil vessel. As a mendicant, he soon fell in with Mahavira, who had recently commenced his life as an ascetic. After accompanying Mahavira on his travels for at least six years, Gosala came to feel that he was spiritually more advanced than his master and left to undertake the practice of austerities on his own. After he gained magic powers, he challenged his master and gathered his own disciples.

Both the Jain and Buddhist sources agree that Gosala taught a form of fatalism that they saw as dangerously wrong. A Buddhist source says that he taught that people are good or bad not because of their own efforts but because of fate. No matter how wise or righteous a person, he or she can do nothing about his or her karma or alter the course of transmigration. "Just as a ball of string, when it is cast forth, will spread out just as far and no farther than it can unwind, so both fools and wise alike, wandering in transmigration exactly for the allotted term, shall then, and only then, make an end of pain."* Some people reach perfection, but not by their own efforts; rather they are individuals who have through the course of numerous rebirths over hundreds of thousands of years rid themselves of bad karma.

The Jains claimed that Gosala lived with a potter woman, violating the celibacy expected of ascetics and moreover teaching that sexual relations were not sinful. The followers of Gosala, a Buddhist source stated, wore no clothing and were very particular about the food they accepted, refusing food specially prepared for them, food in a cooking pan, and food from couples or women with children. Like other ascetics, Gosala's followers owned no property, carrying the principle further than the Jains, who allowed the possession of a food bowl. Instead they made a bowl from the palms of their hands, giving them the name "hand lickers."

Jain sources report that after sixteen years of separation, Mahavira happened to come to the town where Gosala lived. When Gosala heard that Mahavira spoke contemptuously of him, he and his followers went to Mahavira's lodgings, and the two sides came to blows. Soon thereafter Gosala became unhinged, gave up all ascetic restraint, and after six months of singing, dancing, drinking, and other riotous living died, though not before telling his disciples, the Jains report, that Mahavira was right. Doubt is cast on this version of his end by the fact that for centuries to come, Gosala's followers, called the Ajivikas, were an important sect in several parts of India. Ashoka honored them among other sects and dedicated some caves to them.

Ascetics of many sects in early India saw clothing as a comfort to be renounced. (Dinodia Picture Agency)

QUESTIONS FOR ANALYSIS

1. How would Gosala's own followers have described his life? What sorts of distortions are likely in a life known primarily from the writings of rivals?
2. How would the early Indian economy have been affected by the presence of ascetic mendicants?

*A. F. R. Hoernle, "Ajivikas," in *Encyclopedia of Religion and Ethics,* vol. 1, ed. James Hastings (Edinburgh: T. & T. Clark, 1908), p. 262.

Although he accepted the Indian idea of reincarnation, the Buddha denied the integrity of the individual self or soul. He saw human beings as a collection of parts, physical and mental. As long as the parts remain combined, that combination can be called "I." When that combination changes, as at death, the various parts remain in existence, ready to become the building blocks of different combinations. According to Buddhist teaching, life is passed from person to person as a flame is passed from candle to candle.

The success of Buddhism was aided by the Buddha's teaching that everyone, noble and peasant, educated and ignorant, male and female, could follow the Eightfold Path. Buddhism differed from Brahmanism and later Hinduism in that it in effect ignored the caste system. Moreover, the Buddha was extraordinarily undogmatic.

Convinced that each person must achieve enlightenment on his or her own, he emphasized that the path was important only because it led the traveler to enlightenment, not for its own sake. He compared it to a raft, essential to cross a river but useless once on the far shore. There was no harm in honoring local gods or observing traditional ceremonies, as long as one remembered the goal of enlightenment and did not let sacrifices become snares or attachments.

Like Mahavira, the Buddha formed a circle of disciples, primarily men but including some women as well. He continually reminded them that each person must reach ultimate fulfillment by individual effort, but he also recognized the value of a group of people striving together for the same goal.

The Buddha's followers transmitted his teachings orally

Men Worshiping at a Stupa The frieze on this pillar from the first century C.E. depicts a stupa (the round building in the center). Stupas housed relics of the Buddha and attracted pilgrims and worshipers. Here both humans and winged heavenly beings are praying, bringing offerings, and making music. *(Eliot Elisofon Collection, Harry Ransom Humanities Center, University of Texas, Austin)*

until they were written down in the second or first century B.C.E. as sutras. The form of monasticism that developed among the Buddhists was less strict than that of the Jains. Buddhist monks moved about for eight months of the year (except the rainy season), consuming only one meal a day obtained by begging, but they could bathe and wear clothes. Within a few centuries, Buddhist monks began to overlook the rule that they should travel. They set up permanent monasteries, generally on land donated by kings or other patrons. Orders of nuns also appeared, giving women the opportunity to seek truth in ways men had traditionally done. The main ritual that monks and nuns performed in their monastic establishments was the communal recitation of the sutras. Lay Buddhists could aid the spread of the Buddhist teachings by providing food for monks and support for their monasteries, and could pursue their own spiritual progress by adopting practices such as abstaining from meat and alcohol.

Because there was no ecclesiastical authority like that developed by early Christian communities, early Buddhist communities developed several divergent traditions and came to stress different sutras. One of the most important of these, associated with the monk-philosopher Nagarjuna (fl. ca 150–250 C.E.), is called **Mahayana,** or "Great Vehicle," because it is a more inclusive form of the religion. It drew on a set of discourses allegedly given by the Buddha and kept hidden by his followers for centuries. One branch of Mahayana taught that reality is "empty" (that is, nothing exists independently, of itself). Another branch held that ultimate reality is consciousness, that everything is produced by the mind.

Just as important as the metaphysical literature of Mahayana Buddhism was its devotional side, influenced by the religions then prevalent in Central Asia. The Buddha became deified and placed at the head of an expanding pantheon of other Buddhas and bodhisattvas. Bodhisattvas were Buddhas-to-be who had stayed in the world after enlightenment to help others on the path to salvation. These Buddhas and bodhisattvas became objects of veneration, especially the Buddha Amitabha and the bodhisattva Avalokitesvara (Guanyin in Chinese, Kannon in Japanese). With the growth of Mahayana, Buddhism attracted more and more laypeople.

Buddhism remained an important religion in India until about 1200 C.E., but thereafter it declined, and the number of Buddhists in India today is small. In Sri Lanka and Nepal, however, Buddhism never lost its hold. Moreover, many elements of Buddhist philosophy were absorbed into Indian thought.

Queen Maya's Dream   The stupa erected at Bharhut in the second century B.C.E. depicts stories of the Buddha's previous lives and events in his life as Shakyamuni. Depicted in this nineteen-inch-tall panel is the legend of his conception. As a lamp flickers at Queen Maya's bedside, a large white elephant hovers above her before descending into her side. (*Government of India, Department of Archaeology*)

Hinduism

Both Buddhism and Jainism were direct challenges to the old Brahmanic religion. Both rejected animal sacrifice, which by then was a central element in Brahmanic power. Although Buddhist and Jain monks still had Brahmans perform life cycle rituals for them, their teachings did not place much weight on these rituals. Even more important, both religions tacitly rejected the caste system, accepting people of any caste into their ranks. In response to this challenge, over the next several centuries (ca 400 B.C.E.–200 C.E.) the Brahmanic religion evolved in a more devotional direction, today commonly called Hinduism. In Hinduism Brahmans retained their high social status, but it became possible for individual worshipers to have more direct contact with the gods, showing their devotion to them without the aid of priests as intermediaries. The bedrock of Hinduism is the belief that the Vedas are sacred revelations and that a specific caste system is implicitly prescribed in them. Hinduism assumes that there are innumerable legitimate ways of worshiping the supreme principle of life. Consequently, it readily incorporates new sects, doctrines, beliefs, rites, and deities.

Hinduism is a guide to life, the goal of which is to reach union with brahman, the ground of all being. There are four steps in this search, progressing from study of the Vedas in youth to complete asceticism in old age. In their quest for brahman, people are to observe **dharma,** the moral law. Dharma stipulates the legitimate pursuits of Hindus: material gain, as long as it is honestly and honorably achieved; pleasure and love, for the per-

petuation of the family; and *moksha,* release from the wheel of life and unity with brahman. Hinduism, recognizing the need for material gain and pleasure, allows a joyful embracing of life.

After the third century B.C.E., Hinduism began to emphasize the roles and personalities of thousands of powerful gods. Brahma, the creator; Shiva, the cosmic dancer who both creates and destroys; and Vishnu, the preserver and sustainer of creation, are three main male deities. Female deities included Lakshmi, goddess of wealth, and Saraswati, goddess of learning and music. People could reach brahman by devotion to personal gods, usually represented by images. A worshiper's devotion to one god did

Shiva   One of the three most important Vedic gods, Shiva represented both destruction and procreation. Here Shiva, mounted on a bull and carrying a spear, attacks the demon Andhaka. Shiva is seen as a fierce and bloodthirsty warrior. *(C. M. Dixon/Photo Resources)*

not entail denial of other deities; ultimately all were manifestations of the divine force that pervades the universe.

A central ethical text of Hinduism is the *Bhagavad Gita*, a part of the world's longest ancient epic, the *Mahabharata*. The *Bhagavad Gita* offers guidance on the most serious problem facing a Hindu—how to live in the world and yet honor dharma and thus achieve release. The heart of the *Bhagavad Gita* is the spiritual conflict confronting Arjuna, a human hero about to ride into battle against his kinsmen. As he surveys the battlefield, struggling with the grim notion of killing his relatives, Arjuna voices his doubts to his charioteer, none other than the god Krishna. When at last Arjuna refuses to spill his family's blood, Krishna instructs him, as he has instructed generations of Hindus, on the true meaning of Hinduism.

You grieve for those beyond grief,
and you speak words of insight;
but learned men do not grieve
for the dead or the living.

Never have I not existed,
nor you, nor these kings;
and never in the future
shall we cease to exist.

Just as the embodied self
enters childhood, youth, and old age,
so does it enter another body;
this does not confound a steadfast man.

Contacts with matter make us feel
heat and cold, pleasure and pain.
Arjuna, you must learn to endure
fleeting things—they come and go!

When these cannot torment a man,
when suffering and joy are equal
for him and he has courage,
he is fit for immortality.

Nothing of nonbeing comes to be,
nor does being cease to exist;
the boundary between these two
is seen by men who see reality.

Indestructible is the presence
that pervades all this;
no one can destroy
this unchanging reality.

Our bodies are known to end,
but the embodied self is enduring,
indestructible, and immeasurable;
therefore, Arjuna, fight the battle!

He who thinks this self a killer
and he who thinks it killed,
both fail to understand;
it does not kill, nor is it killed.

It is not born,
it does not die;
having been,
it will never not be;
unborn, enduring,
constant, and primordial,
it is not killed
when the body is killed.[3]

Krishna then clarifies the relationship between human reality and the eternal spirit. He explains compassionately to Arjuna the duty to act—to live in the world and carry out his duties as a warrior. Indeed, the *Bhagavad Gita* emphasizes the necessity of action, which is essential for the welfare of the world. Arjuna makes it the warrior's duty to wage war in compliance with his dharma. Only those who live within the divine law without complaint will be released from rebirth. One person's dharma may be different from another's, but both must follow their own dharmas.

Early in India's history, Hinduism provided a complex and sophisticated philosophy of life and a religion of enormous emotional appeal. Hinduism also inspired the preservation, in Sanskrit and the major regional languages of India, of literary masterpieces. Among these are the *Puranas,* which are stories of the gods and great warrior clans, and the *Mahabharata* and *Ramayana,* which are verse epics of India's early kings. Hinduism also validated the caste system, adding to the stability of everyday village life, since people all knew where they stood in society.

INDIA AND THE WEST (CA 513–298 B.C.E.)

In the late sixth century B.C.E., west India was swept up in events that were changing the face of the ancient Near East. During this period the Persians were creating an empire that stretched from the west coast of Anatolia to the Indus River (see pages 47–48). India became involved in these events when the Persian emperor Darius conquered the Indus Valley and Kashmir about 513 B.C.E.

Persian control did not reach eastward beyond the Punjab. Even so, it fostered increased contact between India and the Middle East and led to the introduction of new ideas, techniques, and materials into India. From

Persian administrators Indians learned more about how to rule large tracts of land and huge numbers of people. They also learned the technique of minting silver coins, and they adopted the Persian monetary standard to facilitate trade with other parts of the empire. Even states in the Ganges Valley, which were never part of the Persian Empire, adopted the use of coinage.

Another result of contact with Persia was introduction of the Aramaic script, used to write the official language of the Persian Empire. To keep records and publish proclamations just as the Persians did, Indians in northwest India adapted the Aramaic script for writing several local languages (elsewhere, Indians developed the Brahmi script, the ancestor of the script used for modern Hindi). In time the sacred texts of the Buddhists and the Jains, as well as the epics and other literary works, all came to be recorded.

The Persian Empire in turn succumbed to Alexander the Great, and in 326 B.C.E. Alexander led his Macedonian and Greek troops through the Khyber Pass into the Indus Valley (see page 125). The India that Alexander encountered was composed of many rival states. He defeated some of these states in the northwest and heard reports of others. Porus, king of west Punjab, fought Alexander with a battalion of two thousand war elephants and after being defeated agreed to become a subordinate king under Alexander. Alexander had heard of the sophistication of Indian philosophers and summoned some to instruct him or debate with him.

The Greeks were impressed with Taxila, a major center of trade in the Punjab (see Map 3.1), and described it as "a city great and prosperous, the biggest of those between the Indus River and the Hydaspes [the modern Jhelum River]—a region not inferior to Egypt in size, with especially good pastures and rich in fine fruits."[4] From Taxila, Alexander followed the Indus River south, hoping to find the end of the world. His men, however, mutinied and refused to continue. When Alexander turned back, he left generals in charge of the regions he had conquered; Seleucus was put in charge of the eastern region.

THE MAURYAN EMPIRE (CA 322–185 B.C.E.)

The one to benefit most from Alexander's invasion was Chandragupta, the ruler of a growing state in the Ganges Valley. He took advantage of the crisis caused by Alexander's invasion to expand his territories, and by 322 B.C.E. he had made himself sole master of north India. In 304

B.C.E. he defeated the forces of Seleucus. In the wake of this battle, Seleucus surrendered the easternmost provinces to Chandragupta, who in return gave him five hundred war elephants and concluded a treaty of alliance with him. In this way Chandragupta not only defeated one of the mightiest of Alexander's lieutenants (see Chapter 5) but also entered the world of Hellenistic politics.

The Mauryan Empire founded by Chandragupta stretched from the Punjab in the west to Bengal in the east. With stunning effectiveness, Chandragupta applied the lessons learned from Persian rule. He adopted the Persian practice of dividing the area into provinces. Each province was assigned a governor, most of whom were drawn from Chandragupta's own family. He established a complex bureaucracy to see to the operation of the state and a bureaucratic taxation system that financed public services through taxes on agriculture. He also built a regular army, complete with departments for everything from naval matters to the collection of supplies.

From his capital at Pataliputra in the Ganges Valley (now Patna in Bihar), Chandragupta sent agents to the provinces to oversee the workings of government and to keep him informed of conditions in his realm. For the first time in Indian history, one man governed most of the subcontinent, exercising control through delegated power. In designing his bureaucratic system, Chandragupta enjoyed the able assistance of his great minister Kautilya, who wrote a treatise on how a king should seize, hold, and manipulate power, rather like the Legalist treatises produced in China later that century (see Chapter 4). The king was urged to use propaganda to gain support, for instance, to disguise secret agents to look like gods so that people would be awed when they saw him in their company. The king was also alerted to the fact that all his immediate neighbors were his enemies but the princes directly beyond them were his natural friends. When a neighboring prince was in trouble, that was the perfect time to attack him. Interstate relations were likened to the law of the fish: the large swallow the small.

Megasthenes, a Greek ambassador sent by Seleucus to Chandragupta's court at Pataliputra, left a lively description of life there. He described the city as square and surrounded by wooden walls, 22 miles on each side, with 570 towers and 64 gates. It had a university, a library, and magnificent palaces, temples, gardens, and parks. The king personally presided over court sessions where legal cases were heard and petitions received. The king claimed for the state all mines and forests, and there were large state farms, granaries, shipyards, and spinning and weaving factories. Even prostitution was controlled by the state.

Megasthenes described Chandragupta as afraid of treachery, especially assassination. According to Megasthenes:

Attendance on the king's person is the duty of women, who indeed are bought from their fathers. Outside the gates of the palace stand the bodyguards and the rest of the soldiers. . . . Nor does the king sleep during the day, and at night he is forced at various hours to change his bed because of those plotting against him. Of his non-military departures from the palace one is to the courts, in which he passes the day hearing cases to the end, even if the hour arrives for attendance on his person. . . . When he leaves to hunt, he is thickly surrounded by a circle of women, and on the outside by spear-carrying bodyguards. The road is fenced off with ropes, and to anyone who passes within the ropes as far as the women death is the penalty.[5]

Those measures apparently worked, and Chandragupta lived a long life. According to Jain tradition, Chandragupta became a Jain ascetic and died a peaceful death in 298 B.C.E. Although he personally adopted a nonviolent philosophy, he left behind a kingdom with the military might to maintain order and defend India from invasion.

The Reign of Ashoka (ca 269–232 B.C.E.)

The years after Chandragupta's death were an epoch of political greatness, thanks largely to Ashoka, one of India's most remarkable figures. The grandson of Chandragupta, Ashoka extended the Mauryan Empire to its farthest limits. The era of Ashoka was enormously important in the religious history of the world, because Ashoka embraced Buddhism, helped to establish it as an important religion in India, and promoted its spread beyond India.

As a young prince, Ashoka served as governor of two prosperous provinces where Buddhism flourished. At the death of his father about 274 B.C.E., Ashoka rebelled against his older brother, the rightful king, and after four years of fighting succeeded in his bloody bid for the throne. Crowned king, Ashoka ruled intelligently and energetically. He was equally serious about his pleasures, especially those of the banquet hall and harem.

In the ninth year of his reign, 261 B.C.E., Ashoka conquered Kalinga, the modern state of Orissa, on the east coast of India. In a grim and savage campaign, Ashoka reduced Kalinga by wholesale slaughter. As Ashoka himself admitted, "One hundred and fifty thousand were forcibly abducted from their homes, 100,000 were killed in battle, and many more died later on."[6] Instead of exulting like a conqueror, however, Ashoka was consumed with remorse and revulsion at the horror of war. He embraced Buddhism and used the machinery of his empire to spread Buddhist teachings throughout India. He supported the doctrine of not hurting humans or animals, then spreading among religious people of all sects, and banned animal sacrifices and any killing of certain species. In place of hunting expeditions, he took pilgrimages. Two years after his conversion, he undertook a 256-day pilgrimage to all the holy sites of Buddhism, and on his return he began his missionary activity, sending missionaries to all known countries. Buddhist tradition also credits him with erecting throughout India 84,000 stupas (Buddhist reliquary mounds), among which the ashes or other bodily remains of the Buddha were distributed, beginning the association of Buddhism with monumental art and architecture.

Ashoka's remarkable crisis of conscience, like the later conversion to Christianity of the Roman emperor Constantine (see pages 174–175), affected the way he ruled. He emphasized compassion, nonviolence, and adherence to dharma. He appointed officials to oversee the moral welfare of the realm and required local officials to govern humanely. He may have perceived dharma as a kind of civic virtue, a universal ethical model capable of uniting the diverse peoples of his extensive empire. Ashoka erected stone pillars, on the Persian model, with inscriptions to inform the people of his policies. He also had long inscriptions carved into large rock surfaces near trade routes. In one inscription he spoke to his people like a father:

Whatever good I have done has indeed been accomplished for the progress and welfare of the world. By these shall grow virtues namely: proper support of mother and father, regard for preceptors and elders, proper treatment of Brahmans and ascetics, of the poor and the destitute, slaves and servants.[7]

These inscriptions are the earliest fully dated Indian texts. (Until the script in which they were written was deciphered in 1837, nothing was known of Ashoka's achievements.) The pillars on which they are inscribed are also the first examples of Indian art to survive since the end of the Indus civilization.

Ashoka felt the need to protect his new religion and to keep it pure. Warning Buddhist monks that he would not tolerate *schism*—divisions based on differences of opinion about doctrine or ritual—he threw his support to religious orthodoxy. According to Buddhist tradition, a great council of Buddhist monks was held at Pataliputra,

Ashokan Pillar   The best preserved of the pillars that King Ashoka erected in about 240 B.C.E. is this one in the Bihar region, near Nepal. The solid shaft of polished sandstone rises thirty-two feet in the air. It weighs about fifty tons, making its erection a remarkable feat of engineering. Like other Ashokan pillars, it is inscribed with accounts of Ashoka's political achievements and instructions to his subjects on proper behavior. These pillars are the earliest extant examples of Indian writing and a major historical source for the Mauryan period. *(Borromeo/Art Resource, NY)*

where the earliest canon of Buddhist texts was codified. At the same time, Ashoka honored India's other religions, even building shrines for Hindu and Jain worshipers. In one edict he banned rowdy popular fairs, allowing only religious gatherings.

Despite his devotion to Buddhism, Ashoka never neglected his duties as emperor. He tightened the central government of the empire and kept a close check on local officials. He also built roads and rest spots to improve communication within the realm. Ashoka himself described this work: "On the highways Banyan trees have been planted so that they may afford shade to men and animals; mango-groves have been planted; watering-places have been established for the benefit of animals and men."[8] These measures also facilitated the march of armies and the armed enforcement of Ashoka's authority. Ashoka's efforts were eminently successful: during his reign India enjoyed peace, prosperity, and humane rule.

Ashoka's inscriptions indirectly tell us much about the Mauryan Empire. He directly administered the central part of the empire, focusing on Magadha. Beyond it were four large provinces, under princes who served as viceroys, each with its own sets of smaller districts and officials. The interior of south India was described as inhabited by undefeated forest tribes. Farther south, along the coasts, were peoples Ashoka maintained friendly relations with but did not rule, such as the Cholas and Pandyas. Relations with Sri Lanka were especially close under Ashoka, and the king sent a branch of the tree under which the Buddha gained enlightenment to the Sri Lankan king. According to Buddhist legend, Ashoka's son Mahinda traveled to Sri Lanka to convert the people there.

Ashoka ruled for thirty-seven years. After he died in about 232 B.C.E., the Mauryan dynasty went into decline, and India broke up into smaller units, much like those in existence before Alexander's invasion. Even though Chandragupta had instituted bureaucratic methods of centralized political control and Ashoka had vigorously pursued the political and cultural integration of the empire, the institutions they created were not entrenched enough to survive periods with weaker kings. For much of subsequent Indian history, political unity would be the exception rather than the rule. By this time, however, key elements of Indian culture—the caste system; the religious traditions of Hinduism, Buddhism, and Jainism; and the great epics and legends—had given India a cultural unity strong enough to endure even without political unity.

REGIONAL DEVELOPMENTS (200 B.C.E.–300 C.E.)

After the Mauryan dynasty collapsed in 184 B.C.E., a series of foreign powers dominated the Indus Valley and adjoining regions. The first were hybrid Indo-Greek states, ruled by the inheritors of Alexander's defunct empire stationed in what is now Afghanistan. King Menander (fl. 160–135 B.C.E.) is remembered because a profound conversation between him and the Buddhist monk Nagasena was recorded as the *Questions of King Milenda.* The city of Taxila became a major center of trade, culture, and education, fusing elements of Greek and Indian culture.

The great, slow movement of nomadic peoples out of East Asia that brought the Scythians to the Middle East brought the Shakas to northwest India. They controlled the region from about 94 to 20 B.C.E., when they were displaced by a new nomadic invader, the Kushans, who ruled the region of today's Afghanistan, Pakistan, and west India as far south as Gujarat. Their king Kanishka (r. ca 78–ca 103 C.E.) is known from Buddhist sources. The famous silk trade from China to Rome passed through his territory.

We know less about what was happening in east and south India in this period, but it is apparent that political division into competing states in India did not lead to cultural or economic decline. During the Kushan period, Greek culture had a considerable impact on Indian art. Indo-Greek artists and sculptors working in India adorned Buddhist shrines, modeling the earliest representation of the Buddha on Hellenistic statues of Apollo. Another contribution from the Indo-Greek states was coins cast with images of the king, which came to be widely adopted by Indian rulers, aiding commerce and adding evidence to the historical record. Cultural exchange also went in the other direction as well. Old Indian animal folktales were translated into Syriac and Greek, and from that source eventually made their way to Europe as well.

During these centuries there were significant advances in science, mathematics, and philosophy. Nagarjuna (fl. ca 50–150 C.E.) was a major theorist of Mahayana Buddhism, who developed sophisticated theories of the nature of reality and debated them directly with Brahman priests. This was also the period when Indian law was codified. The **Code of Manu,** which lays down family, caste, and commercial law, was compiled in the second or third century C.E.

Regional cultures tend to flourish when there is no dominant, unifying state. In south India the third century

Kushan Girl   The young woman on this second-century C.E. stone sculpture wears bracelets, necklaces, and earrings. She is carrying a platter of food, perhaps for a feast. *(Courtesy, Archaeological Museum, Mathura)*

B.C.E. to the third century C.E. is considered the classical period of Tamil culture, when many great works of literature were written under the patronage of the regional kings. Some of these poems take a hard look at war.

Harvest of War

Great king
you shield your men from ruin,
so your victories, your greatness
are bywords.

Loose chariot wheels
lie about the battleground
with the long white tusks
of bull-elephants.

Flocks of male eagles
eat carrion
with their mates.

Headless bodies
dance about
before they fall
to the ground.

Blood glows,
like the sky before nightfall,
in the red center
of the battlefield.

Demons dance there.
And your kingdom
is an unfailing harvest
of victorious wars.[9]

South India in this period was also the center of active seaborne trade, with networks reaching all the way to Rome. Indian sailing technology was highly advanced, and much of this trade was in the hands of Indian merchants. Roman traders based in Egypt followed the routes already used by Arab traders, sailing with the monsoon from the Red Sea to the west coast of India in about two weeks, returning about six months later when the direction of the winds reversed. In the second half of the first century C.E. a Greek merchant involved in this trade reported that the traders sold coins, topaz, coral, crude glass, copper, tin, and lead and bought pearls, ivory, silk (probably originally from China), jewels of many sorts (probably many from Southeast Asia), and above all cinnamon and pepper. More Roman gold coins of the first and second centuries C.E. have been found near the southern tip of India than in any other area. The local rulers had slits made across the image of the Roman emperor to show that his sovereignty was not recognized, but they had no objection to the coins circulating. (By contrast, the Kushan rulers in the north had Roman coins melted down to use to make coins with their own images on them.)

Even after the fall of Rome, many of the traders on the southwest coast of India remained. These diasporic communities of Christians and Jews lived in the coastal cities into modern times. When Vasco da Gama, the Portuguese explorer, reached Calicut in 1498, he found a local Jewish merchant who was able to interpret for him.

SUMMARY

Many of the cultural elements that unify India date to the ancient period discussed in this chapter. Although India never had a single language and only periodically had a centralized government, certain ideas and cultural practices gave India a distinct identity. These included the core ideas of Brahmanism, the caste system, and the story cycles recorded in the great epics. These cultural elements spread through trade and other contact, even when the subcontinent was divided into hostile kingdoms. India also was in contact with the outside world from the time of the Indus civilization on. Just as India came to absorb some Persian bureaucratic techniques and Greek artistic styles, other regions borrowed crops, textiles, inventions, and religious ideas from India.

KEY TERMS

Harappan	brahman
Aryans	Four Noble Truths
Rigveda	Eightfold Path
raja	nirvana
Brahmans	Mahayana
caste system	dharma
varna	Code of Manu
outcastes	
samsara	
karma	
moksha	

NOTES

1. *Rigveda* 10.90, translated by A. L. Basham, in *The Wonder That Was India* (New York: Grove Press, 1954), p. 241.
2. J. Mascaro, trans., *The Upanishads* (London: Penguin Books, 1965), pp. 117–118.
3. B. S. Miller, trans., *The Bhagavad-gita: Krishna's Counsel in Time of War* (New York: Columbia University Press, 1986), pp. 31–32.
4. Arrian, *Anabasis* 5.8.2; Plutarch, *Alexander* 59.1. Translated by John Buckler.
5. *Strabo,* 15.1.55. Translated by John Buckler.
6. Quoted in H. Kulke and D. Rothermund, *A History of India,* 3d ed. (London: Routledge, 1998), p. 62.
7. Quoted in B. G. Gokhale, *Asoka Maurya* (New York: Twayne Publishers, 1966), p. 169.
8. Quoted ibid., pp. 168–169.
9. A. K. Ramanujan, ed. and trans., *Poems of Love and War: From the Eight Anthologies and the Ten Long Poems of Classical Tamil* (New York: Columbia University Press, 1985), p. 115.

SUGGESTED READING

Much splendid work has been done on the geographical background of ancient Indian society. See, in particular, G. Johnson, *Cultural Atlas of India* (1996), and J. Schwartzberg, ed., *An Historical Atlas of South Asia* (1978), the epitome of what a historical atlas should be. The contents of both range well into contemporary times. Useful general reference works on India include A. T. Embree, ed., *Encyclopedia of Asian History* (1989), and F. Robinson, ed., *The Cambridge Encyclopedia of India* (1989). On Indian art, see S. L. Huntington, *The Art of Ancient India* (1985); J. C. Harle, *The Art and Architecture of the Indian Subcontinent* (1986); and V. Dehejia, *Indian Art* (1997). Good translations of Indian literature discussed in the chapter are listed in the Notes. For an overview of Indian literature, see E. Dimock, Jr., et al., *The Literatures of India* (1974).

Among the best general histories of India are H. Kulke and D. Rothermund, *A History of India,* 3d ed. (1998); A. L. Basham, *The Wonder That Was India,* 3d rev. ed. (1968); R. Thapar, *History of India* (1966); and B. Stein, *A History of India* (1998). Also rewarding are R. Thapar, *Ancient Indian Social History* (1978); Z. Liu, *Ancient India and Ancient China* (1988); S. F. Mahmud, *A Concise History of Indo-Pakistan,* 2d ed. (1988); H. Scharff, *The State in Indian Tradition* (1989), which covers the period from the Aryans to the Muslims; and N. N. Bhattacharya, *Ancient Indian History and Civilization* (1988), which focuses on India before 1000 C.E.

Work on the Indus civilization continues at a rapid pace. See G. L. Possehl, ed., *Harappan Civilization: A Recent Perspective* (1993); G. L. Possehl and M. H. Ravel, *Harappan Civilization and Rojdi* (1989); and J. M. Kenoyer, *Ancient Cities of the Indus Valley Civilization* (1998). Trade between the Indus and Mesopotamian civilizations is treated in E. C. L. During Caspers, "Sumer, Coastal Arabia and the Indus Valley in Protoliterate and Early Dynastic Eras," *Journal of Economic and Social History of the Orient* 22 (1979): 121–135, and S. Ratnagar, *Encounters: The Westerly Trade of the Harappa Civilization* (1981).

For the Aryans and the Vedic period, see N. R. Banerjee, *The Iron Age in India* (1965), and C. Chakraborty, *Common Life in the Rig-veda and Atharvaveda* (1977). D. K. Chakrabarti, *The Early Use of Iron in India* (1992), uses archaeological evidence to prove that the ancient Indians used iron far earlier than previously thought. The question of the origins of the Aryans is analyzed in depth in C. Renfew, *Archaeology and Language: The Puzzle of Indo-European Origins* (1987). The polemical side of the debate can be seen from K. Elst, *Update on the Aryan Invasion Debate* (1999).

An excellent introduction to Indian religion, philosophy, and intellectual history is A. Embree, ed., *Sources of Indian Tradition,* 2d ed. (1988), which provides translations of major sources. Another excellent source of translated documents is D. Lopez, ed., *Religions of India in Practice* (1998). A broad overview of Indian religion is provided by J. Koller, *The Indian Way* (1982). P. S. Jaini, *The Jaina Path of Purification* (1979), and T. Hopkins, *Hindu Religious Tradition* (1971), cover two of the major religions, to which should be added K. K. Klostermaier, *A Survey of Hinduism* (1989), and K. H. Potter, *Guide to Indian Philosophy* (1988).

Buddhism is such a popular topic that the bibliography is virtually endless. H. Akira, *A History of Indian Buddhism* (1990), treats the early history of the Buddha and his followers. R. Robinson and W. Johnson, *The Buddhist Religion,* 4th ed. (1996), offers a comprehensive overview. See also D. Lopez, *The Story of the Buddha: A Concise Guide to Its History and Teachings* (2001). Still unsurpassed for its discussion of the relations between Buddhism and Hinduism is the grand work of C. N. Eliot, *Hinduism and Buddhism,* 3 vols. (reprint 1954), which traces the evolution of theistic ideas in both religions. C. Humphreys has written extensively about Buddhism. The student may wish to consult his *Buddhism* (1962), *Exploring Buddhism* (1975), or *The Wisdom of Buddhism,* rev. ed. (1979). More recent is D. Fox, *The Heart of Buddhist Wisdom* (1985). A well-illustrated volume is H. Bechert and R. Gombrich, ed., *The World of Buddhism* (1984).

Among the numerous works describing India's relations with the Persian Empire and Alexander the Great are several titles cited in the Suggested Reading for Chapters 2 and 5. P. H. L. Eggermont, *Alexander's Campaigns in Sind and Baluchistan* (1975), focuses solely on Alexander's activities in India. A. J. Dani, *The Historic City of Taxila* (1988), uses anthropological and historic evidence to study this important city and its influence.

On the reigns of Chandragupta and Ashoka, see R. K. Mookerji, *Chandragupta Maurya and His Times,* rev. ed. (1966), and R. Thapar, *Asoka and the Decline of the Mauryas* (1961), as well as her *Mauryas Revisited* (1987). J. C. Heesterman, "Kautilya and the Ancient Indian State," *Wiener Zeitschrift* 15 (1971): 5–22, analyzes the work and thought of Chandragupta's great minister of state.

For the Gupta period, see O. P. Singh Bhatia, trans., *The Imperial Guptas* (1962), and B. Smith, ed., *Essays on Gupta Culture* (1983). In a series of works, S. K. Maity covers many facets of the period: *Gupta Civilization: A Study* (1974), *The Imperial Guptas and Their Times* (1975), and *Economic Life in North India in the Gupta Period* (1975). Good treatments of Indian society and daily life in this period can be found in J. Auboyer, *Daily Life in Ancient India from Approximately 200 B.C. to A.D. 700* (1965).

RAMA AND SITA

The Ramayana, *an epic poem of about fifty thousand verses, is attributed to the third-century* B.C.E. *poet Valmiki. Its main character, Rama, the oldest son of a king, is an incarnation of the great god Vishnu. As a young man, he wins the princess Sita as his wife when he alone among her suitors proves strong enough to bend a huge bow. Rama and Sita love each other deeply, but court intrigue disturbs their happy life. After the king announces that he will retire and consecrate Rama as his heir, his beautiful junior wife, wishing to advance her own son, reminds the king that he has promised her a favor of her choice. She then asks to have him appoint her son heir and to have Rama sent into the wilderness for fourteen years. The king is forced to consent, and Rama obeys his father.*

The passage below gives the conversations between Rama and Sita after Rama learns he must leave. In subsequent parts of the very long epic, the lovers undergo many other tribulations, including Sita's abduction by the lord of the demons, the ten-headed Ravana, and her eventual recovery by Rama with the aid of monkeys.

The Ramayana *eventually appeared in numerous versions in all the major languages of India. Hearing it recited was said to bring religious merit. Sita, passionate in her devotion to her husband, has remained the favorite Indian heroine. Rama, Sita, and the monkey Hanuman are cult figures in Hinduism, with temples devoted to their worship.*

"For fourteen years I must live in Dandaka, while my father will appoint Bharata prince regent. I have come to see you before I leave for the desolate forest. You are never to boast of me in the presence of Bharata. Men in power cannot bear to hear others praised, and so you must never boast of my virtues in front of Bharata. . . . When

I have gone to the forest where sages make their home, my precious, blameless wife, you must earnestly undertake vows and fasts. You must rise early and worship the gods according to custom and then pay homage to my father Dasaratha, lord of men. And my aged mother Kausalya, who is tormented by misery, deserves your respect as well, for she has subordinated all to righteousness. The rest of my mothers, too, must always receive your homage. . . . My beloved, I am going to the great forest, and you must stay here. You must do as I tell you, my lovely, and not give offense to anyone."

So Rama spoke, and Sita, who always spoke kindly to her husband and deserved kindness from him, grew angry just because she loved him, and said, "My lord, a man's father, his mother, brother, son, or daughter-in-law all experience the effects of their own past deeds and suffer an individual fate. But a wife, and she alone, bull among men, must share her husband's fate. Therefore I, too, have been ordered to live in the forest. It is not her father or mother, not her son or friends or herself, but her husband, and he alone, who gives a woman permanent refuge in this world and after death. If you must leave this very day for the trackless forest, Rama, I will go in front of you, softening the thorns and sharp *kusa* grass. Cast out your anger and resentment, like so much water left after drinking one's fill. Do not be reluctant to take me, my mighty husband. There is no evil in me. The shadow of a husband's feet in any circumstances surpasses the finest mansions, an aerial chariot, or even flying through the sky. . . . O Rama, bestower of honor, you have the power to protect any other person in the forest. Why then not me? . . .

"If I were to be offered a place to live in heaven itself, Rama, tiger among men, I would refuse it if you were not there. I will go to the trackless forest teeming with deer, monkeys, and elephants, and live there as in my father's house, clinging to your feet alone, in strict self-discipline. I love no one else; my heart is so attached to you that were we to be parted I am resolved to die. Take me, oh please grant my request. I shall not be a burden to you." . . .

When Sita finished speaking, the righteous prince, who knew what was right and cherished it, attempted to dissuade her. . . .

"Sita, give up this notion of living in the forest. The name 'forest' is given only to wild regions where hardships abound. . . . There are lions that live in mountain caves; their roars are redoubled by mountain torrents and are a painful thing to hear—the forest is a place of pain. At night worn with fatigue, one must sleep upon the ground on a bed of leaves, broken off of themselves—the forest is a place of utter pain. And one has to fast, Sita, to the limit of one's endurance, wear clothes of barkcloth and bear the burden of matted hair. . . . There are many creeping creatures, of every size and shape, my lovely, ranging aggressively over the ground. . . . Moths, scorpions, worms, gnats, and flies continually harass one, my frail Sita—the forest is wholly a place of pain. . . ."

Sita was overcome with sorrow when she heard what Rama said. With tears trickling down her face, she answered him in a faint voice. . . . "If from feelings of love I follow you, my pure-hearted husband, I shall have no sin to answer for, because my husband is my deity. My union with you is sacred and shall last even beyond death. . . . If you refuse to take me to the forest despite the sorrow that I feel, I shall have no recourse but to end my life by poison, fire, or water."

Though she pleaded with him in this and every other way to be allowed to go, great-armed Rama would not consent to taking her to the desolate forest. And when he told her as much, Sita fell to brooding, and drenched the ground, it seemed, with the hot tears that fell from her eyes. . . . She was nearly insensible with sorrow when Rama took her in his arms and comforted her. . . . "Without knowing your true feelings, my lovely, I could not consent to your living in the wilderness, though I am perfectly capable of protecting you. Since you are determined to live with me in the forest, Sita, I could no sooner abandon you than a self-respecting man his reputation. . . . My father keeps to the path of righteousness and truth, and

Rama and Sita in the forest, from a set of miniature paintings done in about 1600. (*National Museum, New Delhi*)

I wish to act just as he instructs me. That is the eternal way of righteousness. Follow me, my timid one, be my companion in righteousness. Go now and bestow precious objects on the brahmans, give food to the mendicants and all who ask for it. Hurry, there is no time to waste."

Finding that her husband had acquiesced in her going, the lady was elated and set out at once to make the donations.

QUESTIONS FOR ANALYSIS

1. What can you infer about early Indian family life and social relations from this story?

2. What do Sita's words and actions indicate about women's roles in Indian society of the time?

3. What do you think accounts for the continuing popularity of the story of Rama throughout Indian history?

Source: The Ramayana of Valmiki: An Epic of India, vol. 2: *Ayodhyakanda,* trans. Sheldon I. Pollock, ed. Robert P. Goldman (Princeton, N.J.: Princeton University Press, 1986), pp. 134–142, modified slightly. Copyright © 1986 by Princeton University Press. Reprinted by permission of Princeton University Press.

This nearly foot-tall ivory cup is inlaid with turquoise from the tomb (ca 1200 B.C.E.) of a Shang royal consort. (© *Cultural Relics Data Center of China*)

CHINA'S CLASSICAL AGE, TO 256 B.C.E.

The early development of China's civilization occurred with little contact with the other early civilizations of Eurasia. The reasons for China's relative isolation were geographic: communication between the Middle East or India and East Asia was very difficult, impeded by high mountains and vast deserts. Thus, in comparison to India and the ancient Middle East, there was less cross-fertilization through trade and other contact with other comparably advanced civilizations. Moreover, there were no cultural breaks comparable to the rise of the Aryans in India or the Assyrians in the Middle East; there were no new peoples and no new languages.

The impact of early China's relative isolation is found in many distinctive or unique features of its culture. Perhaps the most important of these is its writing system. Unlike the other major societies of Eurasia, China retained a logographic writing system, with a separate symbol for each word. This writing system shaped not only Chinese literature and thought but also key social and political processes, such as the nature of the ruling class and the way Chinese interacted with non-Chinese.

Chinese history is discussed in terms of a succession of dynasties. The Shang Dynasty (ca 1500–ca 1050 B.C.E.) was the first to have writing, metalworking, cities, and chariots. The Shang kings played priestly roles, serving as intermediaries with both their royal ancestors and the high god Di. The Shang were overthrown by one of their vassal states, the Zhou (ca 1050–256 B.C.E.). The Zhou rulers set up a decentralized, feudal governmental structure. After several centuries, this structure evolved into a multistate system. As warfare between the states intensified from the sixth century B.C.E. on, social and cultural change also quickened. Aristocratic privileges declined, and China entered one of its most creative periods, when the philosophies of Confucianism, Daoism, and Legalism were developed.

- How did China's geography influence its development?
- In what ways did ancient and classical China resemble other early civilizations?
- What effects did China's retaining a logographic writing system have on its culture?
- What were the key contributions of the ancient and classical periods to the later development of Chinese civilization?

These are the questions addressed in this chapter.

THE LAND AND ITS CHALLENGE

The term *China,* like the term *India,* does not refer to the same geographical entity at all points in history. But the historical China, also called China proper, was smaller than present-day China, not larger like the historical India. The contemporary People's Republic of China includes territories like Tibet, Inner Mongolia, Turkestan, and Manchuria that were not in premodern times inhabited by Chinese or ruled directly by Chinese states (see Map 4.1).

China proper, about a thousand miles north to south and east to west, occupies much of the temperate zone of East Asia. The northern part, drained by the Yellow River, is colder, flatter, and more arid than the south. Rainfall in many areas is less than twenty inches a year, making it well suited to crops like wheat and millet. The dominant soil is **loess**—fine wind-driven earth that is fertile and easy to work even with primitive tools. Because so much of the loess ends up as silt in the Yellow River, the riverbed rises, and the river has to be diked and easily floods. Drought is another perennial problem for farmers in the north. The Yangzi River is the dominant feature of the warmer, wetter, and more lush south, a region well suited to rice cultivation and double cropping. The Yangzi and its many tributaries are navigable, so boats were traditionally the preferred means of transportation in the south.

Mountains, deserts, and grasslands separated China proper from other early civilizations. Between China and India lay Tibet, with its vast mountain ranges and high plateaus. North of Tibet are great expanses of desert

MAP 4.1 China Under the Shang and Zhou Dynasties   Chinese civilization developed in the temperate regions drained by the Yellow and Yangzi Rivers. The early Zhou government controlled larger areas than the Shang did, but the independent states of the Warring States Period were more aggressive about pushing out their frontiers, greatly extending the geographical boundaries of Chinese civilization.

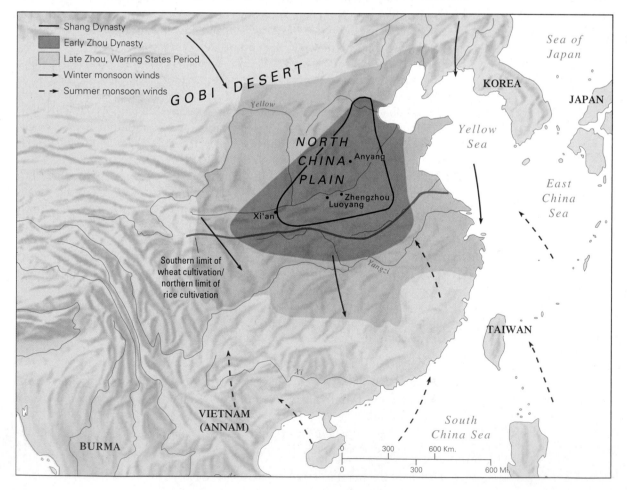

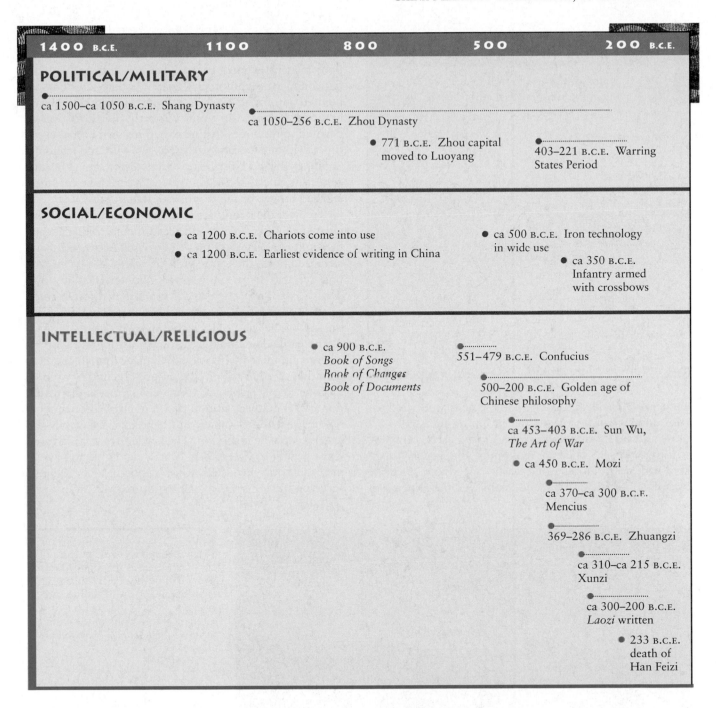

1400 B.C.E.	1100	800	500	200 B.C.E.

POLITICAL/MILITARY

ca 1500–ca 1050 B.C.E. Shang Dynasty

ca 1050–256 B.C.E. Zhou Dynasty

771 B.C.E. Zhou capital moved to Luoyang

403–221 B.C.E. Warring States Period

SOCIAL/ECONOMIC

ca 1200 B.C.E. Chariots come into use

ca 1200 B.C.E. Earliest evidence of writing in China

ca 500 B.C.E. Iron technology in wide use

ca 350 B.C.E. Infantry armed with crossbows

INTELLECTUAL/RELIGIOUS

ca 900 B.C.E. *Book of Songs* *Book of Changes* *Book of Documents*

551–479 B.C.E. Confucius

500–200 B.C.E. Golden age of Chinese philosophy

ca 453–403 B.C.E. Sun Wu, *The Art of War*

ca 450 B.C.E. Mozi

ca 370–ca 300 B.C.E. Mencius

369–286 B.C.E. Zhuangzi

ca 310–ca 215 B.C.E. Xunzi

ca 300–200 B.C.E. *Laozi* written

233 B.C.E. death of Han Feizi

where nothing grows except in rare oases, and north of them stretch grasslands from Ukraine to eastern Siberia. Chinese civilization did not spread into any of these Inner Asian regions, above all because they were not suited to crop agriculture. Inner Asia, where raising animals is a more productive use of land than planting crops, became the heartland of China's traditional enemies, such as the **Xiongnu** and Mongols.

CHINA'S EARLIEST CIVILIZATIONS, TO 1050 B.C.E.

Chinese myths and legends, like those of other early civilizations, reveal what the Chinese considered to be their central and distinctive values. In the form in which these myths have been preserved, China was fashioned not by gods but by brilliant human beings who invented the key

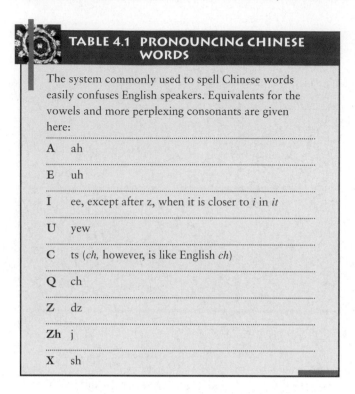

TABLE 4.1 PRONOUNCING CHINESE WORDS

The system commonly used to spell Chinese words easily confuses English speakers. Equivalents for the vowels and more perplexing consonants are given here:

A	ah
E	uh
I	ee, except after z, when it is closer to *i* in *it*
U	yew
C	ts (*ch,* however, is like English *ch*)
Q	ch
Z	dz
Zh	j
X	sh

elements of civilization. The earliest ones were credited with domesticating animals and inventing the family, the plow and hoe, bows and arrows, boats, carts, ceramics, writing, and silk. The trio Yao, Shun, and Yu are associated with the beginning of dynastic rule. Yao devised the calendar, instituted rituals, and established the principle of rule by the worthy: when it was time to turn over power, he bypassed his own less worthy son in favor of Shun, a poor peasant of unsurpassed filial devotion to his blind father and evil stepmother. To deal with floods, Shun appointed an official, Yu, who zealously dredged the channels that became the rivers of north China. Yu was so devoted to his duties that he passed his own home several times without pausing to greet his wife and children. Shun recognized Yu's abilities and selected him as his successor. As ruler, Yu divided the realm into nine provinces and had bronze vessels cast using earth from each one. After Yu died, the people ignored the successor he had designated and asked Yu's son to lead them, making Yu and his son the two kings of the Xia Dynasty. According to ancient traditions, the fourteenth Xia ruler was a tyrant who was deposed by a subordinate who founded his own dynasty, the Shang, which in turn lasted through thirty rulers until a self-indulgent and obstinate king was overthrown by the ruler of the vassal state of Zhou.

The early Chinese conception of history and cosmology seen in these myths was much more human-centered than that of other major civilizations. Technology played a major role: what made China civilized was the invention of agriculture, writing, flood control, bronze technology, silk, and ceramics. But hereditary monarchy was just as crucial an invention. The key figures were virtuous kings willing to delegate to officials and able to pass on their authority to their sons. Modern archaeologists agree on the importance of agriculture, writing, bronze,

Yellow River Valley The Yellow River acquired its name because the silt it carries gives it a muddy look. The earth of the north China plain is predominantly wind-borne and river-borne loess soil, which led early Chinese also to think of the earth as yellow. (*China Tourism Photo Library, Hong Kong*)

Painted Pottery Figure   The Neolithic cultures of northwest China in the third millennium B.C.E. decorated pottery with red and black paint. Most of the finds are jars decorated with geometric designs, but there are occasionally images of human beings, animals, and fish. Some scholars speculate that this image depicts a shaman wearing face paint. Note the snake depicted climbing the back of its head. (© *Museum of Far Eastern Antiquities*)

and state formation to the story of Chinese civilization but also give weight to ritual and religion. Moreover, rather than concentrate narrowly on the direct predecessors of the Shang kings, they have shown that both in Shang times and in the millennium before them, China proper was home to many distinct cultures, all of which played a part in the evolution of Chinese civilization.

The Neolithic Age

From about 10,000 B.C.E. agriculture was practiced in China, apparently originating independently of somewhat earlier developments in Egypt and Mesopotamia, but perhaps influenced by developments in Southeast Asia, where rice cultivation began earlier than in China. By 5000 B.C.E. there were Neolithic village settlements in several regions of China. The primary Neolithic crops were drought-resistant millet, grown in the loess soils of the region drained by the Yellow River, and rice, grown in the wetlands of the lower reaches of the Yangzi River, where it was supplemented by fish. In both areas pigs, dogs, and cattle were domesticated, and by 3000 B.C.E. sheep had become important in the north and water buffalo in the south.

Over the course of the fifth to third millennia B.C.E., many distinct regional Neolithic cultures emerged. For instance, in the northwest during the fourth and third millennia B.C.E., people made fine red pottery vessels decorated in black pigment with bold designs, including spirals,

sawtooth lines, and zoomorphic stick figures. At the same time in the east, pottery was rarely painted but was made into distinctive shapes, including three-legged, deep-bodied tripods. Jade ornaments, blades, and ritual objects, sometimes of extraordinary craftsmanship, have been found in several eastern sites but are rare in western ones.

Over time Neolithic cultures came to share more by way of material culture and social and cultural practices. Many practices related to treatment of the dead spread out of their original area, including use of coffins, ramped chambers, large numbers of grave goods, and divination based on interpreting cracks induced by heat in cattle bones. Fortified walls, made of rammed earth, came to be built around settlements in many areas, suggesting not only increased contact but also increased conflict.

The Shang Dynasty (ca 1500–ca 1050 B.C.E.)

After 2000 B.C.E. a Bronze Age civilization appeared in north China with the traits found in Bronze Age civilizations elsewhere, such as writing, metalworking, domestication of the horse, class stratification, and cult centers. Perhaps the first stage of this transition should be identified as the Xia Dynasty, traditionally said to precede the Shang, but no sites from that period have yielded written documents. The Shang Dynasty, however, is well documented in the divination texts excavated from Shang royal tombs.

Shang civilization was not as densely urban as Mesopotamia, but Shang kings ruled from large settlements. The best excavated is **Anyang,** from which the Shang kings ruled for more than two centuries. At the center of Anyang were large palaces, temples, and altars. These buildings were constructed on rammed-earth foundations (a feature of Chinese building practice that would last for centuries). Outside the central core were industrial areas where bronzeworkers, potters, stone carvers, and other artisans lived and worked. Many homes were built partly below ground level, probably as a way to conserve heat. Beyond these urban settlements were farming areas and large forests. Deer, bears, tigers, wild boars, elephants, and rhinoceros were still plentiful in north China in this era.

The divinatory texts found in the royal tombs outside Anyang show that Shang kings—the ones posing the questions in these texts—were military chieftains. The king regularly sent out armies of three thousand to five thousand men on campaigns, and when not at war they would go on hunts lasting for months. They fought rebellious vassals and foreign tribes, but the situation constantly changed as vassals became enemies and enemies accepted offers of alliance. War booty was an important source of the king's revenue, especially the war captives who could be made into slaves. Captives not needed as slaves might end up as sacrificial victims—or perhaps the demands of the gods and ancestors for sacrifices were a motive for going to war.

Bronze technology gave Shang warriors improved weapons. Bronze-tipped spears and halberds were widely used. Bronze was also used for the fittings of the chariots that came into use around 1200 B.C.E., probably as a result of diffusion across Asia. The chariot provided commanders with a mobile station from which they could supervise their troops; it also gave archers and soldiers armed with long halberds increased mobility.

Shang power did not rest solely on military supremacy. The Shang king was also the high priest, the one best qualified to offer sacrifices to the royal ancestors and the high god Di. Royal ancestors were viewed as able to intervene with Di, send curses, produce dreams, assist the king in battle, and so on. The king communicated with his ancestors by interpreting the cracks made in heated cattle bones or tortoise shells, prepared for him by professional diviners.

Shang palaces were undoubtedly splendid but were constructed of perishable material like wood, and nothing of them remains today, unlike the stone buildings and monuments so characteristic of the ancient West. What

Shang Oracle Bone
To communicate with their ancestors or the high gods, Shang kings employed diviners. After the ruler posed a yes or no question, the diviner applied a hot point to a prepared bone, usually a cattle scapula bone. The direction of the cracks indicated whether the god's answer was yes or no. Sometimes the diviners, to keep records, would record the question and answer on the other side of the bone. On the bone shown here, the question related to a hunt. Other questions commonly posed concerned weather, travel, illness, and dreams. *(Lowell Georgia/Photo Researchers)*

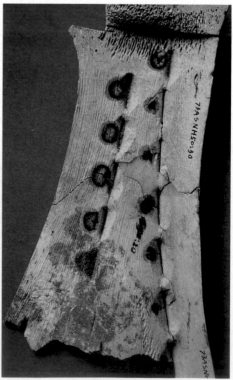

Royal Tomb at Anyang   Eleven large tombs and more than a thousand small graves have been excavated at the royal burial ground at Anyang. This grave, about sixty feet deep and three hundred feet long, would have taken thousands of laborers many months to complete. But even more wealth was expended to fill it with bronze, stone, pottery, jade, and textile grave goods. Human victims were also placed in it. *(Academia Sinica, Taiwan)*

has survived are the lavish underground tombs built for Shang kings and their consorts. The one royal tomb not to have been robbed before it was excavated was for Lady Hao, one of the many wives of the king Wu Ding (ca 1200 B.C.E.). Although one of the smaller royal tombs (about 13 by 18 feet at the mouth and about 25 feet deep) and not in the main royal cemetery, it was nonetheless filled with an extraordinary array of sacrificial goods. Human beings were sacrificed at her tomb (the 16 human skeletons included both males and females, children and adults), but not on as great a scale as at some of the larger tombs. Rather it was the burial of a profusion of valuable objects that was the most striking feature of this tomb, which contained 460 bronze objects (including more than 200 ritual vessels, more than 130 weapons, 23 bells, 27 knives, 4 mirrors, and 4 tigers or tiger heads), nearly 750 jade objects, some 70 stone sculptures, nearly 500 bone hairpins, more than 20 bone arrowheads, and 3 ivory carvings. Others, however, were

apparently tribute sent to the capital from distant places. More than 20 different types of ritual vessels were buried in the tomb, of which about 60 had Lady Hao's name inscribed on them. The weapons found in this tomb are only one sign that Lady Hao took an interest in military affairs. From inscribed bones found elsewhere at Anyang, we know that she led military campaigns, once with 13,000 troops against the Qiang to the west, at other times against the Fu Fang in the northwest, the Ba Fang in the southwest, and the Yi in the east.

In addition to objects of value or practical use, the Shang interred human beings in royal tombs, sometimes dozens of them. Many were war captives, offered as sacrifices. Others were the king's followers, retainers, and servants, who had voluntarily decided to accompany him in death. Early Shang graves rarely had more than three victims or followers accompanying the main occupant, but over time the practice grew. The late Shang tomb for the king who reigned about 1200 B.C.E. contained the

Owl-Shaped Shang Bronze   This 18-inch-tall bronze vessel in the shape of an owl was one of more than two hundred bronze ritual vessels buried in about 1200 B.C.E. in the tomb of Lady Hao, a consort of the Shang king Wu Ding. (© *Cultural Relics Data Center of China*)

Jade Figure   Among the valuables placed in royal Shang tombs were many jade objects, such as this figure, 2¾ inches tall. Since Neolithic times, jade has had the place in China occupied by gold in many other cultures: it is valued for its beauty, rarity, and endurance. This figure was one of seven hundred jade pieces in the tomb of Lady Hao (see page 85). (© *Cultural Relics Data Center of China*)

remains of 90 followers, 74 human sacrifices, 12 horses, and 11 dogs. The sacrificial victims are recognizable because they were decapitated, cut at the waist, or otherwise put to death by mutilation. Those who voluntarily followed their king to the grave generally had their own ornaments and might also have had coffins and grave goods such as weapons.

Shang rulers had to have the ability to mobilize thousands of laborers to dig the 30- to 40-foot pits for these tombs, then later fill in the site by ramming earth. Ramming earth was also used to construct city walls. It has been estimated that even with 10,000 laborers working to move and ram the earth, the 60-foot-wide and 30-foot-high wall at Zhengzhou would not have been completed in less than 10 years.

Shang society was marked by sharp status distinctions. The Shang royal family and aristocracy lived in large houses built on huge platforms of rammed earth. The king and other noble families had family and clan names transmitted along patrilineal lines, from father to son. Kingship similarly passed along patrilines, from elder to younger brother and father to son, but never to or through sisters or daughters. The kings and the aristocracy owned slaves, many of whom had been captured in war. In the urban centers there were substantial numbers of craftsmen who worked in stone, bone, and bronze.

Shang farmers were essentially serfs of the aristocrats. Their life was not that different from that of their Neolithic ancestors, and they worked the fields with similar stone tools. They usually lived in small, compact villages surrounded by fields. Some new crops became common in Shang times, most notably wheat, which had spread from West Asia. Shang farmers themselves probably deserve the credit for discovering how to make silk from the cocoons of silkworms, which liked to feed on mulberry trees. Because of its beauty, strength, and light weight, silk became an important item of long-distance trade even in ancient times. Recently silk from Shang China was discovered in an Egyptian tomb.

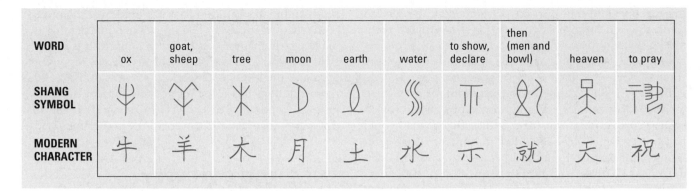

WORD	ox	goat, sheep	tree	moon	earth	water	to show, declare	then (men and bowl)	heaven	to pray
SHANG SYMBOL	ψ	ϒ	朩	D	♀	⁓⁓⁓	示	就	天	祝
MODERN CHARACTER	牛	羊	木	月	土	水	示	就	天	祝

FIGURE 4.1 The Origins of Chinese Writing   The modern Chinese writing system (bottom row) evolved from the script employed by diviners in the Shang period (upper row). *(Source: Adapted from Patricia Buckley Ebrey,* The Cambridge Illustrated History of China *[Cambridge: Cambridge University Press, 1996], p. 26. Reprinted by permission of Cambridge University Press.)*

Writing   The survival of divination texts inscribed on bones from Shang tombs demonstrates that writing was already a major element in Chinese culture by 1200 B.C.E. Writing must have been developed earlier, but the early stages cannot be traced, probably because writing was done on perishable materials like wood, bamboo, or silk. The earliest possible signs of writing are the symbols or emblems inscribed on late Neolithic pots and the symbols cast into early Shang bronzes. Not until the oracle bones from the late Shang period, however, is there evidence of full sentences.

Once writing was invented, it had profound effects on China's culture and government. A written language made possible a bureaucracy capable of keeping records and conducting correspondence with commanders and governors far from the palace. Hence literacy became the ally of royal rule, facilitating communication with and effective control over the realm. Literacy also preserved the learning, lore, and experience of early Chinese society and facilitated the development of abstract thought.

The Chinese script was **logographic,** like ancient Egyptian and Sumerian, meaning that each word was represented by a single symbol. In the Chinese case, some of these symbols were pictures, but for the names of abstract concepts other methods were adopted. Sometimes the symbol for a different word was borrowed because the two words were pronounced alike. Sometimes two different symbols were combined; for instance, to represent different types of trees, the symbol for tree could be combined with another symbol borrowed for its pronunciation (see Figure 4.1).

In western Eurasia logographic scripts were eventually modified or replaced by phonetic scripts, but that never happened in China (although, because of changes in the spoken language, today many words are represented by two or three characters rather than a single one). Because China retained its early logographic writing system, many years were required to gain full mastery of reading and writing, which added to the prestige of education.

Why did China retain a logographic writing system, even after encounters with phonetic ones? Although phonetic systems have many real advantages, especially with respect to ease of learning to read, there are some costs to dropping a logographic system. Those who learned to read Chinese could communicate with a wider range of people than those who read scripts based on speech. Since characters did not change when the pronunciation changed, educated Chinese could read texts written centuries earlier without the need for them to be translated. Moreover, as the Chinese language developed regional variants, readers of Chinese could read books and letters by contemporaries whose oral language they could not comprehend. Thus the Chinese script played a large role in holding China together and fostering a sense of connection with the past. In addition, many of China's neighbors (Japan, Korea, and Vietnam, in particular) adopted the Chinese script, allowing communication through writing between people whose languages were totally unrelated. In this regard, the Chinese language was like Arabic numerals, which have the same meaning however they are read.

Bronzes   As in Egypt, Mesopotamia, and India, the development of more complex forms of social organization in Shang China coincided with the mastery of metalworking, specifically bronze. The bronze industry required central coordination of a large labor force to mine, refine, and transport copper, tin, and lead ores and to produce and transport charcoal. It also required technically skilled artisans to make clay models, construct ceramic piece molds, and assemble and finish each vessel, some of which weighed over one thousand pounds.

Bronze, in Shang times, was used more for ritual than for war. Most surviving Shang bronze objects are vessels such as cups, goblets, steamers, and cauldrons that would have originally have been used during sacrificial ceremonies but that have survived because they were buried in tombs. They were beautifully formed in a great variety of shapes and sizes. Complex designs were achieved through mold casting and prefabrication of parts. For instance, legs, handles, and other protruding members were cast first before the body was cast onto them.

The decoration on Shang bronzes seems to say something interesting about Shang culture, but scholars cannot agree just what it says. In the art of ancient Egypt, Assyria, and Babylonia, representations of agriculture (domesticated plants and animals) and of social hierarchy (kings, priests, scribes, and slaves) are very common, matching our understandings of the social, political, and economic development of those societies. In Shang China, by contrast, images of wild animals predominate. Some animal images readily suggest possible meanings. Jade cicadas were sometimes found in the mouths of the dead, and images of cicadas on bronzes are easy to interpret as images evocative of rebirth in the realm of ancestral spirits, as cicadas spend years underground before emerging. Birds, similarly, suggest to many the idea of messengers that can communicate with other realms, especially ones in the sky. More problematic is the most common image, the stylized animal face called the **taotie**. To some it is a monster—a fearsome image that would scare away evil forces. Others imagine a dragon—an animal whose vast powers had more positive associations. Some hypothesize that it reflects masks used in rituals. Others associate it with animal sacrifices, totemism, or shamanism. Still others see these images as hardly more than designs.

Bronze technology spread beyond Shang territories into areas the Shang would have considered enemy lands. A striking example was discovered in 1986 in the western province of Sichuan. There a bronze-producing culture contemporaneous with the late Shang had markedly different religious and artistic practices. This culture did not practice human sacrifice, but two sacrificial pits contained the burned remains of elephant tusks and a wide range of gold, bronze, jade, and stone objects. Among them were a life-size statue and many life-size bronze heads, all with angular facial features and enormous eyes. The heads may have been used to top wood or clay statues. Some of the

heads and masks had thin layers of gold over the bronze. Some scholars speculate that figures of humans were used in place of humans in a sacrificial ceremony. It is also possible that the statues with the bronze heads represented gods and the local people felt for some reason that these representations had to be burned and buried. Archaeologists are continuing to excavate in this region, and new discoveries may lead to answers to these questions.

THE ZHOU DYNASTY (CA 1050–256 B.C.E.)

The Shang campaigned constantly against enemies. To the west were the fierce Qiang, considered barbarian tribesmen by the Shang and perhaps speaking an early form of Tibetan. Between the Shang capital and the Qiang was a frontier state called Zhou, which seems to have both inherited cultural traditions from the Neolithic cultures of the northwest and absorbed most of the material culture of the Shang. In about 1050 B.C.E., the Zhou rose against the Shang and defeated them in battle.

Zhou Politics

The early Zhou period is the first one for which transmitted texts exist in some abundance. The **Book of Documents** describes the Zhou conquest of the Shang as the victory of just and noble warriors over decadent courtiers who were led by a dissolute, sadistic king. At the same time, these documents show that the Zhou recognized the Shang as occupying the center of the world, were eager to succeed to that role rather than dispute it, and saw history as a major way to legitimate power. Thus, like many of the invaders in Mesopotamia, the Zhou built on the accomplishments of their predecessors. The three early Zhou rulers who are given the most praise are King Wen (the "cultured" or "literate" king), who expanded the Zhou domain; his son King Wu (the "martial" king), who conquered the Shang; and Wu's brother, the Duke of Zhou, who consolidated the conquest and served as loyal regent for Wu's heir. Besides these transmitted texts, hundreds of inscriptions on ritual bronzes have survived, some of which record benefactions from the king and mention the services that had earned the king's favor.

Like the Shang kings, the Zhou kings sacrificed to their ancestors, but they also sacrificed to Heaven. The *Book of Documents* assumes a close relationship between Heaven and the king, who was called the Son of Heaven. Heaven gives the king a mandate to rule only as long as he rules in the interests of the people. Thus it was because the last king of the Shang had been decadent and cruel that Heaven took the mandate away from him and entrusted it to the virtuous Zhou kings. Humanity needs such a king to mediate between it and Heaven. Because this theory of the **Mandate of Heaven** does not seem to have had any place in Shang cosmology, it may have been elaborated by the early Zhou rulers as a kind of propaganda to win over the conquered subjects of the Shang. Whatever its origins, it remained a central feature of Chinese political ideology from the early Zhou period on.

Rather than attempt to rule all of their territories directly, the early Zhou rulers set up a decentralized, feudal system. They sent out relatives and trusted subordinates with troops to establish walled garrisons in the conquered territories. These vassals were generally able to pass their positions on to a son, so that in time the domains became hereditary fiefs. By 800 B.C.E. there were about two hundred lords with domains large and small, of which only about twenty-five were large enough to matter much in interstate politics. Each lord appointed officers to serve him in ritual, administrative, or military capacities. These posts and their associated titles tended to become hereditary as well. Each domain thus came to have noble families with patrimonies in offices and associated lands.

The decentralized rule of the early Zhou period had from the beginning carried within it the danger that the regional lords would become so powerful that they would no longer obey the commands of the king. As generations passed and ties of loyalty and kinship grew more distant, this indeed happened. In 771 B.C.E. the Zhou king was killed by an alliance of Rong tribesmen and Zhou vassals. One of his sons was put on the throne, and then for safety's sake the capital was moved east out of the Wei River valley to modern Luoyang, just south of the Yellow River in the heart of the central plains (see Map 4.1).

The revived Zhou Dynasty never fully regained control over its vassals, and China entered a prolonged period without a strong central authority. For a couple of centuries a code of chivalrous or sportsmanlike conduct still regulated warfare between the states: one state would not attack another while it was in mourning for its ruler; during battles one side would not attack before the other side had time to line up; ruling houses were not wiped out, so that a successor could continue to sacrifice to their ancestors; and so on. Thereafter, however, such niceties were abandoned and China entered a period of nearly constant conflict called the **Warring States Period** (403–221 B.C.E.). By the third century B.C.E. there were only seven important states remaining. These states were much more centralized than their early Zhou predecessors. The kings of these states had eliminated indirect control through vassals and in its place had dispatched royal officials to remote cities, controlling them from a distance through the transmission of documents and dismissing them at will.

Zhou Society

Over the course of the eight centuries of the Zhou Dynasty, Chinese society underwent radical changes. Early Zhou rule was highly aristocratic. Inherited ranks placed people in a hierarchy ranging from the king to the rulers of states with titles like duke and marquis, the hereditary lords of the individual states, the hereditary great officials of the states, the lower ranks of the aristocracy (men who could serve either in military or civil capacities, known as **shi**), and finally to the ordinary people (the farmers, craftsmen, and traders). Patrilineal family ties were very important in this society, and at the upper reaches at least, sacrifices to ancestors were one of the key rituals that were used to forge social ties.

Glimpses of what life was like at various social levels in the early Zhou Dynasty can be found in the **Book of Songs,** which contains the earliest Chinese poetry. Some of the songs are hymns used in court religious ceremonies, such as offerings to ancestors, and reveal aspects of religious practice, such as the use of a grandson of the deceased to impersonate him during the ceremony. Others clearly had their origins in folk songs. Some of these folk songs depict farmers at work clearing fields, plowing and planting, gathering mulberry leaves for silkworms, spinning and weaving. The seasons set the pace for rural life, and the songs contain many references to seasonal changes, such as the appearance of insects like grasshoppers and crickets. Farming life involved not merely the cultivation of crops like millet, hemp (for cloth), beans, and vegetables, but also hunting small animals and collecting grasses and rushes to make rope and baskets.

Many of the folk songs are love songs that depict a more informal pattern of courtship than prevailed in later China. One stanza reads:

Please, Zhongzi,
Do not leap over our wall,
Do not break our mulberry trees.
It's not that I begrudge the mulberries,
But I fear my brothers.
You I would embrace,
But my brothers' words—those I dread.[1]

There were also songs of complaint, such as this one in which soldiers protest:

Which plant is not brown?
Which man is not sad?
Have pity on us soldiers,
Treated as though we were not men![2]

Other songs in this collection are court odes that reveal attitudes of the aristocrats. One such ode expresses a deep distrust of women's involvement in politics:

Clever men build cities,
Clever women topple them.
Beautiful, these clever women may be
But they are owls and kites.
Women have long tongues
That lead to ruin.
Disorder does not come down from heaven;
It is produced by women.[3]

Part of the reason for distrust of women in politics was the practice of concubinage. Rulers regularly demonstrated their power and wealth by accumulating large numbers of concubines and thus would have children by several women. In theory, succession went to the eldest son of the wife, then younger sons by her, and only in their absence sons of concubines, but in actual practice, the ruler of a state or head of a powerful ministerial family could select a son of a concubine to be his heir if he wished. This led to much scheming for favor among the various sons and their mothers and the common perception that women were incapable of taking a disinterested view of the larger good.

The economic growth of the Zhou period is evident in the appearance of cities all over north China. Thick earthen walls were built around the palaces and ancestral temples of the ruler and other aristocrats, and often an outer wall was added to protect the artisans, merchants, and farmers who lived outside the inner wall. Accounts of

Bronze Relief of Hunters   Hunting provided an important source of food in the Zhou period, and hunters were often depicted on inlaid bronzes of the period. *(The Avery Brundage Collection/Laurie Platt Winfrey, Inc.)*

sieges launched against these walled citadels, with scenes of the scaling of walls and the storming of gates, are central to descriptions of military confrontations in this period.

By the Warring States Period, the old aristocratic social structure of the Zhou was being undermined by the effects of intense competition between the states and advances in military technology. Large, well-drilled infantry armies also became a potent military force in this period, able to withstand and defeat chariot-led forces. By 300 B.C.E. states were sending out armies of a couple hundred thousand drafted foot soldiers, usually accompanied by horsemen. Adding to the effectiveness of armies of drafted foot soldiers was the development of the **crossbow.** The trigger of a crossbow is an intricate bronze mechanism that allowed a foot soldier to shoot farther than a horseman carrying a light bow. One text of the period reports that a skilled soldier with a powerful crossbow and a sharp sword was the match of a hundred ordinary men. To defend against crossbows, soldiers began wearing armor and helmets. Most of the armor was made of leader strips tied with cords. Helmets were sometimes made of iron.

The introduction of cavalry in this period also reduced the need for a chariot-riding aristocracy. Shooting bows and arrows from horseback was first perfected by non-Chinese peoples to the north of China proper, who at that time were making the transition to a nomadic pastoral economy. The northern state of Jin, to defend itself from the attacks of these horsemen, developed its own cavalry armies. Once it started using them against other Chinese states, they naturally had to master the new technology in turn. From this time on, acquiring and pasturing horses was a key component of military preparedness.

Because these developments made commoners and craftsmen central to the success of their armies, rulers of the warring states tried to find ways to increase their populations. To increase agricultural output, they brought new land into cultivation, drained marshes, and dug irrigation channels. By the sixth century B.C.E. rulers were surveying their land and beginning to try to tax farmers. They wanted to undermine the power of lords over their subjects in order to get direct access to the peasants' labor power. Serfdom thus gradually declined. Registering populations led to the extension of family names to commoners at an earlier date than anywhere else in the world.

To encourage trade, rulers began casting coins. The development of iron technology in the early Zhou Dynasty also promoted economic expansion. By the fifth century iron was being widely used for both farm tools and weapons. By the third century the largest smelters

employed two hundred or more workmen. A new powerful group also emerged in society—the rich who had acquired their wealth through trade or industry rather than inheritance or political favor. Merchants were another important new group in society, and late Zhou texts frequently mention cross-regional trade in objects such as furs, copper, dyes, hemp, salt, and horses.

Within elite strata as well, social mobility increased in this period. Rulers more often sent out their own officials rather than delegate authority to hereditary lesser lords. This trend toward centralized bureaucratic control created opportunities for social advancement for those on the lower end of the old aristocracy (the shi), valued for their ability more than their birth. Competition among such men guaranteed rulers a ready supply of able and willing subordinates, and competition among rulers for talent meant that ambitious men could be selective in deciding where to offer their services. (See the feature "Individuals in Society: Guan Zhong.")

The development of infantry armies also created the need for a new type of general, and rulers became less willing to let men lead troops merely because of aristocratic birth. Treatises on the art of war described the ideal general as a master of maneuver, illusion, and deception. *The Art of War,* attributed to Sun Wu, is thought to have appeared between 453 and 403 B.C.E. Master Sun analyzed battle tactics and ways to win wars without combat by deceiving the enemy. He argued that heroism is a useless virtue that leads to needless deaths. But discipline is essential, and he insisted that the entire army had to be trained to follow the orders of its commanders without questioning them.

Archaeology provides ample evidence of changes in material and religious culture throughout Zhou times. The practice of burying the living with the dead steadily declined, but a ruler who died in 433 B.C.E. still had his female musicians buried with him, and not until 384 B.C.E. did the king of Qin outlaw the practice in his state. Bronze ritual vessels continued to be buried in the tombs of rulers, but their styles had radically changed. Music played a major role in court entertainment, and bells are among the most impressive bronze objects of the period.

Social groups that had been considered barbarian or semibarbarian among the early Zhou were more and more brought into the cultural sphere of the Central States, the core region of China. These were the states on the periphery, with room to expand. By the fourth and third centuries B.C.E., they were the most powerful of the states. For instance, the southern state of Chu expanded rapidly in the Yangzi Valley, defeating and absorbing fifty

Bells of the Marquis of Yi   Music played a central role in court life in ancient China. The tomb of a minor ruler who died about 400 B.C.E. contained 124 musical instruments, including drums, flutes, mouth organs, pan pipes, zithers, a set of 32 chime stones, and this 64-piece bell set. The bells bear inscriptions that name the two tones each bell could make, depending on where it was struck. Five men, using poles and mallets, and standing on either side of the set of bells, would have played the bells by hitting them from outside. (© *Cultural Relics Data Center of China*)

or more small states as it extended its reach north to the heartland of Zhou and east to absorb the old states of Wu and Yue. By the late Zhou period, Chu was on the forefront of cultural innovation and produced the greatest literary masterpieces of the era, the *Songs of Chu,* a collection of fantastical poems full of images of elusive deities and shamans who can fly through the spirit world.

THE GOLDEN AGE OF CHINESE PHILOSOPHY

Known as the time when the "Hundred Schools of Thought" contended, the late Zhou period was one of intellectual flowering. During the same period in which Indian sages and mystics were developing religious speculation about karma, souls, and eons of time, Chinese thinkers were arguing about the ideal forms of social and political organization and man's connections to nature.

The constant warfare of the period helped rather than hindered intellectual creativity. People wanted solutions to the disorder they saw around them. Rulers and high officials took advantage of the destruction of states to recruit newly unemployed men to serve as their advisers and court assistants. Lively debate often resulted as these strategists proposed court policies and defended their

ideas against challengers. Followers took to recording their teachers' ideas, and the circulation of these "books" (rolls of silk, or strips of wood or bamboo tied together) served further to stimulate debate.

Confucius and His Followers

Confucius (traditional dates, 551–479 B.C.E.) was the first and most important of the men of ideas seeking to influence the rulers of the day. As a young man, Confucius served in the court of his home state of Lu without gaining much influence. After leaving Lu, he set out with a small band of students and wandered through neighboring states in search of a ruler who would take his advice. Although he yearned for a ruler to serve devotedly, he spent most of his life teaching the sons of the aristocracy.

Confucius's ideas are known to us primarily through the sayings recorded by his disciples in the *Analects*. The thrust of his thought was ethical rather than theoretical or metaphysical. He talked repeatedly of an ideal age in the early Zhou Dynasty, which he conceived of as a perfect society in which everyone was devoted to fulfilling his or her role: superiors looked after those dependent on them, inferiors devoted themselves to the service of their superiors, parents and children, husbands and wives, all wholeheartedly embraced what was expected of them.

GUAN ZHONG

By the time of Confucius, the success of states was often credited more to the lord's astute advisers than to the lord himself. To Confucius, the most praiseworthy political adviser was Guan Zhong (ca 720–645 B.C.E.), the genius behind the rise of the state of Qi, in eastern China.

The earliest historical sources to recount Guan Zhong's accomplishments are the "commentaries" compiled in the Warring States Period to elaborate on the dry chronicle known as the *Spring and Autumn Annals.* The *Zuo Commentary,* for instance, tells us that in the year 660 B.C.E. Guan Zhong advised Duke Huan to aid the small state of Xing, then under attack by the non-Chinese Rong tribes: "The Rong and the Di are wolves who cannot be satiated. The Xia (Chinese) states are kin who should not be abandoned." In 652 B.C.E., it tells us, Guan Zhong urged the duke to maintain the respect of the other states by refusing the offer of the son of a recently defeated state's ruler to ally himself with Qi if Qi would help him depose his father. Because the duke regularly listened to Guan Zhong's sound advice, Qi brought the other states under its sway and the duke came to be recognized as the first *hegemon,* or leader of the alliance of states.

Guan Zhong was also credited with strengthening the duke's internal administration. He encouraged the employment of officials on the basis of their moral character and ability rather than their birth. He introduced a system of drafting commoners for military service. In the history of China written by Sima Qian in about 100 B.C.E., Guan Zhong is also given credit for enriching Qi by promoting trade, issuing coins, and standardizing merchants' scales. He was credited with the statement, "When the granaries are full, the people will understand ritual and moderation. When they have enough food and clothing, they will understand honor and disgrace."

Sima Qian's biography of Guan Zhong emphasizes his early poverty and the key role played by a friend, Bao Shuya, who recognized his worth. As young men, both Bao and Guan Zhong served brothers of the duke of Qi. When this duke was killed and a messy succession struggle followed, Bao's patron won out and became the next duke, while Guan Zhong's patron had to flee and in the end was killed. Bao, however, recommended Guan Zhong to the new duke, Duke Huan, and Guan Zhong took up a post under him.

The inlaid decoration on bronze vessels of the Warring States Period often shows people engaged in warfare, hunting, preparing food, performing rituals, and making music. (© Courtesy, Sichuan Museum)

In the *Analects,* one of Confucius's disciples thought that Guan Zhong's lack of loyalty to his first lord made him a man unworthy of respect: "When Duke Huan killed his brother Jiu, Guan Zhong was unable to die with Jiu but rather became prime minister to Duke Huan." Confucius disagreed: "Guan Zhong became prime minister to Duke Huan and made him hegemon among the lords, uniting and reforming all under Heaven. The people, down to the present, continued to receive benefits from this. Were it not for Guan Zhong our hair would hang unbound and we would fold our robes on the left [that is, live as barbarians]."*

A book of the teachings associated with Guan Zhong, the *Guanzi,* was in circulation by the late Warring States Period. Although it is today not thought to reflect the teachings of the historical Guan Zhong, the fact that later statecraft thinkers would borrow his name is an indication of his fame as a great statesman.

QUESTIONS FOR ANALYSIS

1. How did the form of government promoted by Guan Zhong differ from the early Zhou political system?
2. What can one infer about Chinese notions of loyalty from the story of Guan Zhong and his friend Bao Shuya?
3. Did Guan Zhong and Confucius share similar understandings of the differences between Chinese and barbarians?

*Analects, 14.18. Translated by Patricia Ebrey.

Confucius considered the family the basic unit of society. He extolled **filial piety,** which to him meant more than just reverent obedience of children toward their parents.

The Master said, "You can be of service to your father and mother by remonstrating with them tactfully. If you perceive that they do not wish to follow your advice, then continue to be reverent toward them without offending or disobeying them; work hard and do not murmur against them."[4]

The relationship between father and son was one of the five cardinal relationships stressed by Confucius. The others were between ruler and subject, husband and wife, elder and younger brother, and friend and friend. Mutual obligations of a hierarchical sort underlay the first four of these relationships—the senior leads and protects, the junior supports and obeys. The exception was the relationship between friends, which was conceived in terms of the mutual obligations between equals.

A man of moderation, Confucius was an earnest advocate of gentlemanly conduct. He redefined the term *gentleman* (*junzi*) to mean a man of moral cultivation rather than a man of noble birth. He repeatedly urged his followers to aspire to be gentlemen of integrity and duty, rather than petty men intent on personal gain. The gentleman, he said, "feels bad when his capabilities fall short of the task. He does not feel bad when people fail to recognize him."[5] Confucius did not advocate social equality, but his teachings minimized the importance of class distinctions and opened the way for intelligent and talented people to rise in the social scale.

The Confucian gentleman found his calling in service to the ruler. Loyal advisers should encourage their rulers to govern through ritual, virtue, and concern for the welfare of their subjects, and much of the *Analects* concerns the way to govern well.

The Master said, "Lead the people by means of government policies and regulate them through punishments, and they will be evasive and have no sense of shame. Lead them by means of virtue and regulate them through rituals and they will have a sense of shame and moreover have standards."[6]

To Confucius the ultimate virtue was **ren,** a term that has been translated as perfect goodness, benevolence, humanity, human-heartedness, and nobility. A person of ren cares about others and acts accordingly.

Zhonggong asked about humanity. The Master said, "When you go out, treat everyone as if you were welcoming a great guest. Employ people as though you were conducting a great sacrifice. Do not do unto others what you would not have

them do unto you. Then neither in your country nor in your family will there be complaints against you."[7]

In the Confucian tradition, studying texts came to be valued over speculation, meditation, and mystical identification with deities. Confucius encouraged the men who came to study with him to master the poetry, rituals, and historical traditions that we know today as Confucian classics. Many passages in the *Analects* reveal Confucius's confidence in the power of study:

The Master said, "I am not someone who was born wise. I am someone who loves the ancients and tries to learn from them."

The Master said, "I once spent a whole day without eating and a whole night without sleeping in order to think. It was of no use. It is better to study."[8]

The eventual success of Confucian ideas owes much to Confucius's followers in the two centuries following his death, the most important of whom were Mencius (ca 370–ca 300 B.C.E.) and Xunzi (ca 310–ca 215 B.C.E.).

Mencius, like Confucius, traveled around offering advice to rulers of various states. (See the feature "Listening to the Past: The Book of Mencius" on pages 102–103.) Over and over he tried to convert them to the view that the ruler able to win over the people through benevolent government would succeed in unifying "all under Heaven." Mencius proposed concrete political and financial measures for easing tax burdens and otherwise improving the people's lot. Men willing to serve an unworthy ruler earned his contempt, especially when they worked hard to fill his coffers or expand his territory. With his disciples and fellow philosophers, Mencius also discussed other issues in moral philosophy, arguing strongly, for instance, that human nature is fundamentally good, as everyone is born with the capacity to recognize what is right and act on it.

Xunzi, a half century later, took the opposite view of human nature, arguing that people are born selfish and that it is only through education and ritual that they learn to put moral principle above their own interest. Much of what is desirable is not inborn but must be taught.

When a son yields to his father, or a younger brother yields to his elder brother, or when a son takes on the work for his father or a younger brother for his elder brother, their actions go against their natures and run counter to their feelings.

And yet these are the way of the filial son and the principles of ritual and morality.[9]

Neither Confucius nor Mencius had had much actual political or administrative experience, but Xunzi had worked for many years in the court of his home state. Not surprisingly, he showed more consideration than either Confucius or Mencius for the difficulties a ruler might face in trying to rule through ritual and virtue. Xunzi was also a more rigorous thinker than his predecessors and developed the philosophical foundations of many ideas merely outlined by Confucius or Mencius. Confucius, for instance, had declined to discuss gods, portents, and anomalies, and had spoken of sacrificing as if the spirits were present. Xunzi went further and explicitly argued that Heaven does not intervene in human affairs. Praying to Heaven or to gods, he asserted, does not induce them to act. "Why does it rain after a prayer for rain? In my opinion, for no reason. It is the same as raining when you had not prayed."[10]

Even though he did not think praying could bring rain or other benefits from Heaven, Xunzi did not propose abandoning traditional rituals. In contrast to Daoists and Mohists (discussed below), who saw rituals as unnatural or extravagant, Xunzi saw them as an efficient way to attain order in society. Rulers and educated men should continue traditional ritual practices such as complex funeral protocols because the rites themselves have positive effects on performers and observers. Not only do they let people express feelings and satisfy desires in an orderly way, but because they specify graduated ways to perform the rites according to social rank, ritual traditions sustain the social hierarchy. Xunzi compared and contrasted ritual and music: music shapes people's emotions and creates feelings of solidarity, while ritual shapes people's sense of duty and creates social differentiation.

The Confucian vision of personal ethics and public service found a small but ardent following in late Zhou times. In later centuries, rulers came to see men educated in Confucian virtues as ideal advisers and officials. Neither revolutionaries nor toadies, Confucian scholar-officials opposed bad government and upheld the best ideals of statecraft. Confucian political ideals shaped Chinese society into the twentieth century.

The Confucian vision also provided the moral basis for the Chinese family into modern times. Repaying parents and ancestors came to be seen as a sacred duty. Because people owe their very existence to their parents, they should reciprocate by respecting them, making efforts to please them, honoring their memories, and placing the interests of the family line above personal preferences. Since this family line is a patrilineal line from father to son to grandson, placing great importance on it has had the effect of devaluing women.

Mozi

Not long after Confucius died, his ideas were challenged by a man who did not come from the aristocracy but rather, it would seem, from among the master craftsmen. Mozi (ca 450 B.C.E.), perhaps an expert in constructing siege engines, did not talk of the distinction between gentlemen and vulgar "petty men," but rather of "concern for everyone." He also argued strongly for the merit principle, that rulers should choose their advisers on the basis of their ability, not their birth.

The book ascribed to Mozi proposes that every idea be evaluated on the basis of its utility: does it benefit the people and the state? The Confucian stress on ritual and filial piety led to prolonged mourning for parents, which Mozi rejected because it interrupts work, injures health, and thus impoverishes the people and weakens the state. Music, too, Mozi saw as a wasteful extravagance.

Mozi made a similar case against aggressive war, seeing no glory in expansion for its own sake and pointing to the huge losses in weapons, horses, and human lives it causes. The capture of a city, he argued, is not worth the loss of thousands of men. But Mozi was for strong government, and in particular for respect for superiors. He argued that disorder could be eliminated if everyone conformed his beliefs to those of his superior, with the king conforming to Heaven. He believed that Confucius's reference to fate and his failure to discuss gods undermined popular morality.

Mozi had many followers over the next couple of centuries, but his school eventually lost its distinct identity. Certain ideas, such as support for the merit principle and the critique of extravagance, in later centuries were absorbed into Confucian thought. Confucians, however, never accepted Mohist ideas about treating everyone equally, unnatural in their minds, or of applying rigidly utilitarian tests to ritual and music, whose value they saw in very different terms.

Daoism

Confucius and his followers believed in moral effort and statecraft. They thought men of virtue should devote themselves to making the government work to the benefit of the people. Those who came to be labeled Daoists disagreed. They thought striving to make things better generally makes them worse. Daoists defended private life and wanted the rulers to leave the people alone. They sought to go beyond everyday concerns and let their minds wander freely. Rather than making human beings and human actions the center of concern, they focused on the larger scheme of things, the whole natural order identified as **the Way,** or Dao.

Early Daoist teachings are known from two surviving books, the *Laozi* and the *Zhuangzi,* both dating to the third century B.C.E. Laozi, the putative author of the *Laozi,* may not be a historical figure, but the text ascribed to him has been of enduring importance. A recurrent theme in this brief, aphoristic text is the mystical superiority of yielding over assertion and silence over words: "The Way that can be discussed is not the constant Way."[11] The highest good is like water: "Water benefits all creatures but does not compete. It occupies the places people disdain and thus comes near to the Way."[12]

Because purposeful action is counterproductive, the ruler should let people return to a natural state of ignorance and contentment.

Do not honor the worthy,
And the people will not compete.
Do not value rare treasures,
And the people will not steal.
Do not display what others want,
And the people will not have their hearts confused.
A sage governs this way:
He empties people's minds and fills their bellies.
He weakens their wills and strengthens their bones.
Keep the people always without knowledge and without
*　desires,*
For then the clever will not dare act.
Engage in no action and order will prevail.[13]

In the philosophy of the *Laozi,* the people would be better off if they knew less, gave up tools, renounced writing, stopped envying their neighbors, and lost their desire to travel or engage in war.

Zhuangzi (369–286 B.C.E.), the author of the book of the same name, was a historical figure who shared many of the central ideas of the *Laozi,* such as the usefulness of the useless and the relativity of ordinary distinctions. He was proud of his disinterest in politics. In one of his many anecdotes, he reported that the king of Chu once sent an envoy to invite him to take over the government of his

Book Written on Silk　This text of the *Laozi* was excavated from a second-century B.C.E. tomb. *(© Cultural Relics Data Center of China)*

realm. In response Zhuangzi asked the envoy whether a tortoise that had been held as sacred for three thousand years would prefer to be dead with its bones venerated or alive with its tail dragging in the mud. When the envoy agreed that life was preferable, Zhuangzi told the envoy to leave. He preferred to drag his tail in the mud.

The *Zhuangzi* is filled with parables, flights of fancy, and fictional encounters between historical figures, including Confucius and his disciples. A more serious strain of Zhuangzi's thought concerned death. He questioned whether we can be sure life is better than death. People fear what they do not know, the same way a captive girl will be terrified when she learns she is to become the king's concubine. Perhaps people will discover that death has as many delights as life in the palace.

When a friend expressed shock that Zhuangzi was not weeping at his wife's death but rather singing, Zhuangzi explained:

When she first died, how could I have escaped feeling the loss? Then I looked back to the beginning before she had life. Not only before she had life, but before she had form. Not only before she had form, but before she had vital energy. In this confused amorphous realm, something changed and vital energy appeared; when the vital energy was changed, form appeared; with changes in form, life began. Now there is another change bringing death. This is like the progression of the four seasons of spring and fall, winter and summer. Here she was lying down to sleep in a huge room and I followed her, sobbing and wailing. When I realized my actions showed I hadn't understood destiny, I stopped.[14]

Zhuangzi was similarly iconoclastic in his political ideas. In one parable a wheelwright insolently tells a duke that books are useless since all they contain are the dregs of men long dead. The duke, insulted, threatens to execute him if he cannot give an adequate explanation of his remark. The wheelwright replies:

I see things in terms of my own work. When I chisel at a wheel, if I go slow, the chisel slides and does not stay put; if I hurry, it jams and doesn't move properly. When it is neither too slow nor too fast, I can feel it in my hand and respond to it from my heart. My mouth cannot describe it in words, but there is something there. I cannot teach it to my son, and my son cannot learn it from me. So I have gone on for seventy years, growing old chiseling wheels. The men of old died in possession of what they could not transmit. So it follows that what you are reading are their dregs.[15]

To put this another way, truly skilled craftsmen respond to situations spontaneously; they do not analyze or reason or even keep in mind the rules they have mastered.

This strain of Daoist thought denies the validity of verbal reasoning and the sorts of knowledge conveyed through words.

Daoism can be seen as a response to Confucianism, a rejection of many of its basic premises. Nevertheless, over the course of Chinese history, many people felt the pull of both Confucian and Daoist ideas and studied the writings of both schools. Even Confucian scholars who had devoted much of their lives to public service might find that the teachings of the *Laozi* or *Zhuangzi* helped to put their frustrations in perspective. Whereas Confucianism often seems sternly masculine, Daoism is more accepting of feminine principles and even celebrates passivity and yielding. Those drawn to the arts were also often drawn to Daoism, with its validation of spontaneity and freedom. Rulers, too, were drawn to the Daoist notion of the ruler who can have great power simply by being himself without instituting anything.

Legalism

Over the course of the fourth and third centuries B.C.E., the number of surviving states dwindled as one small state after another was conquered. Rulers fearful that their states might be next were ready to listen to political theorists who claimed expertise in the accumulation of power. These theorists, labeled **Legalists** because of their emphasis on the need for rigorous laws, argued that strong government depended not on the moral qualities of the ruler and his officials, as Confucians claimed, but on establishing effective laws and procedures. Legalism, though eventually discredited, laid the basis for China's later bureaucratic government.

In the fourth century B.C.E. the state of Qin, under the leadership of its chief minister, Lord Shang (d. 338 B.C.E.), adopted many Legalist policies. It abolished the aristocracy. Social distinctions were to be based on military ranks determined by the objective criterion of the number of enemy heads cut off in battle. In place of the old fiefs, Qin divided the country into counties and appointed officials to govern them according to the laws decreed at court. To increase the population, migrants were recruited from other states with offers of land and houses. To encourage farmers to work hard and improve their land, they were allowed to buy and sell it. Ordinary farmers were thus freed from serflike obligations to the local nobility, but direct control by the state could be even more onerous. Taxes and labor service obligations were heavy. Travel required a permit, and vagrants could be forced into penal labor service. All families were grouped into mutual responsibility groups of five and ten families; whenever anyone in the group committed a crime, all the others were equally liable unless they reported it.

A book ascribed to Lord Shang heaped scorn on respect for tradition and urged the ruler not to hesitate to institute changes that would strengthen his state: "Wise people create laws while ignorant ones are controlled by them; the worthy alter the rites while the unworthy are held fast by them."[16]

In the century after Lord Shang, Legalism found its greatest exponent in Han Feizi (d. 233 B.C.E.). Han Feizi had studied with the Confucian master Xunzi but had little interest in Confucian values of goodness or ritual. In his writings he warned rulers of the political pitfalls awaiting them. They had to be careful where they placed their trust, for "when the ruler trusts someone, he falls under that person's control."[17] This is true even of wives and concubines, who think of the interests of their sons. Given subordinates' propensities to pursue their own selfish interests, the ruler should keep them ignorant of his intentions and control them by manipulating competition among them. Warmth, affection, or candor could have no place in his relationships with others.

Han Feizi saw the Confucian notion that government could be based on virtue as naive.

Think of parents' relations to their children. They congratulate each other when a son is born, but complain to each other when a daughter is born. Why do parents have these divergent responses when both are equally their offspring? It is because they calculate their long-term advantage. Since even parents deal with their children in this calculating way, what can one expect where there is no parent-child bond? When present-day scholars counsel rulers, they all tell them to rid themselves of thoughts of profit and follow the path of mutual love. This is expecting rulers to go further than parents.[18]

If rulers would make the laws and prohibitions clear and the rewards and punishments automatic, then the officials and common people would be easy to govern. Uniform laws get people to do things they would not

Embroidered Silk From ancient times, silk was one of China's most famous products. Women traditionally did most of the work involved in making silk, from feeding mulberry leaves to the silkworms, to reeling and twisting the fibers, to weaving and embroidering. The embroidered silk depicted here is from a robe found in a fourth-century B.C.E. tomb in central China. The flowing, curvilinear design incorporates dragons, phoenixes, and tigers. *(Jingzhou Museum)*

otherwise be inclined to do, such as work hard and fight wars, essential to the goal of establishing hegemony over all the other states.

The laws of the Legalists were designed as much to constrain officials as to regulate the common people. The third century B.C.E. tomb of a Qin official has yielded statutes detailing the rules for keeping accounts, supervising subordinates, managing penal labor, conducting investigations, and many other responsibilities. Infractions were generally punishable through the imposition of fines.

Legalism saw no value in intellectual debate or private opinion. Divergent views of right and wrong lead to weakness and disorder. The ruler should not allow others to undermine his laws by questioning them. In Legalism, there were no laws above or independent of the wishes of the rulers, ones that might set limits on rulers' actions in the way that natural or divine laws did in Greek thought. Indeed, a ruler's right to exercise the law as he sees fit is demonstrated in the violent deaths of the two leading Legalist thinkers: Lord Shang was drawn and quartered by chariots in 338 B.C.E., and Han Feizi was imprisoned and forced to drink poison in 233 B.C.E.

Rulers of several states adopted some Legalist ideas, but only the state of Qin systematically followed them. The extraordinary but brief success Qin had with these policies is discussed in Chapter 7.

Other Schools of Thought

Confucians, Mohists, Daoists, and Legalists had the greatest long-term impact on Chinese civilization, but the late Zhou "Hundred Schools of Thought" also included everything from logicians, hedonists, and utopians, to agriculturalists who argued that no one should eat who does not farm, and hermits who justified withdrawal from social life.

Cosmological speculation formed one important strain of early Chinese thought. The concepts of **yin and yang** are found in early form in the divination manual the *Book of Changes,* but late Zhou theorists developed much more elaborate theories based on them. Yin is the feminine, dark, receptive, yielding, negative, and weak; yang is the masculine, bright, assertive, creative, positive, and strong. Yin and yang are complementary poles rather than distinct entities or opposing forces. The movement of yin and yang accounts for the transition from day to night and from summer to winter. These models based on observation of nature were extended to explain not only phenomena we might classify as natural, such as illness, storms, or earthquakes, but also social phenomena, such as the rise and fall of states or conflict in families. In

Dagger Depicting Taiyi   Recent archaeological excavations of manuscripts from the Warring States Period have given us a much clearer understanding of religious beliefs and practices in early China. The deity Taiyi ("Grand One"), depicted on this late-fourth-century B.C.E. dagger, was the god of the pole star. Sacrifices were made to Taiyi to avert evil or gain his protection in battle. *(From Michael Loewe and Edward Shaughnessy, eds.,* Cambridge History of Ancient China *[New York: Cambridge University Press, 1999])*

all these realms, when the balance between yin and yang gets disturbed, unwanted things happen.

In recent decades archaeologists have further complicated our understanding of early Chinese thought by unearthing records of the popular religion of the time— astrological manuals, handbooks of lucky and unlucky days, medical prescriptions, exercises, and ghost stories. The tomb of an official who died in 316 B.C.E. has records of divinations showing that illness was seen as the result of unsatisfied spirits or malevolent demons, best dealt with through exorcisms or offering sacrifices to the god Taiyi (Grand One). Taiyi was an astral deity, sometimes depicted on weapons of the period as well.

SUMMARY

By 200 B.C.E. Chinese civilization had passed through several distinct phases. After a long Neolithic period, China entered the Bronze Age with the Shang Dynasty. In Shang times, the kings served also as priests, and great wealth was invested in extraordinarily complex bronze ritual vessels. From Shang times on, the Chinese language has been written in a logographic script, which shaped the ways people have become educated and the value assigned to education.

The Zhou Dynasty, which overthrew the Shang in about 1050 B.C.E., parceled out their territory to lords in a feudal manner. These fiefs gradually came to act like independent states, so by 500 B.C.E. China is best thought of as a multistate society. Social and cultural change was particularly rapid under these conditions of intense competition.

The period from 500 to 200 B.C.E. was the golden age of Chinese philosophy. Confucius and his followers advocated a deeply moral view of the way to achieve order through the cultivation of virtues by everyone from the ruler on down. Mozi contended that every idea should be evaluated on the basis of its utility for the common good and objected to hereditary privilege and aggressive warfare on these grounds. Daoists like Laozi and Zhuangzi looked beyond the human realm to the entire cosmos and spoke of the relativity of concepts such as good and bad and life and death. The Legalists were hardheaded men who heaped ridicule on the idea that a ruler could get his people to be good by being good himself and proposed instead clear laws with strict rewards and punishments. Chinese thought in later centuries was profoundly shaped by the ideas espoused by these early thinkers.

KEY TERMS

loess	crossbow
Xiongnu	filial piety
Anyang	ren
logographic	the Way
taotie	Legalists
Book of Documents	yin and yang
Mandate of Heaven	
Warring States Period	
shi	
Book of Songs	

NOTES

1. Patricia Buckley Ebrey, ed., *Chinese Civilization: A Sourcebook,* 2d ed. (New York: Free Press/Macmillan, 1993), p. 11.
2. Ibid., p. 13.
3. Patricia Buckley Ebrey, *The Cambridge Illustrated History of China* (Cambridge: Cambridge University Press, 1996), p. 34.
4. Ebrey, *Chinese Civilization,* p. 21.
5. Ibid., p. 19.
6. Ibid., p. 21.
7. Ibid.
8. *Analects* 7.19, 15.30. Translated by Patricia Ebrey.
9. Ebrey, *Chinese Civilization,* p. 26.
10. Ibid., p. 24, modified.
11. Ibid., p. 27.
12. Ibid., p. 28, modified.
13. Ibid., p. 28.
14. Ibid., p. 31.
15. Ibid.
16. Ibid., p. 33.
17. Ibid.
18. Ibid., p. 35.

SUGGESTED READING

Among the most interesting and accessible general histories of China are R. Huang's lively, interpretive *China: A Macro History* (1988), J. Gernet's solid *A History of Chinese Civilization* (1989), C. Schirokaur's popular and balanced textbook *A Brief History of Chinese Civilization* (1991), C. Hucker's *China's Imperial Past* (1975), and P. Ebrey's attractive *Cambridge Illustrated History of China* (1996). For premodern history, see also V. Hansen, *The Open Empire: A History of China to 1600* (2000). P. Ropp, ed., *Heritage of China: Contemporary Perspectives on Chinese Civilization* (1990), offers readers essays on religion, thought, family, art, and other topics. For translations of Chinese writings providing insights into Chinese society and culture, see P. Ebrey, *Chinese Civilization: A Sourcebook* (1993) and W. de Bary and I. Bloom, *Sources of Chinese Tradition* (1999). An introduction to Chinese history through biographies of key individuals is provided by J. Wills, Jr., *Mountain of Fame: Portraits in Chinese History* (1994). A recent well-illustrated topical volume is E. Shaunhessey, *China: Empire and Civilization* (2000).

Useful reference works for China include B. Hook and D. Twitchett, eds., *The Cambridge Encyclopedia of China* (1991); H. T. Zurndorfer, *China Bibliography* (1995); and A. Embree, ed., *Encyclopedia of Asian History* (1988). For historical maps and well-illustrated topical essays, see C. Blunden and M. Elvin, *Cultural Atlas of China* (1983). Many fine surveys of art are available, including L. Sickman and A. Soper, *The Art and Architecture of China* (1978);

J. Rawson, ed., *The British Museum Book of Chinese Art* (1992), and, most recently, R. Thorp and R. Vinograd, *Chinese Art and Culture* (2001).

For early China, the most authoritative volume is M. Loewe and E. Shaunhessey, *The Cambridge History of Ancient China: From the Origins of Civilization to 221 B.C.* (1999). The journal *Early China* often reports on important new archaeological finds. The foremost authority on the archaeology of early China is K. C. Chang. See his *Archeology of Ancient China,* 4th ed. (1986), *Shang Civilization* (1986), and *Art, Myth, and Ritual: The Path to Political Authority in Ancient China* (1983). For the development of the Chinese writing system, see W. Boltz, *The Origin and Early Development of the Chinese Writing System* (1994). For a comparative perspective on prehistory and the ancient period, see Gina L. Barnes, *The Rise of Civilization in East Asia* (1993). Sarah Allan examines Shang cosmology and Zhou myths in *The Shape of the Turtle: Myth, Art, and Cosmology in Early China* (1991). For ancient art and technology, see W. Fong's lavishly illustrated *Great Bronze Age of China* (1980) and Jessica Rawson's *Ancient China: Art and Archeology* (1980).

For the Zhou period, see M. Lewis, *Sanctioned Violence in Early China* (1990); C. Hsu and K. Linduff, *Western Chou Civilization* (1988); and X. Li, *Eastern Zhou and Qin Civilizations* (1985).

Good overviews of the intellectual flowering of the Warring States Period include A. C. Graham, *Disputers of the Tao: Philosophical Argument in Ancient China* (1989); Benjamin Schwartz, *The World of Thought in Ancient China* (1985); M. Lewis, *Writing and Authority in Early China* (1999); and, more briefly, F. W. Mote, *Intellectual Foundations of China* (1989). James Legge did a complete translation of *The Chinese Classics,* 5 vols. (1960), in the nineteenth century. More recent translators include A. Waley, D. C. Lau, and B. Watson. For Waley, see *Analects of Confucius* (1938) and *Book of Songs* (1937). Lau translated *Confucius: The Analects* (1979), *Tao Te Ching: Chinese Classics* (1982), and *Mencius* (1970). Watson has published *The Tso Chuan: Selections from China's Oldest Narrative History* (1989), *The Complete Works of Chuang Tzu* (1968), and *Basic Writings of Mo Tzu, Hsun Tzu, and Han Fei Tzu* (1967). For military thinking, see R. Ames, trans., *Sun-tzu: The Art of War* (1993).

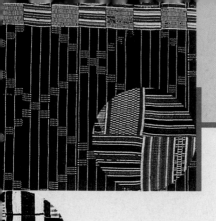

LISTENING TO THE PAST

THE BOOK OF MENCIUS

*T*he book that records the teachings of Mencius *(ca 370–ca 300 B.C.E.) was modeled on the* Analects *of Confucius. It presents, in no particular order, conversations between Mencius and several rulers, philosophers, and disciples. Unlike the* Analects, *however, the* Book of Mencius *includes extended discussions of particular points, suggesting that Mencius had a hand in recording the conversations.*

Mencius had an audience with King Hui of Liang. The king said, "Sir, you did not consider a thousand *li* too far to come. You must have some ideas about how to benefit my state."

Mencius replied, "Why must Your Majesty use the word 'benefit'? All I am concerned with are the benevolent and the right. If Your Majesty says, 'How can I benefit my state?' your officials will say, 'How can I benefit my family,' and officers and common people will say, 'How can I benefit myself?' Once superiors and inferiors are competing for benefit, the state will be in danger.

"When the head of a state of ten thousand chariots is murdered, the assassin is invariably a noble with a fief of a thousand chariots. When the head of a fief of a thousand chariots is murdered, the assassin is invariably head of a subfief of a hundred chariots. Those with a thousand out of ten thousand, or a hundred out of a thousand, had quite a bit. But when benefit is put before what is right, they are not satisfied without snatching it all. By contrast, there has never been a benevolent person who neglected his parents or a righteous person who put his lord last. Your Majesty perhaps will now also say, 'All I am concerned with are the benevolent and the right.' Why mention 'benefit'?"

After seeing King Xiang of Liang, Mencius said to someone, "When I saw him from a distance, he did not look like a ruler, and when I got closer, I saw nothing to command respect. But he asked, 'How can the realm be settled?'

"I answered, 'It can be settled through unity.'

"'Who can unify it?' he asked.

"I answered, 'Someone not fond of killing people.'

"'Who could give it to him?'

"I answered, 'Everyone in the world will give it to him. Your Majesty knows what rice plants are? If there is a drought in the seventh and eighth months, the plants wither, but if moisture collects in the sky and forms clouds and rain falls in torrents, the plants suddenly revive. This is the way it is; no one can stop the process. In the world today there are no rulers disinclined toward killing. If there were a ruler who did not like to kill people, everyone in the world would crane their necks to catch sight of him. This is really true. The people would flow toward him the way water flows down. No one would be able to repress them.'"

After an incident between Zou and Lu, Duke Mu asked, "Thirty-three of my officials died but no common people died. I could punish them, but I could not punish them all. I could refrain from punishing them, but they did angrily watch their superiors die without saving them. What would be the best course for me to follow?"

Mencius answered, "When the harvest failed, even though your granaries were full, nearly a thousand of your subjects were lost—the old and weak among them dying in the gutters, the able-bodied scattering in all directions. Your officials never reported the situation, a case of superiors callously inflicting suffering on their subordinates. Zengzi said, 'Watch out, watch out! What you do will be done to you.' This was the first chance the people had to pay them back. You should not resent them. If Your Highness practices benevolent government, the common people will love their superiors and die for those in charge of them."

102

Opening page of a 1617 edition of the *Book of Mencius. (Rare Books Collections, Harvard-Yenching Library, Harvard University)*

King Xuan of Qi asked, "Is it true that Tang banished Jie and King Wu took up arms against Zhou?"

Mencius replied, "That is what the records say."

"Then is it permissible for a subject to assassinate his lord?"

Mencius said, "Someone who does violence to the good we call a villain; someone who does violence to the right we call a criminal. A person who is both a villain and a criminal we call a scoundrel. I have heard that the scoundrel Zhou was killed, but have not heard that a lord was killed."

King Xuan of Qi asked about ministers.

Mencius said, "What sort of ministers does Your Majesty mean?"

The king said, "Are there different kinds of ministers?"

"There are. There are noble ministers related to the ruler and ministers of other surnames."

The king said, "I'd like to hear about noble ministers."

Mencius replied, "When the ruler makes a major error, they point it out. If he does not listen to their repeated remonstrations, then they put someone else on the throne."

The king blanched. Mencius continued, "Your Majesty should not be surprised at this. Since you asked me, I had to tell you truthfully."

After the king regained his composure, he asked about unrelated ministers. Mencius said, "When the king makes an error, they point it out. If he does not heed their repeated remonstrations, they quit their posts."

Bo Gui said, "I'd like a tax of one part in twenty. What do you think?"

Mencius said, "Your way is that of the northern tribes. Is one potter enough for a state with ten thousand households?"

"No, there would not be enough wares."

"The northern tribes do not grow all the five grains, only millet. They have no cities or houses, no ritual sacrifices. They do not provide gifts or banquets for feudal lords, and do not have a full array of officials. Therefore, for them, one part in twenty is enough. But we live in the central states. How could we abolish social roles and do without gentlemen? If a state cannot do without potters, how much less can it do without gentlemen. Those who want to make government lighter than it was under Yao and Shun are to some degree barbarians. Those who wish to make government heavier than it was under Yao and Shun are to some degree [tyrants like] Jie."

Gaozi said, "Human nature is like whirling water. When an outlet is opened to the east, it flows east; when an outlet is opened to the west, it flows west. Human nature is no more inclined to good or bad than water is inclined to east or west."

Mencius responded, "Water, it is true, is not inclined to either east or west, but does it have no preference for high or low? Goodness is to human nature like flowing downward is to water. There are no people who are not good and no water that does not flow down. Still, water, if splashed, can go higher than your head; if forced, it can be brought up a hill. This isn't the nature of water; it is the specific circumstances. Although people can be made to be bad, their natures are not changed."

QUESTIONS FOR ANALYSIS

1. Does Mencius give consistent advice to the kings he talks to?

2. Do you see a link between Mencius's views on human nature and his views on the true king?

3. What role does Mencius see for ministers?

Source: Patricia Buckley Ebrey, ed., *Chinese Civilization: A Sourcebook,* 2d ed. (New York: Free Press/Macmillan, 1993), pp. 22–24. Reprinted with permission of The Free Press, a Division of Simon & Schuster. Copyright © 1993 by Patricia Buckley Ebrey.

Dionysos at sea. Dionysos here symbolizes the Greek
sense of exploration, independence, and love of life.
(Bildarchiv Preussischer Kulturbesitz)

CHAPTER

5

THE GREEK EXPERIENCE

The rocky peninsula of Greece was the home of the civilization that fundamentally shaped Western civilization and nurtured a culture that eventually spread its essence, concepts, and values throughout the world. The Greeks explored questions that continue to concern people to this day. Going beyond mythmaking and religion, the Greeks strove to understand in logical, rational terms both the universe and the place of human beings in it.

The history of the Greeks and their culture is divided into two broad periods. The first is the Hellenic, roughly the time between the arrival of the Greeks (approximately 2000 B.C.E.) and the victory of Philip of Macedon over them in 338 B.C.E. The second is the Hellenistic, the years beginning with the reign of Alexander the Great (336–323 B.C.E.) and ending with the Roman conquest of the Hellenistic East (200–146 B.C.E.).

During the first of these periods, the Greeks developed and spread their culture and people beyond Greece to West Asia, North Africa, and southern Europe. The greatest monuments of the Greeks were profound thoughts set down in terms as fresh and immediate today as they were some twenty-four hundred years ago.

The Hellenistic period saw this civilization burst upon a larger world. In the footsteps of Alexander came others spreading all aspects of Greek culture deeper into western and Central Asia and into western Europe. In the process the Greeks shared their heritage with both emerging societies in Europe and venerable cultures in Asia.

- How did the Greeks develop basic political forms, as different as democracy and tyranny, that have influenced all of later history?
- What did the Greek intellectual triumph entail, and what were its effects?
- What did the spread of Hellenism mean to the Greeks and to the peoples of Asia, Africa, and Europe?
- What did the meeting of West and East hold for the development of economics, religion, philosophy, women's concerns, science, and medicine?

These are the questions we will explore in this chapter.

106

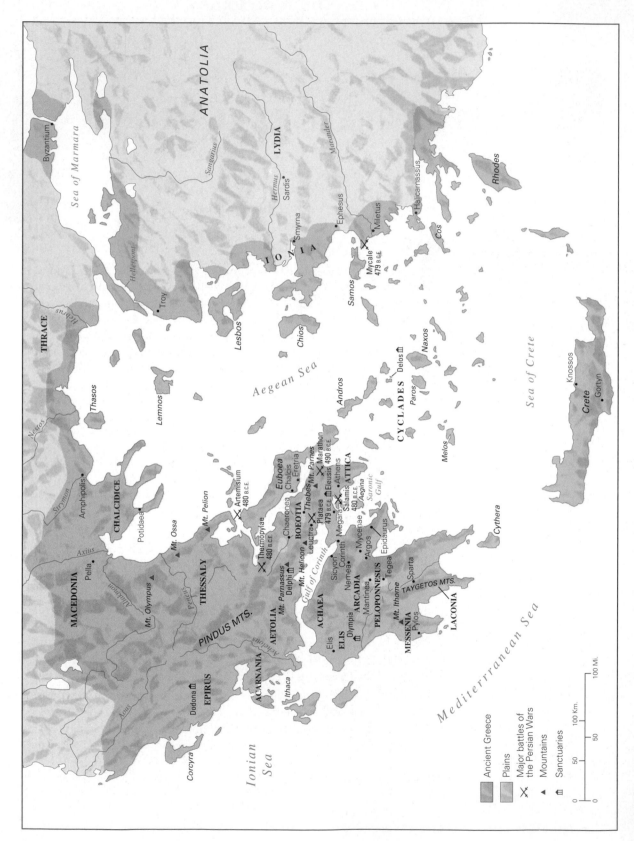

MAP 5.1 Ancient Greece In antiquity the home of the Greeks included the islands of the Aegean and the western shore of Turkey as well as the Greek peninsula itself.

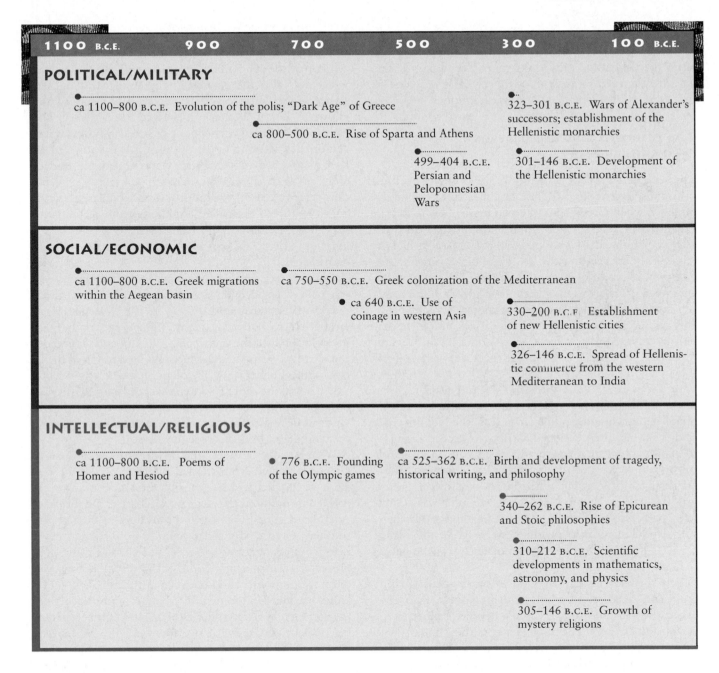

1100 B.C.E.   **900**   **700**   **500**   **300**   **100** B.C.E.

POLITICAL/MILITARY

ca 1100–800 B.C.E. Evolution of the polis; "Dark Age" of Greece

ca 800–500 B.C.E. Rise of Sparta and Athens

499–404 B.C.E. Persian and Peloponnesian Wars

323–301 B.C.E. Wars of Alexander's successors; establishment of the Hellenistic monarchies

301–146 B.C.E. Development of the Hellenistic monarchies

SOCIAL/ECONOMIC

ca 1100–800 B.C.E. Greek migrations within the Aegean basin

ca 750–550 B.C.E. Greek colonization of the Mediterranean

ca 640 B.C.E. Use of coinage in western Asia

330–200 B.C.E. Establishment of new Hellenistic cities

326–146 B.C.E. Spread of Hellenistic commerce from the western Mediterranean to India

INTELLECTUAL/RELIGIOUS

ca 1100–800 B.C.E. Poems of Homer and Hesiod

776 B.C.E. Founding of the Olympic games

ca 525–362 B.C.E. Birth and development of tragedy, historical writing, and philosophy

340–262 B.C.E. Rise of Epicurean and Stoic philosophies

310–212 B.C.E. Scientific developments in mathematics, astronomy, and physics

305–146 B.C.E. Growth of mystery religions

HELLAS: THE LAND

Hellas, as the Greeks call their land, encompassed the Aegean Sea and its islands as well as the Greek peninsula (see Map 5.1). The Greek peninsula itself, stretching in the direction of Egypt and the Near East, is an extension of the Balkan system of mountains. The rivers of Greece are never more than creeks, and most of them go dry in the summer. Greece is, however, a land blessed with good harbors, the most important of which look to the east. The islands of the Aegean serve as steppingstones between the peninsula and Asia Minor.

Despite the beauty of the region, geography acts as an enormously divisive force in Greek life. The mountains of Greece dominate the landscape, cutting the land into many small pockets and isolating areas of habitation. Innumerable small peninsulas open to the sea, which is dotted with islands, most of them small and many uninhabitable. The geographical fragmentation of Greece encouraged political fragmentation. Furthermore, communications were extraordinarily poor. Rocky tracks were far more common than roads, and the few roads were unpaved. Usually a road consisted of nothing more than a pair of ruts cut into the rock to accommodate wheels. These conditions discouraged the growth of great empires.

The Minoans and Mycenaeans (ca 1650–ca 1100 B.C.E.)

The origins of Greek civilization are obscure. Neither historians, archaeologists, nor linguists can confidently establish when Greek-speaking peoples made the Balkan Peninsula of Greece their homeland. All that can now safely be said is that by about 1650 B.C.E. Greeks had established themselves at the great city of Mycenae in the Peloponnesus and elsewhere in Greece. Before then, the area from Thessaly in the north to Messenia in the south was inhabited by small farming communities. Quite probably the Greeks merged with these natives, and from that union emerged the society that modern scholars call "Mycenaean," after Mycenae, the most important site of this new Greek-speaking culture.

By about 1650 B.C.E. the island of Crete was the home of the flourishing and vibrant Minoan culture. The Minoans had occupied Crete from at least the Neolithic period. They had also developed a script, now called Linear A, to express their language in writing. Because Linear A is yet undeciphered, however, only archaeology and art offer clues to Minoan life. The symbol of Minoan culture was the palace. Around 1650 B.C.E. Crete was dotted with palaces, such as those at Mallia on the northern coast and Kato Zakro on the eastern tip of the island. Towering above all others in importance was the palace at Cnossus.

Few specifics are known about Minoan society except that at its head stood a king and his nobles, who governed the lives and toil of Crete's farmers, sailors, shepherds, and artisans. The implements of the Minoans, like those of the Mycenaeans, were bronze, so archaeologists have named this period the Bronze Age. Minoan society was wealthy and, to judge from the absence of fortifications on the island, peaceful. Enthusiastic sailors and merchants, the Minoans traded with Egypt and the cities of the area known today as the Middle East, or Levant. They also established trading posts throughout the Aegean Sea, which brought them into contact with the Mycenaeans on the Greek peninsula.

By about 1650 B.C.E. Greek-speakers were firmly settled at Mycenae, which became a major city and trading center. Later, other Mycenaean palaces and cities developed at Thebes, Athens, Tiryns, and Pylos. As in Crete,

the political unit was the kingdom. The king and his warrior aristocracy stood at the top of society. The seat and symbol of the king's power and wealth was his palace, which was also the economic center of the kingdom. Palace scribes kept records in Greek with a script (now known as Linear B) that was derived from Minoan Linear A. The scribes kept account of taxes and drew up inventories of the king's possessions. Little is known of the king's subjects except that they were the artisans, traders, and farmers of Mycenaean society. The Mycenaean economy was marked by an extensive division of labor, tightly controlled from the palace. At the bottom of the social scale were the slaves, who were normally owned by the king and aristocrats but who also worked for ordinary craftsmen.

Contacts between the Minoans and Mycenaeans were originally peaceful, and Minoan culture flooded the Greek mainland. But around 1450 B.C.E. the Mycenaeans attacked Crete, destroying many Minoan palaces and taking possession of the grand palace at Cnossus. For about the next fifty years the Mycenaeans ruled much of the island until a further wave of violence left Cnossus in ashes. These events are more disputed than understood. Archaeologists cannot determine whether the Mycenaeans at Cnossus were attacked by other Mycenaeans or whether the conquered Minoans rose in revolt.

Whatever the answer, the Mycenaean kingdoms in Greece benefited from the fall of Cnossus and the collapse of its trade. Mycenaean commerce quickly expanded throughout the Aegean, reaching as far abroad as Anatolia, Cyprus, and Egypt. Throughout central and southern Greece Mycenaean culture flourished as never before. Palaces became grander, and citadels were often protected by mammoth stone walls. Prosperity, however, did not bring peace, and between 1300 and 1000 B.C.E. kingdom after kingdom suffered attack and destruction.

Later Greeks accused the Dorians, who spoke a particular dialect of Greek, of overthrowing the Mycenaean kingdoms. Yet some modern linguists argue that the Dorians dwelt in Greece during the Mycenaean period. Archaeologists generally conclude that the Dorians, if not already present, could have entered Greece only long after the era of destruction. Furthermore, not one alien artifact has been found at any of these sites; thus there is no archaeological evidence for outside invaders. Normally, foreign invaders leave traces of themselves—for example, broken pottery and weapons—that are different from those of the attacked. We can conclude, therefore, that no outside intrusion destroyed the Mycenaean world. In fact, the legends preserved by later Greeks tell of grim wars between Mycenaean kingdoms and of the fall of

Mycenaean Lion Hunt
The Mycenaeans were a robust, warlike people who enjoyed the thrill and the danger of hunting. This scene on the blade of a dagger depicts hunters armed with spears and protected by shields defending themselves against charging lions. *(National Archaeological Museum/Archaeological Receipts Fund)*

great royal families. Apparently, Mycenaean Greece destroyed itself in a long series of internecine wars, a pattern that later Greeks would repeat.

The fall of the Mycenaean kingdoms ushered in a period of such poverty, disruption, and backwardness that historians usually call it the "Dark Age" of Greece (ca 1100–800 B.C.E.). Even literacy, which was not widespread in any case, was a casualty of the chaos. Nonetheless, the Greeks survived the storm to preserve their culture and civilization. Greece remained Greek; nothing essential was swept away. Greek religious cults remained vital to the people, and basic elements of social organization continued to function effectively. It was a time of change and challenge, but not of utter collapse.

This period also saw a development of enormous importance for the course of Western civilization. The disruption of Mycenaean societies caused the widespread movement of Greek peoples. Some Greeks sailed to Crete, where they established new communities. The most important line of immigration was east to the shores of Asia Minor. The Greeks arrived during a time when the traditional states and empires had collapsed. Economic hardship was common, and various peoples wandered for years. The age saw both the displacement of peoples throughout the region and ethnic intermixing. Whereas the Sea Peoples (see page 25) had eventually dissolved into their various parts and gone their separate ways, the Greeks spread the culture of their homeland throughout the eastern Mediterranean.

Upon landing in Asia Minor, the Greeks encountered peoples who had been influenced by the older cultures of the region. Furthermore, the Greeks themselves had had long associations with these peoples. Thus they were hardly strangers, nor was Greek culture alien or unknown to the natives. By the end of the Dark Age of Greece, the Greeks had established a string of settlements along a coast already accustomed to them. Their arrival resulted in the spread of Greek culture throughout the area, not through force of arms but because of its freedom of ideas, the right of individuals to express them, and the vitality of Greek social life.

Homer, Hesiod, and the Heroic Past (1100–800 B.C.E.)

The Greeks, unlike the Hebrews, had no sacred book that chronicled their past. Instead they had the *Iliad* and the *Odyssey* to describe a time when gods still walked the earth. And they learned the origin and descent of the gods from the *Theogony,* an epic poem by Hesiod (ca 700 B.C.E.). Instead of authentic history the poems of Homer and Hesiod offered the Greeks an ideal past, a largely legendary Heroic Age. These poems contain scraps of information about the Bronze Age, much about the early Dark Age, and some about the poets' own era. Chronologically, the Heroic Age falls mainly in the period between the collapse of the Mycenaean world and the rebirth of literacy.

The *Iliad* recounts an expedition of Mycenaeans, whom Homer called "Achaeans," to besiege the city of Troy in Asia Minor. The heart of the *Iliad,* however, concerns the quarrel between Agamemnon, the king of Mycenae, and Achilles, the tragic hero of the poem, and how their anger and pride brought suffering to the

Funeral Games   At the end of the *Iliad* Homer describes the funeral games given in honor of Patroclus, the companion of Achilles. The main event was the chariot race, which is shown here. The painter states in the Greek inscription that one of these chariots belonged to Achilles. *(National Archaeological Museum/ Archaeological Receipts Fund)*

Achaeans. The *Odyssey,* probably composed later than the *Iliad,* narrates the adventures of Odysseus, one of the Achaean heroes who fought at Troy, during his voyage home from the fighting.

The splendor of these poems does not lie in their plots, although the *Odyssey* is a marvelous adventure story. Rather, both poems portray engaging but often flawed characters who are larger than life and yet typically human. Homer was also strikingly successful in depicting the great gods, who generally sit on Mount Olympus and watch the fighting at Troy like spectators at a baseball game, although they sometimes participate in the action. Homer's deities are reminiscent of Mesopotamian gods and goddesses. Hardly a decorous lot, the Olympians are raucous, petty, deceitful, and splendid. In short, they are human.

Homer at times portrayed the gods in a serious vein, but he never treated them in a systematic fashion, as did Hesiod, who lived somewhat later than Homer. Hesiod's epic poem, the *Theogony,* traces the descent of Zeus. Hesiod was influenced by Mesopotamian myths, which the Hittites had adopted and spread to the Aegean. Like the Hebrews, however, Hesiod envisaged his *cosmogony*— his account of the way the universe developed—in moral terms. Cronus, the son of Earth and Heaven, like the Mesopotamian Enlil, separated the two and became king of the gods. Zeus, the son of Cronus, defeated his evil father and took his place as king of the gods. He then sired Lawfulness, Right, Peace, and other powers of light and beauty. Thus, in Hesiod's conception, Zeus was the god of righteousness, who loved justice and hated wrongdoing.

In another epic poem, *Works and Days,* Hesiod wrote of his own time and his own village of Ascra in Boeotia, a scenic place set between beautiful mountains and fertile plains. In his will, Hesiod's father had divided his lands between Hesiod and his brother, Perses. Perses bribed the aristocratic authorities to give him the larger part of the inheritance and then squandered his wealth. Undaunted by the injustice of the powerful, Hesiod thundered back:

Bribe-devouring lords, make straight your decisions,
Forget entirely crooked judgments.
He who causes evil to another harms himself.
Evil designs are most evil to the plotter.[1]

Hesiod did not receive justice from the political authorities of the day, but he fully expected divine vindication. Hesiod spoke of Zeus as Jeremiah had spoken of Yahweh, warning that Zeus would see that justice was done and injustice punished. He cautioned his readers that Zeus was angered by those who committed adultery, harmed orphans, and offended the aged.

THE POLIS

After the upheavals that ended the Mycenaean period and the slow recovery of prosperity during the Dark Age, the Greeks developed their basic political and institutional unit, the **polis,** or city-state. Only three city-states were able to muster the resources of an entire region behind them (see Map 5.1): Sparta, which dominated the regions of Laconia and Messenia; Athens, which united the large peninsula of Attica under its rule; and Thebes, which in several periods marshaled the resources of the fertile region of Boeotia. Otherwise, the political pattern of ancient Greece was one of many small city-states, few of which were much stronger or richer than their neighbors.

Physically the term *polis* designated a city or town and its surrounding countryside. The people of a typical polis lived in a compact group of houses within a city. The city's water supply came from public fountains and cisterns. By the fifth century B.C.E. the city was generally surrounded by a wall. The city contained a point, usually elevated, called the **acropolis,** and a public square or marketplace, the *agora.* On the acropolis, which in the early period was a place of refuge, stood the temples, altars, public monuments, and various dedications to the gods of the polis. The agora was originally the place where the warrior assembly met, but it became the political center of the polis. In the agora were porticoes, shops, and public buildings and courts.

The unsettled territory of the polis—arable land, pastureland, and wasteland—was typically its source of wealth. Farmers left the city each morning to work their fields or tend their flocks of sheep and goats, and they returned at night. On the wasteland men often quarried stone or mined for precious metals. Thus the polis was the scene of both urban and agrarian life.

The size of the polis varied according to geographical circumstances. Population figures for Greece are mostly guesswork, because most city-states were too small to need a census. But regardless of its size or wealth, the polis was fundamental to Greek life. The intimacy of the polis was an important factor. The smallness of the polis enabled Greeks to see how the individual fitted into the

Polis of Argos   This view of modern Argos remarkably illustrates the structure of an ancient polis. Atop the hill in the background are the remains of the ancient acropolis. At its foot to the right are foundations of ancient public and private buildings, spreading beyond which are modern houses, situated where ancient houses were located. The trees and cut grain in the foreground were also major features of the *chora,* the agricultural basis of the polis. *(John Buckler)*

overall system—how the human parts made up the social whole. These simple facts go far to explain why the Greek polis was fundamentally different from the great empires of Persia and China. The Greeks knew their leaders and elected them to limited terms of office. They were unlike the subjects of the Mauryan Empire or the Han Dynasty, who might spend their entire lives without ever seeing their emperors. One result of these factors was the absence in Greek politics of a divine emperor. Another was the lack of an extensive imperial bureaucracy and a standing army. The ancient Greeks were their own magistrates, administrators, and soldiers.

Instead of a standing army, the average polis relied on its own citizens for protection. Very rich citizens often served as cavalry. However, the heavily armed infantry was the backbone of the army. The foot soldiers, or **hoplites,** provided their own equipment and were basically amateurs. When in battle, they stood in several dense lines, in which cohesion and order became as valuable as courage.

The polis could be governed in any of several ways. In a **monarchy,** a term derived from the Greek for "the rule of one man," a king represented the community, reigning according to law and respecting the rights of the citizens. Or the **aristocracy** could govern the state. A literal political translation of this term means "power in the hands of the best." Or the running of the polis could be the duty and prerogative of an **oligarchy,** which literally means "the rule of a few"—in this case a small group of

wealthy citizens, not necessarily of aristocratic birth. Or the polis could be governed as a **democracy,** through the rule of the people, a concept that in Greece meant that all citizens, regardless of birth or wealth, administered the workings of government. How a polis was governed depended on who had the upper hand. When the wealthy held power, they usually instituted oligarchies; when the people could break the hold of the rich, they established democracies. Still another form of Greek government was **tyranny,** rule by a tyrant, a man who had seized power by extralegal means, generally by using his wealth to gain a political following that could topple the existing government.

Because the bonds that held the polis together were so intimate, Greeks were extremely reluctant to allow foreigners to share fully in its life. An alien, even someone Greek by birth, could almost never expect to be made a citizen. Nor could women play a political role. Women participated in the civic cults and served as priestesses, but the polis had no room for them in state affairs. This exclusiveness doomed the polis to a limited horizon.

Although each polis was jealous of its independence, some Greeks banded together to create leagues of city-states. Here was the birth of Greek federalism, a political system in which several states formed a central government while remaining independent in their internal affairs. United in a league, a confederation of city-states was far stronger than any of the individual members and better able to withstand external attack.

Early Greek Warfare Before the hoplites became the backbone of the army, wealthy warriors rode into battle in a chariot, dismounted, and engaged the enemy. This scene, almost a photograph, shows on the left the warrior protecting the chariot before it returns to the rear. The painter has caught the lead horses already beginning the turn. *(Courtesy of the Ure Museum of Greek Archaeology, University of Reading)*

The passionate individualism of the polis proved to be another serious weakness. The citizens of each polis were determined to remain free and autonomous. Rarely were the Greeks willing to unite in larger political bodies. The political result in Greece, as in Sumer, was almost constant warfare. The polis could dominate, but unlike Rome it could not incorporate.

THE ARCHAIC AGE (800–500 B.C.E.)

The maturation of the polis coincided with one of the most vibrant periods of Greek history, an era of extraordinary expansion geographically, artistically, and politically. Greeks ventured as far east as the Black Sea and as far west as Spain (see Map 5.2). With the rebirth of literacy, this period also witnessed a tremendous literary flowering as poets broke away from the heroic tradition and wrote about their own lives. Politically these were the years when Sparta and Athens—the two poles of the Greek experience—rose to prominence.

Overseas Expansion

Between 1100 and 800 B.C.E. the Greeks not only recovered from the breakdown of the Mycenaean world but also grew in wealth and numbers. This new prosperity brought with it new problems. Greece is a small and not especially fertile country. The increase in population meant that many men and their families had very little land or none at all. Land hunger and the resulting social and political tensions drove many Greeks to seek new homes outside Greece (see Map 5.2).

From about 750 to 550 B.C.E., Greeks from the mainland and Asia Minor traveled throughout the Mediterranean and even into the Atlantic Ocean in their quest for new land. They sailed in the greatest numbers to Sicily and southern Italy, where there was ample space for expansion. They also sailed farther west to Sardinia, southern France and Spain, and even the Canary Islands. In Sicily they found the Sicels, who had already adopted many Carthaginian customs, including a nascent urban culture. Fiercely independent, they greeted the coming of the Greeks just as they had the arrival of the Carthaginians. They welcomed Greek culture but not Greek

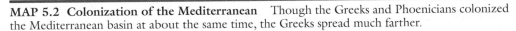

MAP 5.2 Colonization of the Mediterranean Though the Greeks and Phoenicians colonized the Mediterranean basin at about the same time, the Greeks spread much farther.

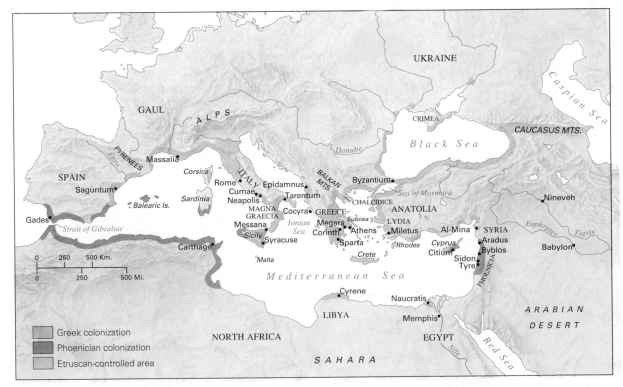

demands for their land. Nonetheless, the two peoples made a somewhat uneasy accommodation. There was enough land in Sicily for Greeks and Sicels alike, so both flourished, albeit not always peacefully.

In southern Italy the Greeks encountered a number of Indo-European peoples. They were for the most part rural and enjoyed few material comforts. Some of their villages were evolving into towns, but in the mountains looser tribal units prevailed. They both welcomed Greek culture, and the Greeks found it easy to establish prosperous cities without facing significant local hostility.

Some adventurous Greeks sailed to Sardinia and the southern coast of modern France. In Sardinia they established outposts that were originally trading ports, meant primarily for bartering with the natives. Commerce was so successful that some Greeks established permanent towns there. Greek influence, in terms of physical remains and the ideas that they reflect, was far stronger on the island than was recognized even a few years ago. From these new outposts Greek influence extended to southern France. The modern city of Marseilles began as a Greek colony and later sent settlers to southern Spain.

One of the most remarkable aspects of the sense of adventure of the Greeks is seen from their remains on the Canary Islands in the Atlantic Ocean. Their settlements on some of the islands took their culture beyond the Mediterranean for the first time. The presence of these pioneers widened the geographical and intellectual horizons of the Greek world. In the process, the Greeks of the Canary Islands introduced their culture to a part of Africa that had not even heard of them. This era of colonization not only spread Greek settlers over much of the western Mediterranean and beyond but also passed on the Hellenic legacy to the rest of the Mediterranean and even to a part of western Africa. Above all, Rome would later fall heir to this heritage.

The Growth of Sparta

During the Lyric Age the Spartans expanded the boundaries of their polis and made it the leading power in Greece. Like other Greeks, the Spartans faced the problems of overpopulation and land hunger. Unlike other Greeks, they solved these problems by conquest, taking control of the rich, fertile region of Messenia after a twenty-year war that ended about 715 B.C.E. They made the Messenians *helots,* or state serfs, who after decades of harsh Spartan treatment rose in revolt.

When the revolt was finally squashed after some thirty years of fighting, Sparta underwent a social transforma-

tion. Non-nobles demanded rights equal to those of the nobility. The aristocrats agreed to remodel the state in a pattern called the Lycurgan regimen after Lycurgus, a legendary lawgiver. Politically, all Spartan men were given equal rights. Two kings ruled, assisted by a council of nobles. Executive power lay in the hands of five overseers elected by the people. Economically, the helots did all the work of the polis; Spartan citizens were supposed to devote their time exclusively to military training.

In the Lycurgan system every citizen owed primary allegiance to Sparta. Suppression of the individual together with emphasis on military prowess led to a barracks state. Family life itself was sacrificed to the polis. Once Spartan boys reached the age of twelve, they were enrolled in separate companies with other boys their age. They slept outside on reed mats and underwent rugged physical and military training until age twenty-four, when they became frontline soldiers. For the rest of their lives, Spartan men kept themselves prepared for combat. Their military training never ceased, and the older men were expected to be models of endurance, frugality, and sturdiness to the younger men. In battle Spartans were supposed to stand and die rather than retreat. An anecdote about one Spartan mother sums up Spartan military values. As her son was setting off to battle, the mother handed him his shield and advised him to come back either victorious, carrying the shield, or dead, being carried on it. In the Lycurgan regimen Spartan men were expected to train vigorously, disdain luxury and wealth, do with little, and like it.

Similar rigorous requirements applied to Spartan women, who may have been unique in all of Greek society. They were prohibited from wearing jewelry or ornate clothes. They too exercised strenuously in the belief that hard physical training promoted the birth of healthy children. Yet they were hardly oppressed. They enjoyed a more active and open public life than most other Greek women, even though they could neither vote nor hold office. They were far more emancipated than many other Greek women in part because Spartan society felt that mothers and wives had to be as hardy as their sons and husbands. Sparta was not a place for weaklings, male or female. Spartan women saw it as their privilege to be the wives and mothers of victorious warriors, and on several occasions their own courage became legendary. They had a reputation for an independent spirit and self-assertion. This position stemmed not only from their genuine patriotism but also from their title to much Spartan land. For all of these reasons, they shared a footing with Spartan men that most other Greek women lacked in their own societies.

Along with the emphasis on military values for both sexes, the Lycurgan regimen had another purpose as well: it served to instill in society the civic virtues of dedication to the state and a code of moral conduct. These aspects of the Spartan system were generally admired throughout the Greek world.

The Evolution of Athens

Like Sparta, Athens faced serious social and economic problems, but it responded in a very different way by creating one of the most thoroughgoing democracies of ancient Greece. In the early sixth century B.C.E. the aristocracy was governing Athens oppressively. Noble landowners had all the best land and governed the polis. They used their power to seize the land of smaller landowners, selling debtors into slavery or sending them to exile. Solon, himself an aristocrat, grew alarmed by these trends. With the respect of both nobles and peasants, he was elected by the nobles as chief magistrate around 594 B.C.E. and given broad powers to reform the state.

Solon freed those who had been enslaved for debt, recalled the exiles, canceled debts for land, and banned enslavement for debtors. He allowed all citizens to join the aristocratic assembly that elected leaders and then, refusing the offer to take power as tyrant, left Athens.

Solon's reforms did not completely solve social problems in Athens. It was not until 508 B.C.E. that Cleisthenes further reorganized the state and created Athenian democracy. He did so with the full approval of the Athenian people; he presented every innovation to the assembly for discussion and ratification.

Cleisthenes created the **deme,** a local unit, to serve as the basis of his political system. Citizenship was tightly linked to the deme, for each deme kept the roll of those within its jurisdiction who were admitted to citizenship. Cleisthenes grouped all the demes into ten tribes, which thus formed the link between the demes and the central government. The central government included an assembly of all citizens and a new council of five hundred members.

The democracy functioned on the idea that all full citizens, the *demos,* were sovereign. Yet not all citizens could take time from work to participate in government. Therefore, they delegated their power to other citizens by creating various offices to run the democracy. The most prestigious of them was the board of ten archons, who were charged with handling legal and military matters. Legislation was in the hands of two bodies, the *boule,* or council, composed of five hundred members, and the *ecclesia,* the assembly of all citizens. The boule was perhaps the major institution of the democracy. By supervising the various committees of government and proposing bills to the assembly, it guided Athenian political life and held the democracy together. The ecclesia, however, had the final word. Open to all male citizens over eighteen years of age, this assembly could accept, amend, or reject bills put before it. Every member could express his opinion on any subject on the agenda. A simple majority vote was needed to pass or reject a bill.

Athenian democracy was to prove an inspiring model by demonstrating that a large group of people, not just a few, could efficiently run the affairs of state. Yet it must not be thought of in modern terms. While any citizen could theoretically enjoy political power, most important offices were held by aristocrats. Furthermore, the polis denied citizenship rights to many people, including women and slaves. Nevertheless, Athenian democracy has proved an inspiring model in that every citizen was expected to vote and to serve. The people were the government. It is this idea that the state exists for the good of the citizen, whose duty it is to serve it well, that has made Athenian democracy so compelling.

Yet Athenian democracy also had a dark side. Because comparatively few people actually exercised power, they could sometimes take advantage of their positions to dominate Athens. In periods of crisis some unscrupulous politicians suppressed political rights and even freedom of speech. These situations were rare, but the ancient Athenians, like modern Americans, balanced the desire for liberty with the need for security.

THE CLASSICAL PERIOD (500–338 B.C.E.)

In the years from 500 to 338 B.C.E. Greek civilization reached its highest peak in politics, thought, and art. In this period the Greeks beat back the armies of the Persian Empire. Then, turning their spears against one another, they destroyed their own political system in a century of warfare. Some thoughtful Greeks felt prompted to record and analyze these momentous events; the result was the creation of history. This era also saw the flowering of philosophy, as Greek thinkers began to ponder the nature and meaning of the universe and human experience. The Greeks also invented drama, and Greek architects reached the zenith of their art. Because Greek intellectual and artistic efforts attained their fullest and finest expression in these years, this age is called the classical period.

The Deadly Conflicts (499–404 B.C.E.)

One of the hallmarks of the classical period was warfare. In 499 B.C.E. the Greeks of West Asia, with the feeble help of Athens, rebelled against the Persian Empire. In 490 B.C.E. the Persians struck back at Athens but were beaten off at the Battle of Marathon, a small plain in Attica (see Map 5.1). In 480 B.C.E. the Persian king Xerxes retaliated with a mighty invasion force. Facing this emergency, many of the Greeks united to resist the invaders. The Spartans provided the overall leadership and commanded the Greek armies. The Athenians, led by the wily Themistocles, provided the heart of the naval forces.

In a series of hard-fought battles at the pass of Thermopylae and in the waters off Artemisium in 480 B.C.E., the Greeks retreated after heavy losses, but that autumn they decisively defeated the enemy at the naval battle of Salamis. In 479 B.C.E. they routed the last Persian forces at Plataea. These victories meant that the Greeks remained free to develop their particular genius. Their political forms and intellectual concepts would be the heritage of the West.

In 478 B.C.E. the victorious Athenians and their allies formed the **Delian League,** a grand naval alliance aimed at liberating Ionia from Persian rule. But Athenian success had a sinister side. While the Athenians drove the Persians out of the Aegean, they also became increasingly imperialistic, even to the point of turning the Delian League into an Athenian empire. Under their great leader Pericles (ca 494–429 B.C.E.), the Athenians grew so powerful and aggressive that they alarmed Sparta and its allies. A short war ending in 445 B.C.E. settled nothing, and in 431 B.C.E. Athenian imperialism finally drove Sparta to another conflict. At the outbreak of this conflict, the Peloponnesian War, a Spartan ambassador warned the Athenians: "This day will be the beginning of great evils for the Greeks." Few have ever spoken more prophetically. The Peloponnesian War lasted a generation (431–404 B.C.E.) and brought in its wake fearful plagues, famines, civil wars, widespread destruction, and huge loss of life. Finally, in 404 B.C.E. the Athenians surrendered, but by then the war had dealt Greek civilization a serious blow.

One positive development stemming from these events was the beginning of historical writing in the West. Just as Sima Qian during the Han Dynasty wrote a comprehensive history of China (see page 187), so Herodotus (ca 485–425 B.C.E.) and Thucydides (ca 460–ca 399 B.C.E.) left vivid, generally accurate accounts of Greek events. Their writings were not the chronicles or king lists of the Near East but analyses of what happened and why, with great emphasis on cause and effect and the role of individuals in important events. For the first time in the West, some men felt that the deeds of human beings were important enough to be recorded, understood, and instructive to others.

Athenian Arts in the Age of Pericles

In the last half of the fifth century B.C.E. Pericles turned Athens into the showplace of Greece by turning the Acropolis into a monument for all time. The planning of the architects and the skill of the workmen who erected these buildings were both very sophisticated. Visitors approaching the Acropolis first saw the Propylaea, the ceremonial gateway, a building of complicated layout and grand design whose Doric columns seemed to hold up the sky. On the right was the small temple of Athena Nike, whose dimensions harmonized with those of the Propylaea. The temple was built to commemorate the victory over the Persians, and the Ionic frieze above its columns depicted the struggle between the Greeks and the Persians. Here for all the world to see was a tribute to Athenian and Greek valor—and a reminder of Athens's part in the victory.

To the left of the visitors, as they passed through the Propylaea, stood the Erechtheum, an Ionic temple that housed several ancient shrines. On its southern side was the famous Portico of the Caryatids, a porch whose roof was supported by statues of Athenian maidens. As visitors walked on, they obtained a full view of the Parthenon, thought by many to be the perfect Doric temple. The Parthenon was the chief monument to Athena and her city. The sculptures that adorned the temple portrayed the greatness of Athens and its goddess.

In many ways the Athenian Acropolis is the epitome of Greek art and its spirit. Although the buildings were dedicated to the gods and most of the sculptures portrayed gods, these works nonetheless express the Greek fascination with the human and the rational. Greek deities were anthropomorphic, and Greek artists portrayed them as human beings. While honoring the gods, Greek artists were thus celebrating human beings. They captured the noblest aspects of human beings: their reason, dignity, and promise.

Other aspects of Athenian cultural life were as rooted in the life of the polis as were the architecture and sculpture of the Acropolis. The development of drama was tied to the religious festivals of the city. The Athenian dramatists were the first artists in Western society to examine such basic questions as the rights of the individual, the demands of society on the individual, and the nature of good and evil. Conflict is a constant element in Athen-

The Acropolis of Athens These buildings embody the noblest spirit of Greek architecture. At the right rises the Parthenon, the temple that honored Athena and Athens alike. The Erechtheum stands next to it and to its left the Propylaea and the small temple of Athena Nike. Despite the ravages of time, they abide today in their silent grandeur. *(Spyros Spyrou Photo Gallery, Aegina)*

ian drama. The dramatists used their art to portray, understand, and resolve life's basic conflicts.

Aeschylus (525–456 B.C.E.), the first of the great Athenian dramatists, was also the first to express the agony of the individual caught in conflict. In his trilogy of plays, *The Oresteia,* Aeschylus deals with the themes of betrayal, murder, and reconciliation, urging that reason and justice be applied to reconcile fundamental conflicts. The final play concludes with a prayer that civil dissension never be allowed to destroy the city and that the life of the city be one of harmony and grace.

Sophocles (496–406 B.C.E.) also dealt with matters personal and political. In *Antigone* he expresses the precedence of divine law over human defects and touches on the need for recognition of the law and adherence to it as a prerequisite for a tranquil state.

Sophocles' masterpieces have inspired generations of playwrights. Perhaps his most famous plays are *Oedipus the King* and its sequel, *Oedipus at Colonus. Oedipus the*

King is the ironic story of a man doomed by the gods to kill his father and marry his mother. Try as he might to avoid his fate, Oedipus's every action brings him closer to its fulfillment. When at last he realizes that he has carried out the decree of the gods, Oedipus blinds himself and flees into exile. In *Oedipus at Colonus* Sophocles dramatizes the last days of the broken king, whose patient suffering and uncomplaining piety win him an exalted position. In the end the gods honor him for his virtue. The interpretation of these two plays has been hotly debated, but Sophocles seems to be saying that human beings should obey the will of the gods, even without fully understanding it, for the gods stand for justice and order.

Euripides (ca 480–406 B.C.E.), the last of the three great Greek tragic dramatists, also explored the theme of personal conflict within the polis and sounded the depths of the individual. With Euripides drama entered a new, and in many ways more personal, phase. To him the gods were far less important than human beings. The essence of Euripides' tragedy is the flawed character—men and women who bring disaster on themselves and their loved ones because their passions overwhelm reason. Although Euripides' plays were less popular in his lifetime than were those of Aeschylus and Sophocles, Euripides was a dramatist of genius whose work later had a significant impact on Roman drama.

Writers of comedy treated the affairs of the polis bawdily and often coarsely. Even so, their plays too were performed at religious festivals. The comic playwrights dealt primarily with the political affairs of the polis and the conduct of its leading politicians. Best known are the comedies of Aristophanes (ca 445–386 B.C.E.), an ardent lover of his city and a merciless critic of cranks and quacks. He lampooned eminent generals, at times depicting them as morons. He commented snidely on Pericles, poked fun at Socrates, and hooted at Euripides. Like Aeschylus, Sophocles, and Euripides, Aristophanes used his art to dramatize his ideas on the right conduct of the citizen and the value of the polis.

Perhaps never were art and political life so intimately and congenially bound together as at Athens. Athenian art was the product of deep and genuine love of the polis. It was aimed at bettering the lives of the citizens and the quality of life in the state.

Daily Life in Periclean Athens

In sharp contrast with the rich intellectual and cultural life of Periclean Athens stands the simplicity of its material life. The Athenians—and in this respect they were typical of Greeks in general—lived very happily with comparatively few material possessions. In the first place, there were very few material goods to own. The thousands of machines, tools, and gadgets considered essential for modern life had no counterparts in Athenian life. Common items of the Greek home included pottery, metal utensils for cooking, tools, luxury goods such as jewelry, and a few other things. These items they had to buy from craftsmen. Whatever else they needed, such as clothes and blankets, they produced at home.

The Athenian house was rather simple. Whether large or small, the typical house consisted of a series of rooms built around a central courtyard, with doors opening onto the courtyard. Many houses had bedrooms on an upper floor. Artisans and craftsmen often set aside a room to use as a shop or work area. The two principal rooms were the men's dining room and the room where the women worked wool. Other rooms included the kitchen and bathroom. By modern standards there was not much

furniture. In the men's dining room were couches, a sideboard, and small tables. Cups and other pottery were often hung on the wall from pegs.

In the courtyard were the well, a small altar, and a washbasin. If the family lived in the country, the stalls of the animals faced the courtyard. Country dwellers kept oxen for plowing, pigs for slaughtering, sheep for wool, goats for cheese, and mules and donkeys for transportation. Even in the city chickens and perhaps a goat or two roamed the courtyard together with dogs and cats.

Cooking, done over a hearth in the house, provided welcome warmth in the winter. Baking and roasting were done in ovens. Food consisted primarily of various grains, especially wheat and barley, as well as lentils, olives, figs, and grapes. Garlic and onion were popular garnishes, and wine was always on hand. These foods were stored at home in large jars; with them the Greek family sometimes ate fish, chicken, and vegetables. Women ground wheat into flour, baked it into bread, and on special occasions made honey or sesame cakes. The Greeks used olive oil for cooking, as families still do in modern Greece; they also used it as an unguent and as lamp fuel.

By American standards the Greeks did not eat much meat. On special occasions, such as important religious festivals, the family ate the animal sacrificed to the god and gave the god the exquisite delicacy of the thighbone wrapped in fat. The only Greeks who consistently ate meat were the Spartan warriors. They received a small portion of meat each day, together with the infamous Spartan black broth, a ghastly concoction of pork cooked in blood, vinegar, and salt. One Greek, after tasting the broth, commented that he could easily understand why the Spartans were so willing to die.

In the city a man might support himself as a craftsman—a potter, bronzesmith, sailmaker, or tanner—or he could contract with the polis to work on public buildings, such as the Parthenon and Erechtheum. Men without skills worked as paid laborers but competed with slaves for work. Slaves were usually foreigners and often barbarians. By "barbarians" the Greeks meant people whose native language was not Greek. Citizens, slaves, and barbarians were paid the same amount for their work.

Slavery was commonplace in Greece, as it was throughout history. In its essentials Greek slavery resembled Mesopotamian slavery. Slaves received some protection under the law and could buy their freedom. On the other hand, masters could mistreat or neglect their slaves, although killing them was illegal. Most slaves in Athens served as domestics and performed light labor around the house. Nurses for children, teachers of reading and writing, and guardians for young men were often slaves.

The lives of these slaves were much like those of their owners. Other slaves were skilled workers, who could be found working on public buildings or in small workshops.

The importance of slavery in Athens must not be exaggerated. Athenians did not own huge gangs of slaves as did Roman owners of large estates. Slave labor competed with free labor and kept wages down, but it never replaced the free labor that was the mainstay of the Athenian economy.

Most Athenians supported themselves by agriculture, but unless the family was fortunate enough to possess holdings in a plain more fertile than most of the land, they found it difficult to reap a good crop from the soil. Many people must have consumed nearly everything they raised. Attic farmers were free and, though hardly prosperous, by no means destitute. They could usually expect yields of five bushels of wheat and ten of barley per acre for every bushel of grain sown. A bad harvest meant a lean year. Farmers usually grew more barley than wheat because of the nature of the soil. Wherever possible farmers also cultivated vines and olive trees.

The social condition of Athenian women has been the subject of much debate and little agreement. One of the difficulties is the fragmentary nature of the evidence. Women appear frequently in literature and art, often in idealized roles, but seldom in historical contexts of a wider and more realistic nature. This is due in part to the fact that most Greek historians of the time recounted primarily the political, diplomatic, and military events of the day, events in which women seldom played a notable part. Yet that does not mean that women were totally invisible in the life of the polis. It indicates instead that ancient sources provide only a glimpse of how women affected the society in which they lived. Greek wives, for example, played an important economic and social role by their management of the household. Perhaps the best way to describe the position of the free woman in Greek society is to use the anthropologist's term *liminal,* which means in this case that although women lacked official power, they nonetheless played a vital role in shaping the society in which they lived. The same situation had existed in Hammurabi's Babylonia, and it would later recur in the Hellenistic period. The mere fact that Athenian and other Greek women did not sit in the assembly does not mean that they did not influence public affairs.

The status of a free woman of the citizen class was strictly protected by law. Only her children, not those of foreigners or slaves, could be citizens. Only she was in charge of the household and the family's possessions. Yet the law protected her primarily to protect her husband's interests. Raping a free woman was a lesser crime than seducing her, because seduction involved the winning of her affections. This law was concerned not with the husband's feelings but with ensuring that he need not doubt the legitimacy of his children.

Women in Athens and elsewhere in Greece received a certain amount of social and legal protection from their dowries. Upon marriage, the bride's father gave the couple a gift of land or money, which the husband administered. However, it was never his, and in the rare cases of divorce, it returned to the wife's domain. The same is often true in Greece today among the upper class.

Ideally, respectable women lived a secluded life in which the only men they saw were relatives. How far this ideal was actually put into practice is impossible to say. At least Athenian women seem to have enjoyed a social circle of other women of their own class. They also attended public festivals, sacrifices, and funerals. Nonetheless, prosperous and respectable women probably spent much of their time in the house. A white complexion—a sign that a woman did not have to work in the fields—was valued highly.

Courtesans lived the freest lives of all Athenian women. Although some courtesans were simply prostitutes, others added intellectual accomplishments to physical beauty. In constant demand, cultured courtesans moved freely in male society. Their artistic talents and intellectual abilities appealed to men who wanted more than sex.

A woman's main functions were to raise the children, oversee the domestic slaves and hired labor, and together with her maids work wool into cloth. The women washed the wool in the courtyard and then brought it into the women's room, where the loom stood. They spun the wool into thread and wove the thread into cloth. They also dyed wool at home and decorated the cloth by weaving in colors and designs. The woman of the household either did the cooking herself or directed her maids. In a sense, poor women lived freer lives than did wealthier women. They performed manual labor in the fields or sold goods in the agora, going about their affairs much as men did.

A distinctive feature of Athenian life and of Greek life in general was acceptance of homosexuality. The Greeks accepted the belief that both homosexual and heterosexual practices were normal parts of life. They did not think that homosexual practices created any particular problems for those who engaged in them.

No one has satisfactorily explained how the Greek attitude toward homosexual love developed or determined how common homosexual behavior was. Homosexuality was probably far more common among the aristocracy

PERIODS OF GREEK HISTORY

PERIOD	SIGNIFICANT EVENTS	MAJOR WRITERS
Bronze Age 1650–1100 B.C.E.	Arrival of the Greeks in Greece Rise and fall of the Mycenaean kingdoms	
Dark Age 1100–800 B.C.E.	Greek migrations within the Aegean basin Social and political recovery Evolution of the polis Rebirth of literacy	Homer Hesiod
Archaic Age 800–500 B.C.E.	Rise of Sparta and Athens Colonization of the Mediterranean basin Flowering of lyric poetry Development of philosophy and science in Ionia	Archilochus Sappho Tyrtaeus Solon Anaximander Heraclitus
Classical Period 500–338 B.C.E.	Persian wars Growth of the Athenian Empire Peloponnesian War Rise of drama and historical writing Flowering of Greek philosophy Spartan and Theban hegemonies Conquest of Greece by Philip of Macedonia	Herodotus Thucydides Aeschylus Sophocles Euripides Aristophanes Plato Aristotle

than among the lower classes. Even among the aristocracy attitudes toward homosexuality were complex and sometimes conflicting. Most people saw homosexual love affairs among the young as a stage in the development of a mature heterosexual life. Warrior aristocracies generally emphasized the physical side of the relationship in the belief that warriors who were also lovers would fight all the harder to impress and to protect each other. Whatever their intellectual content, homosexual love affairs were also overtly sexual.

Greek Religion

Greek religion is extremely difficult for modern people to understand, largely because of the great differences between Greek and modern cultures. In the first place, it is not even easy to talk about "Greek religion," since the Greeks had no uniform faith or creed. Although the Greeks usually worshiped the same deities—Zeus, Hera, Apollo, Athena, and others—the cults of these gods and goddesses varied from polis to polis. The Greeks had no

sacred books such as the Bible, and Greek religion was often a matter more of ritual than of belief. Nor did cults impose an ethical code of conduct. Greeks did not have to follow any particular rule of life, practice certain virtues, or even live decent lives in order to participate. Unlike the Egyptians and Hebrews, the Greeks lacked a priesthood as the modern world understands the term. In Greece priests and priestesses existed to care for temples and sacred property and to conduct the proper rituals, but not to make religious rules or doctrines, much less to enforce them. In short, there existed in Greece no central ecclesiastical authority and no organized creed.

Although temples to the gods were common, they were unlike modern churches or synagogues in that they were not normally places where a congregation met to worship as a spiritual community. Instead, the individual Greek either visited the temple occasionally on matters of private concern or walked in a procession to a particular temple to celebrate a particular festival. In Greek religion the altar, which stood outside the temple, was important; when the Greeks sought the favor of the gods, they offered them sacrifices. Greek religious observances were generally cheerful. Festivals and sacrifices were frequently times for people to meet together socially, times of high spirits and conviviality rather than of pious gloom. By offering the gods parts of the sacrifice while consuming the rest themselves, worshipers forged a bond with the gods.

The most important members of the Greek pantheon were Zeus, the king of the gods, and his consort, Hera. Although they were the mightiest and most honored of the deities who lived on Mount Olympus, their divine children were closer to ordinary people. Apollo was especially popular. He represented the epitome of youth, beauty, benevolence, and athletic skill. He was also the god of music and culture and in many ways symbolized the best of Greek culture. His sister Athena, who patronized women's crafts such as weaving, was also a warrior-goddess. Best known for her cult at Athens, to which she gave her name, she was highly revered throughout Greece, even in Sparta, which eventually became a fierce enemy of Athens. Artemis was Apollo's elder sister. A virgin and a huntress, she oversaw women's passage from virginity to marriage. Paradoxically, though a huntress, she also protected wildlife. There was something wild and free about her. Other divinities watched over every aspect of human life.

The Greeks also honored some heroes. A hero was born of a union of a god and a mortal and was an intermediate between the divine and the human. A hero displayed his divine origins by performing deeds beyond the ability of human beings. Herakles (or Hercules) was easily the greatest of them. He successfully fulfilled twelve labors, all of which pitted him against mythical opponents or tasks. Like other heroes, he protected mortals from supernatural dangers. The Greeks created other divinities with various purposes and powers, but in the hero, they believed, human beings could partake of divinity.

Besides the Olympian gods, each polis had its own minor deities, each with his or her own local cult. In many instances Greek religion involved the official gods and goddesses of the polis and their cults. The polis administered the cults and festivals, and all were expected to participate in this civic religion, regardless of whether they even believed in the deities being worshiped. Participating unbelievers, who seem to have been a small minority, were not considered hypocrites. Rather, they were seen as patriotic, loyal citizens who in honoring the gods also honored the polis. If this attitude seems contradictory, an analogy may help. Before baseball games Americans stand at the playing of the national anthem, whether they are Democrats, Republicans, or neither, and whether they agree or disagree with the policies of the current administration. They honor their nation as represented by its flag, in somewhat the same way an ancient Greek honored the polis and demonstrated solidarity with it by participating in the state cults.

Some Greeks turned to mystery religions like those of the Eleusinian mysteries in Attica and of Trophonios in Boeotia. These mystery religions in some ways foreshadowed aspects of early Christian practices by their rites of initiation, their acceptance of certain doctrines, and generally their promise of life after death. The basic concept of these cults was to unite individuals in an exclusive religious society with particular deities. Those who joined them went through a period of preparation in which they learned the essential beliefs of the cult and its necessary rituals. Once they had successfully undergone initiation, they were forbidden to reveal the secrets of the cult. Consequently, modern scholars know comparatively little about their tenets. Although the mystery religions were popular until the coming of Christianity in the Roman Empire, relatively few except the wealthy could afford the luxuries of time and money to join them.

For most Greeks religion was quite simple and close to nature. They believed in the supernatural. The religion of the common people was a rich combination of myth, ritual, folklore, and cult. They believed in a world of deities who were all around them. A single example can give an idea of the essence of this religion, its bond with nature, and its sense of ethics and propriety. Whereas no one today would think much about wading across a stream, Hesiod would have considered it sacrilegious. He advises the traveler who encounters a stream:

Never cross the beautifully flowing water of an overflowing
*   river on foot,*
until having looked into the lovely stream and having
*   washed your hands in the very lovely, clear waters,*
you offer a prayer. Whoever crosses a river and with hands
*   unwashed of evil,*
to him the gods will wreak vengeance and will give him
*   pain.*[2]

Though Greek religion in general was individual or related to the polis, the Greeks also shared some Pan-Hellenic festivals, the chief of which were held at Olympia in honor of Zeus and at Delphi in honor of Apollo. The festivities at Olympia included the famous games, athletic contests that have inspired the modern Olympic games. Held every four years, these games were for the glory of Zeus. They attracted visitors from all over the Greek world and lasted well into Christian times. The Pythian games at Delphi were also held every four years, but these contests differed from the Olympic games by including musical and literary contests. Both the Olympic and the Pythian games were unifying factors in Greek life, bringing Greeks together culturally as well as religiously.

The Flowering of Philosophy

The myths and epics of the Mesopotamians, Aryans, and others provide ample testimony that speculation about the origin of the universe and of humankind did not begin with the Greeks. The signal achievement of the Greeks was the willingness of some to treat these questions in rational rather than mythological terms. Although Greek philosophy did not fully flower until the classical period, Ionian thinkers had already begun to ask what the universe was made of. These men are called the Pre-Socratics, for their work preceded the philosophical revolution begun by the Athenian Socrates. Taking individual facts, they wove them into general theories. Despite appearances, they concluded, the universe was actually simple and subject to natural laws. Drawing on their observations, they speculated about the basic building blocks of the universe.

The first of these Pre-Socratic thinkers, Thales (ca 600 B.C.E.), differed from wise men elsewhere because he concluded that natural phenomena could be explained in natural terms, not by the actions of gods. He sought a basic element of the universe from which all else sprang. He surmised that it was water. Although he was wrong, the way in which he asked the question was momentous: it was the beginning of the scientific method. Other Pre-Socratics continued Thales' work. Anaximander was the first to use general concepts, which are essential to abstract thought. He concluded that the basic element of the universe was the "boundless"—something infinite and indestructible. Heraclitus (ca 500 B.C.E.) declared the primal element to be fire, which is ever changing and eternal. Democritus (ca 460 B.C.E.) created the atomic theory that the universe is made up of invisible, indestructible particles. The culmination of Pre-Socratic thought was the theory that four simple substances make up the universe: fire, air, earth, and water.

With this impressive heritage behind them, the philosophers of the classical period ventured into new areas of speculation. This development was partly due to the work of Hippocrates (second half of the fifth century B.C.E.), the father of medicine. Like Thales, Hippocrates sought natural explanations for natural phenomena. Basing his opinions on empirical knowledge, not on religion or magic, he taught that natural means could be employed to fight disease. But Hippocrates broke away from the mainstream of Ionian speculation by declaring that medicine was a separate craft—just as ironworking was—that had its own principles.

The distinction between natural science and philosophy on which Hippocrates insisted was also promoted by the Sophists, who traveled the Greek world teaching young men. Despite differences of opinion on philosophical matters, the Sophists all agreed that human beings were the proper subject of study. They also believed that excellence could be taught, and they used philosophy and rhetoric to prepare young men for life in the polis. The Sophists laid great emphasis on logic and the meanings of words. They criticized traditional beliefs, religion, rituals, and myth and even questioned the laws of the polis. In essence, they argued that nothing is absolute, that everything is relative.

One of those whom contemporaries thought was a Sophist was Socrates (ca 470–399 B.C.E.), who sprang from the class of small artisans. Socrates spent his life in investigation and definition. Not, strictly speaking, a Sophist, because he never formally taught or collected fees from anyone, Socrates shared the Sophists' belief that human beings and their environment are the essential subjects of philosophical inquiry. His approach when posing ethical questions and defining concepts was to start with a general topic or problem and to narrow the matter to its essentials. He did so by continuous questioning, conducting a running dialogue with his listeners. Never did he lecture. Socrates thought that by constantly pursuing excellence, an essential part of which was knowledge, human beings could approach the supreme good and thus find true happiness. Yet in 399 B.C.E. Socrates was brought to trial, convicted, and executed on charges of corrupting the youth of the city and introducing new gods.

Socrates' student Plato (427–347 B.C.E.) carried on his master's search for the truth. Unlike Socrates, Plato wrote down his thoughts and theories and founded a philosophical school, the Academy. Most people rightly think of Plato as a philosopher. Yet his writings were also literary essays of great charm. They drew out characters, locales, and scenes from ordinary life that otherwise would have been lost to posterity. In addition, Plato used satire, irony, and comedy to relay his thoughts. Behind the elegance of his literary style, however, stand the profound thoughts of a brilliant mind grappling with the problems of his own day and the eternal realities of life. The destruction and chaos of the Peloponnesian War prompted him to ask new and different questions about the nature of human society. He pondered where, why, and how the polis had gone wrong. He gave serious thought to the form that it should take. In these considerations Plato was not only a philosopher but a political scientist and a utopian.

Plato tried to show that a life of ignorance was wretched. From education, he believed, came the possibility of determining an all-comprising unity of virtues that would lead to an intelligent, moral, and ethical life. Plato concluded that only divine providence could guide people to virtue. In his opinion, divine providence was one intelligible and individualistic being. In short, he equated god with the concept of good.

Plato developed the theory that all visible, tangible things are unreal and temporary, copies of "forms" or "ideas" that are constant and indestructible. Only the mind, not the senses, can perceive eternal forms. In Plato's view the highest form is the idea of good. He discussed these ideas in two works. In *The Republic* Plato applied his theory of forms to politics in an effort to describe the ideal polis. His perfect polis was utopian; it aimed at providing the greatest good and happiness to all its members. Plato thought that the ideal polis could exist only if its rulers were philosophers and were devoted to educating their people. He divided society into rulers, guardians of the polis, and workers. The role of individuals in each category would be decided by their education, wisdom, and ability. In Plato's republic men and women would be equal to one another, and women could become rulers. The utopian polis would be a balance, with each individual doing what he or she could to support the state and with each receiving from the state his or her just due. In *The Laws,* however, Plato drew a more authoritarian picture of government and society, one not so very different from that of twentieth-century dictatorship.

A student of Plato, Aristotle (384–322 B.C.E.) went far beyond him in striving to understand the universe. The range of Aristotle's thought is staggering. Everything in human experience was fit subject for his inquiry. In *Politics* Aristotle followed Plato's lead by writing about the ideal polis, approaching the question more realistically than Plato had done. In *Politics* and elsewhere, Aristotle stressed moderation, concluding that the balance of the ideal state depended on people of talent and education who could avoid extremes.

Aristotle was both a philosopher and a scientist. He became increasingly interested in the observation and explanation of natural phenomena. He used logic as his method of scientific discussion, and he attempted to bridge the gap that Plato had created between abstract truth and concrete perception. He argued that the universe was finite, spherical, and eternal. He discussed an immaterial being that was his conception of god. Yet his god neither created the universe nor guided it. The inconsistencies of Aristotle on these matters are obvious. His god was without purpose. Yet for him scientific endeavor, the highest attainable form of living, reached the divine.

Aristotle expressed the heart of his philosophy in *Physics* and *Metaphysics*. In those masterful works he combined empiricism, or observation, and speculative method. In *Physics* he tried to explain how natural physical phenomena interact and how their interactions lead to the results that people see around them daily. He postulated four principles: matter, form, movement, and goal. A seed, for example, possesses both matter and an encoded form. Form determines whether a plant will be a rose or poison ivy. Growth represents movement, and the mature plant the goal of the seed. Although Aristotle considered nature impersonal, he felt that it had its own purposes. In a sense, this notion is a rudimentary ancestor of the concept of evolution.

In *On the Heaven* Aristotle took up the thread of Ionian speculation. His theory of cosmology added ether to air, fire, water, and earth as building blocks of the universe. He concluded that the universe revolves and that it is spherical and eternal. He wrongly thought that the earth is the center of the universe and that the stars and planets revolve around it.

Aristotle possessed one of history's keenest and most curious philosophical minds. While rethinking the old topics explored by the Pre-Socratics, he created whole new areas of study. In short, he tried to learn everything possible about the universe and everything in it.

From Polis to Monarchy (404–323 B.C.E.)

Immediately after the Peloponnesian War, with Athens humbled, Sparta began striving for empire over the Greeks. The arrogance and imperialism of the Spartans turned their former allies against them. Even with Persian help Sparta could not maintain its hold on Greece. In 371 B.C.E. on the plain of Leuctra in Boeotia, a Theban army under the command of Epaminondas destroyed the flower of the Spartan army on a single summer day. But the Thebans were unable to bring peace to Greece. In 362 B.C.E. Epaminondas was killed in battle, and a period of stalemate set in. The Greek states were virtually exhausted.

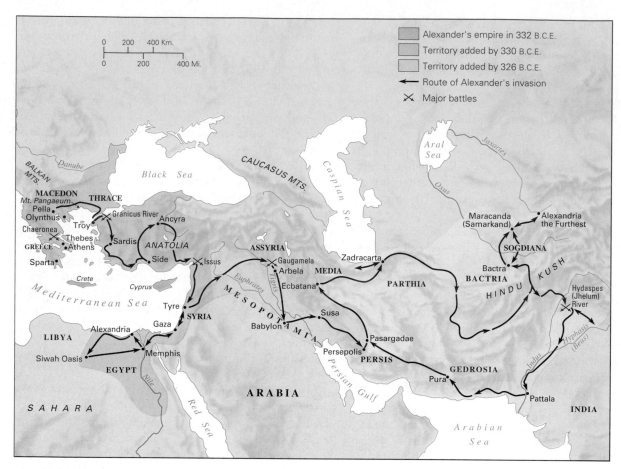

MAP 5.3 Alexander's Conquests   This map shows the course of Alexander's invasion of the Persian Empire and the speed of his progress. More important than the great success of his military campaigns was his founding of Hellenistic cities in the East.

The man who turned the situation to his advantage was Philip II, king of Macedonia (359–336 B.C.E.). Throughout most of Greek history Macedonia, which bordered Greece in the north (see Map 5.3), had been a backward, disunited kingdom, but Philip's genius and courage turned it into a major power. One of the ablest statesmen of antiquity, Philip united his powerful kingdom, built a redoubtable army, and pursued his ambition with drive and determination. His horizon was not limited to Macedonia, for he realized that he could turn the rivalry and exhaustion of the Greek states to his own purposes. By clever use of his wealth and superb army, Philip won control of the northern Aegean and awakened fear in Athens, which had vital interests there. A comic playwright depicted one of Philip's ambassadors warning the Athenians:

Do you know that your battle will be with men
Who dine on sharpened swords,
And gulp burning firebrands for wine?
Then immediately after dinner the slave
Brings us dessert—Cretan arrows
Or pieces of broken spears.
We have shields and breastplates for
Cushions and at our feet slings and arrows,
And we are crowned with catapults.[3]

In 338 B.C.E. a combined Theban-Athenian army met Philip's veterans at the Boeotian city of Chaeronea. Philip's army won a hard-fought victory: he had conquered Greece and put an end to Greek freedom. Because the Greeks could not put aside their quarrels, they fell to an invader.

Alexander at the Battle of Issus   At left, Alexander the Great, bareheaded and wearing a breast-plate, charges King Darius, who is standing in a chariot. The moment marks the turning point of the battle, as Darius turns to flee from the attack. *(National Museum, Naples/Alinari/Art Resource, NY)*

Philip used his victory to unite the Greek states with his Macedonian kingdom to form the League of Corinth. He hoped to bring unity and harmony to both Greeks and Macedonians for the first time in history. He also proclaimed that the mission of this union was to liberate the Greeks of Asia from Persian control. Although Greeks and Macedonians alike prepared for a massive invasion of the Persian Empire, Philip fell to an assassin's dagger in 336 B.C.E. His young son Alexander, soon to be known as "the Great," ascended the Macedonian throne and vowed to carry on Philip's mission. Alexander proclaimed to all that the invasion of Persian territory was to be a great crusade, a mighty act of revenge for the Persian invasion of Greece in 480 B.C.E. Despite his youth, Alexander was well prepared to lead the attack. In 334 B.C.E. he led an army of Macedonians and Greeks into western Asia. In the next three years he won three major battles—at the Granicus River, at Issus, and at Gaugamela—victories that stand almost as road signs marking his march to the east (see Map 5.3). Having overthrown the Persian Empire, he crossed the Indus River in 326 B.C.E. and entered In-

dia, where he saw hard fighting. Finally, at the Hyphasis River his troops refused to go farther. Still eager to explore the limits of the world, Alexander turned south to the Arabian Sea and then west. In 324 B.C.E. a long, hard march brought him back to his camp at Susa. The great crusade was over, and Alexander himself died the next year in Babylon.

The political result of Alexander's premature death was chaos. Since several of the chief Macedonian officers aspired to Alexander's position as emperor and others opposed these ambitions, civil war lasting forty-three years tore Alexander's empire apart. By the end of this conflict, the most successful generals had carved out their own small and more or less stable monarchies.

Ptolemy immediately seized Egypt and transformed the native system of administration by appointing Greeks and Macedonians to the chief bureaucratic positions. Meanwhile, Seleucus won the bulk of Alexander's empire; his monarchy extended from western Asia to India. In the third century B.C.E., however, the eastern parts of Seleucus's monarchy gained their independence: the

Theater of Stratos Excavation of this theater in Stratos, a major city in northwestern Greece, began only in 1994. Not a city in the mainstream of Greek affairs, Stratos nevertheless shared the love and appreciation of the arts that stamped all of Greek culture. Even in its partially excavated state, the theater boasts the remains of a stone building in the foreground, the orchestra, and behind it the seats. Beyond its many architectural refinements, the theater is of interest because most Greek plays were staged in small theaters such as this. *(John Buckler)*

Parthians came to power in Iran, and the Greeks created a monarchy of their own in Bactria. Antigonus maintained control of the Macedonian monarchy in Europe. Until the arrival of the Romans in the eastern Mediterranean in the second century B.C.E., these great monarchies were often at war with one another, but without winning any significant political or military advantage. In that respect, the Hellenistic monarchy was no improvement on the Greek polis.

Despite the disintegration of his empire, Alexander was instrumental in changing the face of politics in the eastern Mediterranean. His campaign swept away the Persian Empire, which had ruled the East for over two hundred years. In its place he established a Macedonian monarchy. More important in the long run was his founding of new cities and military colonies, which scattered Greeks and Macedonians throughout the East (see Map 5.3). Thus the practical result of Alexander's campaign was to open the East to the tide of Hellenism.

THE SPREAD OF HELLENISM

When the Greeks and Macedonians entered Asia Minor, Egypt, and the more remote East, they encountered civilizations older than their own. In some ways the Eastern cultures were more advanced than the Greek, in others less so. Thus this third great tide of Greek migration differed from preceding waves, which had spread over land that was uninhabited or inhabited by less-developed peoples.

How did Hellenism and the cultures of the East affect one another? What did the meeting of East and West entail for the history of the world?

Cities and Kingdoms

A major development of the Hellenistic kingdoms, the resurgence of monarchy had many repercussions. For most Greeks, monarchs were something out of the heroic past, something found in Homer's *Iliad* but not in daily life.

Most Hellenistic kingdoms encompassed numerous different peoples who had little in common. Hellenistic kings thus attempted to create a ruler cult that linked the king's authority with that of the gods and to establish an easily understandable symbol of political and religious unity within the kingdom.

Monarchy included royal women, who began to play an active part in political and diplomatic life. Some of them did so in their own right, others by manipulating their husbands. Many Hellenistic queens have been depicted as willful or ruthless, especially in power struggles over the throne. In some cases, those charges are accurate. Yet for the most part, queens served as examples that women were as capable of shouldering vast responsibilities and performing them successfully as men were. (See the feature "Individuals in Society: Queen Cratesicleia's Sacrifice.")

Hellenistic kings needed large numbers of Greeks to run their kingdoms. Without them, royal business would have ground to a halt, and the conquerors would soon have been swallowed up by the far more numerous conquered population. Obviously, then, the kings had to encourage Greeks to immigrate and build new homes. Since Greek civilization was urban, the kings continued Alexander's policy of establishing cities throughout their kingdoms in order to entice Greeks to immigrate. Yet the creation of these cities posed a serious political problem that the Hellenistic kings failed to solve.

To the Greeks civilized life was unthinkable without the polis, which was far more than a mere city. The Greek polis was by definition **sovereign.** It was an independent, autonomous state run by its citizens, free of any outside power or restraint. Hellenistic kings, however, refused to grant sovereignty to their cities. They gave their cities all the external trappings of a polis. Each had an assembly of citizens, a council to prepare legislation, and a board of magistrates to conduct the city's political business. But these cities could not pursue their own foreign policy, wage their own wars, or govern their own affairs without interference from the king, who often placed his own officials in the cities to see that his decrees were followed. There were no constitutional links between city and king. The city was simply his possession. Its citizens had no voice in how the kingdom was run and no rights except for those the king granted.

In many respects the Hellenistic city resembled a modern city. It was a cultural center with theaters, temples,

The Main Street of Pergamum   No matter where in old Greece they had come from, all Greeks would immediately feel at home walking along this main street in Pergamum. They would all see familiar sights. To the left is the top of the theater where they could watch the plays of the great dramatists, climb farther to the temple, and admire the fortifications on the right. *(Fatih Cimok/A Turizm Yayinlari Ltd.)*

and libraries—a seat of learning and a place where people could find amusement. The Hellenistic city was also an economic center—a marketplace, a scene of trade and manufacturing. In short, the Hellenistic city offered cultural and economic opportunities but did not foster a sense of united, integrated enterprise.

Hellenistic kings tried to make the kingdom the political focus of citizens' allegiance. If the king could secure the frontiers of his kingdom, he could give it a geographical identity. He could then hope that his subjects would direct their primary loyalty to the kingdom rather than to a particular city. However, the kings' efforts to fix their borders led only to sustained warfare, and rule by force became the chief political principle of the Hellenistic world (see Map 5.4).

Border wars were frequent and exhausting. The Seleucids and Ptolemies, for instance, waged five wars for the possession of southern Syria. Other kings followed Alexander's example and waged wars to reunify his empire under their own authority. By the third century B.C.E., a weary balance of power was reached, but only as the result of stalemate, not any political principle.

The Hellenistic city remained the basic social and political unit in the Hellenistic East until the sixth century C.E. Cities were the chief agents of Hellenization, and their influence spread far beyond their walls. Roman rule in the Hellenistic East would later be based on this urban culture. In broad terms, Hellenistic cities were remarkably successful.

The Greeks and the Opening of the East

If the Hellenistic kings failed to satisfy the Greeks' political yearnings, they nonetheless succeeded in giving them unequaled economic and social opportunities. The ruling dynasties of the Hellenistic world were Macedonian,

MAP 5.4 The Hellenistic World   After Alexander's death, no single commander could hold his vast conquests together, resulting in the empire's breakup into several kingdoms and leagues.

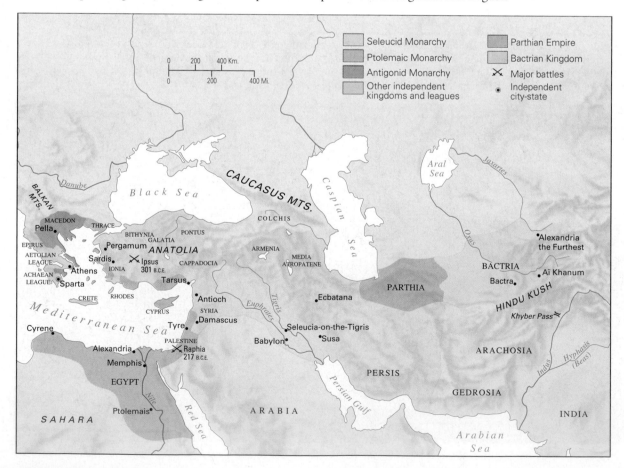

QUEEN CRATESICLEIA'S SACRIFICE

Hellenistic queens were hardly ordinary women, but they were women nonetheless. The Spartan Cratesicleia combined in herself the duties of queen mother to her homeland and mother of her own family. Her finest hour came in 225 B.C.E., when Sparta tried to reassert itself as a major power. As was seen on page 123, Epaminondas and the Thebans had shattered Spartan might. Yet in the late third century B.C.E., Cratesicleia's son, King Cleomenes, made a valiant effort to restore Sparta's fortunes. He tried to win control of the Peloponnesus and stoutly opposed King Antigonus of Macedonia, who drove him back to Sparta. At this point Ptolemy, son of the Macedonian Lagus and king of Egypt, offered to help, but at a high and humiliating price.

Now, Ptolemy the king of Egypt promised Cleomenes aid and assistance, but demanded his mother [Cratesicleia] and his children as hostages. For a long time, therefore, he was ashamed to tell his mother, and though he often went to her and was at the very point of letting her know, he held his peace, so that she on her part became suspicious and enquired of his friends whether there was not something that he wished to tell her but hesitated to do so. Finally, when Cleomenes plucked up courage to speak to the matter, his mother burst into a hearty laugh and said: "Was this the thing that you often had a mind to tell me but lost your courage? Hurry, put me on board a ship, and send this frail body wheresoever you think it will be of most use to Sparta, before old age destroys it sitting idly here."

Accordingly, when all things were ready, they came to Taenarus [a harbor in Laconia] by land, while the army escorted them under arms. And as Cratesicleia was about to embark, she drew Cleomenes aside by himself into the temple of Poseidon, and after embracing and kissing him in his anguish and deep trouble, said: "Come, king of the Spartans, when we go forth let no one see us weeping or doing anything unworthy of Sparta. For this lies in our power, and this alone; but as for the issues of Tyche [Fortune], we shall have what the deity may grant." After saying this, she composed herself and proceeded to the ship with her little grandson, and bade the captain to put to sea with all speed. And when she arrived in Egypt, and learned that Ptolemy was receiving embassies and proposals from Antigonus, and heard that although the Achaeans invited Cleomenes to make peace with them, he was afraid on her account to end the war without the consent of Ptolemy, she sent word to him that he must do what was fitting and advantageous for Sparta, and not, because of one old woman and a little boy, be ever in fear of Ptolemy.

With the time and the military support bought in large part by Cratesicleia's sacrifice, Cleomenes renewed the war against the Macedonians. Yet at the Battle of Sellasia in 222 B.C.E., Antigonus defeated him, forcing him to flee to Ptolemy in Egypt. There in defeat and disgrace, he died the victim of a palace plot. Plutarch recounts Ptolemy's response:

When Ptolemy learned of these events, he gave orders that the body of Cleomenes should be flayed and hung up, and that his children, his mother, and the women who were with her, should be killed. . . . And Cratesicleia herself was not one bit dismayed at death, but asked only one favor, that she might die before the children died. However, when they arrived at the place of execution, first the children were murdered before her eyes, and then Cratesicleia herself was killed, making only this one cry at sorrows so great: "O children, where have you gone?"

Though horrified, she nonetheless met her death with dignity and without fear. Plutarch ends the story by observing: "Virtue cannot be outraged by the might of Tyche," or, it can be said, by human barbarity.

From Corone (shown here in an 1829 sketch) Cratesicleia did her duty by sailing as a hostage to Egypt. (Boccuet in *Expédition scientifique de Moree*)

QUESTIONS FOR ANALYSIS

1. Was Cratesicleia's valor any greater or less than that of Spartan soldiers who defended the state on the battlefield?
2. What does this episode tell us about the tradition of Spartan patriotism?
3. Was Cleomenes justified in putting his family in such jeopardy?

Source: Quotations reprinted by permission of the publishers and Trustees of the Loeb Classical Library from *Plutarch: Vol. X— Plutarch Lives,* trans. B. Perrin (Cambridge, Mass.: Harvard University Press, 1921). The Loeb Classical Library® is a registered trademark of the President and Fellows of Harvard College.

Ladies Chatting   In the Hellenistic period, art gracefully embraced the ordinary. This terra-cotta group has captured two well-dressed ladies in intimate conversation. This small piece is realistic in depicting the women, the styles of their clothes, and even their varied colors. *(British Museum/Michael Holford)*

and Greeks filled all important political, military, and diplomatic positions. They constituted an upper class that sustained Hellenism. Besides building Greek cities, Hellenistic kings offered Greeks land and money as lures to further immigration.

The Hellenistic monarchy, unlike the Greek polis, did not depend solely on its citizens to fulfill its political needs. Talented Greeks could expect to rise quickly in the government bureaucracy. Appointed by the king, these administrators held their jobs year after year and had ample time to evolve new administrative techniques. The needs of the Hellenistic monarchy and the opportunities it offered thus gave rise to a professional corps of Greek administrators.

Greeks and Macedonians also found ready employment in the armies and navies of the Hellenistic monarchies. Alexander had proved the Greco-Macedonian style of warfare to be far superior to that of the Easterners, and Alexander's successors, themselves experienced officers, realized the importance of trained Greek and Macedonian soldiers. Moreover, Hellenistic kings were extremely reluctant to allow the native populations to serve in the army, fearing military rebellions among their conquered subjects. The result was the emergence of professional armies and navies consisting entirely of Greeks and Macedonians.

Greeks were able to dominate other professions as well. The kingdoms and cities recruited Greek writers and artists to bring Greek culture to Asian soil. Archi-

tects, engineers, and skilled craftsmen found their services in great demand. If Hellenistic kingdoms were to have Greek cities, those cities needed Greek buildings—temples, porticoes, gymnasia, theaters, fountains, and houses. Architects and engineers were sometimes commissioned to design and build whole cities, which they laid out in checkerboard fashion. An enormous wave of construction took place under the Hellenistic monarchs.

New opportunities opened for women as well, owing in part to the examples of the queens. More women than ever before received educations that enabled them to enter medicine and other professions. Literacy among women increased dramatically, and their options expanded accordingly. Some won fame as poets, while others studied with philosophers and contributed to the intellectual life of the age. Women also began to participate in politics on a limited basis. They served in civil capacities, for which they often received public acknowledgment. A few women received honorary citizenship from foreign cities because of aid given in times of crisis. As a rule, however, these developments touched only wealthy women, and not all of them. Although some poor women were literate, most were not.

The major reason for the new prominence of women was their increased participation in economic affairs. During the Hellenistic period some women took part in commercial transactions. They still lived under legal handicaps. In Egypt, for example, a Greek woman needed a male guardian to buy, sell, or lease land, to borrow money, and to represent her in other transactions. Yet often the guardian was present only to fulfill the letter of the law. The woman was the real agent and handled the business being transacted. In Hellenistic Sparta, women accumulated large fortunes and vast amounts of land. Spartan women, however, were exceptional. In most other areas, even women who were wealthy in their own right were formally under the protection of their male relatives.

Despite the opportunities they offered, the Hellenistic monarchies were hampered by their artificial origins. Their failure to win the political loyalty of their Greek subjects and their policy of wooing Greeks with lucrative positions encouraged a feeling of uprootedness and self-serving individualism among Greek immigrants. Once a Greek had left home to take service with, for instance, the army or the bureaucracy of the Ptolemies, he had no incentive beyond his pay and the comforts of life in Egypt to keep him there. If the Seleucid king offered him more money or a promotion, he might well accept it and take his talents to Asia Minor, where he could find the same sort of life and environment.

As long as Greeks continued to replenish their professional ranks, the Hellenistic kingdoms remained strong. In the process they drew an immense amount of talent from the Greek peninsula, draining the vitality of the Greek homeland. However, the Hellenistic monarchies could not keep recruiting Greeks forever, in spite of their wealth and willingness to spend lavishly. In time, the huge surge of immigration slowed greatly. Even then, the Hellenistic monarchs were reluctant to recruit Easterners to fill posts normally held by Greeks. The result was at first the stagnation of the Hellenistic world and finally, after 202 B.C.E., its collapse in the face of the young and vigorous Roman republic.

Greeks and Easterners

The Greeks in the East were a minority, but Hellenistic monarchies were remarkably successful in at least partially Hellenizing Easterners and spreading a uniform culture throughout the East. Indeed, the Near East had seen nothing comparable since the days when Mesopotamian culture had spread throughout the area. The spread of Greek culture, however, was wider than it was deep. At best it was a veneer, thicker in some places than in others. Hellenistic kingdoms were never entirely unified in language, customs, and thought. Greek culture took firmest hold along the shores of the Mediterranean, but in the Far East, in Persia and Bactria, it eventually gave way to Eastern cultures.

The Ptolemies in Egypt made no effort to spread Greek culture, and unlike other Hellenistic kings they were not city builders. Indeed, they founded only the city of Ptolemais near Thebes. At first the native Egyptian population, the descendants of the pharaoh's people, retained their traditional language, outlook, religion, and way of life. Initially untouched by Hellenism, the natives continued to be the foundation of the state: they fed it by their labor in the fields and financed its operations with their taxes.

Greek Influence Abroad This stunning gold comb is a remarkable combination of Greek and Eastern details. The art is almost purely Greek. The mounted horseman is clothed with largely Greek armor, but he attacks an Eastern enemy. The horseman's companion is also Eastern. This splendid piece of art testifies to the exchange of artistic motifs and styles in the eastern Mediterranean basin. *(Hermitage, Leningrad)*

SPREAD OF HELLENISM

338 B.C.E.	Battle of Chaeronea: Philip II of Macedonia conquers Greece
336 B.C.E.	Alexander the Great inherits Macedonian crown
334–330 B.C.E.	Alexander overthrows the Persian Empire
330–326 B.C.E.	Alexander conquers Bactria
326 B.C.E.	Alexander enters India; troops mutiny at the Hyphasis River
323 B.C.E.	Alexander dies in Babylon at the age of thirty-two
323–275 B.C.E.	Alexander's empire divided: new dynasties founded by Ptolemy I (Egypt), Antigonus Gonatar (Macedonia, Asia Minor), and Seleucus I (Mesopotamia)
3d century B.C.E.	Development of the Hellenistic city
ca 300–250 B.C.E.	Diffusion of philosophy; new schools founded by Epicurus and Zeno
ca 300–200 B.C.E.	Scientific advances by Euclid, Archimedes, Eratosthenes, and Aristarchus of Samos

The bureaucracy of the Ptolemies was ruthlessly efficient, and the native population was viciously and cruelly exploited. Even in times of hardship the king's taxes came first, although payment might mean starvation for the natives. Their desperation was summed up by one Egyptian, who scrawled the warning: "We are worn out; we will run away."[4]

Throughout the third century B.C.E., the Greek upper class in Egypt had little to do with the native population. But in the second century B.C.E., Greeks and native Egyptians began to intermarry and mingle their cultures and languages. Some natives adopted Greek customs and language and began to play a role in the administration of the kingdom and even to serve in the army. While many Greeks and Egyptians remained aloof from each other, the overall result was the evolution of a widespread Greco-Egyptian culture.

Meanwhile, the Seleucid kings established many cities and military colonies in western Asia Minor and along the banks of the Tigris and Euphrates Rivers in order to nurture a vigorous and large Greek population. The Seleucids had no elaborate plan for Hellenizing the native population, but the arrival of so many Greeks was bound to have an impact. Seleucid military colonies were generally founded near native villages, thus exposing Easterners to all aspects of Greek life. In Asia Minor and Syria, numerous native villages and towns developed along Greek lines, and some of them became Hellenized cities. Farther east, the Greek kings who replaced the Seleucids in the third century B.C.E. spread Greek culture to their neighbors, even into the Indian subcontinent.

For Easterners the prime advantage of Greek culture was its very pervasiveness. The Greek language became the common speech of the East. A common dialect called **koine** even influenced the speech of peninsular Greece itself. Greek became the speech of the royal court, bureaucracy, and army, and any Easterner who wanted to compete in business had to learn it. As early as the third century B.C.E., some Greek cities were giving citizenship to Hellenized natives.

The vast majority of Hellenized Easterners, however, took only the externals of Greek culture while retaining the essentials of their own way of life. A prime illustration is the impact of Greek culture on the Jews. Jews in Hellenistic cities were allowed to attend to their religious and internal affairs without interference from the Greek municipal government. They obeyed the king's commands, but there was virtually no royal interference with the Jewish religion. Indeed, the Greeks were always reluctant to tamper with anyone's religion. (See the feature "Listening to the Past: Antiochus III Meets the Jews" on pages 140–141.)

Some Jews were given the right to become full citizens of Hellenistic cities, but few exercised that right. Citizenship would have obligated them to worship the gods of the city—a practice few Jews chose to follow. But Jews living in Hellenistic cities often embraced a good deal of Hellenism. So many Jews learned Greek, especially in Alexandria, that the Old Testament was translated into Greek. Yet no matter how much of Greek culture or its externals Jews borrowed, most remained attached to their religion. Thus, in spite of Hellenistic trappings, Hellenized Jews remained Jews at heart.

Though Greeks and Easterners adapted to each other's ways, there was never a true fusion of cultures. Nonetheless, each found useful things in the civilization of the other, and the two fertilized each other. This mingling of Greek and Eastern elements is what makes Hellenistic culture unique.

Developments in the Western Mediterranean

While Hellenism made new and broader strides in the East, far more complicated and imperfectly understood developments occurred in the western Mediterranean. A survey of the region reveals a wealth of peoples and cultures, some already settled in the area and others moving into it. One group of peoples usually called Berbers were Libyans, Numidians, and Moors, who settled the area of modern Algeria, Morocco, and Tunisia. They also made contact with Sicily and Spain to the north. Even by today's standards the western Mediterranean was a small world. Into this world had come the Phoenicians from the east, planting trading stations and spreading their customs primarily along the coast. To the north the Iberians, Celtiberians, and Celts, all Indo-European-speakers, moved into modern Spain and Portugal. In the eighth century B.C.E. they began mining the rich mineral deposits of these regions, which soon attracted the Phoenicians and later the Greeks. In southern France Ligurian and Celto-Ligurian peoples arrived from the east, sometimes in organized confederations. As early as the seventh century B.C.E. they extended contact beyond their immediate neighbors to the Greeks in southern Italy.

In Italy a pre-Indo-European people first occupied the land, but little is known of them. The arrival of Italic folk, who spoke a variety of related dialects, occurred perhaps as early as 1000 B.C.E. They overwhelmed the native population and transformed the way of life of the peninsula. In the process they encountered the Etruscans, one of the most mysterious peoples of antiquity, and came into contact with the Greeks, who had long established themselves in the south. For historical purposes the importance of these social contacts can be best understood by treating them in the context of the rise of Rome (see Chapter 6). Here it is sufficient to recognize that even at this early period, the Mediterranean world was drawing closer together.

THE ECONOMIC SCOPE OF THE HELLENISTIC WORLD

The Hellenistic period did not see a revolution in the way people lived and worked. The material demands of Hellenistic society remained as simple as those of Athenian society in the fifth century B.C.E. Clothes and furniture were essentially unchanged, as were household goods, tools, and jewelry. Yet Alexander and his successors brought the East fully into the sphere of Greek economics, linking East and West in a broad commercial network. The spread of Greeks throughout the East created new markets and stimulated trade. The economic unity of the Hellenistic world, like its cultural bonds, would later prove valuable to the Romans.

Commerce

Alexander's conquest of the Persian Empire had immediate effects on trade. In the Persian capitals Alexander had found vast sums of gold, silver, and other treasure. This wealth financed the creation of new cities, the building of roads, and the development of harbors. Most of the great monarchies coined their money on the Attic standard. Traders were less in need of moneychangers than in the days when each major power coined money on a different standard of value. As a result of Alexander's conquests, geographical knowledge of the East increased dramatically. The Greeks spread their law and methods of transacting business throughout the East. In bazaars, ports, and trading centers Greeks learned of Eastern customs and traditions while spreading knowledge of their own culture.

The Seleucid and Ptolemaic dynasties traded as far afield as India, Arabia, and sub-Saharan Africa. Overland trade with India and Arabia was conducted by caravan and was largely in the hands of Easterners. The caravan trade never dealt in bulk items or essential commodities; only luxury goods could be transported in this very expensive fashion. Once the goods reached the Hellenistic monarchies, Greek merchants took a hand in the trade.

The caravan trade linked China to the Mediterranean world. Goods flowed into Egypt and the excellent harbors of Palestine, Phoenicia, and Syria and from there to Greece, Italy, and Spain. Over these routes came luxury goods that were light, rare, and expensive, including gold, silver, ivory, precious stones, spices, and a host of other goods. Most important were tea and, especially, silk, which is why the route came to be called the **Great Silk Road.** The Greeks and Macedonians sent east manufactured goods, especially metal weapons, cloth, wine, and olive oil. These routes actually date to earlier times, but they became more prominent—and business practices became more standard—in the Hellenistic period. The importance of the trade is demonstrated by the fact that it continued even in the chaos that followed Alexander's death.

In the early Hellenistic period, the Seleucids and Ptolemies ensured that the caravan trade proceeded efficiently. Later in the period—a time of increased war and confusion—they left the caravans unprotected. Taking advantage of this situation, Palmyra in the Syrian Desert and Nabataean Petra in Arabia arose as caravan states. Such states protected the caravans from bandits and marauders and served as dispersal areas for caravan goods.

The Ptolemies discovered how to use monsoon winds to establish direct contact with India. One hardy merchant left a firsthand account of sailing this important maritime route:

Hippalos, the pilot, observing the position of the ports and the conditions of the sea, first discovered how to sail across the ocean. Concerning the winds of the ocean in this region, when with us the Etesian winds begin, in India a wind between southwest and south, named for Hippalos, sets in from the open sea. From then until now some mariners set forth from Kanes and some from the Cape of Spices. Those sailing to Dimurikes [in southern India] throw the bow of the ship farther out to sea. Those bound for Barygaza and the realm of the Sakas [in northern India] hold to the land no more than three days; and if the wind remains favorable, they hold the same course through the outer sea, and they sail along past the previously mentioned gulfs.[5]

Although this sea route never replaced overland caravan traffic, it kept direct relations between East and West alive, stimulating the exchange of ideas as well as goods.

More economically important than the exotic caravan trade were commercial dealings in essential commodities like raw materials, grain, and industrial products. The Hellenistic monarchies usually raised enough grain for their own needs as well as a surplus for export. For the cities of Greece and the Aegean this trade in grain was essential, because many of them could not grow enough.

The large-scale wars of the Hellenistic period often interrupted both the production and the distribution of grain. In addition, natural calamities, such as excessive rain or drought, frequently damaged harvests. Throughout the Hellenistic period, famine or severe food shortage remained a grim possibility.

The Greek cities paid for their grain by exporting olive oil and wine. Another significant commodity was fish, which for export was salted, pickled, or dried. This trade was doubly important because fish provided poor people with an essential element of their diet. Also important was the trade in honey, dried fruit, nuts, and vegetables. Of raw materials, wood was high in demand, but little trade occurred in manufactured goods.

Slaves were a staple of Hellenistic trade. The wars provided prisoners for the slave market; to a lesser extent, so did kidnapping and capture by pirates. The number of slaves involved cannot be estimated, but there is no doubt that slavery flourished. Both old Greek states and new Hellenistic kingdoms were ready slave markets, as was Rome when it emerged triumphant from the Second Punic War (see page 149). Only the Ptolemies discouraged both the trade and slavery itself, and they did so only for economic reasons. Their system had no room for slaves, who would only have competed with free labor. Otherwise, slave labor was to be found in the cities and temples of the Hellenistic world, in the factories and fields, and in the homes of wealthy people. Slaves were vitally important to the Hellenistic economy.

Industry and Agriculture

Although demand for goods increased during the Hellenistic period, no new techniques of production appear to have developed. Manual labor, not machinery, continued to turn out the agricultural produce, raw materials, and few manufactured goods the Hellenistic world used. Nowhere was this truer than in mining.

Invariably miners were slaves, criminals, or forced laborers. The conditions under which they worked were frightful. The Ptolemies ran their gold mines along typically harsh lines. One historian gives a grim picture of the miners' lives:

The kings of Egypt condemn [to the mines] those found guilty of wrong-doing and those taken prisoner in war, those who were victims of false accusations and were put into jail because of royal anger. . . . The condemned—and they are very many—all of them are put in chains, and they work persistently and continually, both by day and throughout the night, getting no rest, and carefully cut off from escape.[6]

The Ptolemies even condemned women and children to work in the mines. The strongest men lived and died swinging iron sledgehammers to break up the gold-bearing quartz rock. Others worked underground, following the seams of quartz; laboring with lamps bound to their foreheads, they were whipped by overseers if they slacked off. Once the diggers had cut out blocks of quartz, young boys gathered up the blocks and carried them outside. All of them—men, women, and boys—worked until they died.

Apart from gold and silver, which were used primarily for coins and jewelry, iron was the most important metal and saw the most varied use. Even so, the method of its production never became very sophisticated.

Although new techniques of production and wider use of machinery did not develop, the volume of goods produced increased in the Hellenistic period. Small manufacturing establishments existed in nearly all parts of the Hellenistic world.

Just as all kings concerned themselves with trade and industry, they also paid special attention to agriculture. Much of their revenue was derived from the produce of royal lands, rents paid by the tenants of royal lands, and taxation of agricultural lands. Some Hellenistic kings even sought out and supported agricultural experts. The Ptolemies, who made the greatest strides in agriculture, sponsored experiments to improve seed grain. Hellenistic authors wrote handbooks discussing how farms and large estates could most profitably be run. Whether these efforts had any impact on the average farmer is difficult to determine, and there is no evidence that agricultural productivity increased.

RELIGION IN THE HELLENISTIC WORLD

In religion the Greeks and Easterners shared their traditions without one dominating the other. They noticed similarities among their respective deities and assumed that they were worshiping the same gods in different garb. The tendency toward religious universalism and personal immortality would prove significant when the Hellenistic world was united politically under the sway of Rome.

At first the Hellenistic period saw the spread of Greek religious cults throughout the East. When Hellenistic kings founded cities, they built temples and established new cults and priesthoods for the old Olympian gods. These cults enjoyed the prestige of being the religion of the conquerors, and they were supported by public money. Still, the Greek cults were attractive only to those socially aspiring Easterners who adopted Greek culture for personal advancement. Indeed, the Greeks themselves felt little genuine attachment to the new cults.

Greek cults suffered from some severe shortcomings. They were primarily concerned with ritual, and participation in them did not even require belief. As a result they could not satisfy deep religious feelings or spiritual yearnings. Educated and thoughtful Greeks turned, at first, to philosophy as a guide for life. Others turned to superstition, magic, or astrology. Still others spoke of *Tyche,* which means "fate," "chance," "doom"—a capricious and sometimes malevolent force.

By the second century B.C.E., after a century of exposure to Eastern religions, Greeks began to adopt one of the Eastern "mystery religions," so called because they featured a body of ritual not to be divulged to anyone not initiated into the cult. These mystery cults incorporated aspects of both Greek and Eastern religions and had a broad appeal to people of both groups. Since the Greeks were already familiar with old mystery cults, such as the Eleusinian Mysteries in Attica, the new cults did not strike them as alien or barbarian. And these new religions enjoyed one tremendous advantage over the old Greek mystery cults. The Greek cults had been tied to one place, forcing people to make pilgrimages to the sacred site to become initiated. The new religions were spread throughout the Hellenistic world.

The mystery religions all claimed to save their adherents from the worst that fate could do and promised life for the soul after death. They all shared the belief that by means of rites of initiation, devotees became united with a particular god, who had died and risen from the dead. The god's sacrifice and victory over death saved the devotee from eternal death. Like the old Greek cults, these religions required a period of preparation and then a ritual initiation that was usually of great emotional intensity.

The two Eastern cults that took the Hellenistic world by storm were the Egyptian cults of Serapis and Isis. Serapis, invented by King Ptolemy, combined elements of the Egyptian god Osiris with aspects of the Greek gods Zeus, Pluto (prince of the underworld), and Asclepius (god of medicine). Serapis was believed to be the judge of souls, who rewarded virtuous and righteous people with eternal life. Many Hellenistic Greeks thought of him as Zeus. The cult of Isis enjoyed even wider appeal. Isis, wife of Osiris, was claimed to have conquered Tyche and promised to save any mortal who came to her. She became the most important goddess in the Hellenistic world, and her worship was very popular among women due to her role as goddess of marriage, conception, and childbirth. Her priests claimed that she had bestowed on humanity the gift of civilization and had founded law and literature.

Tyche   This statue depicts Tyche as the city-goddess of Antioch, a new Hellenistic foundation of the Seleucid king Antiochus. Some Hellenistic Greeks worshiped Tyche in the hope that she would be kind to them. Philosophers tried to free people from her whimsies. Antiochus tried to win her favor by honoring her. *(Photo Vatican Museums)*

HELLENISTIC THOUGHT

The Hellenistic world was a time of uncertainty and instability, and the growing popularity of the mystery religions reflected a desire for a spiritual answer to the problem of Tyche. These same trends left their mark on the thinking of the period, as new schools of philosophy tried to develop their own answers to the questions of how humans relate to the world and to one another. At the same time, the meeting of Greek and Eastern thinking contributed to a surge in scientific knowledge.

Philosophy

Philosophy during the Hellenic period had been the exclusive province of the wealthy, for only they had had leisure enough to pursue philosophical study. During the Hellenistic period, however, philosophy reached out to touch the lives of more men and women than ever before. One reason was that, with the decline of the ideal of the polis, politics no longer offered people an intellectual outlet. Second, much of Hellenistic life, especially in the new cities of the East, seemed unstable and without venerable traditions. Many people in search of something permanent turned to philosophy. Finally, the decline of traditional religion and the growing belief in Tyche led many Greeks to look to philosophy to protect them against the worst that Tyche could do.

Philosophers became more numerous, and they developed several different schools of thought. Although these philosophers felt a good deal of rivalry, all shared the idea that people could be truly happy—could deal successfully with Tyche—only when they had turned their backs on the world and focused their full attention on one enduring thing. They differed chiefly on what that enduring thing was.

Epicurus (340–270 B.C.E.) based his view of life on scientific theories and put forward a naturalistic theory of the universe. The gods, he said, had no effect on human life. He argued that the principal good of human life is pleasure, which is the absence of pain. Hardly a promoter of drunken revels or sexual dissipation, Epicurus taught that individuals can most easily attain peace and serenity by rejecting the world and examining their personal feelings. He urged people to ignore politics, which could cause emotional upheaval that would disturb the soul.

Zeno (335–262 B.C.E.) founded a school of thought called **Stoicism** that rejected the passivity of the Epicureans. Zeno and his followers thought that people could be happy only if they lived in accordance with nature. They also said that people should participate in politics, but they did not advocate attempts to change the political order. Rather, the Stoic, like an actor in a play, plays an assigned part but does not try to change the play. What matters is not what a person achieves in life, but whether he or she lives a virtuous life. Stoics believed that all people are brothers and all are governed by one natural law. Rome adopted this Stoic concept of a universal state governed by natural law.

Hellenistic Science

Hellenistic culture achieved its greatest triumphs in science, and these achievements resulted from contributions by both East and West. The Babylonians, who had scanned the skies for centuries, provided the foundation of Hellenistic astronomy. The most notable Hellenistic astronomer was Aristarchus of Samos (ca 310–230 B.C.E.), who concluded that the sun is far larger than the earth and the stars are exceedingly distant. Breaking with Aristotle, his teacher, he said that the sun, not the earth, was the center of the solar system. In the second century C.E., however, mathematician and astronomer Claudius Ptolemy accepted Aristotle's view, and the earth-centered universe prevailed for the next fourteen hundred years.

In geometry Hellenistic thinkers discovered little that was new, but Euclid (ca 300 B.C.E.) compiled a valuable textbook of existing knowledge. *The Elements of Geometry* became the standard introduction to the field.

The greatest thinker of the period was Archimedes (ca 287–212 B.C.E.), also a skilled inventor. From his home in Syracuse in Sicily, he watched Rome rise as a power. To thwart the Roman conquest of his city, he invented a catapult that hurled rocks large enough to sink ships and grappling devices that lifted ships out of the water. In peacetime he invented the Archimedean screw to raise water from a lower to a higher level and a compound pulley to lift heavy weights. His chief interest, however, lay in pure mathematics, and he researched and wrote in many areas, including mechanics. He also founded the science of hydrostatics and discovered the principle that the weight of a solid floating in a liquid is equal to the weight of the liquid displaced by the solid.

One of Archimedes' colleagues, Eratosthenes (285–ca 204 B.C.E.), served as librarian of the great royal library in Alexandria, Egypt. While there he calculated the circumference of the earth at about 24,675 miles—only 185 miles off the actual circumference. Interested in geography, he argued that a ship could sail from Spain either around Africa or directly westward and eventually reach India. Not until the fifteenth century C.E. was this idea proved.

The study of botany also originated in the Hellenistic period when Theophrastus (ca 372–288 B.C.E.), another student of Aristotle, studied the botanical information made available by Alexander's penetration into the East. In his two books he classified plants and accurately described their parts. He detected the process of germination and realized the importance of climate and soil to plants. Some of his findings made their way into agricultural handbooks, but for the most part Hellenistic science did not carry botany any further.

In fact Hellenistic science did not exploit many of its remarkable discoveries. Although scientists of the period invented machines such as an air gun, a water organ, and even a steam engine, they did not develop them as labor-saving devices. The explanation may be that they saw no need for such machines since slave labor was abundant. Still, later scientists preserved the discoveries of Hellenistic science for modern times.

One practical area in which Hellenistic science did flourish was medicine. Herophilus, who lived in the first half of the third century B.C.E., approached the study of medicine in a systematic fashion. He dissected dead bod-

An Unsuccessful Delivery   This funeral stele depicts a mother who has perhaps lost her own life as well as her baby's. Maternal and infant mortality were quite common in antiquity. A similar stele elsewhere bears the heartbreaking words attributed to the mother by her grieving family: "All my labor could not bring the child forth; he lies in my womb, among the dead." *(National Archaeological Museum, Athens/Archaeological Receipts Fund)*

ies and measured what he observed. He discovered the nervous system and studied the brain. His work and that of his Dogmatic school of medicine improved knowledge of anatomy, which led to better surgical tools and techniques. Another school of medicine, the Pragmatists, arose in opposition. They concentrated on the observation and cure of illnesses and put more emphasis on the use of drugs and medicines.

Despite these medical advances, Hellenistic medicine had its dark side. Many physicians were moneygrubbers, fools, or quacks. Still others claimed to cure illness through incantations and magic.

SUMMARY

In a comparatively brief span of time the Greeks progressed from a primitive folk—backward and rude compared with their Near Eastern neighbors—to one of the most influential peoples of history. These originators of science and philosophy asked penetrating questions about the nature of life and society and came up with deathless responses to many of their own questions. Greek achievements range from the development of sophisticated political institutions to the creation of a stunningly rich literature.

Greek civilization was in full bloom when Alexander the Great launched his crusade against the Persian Empire in 334 B.C.E. Though bent on military conquest alone, Alexander nonetheless opened the cultural world of the ancient Near East to the Greeks and Macedonians as never before. They poured into Egypt and into western and even Central Asia. Not only did West meet East, but the two also combined to create a new cosmopolitan world that mingled political, social, and religious ideas. Further Greek exploration to the west pushed back the physical and intellectual frontiers until the Hellenistic world in its broadest sense stretched from Gibraltar to India. For the first time in history, vast reaches of the globe shared at least some aspects of the same culture.

KEY TERMS

polis	tyranny
acropolis	deme
hoplites	Delian League
monarchy	sovereign
aristocracy	koine
oligarchy	Great Silk Road
democracy	Stoicism

NOTES

1. Hesiod, *Works and Days* 263–266. John Buckler is the translator of all uncited quotations from foreign languages in Chapter 5.
2. Ibid., 737–741.
3. J. M. Edmonds, *The Fragments of Attic Comedy* (Leiden: E. J. Brill, 1971), 2.366–369, Mnesimachos frag. 7.
4. Quoted in W. W. Tarn and G. T. Griffith, *Hellenistic Civilisation*, 3d ed. (London: Edward Arnold, 1959), p. 199.
5. *Periplous of the Erythraian Sea* 57.
6. Diodoros 3.12.2–3.

SUGGESTED READING

Translations of the most important writings of the Greeks and Romans can be found in the Loeb Classical Library published by Harvard University Press. Paperback editions of the major Greek and Latin authors are available in the Penguin Classics. Translations of documents include C. Fornara, *Translated Documents of Greece and Rome,* vol. 1 (1977); P. Harding, vol. 2 (1985); S. M. Burstein, vol. 3 (1985); and M. M. Austin, *The Hellenistic World from Alexander to the Roman Conquest* (1985).

Among the general treatments of the period is J. Boardman et al., *The Cambridge Ancient History,* vols. 3–7 (1982–1994), which covers both the classical and Hellenistic periods. More general are J. K. Davies, *Democracy and Classical Greece* (1993), and F. W. Walbank, *The Hellenistic World,* rev. ed. (1993).

Books on early Greece include C. G. Thomas, *Myth Becomes History* (1993), an excellent treatment of early Greece and modern attitudes toward it. R. Osborne, *Greece in the Making* (1996), surveys developments from 1200 to 479 B.C.E. S. Nelson, *God and the Land* (1998), explores the economic and religious significance of agriculture. R. Gotshalk, *Homer and Hesiod* (2000), provides a good account of their poetry and purposes in writing. L. H. Wilson, *Sappho's Sweetbitter Songs* (1996), deals with female and male relations in terms of her poetry. Some of the most original and substantial recent work on the polis appears in M. H. Hansen and K. Raaflaub, eds., *Studies in the Ancient Greek Polis* (1995) and *More Studies in the Ancient Greek Polis* (1996). Related is F. de Polignac, *Cults, Territory, and the Origins of the Greek State* (1995). A. J. Graham, *Colony and Mother City in Ancient Greece,* rev. ed. (1984), gives a good but somewhat dated account of Greek colonization. C. Roebuck, *Economy and Society in the Early Greek World* (1984), though also dated, is still a reliable treatment of the topic. W. Burkert, *The Orientalizing Revolution* (1992), is a masterful discussion of Near Eastern influence on early Greek culture. A good survey of early Sparta is S. Hodkinson, *Property and Wealth in Classical Sparta* (2000), which discusses many aspects of Spartan life. The Athenian democracy has become an overworked and sterile subject, but the best treatments are M. Ostwald, *From Popular Sovereignty to the Sovereignty of Law* (1986), and especially M. H. Hansen, *The Athenian Democracy in the Age of Demosthenes* (1991).

Useful studies of fifth-century B.C. Greece include M. McGregor, *The Athenians and Their Empire* (1987); M. C. Miller, *Athens and Persia in the Fifth Century B.C.* (1997); and E. Badian, *From Plataea to Potidaea* (1993), a challenging collection of essays on major aspects of the period. The fourth century B.C.E. has been one of the most fertile fields of recent research. P. Cartledge, *Agesilaos and the Crisis of Sparta* (1987), treats Spartan government and society in its period of greatness and collapse. J. Buckler, *The Theban Hegemony, 371–362 B.C.* (1980), examines the period of the Theban ascendancy, and his *Philip II and the Sacred War* (1989) studies the ways in which Philip of Macedonia used Greek politics to his own ends. J. Cargill, *The Second Athenian League* (1981), traces Athens's generally successful foreign policy during the century. G. Cawkwell, *Philip of Macedon* (1978), provides the best study of the king, and A. B. Bosworth, *Conquest and Empire* (1988), is a magisterial study of Alexander the Great, which reveals a ruthless but brilliant conqueror. F. L. Holt, *Alexander the Great and Bactria* (1988), discusses the formation of a Greco-Macedonian frontier in Central Asia.

Greek social life is a recent theme of continuing interest among classical scholars. R. Just, *Women in Athenian Law and Life* (1988), explores topics such as daily life, the family, and women's role in society, as do C. B. Patterson, *The Family in Greek History* (1998), and S. B. Pomeroy, *Families in Classical and Hellenistic Greece* (1997). M. Golden, *Children and Childhood in Ancient Athens* (1993), studies a neglected topic, as does Z. H. Archibald et al., *Hellenistic Economics* (2001). M. Golden, *Sport and Society in Ancient Greece* (1998), places athletics in its social context, and Y. Garlan, *Slavery in Ancient Greece* (1988), gives a balanced interpretation of this difficult subject.

Much new work has focused on the spread of Hellenism throughout the Near East. Very extensive is A. Kuhrt and S. Sherwin-White, eds., *Hellenism in the East* (1988), which treats a broad range of topics, including biblical studies, Christianity, and Islam. A. E. Samuel, *The Promise of the West* (1988), studies connections among Greek, Roman, and Jewish culture. A. K. Bowman, *Egypt After the Pharaohs* (1986), gives an account of the Greeks' and Macedonians' impact on Egyptian society. R. A. Billows, *Antigonus the One-Eyed and the Creation of the Hellenistic State* (1990), examines the career of the one man who most nearly reunited Alexander's empire, and G. M. Cohen, *The Hellenistic Settlements in Europe, the Islands, and Asia Minor* (1996), ably studies the impact of the Greeks on the world around them.

Studies of Greek religion in general are P. N. Hunt, ed., *Encyclopedia of Classical Mystery Religions* (1993), which includes more than a thousand entries on mystery religions. J. D. Mikalson, *Athenian Popular Religion* (reprint 1987), opens an avenue to Greek popular religion in general, and his *Religion in Hellenistic Society* (1998) extends his studies into later Greek society. W. Burkert, *Greek Religion* (1987), is a masterful study of the topic. A. W. Bulloch et al., *Images and Ideologies* (1993), is a broad-ranging treatment of all important intellectual aspects of Hellenistic history. S. K. Heyob, *The Cult of Isis Among Women in the Graeco-Roman World* (1975), and J. G. Griffiths, *The Origins of Osiris and His Cult* (1980), treat this influential pair of deities. L. H. Feldman, *Jew and Gentile in the Ancient World* (1993), argues that the pagan response to Judaism was not as negative as is often thought. Lastly, P. Franklin, *Magic in the Ancient World* (1997), is a fresh treatment of a neglected subject.

G. Vlastos, *Studies in Greek Philosophy,* vols. 1 and 2 (1995–1996), covers philosophy from the Pre-Socratics to Plato. R. W. Sharples, *Stoics, Epicureans, Sceptics* (1996), provides a good synthesis of these three major philosophies. P. Kingsley, *Ancient Philosophy* (1996), studies the effects of myth and magic on the development of Greek philosophy. A novel approach to the topic is J. K. Ward, ed., *Feminism in Ancient Philosophy* (1996). G. E. R. Lloyd, *Greek Science After Aristotle* (1963), is a solid survey of Hellenistic science.

ANTIOCHUS III MEETS THE JEWS

*E*ver since the days of the pharaohs and the Hittites the Levant, the area known today as the Middle East, has served as a battleground between the Egyptians and any major power to their north. The peoples in this area were perennially caught between their more powerful neighbors on either side. Nothing changed in the Hellenistic period. Around 200 B.C.E. Antiochus III, king of the Seleucid empire, drove the Ptolemies from Syria and Palestine. In his victory he encountered the Jews, a people theretofore unfamiliar to him. The Jews, who had long been discontented with Ptolemaic rule, eagerly welcomed Antiochus, and he responded to them with equal enthusiasm. The Hellenized Jewish historian Josephus (37/38–100 C.E.), in his work* Jewish Antiquities *(12.138–153), preserves three royal documents in which Antiochus officially instructs his governor of the area, also named Ptolemy, of the benefits that he had conferred on the Jews and his reasons for having done so.*

"King Antiochus [III] to Ptolemy, greetings. Since the Jews, when we entered their country, at once displayed their enthusiasm for us, and when we arrived at their city received us magnificently and came to meet us with their senate, and have provided abundant supplies to our soldiers and elephants, and assisted us in expelling the Egyptian garrison in the citadel, we thought it right on our part to repay them for these services and to restore their city which had been destroyed by the accidents of war, and to repeople it by bringing back to it those who have been scattered abroad. In the first place we have decided because of their piety to provide them with an allowance for sacrifices consisting of sacrificial animals, wine, olive oil and frankincense, to the value of 20,000 silver pieces, and sacred artabas of finest flour in accordance with their native law, and 1,460 medimni of wheat, and 375 medimni of salt. I wish these grants to be made to them in accordance with my instructions, and the work on the Temple to be completed together with the stoas and anything else which needs to be built. The timber required for the woodwork shall be brought from Judaea itself, from the other nations and from Lebanon, and no one shall charge any duty on it. Similarly for the other materials needed for repairing the Temple in a more splendid way. All the people of the nation shall govern themselves in accordance with their ancestral laws, and the senate, the priests, the scribes of the Temple and the Temple-singers shall be exempted from the poll-tax, the crown-tax and the salt-tax. To hasten the repeopling of the city, I grant to the present inhabitants and to those who come back before the month of Hyperberetaeus [ca October] freedom from taxes for three years. We also remit for the future one third of their taxes to make good the injuries they have sustained. As for all those who were carried away from their city and are now slaves, I grant their freedom to them and to their children, and order the restoration of their property to them."

Such was the content of the letter. And out of respect for the Temple he issued a proclamation throughout the whole kingdom in the following terms: "No foreigner shall be allowed to enter the precinct of the Temple which is forbidden to the Jews, except for those who are accustomed to doing so after purifying themselves in accordance with ancestral custom. Nor shall anyone bring into the city the flesh of horses, mules, wild or tame asses, leopards, foxes, and hares, and generally of any of the animals forbidden to the Jews. Nor is it allowed to bring in their skins, nor even to rear any of these animals in the city. Only the sacrificial animals used by their ancestors,

Coin of Antiochus III. *(British Museum/ Michael Holford)*

necessary for a propitious sacrifice to God, shall they be allowed to use. Whoever transgresses any of these rules shall pay to the priests a fine of 3,000 drachmas of silver."

He also gave witness to our piety and good faith when during his stay in the upper satrapies he heard of the revolt of Phrygia and Lydia, and wrote to Zeuxis, his general and one of his closest "friends," with instructions to send some of our people from Babylon to Phrygia. He writes as follows: "King Antiochus to Zeuxis, his father, greetings. If you are in good health, it is well; I too am in good health. On hearing that the people in Lydia and Phrygia are in revolt, I thought this required great attention on my part, and after discussing with my friends what ought to be done, I resolved to move 2,000 Jewish families with their chattels from Mesopotamia and Babylonia to the strongholds and the most strategic places. For I am convinced that they will be loyal guardians of our interests because of their piety to God, and I know that my ancestors have given witness to their loyalty and eagerness for what they are asked to do. I wish therefore to transfer them, although this is a laborious task, with the promise that they shall use their own laws. When you have brought them to the places I have mentioned, you will give them each a place to build a house and a plot of land to cultivate and plant vines, and you will grant them exemption from taxes on agricultural produce for ten years. Until such time as they obtain produce from the soil, corn shall be measured out to them to feed their servants. To those who perform services [?] shall be provided everything they need, so that by receiving this favour from us they might show themselves more devoted to our interests. Show concern for their people as much as possible, so that it may not be troubled by anyone." Concerning the friendliness of Antiochus the Great towards the Jews let the proofs we have given suffice.

QUESTIONS FOR ANALYSIS

1. What were the principal reasons for Antiochus's kindness to the Jews?

2. Did his actions show genuine respect for Jewish religion and tradition?

3. Did Antiochus use the Jews as political pawns, or was he sincerely concerned for them as loyal subjects?

Source: Reprinted by permission of the publishers and the Trustees of the Loeb Classical Library from *Josephus: Volume IX—Jewish Antiquities,* Loeb Classical Library Volume L 365, trans. Ralph Marcus (Cambridge, Mass.: Harvard University Press, 1943, 1998). The Loeb Classical Library® is a registered trademark of the President and Fellows of Harvard College.

The Roman Forum. *(Josephine Powell)*

6 THE GLORY OF ROME

Who is so thoughtless and lazy that he does not want to know in what way and with what kind of government the Romans in less than 53 years conquered nearly the entire inhabited world and brought it under their rule—an achievement previously unheard of?"[1] This question was first asked by Polybius, a Greek historian who lived in the second century B.C.E. With keen awareness Polybius realized that the Romans were achieving something unique in world history.

What was that achievement? Rome was not the first to create a huge empire. The Persians and the Han emperors had done the same thing. Chandragupta and his successors had likewise brought many peoples under their rule. The Romans themselves admitted that in matters of art, literature, philosophy, and culture they learned from the Greeks. Rome's achievement lay in the ability of the Romans not only to conquer peoples but to incorporate them into the Roman system. Rome succeeded where the Greek polis had failed. Unlike the Greeks, who refused to share citizenship, the Romans extended their citizenship first to the Italians and later to the peoples of the provinces. With that citizenship went Roman government and law. Rome created a world state that embraced the entire Mediterranean area. For the first and second centuries C.E. the lot of the Mediterranean world was the Roman peace—the pax Romana, a period of security, order, harmony, flourishing culture, and expanding economy. It was a period that saw the wilds of Gaul, Spain, Germany, and eastern Europe introduced to Greco-Roman culture.

Nor was Rome's achievement limited to the ancient world. By the third century C.E., when the empire began to give way to the medieval world, the greatness of Rome and its culture had left an indelible mark on the ages to come. Rome's law, language, and administrative practices were a precious heritage to medieval and modern Europe.

- How did Rome rise to greatness?
- What effects did the conquest of the Mediterranean have on the Romans themselves?
- How did the Roman emperors govern the empire, and how did they spread Roman influence into northern Europe?
- Why did Christianity, originally a minor local religion, sweep across the Roman world to change it fundamentally?

143

- How did the Roman Empire meet the grim challenge of barbarian invasion and subsequent economic decline?

These are the questions we will answer in this chapter.

THE LAND AND THE SEA

To the west of Greece the boot-shaped peninsula of Italy, with Sicily at its toe, occupies the center of the Mediterranean basin. As Map 6.1 shows, Italy and Sicily thrust southward toward Africa: the distance between southwestern Sicily and the northern African coast is at one point only about a hundred miles. Italy and Sicily literally divide the Mediterranean into two basins and form the focal point between the halves.

Like Greece and other Mediterranean lands, Italy enjoys a genial, almost subtropical climate. The winters are rainy, but the summer months are dry. Because of the climate the rivers of Italy usually carry little water during the summer, and some go entirely dry. Thus Italian rivers never became major thoroughfares for commerce and communication.

In the north of Italy the Apennine Mountains break off from the Alps and form a natural barrier. The Apennines hindered but did not prevent peoples from invading Italy from the north. North of the Apennines lies the Po Valley, an important part of modern Italy. In antiquity this valley did not become Roman territory until late in the history of the republic. From the north the Apennines run southward the entire length of the Italian boot; they virtually cut off access to the Adriatic Sea, inducing Italy to look west to Spain and Carthage rather than east to Greece.

Even though most of the land is mountainous, the hill country is not as inhospitable as are the Greek highlands. In antiquity the general fertility of the soil provided the basis for a large population. Nor did the mountains of Italy so carve up the land as to prevent the development of political unity. Geography proved kinder to Italy than to Greece.

In their southward course the Apennines leave two broad and fertile plains, those of Latium and Campania. These plains attracted settlers and invaders from the time when peoples began to move into Italy. Among these peoples were the Romans, who established their city on the Tiber River in Latium. The Tiber provided Rome with a constant source of water. Located at an easy crossing point on the Tiber, Rome stood astride the main avenue of communication between northern and southern Italy. The seven hills of Rome were defensible and safe from the floods of the Tiber. Rome was in an excellent position to develop the resources of Latium and maintain contact with the rest of Italy.

THE ETRUSCANS AND THE ROMAN CONQUEST OF ITALY (750–290 B.C.E.)

According to Roman legend, Romulus and Remus founded Rome in 753 B.C.E. From then until 509 B.C.E. the Romans lived under the rule of Etruscan kings and embraced many Etruscan customs. They adopted the

Sarcophagus of Lartie Seianti The woman portrayed on this lavish sarcophagus is the noble Etruscan Lartie Seianti. Although the sarcophagus is her place of burial, she is portrayed as in life, comfortable and at rest. The influence of Greek art on Etruscan is apparent in almost every feature of the sarcophagus. *(Archaeological Museum, Florence/Nimatallah/Art Resource, NY)*

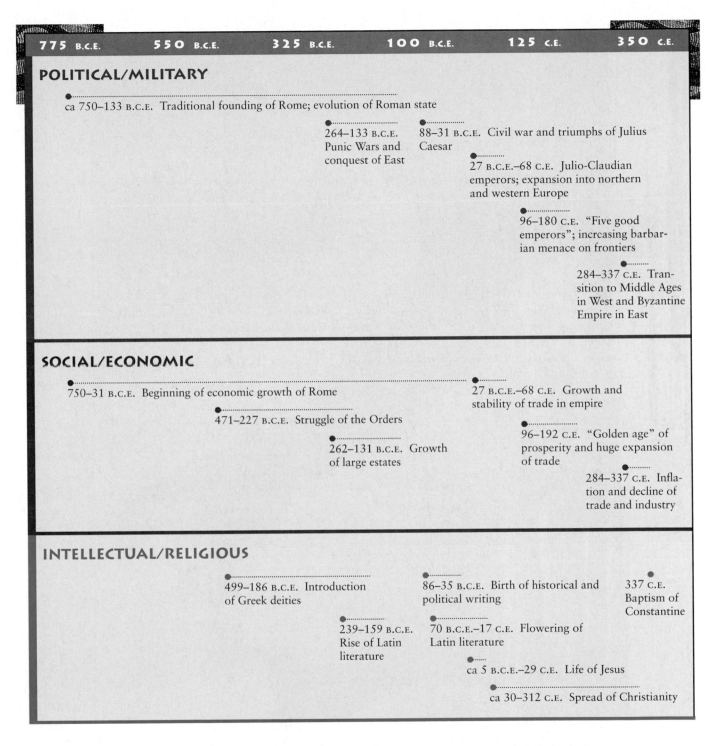

| 775 B.C.E. | 550 B.C.E. | 325 B.C.E. | 100 B.C.E. | 125 C.E. | 350 C.E. |

POLITICAL/MILITARY

ca 750–133 B.C.E. Traditional founding of Rome; evolution of Roman state

264–133 B.C.E. Punic Wars and conquest of East

88–31 B.C.E. Civil war and triumphs of Julius Caesar

27 B.C.E.–68 C.E. Julio-Claudian emperors; expansion into northern and western Europe

96–180 C.E. "Five good emperors"; increasing barbarian menace on frontiers

284–337 C.E. Transition to Middle Ages in West and Byzantine Empire in East

SOCIAL/ECONOMIC

750–31 B.C.E. Beginning of economic growth of Rome

471–227 B.C.E. Struggle of the Orders

262–131 B.C.E. Growth of large estates

27 B.C.E.–68 C.E. Growth and stability of trade in empire

96–192 C.E. "Golden age" of prosperity and huge expansion of trade

284–337 C.E. Inflation and decline of trade and industry

INTELLECTUAL/RELIGIOUS

499–186 B.C.E. Introduction of Greek deities

86–35 B.C.E. Birth of historical and political writing

337 C.E. Baptism of Constantine

239–159 B.C.E. Rise of Latin literature

70 B.C.E.–17 C.E. Flowering of Latin literature

ca 5 B.C.E.–29 C.E. Life of Jesus

ca 30–312 C.E. Spread of Christianity

Etruscan alphabet, which the Etruscans themselves had adopted from the Greeks and which the Romans later passed on to medieval Europe. In this period Rome enjoyed contacts with the larger Mediterranean world, including trade in metalwork and Greek vases. The city began to grow, and between 575 and 550 B.C.E. temples and public buildings began to grace the city. The temple of Jupiter Optimus Maximus (Jupiter the Best and Greatest) became the religious center of the city. The Forum, on the site of a former cemetery, began to serve as a public meeting place, like a Greek agora. The Etruscans had found Rome a collection of villages and made it a city.

According to tradition, in 509 B.C.E. the Romans expelled an Etruscan king from the city and founded the

Rome

0   500   1000 M.
0   1500   3000 Ft.

FIELD OF MARS

Tiber

JANICULUM

CAPITOLINE MT.

QUIRINAL HILL

VIMINAL HILL

ESQUILINE MT.

Senate House

Forum

Regia

Temple of Jupiter

PALATINE MT.

Circus Maximus

AVENTINE MT.

CAELIAN MT.

A L P S

Po

A P E N N I N E S

Arno

ETRURIA

UMBRIA

PICENUM

Tiber

SABINI

AEQUI

VESTINI

Veii

Rome

LATIUM

SAMNIUM

CAMPANIA

APULIA

CALABRIA

LUCANIA

Tarentum

CORSICA

SARDINIA

Tyrrhenian Sea

BRUTTIUM

A d r i a t i c   S e a

Messana

SICILY

Syracuse

M e d i t e r r a n e a n   S e a

Carthage

Cape Bon

NORTH AFRICA

0   50   100 Km.
0   50   100 Mi.

━━━ Roman boundary before the Punic Wars
─── Roman boundary before Augustus
─── Roman internal regional divisions
─── Major road

republic. In the years that followed, the Romans expanded throughout the Italian peninsula as a result of their tenacious fighting and their skillful diplomacy. The growth of Roman power was slow. It took a century to drive the Etruscans fully out of Latium. Around 390 B.C.E. the Romans suffered a setback when a new people, the Celts—or Gauls, as the Romans called them—swept aside a Roman army and sacked Rome. They agreed to abandon the city in return for a thousand pounds of gold.

From 390 to 290 B.C.E. the Romans regrouped and began their drive to empire. They reorganized their army to create the mobile legion, a flexible unit capable of fighting on either broken or open ground. First they brought Latium and their Latin allies fully under their control (see Map 6.1). Then they defeated the Samnites after a long conflict and gained southern Italy.

In this expansion Rome's success in diplomacy and politics was vitally important. Like Cyrus the Persian and unlike the Greeks, they proved generous victors. They shared with other Italian cities political power and degrees of citizenship. While all allied peoples were not given the right to vote or hold office, they were allowed to run local affairs, and Latin allies could gain full citizenship by moving to Rome. The unwillingness of the Greek polis to share its citizenship condemned it to a limited horizon. By contrast, the extension of Roman citizenship gave Rome additional manpower and wealth.

THE ROMAN REPUBLIC

The Romans summed up their political existence in a single phrase: *senatus populusque Romanus,* "the Roman senate and the people." The real genius of the Romans lay in the fields of politics and law. Unlike the Greeks, they did not often speculate on the ideal state or on political forms. Instead, they realistically met actual challenges and created institutions, magistracies, and legal concepts to deal with practical problems. Change was consequently commonplace in Roman political life; thus the constitution of 509 B.C.E. was far simpler than that of 27 B.C.E. Moreover, the Roman constitution was not a single written document but a set of traditional beliefs, customs, and laws.

MAP 6.1 **Italy and the City of Rome**   The geographical configuration of the Italian peninsula shows how Rome stood astride north-south communication routes and how the state that united Italy stood poised to move into Sicily and northern Africa.

The Roman State and Social Conflict

In the early republic social divisions determined the shape of politics. Political power was in the hands of the aristocracy—the **patricians,** who were wealthy landowners. Patrician families formed clans, as did aristocrats in early Greece. They dominated the affairs of state, provided military leadership in times of war, and monopolized knowledge of law and legal procedure. The common people of Rome, the **plebeians,** had few of the patricians' advantages. Some plebeians formed their own clans and rivaled the patricians in wealth, but most plebeians were poor. They were the artisans, small farmers, and landless urban dwellers. The plebeians, rich and poor alike, were free citizens with a voice in politics. Nonetheless, they were overshadowed by the patricians.

Perhaps the greatest institution of the republic was the **senate,** which had originated under the Etruscans as a council of noble elders who advised the king. During the republic the senate advised the consuls and other magistrates. Because the senate sat year after year, while magistrates changed annually, it provided stability and continuity. It also served as a reservoir of experience and knowledge. Technically, the senate could not pass legislation; it could only offer its advice. But increasingly, because of the senate's prestige, its advice came to have the force of law.

The Romans created several assemblies through which the people elected magistrates and passed legislation. Patricians generally dominated, but in 471 B.C.E. the plebeians won the right to meet in an assembly of their own, the *concilium plebis,* and to pass ordinances.

The chief magistrates of the republic were two consuls, elected for one-year terms. At first the consulship was open only to patricians. The consuls commanded the army in battle, administered state business, and supervised financial affairs. In effect, they and the senate ran the state.

In 366 B.C.E. the Romans created the office of **praetor,** and in 227 B.C.E. the number of praetors was increased to four. When the consuls were away from Rome, the praetors could act in their place. The praetors dealt primarily with the administration of justice. When a praetor took office, he issued a proclamation declaring the principles by which he would interpret the law. These proclamations became very important because they usually covered areas where the law was vague and thus helped clarify the law.

After the age of overseas conquest (see pages 149–151), the Romans divided the Mediterranean area into **provinces** governed by former consuls and former praetors. Because of their experience in Roman politics, they

THE ROMAN REPUBLIC

509 B.C.E.	Founding of the Roman republic
471 B.C.E.	Plebeians win official recognition of their assembly, the *concilium plebis*
ca 450 B.C.E.	Law of the Twelve Tables
390 B.C.E.	Gauls sack Rome
390–290 B.C.E.	Rebuilding of Rome Reorganization of the army Roman expansion in Italy
287 B.C.E.	Legislation of the *concilium plebis* made binding on entire population
264–241 B.C.E.	First Punic War: Rome defeats Carthage, acquires Sicily
218–202 B.C.E.	Second Punic War: Scipio defeats Hannibal Rome dominates the western Mediterranean
200–148 B.C.E.	Rome conquers the Hellenistic East
149–146 B.C.E.	Third Punic War: destruction of Carthage and Corinth
133–121 B.C.E.	The Gracchi introduce land reform but are murdered
107 B.C.E.	Marius becomes consul and begins the professionalization of the army
91–88 B.C.E.	War with Rome's Italian allies
88–27 B.C.E.	Era of civil war
45 B.C.E.	Julius Caesar defeats Pompey's forces and becomes dictator
44 B.C.E.	Assassination of Julius Caesar
31 B.C.E.	Augustus defeats Antony and Cleopatra at Actium

were well suited to administer the affairs of the provincials and to fit Roman law and custom into new contexts.

The development of law was one of the Romans' most splendid achievements. Roman law began as a set of rules that regulated the lives and relations of citizens. This civil law, or **ius civile,** consisted of statutes, customs, and forms of procedure. Roman assemblies added to the body of law, and praetors interpreted it. The spirit of the law aimed at protecting the property, lives, and reputations of citizens; redressing wrongs; and giving satisfaction to victims of injustice.

As the Romans came into more frequent contact with foreigners, they had to devise laws to deal with disputes between Romans and foreigners and between foreigners living under Roman jurisdiction. In these instances, where there was no precedent to guide the Romans, the legal decisions of the praetors proved of immense importance. The praetors adopted aspects of other legal systems and resorted to the law of equity—what they thought was right and just to all parties. Free, in effect, to determine law, the praetors enjoyed a great deal of flexibility. This situation illustrates the practicality and the genius of the Romans. By addressing specific, actual circumstances the praetors developed a body of law, the *ius gentium,* "law of peoples," that applied to Romans and foreigners and that laid the foundation for a universal conception of law. By the time of the late republic, Roman jurists were reaching decisions on the basis of the

Stoic concept of **ius naturale,** "natural law," a universal law that could be applied to all societies.

Another important aspect of early Roman history was a great social conflict, usually known as the **Struggle of the Orders,** which developed between patricians and plebeians. What the plebeians wanted was real political representation and safeguards against patrician domination. The plebeians' efforts to obtain recognition of their rights are the crux of the Struggle of the Orders.

Rome's early wars gave the plebeians the leverage they needed: Rome's survival depended on the army, and the army needed the plebeians. The first showdown between plebeians and patricians came, according to tradition, in 494 B.C.E. To force the patricians to grant concessions, the plebeians seceded from the state; they literally walked out of Rome and refused to serve in the army. The plebeians' general strike worked. Because of it the patricians made important concessions. One of these was social. In 445 B.C.E. the patricians passed a law, the *lex Canuleia,* that for the first time allowed patricians and plebeians to marry each other. Furthermore, the patricians recognized the right of plebeians to elect their own officials, the **tribunes.** The tribunes in turn had the right to protect the plebeians from the arbitrary conduct of patrician magistrates. The tribunes brought plebeian grievances to the senate for resolution. The plebeians were not bent on undermining the state. Rather, they used their gains only to win full equality under the law.

The law itself was the plebeians' next target. Only the patricians knew what the law was, and only they could argue cases in court. All too often they had used the law for their own benefit. The plebeians wanted the law codified and published. The result of their agitation was the Law of the Twelve Tables. Later still, the plebeians forced the patricians to publish legal procedures as well. The plebeians had broken the patricians' legal monopoly and henceforth enjoyed full protection under the law.

The decisive plebeian victory came in 367 B.C.E. after rich plebeians joined the poor to mount a sweeping assault on patrician privilege. Wealthy plebeians demanded that the patricians allow them access to all the magistracies of the state. The senate did approve a law that stipulated that one of the two consuls had to be a plebeian. Though decisive, this victory did not automatically end the Struggle of the Orders. That happened only in 287 B.C.E. with the passage of a law, the *lex Hortensia,* that gave the resolutions of the concilium plebis the force of law for patricians and plebeians alike.

The Struggle of the Orders resulted in a Rome stronger and better united than before. It could have led to class warfare and anarchy, but again certain Roman traits triumphed. The values fostered by their social structure predisposed the Romans to compromise, especially in the face of common danger. Important, too, were Roman patience, tenacity, and a healthy sense of the practical. These qualities enabled both sides to keep working until they had resolved the crisis. The Struggle of the Orders ended in 287 B.C.E. with a new concept of Roman citizenship. All citizens shared equally under the law. Theoretically, all could aspire to the highest political offices. Patrician or plebeian, rich or poor, Roman citizenship was equal for all.

The Age of Overseas Conquest (282–146 B.C.E.)

In 282 B.C.E. Rome embarked on a series of wars that left it ruler of the Mediterranean world. These wars did not result from a grandiose strategy for world conquest. In many instances the Romans did not even initiate military action; they simply responded to events. Although they sometimes declared war reluctantly, they always felt a need to dominate, to eliminate any threat.

After Rome won the Samnite wars, the Greek city of Tarentum felt threatened by growing Roman power. Tarentum invited help from Pyrrhus, the king of Epirus in Greece. He won two furious battles against the Romans but suffered heavy losses (hence the phrase "Pyrrhic victory") and was finally driven out by the Roman army.

The next battleground for Rome was nearby Sicily, long the target of the Phoenician city of Carthage in North Africa (see Map 6.2). The struggle for control of Sicily produced the First Punic War, which lasted for twenty-three years (264–241 B.C.E.). The Romans quickly learned that they could not conquer Sicily unless they controlled the sea. Although they lacked a fleet and hated the sea, the Romans, with grim resolution, built a navy and then won six of seven major naval battles against the Carthaginians. In 241 B.C.E. Rome took control of Sicily, which became its first real province. Rome's resources, manpower, and determination had proved decisive.

But the First Punic War was a beginning, not an end. Carthage, still a formidable enemy, expanded its army led by a brilliant general, Hannibal (ca 247–183 B.C.E.). Realizing the advantage of swift mobile forces and an innovator in tactics, Hannibal moved against Rome. During the Second Punic War, in 218 B.C.E. he led his troops—infantry, cavalry, and elephants—on a thousand-mile march across southern France and over the Alps to carry the fighting to the gates of Rome. He won three major victories, inflicting some forty thousand casualties on Rome's army at the Battle of Cannae in 216 B.C.E. He

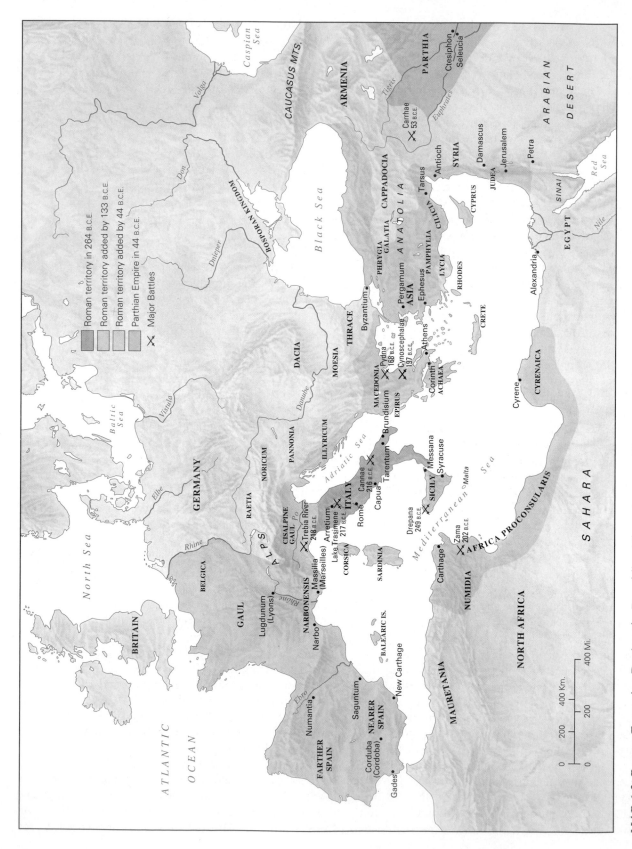

MAP 6.2 Roman Expansion During the Republic The main spurt of Roman expansion occurred between 264 and 133 B.C.E., when most of the Mediterranean fell to Rome, followed by the conquest of Gaul and the eastern Mediterranean by 44 B.C.E.

also spread devastation across the Italian countryside. But he could not break Rome's iron circle of Latium, Etruria, and Samnium, and Rome and its Italian allies fought back.

The Roman general Scipio Africanus (ca 236–ca 183 B.C.E.) copied Hannibal's mobile warfare to wrest Spain from Carthage's control. The Roman fleet dominated the seas, preventing Carthage from sending reinforcements to Hannibal in Italy. Then Scipio landed in North Africa and threatened Carthage itself. Hannibal hurried back, and in 202 B.C.E., near the town of Zama, Scipio defeated Hannibal in one of history's most decisive battles. Scipio's victory ensured that Rome's heritage would be passed on to the Western world.

One more conflict between Rome and Carthage remained. The Third Punic War ended in 146 B.C.E. when Scipio's grandson destroyed Carthage. When Rome took complete control of Spain in 133 B.C.E., it dominated the western Mediterranean.

Even in the midst of this bitter series of conflicts, the Romans began to reach to the east. During the Second Punic War, the king of Macedonia had made an alliance with Carthage. Roman legions moved east to settle accounts and quickly conquered Macedonia, Greece, and the Seleucid monarchy. By 146 B.C.E. the Romans stood unchallenged in the eastern Mediterranean and had turned many states into provinces. (See the feature "Listening to the Past: Titus Flamininus and the Liberty of the Greeks" on pages 178–179.) In 133 B.C.E. the king of Pergamum in Asia Minor willed his kingdom to Rome when he died. The Ptolemies of Egypt meekly obeyed Roman wishes. The Mediterranean had become *mare nostrum,* "our sea."

Old Values and Greek Culture

Rome had conquered the Mediterranean world, but some Romans considered that victory a misfortune. The historian Sallust (86–34 B.C.E.), writing from hindsight, complained that the acquisition of an empire was the beginning of Rome's troubles:

But when through labor and justice our Republic grew powerful, great kings defeated in war, fierce nations and mighty peoples subdued by force, when Carthage the rival of the Roman people was wiped out root and branch, all the seas and lands lay open, then fortune began to be harsh and to throw everything into confusion. The Romans had easily borne labor, danger, uncertainty, and hardship. To them leisure, riches—otherwise desirable—proved to be burdens and torments. So at first money, then desire for power, grew great. These things were a sort of cause of all evils.[2]

Triumphal Column of Caius Duilius   This curious monument celebrates Rome's first naval victory in the First Punic War. In the battle Caius Duilius destroyed fifty Carthaginian ships. He then celebrated his success by erecting this column that portrays the prows of the enemy ships projecting from the column. *(Alinari/Art Resource, NY)*

Sallust was not alone in his feelings. At the time, some senators had opposed the destruction of Carthage on the grounds that fear of their old rival would keep the Romans in check. In the second century B.C.E. the Romans learned that they could not return to what they fondly considered a simple life. They were world rulers. The responsibilities they faced were complex and awesome. They had to change their institutions, social patterns, and way of thinking to meet the new era. They were in fact building the foundations of a great imperial system.

How did the Romans of the day meet these challenges? How did they lead their lives and cope with these momentous changes? Obviously there are as many answers to these questions as there were Romans. Yet two attitudes represent the major trends of the second century B.C.E. One was a longing for the good old days and an idealized view of the traditional agrarian way of life. The other was an embracing of the new urban life, with its eager acceptance of Greek culture.

In Roman society ties within the family were very strong. The head of the family was the **paterfamilias,** a term that means far more than merely "father." The paterfamilias was the oldest dominant male of the family. He held nearly absolute power over the lives of his wife and children as long as he lived. He could legally kill his wife for adultery or divorce her at will. He could kill his children or sell them into slavery. He could force them to marry against their will. Until the paterfamilias died, his sons could not legally own property. At his death, the wife and children of the paterfamilias inherited his property.

Despite his immense power, the paterfamilias did not necessarily act alone or arbitrarily. To deal with important family matters, he usually called a council of the adult males. In this way the leading members of the family aired their views. In these councils the women of the family had no formal part, but it can safely be assumed that they played an important role behind the scenes. Although the possibility of serious conflicts between a paterfamilias and his grown sons is obvious, no one in ancient Rome ever complained about the institution. Perhaps in practice the paterfamilias preferred to be lenient rather than absolute.

In the traditional Roman family, the wife was the matron of the family, a position of authority and respect. The virtues expected of a Roman matron were fidelity, chastity, modesty, and dedication to the family. She ran the household. She supervised the domestic slaves, planned the meals, and devoted a good deal of attention to her children. In wealthy homes during this period, the matron had begun to employ a slave as a wet nurse, but most ordinary Roman women nursed their babies and bathed and swaddled them daily. After the age of seven, sons—and in many wealthy households daughters too—began to undertake formal education.

The agricultural year followed the sun and the stars—the farmer's calendar. Farmers used oxen and donkeys to pull the plow, collecting the dung of the animals for fertilizer. The main money crops, at least for rich soils, were wheat and flax. Forage crops included clover, vetch, and alfalfa. Prosperous farmers raised olive trees chiefly for the oil. They also raised grapevines for the production of wine. Harvests varied depending on the soil, but farmers could usually expect yields of 5½ bushels of wheat or 10½ bushels of barley per acre.

An influx of slaves came about from Rome's wars and conquests. Prisoners from Spain, Africa, and the Hellenistic East and even some blacks and other prisoners from Hannibal's army came to Rome as the spoils of war. The Roman attitude toward slaves and slavery had little in common with modern views. To the Romans slavery was a misfortune that befell some people, but it did not entail any racial theories. Races were not enslaved because the Romans thought them inferior. The black African slave was treated no worse—and no better—than

Scene of the Life of a Child   This scene depicts the life of Marcus Cornelius from infancy to playing with his ponies to death. The entire scene suggests a pleasant and loving, if brief, childhood. *(Giraudon/Art Resource, NY)*

the Spaniard. Indeed, some slaves were valued because of their physical distinctiveness: black Africans and blond Germans were particular favorites. For the talented slave, the Romans always held out the hope of eventual freedom. **Manumission**—the freeing of individual slaves by their masters—became so common that it had to be limited by law. Not even Christians questioned the institution of slavery. It was just a fact of life.

For most Romans, religion played an important part in life. Originally the Romans thought of the gods as invisible, shapeless natural forces. Only through Etruscan and Greek influence did Roman deities take on human form. Jupiter, the sky-god, and his wife, Juno, became equivalent to the Greek Zeus and Hera. Mars was the god of war but also guaranteed the fertility of the farm and protected it from danger. The gods of the Romans were not loving and personal. They were stern, powerful, and aloof. But as long as the Romans honored the cults of their gods, they could expect divine favor.

In addition to the great gods, the Romans believed in spirits who haunted fields, forests, crossroads, and even the home itself. Some of the deities were hostile; only magic could ward them off. The spirits of the dead, like ghosts in modern horror films, frequented places where they had lived. They, too, had to be placated but were ordinarily benign. As the poet Ovid (43 B.C.E.–17 C.E.) put it:

The spirits of the dead ask for little.
They are more grateful for piety than for an
    expensive gift—
Not greedy are the gods who haunt the Styx below.
A rooftile covered with a sacrificial crown,
Scattered kernels, a few grains of salt,
Bread dipped in wine, and loose violets—
These are enough.
Put them in a potsherd and leave them in the middle of
    the road.[3]

A good deal of Roman religion consisted of rituals such as those Ovid describes. These practices lived on long after the Romans had lost interest in the great gods. Even Christianity could not entirely wipe them out. Instead, Christianity was to incorporate many of these rituals into its own style of worship.

By the second century B.C.E. the ideals of traditional Roman society came into conflict with a new spirit of wealth and leisure. The conquest of the Mediterranean world and the spoils of war made Rome a great city. Roman life, especially in the cities, was changing and becoming less austere. The spoils of war went to build baths, theaters, and other places of amusement. Simultaneously, the new responsibilities of governing the world produced in Rome a sophisticated society. Romans developed new tastes and a liking for Greek culture and literature. They began to learn the Greek language. Hellenism dominated the cultural life of Rome.

The new Hellenism profoundly stimulated the growth and development of Roman art and literature. After conquering the Hellenistic East, the Romans brought back Greek paintings and sculptures to grace temples, public buildings, and private homes. Roman artists copied many aspects of Greek art, but their emphasis on realistic portraiture carried on a native tradition. Similarly, Roman writers such as Plautus (ca 254–184 B.C.E.) and Terence (ca 195–159 B.C.E.) followed Greek models for their plays but put their own Roman stamp on them. All of early Roman literature was derived from the Greeks, but it managed in time to flourish in its own voice because it had something of its own to say.

The conquest of the Mediterranean world brought the Romans leisure, and Hellenism influenced how they

African Acrobat Conquest and prosperity brought exotic pleasure to Rome. Every feature of this sculpture is exotic. The young African woman and her daring gymnastic pose would catch anyone's attention. To add to the spice of her act, she performs using a live crocodile as her platform. Americans would have loved it. *(Courtesy of the Trustees of the British Museum)*

Roman Table Manners This mosaic is a floor that can never be swept clean. It whimsically suggests what a dining room floor looked like after a lavish dinner and also tells something about the menu: a chicken head, a wishbone, and remains of various seafood, vegetables, and fruit are easily recognizable. *(Museo Gregoriano Profano, Vatican Museums/Scala/ Art Resource, NY)*

Dressing of the Bride Preparing for a wedding was an occasion for fun and ceremony. On the night before the event the bride tried on her wedding dress for a favorable omen. The next morning she was fastidiously dressed by her mother or under her mother's supervision. Here a sister or maid arranges the bride's hair, over which was later placed her veil, normally crowned with flowers that the girl had picked herself. *(Erich Lessing/Art Resource, NY)*

spent their free time. During the second century B.C.E. the Greek custom of bathing became a Roman passion and an important part of the day. In the early republic Romans had bathed infrequently, especially in the winter. Now large buildings containing pools and exercise rooms went up in great numbers, and the baths became an essential part of the Roman city. Architects built intricate systems of aqueducts to supply the bathing establishments with water. Conservatives railed at this Greek cus-

tom, calling it a waste of time and an encouragement to idleness. But the baths were socially important places where men and women went to see and be seen. Social climbers tried to talk to the "right people" and wangle invitations to dinner; politicians took advantage of the occasion to discuss the affairs of the day.

Did Hellenism and new social customs corrupt the Romans? Perhaps the best answer is this: the Roman state and the empire it ruled continued to exist for six more centuries. Rome did not collapse; the state continued to prosper. The golden age of Roman literature was still before it. The high tide of Roman prosperity still lay in the future. The Romans did not like change but took it in stride. That was part of their practical turn of mind and their strength.

The Late Republic (133–31 B.C.E.)

The wars of conquest created serious problems for the Romans. Some of the most pressing were political. The republican constitution had suited the needs of a simple city-state but was inadequate to meet the requirements of Rome's new position in international affairs (see Map 6.2). Sweeping changes and reforms were necessary to make it serve the demands of empire. A system of provincial administration had to be established. Armies had to be provided for defense, and a system of tax collection had to be created.

Other political problems were equally serious. During the wars Roman generals commanded huge numbers of troops for long periods of time. Men such as Scipio Aemilianus were on the point of becoming too mighty for the state to control. Although Rome's Italian allies had borne much of the burden of the fighting, they received fewer rewards than did Roman officers and soldiers. Italians began to agitate for full Roman citizenship and a voice in politics.

There were serious economic problems, too. Hannibal's operations and the warfare in Italy had left the countryside a shambles. The movements of numerous armies had disrupted agriculture. The prolonged fighting had also drawn untold numbers of Roman and Italian men away from their farms for long periods. The families of these soldiers could not keep the land under full cultivation. The people who defended Rome and conquered the world for Rome became impoverished for having done their duty. These problems, complex and explosive, largely account for the turmoil of the closing years of the republic.

When the legionaries returned home, they found that their farms looked like those of the people they had conquered. Many chose to sell their land; they found ready buyers in those who had become incredibly rich through the wars of conquest. These wealthy men created huge estates called **latifundia.** Landless veterans moved to the cities, especially Rome, but most could find no work. Those who did work received meager pay kept low by competition from slave labor. These changes threatened Rome's army, as landless men were forbidden to serve.

The landless veterans were willing to follow any leader who promised help. Tiberius Gracchus (163–133 B.C.E.)

emerged. An aristocrat, Tiberius was appalled that Rome's soldiers "fight and die to support others in luxury" and decried the fact that "they are styled masters of the world, [but] they have not a single clod of earth that is their own."[4] Elected tribune of the people in 133 B.C.E., Tiberius proposed dividing public land among the poor, but his sensible plan was thwarted by wealthy aristocrats. A group of senators murdered Tiberius, launching a long era of political violence that would destroy the republic.

Still, Tiberius's land bill became law, and his brother Gaius Gracchus (153–121 B.C.E.) led the fight for further reforms. He passed a law providing the urban poor with cheap grain and urged that poor Romans be sent to colonize southern Italy. When he proposed giving full citizenship rights to all Italians, senators once again tried to stem the tide of reform by murder.

The next reforming leader was Gaius Marius, who unlike the Gracchus brothers was not part of the traditional Roman aristocracy. In 107 B.C.E. he recruited the landless into the army he needed to campaign against a rebel king in North Africa. When the soldiers returned home, they expected Marius to deliver on the land he had promised them. The senate, however, refused to enact Marius's bill. From then on, Roman soldiers looked to their commanders, not the senate or the state, to protect their interests.

Soon after, in 91 B.C.E., a bitter war erupted between the Romans and their allies over the issue of full citizenship for Italians. In 88 B.C.E. the Roman general Sulla ended the war and made himself dictator. Although he stepped down nine years later and tried to restore the republican constitution, it was too late. Once the senate and other institutions of the Roman state had failed to meet the needs of the empire, once they had lost control of their generals and armies, and once the soldiers had put their faith in generals rather than the state, the republic was doomed.

The history of the late republic is the story of the power struggles of some of Rome's most famous figures: Julius Caesar, Pompey, Augustus, Marc Antony, and Cicero. (See the feature "Individuals in Society: Cicero.") A man of boundless ambition, Pompey used military success in Spain to force the senate to allow him to run for consul. In 59 B.C.E. he was joined in a political alliance called the **First Triumvirate** by Crassus, another ambitious politician, and Julius Caesar (100–44 B.C.E.). Born of a noble family, Caesar was a cultivated man, an able general, and a brilliant politician with unbridled ambition. Recognizing that military service was the road to power, Caesar led an army in Spain, winning the respect and affection of his troops with his courage. Brave,

Julius Caesar This realistic bust of Caesar captures all of the power, intensity, and brilliance of the man. It is a study of determination and an excellent example of Roman portraiture. *(National Archaeological Museum, Naples/Alinari/Art Resource, NY)*

tireless, and a superb strategist, he moved next to conquer all of Gaul (modern France). By 49 B.C.E. the First Triumvirate had collapsed. Crassus had died in battle, and Caesar and Pompey, each suspecting the other of treachery, were engaged in a bloody civil war. Pompey had the official support of the government, but Caesar defeated him in 45 B.C.E.

Making himself dictator, Caesar was determined to enact basic reforms. He extended citizenship to many of the provincials (people outside Italy) who had supported him. To relieve the pressure of Rome's growing population, he sent eighty thousand poor and jobless people to plant colonies in Gaul, Spain, and North Africa. These new communities—formed of Roman citizens, not subjects—helped spread Roman culture.

In 44 B.C.E. a group of conspirators assassinated Caesar and set off another round of civil war. His grand-nephew and heir, the eighteen-year-old Octavian, joined with two of Caesar's followers, Marc Antony and Lepidus, in the Second Triumvirate. They defeated Caesar's murderers but soon had a falling-out. Octavian forced Lepidus out of office and waged war against Antony, who

had become allied with Cleopatra, queen of Egypt. In 31 B.C.E., with the might of Rome at his back, Octavian met and defeated the combined forces of Antony and Cleopatra at the Battle of Actium in Greece. His victory ended an age of civil war that had lasted since the days of Sulla. For this success the senate in 27 B.C.E. voted Octavian the name *Augustus.*

THE PAX ROMANA

When Augustus put an end to the civil wars that had raged since 88 B.C.E., he faced monumental problems of reconstruction. He could easily have declared himself dictator, as Caesar had done, but the thought was repugnant to him. Augustus was neither an autocrat nor a revolutionary. His solution, as he put it, was to restore the republic. But was that possible? Some eighteen years of anarchy and civil war had shattered the republican constitution. From 29 to 23 B.C.E., Augustus toiled to heal Rome's wounds. The first problem facing him was to rebuild the constitution and the organs of government. Next he had to demobilize much of the army and care for the welfare of the provinces. Then he had to meet the danger of barbarians at Rome's European frontiers. Augustus was highly successful in meeting these challenges. The world came to know this era as the **pax Romana,** the Roman peace. His gift of peace to a war-torn world sowed the seeds of the empire's golden age.

Augustus's Settlement (31 B.C.E.–14 C.E.)

Augustus claimed that in restoring constitutional government he was also restoring the republic. Typically Roman, he preferred not to create anything new; he intended instead to modify republican forms and offices to meet new circumstances. Augustus expected the senate to administer some of the provinces, continue to be the chief deliberative body of the state, and act as a court of law. But he did not give the senate enough power to become his partner in government. As a result, the senate could not live up to the responsibilities that Augustus assigned. Many of its prerogatives shifted by default to Augustus and his successors.

Augustus's own position in the restored republic was something of an anomaly. He could not simply surrender the reins of power, for someone else would have seized them. But how was he to fit into a republican constitution? Again Augustus had his own answer. He became **princeps civitatis,** the "First Citizen of the State." This prestigious title carried no power; it indicated only that

INDIVIDUALS IN SOCIETY

CICERO

Bust of Cicero from the first century B.C.E. (Alinari/Art Resource, NY)

In republican Rome entry of a "new man" into the exalted rank of senator was possible but also difficult and infrequent. The families that had traditional hold on power in the senate formed an exclusive circle, jealous of their power and proud of their prestige. They provided the leadership of the republic and were very reluctant to allow social inferiors to join their ranks. Few men from the lower classes were admitted. Those few who were ultimately accepted into this rarefied air needed outstanding ability, wealth, a good education, social graces, and a noble patron. Cicero was one of those who possessed all of these advantages.

Marcus Tullius Cicero was born on January 3, 106 B.C.E., in Arpinum, southwest of Rome. He was of equestrian rank, which means that his social standing was inferior to that of the senators. Furthermore, not having been born in Rome, he was an outsider. Yet his father was intelligent, ambitious, and foresighted. He sent Cicero and his brother to Rome for an education. Rome was the place to make a reputation, and Cicero made good use of the opportunity. He studied philosophy and rhetoric there and laid the foundations of his later career.

From 90 to 89 B.C.E. he served in the Roman army, which gave him firsthand knowledge of military affairs. Although the dream of military glory remained with him always, his martial ability was that of a subordinate, not a leader.

After his military service Cicero turned to the study of law, which was a lucrative avenue to a political career. He won his first case in 81 B.C.E. and immediately earned a reputation for knowledge of the law, reasoned argument, and eloquent speaking. His victory may have annoyed Sulla, because it legally demonstrated the weakness of his dictatorship. In 79 B.C.E. Cicero traveled first to Athens and then to Rhodes to continue his study of philosophy and oratory. He was honing the skills that would establish his reputation and make his career.

Cicero returned to Rome to enter politics after Sulla's death in 78 B.C.E. Success was immediate. He became praetor of Sicily in 66 B.C.E., which gave him direct experience with Roman administration. He also earned a reputation as a man who honored Rome's traditional values. He was politically conservative and thus acceptable to many senators. The height of his political career came in 63 B.C.E., when he was elected consul. He was the first *novus homo* (new man) to be elected to the consulship in thirty-one years.

Cicero took no active part in the revolution that brought down the republic. Instead, he tried to stop it. He urged peace and a return to the traditional government, what he called "concord of the orders," an attempt to reconcile the warring factions. His plan fell on deaf ears. Events had escalated beyond him, and now only politicians with armies could decide the fate of the republic. He took no part in Caesar's assassination but nonetheless made several influential enemies. One of them, Marc Antony, ordered his execution. Cicero made a halfhearted attempt to escape, but Roman soldiers caught him and murdered him on December 7, 43 B.C.E. He died with dignity and courage.

Cicero exhibited little military talent, fair but not brilliant administrative skills, and mediocre political abilities. Why does history remember him? Most Romans respected him for his dedication to Rome and its laws. Posterity has honored him for his writings, which have endured. He was a literary genius whose Latin prose was never equaled, even in antiquity. His essays on politics and philosophy explore the nature and functioning of proper, stable government and an attempt to understand the universe and people's place in it. The finest tribute to him was one he never heard. The emperor Augustus once called him "a learned man . . . and a lover of his country."

QUESTIONS FOR ANALYSIS

1. Was Cicero's ideal of "concord of the orders" a realistic ideal in his day?
2. For all of his fame and talent, how successful was Cicero in practical politics, and what did he achieve?

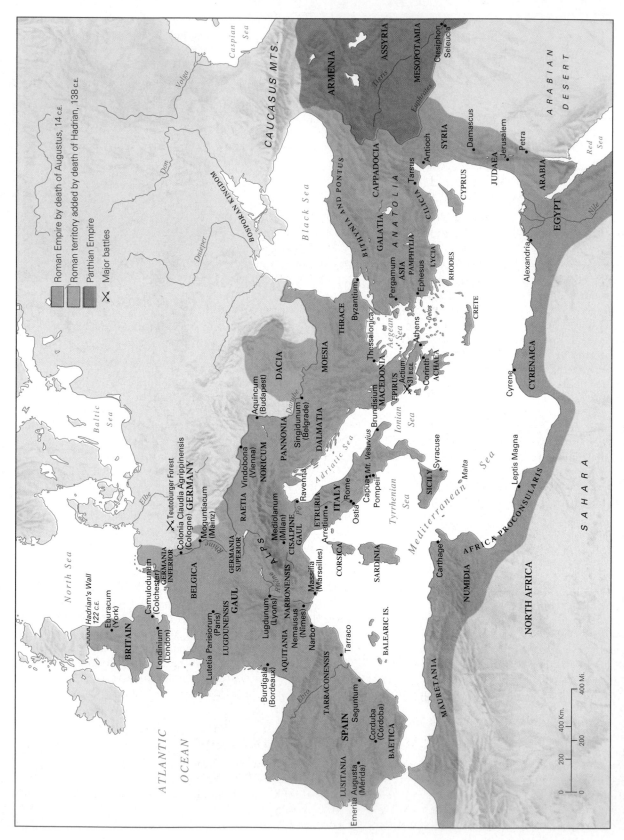

MAP 6.3 Roman Expansion Under the Empire Following Roman expansion during the republic, Augustus added vast tracts of Europe to the Roman Empire, which the emperor Hadrian later enlarged by assuming control over parts of central Europe, the Near East, and North Africa.

Augustus was the most distinguished of all Roman citizens. In effect, it designated Augustus as the first among equals—a little "more equal" than anyone else. His real power resided in the multiple magistracies he held and in the powers granted him by the senate. As consul he had no more constitutional and legal power than his fellow consuls, but he was consul every year. In addition, Augustus held many magistracies that his fellow consuls did not. The senate also voted him the full power of the tribunes, giving him the right to call the senate into session, present legislation to the people, and defend their rights. Along with all these other powers, Augustus had control of the army, which he made a permanent, standing organization. Although he carefully kept this power in the background, it was there. Augustus did not restore the republic, but he did create a constitutional monarchy. Without saying so, he created the office of emperor.

Augustus's title as commander of the Roman army was *imperator*, the title with which Rome customarily honored a general after a major victory, and it came to mean "emperor" in the modern sense of the term. Augustus governed the provinces where troops were needed for defense. The frontiers were his special concern. There Roman legionaries held the German barbarians at arm's length. Augustus made sure that Rome went to war only at his command. He controlled deployment of the Roman army and paid its wages. He granted it bonuses and gave veterans retirement benefits. To employ Rome's surplus of soldiers, he also founded at least forty new colonies, which, like Julius Caesar's, were a significant tool in the spread of Roman culture. Thus he avoided the problems with the army that the old senate had created for itself. Augustus never shared control of the army, and no Roman found it easy to defy him militarily.

Augustus, however, failed to solve a momentous problem. He never found a way to institutionalize his position with the army. The ties between the princeps and the army were always personal. The army was loyal to the princeps but not necessarily to the state. The Augustan principate worked well at first, but by the third century C.E. the army would make and break emperors at will. Nonetheless, it is a measure of Augustus's success that his settlement survived as long and as well as it did.

Administration and Expansion Under Augustus

In the areas under his immediate jurisdiction, Augustus put provincial administration on an orderly basis and improved its functioning. Believing that the cities of the empire should look after their own affairs, he encouraged local self-government and urbanism. Augustus respected local customs and ordered his governors to do the same.

As a spiritual bond between the provinces and Rome, Augustus encouraged the cult of Roma, goddess and guardian of the state. In the Hellenistic East, where king worship was an established custom, the cult of *Roma et Augustus* (Rome and Augustus) grew and spread rapidly. Augustus then introduced it in the West. By the time of his death in 14 C.E., nearly every province in the empire could boast an altar or a shrine to Roma et Augustus. In the West it was not the person of the emperor who was worshiped but his *genius*—his guardian spirit. In praying for the good health and welfare of the emperor, Romans and provincials were praying for the empire itself. The cult became a symbol of Roman unity.

For the history of Western civilization, one of the most momentous aspects of Augustus's reign was Roman expansion into the wilderness of northern and western Europe (see Map 6.3). Carrying on Caesar's work, Augustus pushed Rome's frontier into the region of modern Germany.

Augustus began his work in the west and north by completing the conquest of Spain. In Gaul, apart from minor campaigns, most of his work was peaceful. He founded twelve new towns, and the Roman road system linked new settlements with one another and with Italy. But the German frontier, along the Rhine River, was the scene of hard fighting. In 12 B.C.E. Augustus ordered a major invasion of Germany beyond the Rhine. In 9 C.E. Augustus's general Varus lost some twenty thousand troops at the Battle of the Teutoburger Forest. Thereafter the Rhine remained the Roman frontier.

Meanwhile more successful generals extended the Roman standards as far as the Danube. Roman legions penetrated the area of modern Austria, southern Bavaria, and western Hungary. The regions of modern Serbia, Bulgaria, and Romania fell. Within this area the legionaries built fortified camps. Roads linked these camps with one another, and settlements grew up around the camps. Amid the vast expanse of forests, Roman towns, trade, language, and law began to exert a civilizing influence on the barbarians. Many military camps became towns, and many modern European cities owe their origins to the forts of the Roman army. For the first time, the barbarian north came into direct, immediate, and continuous contact with Mediterranean culture. The arrival of the Romans often provoked resistance from barbarian tribes that simply wanted to be left alone. In other cases the prosperity and wealth of the new Roman towns lured

Boscoreale Cup   The central scene lavishly depicted on the side of a silver cup shows Augustus seated in majesty. In his right hand he holds an orb that represents his position as master of the world. The scroll in his left hand symbolizes his authority as lawgiver. On his right is a group of divinities who support his efforts, on his left a group of barbarians who have submitted to Rome. *(Louvre/R.M.N./Art Resource, NY)*

barbarians eager for plunder. The Romans maintained peaceful relations with the barbarians whenever possible, but Roman legions remained on the frontier to repel hostile barbarians. The result was the evolution of a consistent, systematic frontier policy.

Literary Flowering

The Augustan settlement's gift of peace inspired a literary flowering unparalleled in Roman history. The tone and ideal of Roman literature, like that of the Greeks, was humanistic and worldly. Roman poets and prose writers celebrated the dignity of humanity and the range of its accomplishments. They stressed the physical and emotional joys of a comfortable, peaceful life.

Virgil (70–19 B.C.E.), Rome's greatest poet, wrote the *Aeneid,* an epic poem that is the equivalent of the *Iliad* and *Odyssey* of Greece. The poem marries the traditional Roman tradition of the founding of Rome by Romulus with the legend of Aeneas, a Trojan hero who escaped to Italy at the fall of Troy. In doing so he connected Rome with Greece's heroic past.

Livy's history of Rome is the prose counterpart of the *Aeneid.* Livy (59 B.C.E.–17 C.E.) received training in Latin literature, rhetoric, and philosophy. He loved and admired the heroes and great deeds of the republic, but he was also a friend of Augustus and a supporter of the principate. He especially approved of Augustus's efforts to restore republican virtues.

The poet Horace (65–8 B.C.E.) rose from humble beginnings to friendship with Augustus—who, along with many of his friends, actively encouraged the writers who created this literary flowering. One of his finest odes commemorates Augustus's victory over Antony and Cleopatra at Actium in 31 B.C.E.

THE COMING OF CHRISTIANITY

During the reign of Tiberius (14–37 C.E.), perhaps in 29 C.E., Pontius Pilate, prefect of Judaea—the Roman province formed of the old kingdom of Judah—condemned Jesus of Nazareth to death. Jesus lived in a troubled time when Roman rule aroused hatred and unrest among the Jews. This climate of hostility formed the backdrop of his ministry.

The Roman civil wars had touched the eastern Mediterranean world, as local populations—including the Jews—took sides in the fighting and both caused and suffered damage. Augustus's peace was less celebrated here than in Rome, as the Jews resented the embrace of Greek culture by his handpicked king, Herod (ca 73–4 B.C.E.). When Herod died, civil war erupted, and the Roman army was needed to restore order. Augustus then put a Roman official, a prefect who reported directly to him, in charge of the province. Resentment of Roman troops and tax collectors sharpened.

Two movements spread among the Jews. First was the rise of the Zealots, resolute in the worship of Yahweh and savage in their attempts to throw off the Roman yoke. Second was the rise of a militant apocalyptic sentiment. The old Jewish belief in the coming of the **Messiah** became more fervent and widespread. People believed that this savior would destroy the Roman Empire and usher in a period of happiness and plenty for the Jews. One who prophesied the coming of the Messiah was John the Baptist. At the same time, the sect described in the Dead Sea Scrolls, probably the Essenes, prepared themselves for the end of the world.

The spiritual ferment of the time extended beyond Judaea. Roman pagans—those who believed in the Greco-Roman gods—were undergoing a turbulent

Pontius Pilate and Jesus   This Byzantine mosaic from Ravenna illustrates a dramatic moment in Jesus' trial and crucifixion. Jesus stands accused before Pilate, but Pilate symbolically washes his hands of the whole affair. *(Scala/Art Resource, NY)*

time as well. Paganism at the time of Jesus' birth can be divided into three broad types: the official state religion of Rome, the traditional Roman cults of hearth and countryside, and the new mystery religions that flowed from the Hellenistic East. The formal state religion, full of ritual and grand spectacle, reflected a bond between the gods and the people, a religious contract for the well-being of the empire, but it provided little emotional or spiritual comfort. Many Romans turned to the old cults of home and countryside. These popular cults brought Romans back in touch with nature but did not satisfy the need for a religion that was more immediate

and personal. Many people in the Roman Empire found that need met by the Hellenistic mystery cults (see pages 135–136). While these religions met people's spiritual needs, none was truly international and open to everyone, as each excluded some people for various reasons.

Into this climate of Roman religious yearning, political severity, fanatical Zealotry, and Messianic hope came Jesus of Nazareth (ca 5 B.C.E.–29 C.E.). He was raised in Galilee, stronghold of the Zealots. Yet Jesus himself was a man of peace. Jesus urged his listeners to love God as their father and one another as God's children.

Jesus' teachings were Jewish. He declared that he would change not one jot of the Jewish law. His major deviation from orthodoxy was his insistence that he taught in his own name, not in the name of Yahweh. Was he then the Messiah? A small band of followers thought so, and Jesus claimed that he was. But Jesus had his own conception of the Messiah. Jesus would not destroy the Roman Empire. He told his disciples flatly that they were to "render unto Caesar the things that are Caesar's." Jesus would establish a spiritual kingdom, not an earthly one. Repeatedly he told his disciples that his kingdom was "not of this world," but one of eternal happiness in a life after death.

Of Jesus' life and teachings the prefect Pontius Pilate knew little and cared even less. All that concerned him was the maintenance of peace and order. The crowds following Jesus at the time of the Passover, a highly emotional time in the Jewish year, alarmed Pilate, who faced a volatile situation. To avert riot and bloodshed, Pilate condemned Jesus to death. After being scourged, he was hung from a cross until he died in the sight of family, friends, enemies, and the merely curious.

Once Pilate's soldiers had carried out the sentence, the entire matter seemed to be closed. Then on the third day after Jesus' crucifixion, an odd rumor began to circulate in Jerusalem. Some of Jesus' followers were saying he had risen from the dead, while others accused them of having stolen his body. For the earliest Christians and for generations to come, the resurrection of Jesus became a central element of faith—and more than that, a promise: Jesus had triumphed over death, and his resurrection promised all Christians immortality.

The memory of Jesus and his teachings sturdily survived. Believers in his divinity met in small assemblies or congregations, often in each other's homes to discuss the meaning of Jesus' message. These meetings always took place outside the synagogue. They included such orthodox Jews as the Pharisees. These earliest Christians were clearly defining their faith to fit the life of Jesus into an orthodox Jewish context. Only later did these congregations evolve into what can be called a church with a formal organization and set of beliefs. One of the first significant events occurred in Jerusalem on the Jewish festival of Pentecost, when Jesus' followers assembled. They were joined by Jews from many parts of the world, including some from as far away as Parthia to the east, Crete to the west, Rome, and Ethiopia. These early followers were Hellenized Jews, many of them rich merchants. They were in an excellent position to spread the Word throughout the known world.

The catalyst in the spread of Jesus' teachings and the formation of the Christian church was Paul of Tarsus, a Hellenized Jew who was comfortable in both the Roman and Jewish worlds. He had begun by persecuting the new sect, but on the road to Damascus he was converted to belief in Jesus. He was the single most important figure responsible for changing Christianity from a Jewish sect into a separate religion. Paul was familiar with Greek philosophy, and he had actually discussed the tenets of the new religion with Epicurean and Stoic philosophers in Athens. Indeed, one of his seminal ideas may have stemmed from the Stoic concept of the unity of mankind. He proclaimed that the mission of Christianity was "to make one of all the folk of men." His vision was to include all the kindred of the earth. That concept meant that he urged the Jews to include non-Jews in the faith. He was the first to voice a universal message of Christianity.

Paul's vision was both bold and successful. When he traveled abroad, he first met with the leaders of the local synagogue, then went among the people. He applied himself especially to the Greco-Romans, whom he did not consider common or unclean because they were not Jews. He went so far as to say that there were no differences between Jews and Gentiles, which in orthodox Jewish thought was not only revolutionary but also heresy. Paul found a ready audience among the Gentiles, who converted to the new religion with surprising enthusiasm. A significant part of this process was the acceptance of Gentile women into the faith. The reasons for this were several. First, intermarriage between Greeks and Jews was common. More important, Christianity gave women more rights than they could expect from either paganism or Judaism. For women Christianity was a source of liberation.

Christianity was attractive to many because it gave the Roman world a cause. Hellenistic philosophy had attempted to make men and women self-sufficient: people who became indifferent to the outside world could no longer be hurt by it. That goal alone ruled out any cause except the attainment of serenity. The Romans, never innovators in philosophy, merely elaborated this lonely and austere message. Instead of passivity, Christianity stressed the ideal of striving for a goal. Each and every Christian, no matter how poor or humble, supposedly worked to realize the triumph of Christianity on earth. This was God's will, a sacred duty for every Christian. By spreading the Word of Christ, Christians played their part in God's plan. No matter how small, the part each Christian played was important. Since this duty was God's will, Christians believed that the goal would be achieved. The

The Catacombs of Rome
The early Christians used underground crypts and rock chambers to bury their dead. The bodies were placed in these galleries and then sealed up. The catacombs became places of pilgrimage, and in this way the dead continued to be united with the living. *(Catacombe di Priscilla, Rome/Scala/Art Resource, NY)*

Christian was not discouraged by temporary setbacks, believing Christianity to be invincible.

Christianity gave its devotees a sense of community. No Christian was alone. All members of the Christian community strove toward the same goal of fulfilling God's plan. Each individual community was in turn a member of a greater community. And that community, the Church General, was indestructible.

So Christianity's attractions were many, from forgiveness of sin to an exalted purpose for each individual. Its insistence on the individual's importance gave solace and encouragement, especially to the poor and meek. Its claim to divine protection fed hope in the eventual success of the Christian community. Christianity made participation in the universal possible for everyone. The ultimate reward promised by Christianity was eternal bliss after death.

THE GOLDEN AGE

For fifty years after Augustus's death the dynasty that he established—known as the Julio-Claudians because all were members of the Julian and Claudian clans—provided the emperors of Rome. Two, Caligula and Nero, were weak and frivolous men who exercised their power stupidly and brought misery to the empire. But two others, Tiberius and Claudius, were sound rulers and able administrators, and during their reigns the empire largely prospered. One of their most momentous achievements was Claudius's creation of an imperial bureaucracy of professional administrators. The numerous duties and immense reponsibilities of the emperor prompted Claudius to delegate power. He created a simple, workable system that enabled him and later emperors to rule more easily and efficiently.

In 68 C.E. Nero's inept rule led to military rebellion and his death, followed by widespread disruption. The next year four men claimed the position of emperor, and several armies marched on Rome to back their claims. The winner was Vespasian, who entered Rome in 70 and restored order.

By establishing the Flavian dynasty (named after his clan), Vespasian turned the principate into an open and admitted monarchy. The Flavians (69–96 C.E.) carried on Augustus's work on the frontiers, gave the Roman world peace, and kept the legions in line. Their work paved the way for the era of the **five good emperors,** the golden age of the empire (96–180 C.E.).

Beginning in the second century C.E., the era of the five good emperors was a period of almost unparalleled prosperity for the empire. Wars generally ended in victories and were confined to the frontiers. The five good emperors—Nerva, Trajan, Hadrian, Antoninus Pius, and Marcus Aurelius—were among the noblest, most dedicated, ablest men in Roman history.

Under the Flavians the principate became a full-blown monarchy, and by the time of the five good emperors the principate was an office with definite rights, powers, and prerogatives. In the years between Augustus and the era of the five good emperors, the emperor had become an indispensable part of the imperial machinery. In short, without the emperor the empire would quickly have fallen to pieces. Augustus had been monarch in fact but not in theory; during their reigns, the five good emperors were monarchs in both.

The five good emperors were not power-hungry autocrats. The concentration of power was the result of empire. The easiest and most efficient way to run the Roman Empire was to invest the emperor with vast powers. Furthermore, Roman emperors on the whole proved to be effective rulers and administrators. As capable and efficient emperors took on new tasks and functions, the emperor's hand was felt in more areas of life and government. The five good emperors were benevolent and exercised their power intelligently, but they were absolute kings all the same. Lesser men would later throw off the façade of constitutionality and use this same power in a despotic fashion.

One of the most significant changes in Roman government since Augustus's day was the enormous growth of the imperial bureaucracy created by Claudius. Hadrian, who became emperor in 117 C.E., reformed this system by putting the bureaucracy on an organized, official basis. He established imperial administrative departments to handle the work formerly done by imperial freedmen. Hadrian also separated civil service from military service. Men with little talent or taste for the army could instead serve the state as administrators. Hadrian's bureaucracy demanded professionalism from its members. Administrators made a career of the civil service. These innovations made for more efficient running of the empire and increased the authority of the emperor—the ruling power of the bureaucracy.

The Roman army had also changed since Augustus's time. The Roman legion had once been a mobile unit, but its duties under the empire no longer called for mobility. The successors of Augustus generally called a halt to further conquests. The army was expected to defend what had already been won. Under the Flavian emperors the frontiers became firmly fixed. Forts and watch stations guarded the borders. Behind the forts the Romans built a system of roads that allowed the forts to be quickly supplied and reinforced in times of trouble. The army had evolved into a garrison force, with legions guarding specific areas for long periods.

The personnel of the legions was also changing. Italy could no longer supply all the recruits needed for the army. Increasingly, only the officers came from Italy and from the more Romanized provinces. The legionaries were mostly drawn from the less civilized provinces, especially the ones closest to the frontiers. In the third century C.E. the barbarization of the army would result in an army indifferent to Rome and its traditions. In the era of the five good emperors, however, the army was still a source of economic stability and a Romanizing agent. Men from the provinces and even barbarians joined the army to learn a trade and to gain Roman citizenship. Even so, the signs were ominous. Veterans from Julius Caesar's campaigns would hardly have recognized Hadrian's troops as Roman legionaries.

LIFE IN THE GOLDEN AGE: IMPERIAL ROME AND THE PROVINCES

Many people, both ancient and modern, have considered these years one of the happiest epochs in Western history. But popular accounts have also portrayed Rome as already decadent by the time of the five good emperors. If Rome was decadent, who kept the empire running? For that matter, can life in Rome itself be taken as representative of life in other parts of the empire? Rome was unique and must be seen as such. Rome no more resembled a provincial city like Cologne than New York resembles Keokuk, Iowa. Only when the uniqueness of Rome is understood in its own right can one turn to the provinces to obtain a full and reasonable picture of the empire under the five good emperors.

Rome was truly an extraordinary city, especially by ancient standards. It was enormous, with a population somewhere between 500,000 and 750,000. Although it could boast of stately palaces, noble buildings, and beautiful residential areas, most people lived in jerrybuilt apartment houses. Fire and crime were perennial problems even after Augustus created fire and urban police forces. Streets were narrow, and drainage was inadequate. During the republic sanitation had been a common problem. Numerous inscriptions record prohibitions against dumping human refuse and even cadavers on the grounds of sanctuaries and cemeteries. Under the empire this situation improved. By comparison with medieval and early modern European cities, Rome was a healthy enough place to live.

Rome was such a huge city that the surrounding countryside could not feed it. Because of the danger of starvation, the emperor, following republican practice, provided the citizen population with free grain for bread and, later, oil and wine. By feeding the citizenry, the emperor prevented bread riots caused by shortages and high prices. For the rest of the urban population who did not enjoy the rights of citizenship, the emperor provided grain at low prices. This measure was designed to prevent speculators from forcing up grain prices in times of crisis. By maintaining the grain supply, the emperor kept the favor of the people and ensured that Rome's poor and idle did not starve.

The emperor also entertained the Roman populace, often at vast expense. The most popular forms of public entertainment were gladiatorial contests and chariot racing. Gladiatorial fighting was originally an Etruscan funerary custom, a blood sacrifice for the dead. Many **gladiators** were criminals; some were the slaves of gladiatorial trainers; others were prisoners of war. Still others were free men who volunteered for the arena. Even women at times engaged in gladiatorial combat. Although some Romans protested gladiatorial fighting, most delighted in it. Not until the fifth century did Christianity put a stop to it.

The Romans were even more addicted to chariot racing than to gladiatorial shows. Two-horse and four-horse chariots ran a course of seven laps, about five miles. Four permanent teams, each with its own color, competed against each other. Some Romans claimed that people cared more about their favorite team than the race itself, but champion drivers won wide accolades. One, who won 1,462 of his 4,257 races, was honored by an inscription that proclaimed him champion of all charioteers.

Ordinary Romans left their own messages for posterity in the inscriptions that grace their graves. They were proud of their work and accomplishments, affectionate toward their families and friends, and eager to be remembered after death. Paprius Vitalis wrote an engaging inscription for his wife: "If there is anything good in the lower regions—I, however, finish a poor life without you—be happy there too, sweetest Thalassia."[5] Other inscriptions reflect individuals' personal philosophies: "All we who are dead below have become bones and ashes, but nothing else"[6] or "I was, I am not, I don't care." Though fond of brutal spectacles, the Romans, like people of all ages, had their loves and dreams.

In the provinces and even on the frontiers, the era of the five good emperors was one of extensive prosperity, especially in western Europe. The Roman army had beaten back the barbarians and exposed them to the civilizing effects of Roman traders. The resulting peace and security opened Britain, Gaul, Germany, and the lands of the Danube to immigration. Agriculture flourished as large tracts of land came under cultivation. Most of this land was in the hands of free tenant farmers. From the

Gladiatorial Games   Though hardly games, these gaudy spectacles often pitted gladiators against rare animals. Many of them, like the lion shown here, were formidable foes. Others, like the ostrich in the background, were probably not too ferocious. (*Galleria Borghese, Rome/Scala/Art Resource, NY*)

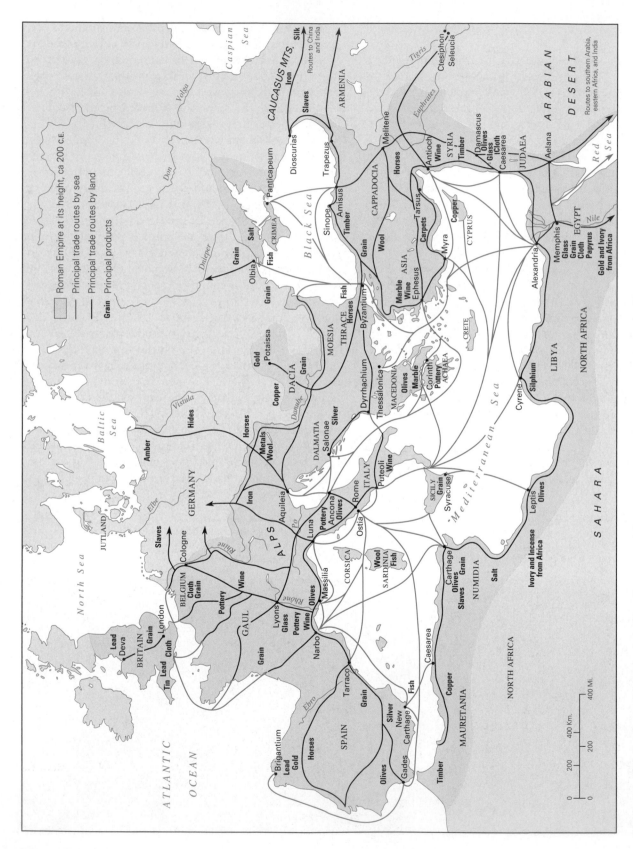

MAP 6.4 The Economic Aspect of the Pax Romana The Roman Empire was not merely a political and military organization but also an intricate economic network through which goods from Armenia and Syria were traded for Western products from as far away as Spain and Britain.

time of Augustus slavery had declined in the empire, as had the growth of latifundia (see page 155). Augustus and his successors encouraged the rise of free farmers. Under the five good emperors this trend continued, and the holders of small parcels of land thrived as never before. The emperors provided loans on easy terms to farmers, enabling them to rent land previously worked by slaves. They also permitted them to cultivate the new lands that were being opened up. Consequently, the small tenant farmer was becoming the backbone of Roman agriculture.

In continental Europe the army was largely responsible for the new burst of expansion. The areas where legions were stationed readily became Romanized. When legionaries retired from the army, they often settled where they had served. Since they had usually learned a trade in the army, they brought essential skills to areas that badly needed trained men. These veterans took their retirement pay and used it to set themselves up in business.

The eastern part of the empire also participated in the boom. The Roman navy had swept the sea of pirates, and Eastern merchants traded throughout the Mediterranean. The flow of goods and produce in the East matched that of the West. Venerable cities like Corinth, Antioch, and Ephesus flourished as rarely before. The cities of the East built extensively, bedecking themselves with new amphitheaters, temples, fountains, and public buildings. For the East this age was the heyday of the city. Life there grew ever richer and more comfortable.

Trade among the provinces increased dramatically. Britain and Belgium became prime grain producers, much of their harvests going to the armies of the Rhine. Britain's wool industry probably got its start under the Romans. Italy and southern Gaul produced wine in huge quantities. Roman colonists introduced the olive to southern Spain and northern Africa, an experiment so successful that these regions produced most of the oil consumed in the western empire. In the East Syrian farmers continued to cultivate the olive, and oil production reached an all-time high. Egypt was the prime grain producer of the East, and tons of Egyptian wheat went to feed the Roman populace. The Roman army in Mesopotamia consumed a high percentage of the raw materials and manufactured products of Syria and Asia Minor. The spread of trade meant the end of isolated and self-contained economies. By the time of the five good emperors, the empire had become an economic as well as a political reality (see Map 6.4).

One of the most striking features of this period was the growth of industry in the provinces. Cities in Gaul and Germany eclipsed the old Mediterranean manufacturing centers. Italian cities were particularly hard hit by this development. Cities like Arretium and Capua had dominated the production of glass, pottery, and bronze ware. Yet in the second century C.E. Gaul and Germany took over the pottery market. Lyons in Gaul, and later Cologne, became the new center of the glassmaking industry. The cities of Gaul were nearly unrivaled in the manufacture of bronze and brass. For the first time in history, northern Europe was able to rival the Mediterranean as a producer of manufactured goods. Europe had entered fully into the economic and cultural life of the Mediterranean world.

The age of the five good emperors was generally one of peace, progress, and prosperity. The work of the Romans in northern and western Europe was a permanent contribution to the history of Western society. This period was also one of consolidation. Roads and secure sea-lanes linked the empire in one vast web. The empire had become a commonwealth of cities, and urban life was its hallmark.

ROME AND THE EAST

Their march to empire and their growing interest in foreign peoples brought the Romans into contact with a world much larger than Europe and the Mediterranean. As early as the late republic, Roman commanders in the East encountered peoples who created order out of the chaos left by Alexander the Great and his Hellenistic successors. This meeting of West and East had two immediate effects. The first was a long military confrontation between the Romans and their Iranian neighbors. Second, Roman military expansion to the east coincided with Chinese expansion to the west, and the surprising result was a period when the major ancient civilizations of the world were in touch with one another (see "China and Rome," pages 189–190).

Romans Versus Iranians

When Roman armies moved into Mesopotamia in 92 B.C.E., they encountered the Parthians, a people who had entered the Iranian Plateau from Central Asia in the time of the Persian kings. The disintegration of Alexander's eastern holdings enabled them to reap the harvest of his victory. They created an empire that once stretched from Armenia and Babylonia in the west to the Hellenistic kingdom of Bactria in the east. They divided their realm into large provinces, or *satrapies,* and created a flexible political organization to administer their holdings. Unlike China, however, Parthia never had a sophisticated

ROMAN HISTORY AFTER AUGUSTUS

PERIOD	IMPORTANT EMPERORS	SIGNIFICANT EVENTS
Julio-Claudians 27 B.C.E.–68 C.E.	Augustus, 27 B.C.E.–14 C.E. Tiberius, 14–37 Caligula, 37–41 Claudius, 41–54 Nero, 54–68	Augustan settlement Beginning of the principate Birth and death of Jesus Expansion into northern and western Europe Creation of the imperial bureaucracy
Year of the Four Emperors 69	Nero Galba Otho Vitellius	Civil war Major breakdown of the concept of the principate
Flavians 69–96	Vespasian, 69–79 Titus, 79–81 Domitian, 81–96	Growing trend toward the concept of monarchy Defense and further consolidation of the European frontiers
Antonines 96–192	Nerva, 96–98 Trajan, 98–117 Hadrian, 117–138 Antoninus Pius, 138–161 Marcus Aurelius, 161–180 Commodus, 180–192	The "golden age"—the era of the "five good emperors" Economic prosperity Trade and growth of cities in northern Europe Beginning of barbarian menace on the frontiers
Severi 193–235	Septimius Severus, 193–211 Caracalla, 198–217 Elagabalus, 218–222 Severus Alexander, 222–235	Military monarchy All free men within the empire given Roman citizenship
"Barracks Emperors" 235–284	Twenty-two emperors in forty-nine years	Civil war Breakdown of the empire Barbarian invasions Severe economic decline
Tetrarchy 284–337	Diocletian, 284–305 Constantine, 306–337	Political recovery Autocracy Legalization of Christianity Transition to the Middle Ages in the West Birth of the Byzantine Empire in the East

bureaucracy. Nonetheless, the loose provincial organization enabled the Parthians to govern the many different peoples who inhabited their realm. The Romans marveled at Parthia's success, as the Greek geographer Strabo (ca 65 B.C.E.–19 C.E.) attests: "and now they rule so much territory and so many people that they have become in a way rivals of the Romans in the greatness of their empire."[7] In the process the Parthians won their place in history as the heirs of the Persian Empire.

Although Augustus sought peace with the Parthians, later Roman emperors, beginning with Nero in 58 C.E., struggled to wrest Armenia and Mesopotamia from them. Until their downfall in 226, the Parthians met the Roman advance to the east with iron and courage.

The Romans found nothing to celebrate in the eclipse of the Parthians, for their place was immediately taken by the Sasanids, a people indigenous to southern Iran. As early as 230 the Sasanids launched a campaign to the west, which the Romans blunted. The setback was only temporary, for in 256 the great Persian king Shapur over-ran Mesopotamia and the Roman province of Syria. Four years later Shapur defeated the legions of the emperor Valerian, whom he took prisoner. Thereafter the Romans and Sasanids fought long, bitter, and destructive wars in western Asia as the Romans battled to save their eastern provinces. Not until the reigns of Diocletian and Constantine was Roman rule again firmly established in western Asia.

Trade and Contact

Although warfare between Roman emperors and Iranian kings disrupted western Asia, it did not prevent the East-West trade that had become firmly established in Hellenistic times (see pages 133–134). Iran served as the crossroads of East and West, and the Parthians eagerly filled the role of middlemen. Chinese merchants sold their wares to the Parthians at the Stone Tower, located in modern Tashkurghan in Afghanistan. The Parthians then carried the goods overland to Mesopotamia or Egypt, where they were shipped throughout the Roman Empire. Silk was still a major shipment from East to West, along with such luxuries as gems, gold, silver, spices, and perfumes. The Romans traded glassware, statuettes, and slaves trained as jugglers and acrobats. The Parthians added exotic fruits, rare birds, ostrich eggs, and other dainties desired in China. (See the feature "Global Trade: Pottery" on pages 170–171.)

Rarely did a merchant travel the entire distance from China to Mesopotamia. The Parthians tried to prevent the Chinese and Romans from making direct contact—and thus learning how large a cut the Parthians took in commercial transactions. The trade fostered urban life in Parthia, as cities arose and prospered. The Parthians themselves became important consumers of goods, contributing to the volume of trade and reinforcing East-West commercial ties.

More than goods passed along these windswept roads. Ideas, religious lore, and artistic inspiration also traveled the entire route. A fine example of how ideas and artistic influence spread across long distances is a Parthian coin that caught the fancy of an artist in China. The coin bore an inscription—a practice the Parthians had adopted from the Greeks—and although the artist could not read it, he used the lettering as a motif on a bronze vessel. Similarly, thoughts, ideas, and literary works found ready audiences; Greek plays were performed at the court of the Parthian king. At a time when communication was difficult and often dangerous, trade routes were important avenues for the spread of knowledge about other societies.

This was also an era of exciting maritime exploration. Roman ships sailed from Egyptian ports to the mouth of the Indus River, where they traded local merchandise and wares imported by the Parthians. Merchants who made the voyage had to contend with wind, shoal waters, and pirates. Despite such dangers and discomforts, hardy mariners pushed into the Indian Ocean and beyond, reaching Malaya, Sumatra, and Java.

Direct maritime trade between China and the West began in the second century C.E. The period of this contact coincided with the era of Han greatness in China. It was the Han emperor Wu Ti who took the momentous step of opening the Silk Road to the Parthian empire. Indeed, a later Han emperor sent an ambassador directly to the Roman Empire by sea. The ambassador, Kan Ying, sailed to the Roman province of Syria, where during the reign of the Roman emperor Nerva (96–98) he became the first Chinese official to have a firsthand look at the Greco-Roman world. Kan Ying enjoyed himself thoroughly, and in 97 delivered a fascinating report of his travels to his emperor:

The inhabitants of that country are tall and well-proportioned, somewhat like the Chinese, whence they are called Ta-ts'in. *The country contains much gold, silver, and rare precious stones . . . corals, amber, glass . . . gold embroidered rugs and thin silk-cloth and asbestos cloth. All the rare gems of other foreign countries come from there. They make coins of gold and silver. Ten units of silver are worth one of gold. They traffic by sea with An-hsi (Parthia) and Tien-chu (India), the profit of which trade is ten-fold. They are honest in their transactions and there are no double prices. Cereals are always cheap. . . . Their kings always desired to send embassies to China, but the An-hsi (Parthians) wished to carry on trade with them in Chinese silks, and it is for this reason that they were cut off from communication.*[8]

THE EMPIRE IN CRISIS

The era of the five good emperors gave way to a period of chaos and stress. During the third century C.E. the Roman Empire was stunned by civil wars and barbarian invasions. By the time peace was restored, the economy was shattered, cities had shrunk in size, and agriculture was becoming manorial. In the disruption of the third century and the reconstruction of the fourth, the medieval world had its origins.

GLOBAL TRADE
POTERY

Today we often consider pottery in utilitarian and decorative terms, but it served a surprisingly large number of purposes in the ancient world. Families used earthen pottery for cooking and tableware, for storing grains and liquids, and for lamps. On a larger scale pottery was used for the transportation and protection of goods traded overseas.

The creation of pottery dates back to the Neolithic period. Pottery required few resources to make, as potters needed only abundant sources of good clay and wheels upon which to throw their vessels. Once

made, the pots were baked in specially constructed kilns. Although the whole process was relatively simple, skilled potters formed groups that made utensils for entire communities. Later innovations occurred when the artisans learned to glaze their pots by applying a varnish before baking them in a kiln.

The earliest potters focused on coarse ware: plain plates, cups, and cooking pots that remained virtually unchanged throughout antiquity. Increasingly, however, potters began to decorate these pieces with simple designs. In this way pottery became both functional and decorative. One of the most popular pieces was the amphora, a large two-handled jar with

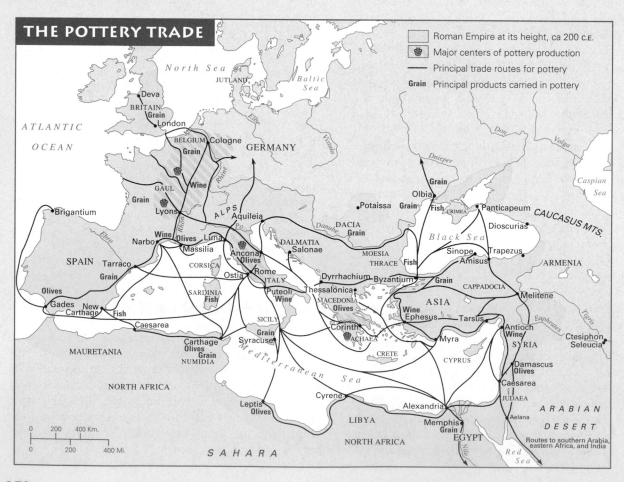

THE POTTERY TRADE

Roman Empire at its height, ca 200 C.E.

Major centers of pottery production

Principal trade routes for pottery

Grain Principal products carried in pottery

The Greeks captured Troy by concealing themselves in a wooden horse, which the Trojans pulled into the city. On this piece from a pot found in Mykonos, probably dating to the seventh century B.C.E., Greeks have just launched their attack from inside the horse. (Archaeological Receipts Fund, Athens)

a wide mouth, a round belly, and a base. It became the workhorse of maritime shipping because it protected contents from water and rodents, was easy and cheap to produce, and could be reused. Amphoras contained goods as different as wine and oil, spices and unguents, dried fish and pitch. The amphora's dependability and versatility kept it in use from the fourth century B.C.E. to the beginning of the Middle Ages.

In classical Greece individual potters sold their wares directly to local customers or traders; manufacturer and buyer alone determined the quantity of goods for sale and their price. In the Hellenistic and Roman periods amphoras became common throughout the Mediterranean and carried goods eastward to the Black Sea, Persian Gulf, and Red Sea. The Ptolemies of Egypt sent amphoras and their contents even farther, to Arabia, eastern Africa, and India. Thus merchants and mariners who had never seen the Mediterranean depended on these containers.

Other pots proved as useful as the amphora, and all became a medium of decorative art. By the eighth century B.C.E. Greek potters and artists began to decorate their wares by painting them with patterns and scenes from mythology, legend, and daily life. They portrayed episodes such as the chariot race at Patroclus's funeral (see page 110) or battles from the *Iliad* (see page 112). Some portrayed the gods, such as

Dionysos at sea (see page 104). These images widely spread knowledge of Greek religion and culture. In the West, especially the Etruscans in Italy and the Carthaginians in North Africa eagerly welcomed the pots, their decoration, and their ideas. The Hellenistic kings shipped these pots as far east as China. Pottery thus served as a cultural exchange among people scattered across huge portions of the globe.

The Romans took the manufacture of pottery to an advanced stage by introducing a wider range of vessels for new purposes. The Roman ceramic trade spread from Italy throughout the Mediterranean. The Roman army provides the best example of how this ordinary industry affected the broader culture. Especially on the European frontiers the army used its soldiers to produce the pottery it needed. These soldiers made their own Italian *terra sigallata,* which was noted for its smooth red glaze. Native potters immediately copied this style, thus giving rise to local industries. Indeed, terra sigallata remained the dominate pottery style in northern Europe until the seventh century C.E. When Roman soldiers retired, they often settled where they had served, especially if they could continue their trades. Such ordinary Romans added local ideas to their craft. This exchange resulted in a culture that was becoming European, rather than just Roman, and extended into Britain, France, the Low Countries, and southern Germany.

Civil Wars and Invasions in the Third Century

After the death of Marcus Aurelius, the last of the five good emperors, his son Commodus, a man totally unsuited to govern the empire, came to the throne. His misrule led to his murder and a renewal of civil war. After a brief but intense spasm of fighting, the African general Septimius Severus defeated other rival commanders and established the Severan dynasty (193–235 C.E.). Although Septimius Severus was able to stabilize the empire, his successors proved incapable of disciplining the legions. When the last of the Severi was killed by one of his own soldiers, the empire plunged into still another grim, destructive, and this time prolonged round of civil war.

Over twenty different emperors ascended the throne in the forty-nine years between 235 and 284, and many rebels died in the attempt to seize power. So many military commanders seized rule that the middle of the third century has become known as the age of the barracks emperors. The Augustan principate had become a military monarchy, and that monarchy was nakedly autocratic.

The first and most disastrous result of the civil wars was trouble on the frontiers. It was Rome's misfortune that this era of anarchy coincided with immense movements of barbarian peoples, still another example of the effects of mass migrations in ancient history, this time against one of the best organized empires of antiquity. Historians still dispute the precise reason for these migrations, though their immediate cause was pressure from tribes moving westward across Asia. In the sixth century C.E. Jordanes, a Christianized Goth, preserved the memory of innumerable wars among the barbarians in his *History of the Goths*. Goths fought Vandals; Huns fought Goths. Steadily the defeated and displaced tribes moved toward the Roman frontiers. Finally, like "a swarm of bees"—to use Jordanes's image—the Goths burst into Europe in 258 C.E.

When the barbarians reached the Rhine and Danube frontiers, they often found huge gaps in the Roman defenses. During much of the third century C.E. bands of Goths devastated the Balkans as far south as Greece. The Alamanni, a Germanic people, at one point entered Italy and reached Milan before they were beaten back. Meanwhile, the Franks, still another Germanic folk, invaded eastern and central Gaul and northeastern Spain. Saxons from Scandinavia sailed into the English Channel in search of loot. In the East the Sasanids overran Mesopotamia. If the Roman army had been guarding the borders instead of creating and destroying emperors, none of these invasions would have been possible. The bar-

racks emperors should be credited with one accomplishment, however: they fought barbarians when they were not fighting one other. Only that kept the empire from total ruin.

Reconstruction Under Diocletian and Constantine (284–337 C.E.)

At the close of the third century C.E. the emperor Diocletian (r. 284–305) put an end to the period of turmoil. Repairing the damage done in the third century was the major work of the emperor Constantine (r. 306–337) in the fourth. But the price was high.

Under Diocletian, the princeps became *dominus*—"lord." The emperor claimed that he was "the elect of God"—that he ruled because of God's favor. Constantine even claimed to be the equal of Jesus' first twelve followers.

No mere soldier but rather an adroit administrator, Diocletian gave serious thought to the empire's ailments. He recognized that the empire and its difficulties had become too great for one man to handle. He also realized that during the third century provincial governors had frequently used their positions to foment or participate in rebellions. To solve the first of these problems, Diocletian divided the empire into a western and an eastern half. Diocletian assumed direct control of the eastern part; he gave the rule of the western part to a colleague, along with the title *augustus,* which had become synonymous with *emperor.* Diocletian and his fellow augustus further delegated power by appointing two men to assist them. Each man was given the title *caesar* to indicate his exalted rank. Although this system is known as the **Tetrarchy** because four men ruled the empire, Diocletian was clearly the senior partner and final source of authority.

Each half of the empire was further split into two prefectures, each governed by a prefect responsible to an augustus. Diocletian reduced the power of the old provincial governors by dividing provinces into smaller units. He organized the prefectures into small administrative units called *dioceses,* which were in turn subdivided into small provinces. Provincial governors were also deprived of their military power, retaining only their civil and administrative duties.

Diocletian's political reforms were a momentous step. The Tetrarchy soon failed, but Diocletian's division of the empire into two parts became permanent. Constantine and later emperors tried hard but unsuccessfully to keep the empire together. Throughout the fourth century C.E. the eastern and the western sections drifted apart. In later centuries the western part witnessed the

The Arch of Constantine   To celebrate the victory that made him emperor, Constantine built his triumphal arch in Rome. Rather than decorate the arch with the inferior work of his own day, Constantine plundered other Roman monuments, including those of Trajan and Marcus Aurelius. (*C. M. Dixon/Photo Resources*)

fall of Roman government and the rise of barbarian kingdoms, while the eastern empire evolved into the majestic Byzantine Empire.

The most serious immediate matters confronting Diocletian and Constantine were economic, social, and religious. They needed additional revenues to support the army and the imperial court. Yet the wars and the barbarian invasions had caused widespread destruction and poverty. The fighting had struck a serious blow to Roman agriculture, which the emperors tried to revive. Christianity had become too strong either to ignore or to crush. The responses to these problems by Diocletian, Constantine, and their successors helped create the economic and social patterns that medieval Europe inherited.

The barracks emperors had dealt with economic hardship by depreciating the currency, cutting the silver content of coins until money was virtually worthless. As a result, the entire monetary system fell into ruin. In Egypt governors had to order bankers to accept imperial money. The immediate result was crippling inflation throughout the empire.

The empire was less capable of recovery than in earlier times. Wars and invasions had disrupted normal commerce and the means of production and had hit the cities especially hard. Markets were disrupted, and travel became dangerous. Craftsmen, artisans, and traders rapidly left devastated regions. Cities were no longer places where trade and industry thrived. The devastation of the countryside increased the difficulty of feeding and supplying the cities. So extensive was the destruction that many wondered whether the ravages could be repaired at all.

The response of Diocletian and Constantine to these problems was marked by compulsion, rigidity, and loss of individual freedom. Diocletian's attempt to curb inflation illustrates the methods of absolute monarchy. In a move unprecedented in Roman history, he issued an edict that fixed maximum prices and wages throughout the empire. The measure proved a failure because it was unrealistic as well as unenforceable.

With the monetary system in ruins, most imperial taxes became payable in kind—that is, in goods or produce instead of money. The major drawback of payment in kind is its demands on transportation. Goods have to be moved from where they are grown or manufactured to where they are needed. Accordingly, the emperors locked into their occupations all people involved in the growing, preparation, and transportation of food and essential commodities. A baker or shipper could not go into any other business, and his son took up the trade at his death. The late Roman Empire had a place for everyone, and everyone had a place.

The late Roman heritage to medieval Europe is most evident in agriculture. During the third century C.E. many free tenant farmers were killed or abandoned farms that had been ravaged in the fighting. Consequently, large tracts of land lay deserted. Great landlords with ample resources began to reclaim land and amass the huge estates that were the forerunners of medieval manors. In return for the protection and security that landlords could offer, free men and their families became the landlords' clients. To ensure a steady supply of labor for themselves, the landlords bound the free men to the soil. Henceforth they worked their patrons' land, not their own, and could not move elsewhere. Free men and women were in effect becoming serfs.

The Acceptance of Christianity

In religious affairs Constantine took the decisive step of recognizing Christianity as a legitimate religion. No longer would Christians suffer persecution for their beliefs as they had occasionally experienced earlier. Constantine himself died a Christian in 337. Why had the pagans persecuted Christians in the first place? Polytheism is by nature tolerant of new gods and accommodating in religious matters. Why was Christianity singled out for violence? These questions are still matters of scholarly debate, but some broad answers can be given.

A splendid approach to these problems has come from the eminent Italian scholar Marta Sordi.[9] Confronting a very complicated topic, she offers evidence that the Christians exaggerated the degree of pagan hostility to them and that most of the gory stories about the martyrs are fictitious. There were indeed some cases of pagan persecution of the Christians, but with few exceptions they were local and sporadic. Even Nero's notorious persecution was temporary and limited to Rome. No constant persecution of Christians occurred. Instead, pagans and Christians alike enjoyed long periods of tolerance and even friendship. Nonetheless, some pagans thought that Christians were atheists because they scorned the traditional pagan gods. Christians in fact either denied the existence of pagan gods or called them evil spirits. They went so far as to urge people not to worship pagan gods. In turn pagans, who believed in their gods as fervently as the Christians believed in their one god, feared that the gods would withdraw their favor from the Roman Empire because of Christian blasphemy.

At first many pagans genuinely misunderstood Christian practices and rites. Even educated and cultured people like the historian Tacitus opposed Christianity because they saw it as a bizarre new sect. Tacitus believed that Christians hated the whole human race. As a rule, early Christians kept to themselves. Romans distrusted and feared their exclusiveness, which seemed unsociable and even subversive. They thought the Lord's Supper, at which Christians said that they ate and drank the body and blood of Jesus, was an act of cannibalism. Pagans also thought that Christians indulged in immoral and indecent rituals. They considered Christianity one of the worst of the Eastern mystery cults, for one of the hallmarks of many of those cults was disgusting rituals.

Another source of misunderstanding was that the pagans did not demand that Christians *believe* in pagan gods. Greek and Roman religion was never a matter of belief or ethics. It was purely a religion of ritual. One of the clearest statements of pagan theological attitudes comes from the Roman senator Symmachus in the later fourth century C.E.: "We watch the same stars; heaven is the same for us all; the same universe envelops us: what importance is it in what way anyone looks for truth? It is impossible to arrive by one route at such a great secret."[10] Yet Roman religion was inseparable from the state. An attack on one was an attack on the other. The Romans were being no more fanatical or intolerant than the eighteenth-century English judge who declared the Christian religion part of the law of the land. All the pagans expected was performance of the ritual act, a small token of sacrifice. Those Christians who sacrificed went free, no matter what they personally believed.

As time went on, pagan hostility decreased. Pagans realized that Christians were not working to overthrow the state and that Jesus was no rival of Caesar. The emperor Trajan forbade his governors to hunt down Christians. Trajan admitted that he thought Christianity an abomination, but he preferred to leave Christians in peace.

The stress of the third century, however, seemed to some emperors the punishment of the gods. What else could account for such anarchy? With the empire threatened on every side, a few emperors thought that one way to appease the gods was by offering them the proper sacrifices. Such sacrifices would be a sign of loyalty to the empire, a show of Roman solidarity and religious piety. Consequently, a new wave of persecutions began out of desperation. Although the Christians depicted the emperor Diocletian as a fiend, he persecuted them in the hope that the gods would restore their blessings on Rome. Yet even these persecutions were never very widespread or long-lived; most pagans were not greatly sympathetic to the new round of persecutions. Pagan and Christian alike must have been relieved when Constantine legalized the Christian religion.

In time the Christian triumph would be complete. In 380 the emperor Theodosius made Christianity the official religion of the Roman Empire. At that point Christians began to persecute the pagans for their beliefs. History had come full circle.

The Construction of Constantinople

The triumph of Christianity was not the only event that made Constantine's reign a turning point in Roman history. Constantine took the bold step of building a new capital for the empire. Constantinople, the New Rome, was constructed on the site of Byzantium, an old Greek city on the Bosporus. Throughout the third century, emperors had found Rome and the West hard to defend. The eastern part of the empire was more easily defensible and escaped the worst of the barbarian devastation. It was wealthy and its urban life still vibrant. Moreover Christianity was more widespread in the East than in the West, and the city of Constantinople was intended to be a Christian center.

Late Antiquity

Recent scholars have identified the period from the third to the eighth centuries C.E. as "late antiquity," arguing that in this time the Mediterranean world witnessed tremendous religious, social, political, and intellectual ferment. The world of the pax Romana, over which Augustus had extended order, harmony, and security, clustered around the Mediterranean Sea. An aristocracy of uniform culture, taste, and language governed that world.

By about 500 C.E., however, a clear political, geographical, and cultural division existed between East and West. The East remained Mediterranean-centered, ruled by a Roman—that is, a Byzantine—emperor (see Chapter 8). It was primarily urban, and the sophisticated life of the populous cities was maintained by a lively trade. In the West Roman imperial power decayed, as did both commerce and cities. Economic life meant agriculture, and the increasingly isolated urban villa was the typical form of organized life.

The most important socioeconomic feature of late antiquity was the enormous and widening gulf between rich and poor. The western senatorial aristocracy, though still open to rising talent from below, was five times more wealthy than senators in the first century. In the East the average senator earned 120,000 gold pieces a year, but a merchant earned only 200 and a peasant a mere 5. An oppressive tax system forced many poor farmers to sell their farms, and fewer and fewer people accumulated more and more land.

The growth of Christianity was another major difference in the world of late antiquity. The religion grew in terms of both numbers of adherents and imperial acceptance. Christians offered a strong sense of community by maintaining their services in the third century, when traditional Roman public ceremonies were declining. Further, church leaders began to play larger roles in civil society. Between 200 and 500, as Roman civil officials neglected or were unable to perform their duties, or as they retreated from the cities for the luxury of their rural estates, Christian officials assumed public responsibilities. They ensured that pipes and aqueducts were repaired, arranged for relief when famine struck, and even organized defenses against barbarian attacks.

The Christianization of the Roman world left its mark on intellectual life as well. The aristocratic culture of late antiquity had sought leisure to develop the mind. By 600 the pagan, educated, senatorial elite had all but disappeared—or become church leaders. These leaders were busy, with little time for leisure. Nor did they wish for their followers to study pagan writers, lest they learn pagan superstitions. In 529 the emperor Justinian (see page 225) prohibited pagans from holding positions in public education. As a result the Academy of Athens, since its founding by Plato a center of education in the eastern Mediterranean, was closed.

SUMMARY

The Romans conquered the Mediterranean world only to find that conquest required them to change their way of life. Politically, their city-state constitution broke down and expired in the wars of the republic. Even so, men like Caesar and later Augustus sought new solutions to the problems confronting Rome. The result was a system of government capable of administering an empire with justice and fairness. Out of the failure of the republic arose the pax Romana of the empire.

The Roman Empire created by Augustus nearly collapsed before being restored by Diocletian and Constantine. Constantine's legalization and patronage of Christianity and his shift of the capital from Rome to Constantinople marked a new epoch in Western history as the ancient world gave way to the medieval. In the process the Roman Empire came into direct contact with its Asian neighbors, sometimes in anger but more often in peace. The force of Rome did not end with its political eclipse. The period known as late antiquity preserved the essence of Greco-Roman civilization and its assimilation of Judeo-Christian culture for the European Middle Ages and ultimately for the world.

The true heritage of Rome is its long tradition of law and freedom. Under Roman law and government, the empire enjoyed relative peace and security for extensive periods of time. Through Rome the best of ancient thought and culture was preserved to make its contribution to modern life. Perhaps no better epitaph for Rome can be found than the words of Virgil:

While rivers shall run to the sea,
While shadows shall move across the valleys of mountains,
While the heavens shall nourish the stars,
Always shall your honor and your name and your fame
endure.[11]

KEY TERMS

patricians	latifundia
plebeians	pax Romana
senate	First Triumvirate
praetor	princeps civitatis
provinces	Messiah
ius civile (civil law)	five good emperors
ius naturale (natural law)	gladiators
Struggle of the Orders	Tetrarchy
tribunes	
paterfamilias	
manumission	

NOTES

1. Polybius, *The Histories* 1.1.5. John Buckler is the translator of all uncited quotations from foreign languages in Chapter 6.
2. Sallust, *War with Catiline* 10.1–3.
3. Ovid, *Fasti* 2.535–539.
4. Plutarch, *Life of Tiberius Gracchus* 9.5–6.
5. *Corpus Inscriptionum Latinarum,* vol. 6 (Berlin: G. Reimer, 1882), no. 9792.
6. Ibid., vol. 6, no. 14672.
7. Strabo, 11.9.2.
8. Quoted in W. H. Schoff, *The Periplus of the Erythraean Sea* (London: Longmans, Green, 1912), p. 276.
9. See M. Sordi, *The Christians and the Roman Empire,* trans. A. Bedini (Norman: University of Oklahoma Press, 1986).
10. Symmachus, *Relations* 3.10.
11. Virgil, *Aeneid* 1.607–609.

SUGGESTED READING

H. H. Scullard gives a broad account of Roman history in *A History of the Roman World, 753–146 B.C.,* 4th ed. (1993). For the Etruscan place in Italian history, a good starting place is H. Barker and T. Rasmussen, *The Etruscans* (1997), and J. F. Hall, ed., *Etruscan Italy* (1998). Various works treat aspects of early Roman history, notably C. J. Smith, *Early Rome and Latium: Economy and Society, c. 1000 to 500 B.C.* (1996), and A. Gtandazzi, *The Foundation of Rome* (1997), which explores the mythology and history of Rome's origins. D. J. Gargola, *Lands, Laws, and Gods* (1995), examines how Roman magistrates regulated the public lands of Rome. Similar is N. Morley, *Metropolis and Hinterland* (1996), a study of how Romans and Italians integrated their economies between 200 B.C.E. and 200 C.E. Military aspects of this development are the concern of A. K. Goldsworthy, *The Roman Army at War, 100 B.C.–A.D. 200* (1996), and C. Brunn, ed., *The Roman Middle Republic, ca. 400–133 B.C.* (2000), though unfortunately many of the chapters in the latter are in foreign languages.

On Roman political developments, the place to start is A. N. Sherwin-White, *Roman Citizenship,* 2d ed. (1973), still a classic work. J. F. Gardner, *Being a Roman Citizen* (1993), is a broad work that includes material on ex-slaves, the lower classes, and much else. E. S. Gruen explores the effects of Greek ideas, literature, and learning on Roman life in *Studies in Greek Culture and Roman Policy* (1996). The topic of Roman intellectual and cultural growth has become a very popular pursuit and is the subject of E. Fantham, *Roman Literary Culture* (1996), and D. Feeney, *Literature and Religion at Rome* (1997).

Some good general treatments of the empire include J. Wacher, ed., *The Roman World,* 2 vols. (1987), and R. MacMullen, *Enemies of the Roman Order* (1993), which treats the ways in which the Romans dealt with aliens and sometimes hostile behavior within the empire. MacMullen's

Romanization in the Time of Augustus (2000) analyzes how the emperor spread Roman concepts throughout the empire. D. Noy, *Foreigners at Rome* (2000), studies the mingling of visitors and natives in the city. D. J. Breeze and B. Dobson, *Roman Officers and Frontiers* (1993), analyzes the careers of officers in the defense of the empire. A. Goldsworthy, *Roman Warfare* (2000), concisely treats warfare from republican to imperial times. B. Isaac, *The Near East Under Roman Rule* (1997), and H. Wolfram, *The Roman Empire and Its Germanic Peoples* (1997), deal with specific but broad parts of the empire.

K. D. White, *Roman Farming* (1970), remains the best treatment of the basic economic activity of most Romans. Work on Roman social history is quickly expanding and producing a wealth of material, including S. Treggiari, *Roman Marriage* (1991); B. Rawson and P. Weaver, *The Roman Family in Italy* (1997); R. A. Baumann, *Women and Politics in Ancient Rome* (1992); and E. Eyben, *Restless Youth in Ancient Rome* (1993). G. A. Williams, *Roman Homosexuality* (1999), is the first systematic study of the subject. Still the best treatment of economics and society combined is M. Rostovtzeff, *The Economic and Social History of the Roman Empire,* 2 vols., rev. ed. (1957).

Social aspects of the empire are the subject of L. A. Thompson, *Romans and Blacks* (1989), while J. Humphrey, *Roman Circuses and Chariot Racing* (1985), covers a favorite Roman sport. C. A. Barton, *The Sorrows of the Ancient Romans* (1993), makes a valiant attempt at explaining the Roman fascination with gladiatorial games. K. R. Bradley, *Slaves and Masters in the Roman Empire* (1988), discusses social controls in a slaveholding society.

Christianity, paganism, Judaism, and their relations have received great attention. The place to start is N. Hyldahl, *The History of Early Christianity* (1997). Other works include J. D. Crossen, *The Historical Jesus* (1992), and J. Meier, *A Marginal Jew* (1992), which examines the Jewish origins of Jesus. On the Gospels and early Christianity, the following works are among the most challenging: J. E. Powell, *The Evolution of the Gospel* (1994), and B. L. Mack, *The Lost Gospel of Q* (1993), which traces the earliest elements of the Gospels. Both S. G. Burnett, *From Christian Hebraism to Jewish Studies* (1996), and J. H. Hexter, *The Judaeo-Christian Tradition,* 2d ed. (1995), deal with Judaism and Christianity in their mutual impact. B. W. Winter, *After Paul Left Corinth* (2001), treats Paul's wider missionary work in the Roman world. L. V. Rutgers, *Subterranean Rome* (2000), serves as a guide to the catacombs. For early Christian society, see D. F. Sawyer, *Women and Religion in the First Christian Centuries* (1996); R. S. Kraemer et al., *Women and Christian Origins* (1998); and H. Moxnes, ed., *Constructing Early Christian Families* (1997).

On Constantine, the man and his significance, see R. MacMullen, *Constantine* (1988), and H. A. Pohlsander, *The Emperor Constantine* (1997). Good introductions to late antiquity are provided by P. Brown, *The World of Late Antiquity, A.D. 150–750* (1989), and R. L. Webste and M. Brown, eds., *The Transformation of the Roman World, A.D. 400–900* (1997).

TITUS FLAMININUS AND THE LIBERTY OF THE GREEKS

After his arrival in Greece in 197 B.C.E., Titus Flamininus defeated the Macedonians in Thessaly. He next sent his recommendations to the Roman senate on the terms of the peace agreement. The following year the senate sent him ten commissioners, who agreed with his ideas. The year 196 B.C.E. was also the occasion when the great Pan-Hellenic Isthmian games were regularly celebrated near Corinth. Many of the dignitaries and the most prominent people of the Hellenistic world were present. Among them was Flamininus, who came neither as a participant in the games nor solely as a spectator of them. Instead, he took the occasion to make a formal announcement about Roman policy. There in Isthmia he officially announced that Rome granted freedom to the Greeks. He assured his audience that Rome had not come as a conqueror. The eminent Greek biographer Plutarch has left a vivid account of the general response to this pronouncement.

Accordingly, at the Isthmian games, where a great throng of people were sitting in the stadium and watching the athletic contests (since, indeed, after many years Greece had at last ceased from wars waged in hopes of freedom, and was now holding festival in time of assured peace), the trumpet signalled a general silence, and the herald, coming forward into the midst of the spectators, made proclamation that the Roman senate and Titus Quintius Flamininus proconsular general, having conquered King Philip and the Macedonians, restored to freedom, without garrisons and without imposts, and to the enjoyment of their ancient laws, the Corinthians, the Locrians, the Phocians, the Euboeans, the Achaeans of Phthiotis, the Magnesians, the Thessalians, and the Perrhaebians. At first, then, the proclamation was by no means generally or distinctly heard, but there was a confused and tumultuous movement in the stadium of people who wondered what had been said, and asked one another questions about it, and called out to have the proclamation made again; but when silence had been restored, and the herald in tones that were louder than before and reached the ears of all, had recited the proclamation, a shout of joy arose, so incredibly loud that it reached the sea. The whole audience rose to their feet, and no heed was paid to the contending athletes, but all were eager to spring forward and greet and hail the saviour and champion of Greece.

And that which is often said of the volume and power of the human voice was then apparent to the eye. For ravens which chanced to be flying overhead fell down into the stadium. The cause of this was the rupture of the air; for when the voice is borne aloft loud and strong, the air is rent asunder by it and will not support flying creatures, but lets them fall, as if they were over a vacuum, unless, indeed, they are transfixed by a sort of blow, as of a weapon, and fall down dead. It is possible, too, that in such cases there is a whirling motion of the air, which becomes like a waterspout at sea with a refluent flow of the surges caused by their very volume.

Be that as it may, had not Titus, now that the spectacle was given up, at once foreseen the rush and press of the throng and taken himself away, it would seem that he could hardly have survived the concourse of so many people about him at once and from all sides. But when they were tired of shouting about his tent, and night was already come, then, with greetings and embraces for any friends and fellow citizens whom they saw, they betook themselves to banqueting and carousing with one another. And here, their pleasure naturally increasing, they moved to reason and discourse about Greece, saying that although she had waged many wars for the sake of her freedom, she had not yet obtained a more secure or more delightful exercise of it than now, when others had striven in her behalf, and she herself, almost without a drop of blood or a pang of grief, had borne away the fairest and most enviable of prizes. Verily, they would say, valour and wisdom are rare things among men, but the rarest of all blessings is the just man. For men like Agesilaüs, or Lysander, or Nicias, or Alcibiades could indeed conduct wars well, and understood how to be victorious commanders in battles by land and sea, but they would not use their successes so as to win legitimate favour and promote the right. Indeed, if one excepts the action at Marathon, the sea-fight at Salamis, Plataea, Thermopylae, and the achievements of Cimon at the Eurymedon and about Cyprus, Greece has fought all her battles to bring servitude upon herself, and every one of her trophies stands as a memorial of her own calamity and disgrace, since she owed her overthrow chiefly to the baseness and contentiousness of her leaders. Whereas men of another race, who were thought to have only slight sparks and insignificant traces of a common remote ancestry, from whom it was astonishing that any helpful word or purpose should be vouchsafed to Greece—these men underwent the greatest perils and hardships in order to rescue Greece and set her free from cruel despots and tyrants.

So ran the thoughts of the Greeks; and the acts of Titus were consonant with his proclamations. For at once he sent Lentulus to Asia to set Bargylia free, and Stertinius to Thrace to deliver the cities and islands there from Philip's garrisons. Moreover, Publius Villius sailed to have a conference with Antiochus concerning the freedom of the Greeks who were under his sway. Titus himself also paid a visit to Chalcis, and then sailed from there to Magnesia, removing their garrisons and restoring to the peoples their constitutions. He was also appointed master of ceremonies for the Nemeian games at Argos, where he conducted the festival in the best possible manner, and once more publicly proclaimed freedom to the Greeks. Then he visited the different cities, establishing among them law and order, abundant justice, concord, and mutual friendliness. He quieted their factions and restored their exiles, and plumed himself on

This coin provides a contemporary profile of Titus Flamininus, which also illustrates Roman realism in portraiture. *(Courtesy of the Trustees of the British Museum)*

his persuading and reconciling the Greeks more than on his conquest of the Macedonians, so that their freedom presently seemed to them the least of his benefactions. . . .

. . . In the case of Titus and the Romans, . . . gratitude for their benefactions to the Greeks brought them, not merely praises, but also confidence among all men and power, and justly too. For men not only received the officers appointed by them, but actually sent for them and invited them and put themselves in their hands. And this was true not only of peoples and cities, nay, even kings who had been wronged by other kings fled for refuge into the hands of Roman officials, so that in a short time—and perhaps there was also divine guidance in this—everything became subject to them. But Titus himself took most pride in his liberation of Greece.

QUESTIONS FOR ANALYSIS

1. Did Titus Flamininus really want peace for the Greeks, or was this a cynical propaganda gesture?

2. What caused Greek political difficulties in the first place?

3. Was the Greek response to Titus Flamininus's proclamation genuine and realistic?

Source: Reprinted by permission of the publishers and the Trustees of the Loeb Classical Library from *Plutarch: Volume X—Parallel Lives.* Loeb Classical Library Volume L 102, trans. B. Perrin (Cambridge, Mass.: Harvard University Press, 1921). The Loeb Classical Library® is a registered trademark of the President and Fellows of Harvard College.

The cave temples of Dunhuang are among the richest depositories of Buddhist art. These three clay statues, which attend the main Buddha in Cave 45 (eighth century C.E.), represent the Buddha's disciple Ananda, a bodhisattva, and a heavenly king. *(© Cultural Relics Data Center of China)*

7

EAST ASIA AND THE SPREAD OF BUDDHISM, CA 200 B.C.E.–800 C.E.

East Asia was transformed over the millennium from 200 B.C.E. to 800 C.E. In 200 B.C.E. there was only one advanced civilization in the region that had writing, iron technology, large cities, and complex state organizations. Over the course of the next several centuries, this situation changed dramatically as war, trade, diplomacy, missionary activity, and pursuit of learning brought increased contact among the peoples of the region. Buddhism came to provide a common set of ideas and visual images for the entire area. Chinese was widely used as an international language outside its native area.

Increased communication stimulated state formation in Central Asia, Tibet, Korea, Manchuria, and Japan. The new states usually adopted political models from China. Nevertheless, by 800 each of these regions was well on its way to developing a distinct political and cultural identity. Ancient China was treated in Chapter 4, but this is the first chapter to treat Korea and Japan.

- What were the consequences of long periods of strong centralized government in China to its own people and to their neighbors?
- How did elements of the cultures of China spread to neighboring lands?
- In what ways was the spread of Buddhism similar to the spread of other world religions?

These questions are addressed in this chapter.

THE AGE OF EMPIRE IN CHINA

In much the same period in which Rome created a huge empire, the Qin and Han rulers in China created an empire on a similar scale. Like the Roman Empire, the Chinese empire was put together through force of arms and held in place by sophisticated centralized administrative machinery.

The Qin Unification (221–206 B.C.E.)

The year 221 B.C.E. marks the beginning of the Chinese empire and has been called "by far the most important single date in Chinese history."[1] That year the state of Qin, the state that had adopted Legalist policies (see

181

Army of the First Emperor The thousands of life-size ceramic soldiers buried in pits about a half mile from the First Emperor's tomb help us imagine the Qin military machine. It was the Qin emperor's concern with the afterlife that led him to construct such a lifelike guard. The soldiers were orginally painted in bright colors, and they held real bronze weapons. *(Robert Harding Picture Library)*

pages 98–99), succeeded in defeating the last of its rivals, thus unifying China for the first time in many centuries. The king of Qin decided that the title "king" was not grand enough and invented the title "emperor" (*huangdi*). He called himself the First Emperor (Shihuangdi) in anticipation of a long line of successors.

The victory of the Qin state owed much to the program of Legalist administrative, economic, and military reforms that had been in place since the mid-fourth century B.C.E. Within Qin the power of the old nobility and the patriarchal family had been undermined to create instead a direct relationship between the ruler and his subjects, based on uniformly enforced laws and punishments.

Once Qin ruled all of China, the First Emperor and his shrewd Legalist minister Li Si embarked on a sweeping program of centralization that touched the lives of nearly everyone in China. To cripple the nobility of the defunct states, the First Emperor ordered them to leave their lands and move to the capital, Xianyang (near modern Xi'an). To administer the territory that had been seized, he dispatched officials, then controlled them through a mass of regulations, reporting requirements, and penalties for inadequate performance. These officials owed their power and positions entirely to the favor of the emperor and had no hereditary rights to their offices.

To harness the enormous human resources of his people, the First Emperor ordered a census of the population. Census information helped the imperial bureaucracy to plan its activities—to estimate the costs of public works, the tax revenues needed to pay for them, and the labor force available for military service and building projects. To make it easier to administer all regions uniformly,

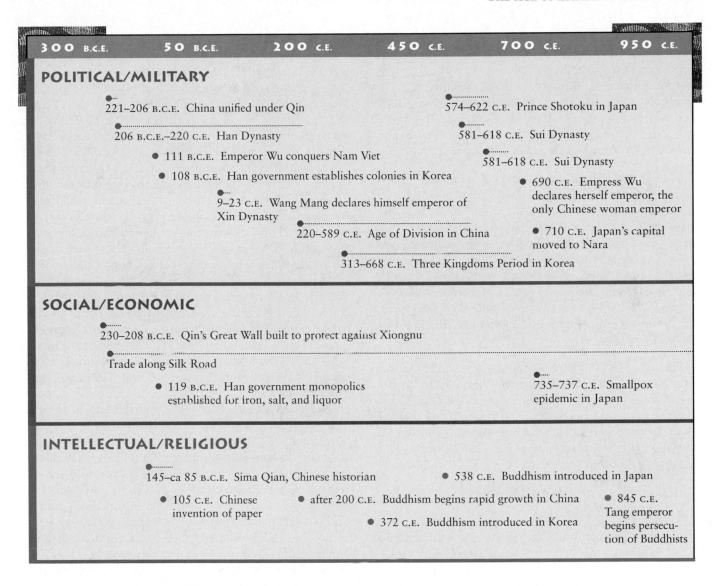

300 B.C.E.	50 B.C.E.	200 C.E.	450 C.E.	700 C.E.	950 C.E.

POLITICAL/MILITARY

221–206 B.C.E. China unified under Qin

206 B.C.E.–220 C.E. Han Dynasty

● 111 B.C.E. Emperor Wu conquers Nam Viet

● 108 B.C.E. Han government establishes colonies in Korea

9–23 C.E. Wang Mang declares himself emperor of Xin Dynasty

220–589 C.E. Age of Division in China

313–668 C.E. Three Kingdoms Period in Korea

574–622 C.E. Prince Shotoku in Japan

581–618 C.E. Sui Dynasty

581–618 C.E. Sui Dynasty

● 690 C.E. Empress Wu declares herself emperor, the only Chinese woman emperor

● 710 C.E. Japan's capital moved to Nara

SOCIAL/ECONOMIC

230–208 B.C.E. Qin's Great Wall built to protect against Xiongnu

Trade along Silk Road

● 119 B.C.E. Han government monopolies established for iron, salt, and liquor

735–737 C.E. Smallpox epidemic in Japan

INTELLECTUAL/RELIGIOUS

145–ca 85 B.C.E. Sima Qian, Chinese historian

● 105 C.E. Chinese invention of paper

● after 200 C.E. Buddhism begins rapid growth in China

● 372 C.E. Buddhism introduced in Korea

● 538 C.E. Buddhism introduced in Japan

● 845 C.E. Tang emperor begins persecution of Buddhists

the script was standardized, along with weights, measures, coinage, even the axle lengths of carts. Private possession of arms was outlawed in order to make it more difficult for subjects to rebel. To make it easier for Qin armies to move rapidly, thousands of miles of roads were built. Investment was also made in canals that could connect rivers, making it possible to travel long distances by boat. Most of the labor on these projects came from peasants performing required corvée labor or convicts working their sentences.

Some twentieth-century Chinese historians glorified the First Emperor as a bold conqueror who let no obstacle stop him, but the traditional evaluation of him was almost entirely negative. For centuries Chinese historians castigated him as a cruel, arbitrary, impetuous, suspicious, and superstitious megalomaniac. Hundreds of thousands of subjects were drafted to build the **Great Wall,** a rammed-earth fortification along the northern border between the Qin realm and the land controlled by the nomadic Xiongnu. After Li Si complained that scholars used records of the past to denigrate the emperor's achievements and undermine popular support, the emperor had all writings other than useful manuals on topics such as agriculture, medicine, and divination collected and burned. As a result of this massive book burning, many ancient texts were lost and others could be only partly reconstructed.

Three times assassins tried to kill the First Emperor, and perhaps in consequence he became obsessed with discovering the secrets of immortality. He spent lavishly on a tomb designed to protect him in the afterlife. Although the central chambers have not yet been excavated, archaeologists have unearthed in nearby pits thousands of life-size terra-cotta figures of armed soldiers and horses lined up to protect him.

Like Ashoka in India a few decades earlier, the First Emperor erected many stone inscriptions to inform his subjects of his goals and accomplishments. But he did not share Ashoka's modesty. On one stone he described the conquest of the other states in this way:

The six states, insatiable and perverse, would not make an end of slaughter, until, pitying the people, the emperor sent troops to punish the wicked and display his might. His penalties were just, his actions true, his power spread far, all submitted to his rule. He wiped out tyrants, rescued the common people, brought peace to the four corners of the earth. His enlightened laws spread far and wide as examples to All Under Heaven until the end of time. Great is he indeed! The whole universe obeys his sagacious will; his subjects praise his achievements and have asked to inscribe them on stone for posterity.[2]

After the First Emperor died in 210 B.C.E., the Qin state unraveled. The Legalist institutions designed to concentrate power in the hands of the ruler made the stability of the government dependent on the strength and character of the emperor. The First Emperor's heir was murdered by his younger brother, and uprisings soon followed.

The Glory of the Han Dynasty (206 B.C.E.–220 C.E.)

The eventual victor in the struggle for power that ensued was Liu Bang, a man who had served the Qin as a minor local official. Liu Bang (known in history as Emperor Gaozu, r. 202–195 B.C.E.) did not disband the centralized government created by the Qin, but he did remove its most unpopular features. Harsh laws were abrogated, taxes were sharply reduced, and a policy of laissez faire was adopted in an effort to promote economic recovery. At first large and nearly autonomous fiefs were given out to the new emperor's relatives, but by the middle of the second century B.C.E. most of these kingdoms had been eliminated, and almost all Han territory was under direct imperial rule. With policies of this sort, relative peace, and the extension of China's frontiers, the Chinese population grew rapidly in the first two centuries of the Han Dynasty. The census of 2 C.E. recorded a population of 58 million, the earliest indication of the large size of China's population.

In contrast to the Qin promotion of Legalism, the Han came to promote Confucianism and recruit officials on the basis of their Confucian learning or Confucian moral qualities. Under the most activist of the Han emperors, Emperor Wu (the "Martial Emperor," r. 141–87 B.C.E.), Confucian scholars were given a privileged position. Emperor Wu decreed that officials should be selected on the basis of Confucian virtues, and he established a national university to train officials in the Confucian classics. As the prestige and influence of government posts rose, men of wealth and local standing throughout the country began to compete to gain recognition for their Confucian learning and character so that they could gain access to office. The Han government's efforts to recruit men trained in the Confucian classics marked the beginning of the Confucian scholar-official system, one of the most distinctive features of imperial China. Chinese officials, imbued with Confucian values, did not comply automatically with the policies of the ruler, seeing their highest duty to maintain their stance as critics of the government. Still, most of those selected as Confucian scholars came from landholding families, much like those who staffed the Roman government. (On the distinctive form of Confucianism that developed in Han times, see page 187.)

The Han government was supported largely by the taxes and labor service demanded of farmers, but this revenue never seemed adequate to its needs. To pay for his military campaigns, Emperor Wu took over the minting of coins, confiscated the land of nobles, sold offices and titles, and increased taxes on private businesses. A widespread suspicion of commerce—from both moral and political perspectives—made it easy to levy especially heavy assessments on merchants. Boats, carts, shops, and other facilities were made subject to property taxes. The worst blow to businessmen, however, was the government's decision to enter into market competition with them by selling the commodities that had been collected as taxes. In 119 B.C.E. government monopolies were established in the production of iron, salt, and liquor. These enterprises had previously been sources of great profit for private entrepreneurs. Large-scale grain dealing also had been a profitable business, which the government now took over under the guise of equitable marketing. Grain was to be bought where it was plentiful and its price low and to be either stored in granaries or transported to areas of scarcity. This procedure was supposed to eliminate speculation in grain, provide more constant prices, and bring profit to the government.

One weakness in the Han system of government lay in the institution of hereditary succession of the throne from father to son. During the last decades of the first century B.C.E., this pattern of succession led to a series of child emperors. **Regents,** generally selected from the families of the boys' mothers, were appointed to rule in their place. One of these regents, Wang Mang, ended up deposing an infant emperor and declared himself emperor of the Xin (New) Dynasty (9–23 C.E.). Though condemned as a usurper, Wang Mang was a learned Confucian scholar who wished to implement policies described in the classics. He renamed offices, asserted state ownership of forests and swamps, built ritual halls, revived public granaries, outlawed slavery, limited private landholdings, and cut court expenses. Some of his policies, such as issuing new coins and nationalizing gold, led to economic turmoil. Matters were made worse when the Yellow River broke through its dikes and shifted course from north to south, driving millions of peasants from their homes as huge regions were flooded. Rebellion broke out, and in the ensuing warfare a Han imperial clansman succeeded in re-establishing the Han Dynasty.

Inner Asia and the Silk Road

The difficulty of defending against the nomadic pastoral peoples to the north is a major reason China came to favor a centralized bureaucratic form of government. From the third century B.C.E. on, China needed a government capable of massive defense.

Beginning long before the Han Dynasty, China's contacts with its northern neighbors had involved both trade and military conflict. China's neighbors sought Chinese products such as silk and lacquer ware. When they did not have goods to trade or trading relations were disrupted, raiding was considered an acceptable alternative in the tribal cultures of the region. Chinese sources speak of defending against raids of "barbarians" from Shang times (ca 1500–ca 1050 B.C.E.) on, but not until the rise of nomadism in the mid-Zhou period (fifth–fourth centuries B.C.E.) did the horsemen of the north become China's main military threat.

The economy of these nomads was based on raising sheep, goats, camels, and horses. Families lived in tents that could be taken down and moved north in summer and south in winter as groups of families moved in search of pasture. Herds were tended on horseback, and everyone learned to ride from a young age. Especially awesome from the Chinese perspective was the ability of nomad horsemen to shoot arrows while riding horseback. The typical social structure of the steppe nomads was fluid, with family and clan units linked through loyalty to tribal chiefs selected for their military prowess. Charismatic tribal leaders could form large coalitions and mobilize the entire society for war.

Xiongnu Metalwork   The metal ornaments of the Xiongnu provide convincing evidence that they were in contact with nomadic pastoralists farther west in Asia, such as the Scythians, who also fashioned metal plaques and buckles in animal designs. This buckle or ornament is made of gold and is about three inches tall. *(The Metropolitan Museum of Art, Gift of J. Pierpont Morgan, 1917. [17.190.1672] Photograph © 1981 The Metropolitan Museum of Art)*

Chinese farmers and Inner Asian herders had such different modes of life that it is not surprising that they had little respect for each other. For most of the imperial period, Chinese farmers looked on the northern non-Chinese horsemen as gangs of bullies who thought robbing was easier than working for a living. The nomads identified glory with military might and viewed farmers as contemptible weaklings.

In the late third century B.C.E. the Xiongnu (known in the West as the Huns) formed the first great confederation of nomadic tribes (see Map 7.1). The Qin's Great Wall was built to defend against them, and the Qin sent out huge armies against them. The early Han emperors tried to make peace with them, offering generous gifts of silk, rice, cash, and even imperial princesses as brides. But these policies were controversial, since critics thought they merely strengthened the enemy. Certainly Xiongnu power did not decline, and in 166 B.C.E. 140,000 Xiongnu raided to within a hundred miles of the Chinese capital.

Emperor Wu decided that China had to push the Xiongnu back. He sent several armies of 100,000 to

300,000 troops deep into Xiongnu territory. These costly campaigns were of limited value since the Xiongnu were a moving target: fighting nomads was not like attacking walled cities. If the Xiongnu did not want to fight the Chinese troops, they simply moved their camps. To try to find allies and horses, Emperor Wu turned his attention west, toward Central Asia. From the envoy he sent into Bactria, Parthia, and Ferghana in 139 B.C.E., the Chinese learned for the first time of other civilized states comparable to China (see Map 7.1). The envoy described Ferghana as an urban society ten thousand li (about three thousand miles) west of China, where grapes were grown for wine and the horses were particularly fine. Concerning Parthia, he was impressed by the use of silver coins stamped with the image of the king's face. These regions,

he reported, were familiar with Chinese products, especially silk, and did a brisk trade in them.

Emperor Wu sent an army into Ferghana and gained recognition of Chinese overlordship in the area, thus obtaining control over the trade routes across Central Asia, commonly called the **Silk Road.** The city-states along this route did not resist the Chinese presence. They could carry out the trade on which they depended more conveniently with Chinese garrisons to protect them than with rival tribes raiding them.

At the same time, Emperor Wu sent troops into northern Korea to establish military districts that would flank the Xiongnu on their eastern border. By 111 B.C.E. the Han government also had extended its rule south into what is now northern Vietnam. Thus during Emperor

MAP 7.1 The Han Empire   The Han Dynasty asserted sovereignty over vast regions from Korea in the east to Central Asia in the west and Vietnam in the south. Once garrisons were established, traders were quick to follow, leading to considerable spread of Chinese material culture in East Asia. Chinese goods, especially silk, were in demand far beyond East Asia, promoting long-distance trade across Eurasia.

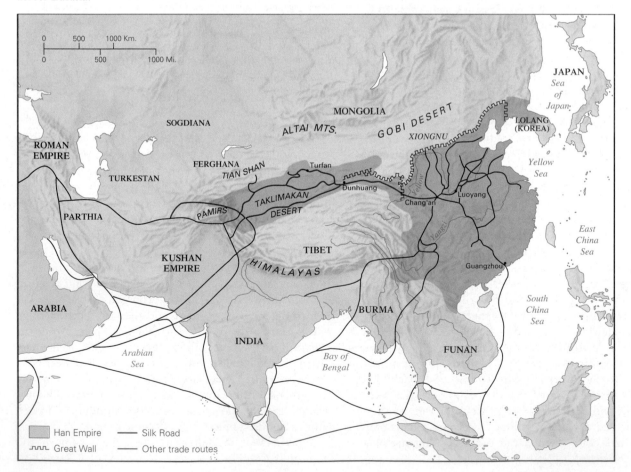

Wu's reign, the territorial reach of the Han state was vastly extended.

During the Han Dynasty, China developed a **tributary system** to regulate contact with foreign powers. States and tribes beyond its borders sent envoys bearing gifts and received gifts in return. Over the course of the dynasty the Han government's outlay on these gifts was huge, perhaps as much as 10 percent of state revenue. In 25 B.C.E., for instance, the government gave tributary states twenty thousand rolls of silk cloth and about twenty thousand pounds of silk floss. Although the tribute system was a financial burden to the Chinese, it reduced the cost of defense and offered China confirmation that it was the center of the civilized world.

The silk given to the Xiongnu and other northern tributaries often entered the trading networks of Sogdian, Parthian, and Indian merchants, who carried it by caravans all the way to Rome. There was a market both for skeins of silk thread and for silk cloth woven in Chinese or Syrian workshops. Caravans returning to China carried gold, horses, and occasionally handicrafts of West Asian origin, such as glass beads and cups. Through the trade along the Silk Road, the Chinese learned of new foodstuffs, including walnuts, pomegranates, sesame, and coriander, all of which came to be grown in China. This trade was largely carried by the two-humped Bactrian camel, which had been bred in Central Asia since the first century B.C.E. With a heavy coat of hair to withstand the bitter cold of winter, each camel could carry about five hundred pounds of cargo.

Maintaining a military presence so far from the center of China threatened to bankrupt the Han government. It tried all sorts of cost-saving policies, such as setting up self-supporting military colonies and recruiting Xiongnu tribes to serve as auxiliary forces, but none of these measures solved the government's financial problems. Vast government horse farms tried to supply the army with horses, but the number of horses was never adequate.

Han Intellectual and Cultural Life

Confucianism made a comeback during the Han Dynasty, but it was a changed Confucianism. Although Confucian texts had fed the First Emperor's bonfires, some dedicated scholars had hidden their books, and others had memorized whole works: one ninety-year-old man was able to recite two books virtually in their entirety. The ancient books recovered in this way came to be regarded as **Confucian classics,** or canonical scriptures, containing the wisdom of the past. Scholars studied them with piety and attempted to make them more useful as sources of moral guidance by writing commentaries on them. Many Confucian scholars specialized in a single classic, with teachers passing on to their disciples their understanding of each sentence in the work. Other Han Confucians went to the opposite extreme, developing comprehensive cosmological theories that explained the world in terms of cyclical flows of yin and yang and the five phases (fire, water, earth, metal, and wood). Some used these theories to elevate the role of the emperor, who alone had the capacity to link the realms of Heaven, earth, and man. Natural disasters such as floods or earthquakes were viewed as portents that the emperor had failed in his role to maintain the proper balance among the forces of Heaven and earth.

Another important intellectual accomplishment of the Han Dynasty was the development of historical writing. The Chinese, like the Greeks, conceived of history as broader and more complex than the mere chronicling of events. Sima Qian (145–ca 85 B.C.E.) wrote a comprehensive history of China from the time of the mythical sage-kings of high antiquity to his own day, dividing his account into a chronology recounting political events, biographies of key individuals, and treatises on subjects such as geography, taxation, and court rituals. Like the Greek Thucydides (see page 116), Sima Qian believed fervently in visiting the sites where history was made, examining artifacts, and questioning people about events. He was also interested in China's geographical variations, local customs, and local history. As an official of the emperor, he had access to important people and documents and to the imperial library. The result of his research, ten years in the making, was ***Records of the Grand Historian,*** a massive work of literary and historical genius.

Sima Qian's work set the standard for Chinese historical writing, although most of the histories modeled after it covered only a single dynasty. The first of these was the work of three members of the Ban family in the first century C.E. The Ban family included China's first woman historian and scholar, Ban Zhao, who not only helped compile the history but also wrote poems and essays, notably *Admonitions for Women,* on the education of girls.

Han men of letters often had varied interests. Zhang Heng (78–139 C.E.), like the Hellenistic philosopher Eratosthenes, delved deeply into astronomy and concluded that the world is round, not flat as many of his contemporaries assumed. Not content to speculate, Zhang Heng built models to test his theories. He even designed a seismograph capable of discerning the direction in which an earthquake was taking place, though not its severity.

Perhaps the most momentous product of Han imagination was the invention of paper, which the Chinese traditionally date to 105 C.E. Scribes had previously written on strips of bamboo and wood. Fine books for the wealthy were written on silk rolls. Cai Lun, to whom the Chinese attribute the invention of paper, worked the fibers of rags, hemp, bark, and other scraps into sheets of paper. Though much less durable than wood, paper was far cheaper than silk and became a convenient means of conveying the written word. By the fifth century paper was in common use, preparing the way for the invention of printing.

Han art and literature reveal a fascination with omens, portents, spirits, immortals, and occult forces. Emperor Wu tried to make contact with the world of gods and immortals through elaborate sacrifices, and welcomed astrologers, alchemists, seers, and shamans to his court. He marveled at stories of the paradise of the Queen Mother of the West and the exploits of the Yellow Emperor, who had taken his entire court with him when he ascended to the realm of the immortals. When Wang Mang was consolidating his power, his allies kept discovering portents that a major change was to take place, an indication that they assumed most people believed in messages from Heaven. Much of this interest in immortality and communicating with the spirit world was absorbed into the emerging religion of Daoism, which also drew on the philosophical ideas of Laozi and Zhuangzi.

Daily Life in Han China

How were ordinary people's lives affected by the creation of a huge bureaucratic empire? The lucky ones who lived in Chang'an or Luoyang, the great cities of the empire, got to enjoy the material benefits of increased long-distance trade and a boom in the production of luxury goods.

The government did not promote trade per se. The Confucian elite, like ancient Hebrew wise men, considered trade necessary but lowly. Agriculture and crafts were more honorable because they produced something, but merchants merely took advantage of others' shortages to make profits as middlemen. This attitude justified the government's takeover of the grain, iron, and salt businesses. Still, the government indirectly promoted commerce by building cities and roads. Cities attracted merchants, who set up shop in stalls in the markets, grouped together according to their wares. All the butchers, for example, congregated in one part of the market, each trying to outsell the others. The markets were also the haunts of entertainers and fortunetellers. People flocked to puppet shows and performances of jugglers and acrobats. Magic shows dazzled the impressionable, and cockfighting appealed to bloody tastes. The markets

also were used for the execution of criminals, to serve as a warning to the onlooking crowd.

Government patronage helped maintain the quality of craftsmanship in the cities. By the beginning of the first century C.E., China had about fifty state-run ironworking factories. These factories smelted iron ore into ingots before turning it over to the craftsmen, who worked it into tools and other articles. Han workmen turned out iron plowshares, agricultural tools with wooden handles, and weapons and armor. Han metalsmiths were massproducing superb crossbows long before the crossbow was dreamed of in Europe.

Iron was replacing bronze in tools, but bronzeworkers still turned out a host of goods. Bronze was prized for jewelry, mirrors, dishes, and spoons. Bronze was also used for minting coins and for precision tools such as carpenters' rules and adjustable wrenches. Surviving bronze gear-and-cog wheels bear eloquent testimony to the sophistication of Han machinery. Han craftsmen also developed lacquer work to a fine art. Because **lacquer** (made from the sap of the lac tree) creates a hard surface that withstands water, it was ideal for cups, dishes, toilet articles, and even parts of carriages.

The bulk of the population in Han times and even into the twentieth century consisted of peasants living in villages of a few hundred households. Since the Han empire, much like the contemporaneous Roman Empire, drew its strength from a large population of free peasants who contributed both taxes and labor services to the state, the government had to try to keep peasants independent and productive. The economic insecurity of small holders was described by one official in 178 B.C.E. in terms that could well have been repeated in most later dynasties:

They labor at plowing in the spring and hoeing in the summer, harvesting in the autumn and storing foodstuff in winter, cutting wood, performing labour service for the local government, all the while exposed to the dust of spring, the heat of summer, the storms of autumn, and the chill of winter. Through all four seasons they never get a day off. They need funds to cover such obligations as entertaining guests, burying the dead, visiting the sick, caring for orphans, and bringing up the young. No matter how hard they work they can be ruined by floods or droughts, or cruel and arbitrary officials who impose taxes at the wrong times or keep changing their orders. When taxes fall due, those with produce have to sell it at half price [to raise the needed cash], and those without [anything to sell] have to borrow [at such high rates] they will have to pay back twice what they borrowed. Some as a consequence sell their lands and houses, even their children and grandchildren.[3]

To fight peasant poverty, the government kept land taxes low, provided relief, aided migration, and promoted improvements in agriculture, such as planting two crops in alternate rows and planting a succession of carefully timed crops. Still, many peasants were left to choose between migration to areas where new lands could be opened and quasi-servile status as the dependents of a magnate. Throughout the Han period, Chinese migrants in search of land to till pushed into frontier areas, expanding Chinese domination at the expense of other ethnic groups, especially in central and south China.

Pressure on small farmers also encouraged technical innovation. The new and more effective plow introduced during the Han period was fitted with two plowshares, guided by a pair of handles, and typically pulled by a pair of oxen. Farmers used fans to blow the chaff from kernels of grain, and they used either mortars and pestles or hand mills to grind grain into flour. The Chinese also developed an elaborate system using long hammers to mill grain and pound earth. Eventually, the hammers were driven by waterpower, long before waterpower was put to this use in Europe. Irrigation was aided by brick-faced wells and pumping devices ranging from a simple pole with an attached bucket and counterweight to a sophisticated machine worked by foot. Chinese metalworking was the most advanced in the world at the time. In contrast to Roman blacksmiths, who hammered heated iron to make wrought iron tools, the Chinese knew how to liquefy iron and pour it into molds, producing tools with a higher carbon content that were harder and more durable.

Smaller and smaller farms were in part a product of the inheritance system. By Han times the common practice in China was equal division of family property among all sons, even if the resulting plots of land were tiny. This was a major change from the primogeniture of the Zhou period, when a single heir, generally the eldest son, succeeded to both aristocratic titles and responsibility to maintain ancestral rites. As free buying and selling of land spread, dividing family property became customary, making downward social mobility due to declining farm sizes quite common.

The Chinese family in Han times was much like the Roman one (see page 152) and the Indian one (see pages 314–315). In all three societies, senior males had great authority, marriages were arranged by parents, and brides normally joined their husbands' families. In Han times the Confucian virtue of filial piety was glorified to an exceptional degree, and the brief *Classic of Filial Piety*, which claimed that filial piety was the root of all virtue, gained wide circulation. The virtues of loyal wives and devoted mothers were extolled in the *Biographies of Exemplary Women*, which told the stories of women from

Plowing with Oxen   Farmers in Han times began to use animal-drawn plows, as depicted here in a stone relief. Improvements in agricultural technology in Han times aided the geographical expansion of Chinese civilization and the growth of the Chinese population. *(From Patricia Buckley Ebrey,* The Cambridge Illustrated History of China, *1996)*

China's past who were notable for giving their husbands good advice, knowing how to educate their sons, and sacrificing themselves when forced to choose between their fathers and husbands. The book also contained a few cautionary tales of scheming, jealous, manipulative women who brought destruction to all around them. Another notable text on women's education was written by the woman scholar Ban Zhao. Her *Admonitions for Women* urged girls to master the seven virtues appropriate to women: humility, resignation, subservience, self-abasement, obedience, cleanliness, and industry.

China and Rome

The empires of China and Rome have often been compared. Both were large, complex states governed by monarchs, bureaucracies, and standing armies. Both reached directly to the people through taxation and conscription policies. Both invested in infrastructure such as roads and waterworks. Both had to work hard to keep land from becoming too concentrated in the hands of wealthy magnates, which would threaten the empires' tax base. In both empires people in areas that came under political domination were attracted to the conquerors' material goods, productive techniques, and other cultural products, which led to gradual cultural assimilation. Both China and Rome had similar frontier problems and tried similar solutions, such as using "barbarian" auxiliaries and settling soldier-colonists.

Nevertheless, the differences between Rome and Han China are worth as much notice as the similarities. The Roman Empire was linguistically and culturally more diverse than China. In China there was only one written language, but in the Roman Empire people still wrote in Greek and several other languages, and people from the East could claim more ancient civilizations. Politically, the dynastic principle was stronger in China than in Rome. Han emperors were never chosen by the army or any institution comparable to the Roman senate, nor were there any republican ideals in China. In contrast to the exclusive notion of the Roman citizen, all those in conquered areas who were willing to assimilate were encouraged to do so. The social and economic structures also differed in the two empires. In Rome slavery was much more important than in China, and merchants were more favored. Over time these differences put Chinese and Roman social and political development on rather different trajectories.

The Fall of the Han and the Age of Division

In the second century C.E. the Han government suffered a series of blows. The succession of child emperors allowed maternal relatives of the emperors to dominate the court. Emperors turned to eunuch palace servants for help in ousting the consort families, only to find that the **eunuchs** were just as difficult to control. In 166 and 169 scholars who had denounced the eunuchs were arrested, killed, or banished from the capital and official life. Then in 184 a millenarian religious sect rose in massive revolt. The armies raised to suppress the rebels soon took to fighting among themselves. In 189 one general slaughtered two thousand eunuchs in the palace and took the Han emperor captive. After years of fighting, a stalemate was reached, with three warlords each controlling distinct territories—one in the north, one in the southeast, and one in the southwest. In 220 one of them forced the

last of the Han emperors to abdicate, formally ending the Han Dynasty.

The period after the fall of the Han Dynasty is often referred to as the **Age of Division** (220–589). A brief reunification from 280 to 316 came to an end when non-Chinese who had been settling in north China since Han times seized the opportunity afforded by the political turmoil to take power. For the next two and a half centuries north China was ruled by one or more non-Chinese dynasties (the Northern Dynasties), while the south was ruled by a sequence of four short-lived Chinese dynasties, all of which were centered in the area of the present-day city of Nanjing (the Southern Dynasties).

One difficulty the rulers of the south faced was that a hereditary aristocracy entrenched itself in the higher reaches of officialdom. These families judged themselves and others on the basis of their ancestors, intermarried only with families of equivalent pedigree, and compiled lists and genealogies of the most eminent families. They saw themselves as maintaining the high culture of the Han, and many excelled in writing poetry or engaging in witty conversation. At the same time many were able to build up great landed estates worked by destitute refugees from the north. At court they often looked on the emperors of the successive dynasties as upstarts—as military men rather than men of culture. (See the feature "Individuals in Society: Tao Qian.")

Constructing a capital at Nanjing, south of the Yangzi River, had a beneficial effect on the economic development of the south. To pay for an army and to support the imperial court and aristocracy in a style that matched their pretensions, the government had to expand the area of taxable agricultural land, whether through settling migrants or converting the local inhabitants into taxpayers. The south, with its temperate climate and ample supply of water, offered nearly unlimited possibilities for such development.

In the north none of the states set up by non-Chinese lasted very long until the Xianbei set up the Northern Wei Dynasty (386–534). During the second half of the fifth century, the Northern Wei rulers adopted a series of policies designed to strengthen the state. To promote agricultural production, they instituted an "equal-field" system to distribute land to peasants. The capital was moved from the northern border near the Great Wall to the ancient city of Luoyang. Chinese-style clothing and customs were adopted at court, and Chinese was made the official language. The tribesmen, who still formed the main military force, saw themselves marginalized by these policies and rebelled in 524. For the next fifty years north China was torn apart by struggles for power.

INDIVIDUALS IN SOCIETY

TAO QIAN

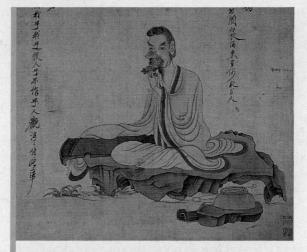

Tao Qian (detail), by Chen Hongshou (1599–1652).
(Honolulu Academy of Arts, Purchase 1954 [1912.1])

One of China's best-loved poets, Tao Qian (365–427), lived during the turbulent period of the Age of Division. Like others of his social class, he was expected to take a post with the government. For a few years Tao worked for two or three of the generals who were busy putting down rebellions in this unsettled period, but he found the work distasteful. After a period at home to mourn his mother according to Confucian norms, he accepted an appointment as magistrate of the county of Pengce, but he held it for only eighty-two days. He is reported to have quit his post rather than entertain a visiting inspector, saying, "How could I bend my waist to this village buffoon for five pecks of rice!"

By the age of forty Tao Qian quit government service altogether and supported himself by farming. Over the next twenty-two years he experienced all the hardships of a farmer's life: the backbreaking work in the fields, crop failure through drought or insect pests, hunger for himself and his family, and, as he grew older, periods of sickness. He was not just any farmer, however, and he maintained social relations with men of education and rank, exchanging visits and poems with them.

In his poems Tao Qian celebrates the quiet life and the pleasures of books, music, and wine:

I try a cup and all my concerns become remote.
Another cup and suddenly I forget even Heaven.
But is Heaven really far from this state?
*Nothing is better than to trust your true self.**

Tao Qian also idealized the farming life, describing its pleasures as a genuine alternative to public service. In his poems he portrays himself as a happy rustic:

Since youth I have not fit the common mold,
Instinctively loving the mountains and hills.
By mistake I fell into the dusty net
And was gone from home for thirty years.
A bird in a cage yearns for its native woods;
A fish in a pond remembers its old mountain pool.
Now I shall clear some land at the edge of the
*   southern wild*
And, clinging to the simple life, return to garden
*   and field,*
To my two-acre lot,
My thatched cottage of eight or nine rooms
With elms and willows shading the back
And peach and plum trees growing in a row in the
*   front.*†

Tao also wrote a eulogy for himself to be read at his funeral:

My rice bin and wine gourd have often been empty. I have worn thin clothing in winter. Yet I have gone happily to draw water from the spring and have sung with a load of firewood on my back. In my humble thatched hut, I performed my chores day and night. As spring and autumn alternated, I busied myself in the fields. I sowed, I plowed. Things grew and multiplied. I pleased myself with the seven string zither. In winter I soaked in the sun, and in summer I bathed in the springs. I have had little rest from my work, yet my mind has always been at leisure. I enjoyed Heaven's gifts and accepted my lot, until I lived out my years.‡

QUESTIONS FOR ANALYSIS

1. Does Tao Qian seem more Confucian or more Daoist?
2. Does Tao reveal much of his personality in his writings? Which traits would have made him appealing to an educated audience?

* From "Drinking Alone in the Rainy Season." Translated by Patricia Ebrey.
† From "On Returning to My Garden and Fields." Translated by Patricia Ebrey.
‡ William H. Nienhauser, Jr., ed., *The Indiana Companion to Traditional Chinese Literature* (Bloomington: Indiana University Press, 1986), p. 676.

For the ordinary person, the Age of Division was notable for the spread of Buddhism, discussed in the following section, and for an increasing proportion of people who were not fully free (slaves, serfs, and the like). The governments after the Han dynasty were not very successful in curbing the tendencies that pushed the poor to accept demeaned status as serfs or soldiers in private armies. In addition, it had long been the custom of the northern pastoral tribes to enslave those they captured; the Northern Wei Dynasty and its successors sometimes enslaved the residents of entire cities. In 554, when the city of Jiangling was taken, 100,000 civilians were enslaved and distributed to generals and officials.

THE SPREAD OF BUDDHISM OUT OF INDIA

In much the same period that Christianity was spreading out of its original home in ancient Israel, Buddhism was spreading beyond India. And just as Christianity was shaped by its contact with cultures in the different areas into which it spread, leading to several distinct forms of Christianity, the forms of Buddhism that spread via Central Asia to China, Korea, and Japan are distinct from those that spread from India to Sri Lanka, Tibet, and Southeast Asia.

Central Asia is a loose term used to refer to the vast area between the ancient civilizations of Persia, India, and China. Modern political borders, in fact, are a product of competition among the British, Russians, and Chinese for empire in the mid-nineteenth century and have relatively little to do with the earlier history of the region. Through most of recorded history, the region was ethnically and culturally diverse; it was home to both urban centers, especially at the oases along the Silk Road, and pastoralists in the mountains and grasslands (see Map 7.2).

Under Ashoka (see pages 71–72) Buddhism began to spread to Central Asia. This continued under the Kushan empire (ca 50–250 C.E.), especially under their greatest king, Kanishka I (ca 100 C.E.). In this region, where the influence of Greek art was strong, artists began to depict the Buddha in human form. Over the next several centuries most of the city-states of Central Asia became centers of Buddhism, from Bamiyan, northwest of Kabul, to Kucha, Khotan, Loulan, Turfan, and Dunhuang (see Map 7.2). Because the remarkable Buddhist civilization of Central Asia was later supplanted by Islam, it was not until early in the twentieth century that European ar-

chaeologists discovered its traces. The main sites yielded not only numerous Buddhist paintings but also thousands of texts in a variety of languages. In Khotan, for instance, an Indian language was used for administrative purposes long after the fall of the Kushan empire. Other texts were in various Persian languages, showing the cultural mix of the region.

The form of Buddhism that spread from Central Asia to China, Japan, and Korea was called Mahayana, which means "Great Vehicle" (see page 67), reflecting the claims of its adherents to a more inclusive form of the religion. One branch of Mahayana taught that reality is "empty" (that is, nothing exists independently, of itself). Emptiness was seen as an absolute, underlying all phenomena, which are themselves transient and illusory. Another branch held that ultimate reality is consciousness, that everything is produced by the mind.

But more important than the metaphysical literature of Mahayana Buddhism was its devotional side, influenced by the Iranian religions then prevalent in Central Asia. The Buddha came to be treated as a god, the head of an expanding pantheon of other Buddhas and bodhisattvas (Buddhas-to-be). These Buddhas and bodhisattvas became objects of worship, especially the Buddha Amitabha and the bodhisattva Avalokitesvara (Guanyin in Chinese, Kannon in Japanese). With the growth of this pantheon, Buddhism became as much a religion for laypeople as for monks and nuns.

The first translators of Buddhist texts into Chinese were not Indians but Parthians, Sogdians, and Kushans from Central Asia. For instance, one of the major interpreters of Buddhism in China was the eminent Central Asian monk Kumarajiva (350–413), from Kucha, who settled in Chang'an and directed several thousand monks in the translation of Buddhist texts.

Why did Buddhism find so many adherents in China during the three centuries after the fall of the Han Dynasty in 220? There were no forced conversions, but still the religion spread rapidly, having something to offer everyone. To Chinese scholars the Buddhist concepts of the transmigration of souls, karma, and nirvana posed a stimulating intellectual challenge. To rulers the Buddhist religion offered a source of magical power and a political tool to unite Chinese and non-Chinese. To the middle and lower classes Buddhism's egalitarianism came as a breath of fresh air. The lower orders of society had as much chance as the elite to live according to the Buddha's precepts, and faith and devotion alone could lead to salvation. For many, regardless of their social status, Buddhism's promise of eternal bliss as the reward for a just and upright life was deeply comforting. In a rough

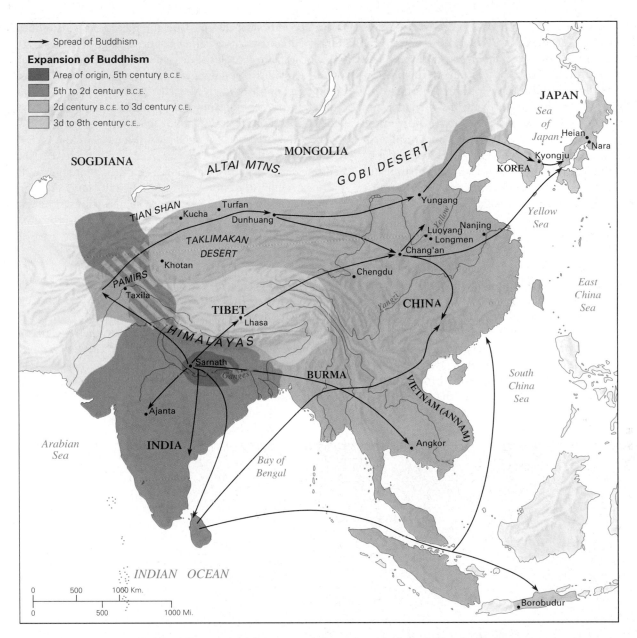

MAP 7.2 The Spread of Buddhism   Buddhism spread throughout India in Ashoka's time and beyond India in later centuries. The different forms of Buddhism found in Asia today reflect this history. The Mahayana Buddhism of Japan came via Central Asia, China, and Korea, with a secondary later route through Tibet. The Theravada Buddhism of Southeast Asia came directly from India and indirectly through Sri Lanka.

and tumultuous age Buddhism's emphasis on kindness, charity, and the value of human life offered hope of a better life on earth. As in India, Buddhism posed no threat to the social order, and the elite who were drawn to Buddhism encouraged its spread to people of all classes. (See

the feature "Listening to the Past: Copying Buddhist Sutras" on pages 206–207.)

The monastic establishment grew rapidly in China. Like their Christian counterparts in medieval Europe, Buddhist monasteries played an active role in social, economic, and political life. By 477 there were said to be 6,478 Buddhist temples and 77,258 monks and nuns in the north. Some decades later south China had 2,846 temples and 82,700 clerics. Given the importance of family lines in China, becoming a monk was a big step, since a man had to give up his surname and take a vow of celibacy, thus cutting himself off from the ancestral cult. Those not ready to become monks or nuns could pursue Buddhist goals as pious laypeople by performing devotional acts and making contributions toward the construction or beautification of temples. Among the most generous patrons were rulers in both north and south.

In China women turned to Buddhism as readily as men. Although incarnation as a female was considered lower than incarnation as a male, it was also viewed as temporary, and women were encouraged to pursue salvation on terms nearly equal to men. Joining a nunnery became an alternative for women who did not want to marry or did not want to stay with their husbands' families in widowhood.

Buddhism had an enormous impact on the visual arts in China, especially sculpture and painting. The merchants and missionaries from Central Asia who brought Buddhism to China also brought ideas about the construction and decoration of temples and the depiction of Buddhas and bodhisattvas. The earlier Chinese had not set up statues of gods in temples, but now they decorated temples with a profusion of images. The great cave temples at Yungang, sponsored by the Northern Wei rulers in the fifth century, contain huge Buddha figures in stone, the tallest a standing Buddha about seventy feet high.

Buddhist temples were just as splendid in the cities. One author described the ceremony held each year on the seventh day of the fourth month at the largest monastery in the northern capital, Luoyang. All the Buddhist statues in the city, more than a thousand altogether, would be brought to the monastery, and the emperor would come in person to scatter flowers as part of the Great Blessing ceremony.

The gold and the flowers dazzled in the sun, and the jewelled canopies floated like clouds; there were forests of banners and a fog of incense, and the Buddhist music of India shook heaven and earth. All kinds of entertainers and trick riders performed shoulder to shoulder. Virtuous hosts of famous monks came, carrying their staves; there were crowds of the Buddhist faithful, holding flowers; horsemen and carriages were packed beside each other in an endless mass.[4]

The Great Buddha This huge Buddha at Yungang in north China is about forty-five feet tall. It is the most massive of some 51,000 Buddhist images carved into the surface of a cliff that extends for over half a mile. Buddhist missionaries from northern India and Afghanistan brought to China the idea of carving images of the Buddha into stone cliffs. The arrival of Buddhism greatly enriched Chinese art traditions, especially sculpture. *(Werner Forman/Art Resource, NY)*

Not everyone was won over by Buddhist teachings. Critics of Buddhism labeled it immoral, unsuited to China, and a threat to the state since monastery land was not taxed. Twice in the north orders were issued to close monasteries and force monks and nuns to return to lay life, but these suppressions did not last long, and no attempt was made to suppress private Buddhist belief.

THE SECOND CHINESE EMPIRE: SUI (581–618) AND TANG (618–907)

In the 570s and 580s, the long period of division in China was brought to an end under the leadership of the Sui Dynasty. Yang Jian, who both founded the Sui Dynasty and oversaw the reunification of China, was from a Chinese family that had intermarried with the non-Chinese elite of the north. He and his successor were both activists. The conquest of the south involved naval as well as land attacks, with thousands of ships on both sides contending for control of the Yangzi River. The Sui reasserted Chinese control over northern Vietnam and campaigned into Korea and against the new force on the steppe, the Turks. The Sui tried to strengthen central control of the government by curtailing the power of local officials to appoint their own subordinates and by instituting competitive written examinations for the selection of officials. Although only a few officials were selected through examinations during the Sui Dynasty, the groundwork was laid for the civil service examinations that came to dominate the lives of educated men in later centuries.

The crowning achievement of the Sui Dynasty was the **Grand Canal,** which connected the Yellow and Yangzi Rivers. The canal facilitated the shipping of tax grain from the recently developed Yangzi Delta to the centers of political and military power in north China. Henceforth the rice-growing Yangzi Valley and south China played an ever more influential role in the country's economic and political life, strengthening China's internal cohesion. Accordingly, maritime trade with Southeast Asia, India, and areas farther west became more important to the Chinese economy and culture.

Despite these accomplishments, the Sui Dynasty lasted for only two reigns. The ambitious projects of the two Sui emperors led to exhaustion and unrest, and in the ensuing warfare Li Yuan, a Chinese from the same northwest aristocratic circles as the founder of the Sui, seized the throne.

The Tang Dynasty (618–907)

The dynasty founded by Li Yuan, the Tang, was one of the high points of traditional Chinese civilization. Especially during this dynasty's first century, China and its capital, Chang'an, were the cultural centers of East Asia, drawing in merchants, pilgrims, missionaries, and students to a degree never matched before or after. This position of strength gave the Chinese the confidence to be open to what they could learn from the outside world, leading to a more cosmopolitan culture than in any other period before the twentieth century.

The first two Tang rulers, Taizu (r. 618–626) and Taizong (r. 626–649), were able monarchs. They extended the equal-field and militia systems of the Northern Dynasties. Using the militia plus auxiliary troops composed of Turks, Tanguts, Khitans, and other non-Chinese led by their own chieftains, they campaigned into Korea, Vietnam, and Central Asia. In 630 the Chinese turned against their former allies the Turks, gaining territory from them and winning for Taizong the title of Great Khan, so that he was for a short period simultaneously head of both the Chinese and the Inner Asian empires.

In the civil sphere Tang accomplishments far outstripped anything known in Europe until the growth of national states in the seventeenth century. Tang emperors subdivided the administration of the empire into departments, much like the numerous agencies of modern governments. They built on Sui precedent, using examinations to select officials. Although only about thirty men were recruited this way each year, the prestige of passing the examinations became so great that more and more men attempted them. Candidates had to master the Confucian classics and the rules of poetry, and they had to be able to discuss practical administrative and political matters. Government schools were founded to prepare the sons of officials and other young men for service as officials.

The mid-Tang Dynasty saw two women—Empress Wu and Consort Yang Guifei—rise to positions of great political power through their hold on rulers. Empress Wu was the consort of the weak and sickly Emperor Gaozong. After Gaozong suffered a stroke in 660, she took full charge. She continued to rule after Gaozong's death, summarily deposing her own two sons and dealing harshly with all opponents. In 690 she proclaimed herself emperor, the only woman who took that title in Chinese history. To gain support, she circulated a Buddhist sutra that predicted the imminent reincarnation of the Buddha Maitreya as a female monarch, during whose reign the world would be free of illness, worry, and disaster. Although despised by later historians as an evil usurper,

Empress Wu was an effective leader who suppressed rebellions, organized aggressive military campaigns, and brought new groups into the bureaucracy. It was not until she was over eighty that members of the court were able to force her out in favor of her son.

Her grandson, the emperor Xuanzong (r. 713–756), in his early years presided over a brilliant court. In his later years, however, after he became enamored of his consort Yang Guifei, he let things slide. This was a period when ample and rounded proportions were much admired in women, and Yang was said to be such a full-figured beauty. The emperor allowed her to place friends and relatives in important positions in the government. One of her favorites was the able general An Lushan, who after getting into a quarrel with Yang's brother over control of the government, rebelled in 755. Xuanzong had to flee the capital, and the troops that accompanied him forced him to have Yang Guifei executed.

But more lay behind this crisis than imperial foolishness. The Tang had outgrown the institutions of the Northern Dynasties, such as the equal-field system. As a result of population growth, in many areas individual allotment holders received only a fraction of the land they were due but still had to pay the standard per capita tax. Peasants fled their allotments, thereby reducing government income. Moreover, as defense problems grew, especially warfare with the Turks and Tibetans, the militia system proved inadequate. A system of military districts had to be established along the borders, and defense was entrusted to professional armies and non-Chinese auxiliary troops. It was because An Lushan commanded one of these armies that he was able to launch an attack on the central government.

The rebellion of An Lushan was devastating to the Tang Dynasty. Peace was restored only by calling on the Uighurs, a Turkish people allied with the Tang, who looted the capital after taking it from the rebels. After the rebellion was finally suppressed in 763, the central government never regained control of the military provinces on the frontiers and had to keep meeting the extortionate demands of the Uighurs. Abandoning the equal-field system and instituting taxes based on actual landholdings helped restore the government's finances, but many military governors came to treat their provinces as hereditary kingdoms and withheld tax returns from the central government. In addition, eunuchs gained increasing power at court and were able to prevent both the emperors and Confucian officials from doing much about them.

Tang Culture

A vibrant, outward-looking culture flourished under the conditions created by reuniting north and south China. The Tang capital cities of Chang'an and Luoyang became great metropolises, with Chang'an and its suburbs growing to more than 2 million inhabitants. The cities

---

Urban Planning Chang'an in Tang times attracted merchants, pilgrims, and students from all over East Asia. The city was laid out on a square grid (*left*) and divided into walled wards, the gates to which were closed at night. Temples were found throughout the city, but trade was limited to two government-supervised markets. In the eighth and ninth centuries the Japanese copied the general plan of Chang'an in designing their capitals—first at Nara, then at Heian, shown on the right. (*From* Cradles of Civilization: China [*Weldon Owen Pty Limited, Australia*])

CHANG'AN

HEIAN (KYOTO)

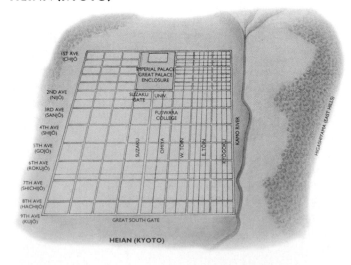

were laid out in rectangular grids and contained a hundred-odd "blocks" inside their walls. Each block was a mini-city divided by many lanes and surrounded by a wall. Like the gates of the city, the gates of each block were locked at night.

In these cosmopolitan cities, knowledge of the outside world was stimulated by the presence of envoys, merchants, and pilgrims who came from the neighboring states in Central Asia, Japan, Korea, and Tibet. Because of the presence of foreign merchants, many religions were practiced, including Nestorian Christianity, Manichaeism, Zoroastrianism, Judaism, and Islam, although none of them spread into the Chinese population the way Buddhism had a few centuries earlier. Foreign fashions in hair and clothing were often copied, and foreign amusements such as polo found followings among the well-to-do. The introduction of new instruments and tunes from India, Iran, and Central Asia brought about a major transformation in Chinese music.

The Tang Dynasty was the great age of Chinese poetry. Skill in composing poetry was tested in the civil service examinations, and educated men had to be able to compose poems at social gatherings. The pain of parting, the joys of nature, and the pleasures of wine and friendship were all common poetic topics. One of Li Bo's (701–762) most famous poems describes an evening of drinking with only the moon and his shadow for company:

A cup of wine, under the flowering trees;
I drink alone, for no friend is near.
Raising my cup I beckon the bright moon,
For he, with my shadow, will make three men.
The moon, alas, is no drinker of wine;
Listless, my shadow creeps about at my side.
. . .
Now we are drunk, each goes his way.
May we long share our odd, inanimate feast,
And we meet at last on the cloudy River of the sky.[5]

Less cheerful but no less talented was Bo Juyi (772–846). He felt the weight of his responsibilities as governor of several small provinces and sympathized with the people whom he governed. At times Bo Juyi worried about whether he was doing his job justly and well:

From these high walls I look at the town below
Where the natives of Pa cluster like a swarm of flies.
How can I govern these people and lead them aright?
I cannot even understand what they say.
But at least I am glad, now that the taxes are in,
To learn that in my province there is no discontent.[6]

In Tang times Buddhism fully penetrated Chinese daily life. Stories of Buddhist origin became widely known,

Woman Playing Polo   Notions of what makes women attractive have changed over the course of Chinese history. The figurines found in Tang tombs reveal that active women, even ones playing polo on horseback like the one shown here, were viewed as appealing. In earlier and later periods, female beauty was identified with slender waists and delicate faces, but in Tang times women were admired for their plump bodies and full faces. *(Chinese. Equestrienne [tomb figure], buff earthenware with traces of polychromy, first half 8th cent., 56.2 × 48.2 cm. Gift of Mrs. Pauline Palmer Wood, 1970.1073. Photograph © 1998, The Art Institute of Chicago)*

and Buddhist festivals, such as the festival for feeding hungry ghosts in the summer, became among the most popular holidays.

Buddhist monasteries had become an important part of everyday life. They ran schools for children. In remote areas they provided lodging for travelers, and in towns they offered literati places to gather for social occasions such as going-away parties. Merchants entrusted their money and wares to monasteries for safekeeping, in effect transforming the monasteries into banks and warehouses. The wealthy often donated money or land to support temples and monasteries, making monasteries among the largest landlords. Formidable in wealth and number, monasteries became influential participants in politics, rivaling the power of the traditional Chinese landed families.

At the intellectual and religious level, Buddhism was developing in a distinctly Chinese direction. Two schools that thrived were Pure Land and Chan. **Pure Land** appealed to laypeople. The simple act of paying homage to the Buddha Amitabha and his chief helper, the compassionate bodhisattva Guanyin, could lead to rebirth in Amitabha's paradise, the Pure Land. Among the educated elite the **Chan** school (known in Japan as Zen) gained popularity. Chan teachings rejected the authority of the sutras and claimed the superiority of mind-to-mind transmission of Buddhist truths. The "northern" tradition emphasized meditation and monastic discipline. The "southern" tradition was even more iconoclastic, holding that enlightenment could be achieved suddenly through insight into one's own true nature, even without prolonged meditation.

In the late Tang period, opposition to Buddhism re-emerged. In addition to concerns about the fiscal impact of removing so much land from the tax rolls and so many men from the labor service force, there were concerns about Buddhism's foreign origins. Probably as China's international position weakened, xenophobia emerged. In 845 the Tang emperor began a full-scale persecution. More than 4,600 monasteries and 40,000 temples and shrines were destroyed, and more than 260,000 Buddhist monks and nuns were forced to return to secular life. Other religious groups were also brought under state control. Although this ban was lifted after a few years, the monastic establishment never fully recovered. Among laypeople Buddhism retained a strong hold, and basic Buddhist ideas like karma and reincarnation had become fully incorporated into everyday Chinese thinking. But Buddhism was never again as central to Chinese life.

THE EAST ASIAN CULTURAL SPHERE

During the millennium from 200 B.C.E. to 800 C.E. China exerted a powerful influence on its immediate neighbors, who began forming states of their own. By Tang times China was surrounded by independent states in Korea, Manchuria, Tibet, the area that is now Yunnan province, Vietnam, and Japan. All of these states were much smaller than China in area and population, making China by far the dominant force politically and culturally until the late nineteenth century. Nevertheless, each of these separate states developed a strong sense of uniqueness and independent identity.

The earliest information about each of these countries is found in Chinese sources. The expansionist tendencies of the Han Dynasty began the process of bringing the knowledge of Chinese civilization to both Korea and Vietnam, but even in those cases much cultural borrowing was entirely voluntary as the elite, merchants, and craftsmen of surrounding areas adopted the techniques, ideas, and practices they found appealing. In Japan much of the process of absorbing elements of Chinese culture was mediated via Korea. In Korea, Japan, and Vietnam the fine arts—painting, architecture, and ceramics, in particular—were all strongly influenced by Chinese models. Tibet, though a thorn in the side of Tang China, was as much in the Indian sphere of influence as the Chinese and thus followed a somewhat different trajectory. Most significant, it never adopted Chinese characters as its written language, nor was it as influenced by Chinese artistic styles as other areas. Moreover the form of Buddhism that became dominant in Tibet came directly from India, not through Central Asia and China.

In each area literate, Chinese-style culture was at first an upper-level overlay over an indigenous cultural base, but in time many products and ideas adopted from China became incorporated into everyday life, ranging from written language to chopsticks and soy sauce. By the eighth century the Chinese language was a written lingua franca among educated people throughout East Asia. Vietnamese, Koreans, and Japanese could communicate in writing when they could not understand each other's spoken languages, and envoys to Chang'an could carry out "brush conversations" with each other. The books that educated people read included the Chinese classics, histories, and poetry, as well as Buddhist texts translated into Chinese.

Korea

Korea is a mountainous peninsula some 600 miles long and 125 to 200 miles wide extending south from Manchuria and Siberia. At its tip it is about 120 miles from Japan (see Map 7.3). Archaeological, linguistic, and anthropological evidence indicates that the Korean people share a common ethnic origin with other peoples of North Asia, including those of Manchuria, Siberia, and Japan. Linguistically they are not related to the Chinese.

Bronze and iron technology spread from China in the Zhou period, and Korean mythology reflects links to China. According to one myth, a royal refugee from the Shang Dynasty founded a dynasty in Korea. During the Warring States Period in China (403–221 B.C.E.), the state of Yan extended into southern Manchuria and a bit of what is now Korea. Through this contact features of China's material culture, such as iron technology, spread to Korea. In about 194 B.C.E. Wiman, an unsuccessful rebel against the Han Dynasty, fled to Korea and set up a state called Choson in what is now northwest Korea and southern Manchuria. In 108 B.C.E. this state was overthrown by the armies of the Han emperor Wu. Four military districts were established there, and Chinese officials were dispatched to govern them.

The Chinese colonies founded at that time served as outposts of Chinese civilization and survived nearly a century after the fall of the Han Dynasty, to 313 C.E. The impact of the Chinese military districts in Korea was similar to that of the contemporary Roman colonies in Britain. Even though the later Korean states were not the direct heirs of the colonies, they retained much that had been introduced by the Chinese. Among the many aspects of Chinese culture that penetrated deeply in this period were names: Korean place names and personal names use Chinese characters.

The Chinese never controlled the entire Korean peninsula. They coexisted with the native Korean kingdom of Koguryo, founded in the first century B.C.E. Chinese sources describe this kingdom as a society of aristocratic tribal warriors who had under them a mass of serfs and slaves, mostly from conquered tribes. After the Chinese colonies were finally overthrown, the kingdoms of Paekche and Silla emerged in the third and fourth centuries C.E. farther south on the peninsula. In all three Korean kingdoms Chinese was used as the language of government and learning.

Buddhism was officially introduced in Koguryo from China in 372 and in the other states not long after. Buddhism placed Korea in a pan-Asian cultural context. Buddhist monks went back and forth between China and Korea. One even made the journey to India and back, and others traveled on to Japan to aid in the spread of Buddhism there.

MAP 7.3 Korea and Japan, ca 600 Korea and Japan are of similar latitude, but Korea's climate is more continental, with harsher winters. Of Japan's four islands, Kyushu is closest to Korea and mainland Asia.

Each of the three main Korean kingdoms had hereditary kings, but their power was curbed by the existence of very strong hereditary elites. For instance, Silla had a Council of Nobles, which made important decisions, and a system of "bone ranks" that determined hereditary status.

When the Sui Dynasty finally reunified China in 589, it attempted to take Korea to re-establish the sort of empire the Han had fashioned. But the Korean kingdoms were

KOREA TO CA 700 C.E.

194 B.C.E.	Wiman establishes Choson
108 B.C.E.–313 C.E.	Chinese colonies in Korea
313–668 C.E.	Three Kingdoms period (Silla, Paekche, and Koguryo)
372 C.E.	Buddhism introduced
668 C.E.	Unification under Silla Chinese models widely adopted

Hunters The Korean elite of the late fifth to early sixth century —the date of this tomb mural— were warriors who took pleasure in hunting. Here men on horses are depicted hunting tigers and deer. The skill and artistry of the painters also testify to the high level attained by Korean artists of the period. *(Courtesy, Yushin Yoo)*

much stronger than their predecessors in Han times, and they repeatedly repulsed Chinese attacks. The Tang government then tried allying itself with one state to fight another. Silla and Tang jointly destroyed Paekche in 660 and Koguryo in 668. With its new resources Silla was able to repel Tang efforts to make Korea a colony but acceded to vassal status. This marks the first political unification of Korea.

For the next century Silla embarked on a policy of wholesale borrowing of Chinese culture and institutions. Annual embassies were sent to Chang'an, and large numbers of students studied in China. The Silla government was modeled on the Tang, although modifications were made to accommodate Korea's more aristocratic social structure.

As in Japan, a powerful force in promoting cultural borrowing from China was the tremendous appeal of Buddhism, known primarily through Chinese texts. The Silla kings spent lavishly on Buddhist monasteries. The stone and brick pagodas and temples built in this period, as well as the stone and bronze Buddhist images, are exceptionally fine. Many Buddhist monks studied in China, and books written by Korean monks were read by Chinese monks as well. The Buddhist master Wonhyo (617–686), for instance, wrote a commentary on the *Awakening of Faith* that was influential in China, and his biography was included in the Chinese collection *Lives of Eminent Monks*.

Vietnam

Vietnam is today classed with the countries to its west as part of Southeast Asia, but its ties are at least as strong to China. The Vietnamese language is part of the Sino-Tibetan family, distantly related to Chinese. Communication between the Guangdong (Canton) region in southernmost China and the Hanoi region and farther south in Vietnam was easy along the coast, even in early times.

The Vietnamese appear in Chinese sources as a people of south China called the Yue, who gradually migrated farther south as the Chinese state expanded. From both Chinese sources and archaeological findings, it is known that the people of the Red River valley in northern Vietnam had achieved a relatively advanced level of Bronze Age civilization by the first century B.C.E. They had learned how to irrigate their rice fields by using the tides that backed up the rivers, but plows and water buffalo as draft animals were still unknown. The bronze heads of their arrows often were dipped in poison to facilitate killing large animals such as elephants, whose tusks were traded to China for iron. Power was held by hereditary tribal chiefs who served as civil, religious, and military leaders, with the king as the most powerful chief.

The collapse of the Qin Dynasty in 206 B.C.E. had an impact on this area because a former Qin general, Zhao Tuo (Trieu Da in Vietnamese), finding himself in the far south, set up his own kingdom of Nam Viet (Nan Yue in Chinese). This kingdom covered much of south China and was ruled by Trieu Da from his capital near the present site of Canton. Its population consisted chiefly of the Viet people. After killing all officials loyal to the Chinese emperor, Trieu Da adopted the customs of the Viet and made himself the ruler of a vast state that extended as far south as modern-day Da Nang.

After almost a hundred years of diplomatic and military duels between the Han Dynasty and Trieu Da and his successors, Nam Viet was conquered in 111 B.C.E. by the Chinese emperor Wu. As in Korea, Chinese administrators were imported to replace the local landed nobility. Chinese political institutions were imposed, and Confucianism became the official ideology. The Chinese language was introduced as the medium of official and literary expression, and Chinese ideographs were adopted as the written form for the Vietnamese spoken language. The Chinese built roads, waterways, and harbors to facilitate communication within the region and to ensure that they maintained administrative and military control over it. Chinese art, architecture, and music had a powerful impact on their Vietnamese counterparts.

Chinese innovations that were beneficial to the Vietnamese were readily integrated into the indigenous culture, but the local elite were not reconciled to Chinese political domination. The most famous early revolt took place in 39 C.E., when two widows of local aristocrats, the Trung sisters, led an uprising against foreign rule. They gathered together the tribal chiefs and their armed followers, attacked and overwhelmed the Chinese strongholds, and had themselves proclaimed queens of an independent Vietnamese kingdom. Three years later a powerful army sent by the Han emperor re-established Chinese rule. The local aristocracy was deprived of all power,

Vietnam was given a centralized Chinese administration, and Chinese influence was resumed.

China retained at least nominal control over northern Vietnam through the Tang Dynasty, and there were no real borders between China proper and Vietnam during this time. The local elite became culturally dual, serving as brokers between the Chinese governors and the native people.

Japan

Japan does not touch China as do Korea, Tibet, and Vietnam. The heart of Japan is four mountainous islands off the coast of Korea (see Map 7.3). Japan's climate ranges from subtropical in the south, which the Pacific bathes in warm currents, to cold winters in the north. Rainfall is abundant, favoring rice production. The long seacoast favors fishing.

Since the land is rugged and lacking in navigable waterways, the Inland Sea, like the Aegean in Greece, was the easiest avenue of communication in early times. Hence the land bordering the Inland Sea developed as the political and cultural center of early Japan. Geography also blessed Japan with a moat—the Korea Strait and the Sea of Japan. Consequently, the Japanese for long periods were free to develop their way of life without external interference.

Japan's creation myths, at least in the form they have been preserved, center on the divine origins of the Japanese imperial family. A divine brother and sister, **Izanagi and Izanami,** came to earth and created the Japanese islands and other gods. Izanami died after giving birth to the god of fire, and Izanagi, like the Greek Orpheus, followed her to the world of the dead. Repelled by her putrifying body, he went to a stream to purify himself, where he gave birth to more deities, above all the sun-goddess,

JAPAN TO CA 800 C.E.

3d century C.E.	Creation of the Yamato state
538	Introduction of Buddhism
604	Shotoku's "Seventeen Article Constitution"
646	Taika Reforms
710	Establishment of Nara as Japan's first capital and first city
710–794	Nara era

Amaterasu, and the storm-god, Susanoo. Their union gave birth to a new generation of gods, but they eventually quarreled, and Susanoo moved to Izumo, where he became the progenitor of a line of rulers who were in constant conflict with the line descended from Amaterasu, the line that became the Japanese imperial family.

From archaeology, however, it is evident that Japan's early development was closely tied to that of the mainland, especially to Korea. Physical anthropologists have discerned several major waves of immigrants into Japan. Wet-field rice was introduced by about 350 B.C.E. During the Han Dynasty in China, some objects of Chinese or Korean manufacture found their way into Japan, an indication that people were traveling back and forth as well.

A Chinese historian wrote one of the earliest reliable descriptions of Japanese life in 297 C.E.:

The land of Wa [Japan] is warm and mild. In winter as in summer the people live on raw vegetables and go barefooted. They live in houses; father and mother, elder and younger, sleep separately. They smear their bodies with pink and scarlet, just as the Chinese use powder. They serve food on bamboo and wooden trays, helping themselves with their fingers.[7]

The society that Chinese sources portray was based on agriculture and dominated by a warrior aristocracy organized into clans, much like Korea. Clad in helmet and armor, these warriors wielded swords and battle-axes and often bows. Some of them rode into battle on horseback.

Each aristocratic clan dominated a particular territory, and the ordinary villagers in the area were treated as subordinates to the warriors. Each clan had its own chieftain, who marshaled clansmen for battle and served as chief priest. Over time these clans fought with each other, and their numbers were gradually reduced through conquest and alliance. By the fifth century or so the chief of the clan that claimed descent from the sun-goddess, located in the Yamato plain around modern Osaka, had come to occupy the position of Great King.

Clans that recognized Yamato dominion continued to exercise local authority, and some clans were given specific military or religious functions to fulfill. In an effort to further centralize the administration of the state, the king created a council of chieftains, who were treated as though they were appointed officials.

The Yamato rulers also used their religion to subordinate the gods of their supporters, much as Hammurabi had used Marduk in Babylonia (see page 13). They established the chief shrine of the sun-goddess near the seacoast, where she could catch the first rays of the rising sun. Cults to other gods also were supported, as long as

they were viewed as subordinate to the sun-goddess. This native religion was called **Shinto,** the Way of the Gods. Much of Shinto's appeal rose from the fact that it was a happy religion. Its rituals celebrated the beauty of nature instead of invoking the hazards of fate or divine wrath, and its festivals were marked by wine, song, and good cheer. Shinto emphasized ritual cleanliness, a form of spiritual purification common in many other religions.

In the fifth and sixth centuries Korea played a major role as the avenue through which Chinese influence reached Japan. Following the Korean example, the Japanese adapted the Chinese systems of writing and record keeping, which allowed for bureaucratic administration along Chinese lines and set the stage for literature, philosophy, and written history.

Buddhism entered Japan this way as well. In 538 a Korean king sent the Yamato court Buddhist images and scriptures. The new religion immediately became a political football. One faction of the ruling clan favored its official adoption, and other factions opposed it. The resulting turmoil, both religious and political, ended only in 587, when members of the pro-Buddhist group defeated their opponents on the battlefield.

The victorious pro-Buddhist faction undertook a sweeping reform of the state, designed to strengthen Yamato rule by introducing Chinese political and bureaucratic practices. The architect of this effort was Prince Shotoku (574–622), the author of the "Seventeen Article Constitution." Issued in 604, this political manifesto upheld the rights of the ruler and commanded his subjects to obey him. It recommended an intricate bureaucracy similar to China's, admonished the nobility to avoid strife and opposition, and urged adherence to Buddhist precepts.

Prince Shotoku was a generous patron of Buddhist temples, sponsoring the magnificent Horyuji Temple and staffing it with clergy from Korea. He also opened direct relations with China, recently unified by the Sui. The Sui emperor was not amused to receive a letter "from the emperor of the sunrise country to the emperor of the sunset country," but during the brief Sui Dynasty Japan sent four missions to China.

Even after Prince Shotoku's death, his policies were pursued. In 645 his supporters gained supremacy, and the following year they proclaimed the Taika Reforms, a bold effort to create a complete imperial and bureaucratic system like that of the Tang empire, down to outlawing private ownership of land and instituting the equal-field system and per capita taxes. The symbol of this new political awareness was the establishment in 710 of Japan's first true city, at **Nara,** north of modern Osaka.

Prince Shotoku   Not only did Prince Shotoku introduce many features of Chinese-style bureaucratic government, but he also sponsored four missions to China. Here he is depicted, along with two attendants, wearing Chinese-style robes and holding the Chinese symbol of office. *(Imperial Household Collection, Kyoto)*

Horyuji Temple   Japanese Buddhist temples, like those in China and Korea, consisted of several buildings within a walled compound. The buildings of the Horyuji Temple (built 670–711, Prince Shotoku's original temple burned down) include the oldest wooden structures in the world and house some of the best early Buddhist sculpture in Japan. The three main buildings depicted here are the pagoda, housing relics; the main hall, with the temple's principal images; and the lecture hall, for sermons. The five-story pagoda could be seen from far away, much like the steeples of cathedrals in medieval Europe. *(The Orion Press)*

Nara, which was modeled on the Tang capital, gave its name to an era that lasted until 794, an era characterized by the avid importation of Chinese ideas and methods. Seven times missions with five hundred to six hundred men were sent on the difficult journey to Chang'an. Chinese and Korean craftsmen were often brought back to Japan, especially to help with the decoration of the many Buddhist temples then under construction. Increased contact with the mainland had unwanted effects as well, such as the great smallpox epidemic of 735–737, which is thought to have reduced the population by 30 percent. (Smallpox did not become an endemic childhood disease in Japan until the tenth or eleventh century.)

The Buddhist monasteries that ringed Nara were both religious centers and wealthy landlords, and the monks were active in the political life of the capital. Copying the policy of the Tang Dynasty in China, the government ordered that every province establish a Buddhist temple with twenty monks and ten nuns to chant sutras and perform other ceremonies on behalf of the emperor and the state.

Many of the temples built during the Nara period still stand, the wood, clay, and bronze statues in them exceptionally well preserved. The largest of these temples was the Todaiji, with its huge (fifty-three feet tall) bronze statue of the Buddha, made from more than a million pounds of metal. When the temple and statue were completed in 752, an Indian monk painted the eyes, and the ten thousand monks present for the celebration had a magnificent vegetarian feast. Objects from the dedication ceremony were placed in a special storehouse, the Shosoin, and about ten thousand of them are still there, including books, weapons, mirrors, screens, and objects of gold, lacquer, and glass, most made in China but some coming via the Silk Road from Central Asia and Persia.

As part of a culture-building process, the Japanese also began writing their own history and poetry. Some books were written entirely in Chinese; others were written in the Japanese language but using Chinese characters to represent each sound, since there was no alphabet. The masterpiece among these books is the *Manyoshu,* a collection of 4,500 mostly short Japanese poems written in Chinese characters borrowed for their sound. Because rhyming is so easy in Japanese, it was not an important feature of poetry, which instead stressed the number of syllables per line. The dominant form was the **tanka,** with thirty-one syllables in five lines of 5-7-5-7-7. The poet Kakinomoto Hitomaro wrote a tanka on the prospect of his own death:

Not knowing I am pillowed
Among the crags of Kamo Mountain
My wife must still be waiting for my return.

When his wife learned of his death, she also wrote a poem:

Never again to meet him in the flesh—
Rise, oh clouds, and spread
Over Ishi River,
That, gazing on you,
I may remember him.[8]

SUMMARY

During the millennium from 200 B.C.E. to 800 C.E., China and India came into contact with each other via the kingdoms of Central Asia. Throughout Asia Buddhism became a major religion, usually coexisting with other religions, including Daoism in China and Shinto in Japan. China's neighbors, notably including Korea, Japan, and Vietnam, began to adopt elements of China's material, political, and religious culture.

In some cases, culture and social forms were spread by force of arms. The Qin, Han, and Tang armies moved into northern Korea, Central Asia, south China, and even northern Vietnam. But military might was not the primary means by which culture spread in this period. Buddhism was not spread by conquest in the way that Christianity and Islam so often were. Moreover Korea and Japan sought out Chinese expertise, believing it to be to their advantage to adopt the most advanced political and economic technologies. Perhaps as a consequence, they could pick and choose, using those elements of the more advanced cultures that suited them, and retaining features of their earlier cultures that they believed superior, in the process developing distinctive national styles.

KEY TERMS

Great Wall	Age of Division
regents	Grand Canal
Silk Road	Pure Land
tributary system	Chan
Confucian classics	Izanagi and Izanami
Records of the Grand	Shinto
Historian	Nara
lacquer	tanka
eunuchs	

NOTES

1. Derk Bodde, "The State and Empire of Ch'in," in M. Loewe and D. Twitchett, eds., *The Cambridge History of China,* vol. 1 (New York: Cambridge University Press, 1986), p. 20.

2. Li Yuning, ed., *The First Emperor of China* (White Plains, N.Y.: International Arts and Sciences Press, 1975), pp. 275–276, slightly modified.

3. Patricia Buckley Ebrey, *The Cambridge Illustrated History of China* (Cambridge: Cambridge University Press, 1996), p. 74.

4. W. F. Jenner, *Memories of Loyang: Yang Hsüan-chih and the Lost Capital (493–534)* (Oxford: Clarendon Press, 1981), p. 208.

5. A. Waley, trans., *More Translations from the Chinese* (New York: Knopf, 1919), p. 27.

6. Ibid., p. 71.

7. R. Tsunoda et al., *Sources of the Japanese Tradition* (New York: Columbia University Press, 1958), p. 6.

8. Martin Collcott, Marius Jansen, and Isao Kumakura, *Cultural Atlas of Japan* (New York: Facts on File, 1988), p. 65.

SUGGESTED READING

Good general histories of China are listed in the Suggested Reading for Chapter 4. For China's relations with the Xiongnu, Xianbei, Turks, and other northern neighbors, see T. Barfield, *Perilous Frontier: Nomadic Empires and China, 221 B.C.–A.D. 1757* (1989), and N. DiCosmo, *Ancient China and Its Enemies: The Rise of Nomadic Power in East Asia* (2002). The nature of the Qin and later empires is analyzed from a fiscal and military standpoint in M. Elvin, *The Pattern of the Chinese Past* (1973). The political and military success of the Qin is the subject of D. Bodde, *China's First Unifier: A Study of the Ch'in Dynasty as Seen in the Life of Li Ssu (280?–208 B.C.)* (1958).

B. Watson has provided two good studies of Sima Qian and his historical work: *Records of the Grand Historian of China* (1961) and *Ssu-ma Ch'ien: Grand Historian of China* (1958). China's most important woman scholar is the subject of N. L. Swann, *Pan Chao: Foremost Woman Scholar of China* (1950). M. Loewe, *Everyday Life in Early Imperial China* (1968), paints a vibrant picture of ordinary life during the Han period, a portrayal that attempts to include all segments of Han society. See also Y. Yu, *Trade and Expansion in Han China: A Study in the Structure of Sino-Barbarian Economic Relations* (1967), and M. Perazzoli-t'Serstevens, *The Han Dynasty,* trans. Janet Seligman (1982). For religion, see Mu-chou Poo, *In Search of Personal Welfare: A View of Ancient Chinese Religion* (1998).

Current scholarship on the turbulent Age of Division after the fall of the Han can be sampled in A. Dien, ed., *State and Society in Early Medieval China* (1990). Also recommended is A. Wright's gracefully written *The Sui Dynasty* (1978). The best short introduction to the topic of Buddhism in China remains Wright's brief *Buddhism in Chinese History* (1959). See also K. Ch'en, *The Chinese Transformation of Buddhism* (1973). E. O. Reischauer provides a glimpse into the social and cultural aspects of Tang Buddhism in his translation, *Ennin's Diary: The Record of a Pilgrimage to China in Search of the Law*, and the companion volume, *Ennin's Travels in T'ang China* (both 1955).

Diverse aspects of the Tang period are explored in two collections of essays: A. Wright and D. Twitchett, eds., *Perspectives on the T'ang* (1973), and J. Perry and B. Smith, eds., *Essays on T'ang Society: The Interplay of Social, Political, and Economic Forces* (1976). On Tang rulership, see H. Wechsler, *Mirror to the Son of Heaven: Wei Cheng at the Court of T'ang T'ai-tsung* (1974). R. W. L. Guisso analyzes the career of China's only empress in *Wu Tse-t'ien and the Politics of Legitimization in T'ang China* (1978). A thorough examination of the economic, political, and military conditions of the early eighth century is found in E. Pulleyblank, *The Background of the Rebellion of An Lu-shan* (1955). For an introduction to Tang poetry, see S. Owen, *The Great Age of Chinese Poetry: The High T'ang* (1981), or one of the many biographies of Tang poets, such as W. Hung, *Tu Fu: China's Greatest Poet* (1952); A. Waley, *The Life and Times of Po Chu-i, 772–846 A.D.* (1949); or C. Hartman, *Han Yü and the T'ang Search for Unity* (1985). For other features of Tang culture, see E. Schafer, *The Golden Peaches of Samarkand* (1963), and J. Gernet, *Buddhism in Chinese Society: An Economic History of the Fifth to the Tenth Centuries* (1995).

On the interconnections among the societies of East Asia, see C. Holcomb, *The Genesis of East Asia, 221 B.C.–A.D. 907* (2001), and W. Cohen, *East Asia at the Center* (2000). For early Korean history, see A. Nahm, *Introduction to Korean History and Culture* (1993), and K. Kim, *A New History of Korea* (1964). P. Lee, ed., *Sourcebook of Korean Civilization* (1993), offers an excellent selection of primary sources.

Good general histories of Japan include P. Varley, *Japanese Culture* (1984); C. Totman, *A History of Japan* (1999); and J. Hall, *Japan from Prehistory to Modern Times* (1970). Still of value is G. Samson, *Japan: A Short Cultural History* (1952). An attractive volume that covers more than history and geography is M. Collcott, M. Jansen, and I. Kumakura, *Cultural Atlas of Japan* (1988). For primary sources, see W. T. de Bary et al., *Sources of Japanese Tradition* (2001), and D. Lu, *Japan: A Documentary History* (1996). The six-volume *Cambridge History of Japan,* ed. J. Hall et al. (1988–1999), offers authoritative accounts of all periods.

W. G. Aston, trans., *Nihongi: Chronicles of Japan from Earliest Times to A.D. 697* (1896, reprint 1990), despite its age, is still the only English translation of the earliest historical chronicle. J. P. Maas, *Antiquity and Anachronism in Japanese History* (1992), makes the bold suggestion that an exaggerated history of antiquity led to a distorted perception of the past. Quite readable is the well-illustrated J. E. Kidder, *Early Buddhist Japan* (1972). J. M. Kitagawa, *Religion in Japanese History* (1966), discusses both Shinto and Buddhism. J. Piggott, *The Emergence of Japanese Kingship* (1999), draws on both archaeology and chronicles to examine the sacred quality of early Japanese rulers.

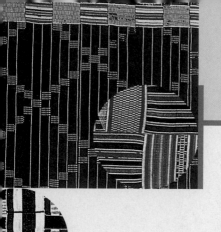

COPYING BUDDHIST SUTRAS

Buddhism was not merely a set of ideas but also a set of practices. In Chinese, Japanese, and Korean monasteries, as in Western ones, monks and nuns, under the direction of the abbot or abbess, would read and copy scriptures as an act of devotion. Pious laypeople might pay to have sutras copied as a means of earning religious merit. Sometimes a copyist attached a statement at the end of a sutra explaining the circumstances that had surrounded the act of copying. Below are two such statements, one from a sutra found in Dunhuang, on the northwest fringe of China proper, dated 550, and the other from Korea, dated 755.

1.

Happiness is not fortuitous: pray for it and it will be found. Results are not born of thin air: pay heed to causes and results will follow. This explains how the Buddhist disciple and nun Daorong—because her conduct in her previous life was not correct—came to be born in her present form, a woman, vile and unclean.

Now if she does not honor the awesome decree of Buddha, how can future consequences be favorable for her? Therefore, having cut down her expenditures on food and clothing, she reverently has had the *Nirvana sutra* copied once. She prays that those who read it carefully will be exalted in mind to the highest realms and that those who communicate its meaning will cause others to be so enlightened.

She also prays that in her present existence she will have no further sickness or suffering, that her parents in seven other incarnations (who have already died or will die in the future) and her present family and close relatives may experience joy in the four elements [earth, water, fire, and air], and that whatever they seek may indeed come to pass. Finally, she prays that all those endowed with knowledge may be included within this prayer. Dated the 29th day of the fourth month of 550.

2.

The copying began on the first day of the eighth month of 754, and was completed on the fourteenth day of the second month of the following year.

One who made a vow to copy the scripture is Dharma master Yongi of Hwangnyong Monastery. His purposes were to repay the love of his parents and to pray for all living beings in the dharma realm to attain the path of the Buddha.

The scripture is made as follows: First scented water is sprinkled around the roots of a paperbark mulberry tree to quicken its growth; the bark is then peeled and pounded to make paper with a clean surface. The copyists, the artisans who make the centerpiece of the scroll, and the painters who draw the images of buddhas and bodhisattvas all receive the bodhisattva ordination and observe abstinence. After relieving themselves, sleeping, eating, or drinking, they take a bath in scented water before returning to the work. Copyists are adorned with new pure garments, loose trousers, a coarse crown, and a deva crown. Two azure-clad boys sprinkle water on their heads and . . . azure-clad boys and musicians perform music. The processions to the copying site are headed by one who sprinkles scented water on their path, another who scatters flowers, a dharma master who carries a censer, and another dharma master who chants Buddhist verses. Each of the copyists carries incense and flowers and invokes the name of the Buddha as he progresses.

This gilt bronze image of Maitreya, not quite three feet tall, was made in Korea in about 600. It depicts the Buddha Maitreya, the Future Buddha who presides over Tushita Heaven. The rounded face, slender body, and gracefully draped robe help convey the idea that the Buddha is neither male nor female, but beyond such distinctions. *(Courtesy, Yushin Yoo)*

Upon reaching the site, all take refuge in the three Jewels (the Buddha, the Dharma, and the Order), make three bows, and offer the *Flower Garland Scripture* and others to buddhas and bodhisattvas. Then they sit down and copy the scripture, make the centerpiece of the scroll, and paint the buddhas and bodhisattvas. Thus, azure-clad boys and musicians cleanse everything before a piece of relic is placed in the center.

Now I make a vow that the copied scripture will not break till the end of the future—even when a major chilicosm [millions of universes] is destroyed by the three calamities, this scripture shall be intact as the void. If all living things rely on this scripture, they shall witness the Buddha, listen to his dharma, worship the relic, aspire to enlightenment without backsliding, cultivate the vows of the Universally Worthy Bodhisattva, and achieve Buddhahood.

QUESTIONS FOR ANALYSIS

1. What common Buddhist beliefs are expressed in both of these statements?

2. What do you make of the emphasis on rituals surrounding copying the sutra in the second statement?

Sources: Patricia Buckley Ebrey, ed., *Chinese Civilization: A Sourcebook* (New York: Free Press, 1993), pp. 102–103; Peter H. Lee, ed., *Sourcebook of Korean Civilization* (New York: Columbia University Press, 1993), pp. 201–202, modified.

Byzantine cross. Justin II gave this cross to Pope John III; it was one of a very few not destroyed in the sack of Rome in 1527. *(Scala/Art Resource, NY)*

THE MAKING OF EUROPE

The centuries between approximately 400 and 900 present a paradox. On the one hand, they witnessed the disintegration of the western Roman Empire, which had been one of humanity's great political and cultural achievements. On the other hand, these five centuries were a creative and seminal period, during which Europeans laid the foundations for medieval and modern Europe. It is not too much to say that this period saw the making of Europe.

The idea of Europe—with the geographical and cultural implications that we in the twenty-first century attach to the word—is actually a fairly recent notion. Classical geographers used the term *Europe* to distinguish it from Africa and Asia, the only other landmasses they knew, and medieval scholars imitated and followed the ancients. Only in the sixteenth century did the word *Europe* enter the common language of educated peoples living in the western parts of the Eurasian landmass and did the continent we call Europe gain a map-based frame of reference.[1] The vision of almost everyone else was provincial, limited by the boundaries of their province or even village. While the peoples living there did not define themselves as European for centuries, a European identity began to be forged in late antiquity and the early medieval period.

The basic ingredients that went into the making of a distinctly European civilization were the cultural legacy of Greece and Rome, the customs and traditions of the Germanic peoples, and the Christian faith. The most important of these was Christianity, because it absorbed and assimilated the other two. It reinterpreted the classics in a Christian sense. It instructed the Germanic peoples and gave them new ideals of living and social behavior. Christianity became the cement that held European society together. As a result, people's understanding of themselves shifted from a social or political one (German, Celt, Roman) to a religious one.

During this period, the Byzantine Empire, centered at Constantinople, served as a protective buffer between Europe and peoples to the east. The Byzantine Greeks preserved the philosophical and scientific texts of the ancient world, which later formed the basis for study in science and medicine, and produced a great synthesis of Roman law, the Justinian *Code*. In the urbane and sophisticated life led at Constantinople, the Greeks set a standard far above the primitive existence of the West.

The civilization later described as European resulted from the fusion of the Greco-Roman heritage, Germanic traditions, Christian faith, and significant elements of Islamic culture (see Chapter 9).

- How did these components act on one another?
- How did they lead to the making of Europe?
- What influence did Byzantine culture have on the making of Europe?

This chapter will focus on these questions.

THE GROWTH OF THE CHRISTIAN CHURCH

In doctrine Christianity was a **syncretic faith.** That is, it absorbed and adopted many of the religious ideas of the eastern Mediterranean world. From Judaism came the concept, unique in the ancient world, of monotheism, belief in one God, together with the rich ethical and moral precepts of the Old Testament Scriptures. From Orphism, a set of sixth-century B.C.E. religious ideas, came the belief that the body is the prison of the soul. From Hellenistic thought derived the notion of the superiority of spirit over matter. Likewise, scholars have noticed the similarity between the career of Jesus and that of the gods of Eastern mystery cults such as Mithra, who died and rose from the dead, and whose followers had a ceremony of communion in which the god's flesh was symbolically eaten. All of these ideas played a part in the formulation of Christian doctrine and in attracting people to it.

With the support of the emperors, the institutional church gradually established an orthodox set of beliefs and adopted a system of organization based on that of the Roman state. Moreover, the church possessed able leaders who launched a dynamic missionary policy. Finally, the church slowly succeeded in assimilating, or adapting, pagan peoples, both Germanic and Roman, to Christianity. These factors help explain the growth of the church in the face of repeated Germanic invasions.

The Church and the Roman Emperors

The church benefited considerably from the emperors' support. In return, the emperors expected the support of the Christian church in maintaining order and unity. After legalizing its practice, Constantine encouraged Christianity throughout his reign. In 380 the emperor Theo-

dosius went further than Constantine and made Christianity the official religion of the empire. Theodosius stripped Roman pagan temples of statues, made the practice of the old Roman state religion a treasonable offense, and persecuted Christians who dissented from orthodox doctrine. Most significant, he allowed the church to establish its own courts. Church courts began to develop their own body of law, called *canon law.* These courts, not the Roman government, had jurisdiction over the clergy and ecclesiastical disputes.

In the fourth century, theological disputes frequently and sharply divided the Christian community. Some disagreements had to do with the nature of Christ. For example, **Arianism,** which originated with Arius (ca 250–336), a priest of Alexandria, denied that Christ was divine and co-eternal with God the Father—two propositions of Orthodox Christian belief. Arius held that God the Father was by definition uncreated and unchangeable. Jesus, however, was born of Mary, grew in wisdom, and suffered punishment and death. Jesus was created by the will of the Father and thus was not co-eternal with the Father. Therefore, Arius reasoned, Jesus the Son must be less than or inferior to the Unbegotten Father, who is incapable of suffering and did not die. This argument implies that Jesus stands somewhere between God the Creator and humanity in need of redemption. Orthodox theologians branded Arius's position a *heresy*—denial of a basic doctrine of faith.

Arianism enjoyed such popularity and provoked such controversy that Constantine, to whom religious disagreement meant civil disorder, interceded. In 325 he summoned a council of church leaders to Nicaea in Asia Minor and presided over it personally. The council produced the Nicene Creed, which defined the Orthodox position that Christ is "eternally begotten of the Father" and of the same substance as the Father. Arius and those who refused to accept the creed were banished, the first case of civil punishment for heresy. This participation of the emperor in a theological dispute within the church paved the way for later emperors to claim that they could do the same.

So active was the emperor Theodosius's participation in church matters that he eventually came to loggerheads with Bishop Ambrose of Milan (339–397). Theodosius ordered Ambrose to hand over his cathedral church to the emperor. Ambrose's response had important consequences for the future:

At length came the command, "Deliver up the Basilica"; I reply, "It is not lawful for us to deliver it up, nor for your Majesty to receive it. . . . It is asserted that all things are

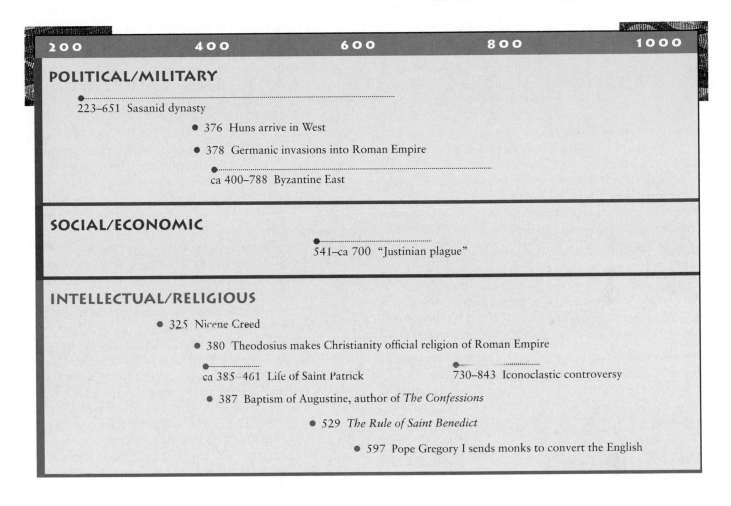

200   400   600   800   1000

POLITICAL/MILITARY

223–651 Sasanid dynasty

376 Huns arrive in West

378 Germanic invasions into Roman Empire

ca 400–788 Byzantine East

SOCIAL/ECONOMIC

541–ca 700 "Justinian plague"

INTELLECTUAL/RELIGIOUS

325 Nicene Creed

380 Theodosius makes Christianity official religion of Roman Empire

ca 385–461 Life of Saint Patrick   730–843 Iconoclastic controversy

387 Baptism of Augustine, author of *The Confessions*

529 *The Rule of Saint Benedict*

597 Pope Gregory I sends monks to convert the English

---

lawful to the Emperor, that all things are his. But do not burden your conscience with the thought that you have any right as Emperor over sacred things. . . . It is written, God's to God and Caesar's to Caesar. The palace is the Emperor's, the Churches are the Bishop's. To you is committed jurisdiction over public, not over sacred buildings."[2]

Throughout the Middle Ages, theologians, canonists, and propagandists repeatedly cited Ambrose's position as the basis for relations between the two powers.

Administration and Leadership

The early church benefited from the administrative abilities of some church leaders and the identification of the authority and dignity of the bishop of Rome with the imperial traditions of the city. The early church organized itself along the lines of the Roman Empire. During the reign of Diocletian (284–305), the empire had been divided for administrative purposes into geograph-

ical units called *dioceses*. Christian bishops made their headquarters, or *sees,* in the urban centers of the old Roman dioceses. A bishop's jurisdiction gradually extended throughout his diocese. The center of his authority was his cathedral, a word deriving from the Latin *cathedra,* meaning "chair."

With imperial power weak, educated people joined and worked for the church in the belief that it was the one institution capable of providing leadership. Bishop Ambrose, the son of the Roman prefect of Gaul, was a trained lawyer and governor of a province. He was typical of Roman aristocrats who held high public office before joining the church and becoming bishops.

After the removal of the imperial capital and the emperor to Constantinople, the bishop of Rome exercised considerable influence in the West, in part because he had no real competitor there. In addition, successive bishops of Rome stressed the special role of that see. They pointed to the importance that Rome had enjoyed in the framework of the old empire. Moreover, according to tradition,

Peter, the chief of Christ's first twelve followers, had lived and been executed in Rome. The popes claimed to be successors to Peter and heirs to his authority, based on Jesus' words: "You are Peter, and on this rock I will build my church. . . . Whatever you declare bound on earth shall be bound in heaven." Theologians call this statement the **Petrine Doctrine.**

The bishops of Rome came to be known as popes—from the Latin *papa,* for "father"—and in the fifth century began to stress their supremacy over other Christian communities and to urge other churches to appeal to Rome for resolution of doctrinal issues. Thus Pope Innocent I (r. 401–417) wrote to the bishops of North Africa:

We approve your action in following the principle that nothing which was done even in the most remote and distant provinces should be taken as finally settled unless it came to the notice of this See, that any just pronouncement might be confirmed by all the authority of this See, and that the other churches might from thence gather what they should teach.[3]

Although Innocent and other popes strongly asserted the primacy of the pope, those assertions were not universally accepted. Local Christian communities and their leaders often exercised decisive authority over their local churches.

Missionary Activity

The word *catholic* derives from a Greek word meaning "general," "universal," or "worldwide." Christ had said that his teaching was for all peoples, and Christians sought to make their faith catholic—that is, believed everywhere. This could be accomplished only through missionary activity. As Saint Paul had written to the Christian community at Colossae in Asia Minor:

You have stripped off your old behavior with your old self, and you have put on a new self which will progress towards true knowledge the more it is renewed in the image of its creator; and in that image there is no room for distinction between Greek and Jew, between the circumcised or the uncircumcised, or between barbarian or Scythian, slave and free man. There is only Christ; he is everything and he is in everything.[4]

Paul urged Christians to bring the "good news" of Christ to all peoples. The Mediterranean served as the highway over which Christianity spread to the cities of the empire (see Map 8.1).

Christian communities were scattered throughout Gaul and Britain during the Roman occupation. The effective beginnings of Christianity in Gaul can be traced to Saint Martin of Tours (ca 316–397), a Roman soldier who, after giving half of his cloak to a naked beggar, had a vision of Christ and was baptized. Martin founded the monastery of Ligugé, the first in Gaul; it became a center for the evangelization of the country districts. In 372 he became bishop of Tours and introduced a rudimentary parish system.

Religion was not a private or individual matter; it was a social affair, and the religion of the chieftain or king determined the religion of the people. Thus missionaries concentrated their initial efforts not on the people, but on kings or tribal chieftains. According to custom, kings negotiated with all foreign powers, including the gods. Because the Christian missionaries represented a "foreign" power (the Christian God), the king dealt with them. Germanic kings accepted Christianity because they believed the Christian God was more powerful than pagan ones and the Christian God would deliver victory in battle; or because Christianity taught obedience to (kingly) authority; or because Christian priests possessed knowledge and a charisma that could be associated with kingly power. Missionaries, therefore, focused their attention on kings. Kings who converted, such as Ethelbert of Kent and the Frankish chieftain Clovis, sometimes had Christian wives. Besides the personal influence a Christian wife exerted on her husband, conversion may have indicated that barbarian kings wanted to enjoy the cultural advantages that Christianity brought,

Ardagh Silver Chalice   This chalice (ca 800) formed part of the treasure of Ardagh Cathedral in County Limerick, Ireland. It has been called "one of the most sumptuous pieces of ecclesiastical metalwork to survive from early medieval Europe." The circular filigree decoration resembles that of Irish manuscript illumination. *(National Museum of Ireland)*

such as literate assistants and an ideological basis for their rule.

Tradition identifies the conversion of Ireland with Saint Patrick (ca 385–461). Born in western England to a Christian family of Roman citizenship, Patrick was captured and enslaved by Irish raiders and taken to Ireland, where he worked for six years as a herdsman. He escaped and returned to England, where a vision urged him to Christianize Ireland. In preparation, Patrick studied in Gaul and in 432 was consecrated a bishop. Patrick's missionary activities followed the existing social pattern: he converted the Irish tribe by tribe, first baptizing the king. In 445, with the approval of Pope Leo I, Patrick established his see in Armagh.

The Christianization of the English really began in 597, when Pope Gregory I sent a delegation of monks under the Roman Augustine to Britain to convert the English. The conversion of the English had far-reaching consequences because Britain later served as a base for the Christianization of the European continent (see Map 8.1). Between the fifth and tenth centuries, the great majority of peoples living on the European continent and the nearby islands accepted the Christian religion—that is, they received baptism, though baptism in itself did not automatically transform people into Christians.

The Germanic peoples were warriors who idealized the military virtues of physical strength, ferocity in battle, and loyalty to the leader. Victors in battle enjoyed the spoils of success and plundered the vanquished. The greater the fighter, the more trophies and material goods he collected. Thus the Germans had trouble accepting the Christian precepts of "love your enemies" and "turn the other cheek," and they found the Christian notions

MAP 8.1 The Spread of Christianity   Originating in Judaea, the southern part of modern Israel and Jordan, Christianity spread throughout the Roman world. Roman sea-lanes and roads facilitated the expansion.

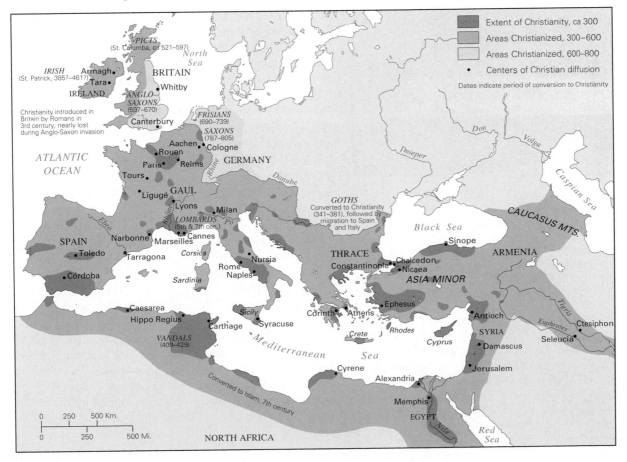

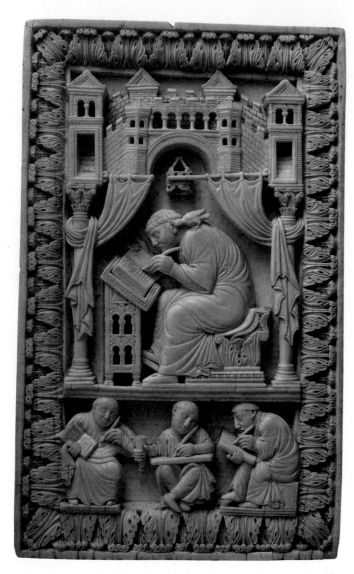

Pope Gregory I (590–604) and Scribes   One of the four "Doctors" (or Learned Fathers) of the Latin church, Gregory is shown in this tenth-century ivory book cover writing at his desk while the Holy Spirit, in the form of a dove, whispers in his ear. Below, scribes copy Gregory's works. *(Kunsthistorisches Museum, Vienna/Art Resource, NY)*

Conversion and Assimilation

In Christian theology, conversion involves a turning toward God—that is, a conscious effort to live according to the Gospel message. How did missionaries and priests get masses of pagan and illiterate peoples to understand and live by Christian ideals and teachings? Through preaching, through assimilation, and through the penitential system.

Preaching aimed at instruction and edification. Instruction presented the basic teachings of Christianity. Edification was intended to strengthen the newly baptized in their faith through stories about the lives of Christ and the saints. Deeply ingrained pagan customs and practices, however, could not be stamped out by words alone or even by imperial edicts. Christian missionaries often pursued a policy of assimilation, easing the conversion of pagan men and women by stressing similarities between their customs and beliefs and those of Christianity. A letter from Pope Gregory I to Augustine of Canterbury in 601 illustrates this policy. The pope instructed Augustine not to tear down the pagan English temples but to destroy the idols and then cleanse the temples with holy water. "In this way," he wrote, "we hope that the people . . . flocking more readily to their accustomed resorts, may come to know and adore the true God."[5]

Similarly, the church joined pagan holidays with Christian occasions. There were two Roman Christians named Valentine, both of whom were martyred for their beliefs in the third century C.E. around the middle of February. The early church converted a mid-February Roman festival called Lupercalia—at which the Romans asked the gods for fertility for themselves, their fields, and their flocks—into Saint Valentine's Day. (It was not until the later Middle Ages that the day became associated with lovers and the exchange of messages and gifts.)

In the early church, confession meant that the sinner *publicly* acknowledged charges laid against him or her and *publicly* carried out the penitential works that the priest or bishop prescribed. For example, an adulterer might have to stand outside the church before services, wearing a sign naming his or her sin and asking for the prayers of everyone who entered. Beginning in the late sixth century, Irish and English missionaries brought the penitential system to continental Europe. The illiterate penitent knelt before the priest, who questioned the penitent about the sins he or she might have committed. The priest then imposed a penance. Penance usually meant fasting for a period of time on bread and water, which was intended as a medicine for the soul. Here is a section of the

of sin and repentance virtually incomprehensible. Sin in Christian thought meant disobedience to the will of God as revealed in the Ten Commandments and the teaching of Christ. Good or "moral" behavior to the barbarians meant the observance of tribal customs and practices. In Germanic society, dishonorable behavior brought social ostracism. The inculcation of Christian ideals took a very long time.

penitential prepared by Archbishop Theodore of Canterbury (668–690), which circulated widely at the time:

If anyone commits fornication with a virgin he shall do penance for one year. If with a married woman, he shall do penance for four years, two of these entire. . . .

A male who commits fornication with a male shall do penance for three years. . . .

Whoever has often committed theft, seven years is his penance, or such a sentence as his priest shall determine, that is, according to what can be arranged with those whom he has wronged. . . .

If a layman slays another with malice aforethought, if he will not lay aside his arms, he shall do penance for seven years; without flesh and wine, three years. . . .

Women who commit abortion before [the fetus] has life, shall do penance for one year or for the three forty-day periods or for forty days, according to the nature of the offense; and if later, that is, more than forty days after conception, they shall do penance as murderesses.[6]

As this sample suggests, writers of penitentials were preoccupied with sexual transgressions.

Penitentials provide an enormous amount of information about the ascetic ideals of early Christianity and about the crime-ridden realities of Celtic and Germanic societies. Penitentials also reveal the ecclesiastical foundations of some modern attitudes toward sex, birth control, and abortion. Unlike the earlier public penances, Celtic forms permitted the repeated reconciliation of the same sinner in a *private* situation involving only the priest and penitent. We do not know whether these severe penances were actually enforced; some scholars believe they were not. In any case, the penitential system contributed to the growth of a different attitude toward religion: formerly public, corporate, and social, religious observances became private, personal, and individual.[7]

CHRISTIAN ATTITUDES TOWARD CLASSICAL CULTURE

Probably the major dilemma the early Christian church faced concerned Greco-Roman culture. In Greek philosophy, art, and architecture, and in Roman law, literature, education, and engineering, the legacy of a great civilization continued. The Christian religion had begun and spread within this intellectual and psychological milieu. What was to be the attitude of Christians to the Greco-Roman world of ideas?

Adjustment

Christians in the first and second centuries believed that Christ would soon fulfill his promise to return and that the end of the world was near. Thus they considered knowledge useless and learning a waste of time, and they preached the duty of Christians to prepare for the Second Coming of the Lord. Good Christians who sought the Kingdom of Heaven by imitating Christ believed they had to disassociate themselves from the "filth" that Roman culture embodied.

Saint Paul (5?–67? C.E.) had written, "The wisdom of the world is foolishness, we preach Christ crucified." And about a century and a half later, Tertullian (ca 160–220), an influential African Christian writer, condemned all secular literature as foolishness in the eyes of God. "What has Athens to do with Jerusalem," he demanded, "the Academy with the Church? We have no need for curiosity since Jesus Christ, nor for inquiry since the gospel."

On the other hand, Christianity encouraged adjustment to the ideas and institutions of the Roman world. Some biblical texts urged Christians to accept the existing social, economic, and political establishment. Specifically addressing Christians living among non-Christians in the hostile environment of Rome, the author of the First Letter of Peter had written about the obligations of Christians:

Always behave honorably among pagans, so that they can see your good works for themselves and, when the day of reckoning comes, give thanks to God for the things which now make them denounce you as criminals. . . .

Accept the authority of every social institution: the emperor, as the supreme authority, and the governors as commissioned by him to punish criminals and praise good citizenship. . . . Have respect for everyone and love for your community; fear God and honour the emperor.[8]

Christians really had little choice. Jewish and Roman cultures were the only cultures early Christians knew; they had to adapt their Roman education to their Christian beliefs. Even Saint Paul believed that there was a good deal of truth in pagan thought, as long as it was correctly understood. The result was compromise, as evidenced by Saint Jerome (340–419). He thought that Christians should study the best of ancient thought because it would direct their minds to God.

The early Christians' adoption of the views of their contemporary world is evidenced as well in Christian attitudes toward women and homosexuality. Jesus considered women the equal of men in his plan of salvation. He

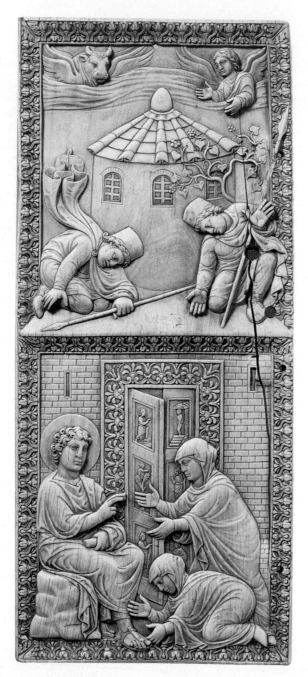

The Marys at the Sepulcher This late-fourth-century ivory panel tells the story (Matthew 28:1–6) of Mary Magdalene and another Mary (*lower*), who went to Jesus' tomb to discover the stone at the entrance rolled away; that an angel had descended from heaven; and in shock the guards assigned (*upper*) to watch the tomb "trembled and became like dead men." The angel told the women that Jesus had risen. The blend of Roman artistic style—in spacing, drapery, men's hair fashion—and Christian subject matter shows the assimilation of classical form and Christian teaching. *(Castello Sforzesco/ Scala/Art Resource, NY)*

attributed no disreputable qualities to women, made no comment on the wiles of women, made no reference to them as inferior creatures. On the contrary, women were among his earliest and most faithful converts. He discussed his mission with them (John 4:21–25), he accepted the ministrations of a reformed prostitute, and women were the first persons to whom he revealed himself after his resurrection (Matthew 28:9–10). The influence of Jewish and Christian writers on the formation of medieval (and modern) attitudes toward women, however, was greater than Jesus' influence.

Jesus' message emphasized love for God and for one's fellow human beings. Later writers tended to stress Christianity as a religion of renunciation and asceticism. Their views derive from Platonic-Hellenistic ideas of the contemporary Mediterranean world. The Hellenistic Jewish philosopher Philo of Alexandria (ca 20 B.C.E.–ca 50 C.E.), for example, held that since the female represented sense perception and the male the higher, rational soul, the female was inferior to the male. Female beauty may come from God, who created everything, the African church father Tertullian wrote, but it should be feared. Women should wear veils, he warned; otherwise, men would be endangered by the sight of them.[9]

The church fathers acknowledged that God had established marriage for the generation of children, but they believed marriage was a concession to weak people who could not bear celibacy. Saint Augustine (see below) considered sexual intercourse a great threat to spiritual freedom. In daily life every act of intercourse was evil, he taught; every child was conceived by a sinful act and came into the world tainted with original sin. Celibacy was the highest good, intercourse little more than animal lust.

Women were considered incapable of writing on the subject, so we have none of their views. The church fathers, by definition, were men. Because many of them experienced physical desire when in the presence of women, misogyny (hatred of women) entered Christian thought. Although early Christian writers believed women the spiritual equals of men, and although Saint Melania, Saint Scholastica (see page 220), and some other women exercised influence as teachers and charismatic leaders, Christianity became a male-centered and sex-negative religion. "The Church Fathers regarded sex as at best something to be tolerated, an evil whose only good was procreation."[10] Until perhaps very recently, this attitude dominated religious thinking on human sexuality.

Toward homosexuality, according to a controversial study, Christians of the first three or four centuries simply imbibed the attitude of the world in which they lived. Many Romans indulged in homosexual activity, and contemporaries did not consider such behavior (or inclinations to it) immoral, bizarre, or harmful. Early Christians, too, considered homosexuality a conventional expression of physical desire and were no more susceptible to anti-homosexual prejudices than pagans were. Some prominent Christians experienced loving same-gender relationships that probably had a sexual element. What eventually led to a change in public and Christian attitudes toward sexual behavior was the shift from the sophisticated urban culture of the Greco-Roman world to the rural culture of medieval Europe.[11]

Synthesis: Saint Augustine

The finest representative of the blending of classical and Christian ideas, and indeed one of the most brilliant thinkers in the history of the Western world, was Saint Augustine of Hippo (354–430). Aside from the scriptural writers, no one else has had a greater impact on Christian thought in succeeding centuries. Saint Augustine was born into an urban family in what is now Algeria in North Africa. His father was a pagan; his mother, Monica, a devout Christian.

Augustine received his basic education in the local school. By modern and even medieval standards, that education was extremely narrow: textual study of the writings of the poet Virgil, the orator-politician Cicero, the historian Sallust, and the playwright Terence. As in the Islamic (see page 266) and Chinese worlds, learning in the Christian West meant memorization. Education in the late Roman world aimed at appreciation of words, particularly those of renowned and eloquent orators.

At the age of seventeen, Augustine went to nearby Carthage to continue his education. There he took a mistress with whom he lived for fifteen years. At Carthage, Augustine began an intellectual and spiritual pilgrimage that led him through experiments with several philosophies and heretical Christian sects. In 383 he traveled to Rome, where he endured not only illness but also disappointment in his teaching: his students fled when their bills were due.

Finally, in Milan in 387, Augustine received Christian baptism. He later became bishop of the seacoast city of Hippo Regius in his native North Africa. He was a renowned preacher to Christians there, a vigorous defender of orthodox Christianity, and the author of over ninety-three books and treatises.

Augustine's autobiography, *The Confessions,* is one of the most influential books in the history of Europe. Written in the form of a prayer, *The Confessions* describes Augustine's moral struggle: the conflict between his spiritual and intellectual aspirations and his sensual and material self.

The Confessions, written in the rhetorical style and language of late Roman antiquity, marks the synthesis of Greco-Roman forms and Christian thought. Many Greek and Roman philosophers had taught that knowledge and virtue are the same—that a person who really knows what is right will do what is right. Augustine rejected this idea. He believed that a person may know what is right but fail to act righteously because of the innate weakness of the human will. He pointed out that people do not always act on the basis of rational knowledge. A learned person can be corrupt and evil.

Augustine's ideas on sin, grace, and redemption became the foundation of all subsequent Christian theology, Protestant as well as Catholic. He wrote that the basic or dynamic force in any individual is the *will,* which he defined as "the power of the soul to hold on to or to obtain an object without constraint." The end or goal of the will determines the moral character of the individual. When Adam ate the fruit forbidden by God in the garden of Eden (Genesis 3:6), he committed "the original sin" and corrupted the will. By concupiscence, or sexual desire, which all humans have, Adam's sin has been passed on by hereditary transmission through the flesh to all humanity. Original sin thus became a common social stain. Because Adam disobeyed God and fell, so all human beings have an innate tendency to sin: their will is weak. But, according to Augustine, God restores the strength of the will through grace (his love, assistance, support), which is transmitted through the sacraments, such as penance, or reconciliation, by the action of the Spirit.

When the Visigothic chieftain Alaric conquered Rome in 410, horrified pagans blamed the disaster on the Christians. In response, Augustine wrote *City of God.* This profoundly original work contrasts Christianity with the secular society in which it existed. *City of God* presents a moral interpretation of the Roman government—in fact, of all history. Filled with references to ancient history and mythology, it remained for centuries the standard statement of the Christian philosophy of history.

According to Augustine, history is the account of God acting in time. Human history reveals that there are two kinds of people: those who live according to the flesh in the City of Babylon and those who live according to the spirit in the City of God. The former will endure eternal hellfire, the latter eternal bliss.

Augustine maintained that states came into existence as the result of Adam's fall and people's inclination to sin. The state is a necessary evil, but it can work for the good by providing the peace, justice, and order that Christians need in order to pursue their pilgrimage to the City of God. The particular form of government—whether monarchy, aristocracy, or democracy—is basically irrelevant. Any civil government that fails to provide justice is no more than a band of gangsters.

Although the state results from a moral lapse—from sin—the church (the Christian community) is not entirely free from sin. The church is certainly not equivalent to the City of God. But the church, which is concerned with salvation, is responsible for everyone, including Christian rulers. Churches in the Middle Ages used Augustine's theory to defend their belief in the ultimate superiority of the spiritual power over the temporal.

CHRISTIAN MONASTICISM

Christianity began and spread as a city religion. Since the first century, however, some especially pious Christians had felt that the only alternative to the decadence of urban life was complete separation from the world. The fourth century witnessed a significant change in the relationship between Christianity and the broader society. Until Constantine's legalization of Christianity, Christians were a persecuted minority. Some were tortured and killed. Christians greatly revered these martyrs, who, like Jesus, suffered and died for their faith. When Christianity was legalized and the persecutions ended, a new problem arose.

Whereas Christians had been a suffering minority, now they came to be identified with the state: non-Christians could not advance in the imperial service. But if Christianity had triumphed, so had "the world," for secular attitudes and values pervaded the church. The church of martyrs no longer existed. Some scholars believe the monasteries provided a way of life for those Christians who wanted to make a total response to Christ's teachings— people who wanted more than a lukewarm Christianity. The monks became the new martyrs. Saint Anthony of Egypt (d. 356), the first monk for whom there is concrete evidence and the person later considered the father of monasticism, went to Alexandria during the last persecution in the hope of gaining martyrdom. Christians believed that monks, like the martyrs before them, could speak to God and that their prayers had special influence with him.

Western Monasticism

Monasticism began in Egypt in the third century. At first individuals and small groups withdrew from cities and organized society to seek God through prayer in caves and shelters in the desert or mountains. Gradually large colonies of monks emerged in the deserts of Upper Egypt. They were called hermits, from the Greek word *eremos,* meaning "desert." Many devout women also were attracted to the monastic life. Although monks (and nuns) led isolated lives and the monastic movement represented the antithesis of the ancient ideal of an urban social existence, ordinary people soon recognized the monks and nuns as holy people and sought them as spiritual guides.

Church leaders did not really approve of **eremitical** life. Hermits sometimes claimed to have mystical experiences—direct communications with God. If hermits could communicate directly with the Lord, what need had they for the priest and the institutional church? The scholarly bishop Basil of Caesarea in Cappadocia in Asia Minor argued that the eremitical life posed the danger of excessive concern with the self and did not provide the opportunity for the exercise of charity, the first virtue of any Christian. Saint Basil and the church hierarchy encouraged **coenobitic monasticism,** communal living in monasteries, which provided an environment for training the aspirant in the virtues of charity, poverty, and freedom from self-deception.

In the fourth, fifth, and sixth centuries, many experiments in communal monasticism were made in Gaul, Italy, Spain, Anglo-Saxon England, and Ireland. The abbey or monastery of Lérins on the Mediterranean Sea near Cannes (ca 410) encouraged the severely penitential and extremely ascetic behavior common in the East, such as long hours of prayer, fasting, and self-flagellation. The Roman-British monk Saint Patrick carried this tradition of harsh self-mortification from Lérins to Ireland in the fifth century, and Irish monastic life followed the ascetic Eastern form. Around 540 the former Roman senator Cassiodorus established a monastery, the Vivarium, on his estate in Italy. Cassiodorus enlisted highly educated and sophisticated men to copy both sacred and secular manuscripts, intending this to be their sole occupation. Cassiodorus started the association of monasticism with scholarship and learning. This developed into a great tradition in the medieval and modern worlds.

The *Rule* of Benedict

In 529 Benedict of Nursia (480–543), who had experimented with both the eremitical and the communal forms of monastic life, wrote a brief set of regulations for the monks who had gathered around him at Monte Cassino between Rome and Naples. Benedict's *Rule* proved highly adaptable and slowly replaced all others.

Cum dombus nifos pluter paraer accipe hbfos.

Saint Benedict   Holding his *Rule* in his left hand, the seated and cowled patriarch of Western monasticism blesses a monk with his right hand. His monastery, Monte Cassino, is in the background. *(Biblioteca Apostolica Vaticana)*

The Rule of Saint Benedict has influenced all forms of organized religious life in the Roman church.

Saint Benedict conceived of his *Rule* as a simple code for ordinary men. It outlined a monastic life of regularity, discipline, and moderation. Each monk had ample food and adequate sleep. Self-destructive acts of mortification were forbidden. In an atmosphere of silence, the monk spent part of the day in formal prayer, which Benedict called the "Work of God." This consisted of chanting psalms and other prayers from the Bible. The rest of the day was passed in study and manual labor. After a year of probation, the monk made three vows.

First, the monk vowed stability: he promised to live his entire life in the monastery of his profession. The object of this vow was to prevent the wandering so common in Saint Benedict's day. Second, the monk vowed conversion of manners—that is, to strive to improve himself and to come closer to God. Third, he promised obedience to the abbot, or head of the monastery.

The Rule of Saint Benedict expresses the assimilation of the Roman spirit into Western monasticism. It reveals the logical mind of its creator and the Roman concern for order, organization, and respect for law. Its spirit of moderation and flexibility is reflected in the patience, wisdom, and understanding with which the abbot is to govern and, indeed, with which life is to be led.

Saint Benedict's *Rule* implies that a person who wants to become a monk or nun need have no previous ascetic experience or even a particularly strong bent toward the religious life. Thus it allowed for the admission of newcomers with different backgrounds and personalities. From Chapter 59, "The Offering of Sons by Nobles or by the Poor," and from Benedict's advice to the abbot—"The abbot should avoid all favoritism in the monastery. . . . A man born free is not to be given higher rank than a slave who becomes a monk" (Chapter 2)—we know that men of different social classes belonged to his monastery. This flexibility helps to explain the attractiveness of Benedictine monasticism throughout the centuries.

The monastic life as conceived by Saint Benedict did not lean too heavily in any one direction. With its division of the day into prayer, study, and manual labor, it struck a balance between asceticism and idleness. It thus provided opportunities for persons of entirely different abilities and talents—from mechanics to gardeners to literary scholars. Benedict's *Rule* contrasts sharply with Cassiodorus's narrow concept of the monastery as a place for aristocratic bibliophiles.

Benedictine monasticism also suited the social circumstances of early medieval society. The Germanic invasions had fragmented European life: the self-sufficient rural estate replaced the city as the basic unit of civilization. A monastery, too, had to be economically self-sufficient. It was supposed to produce from its lands and properties all that was needed for food, clothing, shelter, and liturgical service of the altar. The monastery fitted in—indeed, represented—the trend toward localism. The Benedictine form of religious life also proved congenial to women. Five miles from Monte Cassino at Plombariola, Benedict's twin sister Scholastica (480–543) adapted the *Rule* for the use of her community of nuns. Many other convents for nuns were established in the early Middle Ages.

Benedictine monasticism also succeeded partly because it was so materially successful. In the seventh and eighth centuries, monasteries pushed back forest and wasteland, drained swamps, and experimented with crop rotation. Such Benedictine houses made a significant contribution to the agricultural development of Europe, earning immense wealth in the process. The communal nature of their organization, whereby property was held in common and profits were pooled and reinvested, made this contribution possible.

Finally, monasteries conducted schools for local young people. Some learned about prescriptions and herbal remedies and went on to provide medical treatment for their localities. A few copied manuscripts and wrote books. This training did not go unappreciated in a society desperately in need of it. Local and royal governments drew on the services of the literate men and able administrators the monasteries produced.

Eastern Monasticism

From Egypt, Christian monasticism also spread to the Greek provinces of Syria and Palestine and to Constantinople itself. With financial assistance from the emperor Justinian I (527–565) and from wealthy nobles, monasteries soon spread throughout the empire, with seventy abbeys erected in Constantinople alone. Justinian granted the monks the right to inherit property from private citizens and the right to receive **solemnia,** or annual gifts, from the imperial treasury or from the taxes of certain provinces, and he prohibited lay confiscation of monastic estates. Beginning in the tenth century, the monasteries acquired fields, pastures, livestock, mills, saltworks, and urban rental properties, as well as cash and precious liturgical vessels. The exemption of Byzantine monasteries from state taxes also served to increase monastic wealth.

Monasticism in the Greek Orthodox world differed in fundamental ways from the monasticism that evolved in western Europe. First, while *The Rule of Saint Benedict* gradually became the universal guide for all western European monasteries, each individual house in the Byzantine world developed its own **typikon,** or set of rules for organization and behavior. The *typika* contain regulations about novitiate, diet, clothing, liturgical functions, commemorative services for benefactors, and the election of officials, such as the *hegoumenos,* or superior of the house. Second, while stability in the monastery eventually characterized Western monasticism, many Orthodox monks "moved frequently from one monastery to another or alternated between a coenobitic monastery and a hermit's kellion [cell]."[12] Finally, unlike the West, where monasteries often established schools for the education of the youth of the neighborhood, education never became a central feature of the Greek houses. Monks and nuns had to be literate to perform the services of the choir, and children destined for the monastic life were taught to read and write. In the monasteries where monks or nuns devoted themselves to study and writing, their communities sometimes played important roles in the development of theology and in the intellectual life of the empire. But those houses were very few, and no monastery assumed responsibility for the general training of the local young. Since bishops and patriarchs of the Greek church were recruited only from the monasteries, Greek houses did, however, exercise a cultural influence.

THE MIGRATION OF THE GERMANIC PEOPLES

The migration of peoples from one area to another has been a dominant and continuing feature of world history. The causes of early migrations varied and are not thoroughly understood by scholars. But there is no question that they profoundly affected both the regions to which peoples moved and the regions they left behind.

The *Völkerwanderungen,* or migrations of the Germanic peoples, were important in the decline of the western Roman Empire and in the making of European civilization. Since about 150, Germanic tribes from the regions of the northern Rhine, Elbe, and Oder Rivers had pressed along the Rhine-Danube frontier of the Roman Empire. Some tribes, such as the Visigoths and Ostrogoths, led a settled existence, engaged in agriculture and trade, and accepted Arian Christianity. Other tribes, such as the Angles, Saxons, and Huns, led a nomadic life unaffected by Roman influences.

Why did the Germans migrate? Although many twentieth-century scholars have tried to answer this question, the answer is not known. Perhaps overpopulation and the resulting food shortages caused migration. Perhaps victorious tribes forced the vanquished to move southward. Probably "the primary stimulus for this gradual migration was the Roman frontier, which increasingly offered service in the army and work for pay around the camps."[13]

The Idea of the Barbarian

The Greeks and Romans invented the idea of the **barbarian.** The Romans labeled all peoples living outside the frontiers of the Roman Empire (except the Persians) as barbarians. Geography, rather than ethnic background, determined a people's classification. The Romans also held that peoples outside the empire had no history and were touched by history only when they entered the Roman Empire.

The modern study of ethnography (writing about the formation of ethnic groups) involves the systematic recording of the major characteristics of different human cultures. Scholars today identify three models of ethnic formation among the Germanic peoples who came in contact with the Romans and whom the Romans called barbarians.

First, there were those Germanic peoples whose identity was shaped by a militarily successful or "royal" family. For example, the Salian Franks, Lombards, and Goths attracted and controlled followers from other peoples by getting them to adhere to the cultural traditions of the leading family. Followers assimilated the "kernel family's" legendary traditions and myths, which traced their origins to a family or individual of divine ancestry. The kernel family led these followers from their original territory, won significant victories over other peoples, and settled someplace within the Roman world.

A second model of ethnic formation derives from Central Asian steppe peoples such as the Huns, Avars, and Alans. These were polyethnic, seminomadic, and seden-

tary groups led by a small body of steppe commanders. (The term *steppe* refers to the vast semiarid plain in Russian Siberia.) These peoples constituted large confederations, whose success depended on constant expansion by military victory or the use of terror. Defeat in battle or the death of a leader could lead to the disintegration of the confederation.

The Alamanni and the Slavs represented a third model of barbarian ethnic formation. Because no evidence of collective legends, genealogies, or traditions among these peoples survives, we do not know whether they had a consciousness of collective identity. They were loosely organized, short-lived bands of peoples who lacked centralized leadership. Because the Slavs intermingled with Turko-Tartar, Finnic, Germanic, and Mongol peoples, the early Slavs possessed no ethnic identity.

One fundamental trait characterizes all barbarian peoples: the formation of ethnic groups did not represent a single historical event. Rather, the formation of such peoples was a continuous and changing process extending over long periods of time.[14]

Romanization and Barbarization

By the late third century, a large percentage of military recruits came from the Germanic peoples. Besides army recruits, several types of barbarian peoples entered the empire and became affiliated with Roman government. The *laeti,* refugees or prisoners of war, were settled with their families in areas of Gaul and Italy under the supervision of Roman prefects and landowners. Generally isolated from the local Roman population, the laeti farmed regions depopulated by plague. The men had to serve in the Roman army.

Free barbarian units called **foederati,** stationed near major provincial cities, were a second type of affiliated barbarian group. Research has suggested that rather than giving them land, the Romans assigned the foederati shares of the tax revenues from the region.[15] Living close to Roman communities, the foederati quickly assimilated into Roman culture. In fact, in the fourth century, some foederati rose to the highest ranks of the army and moved in the most cultured and aristocratic circles.

The arrival of the Huns in the West in 376 precipitated the entry of entire peoples, the *gentes,* into the Roman Empire. Pressured by defeat in battle, starvation, or the movement of other peoples, tribes such as the Ostrogoths and Visigoths entered in large numbers, perhaps as many as twenty thousand men, women, and children.[16] Once the Visigoths were inside the empire, Roman authorities exploited their hunger by forcing them to sell

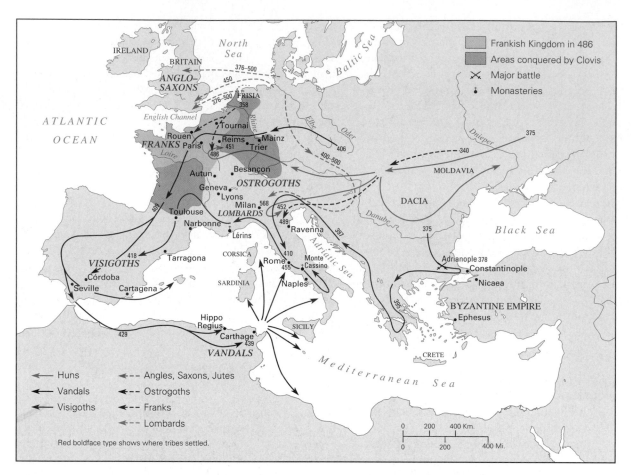

MAP 8.2 The Germanic Migrations   The Germanic tribes infiltrated and settled in all parts of western Europe. The Huns, who were not German ethnically, originated in Central Asia. The Huns' victory over the Ostrogoths led the emperor to allow the Visigoths to settle within the empire, a decision that proved disastrous for Rome.

their own people in exchange for dog flesh: "the going rate was one dog for one Goth." The bitterness of those enslaved was aggravated by the arrival of the Ostrogoths. A huge rebellion erupted, and the Goths crushed the Roman army at Adrianople on August 9, 378.[17] This date marks the beginning of massive Germanic invasions into the empire (see Map 8.2).

Except for the Lombards, whose conquests of Italy persisted into the mid-eighth century, the movements of Germanic peoples on the European continent ended about 600. Between 450 and 565, the Germans established a number of kingdoms, but none except the Frankish kingdom lasted very long. Unlike modern nation-states, the Germanic kingdoms did not have definite geographical boundaries. The Visigoths overran much of southwestern Gaul. Establishing their headquarters at Toulouse,

they exercised a weak domination over Spain until a great Muslim victory at Guadalete in 711 ended Visigothic rule. The Vandals, whose destructive ways are commemorated in the word *vandal,* settled in North Africa. In northern and western Europe in the sixth century, the Burgundians established rule over lands roughly circumscribed by old Roman army camps at Lyons, Besançon, Geneva, and Autun.

In northern Italy, the Ostrogothic king Theodoric (r. 471–526) established his capital at Ravenna and gradually won control of all Italy, Sicily, and the territory north and east of the upper Adriatic. Though attached to the customs of his people, Theodoric pursued a policy of assimilation between Germans and Romans. He maintained close relations with the emperor at Constantinople and attracted to his administration able scholars such

Germanic Bracteate (Gold Leaf) Pendant   This late-fifth-century piece, with the head of Rome above a wolf suckling Romulus and Remus, reflects Germanic assimilation of Roman legend and artistic design. *(Courtesy of the Trustees of the British Museum)*

as Cassiodorus (see page 218). Theodoric's accomplishments were significant, but after his death his administration fell apart.

The most enduring Germanic kingdom was established by the Frankish chieftain Clovis (r. 481–511). Originally only a petty chieftain in northwestern Gaul (modern Belgium), Clovis began to expand his territories in 486. His Catholic wife Clothild worked to convert her husband and supported the founding of churches and monasteries. Clothild typifies the role women played in the Christianization and Romanization of the Germanic kingdoms. Clovis's conversion to orthodox Christianity in 496 won him the crucial support of the papacy and the bishops of Gaul. (See the feature "Listening to the Past: The Conversion of Clovis" on pages 236–237.) As the defender of Roman Catholicism against heretical Germanic tribes, Clovis went on to conquer the Visigoths, extending his domain as far as the Pyrenees and making Paris his headquarters. Because he was descended from the half-legendary chieftain Merovech, the dynasty that Clovis founded has been called Merovingian (see pages 364–365).

The island of Britain, conquered by Rome during the reign of Claudius, shared fully in the life of the Roman Empire during the first four centuries of the Christian era. A military aristocracy governed, and the official religion was the cult of the emperor. Towns were planned in the Roman fashion, with temples, public baths, theaters, and amphitheaters. In the countryside, large manors controlled the surrounding lands. Roman merchants brought Eastern luxury goods and religions—including Christianity—into Britain. The native Britons, a peaceful Celtic people, became thoroughly Romanized. Their language was Latin; their lifestyle was Roman.

After the Roman defeat at Adrianople, however, Roman troops were withdrawn from Britain, leaving it unprotected. The savage Picts from Scotland harassed the north. Teutonic tribes from modern-day Norway, Sweden, and Denmark—the Angles, Saxons, and Jutes—stepped up their assaults. Germans took over the best lands and humbled the Britons. Germanic tribes never subdued Scotland, where the Picts remained strong, or Wales, where the Celts and native Britons continued to put up stubborn resistance.

GERMANIC SOCIETY

After the Germans replaced the Romans, Germanic customs and traditions shaped European society for centuries. What sorts of social, political, and economic life did the Germans have? Scholars are hampered in answering such questions because the Germans did not write and thus kept no written records before their conversion to Christianity. The earliest information about them comes from moralistic accounts by Romans such as the historian Tacitus (see page 174), who was acquainted only with the tribes living closest to the borders of the Roman Empire and imposed Greco-Roman categories of tribes and nations on the Germanic peoples he described.

Kinship, Class, and Law

The Germans had no notion of the state as we use the term; they thought in social, not political, terms. The basic Germanic social unit was the tribe, or *folk*. Members of the folk believed that they were all descended from a common ancestor. Blood united them. Kinship protected them. Law was custom—unwritten and handed down by word of mouth from generation to generation. Custom regulated everything. Members were subject to their tribe's customary law wherever they went, and friendly tribes respected one another's laws.

Germanic tribes were led by kings or tribal chieftains. The chief, recognized as the strongest and bravest in battle, was elected from among the male members of the strongest family. He led the tribe in war, settled disputes among its members, conducted negotiations with outside powers, and offered sacrifices to the gods.

Closely associated with the chief in some southern tribes was the **comitatus,** or "war band." Writing at the end of the first century, Tacitus described the war band as the bravest young men in the tribe. They swore loyalty to the chief, fought with him in battle, and were not supposed to leave the battlefield without him; to do so implied cowardice and disloyalty and resulted in social disgrace. Social egalitarianism existed among members of the war band.

During the migrations of the third and fourth centuries, and as a result of constant warfare, the war band was transformed into a system of stratified ranks. Armbands, first obtained through contact with the Romans, came to be coveted as marks of rank, especially the gold ones reserved for the "royal families." During the Ostrogothic conquest of Italy under Theodoric, warrior-nobles also sought to acquire land, both as a mark of prestige and as a means to power. As land and wealth came into the hands of a small elite class, social inequalities emerged and gradually grew stronger.[18] These inequalities help to explain the origins of the European noble class (see page 396).

As long as custom determined all behavior, the early Germans had no need for written law. Beginning in the late sixth century, however, German tribal chieftains began to collect, write, and publish lists of their customs. Why then? The Christian missionaries who were slowly converting the Germans to Christianity wanted to read about German ways in order to assimilate the tribes to Christianity, and they encouraged German rulers to write their customs down. Moreover, by the sixth century the German rulers needed regulations that applied to the Romans under their jurisdiction as well as to their own people.

Today, if a person holds up a bank, American law maintains that the robber attacks both the bank and the state in which it exists—a sophisticated notion involving the abstract idea of the state. In early Germanic law, all crimes were regarded as crimes against a person.

According to the code of the Salian Franks, every person had a particular monetary value to the tribe. This value was called the **wergeld,** which literally means "man-money" or "money to buy off the spear." Men of fighting age had the highest wergeld, then women of childbearing age, then children, and finally the aged. If a person accused of a crime agreed to pay the wergeld and if the victim and his or her family accepted the payment, there was peace. If the accused refused to pay the

wergeld or if the victim's family refused to accept it, a blood feud ensued. Individuals depended on their kin for protection, and kinship served as a force of social control.

The early law codes are patchwork affairs studded with additions made in later centuries. The law code of the Salian Franks issued by Clovis offers a general picture of Germanic life and problems in the early Middle Ages and is typical of the law codes of other tribes. The **Salic Law** is not really a code of law at all, but a list of tariffs or fines for particular offenses.

If any person strike another on the head so that the brain appears, and the three bones which lie above the brain shall project, he shall be sentenced to 1200 denars, which make 300 shillings. . . .

If any one have killed a free woman after she has begun bearing children, he shall be sentenced to 2400 denars, which make 600 shillings. . . .

If any one shall have drawn a harrow through another's harvest after it has sprouted, or shall have gone through it with a wagon where there was no road, he shall be sentenced to 120 denars, which make 30 shillings.[19]

Germanic law aimed at the prevention or reduction of violence. It was not concerned with abstract justice.

Germanic law differed considerably from Roman law. By the time of the Germanic migrations, Roman law consisted of a mass of imperial edicts, judicial decisions, senatorial enactments, and commentaries of jurists. Roman law included public law, which concerned affairs of the state, and private law, which related to the interests of individuals. It dealt with issues of marriage and the family, commerce and trade, property rights and criminal acts. It was written down. It regulated a complex and sophisticated society, and it involved abstract ideas such as the state and justice. Germanic law was unwritten; it was custom passed down by oral tradition from one generation to the next. Legislation did not consist of new laws issued by a king or chief or made by an assembly. Rather, Germanic law was found in the collective memory of the customs of the folk, and that custom was then applied to a particular situation. Germanic law was attached to the individual person, not to any territory, and the person took his law wherever he went.

As German kings accepted Christianity and as Romans and Germans increasingly intermarried, the distinction between Germanic and Roman law blurred and, in the course of the seventh and eighth centuries, disappeared. The result would be the new feudal law.

Germanic Life

The Germans usually resided in small villages. Climate and geography determined the basic patterns of agricultural and pastoral life. In the flat or open coastal regions, men engaged in animal husbandry, especially cattle raising. Many tribes lived in small settlements on the edges of clearings where they raised barley, wheat, oats, peas, and beans. They tilled their fields with a simple wooden scratch plow and harvested their grains with a small iron sickle. Women ground the kernels of grain with a grindstone and made the resulting flour into a dough that they shaped into flat cakes and baked on clay trays. Much of the grain was fermented into a strong, thick beer. Women performed the heavy work of raising, grinding, and preserving cereals, a mark, some scholars believe, of their low status in a male-dominated society. Women were also responsible for weaving and spinning.

Within the small villages, there were great differences in wealth and status. Free men constituted the largest class. The number of cattle a man possessed indicated his wealth and determined his social status. "Cattle were so much the quintessential indicator of wealth in traditional society that the modern English term 'fee' (meaning cost of goods or services), which developed from the medieval term 'fief,' had its origin in the Germanic term *fihu . . .* , meaning cattle, chattels, and hence, in general, wealth."[20] Free men also shared in tribal warfare. Slaves (prisoners of war) worked as farm laborers, herdsmen, or household servants.

Germanic society was patriarchal: within each household the father had authority over his wives, children, and slaves. The Germans practiced polygamy, and men who could afford them had more than one wife.

Did the Germans produce goods for trade and exchange? Ironworking was the most advanced craft of the Germanic peoples. Much of northern Europe had iron deposits at or near the earth's surface, and the dense forests provided wood for charcoal. Most villages had an oven and smiths who produced agricultural tools and instruments of war—one-edged swords, arrowheads, and shields. In the first two centuries C.E., the quantity and quality of German goods increased dramatically, and the first steel swords were superior to the weapons of Roman troops. German goods, however, were produced for war and the subsistence economy, not for trade. Goods were also used for gift giving, a social custom that conferred status on the giver. Gift giving showed the higher (economic) status of the giver, cemented friendship, and placed the re-

ceiver in the giver's debt.[21] Goods that could not be produced in the village were acquired by raiding and warfare rather than by commercial exchanges. Raids between tribes brought the victors booty; captured cattle and slaves were traded or given as gifts. Warfare determined the economy and the individual's status within Germanic society.

What was the position of women in Germanic society? Did they have, as some scholars contend, a higher status than they were to have later in the Middle Ages? The law codes provide the best evidence. The codes show societies that regarded women as family property. A marriageable daughter went to the highest bidder. A woman of childbearing years had a very high wergeld. The codes also protected the virtue of women. For example, the Salic Law of the Franks fined a man a large amount if he pressed the hand of a woman and even more if he touched her above the elbow. But heavy fines did not stop injury, rape, or abduction. Widows were sometimes seized on the battlefields where their dead husbands lay and were forced to marry the victors.

A few slaves and peasant women used their beauty and their intelligence to advance their positions. The slave Fredegunda, for whom King Chilperic murdered his Visigothic wife, became a queen and held her position after her husband's death.[22]

THE BYZANTINE EAST (CA 400–788)

Constantine (r. 306–337) and later emperors tried to maintain the unity of the Roman Empire, but during the fifth and sixth centuries the western and eastern halves drifted apart. Justinian (r. 527–565) waged long and hard-fought wars against the Ostrogoths and temporarily regained Italy and North Africa. But his conquests had disastrous consequences. Justinian's wars exhausted the resources of the Byzantine state, destroyed Italy's economy, and killed a large part of Italy's population. The wars paved the way for the easy conquest of Italy by the Lombards shortly after Justinian's death. In the late sixth century, the territory of the western Roman Empire came under Germanic sway, while in the East the Byzantine Empire (see Map 8.3) continued the traditions and institutions of the caesars.

Latin Christian culture was only one legacy the Roman Empire bequeathed to the Western world. The Byzantine culture centered at Constantinople was another. The

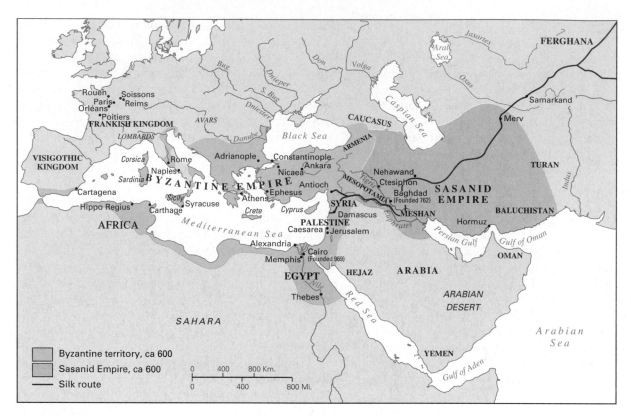

MAP 8.3 The Byzantine Empire, ca 600   The Sasanid kingdom of Persia spanned much of central Asia, while the Byzantine Empire straddled Asia and Europe. The series of wars between the two powers brought neither of them lasting territorial acquisitions; the strife weakened them and paved the way for Islamic conquest in the seventh century.

Byzantine Empire maintained a high standard of living, and for centuries the Greeks were the most civilized people in the Western world. The Byzantine Empire held at bay barbarian peoples who otherwise could have wreaked additional devastation on western Europe, retarding its development. Most important, however, is the role of the Byzantines, together with the Muslims (see pages 232, 268–269), as preservers of the wisdom of the ancient world. Throughout the long years when barbarians in western Europe trampled down the old and then painfully built something new, Byzantium protected the intellectual heritage of Greco-Roman civilization.

While the western parts of the Roman Empire gradually succumbed to Germanic invaders, the eastern or Roman-Byzantine Empire survived Germanic, Persian, and Arab attacks. In 540 the Huns and Bulgars raided Greece. In 559 a force of Huns and Slavs reached the gates of Constantinople. In 583 the Avars, a mounted Mongol people who had swept across Russia and southeastern Europe, seized Byzantine forts along the Danube and also reached the walls of Constantinople. Between 572 and 630 the Greeks were repeatedly at war with the Sasanid Persians (see below). Beginning in 632, the Arabs pressured the Greek empire. Why didn't one or a combination of these enemies capture Constantinople, as the Germans had taken Rome?

The answer lies in the strong military leadership the Greeks possessed, and even more in the city's location and its excellent fortifications. Under the skillful leadership of General Priskos (d. 612), Byzantine armies inflicted a severe defeat on the Avars in 601. Then, after a long war, the well-organized emperor Heraclius I (r. 610–641), helped by dynastic disputes among the Persians and Muslim pressures on them, crushed the Persians at Nineveh in Iraq. The Muslim Arabs now posed the greatest threat to the Byzantines. Why didn't they conquer the city? As a recent scholar explains, "If in the fourth century Constantine had chosen Antioch, Alexandria or Palestinian Caesarea as a capital there could be little doubt that the Roman empire would have gone as swiftly (to the Muslims) as the Persian."[23] The site of Constantinople was not absolutely impregnable—as the Venetians demonstrated in 1204 (see page 375) and as the Ottoman Turks showed in 1453. But it was almost so. Constantinople had the most powerful defenses in the ancient world. Massive triple walls, built by Constantine and Theodosius II (r. 408–450) and kept in good repair, protected the city from sea invasion. Within the walls huge cisterns provided water, and vast gardens and grazing areas supplied vegetables and meat. Such strong fortifications and provisions meant that if attacked by sea, a defending people could hold out far longer than a besieging army.

The site chosen for the imperial capital in the fourth century enabled Constantinople to survive in the eighth century. Because the city survived, the empire, though reduced in territory, endured.[24]

The Sasanid Kingdom of Persia and Byzantium

In 226, Ardashir I (r. 226–243), a member of the Sasanid family indigenous to southern Persia and a vassal of the Parthian king Artabanus V, defeated Artabanus at Hormuz. Ardashir assumed authority over Parthian territories, received the submission of the Kushans and of Turan (modern Pakistan and Baluchistan) in the east and of Merv in the northeast, and founded the Sasanid dynasty, which lasted until 651, when it was overthrown by the Muslims. On the death of the Roman emperor Alexander Severus in 235, Ardashir absorbed the Roman province of Mesopotamia.

Centered in the fertile Tigris-Euphrates Valley, but with access to the Persian Gulf and extending south to Meshan (modern Kuwait), the Sasanid kingdom's economic prosperity rested on agriculture; its location also proved well suited for commerce. A lucrative caravan trade from Ctesiphon north to Merv and then east to Samarkand linked the Sasanid kingdom to the Silk Road and China (see page 186). Persian metalwork, textiles, and glass were exchanged for Chinese silks, and these goods brought about considerable cultural contact between the Sasanids and the Chinese.

Sasanid Persian Plate   Hunting scenes enjoyed great popularity in Sasanid art. This image of King Shapur II (r. 309–379), depicting the ruler with a full beard and elaborately styled hair while hunting lions on horseback, seems reminiscent of ancient Assyrian art (see page 43). Carried across the Central Asian Silk Road and exchanged for Chinese silk, this gilded silver plate came into the possession of a Tang Dynasty official. Chinese desire for things Persian mirrored Western passion for Chinese silk. *(Courtesy of the Middle Eastern Culture Center in Japan)*

Whereas the Parthians had tolerated many religions, the Sasanid Persians made Zoroastrianism the official state religion. Religion and the state were inextricably tied together. The king's power rested on the support of nobles and Zoroastrian **magi** (priests), who monopolized positions in the court and in the imperial bureaucracy. A highly elaborate court ceremonial and ritual exalted the status of the king and emphasized his semidivine pre-eminence over his subjects. (The Byzantine monarchy, the Roman papacy, and the Muslim caliphate subsequently copied aspects of this Persian ceremonial.) Zoroastrianism promoted hostility toward Christians because of what was perceived as their connections to Rome and Constantinople, and the sizable Jewish population in Mesopotamia after the **diaspora** (dispersion of the Jews from Jerusalem between 132 and 135) suffered intermittent persecution.

An expansionist foreign policy brought Persia into frequent conflict with the Roman Empire. Between 337 and 376, the Persians and Romans engaged in three indecisive wars. After the shift of the Roman capital to Constantinople, war repeatedly erupted between the Persians and Byzantines, partly because of Persian persecution of Christians, whom the Greeks sought to defend, and partly because both Persia and Byzantium had interests in Syria and Armenia. Neither side was able to achieve a clear-cut victory. The long wars, financed by higher taxation, on top of the arrival of the bubonic plague (see page 233), compounded discontent in both Byzantine and Persian societies. Political instability, characterized by palace coups, weakened both regimes. Finally, Byzantine persecution of Monophysites and Persian persecution of Christians and Jews created bitterness in those minorities. Thus domestic infirmities eased the way for the Arab sweep across the Persian plains and defeat of the imperial Sasanid army in 642 at Nihawand. The execution of Yazdgird III (r. 632–651) brought an end to the Sasanid dynasty. Persian territories were then absorbed into the Islamic caliphate (see page 244).

Byzantine East and Germanic West

As imperial authority disintegrated in the West during the fifth century, civic functions were performed first by church leaders and then by German chieftains. Meanwhile, in the East, the Byzantines preserved the forms and traditions of the old Roman Empire and even called themselves Romans. Byzantine emperors traced their lines back past Constantine to the emperor Augustus.

The senate that sat in Constantinople carried on the traditions and preserved the glory of the old Roman senate. The army that defended the empire was the direct descendant of the old Roman legions. Even the chariot factions of the Roman Empire lived on under the Greeks, who cheered their favorites as enthusiastically as had the Romans of Hadrian's day.

The position of the church differed considerably in the Byzantine East and the Germanic West. The fourth-century emperors Constantine and Theodosius had wanted the church to act as a unifying force within the empire, but the Germanic invasions made that impossible. The bishops of Rome repeatedly called on the emperors at Constantinople for military support against the invaders, but rarely could the emperors send it. The church in the West steadily grew away from the empire and became involved in social and political affairs. Nevertheless, until the eighth century, the popes, who were often selected by the clergy of Rome, continued to send announcements of their election to the emperors at Constantinople—a sign that the popes long saw themselves as bishops of the Roman Empire.

Because the Western church concentrated on its missionary function, it took centuries for the clergy to be organized. Most church theology in the West came from the East, and the overwhelming majority of popes were of Eastern origin.

We have seen that Ambrose of Milan presented a view typical of the church in the West: that spiritual authority rested with church officials. Such an assertion was virtually unheard-of in the East, where the emperor's jurisdiction over the church was fully acknowledged. The emperor in Constantinople nominated the *patriarch,* as the highest prelate of the Eastern church was called. The Eastern emperor looked on religion as a branch of the state. Religion was such a vital aspect of the social life of the people that the emperor devoted considerable attention to it. He considered it his duty to protect the faith, not only against heathen enemies but also against heretics within the empire. In case of doctrinal disputes, the emperor, following Constantine's example at Nicaea, summoned councils of bishops and theologians to settle problems.

External Threats and Internal Conflicts

The wars of Justinian's reign left the Byzantine Empire economically and demographically weakened. Over the next two centuries, two additional troubles threatened its very survival: foreign invasions and internal theological disputes.

From these foreign invasions certain benefits did result. First, the territories lost to the empire contained peoples of very diverse ethnic origins, languages, and religions. The territories that continued under imperial authority gradually achieved a strong cultural unity. They were Greek in culture and administration, orthodox in religion.

Second, foreign invasions created the need for internal reorganization. The emperors militarized the administration, dividing the empire into **themes,** or military districts, governed by *strategoi,* or generals, who held both civil and military authority. The strategoi were directly responsible to the emperor. This reorganization brought into being a new peasant army. Foreign invasions had broken up the great landed estates of the empire, and the estate land was distributed to peasant soldiers, who equipped and supported themselves from the profits of the land. Formerly, the Byzantine state had relied on foreign mercenaries. Now each theme had an army of native soldiers with a permanent (landed) interest in the preservation of the empire. The government saved the costs of hiring troops and was assured the loyalty of native soldiers.

In addition, some scholars maintain that the military disasters of the period led to an increase in popular piety and devotion to *icons*—images or representations in painting, bas-relief, or mosaic of God the Father, Jesus, the Virgin, or the saints. Since the third century, the church had allowed people to venerate icons. Although all prayer had to be directed to God the Father, Christian teaching held that icons representing the saints fostered reverence and that Jesus and the saints could most effectively plead a cause to God the Father. *Iconoclasts,* those who favored the destruction of icons, argued that people were worshiping the image itself rather than what it signified. This, they claimed, constituted *idolatry,* a violation of the Mosaic prohibition of graven images in the Ten Commandments.

The result of the controversy over icons was a terrible theological conflict that split the Byzantine world for a century. In 730 the emperor Leo III (r. 717–741) ordered the destruction of the images. The removal of icons from Byzantine churches provoked a violent reaction: entire provinces revolted, and the empire and Roman papacy severed relations. Since Eastern monasteries were the fiercest defenders of icons, Leo's son Constantine V (r. 741–775), nicknamed "Copronymous" ("Dung-name") by his enemies, took the war to the monasteries. He seized their property, executed some of the monks, and forced others into the army. Theological disputes and civil disorder over the icons continued intermittently until 843, when the icons were restored.

The implications of the **iconoclastic controversy** extended far beyond strictly theological issues. Iconoclasm raised the question of the right of the emperor to intervene in religious disputes—a central problem in the relations of church and state. Iconoclasm antagonized the pope and served to encourage him in his quest for an alliance with the Frankish monarchy (see page 365). Iconoclasm thus contributed to the end of Byzantine political influence in central Italy. Arab control of the Mediterranean in the seventh and eighth centuries furthered the separation of the Roman and Byzantine churches by dividing the two parts of Christendom. Separation bred isolation. Isolation, combined with prejudice on both sides, bred hostility.

In 1054 a theological disagreement led the bishop of Rome and the patriarch of Constantinople to excommunicate each other. The outcome was a continuing **schism,** or split, between the Roman Catholic and the Greek Orthodox churches. The bitterness generated by iconoclasm contributed to that schism. Finally, the acceptance of icons profoundly influenced subsequent religious art. That art rejected the Judaic and Islamic prohibition of figural representation and continued in the Greco-Roman tradition of human representation.

The Byzantines spread their views to the East by civilizing the Slavs in the Balkans and in Russia. Byzantine missionaries spread the Word of Christ, and one of their triumphs was the conversion of the Russians in the tenth century. The Byzantine missionary Cyril invented a Slavic alphabet using Greek characters, and this script (called the Cyrillic alphabet) is still in use today. Cyrillic script made possible the birth of Russian literature. Similarly, Byzantine art and architecture became the basis and inspiration for Russian forms. The Byzantines were so successful that the Russians claimed to be the successors of the Byzantine Empire. For a time, Moscow was even known as the "Third Rome" (the second Rome being Constantinople).

The Law Code of Justinian

One of the most splendid achievements of the Byzantine emperors was the preservation of Roman law for the medieval and modern worlds. Roman law had developed from many sources—decisions by judges, edicts of the emperors, legislation passed by the senate, and the opinions of jurists expert in the theory and practice of law. By the fourth century, Roman law had become a huge, bewildering mass. Its sheer bulk made it almost unusable. Some laws had become outdated; some repeated or contradicted others.

Justinian and His Attendants This mosaic detail is composed of thousands of tiny cubes of colored glass or stone called *tessarae,* which are set in plaster against a blazing golden background. Some attempt has been made at naturalistic portraiture. *(Scala/Art Resource, NY)*

The emperor Justinian appointed a committee of eminent jurists to sort through and organize the laws. The result was the *Code,* which distilled the legal genius of the Romans into a coherent whole, eliminated outmoded laws and contradictions, and clarified the law itself.

Justinian next set about bringing order to the equally huge body of Roman *jurisprudence,* the science or philosophy of law. To harmonize the often differing opinions of Roman jurists, Justinian directed his jurists to clear up disputed points and to issue definitive rulings. Accordingly, in 533 his lawyers published the *Digest,* which codified Roman legal thought. Then Justinian's lawyers compiled a handbook of civil law, the *Institutes.*

These three works—the *Code, Digest,* and *Institutes*—are the backbone of the **corpus juris civilis,** the "body of civil law," which is the foundation of law for nearly every modern European nation.

Byzantine Intellectual Life

Among the Byzantines, education was highly prized, and because of them many masterpieces of ancient Greek literature survived to influence the intellectual life of the modern world. The literature of the Byzantine Empire was predominately Greek, although Latin was long spoken by top politicians, scholars, and lawyers. Among members of the large reading public, history was a favorite subject. Generations of Byzantines read the historical works of Herodotus, Thucydides, and Polybius.

The most remarkable Byzantine historian was Procopius (ca 500–ca 562), who left a rousing account of Justinian's reconquest of North Africa and Italy. Procopius's *Secret History,* however, is a vicious and uproarious attack on Justinian and his wife, the empress Theodora. (See the feature "Individuals in Society: Theodora of Constantinople.")

THEODORA OF CONSTANTINOPLE

The Empress Theodora, with a halo—symbolic of power in Eastern art. (Scala/Art Resource, NY)

The most notorious woman in Byzantine history, daughter of a circus bear trainer in the hippodrome, Theodora (ca 497–548) grew up in what contemporaries considered a morally corrupt atmosphere. Heredity gave her intelligence, wit, charm, and beauty, which she put to use as a striptease artist and actress. Modern scholars question the tales spread by the historian Procopius's *Secret History* (ca 550) about Theodora's insatiable sexual appetite, but the legend of her sensuality has often influenced interpretations of her.

Theodora gave up her stage career and passed her time spinning wool and discussing theological issues. When Justinian first saw her, he was so impressed by her beauty and wit, he brought her to the court, raised her to the *patriciate* (high nobility), and in 525 married her. When he was proclaimed co-emperor with his uncle Justin on April 1, 527, Theodora received the rare title of *augusta*, empress. Thereafter her name was always linked with Justinian's in the exercise of imperial power.

We know a fair amount about Theodora's public life. With four thousand attendants, she processed through the streets of Constantinople to attend Mass and celebrations thanking God for deliverance from the plague. She presided at imperial receptions for Arab sheiks, Persian ambassadors, Gothic princesses from the West, and barbarian chieftains from southern Russia. Her endowment of hospitals, orphanages, houses for the rehabilitation of prostitutes, and Monophysite churches gave her a reputation for piety and charity. But her private life remains hidden. She spent her days in the silken luxury of the *gynaceum* (women's quarters) among her female attendants and eunuch guards. She took the waters at the sulfur springs in Bithynia, and spent the hot summer months at her palace at Hieron, a small town on the Asiatic shore of the Bosporus. Justinian is reputed to have consulted her every day about all aspects of state policy.

One conciliar occasion stands out. In 532 various elements combined to provoke a massive revolt against the emperor. Shouting N-I-K-A (Victory), rioters swept through the city burning and looting. Justinian's counselors urged flight, but Theodora rose and declared:

For one who has reigned, it is intolerable to be an exile. . . . If you wish, O Emperor, to save yourself, there is no difficulty: we have ample funds and there are the ships. Yet reflect whether, when you have once escaped to a place of security, you will not prefer death to safety. I agree with an old saying that the purple is a fair winding sheet.

Justinian rallied, had the rioters driven into the hippodrome, and ordered between thirty-five thousand and forty thousand men and women executed. The revolt was crushed. When the bubonic plague hit Justinian in 532, Theodora took over his duties. Her influence over her husband and her power in the Byzantine state continued until she died of cancer.

How do we assess this highly complicated woman who played so many roles, who could be ruthless and merciless, political realist and yet visionary, totally loyal to those she loved? As striptease artist? Actress? Politician? Pious philanthropist? Did she learn survival in the brutal world of the hippodrome? To jump from striptease artist and the stage all the way to the imperial throne suggests enormous intelligence. Is Theodora a symbol of that manipulation of beauty and cleverness by which some women (and men) in every age have attained position and power? Were her many charitable works, especially the houses for the rehabilitation of prostitutes, the result of compassion for a profession she knew well? Or were those benefactions only what her culture expected of the rich and famous? With twenty years service to Justinian and the state, is it fair to brand her as "notorious" for what may only have been youthful indiscretions?

QUESTIONS FOR ANALYSIS

1. How would you assess the importance of ceremony in Byzantine life?
2. Since Theodora's name was always linked with Justinian's, was she a co-ruler?

The Byzantines are often depicted as dull and lifeless, but such opinions are hard to defend in the face of Procopius's description of Justinian's character:

For he was at once villainous and amenable; as people say colloquially, a moron. He was never truthful with anyone, but always guileful in what he said and did, yet easily hoodwinked by any who wanted to deceive him. His nature was an unnatural mixture of folly and wickedness.[25]

How much of this is true, how much the hostility of a sanctimonious hypocrite relishing the gossip he spreads, we will never know. Certainly *The Secret History* is robust reading.

In mathematics and geometry, the Byzantines discovered little that was new. Yet they were exceptionally important as catalysts, for they passed Greco-Roman learning on to the Arabs, who assimilated it and made remarkable advances with it. The Byzantines were equally uncreative in astronomy and natural science, but at least they faithfully learned what the ancients had to teach.

Only when science could be put to military use did the Byzantines make advances. The best-known Byzantine scientific discovery was chemical—"Greek fire" or "liquid fire," an explosive compound made of crude oil mixed with resin and sulfur, which was heated and propelled by a pump through a bronze tube. As the liquid jet left the tube, it was ignited. The Byzantines zealously guarded details of Greek fire's composition. The equivalent of a modern flamethrower, it saved Constantinople from Arab assault in 678. In mechanics the Byzantines continued the work of Hellenistic and Roman inventors of artillery and siege machinery.

The Byzantines devoted a great deal of attention to medicine, and the general level of medical competence was far higher in the Byzantine Empire than it was in the medieval West. The Byzantines assimilated the discoveries of Hellenic and Hellenistic medicine but added very few of their own. The basis of their medical theory was Hippocrates' concept of the four humors. Byzantine physicians emphasized the importance of diet and rest

Anicia Juliana (462?–528?)
Daughter of a Byzantine emperor and great benefactor of the church and of the arts, Anicia Juliana commissioned a manuscript of the works of the physician Dioscorides (fl. first century) on herbal medicines, which remained the standard reference work on the subject for centuries. She is shown here seated between two Virtues, Magnanimity and Patience. *(Osterreichische National-bibliothek)*

and relied heavily on herbal drugs. Perhaps their chief weakness was excessive use of bleeding and burning, which often succeeded only in further weakening an already feeble patient.

Greek medical science, however, could not cope with the terrible disease, often called "the Justinian plague," that swept through the Byzantine Empire, Italy, southern France, Iberia, and the Rhine Valley between 541 and approximately 700. Probably originating in northwestern India and carried to the Mediterranean region by ships, the disease was similar to modern forms of bubonic plague. Characterized by high fevers, chills, delirium, and enlarged lymph nodes, or by inflammation of the lungs that caused hemorrhages of black blood, the plague carried off tens of thousands of people. It reappeared in eight- or twelve-year cycles (558–561, 580–582, 599–600, and so on) but killed fewer people each time.

The epidemic had profound political as well as social consequences. It weakened Justinian's military resources, thus hampering his efforts to restore unity to the Mediterranean world (see page 225). Losses from the plague also further weakened Byzantine and Persian forces that had badly damaged each other, contributing to their inability to offer more than token opposition to the Muslim armies when the Arabs swarmed out of Arabia in 634[26] (see page 245).

Still, by the ninth or tenth century, most major Greek cities had hospitals for the care of the sick. The hospital operated by the Pantokrator monastery in Constantinople possessed fifty beds divided into five wards for different illnesses. A female gynecologist practiced in the women's ward. The hospital staff also included an ophthalmologist (specialist in the functions and diseases of the eye), a surgeon who performed hernia repairs, and two general practitioners. The imperial Byzantine government bore the costs of this hospital and others.

Constantinople: The Second Rome

In the tenth century, Constantinople was the greatest city in the Christian world: the seat of the imperial court and administration, a large population center, and the pivot of a large volume of international trade. As a natural geographical entrepôt between East and West, the city's markets offered goods from many parts of the world. About 1060 the Spanish Jew Benjamin of Tudela reported that Constantinople had merchant communities from Babylon, Canaan, Egypt, Hungary, Persia, Russia, Sennar (in the Sudan), and Spain, plus two thousand Jews.

But Constantinople did not enjoy constant political stability. Between the accession of Heraclius in 610 and the fall of the city to Western Crusaders in 1204 (see page 375), four separate dynasties ruled at Constantinople. Imperial government involved such intricate court intrigue, assassinations, and military revolts that the word *byzantine* is sometimes used in English to mean extremely entangled and complicated politics. For example, in 963 the emperor Nicephorus I Phocas married Theophano, the widow of the emperor Romanus II. In 969 Nicephorus was murdered and replaced by his nephew John I Tzimisces, Theophano's lover and an exceptionally able general.

Jewish, Muslim, and Italian merchants controlled most foreign trade. Among the Greeks, commerce faced ancient prejudices, and aristocrats and monasteries usually invested their wealth in real estate, which involved little risk but brought little gain. As in the medieval West and early modern China, rural ideals permeated Byzantine society. The landed aristocracy always held the dominant social position. Merchants and craftsmen, even when they acquired considerable wealth, never won social prominence.

Behind the public life of the imperial court with its assassinations and complicated politics, beyond the noise and bustle of the marketplaces thronged with Venetian and Eastern merchants, and behind the monastery walls enclosing the sophisticated theological debates of the monks, what do we know of the private life of the Greeks in Constantinople? Recent research has revealed a fair amount about the Byzantine *oikos,* or household. The Greek household included family members and servants, some of whom were slaves. Artisans lived and worked in their shops. Clerks, civil servants, minor officials, business people—those who today would be called middle class—commonly dwelt in multistory buildings perhaps comparable to the apartment complexes of modern American cities. Wealthy aristocrats resided in freestanding mansions that frequently included interior courts, galleries, large reception halls, small sleeping rooms, reading and writing rooms, baths, and *oratories,* chapels where all members of the household met for religious services. A complicated system of locks protected most houses from intrusion.

In the homes of the upper classes, the segregation of women seems to have been the first principle of interior design. Private houses contained a *gynaceum,* or women's apartment, where women were kept strictly separated from the outside world (the Muslim harem, discussed on page 256, probably derives from this Greek institution). The fundamental reason for this segregation was the family's honor: "An unchaste daughter is guilty of harming not only herself but also her parents and relatives. That is why you should keep your daughters under lock and key, as if proven guilty or imprudent, in order to avoid venomous bites," as an eleventh-century Byzantine writer put it.[27] Women did not receive outside guests, at least in theory. Although they were allowed at family banquets, they could not attend if wine was served or questionable entertainment was given. To do so gave a husband grounds for divorce.

Marriage served as part of a family's strategy for social advancement. The family and the entire kinship group participated in the selection of brides and grooms. Wealth and social connections were the chief qualities sought in potential candidates. Weddings could take place at home, in the oratory of the bride's house, or in the local church.

SUMMARY

Saint Augustine died in 430 as the Vandals approached the coastal city of Hippo. Scholars have sometimes described Augustine as standing with one foot in the ancient world and one in the Middle Ages. Indeed, Augustine represents the end of ancient culture and the birth of what has been called the Middle Ages. A new and different kind of society was gestating in the mid-fifth century.

The world of the Middle Ages combined Germanic practices and institutions, classical ideas and patterns of thought, Christianity, and a significant dash of Islam (see Chapter 9). Christianity, because it creatively and energetically fashioned the Germanic and classical legacies, was the most powerful agent in the making of Europe. Saint Augustine of Hippo, dogmatic thinker and Christian bishop, embodied the coming world-view. In the Byzantine Empire, a vigorous intellectual life, which preserved Greek scientific and medical knowledge and Roman law, flourished.

KEY TERMS

syncretic faith	comitatus
Arianism	wergeld
Petrine Doctrine	Salic Law
penitentials	magi
eremitical	diaspora
coenobitic monasticism	themes
solemnia	iconoclastic controversy
typikon	schism
barbarian	corpus juris civilis
foederati	

NOTES

1. See J. Hale, *The Civilization of Europe in the Renaissance* (New York: Atheneum, 1994), pp. xix, 3–5.
2. R. C. Petry, ed., *A History of Christianity: Readings in the History of Early and Medieval Christianity* (Englewood Cliffs, N.J.: Prentice-Hall, 1962), p. 70.
3. H. Bettenson, ed., *Documents of the Christian Church* (Oxford: Oxford University Press, 1947), p. 113.
4. Colossians 3:9–11.
5. L. Sherley-Price, trans., *Bede: A History of the English Church and People* (Baltimore: Penguin Books, 1962), pp. 86–87.
6. J. T. McNeill and H. Gamer, trans., *Medieval Handbooks of Penance* (New York: Octagon Books, 1965), pp. 184–197.
7. L. White, "The Life of the Silent Majority," in *Life and Thought in the Early Middle Ages,* ed. R. S. Hoyt (Minneapolis: University of Minnesota Press, 1967), p. 100.
8. 1 Peter 2:11–20.
9. Quoted in V. L. Bullough, *The Subordinate Sex: A History of Attitudes Toward Women* (Urbana: University of Illinois Press, 1973), p. 114.
10. Ibid., pp. 118–119.
11. See J. Boswell, *Christianity, Social Tolerance, and Homosexuality: Gay People in Western Europe from the Beginning of the Christian Era to the Fourteenth Century* (Chicago: University of Chicago Press, 1980), Chaps. 3 and 5, esp. pp. 87, 127–131.
12. A. Talbot, "Monasteries," in *The Oxford Dictionary of Byzantium,* vol. 2, ed. A. P. Kazhdan (New York: Oxford University Press, 1991), p. 1393.
13. T. Burns, *A History of the Ostrogoths* (Bloomington: Indiana University Press, 1984), pp. 18, 21.
14. See Patrick J. Geary, "Barbarians and Ethnicity," in *Late Antiquity: A Guide to the Postclassical World,* ed. G. W. Bowerstock, P. Brown, and O. Grabar (Cambridge, Mass.: Harvard University Press, 1999), pp. 107–129, esp. 107–113.
15. See W. Goffart, *Barbarians and Romans: The Techniques of Accommodation* (Princeton, N.J.: Princeton University Press, 1980), Chap. 3, and esp. Conclusion, pp. 211–230.
16. See P. J. Geary, *Before France and Germany: The Creation and Transformation of the Merovingian World* (New York: Oxford University Press, 1988), pp. 18–25.
17. Ibid., p. 24.
18. Ibid., pp. 108–112.
19. E. F. Henderson, ed., *Select Historical Documents of the Middle Ages* (London: G. Bell & Sons, 1912), pp. 176–189.
20. Geary, *Before France and Germany,* p. 46.
21. Ibid., p. 50.
22. See S. F. Wemple, "Sanctity and Power: The Dual Pursuit of Early Medieval Women," in *Becoming Visible: Women in European History,* 2d ed., ed. R. Bridenthal et al. (Boston: Houghton Mifflin, 1987), pp. 133–136.
23. M. Whittow, *The Making of Byzantium, 600–1025* (Berkeley: University of California Press, 1996), p. 99.
24. Ibid., pp. 99–103.
25. R. Atwater, trans., *Procopius: The Secret History* (Ann Arbor: University of Michigan Press, 1963), bk. 8.
26. W. H. McNeill, *Plagues and Peoples* (New York: Doubleday, 1976), pp. 127–128.

27. Quoted in E. Patlagean, "Byzantium in the Tenth and Eleventh Centuries," in *A History of Private Life.* Vol. 1: *From Pagan Rome to Byzantium,* ed. P. Ariès and G. Duby (Cambridge, Mass.: Harvard University Press, 1987), p. 573.

SUGGESTED READING

J. Herrin's *The Formation of Christendom* (1987) is a fine synthesis of the history of the early Middle Ages. P. Brown, *The World of Late Antiquity, A.D. 150–750,* rev. ed. (1989), which stresses social and cultural change, is a lavishly illustrated and lucidly written introduction to the period. J. Pelikan, *The Excellent Empire: The Fall of Rome and the Triumph of the Church* (1987), describes how interpretations of the fall of Rome have influenced our understanding of Western culture.

J. Pelikan, *Jesus Through the Centuries: His Place in the History of Culture* (1985), discusses the image of Jesus held by various cultures over the centuries. F. Oakley, *The Medieval Experience: Foundations of Western Cultural Singularity* (1974), emphasizes the Christian roots of Western cultural uniqueness. W. Meeks, *The First Urban Christians: The Social World of the Apostle Paul* (1983), provides fascinating material and shows that early Christians came from all social classes. For a solid appreciation of Christian life in a non-Christian society, see M. Mullin, *Called to Be Saints: Christian Living in First Century Rome* (1992). For the conversion of the Germans and other pagan peoples, see R. Fletcher, *The Barbarian Conversion: From Paganism to Christianity* (1997), and R. MacMullen, *Christianity and Paganism in the Fourth to Eighth Centuries* (1997). Students seeking to understand early Christian attitudes on sexuality and how they replaced Roman ones should consult the magisterial work of P. Brown, *The Body and Society: Men, Women, and Sexual Renunciation in Early Christianity* (1988). The profound study of J. Cohen, *"Be Fertile and Increase, Fill the Earth and Master It": The Ancient and Medieval Career of a Biblical Text* (1992), gives a lucid analysis of the church fathers' views on marriage.

The best biography of Saint Augustine is P. Brown, *Augustine of Hippo* (1967), which treats him as a symbol of change. J. B. Russell, *Dissent and Order in the Middle Ages: The Search for Legitimate Authority* (1992), offers a provocative discussion of orthodoxy and heresy.

For the Germans, see, in addition to Burns's work cited in the Notes, H. Wolfram, *History of the Goths,* trans. T. J. Dunlop (1988), which explores Germanic tribal formation and places Gothic history within the context of late Roman society and institutions. F. Lot, *The End of the Ancient World* (1965), emphasizes the economic and social causes of Rome's decline. E. Amt, ed., *Women's Lives in Medieval Europe: A Sourcebook* (1993), is perhaps the best available collection of primary materials on women from biblical times through the thirteenth century.

The phenomenon of monasticism has attracted interest throughout the centuries. The best modern edition of the document is T. Fry et al., eds., *RB 1980: The Rule of St. Benedict in Latin and English with Notes* (1981), which contains a history of Western monasticism and a scholarly commentary on the *Rule.* Especially useful for students is O. Chadwick, *The Making of the Benedictine Ideal* (1981), a short but profound essay that emphasizes the personality of Saint Benedict in the development of the Benedictine ideal. G. Constable, *Medieval Monasticism: A Select Bibliography* (1976), is a useful research tool.

For Byzantium, see J. J. Norwich, *Byzantium: The Early Centuries* (1989), an elegantly written sketch; E. Patlagean, "Byzantium in the Tenth and Eleventh Centuries," in *A History of Private Life.* Vol. 1: *From Pagan Rome to Byzantium* (1987); J. Hussey, *The Byzantine World* (1961); S. Runciman, *Byzantine Civilization* (1956); and A. Bridge, *Theodora: Portrait in a Byzantine Landscape* (1984), a romantic and amusing biography of the courtesan who became empress. A. Harvey, *Economic Expansion in the Byzantine Empire, 900–1200* (1989), should prove useful for research on social and economic change.

THE CONVERSION OF CLOVIS

Modern Christian doctrine holds that conversion is a process, the gradual turning toward Jesus and the teachings of the Christian Gospels. But in the early medieval world, conversion was perceived more as a one-time event determined by the tribal chieftain. If he accepted baptism, the mass conversion of his people followed. The selection here about the Frankish king Clovis is from The History of the Franks *by Gregory, bishop of Tours (ca 504–594), written about a century after the events it describes.*

The first child which Clotild bore for Clovis was a son. She wanted to have her baby baptized, and she kept urging her husband to agree to this. "The gods whom you worship are no good," she would say. "They haven't even been able to help themselves, let alone others. . . . Take your Saturn, for example, who ran away from his own son to avoid being exiled from his kingdom, or so they say; and Jupiter, that obscene perpetrator of all sorts of mucky deeds, who couldn't keep his hands off other men, who had his fun with all his female relatives and couldn't even refrain from intercourse with his own sister. . . .

"You ought instead to worship Him who created at a word and out of nothing heaven, and earth, the sea and all that therein is, who made the sun to shine, who lit the sky with stars, who peopled the water with fish, the earth with beasts, the sky with flying creatures, by whose hand the race of man was made, by whose gift all creation is constrained to serve in deference and devotion the man He made." However often the Queen said this, the King came no nearer to belief. . . .

The Queen, who was true to her faith, brought her son to be baptized. . . . The child was baptized; he was given the name Ingomer; but no sooner had he received baptism than he died in his white robes. Clovis was extremely angry. He began immediately to reproach his Queen. "If he had been dedicated in the name of my gods," he said, "he would have lived without question; but now that he has been baptized in the name of your God he has not been able to live a single day!"

"I give thanks to Almighty God," replied Clotild, "the Creator of all things who has not found me completely unworthy, for He has deigned to welcome into his Kingdom a child conceived in my womb. . . ."

Some time later Clotild bore a second son. He was baptized Chlodomer. He began to ail and Clovis said, "What else do you expect? It will happen to him as it happened to his brother: no sooner is he baptized in the name of your Christ than he will die!" Clotild prayed to the Lord and at His commands the baby recovered.

Queen Clotild continued to pray that her husband might recognize the true God and give up his idol-worship. Nothing could persuade him to accept Christianity. Finally war broke out against the Alamanni and in this conflict he was forced by necessity to accept what he had refused of his own free will. It so turned out that when the two armies met on the battlefield there was a great slaughter and the troops of Clovis were rapidly being annihilated. He raised his eyes to heaven when he saw this, felt compunction in his heart and was moved to tears. "Jesus Christ," he said, "you who Clotild maintains to be the Son of the living God, you who deign to give help to those in travail and victory to those who trust in you, in faith I beg the glory of your help. If you will give me victory over my enemies, and if I may have evidence to that miraculous power which the people dedicated to your name say that they have experienced, then I will believe in you and I will be baptized in your name. I have called upon my own gods, but, as I see only too clearly, they have no intention of helping me. I therefore cannot believe that they possess any power for they do not come to the assistance of those who trust them. I now call upon you. I want to believe in you, but I must first be saved from my enemies." Even as he said this the Alamanni turned their backs and began to run away. As soon as they saw that their King was killed, they submitted to Clovis. "We beg you," they said, "to put an end to this slaughter. We are prepared to obey you." Clovis stopped the war. He made a speech in which he called for peace. Then he went home. He told the Queen how he had won a victory by calling on the name of Christ. This happened in the fifteenth year of his reign (496).

The Queen then ordered Saint Remigius, Bishop of the town of Rheims, to be summoned in secret. She begged him to impart the word of salvation to the King. The Bishop asked Clovis to meet him in private and began to urge him to believe in the true God, Maker of heaven and earth, and to forsake his idols, which were powerless to help him or anyone else. The King replied: "I have listened to you willingly, holy father. There remains one obstacle. The people under my command will not agree to forsake their gods. I will go and put to them what you have just said to me." He arranged a meeting with his people, but God in his power had preceded him, and before he could say a word all those present shouted in unison: "We will give up worshipping our mortal gods, pious King, and we are prepared to follow the immortal God about whom Remigius preaches." This news was reported to the Bishop. He was greatly pleased and he ordered the baptismal pool to be made ready. . . . The baptistry was prepared, sticks of incense gave off clouds of perfume, sweet-smelling candles gleamed bright and the holy place of baptism was filled with divine fragrance. God filled the hearts of all present with such grace that they imagined themselves to have been transported to some perfumed paradise. King Clovis asked that he might be baptized first by the Bishop. Like some new Constantine he stepped forward to the

Ninth-century ivory carving showing Clovis being baptized by Saint Remi. *(Musée Condé, Chantilly/ Laurie Platt Winfrey, Inc.)*

baptismal pool, ready to wash away the sores of his old leprosy and to be cleansed in flowing water from the sordid stains which he had borne so long.

King Clovis confessed his belief in God Almighty, three in one. He was baptized in the name of the Father, the Son and the Holy Ghost, and marked in holy chrism [an anointing oil] with the sign of the Cross of Christ. More than three thousand of his army were baptized at the same time.

QUESTIONS FOR ANALYSIS

1. Who took the initiative in urging Clovis's conversion? What can we deduce from that?

2. According to this account, why did Clovis ultimately accept Christianity?

3. For the Salian Franks, what was the best proof of divine power?

4. On the basis of this selection, do you consider *The History of the Franks* reliable history? Why or why not?

Sources: L. Thorpe, trans., *The History of the Franks by Gregory of Tours* (Harmondsworth, England: Penguin, 1974), p. 159; P. J. Geary, ed., *Readings in Medieval History* (Peterborough, Ontario: Broadview Press, 1991), pp. 165–166.

Arch before the *mihrab* (small niche) in the beautiful mosque of Córdoba, which was begun by Abd al-Rahman I in 795. *(Institut Amatller d'Art Hispanic)*

CHAPTER 9

THE ISLAMIC WORLD, CA 600–1400

Historians have traditionally explained the origins and beginnings of Islam in terms of central Arabia, the region of Mecca and Medina, also known as the Hijaz. Thus, according to Islamic tradition, the background and the impetus for the growth and spread of the religion lies in the Hijaz. Recent research, however, stresses that although Islam traces its geographical beginnings to Arabia, it underwent essential development and achieved distinct form outside Arabia. Historians seek to separate the tradition or legend that grew up around a person or event, which may be widely believed and accepted as truth, from information that is verifiable and provable, which legend sometimes is not.

According to tradition, around 610, in the city of Mecca in what is now Saudi Arabia, a merchant called Muhammad began to have religious experiences. By the time he died in 632, most of Arabia had accepted his creed. A century later, his followers controlled Syria, Palestine, Egypt, Iraq, Persia (present-day Iran), northern India, North Africa, Spain, and part of France. Within another century, Muhammad's beliefs had been carried across Central Asia to the borders of China. In the ninth, tenth, and eleventh centuries, the Muslims created a brilliant civilization centered at Baghdad in Iraq, a culture that profoundly influenced the development of both Eastern and Western civilizations.

- Who were the Arabs?
- What are the main tenets of the Muslim faith?
- What factors account for the remarkable spread of Islam?
- How did the Muslims govern the vast territories they conquered?
- Why did the Shi'ite Muslim tradition arise, and how did the split between Shi'ites and Sunnis affect the course of Islam?
- What position did women hold in Muslim society?
- What features characterized the societies of the great Muslim cities of Baghdad and Córdoba?
- How did the Muslims view Western society and culture?

This chapter explores these questions.

THE ARABS BEFORE ISLAM

The Arabian peninsula, perhaps a third of the size of Europe or the United States, covers about a million square miles. Ancient Greek geographers named the peninsula *Arabia* after the Bedouin Arabs, nomads who grazed their animals in the sparse patches of grass that dotted the vast, semiarid land. Thus *Arab* originally meant a native of Arabia. After Islam spread and peoples of various ethnic backgrounds attached themselves to or intermarried with the Arabs, they assumed an Arab identity. Today, the term *Arab* refers to an ethnic identity; *Arabic* means a linguistic and cultural heritage.

In the sixth century C.E., most Arabs were not nomads; most led a settled existence. In the southwestern mountain valleys of the Arabian peninsula, plentiful rainfall and sophisticated irrigation techniques resulted in highly productive agriculture that supported fairly dense population settlements. In other areas scattered throughout the peninsula, oasis towns based on the cultivation of date palms grew up around underground sources of water. Some oasis towns sustained sizable populations including artisans, merchants, and religious leaders. Some, such as Mecca, according to tradition served as important trading outposts. The presence of the **Ka'ba**, a temple containing a black stone thought to be a god's dwelling place, also attracted pilgrims and enabled Mecca to become the metropolis of western Arabia. Mecca served economic and religious/cultic functions.

Thinly spread over the entire peninsula, the nomadic Bedouins migrated from place to place, grazing their sheep, goats, and camels. Though always small in number, Bedouins were the most important political and military force in the region because of their toughness, solidarity, fighting traditions, possession of horses, and ability to control trade and lines of communication. Between the peoples settled in oasis towns and the Bedouin nomads were seminomads. As the agricultural conditions around them fluctuated, they practiced either settled agriculture or nomadic pastoralism.

For all Arabs, the basic social unit was the *tribe*—a group of blood relations that descended in the male line. The tribe provided protection and support and in turn received members' total loyalty. Like the Germanic peoples in the age of their migrations (see pages 220–221), Arab tribes were not static entities but continually evolving groups. A particular tribe might include both nomadic and sedentary members.

Strong economic links joined all Arab peoples. Nomads and seminomads depended on the agriculturally productive communities for food they could not produce, cloth, metal products, and weapons. Nomads paid for these goods with the livestock, milk and milk products, hides, and hair wanted by oasis towns. Nomads acquired income by serving as desert guides and as guards for caravans. Plundering caravans and extorting protection money also yielded funds.

In northern and central Arabia, tribal confederations dominated by a warrior elite characterized Arab political organization. In the southern parts of the peninsula in the early seventh century, religious aristocracies tended to hold political power. Many oasis or market towns contained members of one holy family who claimed to be servants or priests of the deity who resided in the town, and they served as guardians of the deity's shrine, or *haram*. At the haram, a *mansib*, or cultic leader, adjudicated disputes and tried to get agreements among warrior tribes. All Arabs respected the harams because they feared retribution if the gods' shrines were desecrated and because the harams served as neutral places for arbitration among warring tribes.

The power of the northern warrior class rested on its fighting skills. The southern religious aristocracy, by contrast, depended on its cultic and economic power. Located in agricultural areas that were also commercial centers, the religious aristocracy had a stronger economic base than the warrior-aristocrats. Scholarship has shown that the arbitrator role of the mansib marks a step toward a society governed by law.[1] The political genius of Muhammad was to bind together these different tribal groups into a strong unified state.

MUHAMMAD AND THE FAITH OF ISLAM

No contemporary biography of Muhammad (ca 570–632) survives. The earliest account of his life, by Ibn Ishaq (d. 767), was edited in 833 and based on oral tradition. It was not concerned with factual accuracy as historians today understand that phrase. Rather, the biography sought to provide a model of Muhammad, an example that the Muslim believer should imitate. (Similarly, the sources of information about Jesus—the Christian Gospels and the letters of Saint Paul—were written fifty to seventy-five years after Jesus' death. They represent views traditional in Christian communities at the time they were written, and they had as their purpose the building up of Christian faith and Christian churches, or communities.)

Orphaned at the age of six, Muhammad was brought up by his paternal uncle. As a young man, he became a

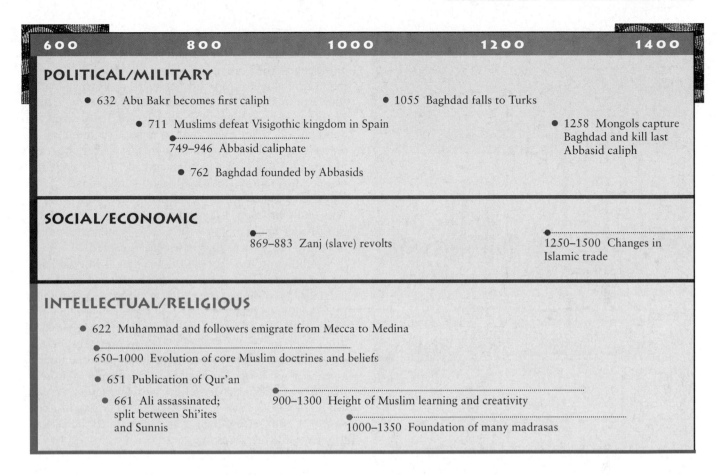

600	800	1000	1200	1400

POLITICAL/MILITARY

- 632 Abu Bakr becomes first caliph
- 711 Muslims defeat Visigothic kingdom in Spain
- 749–946 Abbasid caliphate
- 762 Baghdad founded by Abbasids
- 1055 Baghdad falls to Turks
- 1258 Mongols capture Baghdad and kill last Abbasid caliph

SOCIAL/ECONOMIC

- 869–883 Zanj (slave) revolts
- 1250–1500 Changes in Islamic trade

INTELLECTUAL/RELIGIOUS

- 622 Muhammad and followers emigrate from Mecca to Medina
- 650–1000 Evolution of core Muslim doctrines and beliefs
- 651 Publication of Qur'an
- 661 Ali assassinated; split between Shi'ites and Sunnis
- 900–1300 Height of Muslim learning and creativity
- 1000–1350 Foundation of many madrasas

merchant in the caravan trade. Later he entered the service of a wealthy widow, Khadija, and their subsequent marriage brought him financial security while she lived. Muhammad apparently was extremely pious, self-disciplined, and devoted to contemplation. At about forty, in a cave in the hills near Mecca where he was accustomed to pray, Muhammad had a profound religious experience. In a vision, an angelic being (whom Muhammad later interpreted to be Gabriel, God's messenger) commanded him to preach the revelations that God would be sending him. Muhammad began to preach to the people of Mecca, urging them to give up their idols and submit to the one indivisible God. During his lifetime, Muhammad's followers jotted down his revelations haphazardly. After his death, scribes organized the revelations into chapters. In 651 they published the version of them that Muslims consider authoritative, the **Qur'an** (from an Arabic word meaning "reading" or "recitation"). Muslims revere the Qur'an for its sacred message and for the beauty of its Arabic language.

After the death of Muhammad, two or three centuries passed before Islam emerged as a fixed religious system,

before the emergence of a distinct Muslim identity. Some writers call this early period the Age of Arab Monotheism. Islam had to be differentiated from the other Middle Eastern monotheistic religions, Judaism and Christianity, as the Dome of the Rock mosque in Jerusalem attempts to do in architecture. Theological issues, such as the oneness of God, the role of angels, the prophets, the Scriptures, and Judgment Day, as well as political issues, such as the authority of Muhammad and that of the **caliph** (successor to Muhammad, representative or deputy of God), all had to be worked out. Likewise, legal issues relating to the **hadith,** collections of the sayings of or anecdotes about Muhammad, required investigation. The hadith were organized according to legal topics and communicated by Muhammad's close companions to later transmitters. Muhammad's example as revealed in the hadith became the legal basis for the conduct or behavior of every Muslim. The life of Muhammad, who is also known as the Prophet, provides the "normative example," or *sunna,* for the Muslim believer. Once Islamic theology and law had evolved into a religious system, Muhammad was revealed as the perfect

Qur'an with Kufic Script Kufic takes its name from the town of Kufa, south of Baghdad in Iraq, at one time a major center of Muslim learning. Kufic scripts were angular and derived from inscriptions on stone monuments. *(Mashed Shrine Library, Iran/Robert Harding Picture Library)*

man, the embodiment of the will of God. The Muslim way of life rests on Muhammad's example. It follows that if Muhammad's life represents the perfect embodiment of God's will, criticism of Muhammad is by implication criticism of the Muslim way of life, "at least in its idealized conception."[2]

Islam, the strict monotheistic faith that is based on the teachings of Muhammad, rests on the principle of the absolute unity and omnipotence of Allah, God. The word *Islam* means "submission to God," and *Muslim* means "a person who submits." Thus the community of Muslims consists of people who have submitted to God by accepting his teachings as revealed by Muhammad. Muslims believe that Muhammad was the last of the prophets, completing

the work begun by Abraham, Moses, and Jesus. According to the Qur'an, both Jewish and Christian authorities acknowledged the coming of a final prophet. The Jewish rabbi Kab al-Ahbar, an early convert to Islam and the source of much of the Jewish material in the early Islamic tradition, asserted that "the disciples of Jesus asked, O Spirit of God, will there be another religious community after us?" And, the rabbi reported, Jesus said: "Yes, the community of Ahmad [that is, Muhammad]. It will comprise people who are wise, knowing, devout, and pious."[3]

Muslims believe that they worship the same God as Jews and Christians. Islam's uncompromising monotheism—belief in the oneness of God—spelled the end of paganism everywhere that Islam was accepted.

Monotheism, however, had flourished in Middle Eastern Semitic and Persian cultures for centuries before Muhammad. According to one scholar, "Muhammad was not the founder of Islam; he did not start a new religion." Instead, like the Old Testament prophets, Muhammad came as a reformer. In Jewish, Christian, and Muslim theology, a prophet is not someone who predicts the future; a prophet speaks the word of God. Muhammad insisted that he was not preaching a new message; rather, he was calling people back to the one true God, urging his contemporaries to reform their lives, to return to the faith of Abraham, the first monotheist.[4]

Muhammad's social and political views are inseparable from his religious ideas. Muhammad displayed genius as both political strategist and religious teacher. He gave Arabs the idea of a unique and unified **umma,** or community, which consisted of all those whose primary identity and bond was a common religious faith and commitment, not a tribal tie. The umma was to be a religious and political community led by Muhammad for the achievement of God's will on earth.

In the early seventh century, the southern Arab tribal confederations, which centered on sacred enclaves, lacked cohesiveness and unity and were constantly warring; they recognized no single higher authority. The Islamic notion of an absolute higher authority transcended the boundaries of individual tribal units and fostered the political consolidation of the tribal confederations. All authority came from God *through Muhammad.* Within the umma, the law of God was discerned and applied through Muhammad. Thus Islam centralized authority, both political and religious, in Muhammad's hands.[5]

The Qur'an prescribes a strict code of moral behavior. A Muslim must recite the profession of faith in God and in Muhammad as his prophet: "There is no God but God, and Muhammad is his Prophet." A believer must also pray five times a day, fast and pray during the sacred

Dome of the Rock, Jerusalem
The Syrian (Muslim) architects intended to assert the theological principle that Islam was victorious, completing the revelation of the earlier monotheistic faiths, Judaism and Christianity. They sought to distinguish the octagonal dome from Jewish and Christian shrines but used Byzantine and Sasanid designs. The seven hundred feet of carefully selected Qur'anic inscriptions and vegetal motifs, however, represent distinctly Arabic features. Completed in 691 and revered by Muslims as the site where Muhammad ascended to Heaven, the Dome of the Rock is the oldest surviving Islamic sanctuary and, after Mecca and Medina, the holiest place in Islam. *(Sonia Halliday)*

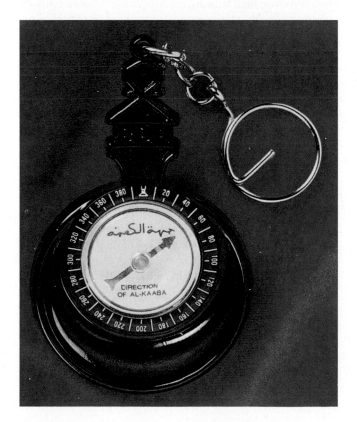

Qibla Compass   Religious precepts inspired Muslims to considerable scientific knowledge. For example, the Second Pillar of Islam requires them to pray five times a day facing the Ka'ba in Mecca. To determine the direction of Mecca, called the *qibla,* Muslims advanced the science of astronomy. Modern worshipers still use the qibla compass. *(Robert Selkowitz)*

month of Ramadan, make a pilgrimage to the holy city of Mecca once during his or her lifetime, and give alms to the Muslim poor. These fundamental obligations are known as the **Five Pillars of Islam,** and they distinguish Islam from Christianity and Judaism.

Islam forbids alcoholic beverages and gambling. It condemns usury in business—that is, lending money and charging the borrower interest—and taking advantage of market demand for products by charging high prices. Some foods, such as pork, are forbidden, a dietary regulation probably adopted from the Mosaic law of the Hebrews.

Most scholars hold that compared with earlier Arab standards, the Qur'an set forth an austere sexual code. Muslim jurisprudence condemned licentious behavior by both men and women, and the status of women improved. About marriage, illicit intercourse, and inheritance, the Qur'an states:

Of . . . women who seem good in your eyes, marry but two, three, or four; and if ye still fear that ye shall not act equitably, then only one. . . .

The whore and the fornicator: whip each of them a hundred times. . . .

The fornicator shall not marry other than a whore; and the whore shall not marry other than a fornicator.[6]

By contrast, Frankish law tended to punish prostitutes, not their clients.

Islam warns about Judgment Day and the importance of the life to come. The Islamic Judgment Day bears a striking resemblance to the Christian one: on that day God will separate the saved and the damned. The Qur'an describes in detail the frightful tortures with which God will punish the damned: scourgings, beatings with iron clubs, burnings, and forced drinking of boiling water. Muhammad's accounts of the heavenly rewards of the saved and the blessed are equally graphic but are different in kind from those of Western Christian theology. The Muslim vision of Heaven features lush green gardens surrounded by refreshing streams. There the saved, clothed in rich silks, lounge on brocade couches, nibbling ripe fruits, sipping delicious beverages, and enjoying the companionship of physically attractive people.

How do those of the Muslim faithful merit the rewards of Heaven? Salvation is by God's grace and choice alone. Because God is all-powerful, he knows from the moment of conception whether a person will be saved. But predestination does not mean that believers have no reason to try to achieve Heaven. Muslims who suffer and die for the faith in battle are ensured the rewards of Heaven. For others, the Qur'anic precepts mark the path to salvation.

THE EXPANSION OF ISLAM

According to Muslim tradition, Muhammad's preaching at first did not appeal to many people. Legend has it that for the first three years he attracted only fourteen believers. Muhammad's teaching constituted social revolution. He preached a revelation that opposed the undue accumulation of wealth and social stratification and that held all men as brothers within a social order ordained by God. Moreover, he urged the destruction of the idols in the Ka'ba at Mecca, a site that drew thousands of devout Arabs annually and thus brought important revenue to the city. The bankers and merchants of Mecca fought him. The townspeople turned against him, and he and his followers were forced to flee to Medina. This *hijra*, or emigration, occurred in 622, and Muslims later dated the beginning of their era from that event. At Medina, Muhammad attracted increasing numbers of believers, and his teachings began to have an impact.

Expansion to the East and the West

By the time Muhammad died in 632, he had welded together all the Bedouin tribes. The crescent of Islam, the Muslim symbol, controlled most of the Arabian peninsula (see Map 9.1). After the Prophet's death, Islam eventually emerged not only as a religious faith but also as a gradually expanding culture of worldwide significance. The roots of that development lay in the geopolitics of the ancient Middle Eastern world.

In the sixth century, two powerful empires divided the Middle East: the Greek-Byzantine empire centered at Constantinople and the Persian-Sasanid empire concentrated at the Ctesiphon (near Baghdad in present-day Iraq). The Byzantine Empire stood for Hellenistic culture and championed Christianity. The Sasanid empire espoused Persian cultural traditions and favored the religious faith known as Zoroastrianism. Although each empire maintained an official state religion, neither possessed religious unity. Both had sizable Jewish populations, and within Byzantium sects whom Orthodox Greeks considered heretical—Monophysites and Nestorians—served as a politically divisive force. Between the fourth and sixth centuries, these two empires had fought each other fiercely to expand their territories and to control (tax) the rich trade coming from Arabia and the Indian Ocean region.

The second and third successors of Muhammad, Umar (r. 634–644) and Uthman (r. 644–656; see page 248), launched a two-pronged attack. One force moved north from Arabia against the Byzantine provinces of Syria and Palestine. The Greek armies there could not halt them (see page 228). From Syria, the Muslims conquered the rich province of Egypt, taking the commercial and intellectual hub of Alexandria in 642. Simultaneously, Arab armies swept into the Sasanid empire, crushing the Persians at al-Qadisiyah (modern-day Kadisiya in southern Iraq). The Muslim defeat of the Persians at Nihawand in 642 signaled the collapse of the Sasanid empire.[7]

The Muslims continued their drive eastward. In the mid-seventh century, they occupied the province of Khurasan, where the city of Merv became the center of Muslim control over eastern Persia and the base for campaigns farther east. By 700 the Muslims had crossed the

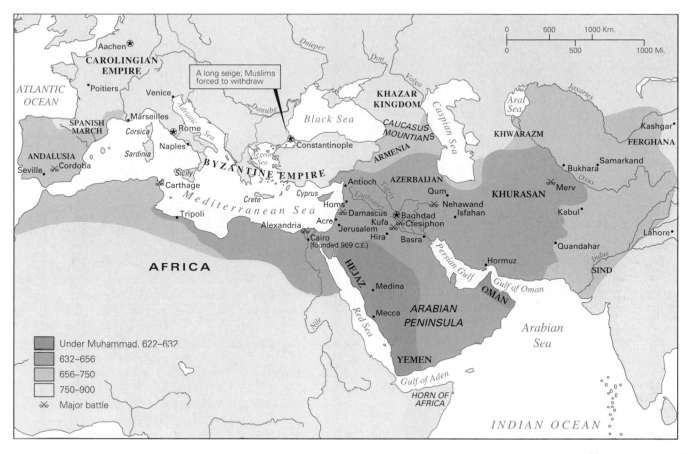

MAP 9.1 The Islamic World, ca 900   The rapid expansion of Islam in a relatively short span of time testifies to the Arabs' superior fighting skills, religious zeal, economic ambition, as well as to their enemies' weakness. Plague, famine, and political troubles in Sasanid Persia contributed to Muslim victory there.

Oxus River and swept toward Kabul, today the capital of Afghanistan. They penetrated Kazakhstan and then seized Tashkent, one of the oldest cities in Central Asia. The clash of Muslim horsemen with a Chinese army at the Talas River in 751 marked the farthest Islamic penetration into Central Asia.

From Makran in southern Persia, a Muslim force marched into the Indus Valley in northern India and in 713 founded an Islamic community at Multan. Beginning in the eleventh century, Muslim dynasties from Ghazni in Afghanistan carried Islam deeper into the Indian subcontinent.

Likewise to the west, Arab forces moved across North Africa, crossed the Strait of Gibraltar, and in 711 at the Guadalete River easily defeated the Visigothic kingdom of Spain. A few Christian princes supported by Merovin-

gian rulers held out in the Cantabrian Mountains, but the Muslims controlled most of Spain until the thirteenth century. From one perspective, the history of the Iberian Peninsula in the Middle Ages is the account of the coexistence and intermingling of Muslims, Christians, and Jews. From another perspective, that history is the story of the *reconquista,* the Christian reconquest of the area (see Map 13.3 on page 378).

Reasons for the Spread of Islam

By the beginning of the eleventh century, the crescent of Islam flew from the Iberian heartlands to northern India. How can this rapid and remarkable expansion be explained? Muslim historians attribute Islamic victories to God's support for the Islamic faith. True, the Arabs

Muezzin Calling People to Prayer A mosque is usually surrounded by an open courtyard containing a fountain for ritual ablutions and a *minaret,* or lofty tower (*left*) surrounded by projecting balconies from which an official, the *muezzin,* summons the faithful to prayer. (*left: Ian Graham; right: R & S Michaud/Woodfin Camp & Associates*)

possessed a religious fervor that their enemies could not equal. Perhaps they were convinced of the necessity of the **jihad,** or holy war. The Qur'an does not precisely explain the concept. Thus modern Islamicists, as well as early Muslims, have debated the meaning of jihad, sometimes called the sixth pillar of Islam. Some students hold that it signifies the *individual* struggle against sin and toward perfection on "the straight path" of Islam. Other scholars claim that jihad has a *social and communal* implication—a militancy as part of a holy war against unbelievers living in territories outside the control of the Muslim community. The Qur'an states, "Fight those in the way of God who fight you. . . . Fight those wheresoever you find them, and expel them

from the place they had turned you out from. . . . Fight until sedition comes to an end and the law of God [prevails]." Similarly, according to the Qur'an, "We shall bestow on who fights in the way of God, whether he is killed or is victorious, a glorious reward" (Qur'an 4:74–76).[8] Since the Qur'an suggests that God sent the Prophet to establish justice on earth, it would follow that justice will take effect only where Islam triumphs. Just as Christians have a missionary duty to spread their faith, so Muslims have the obligation, as individuals and as a community, to extend the power of Islam. For some Islam came to mean the struggle to expand Islam, and those involved in that struggle were assured happiness in the world to come.

The Muslim practice of establishing garrison cities or camps facilitated expansion. Rather than scattering as landlords of peasant farmers over conquered lands, Arab soldiers remained together in garrison cities, where their Arab ethnicity, tribal organization, religion, and military success set them apart from defeated peoples. Situated on the edge of the desert, which afforded a place for quick retreat in case of trouble, new garrison cities such as Al-Fustat in Egypt, Kufa and Basra in Iraq, and Qayrawan (now Kairouan) in North Africa, and old cities such as Merv in Khurasan adapted for garrison use, fostered the development of Muslim identity and society. From a garrison city, armies could be sent forth for further expansion or to crush revolts.

Garrison cities were army camps, the outposts of Muslim society. Gradually, Muslim society became identical with Arab armies. The Muslim surge originated from Medina in Arabia. As Arabs left their homes in Arabia and emigrated to garrison cities to serve Allah as soldiers, the cities grew in size. Muslim society came to mean "the community set up by Arabs in the conquered Middle East, rather than the Arabs who stayed behind in Arabia." Muslims were emigrants, while those who stayed behind were "bedouins," regardless of whether they were pastoralists, agriculturalists, or business people.[9] Garrison cities forged a distinct Muslim identity and served as springboards for future expansion.

All soldiers were registered in the **diwan,** an administrative device adopted from the Persians or Byzantines meaning "register." Soldiers received a monthly ration of food for themselves and their families and an annual cash stipend. In return, they had to be available for military service. Fixed salaries, regular pay, and the lure of battlefield booty attracted more rugged tribesmen from Arabia. Except for the Berbers of North Africa, whom the Arabs could not pacify, Muslim armies initially did not seek to convert or recruit warriors from conquered peoples.[10] Instead, conquered peoples became slaves. In later campaigns, to the east, many recruits were recent converts to Islam from Christian, Persian, and Berber backgrounds. The assurance of army wages secured the loyalty of these very diverse men. Here is an eleventh-century description of the Egyptian army (medieval numbers were always greatly exaggerated):

Each corps has its own name and designation. One group are called Kitamis [a Berber tribe]. These came from Qayrawan in the service of al-Mu'izz li-Din Allah. They are said to number 20,000 horsemen. . . . Another group is called Masmudis. They are blacks from the land of the Masmudis and said to number 20,000 men. Another group are called the Easterners, consisting of Turks and Persians. They are so-called because they are not of Arab origin. Though most of them were born in Egypt, their name derives from their origin. They are said to number 10,000 powerfully built men. Another group are called the slaves by purchase. . . . They are slaves bought for money and are said to number 30,000 men. Another group are called Bedouin. They are from the Hijaz [Hejaz] and are all armed with spears. They are said to number 50,000 horsemen.[11]

Still, in the first two centuries of Muslim expansion, Arab military victories probably resulted more from their enemies' (the Sasanid Persians and the Byzantines; see page 228) weakness than from Arab strength.

Some scholars speculate that the Muslim outburst from Arabia had economic and political, as well as religious and military, causes. The Arab surge may have reflected the economic needs of a people squeezed into a semibarren, overpopulated area and the desire to share in the rich life of the Fertile Crescent. Arab expansion in the seventh and eighth centuries, these scholars argue, was another phase of the infiltration that had taken the ancient Hebrews to the other end of the Fertile Crescent (see Map 1.1 on page 9).

The Muslim conquest of Syria may provide an example of several motives that propelled early Muslim expansion. Situated to the north of the Arabian peninsula, Syria had been under Byzantine-Christian or Roman rule for centuries. Arab caravans knew the market towns of southern Syria and the rich commercial centers of the north, such as Edessa, Aleppo, and Damascus. Syria's economic prosperity may have attracted the Muslims, and perhaps Muhammad saw the land as a potential means of support for the poor who flooded Medina. Syria also contained sites important to the faith: Jerusalem, where Jesus and other prophets mentioned in the Qur'an had lived and preached, and Hebron, the traditional burial place of Abraham, the father of monotheism.[12]

How did conquered peoples perceive the motives of the Muslims? How did the defeated make sense of their new subordinate situations? Defeated peoples almost never commented on the actions and motives of the Arabs. Jews and Christians both tried to minimize the damage done to their former status and played down the gains of their new masters. A scripturally rooted people, they sought explanation in the Bible. Christians regarded the conquering Arabs as God's punishment for their sins, while Jews saw the Arabs as instruments for their deliverance from Greek and Sasanid persecution.[13]

BEGINNINGS OF THE ISLAMIC STATE

Although centered in towns, Islam arose within a tribal society that lacked stable governing institutions. When Muhammad died in 632, he left a large Muslim umma, but this community stood in danger of disintegrating into separate tribal groups. Some tribespeople even attempted to elect new chiefs for their tribes. What provisions did Muhammad make for the religious and political organization of his followers? How was the vast empire that came into existence within one hundred years of his death to be governed?

The Caliphate

Muhammad fulfilled his prophetic mission, but his religious work remained. The Muslim umma had to be maintained and Islam carried to the rest of the world. To achieve these goals, political and military power had to be exercised. But neither the Qur'an nor the Sunna, the account of the Prophet's sayings and conduct in particular situations, offered guidance for the succession (see page 241).

In this crisis, according to tradition, a group of Muhammad's ablest followers elected Abu Bakr (573–634), a close supporter of the Prophet and his father-in-law, and hailed him as *khalifa,* or caliph, an Arabic term combining the ideas of leader, successor, and deputy (of the Prophet). This election marked the victory of the concept of a universal community of Muslim believers. The goals of the Muslim umma were set down in the Qur'an to make the faith revealed to Muhammad the cornerstone of Muslim law, government, and personal behavior.

Because the law of the Qur'an was to guide the community, there had to be an authority to enforce the law. Muslim teaching held that the law was paramount. God is the sole source of the law, and the ruler is bound to obey the law. Government exists not to make law but to enforce it. Muslim teaching also maintained that there is no distinction between the temporal and spiritual domains: social law is a basic strand in the fabric of comprehensive religious law. Thus religious belief and political power are inextricably intertwined: the first sanctifies the second, and the second sustains the first.[14] The creation of Islamic law in an institutional sense took three or four centuries and is one of the great achievements of medieval Islam.

In the two years of his rule (632–634), Abu Bakr governed on the basis of his personal prestige within the Muslim umma. He sent out military expeditions, collected taxes, dealt with tribes on behalf of the entire community, and led the community in prayer. Gradually, under Abu Bakr's first three successors, Umar (r. 634–644), Uthman (r. 644–656), and Ali (r. 656–661), the caliphate emerged as an institution. Umar succeeded in exerting his authority over the Bedouin tribes involved in ongoing conquests. Uthman asserted the right of the caliph to protect the economic interests of the entire umma. Uthman's publication of the definitive text of the Qur'an showed his concern for the unity of the umma. But Uthman's enemies accused him of nepotism—of using his position to put his family in powerful and lucrative jobs—and of unnecessary cruelty. Opposition coalesced around Ali, and when Uthman was assassinated in 656, Ali was chosen to succeed him.

The issue of responsibility for Uthman's murder raised the question of whether Ali's accession was legitimate. Uthman's cousin Mu'awiya, a member of the Umayyad family, who had built a power base as governor of Syria, refused to recognize Ali as caliph. In the ensuing civil war, Ali was assassinated, and Mu'awiya (r. 661–680) assumed the caliphate. Mu'awiya founded the Umayyad Dynasty and shifted the capital of the Islamic state from Medina in Arabia to Damascus in Syria.

When the Umayyad family assumed the leadership of Islam, there was no Muslim state, no formal impersonal institutions of government exercising jurisdiction over a very wide area. Rather, there was "only a federation of regional armies, each one of which was recruited and employed within its own region, maintained from its own revenues, and administered by such local bureaucrats as it contained."[15] Familiar only with tribal relationships with people they knew, the Umayyads depended for governmental services on personal connections, reinforced by marriage alliances, with tribal chiefs. "This preference for personal networks over formal institutions was to become a standard feature of Muslim society."[16]

The first four caliphs were elected by their peers, and the theory of an elected caliphate remained the Islamic legal ideal. Three of the four "patriarchs," as they were called, were murdered, however, and civil war ended the elective caliphate. Beginning with Mu'awiya, the office of caliph was in fact, but never in theory, dynastic. Two successive dynasties, the Umayyad (661–750) and the Abbasid (750–1258), held the caliphate.

From its inception with Abu Bakr, the caliphate rested on the theoretical principle that Muslim political and religious unity transcended tribalism. But tribal connections remained very strong. Mu'awiya sought to enhance the power of the caliphate by making the tribal leaders dependent on him for concessions and special benefits.

At the same time, his control of a loyal and well-disciplined army enabled him to develop the caliphate in an authoritarian direction. Through intimidation he forced the tribal leaders to accept his son Yazid as his heir—thereby establishing the dynastic principle of succession. By distancing himself from a simple life within the umma and withdrawing into the palace that he built at Damascus, and by surrounding himself with symbols and ceremony, Mu'awiya laid the foundations for an elaborate caliphal court. Many of Mu'awiya's innovations were designed to protect him from assassination. A new official, the *hajib,* or chamberlain, restricted access to the caliph, who received visitors seated on a throne surrounded by bodyguards. Beginning with Mu'awiya, the Umayyad caliphs developed court ritual into a grand spectacle.

The assassination of Ali and the assumption of the caliphate by Mu'awiya had another profound consequence. It gave rise to a fundamental division in the umma and in Muslim theology. Ali had claimed the caliphate on the basis of family ties—he was Muhammad's cousin and son-in-law. When Ali was murdered,

his followers argued—partly because of the blood tie, partly because Muhammad had designated Ali **imam,** or leader in community prayer—that Ali had been the Prophet's designated successor. These supporters of Ali were called **Shi'ites,** or *Shi'at Ali,* or simply *Shi'a*—Arabic terms all meaning "supporters" or "partisans" of Ali. In succeeding generations, opponents of the Umayyad Dynasty emphasized their blood descent from Ali and claimed to possess divine knowledge that Muhammad had given them as his heirs.

Other Muslims adhered to the practice and beliefs of the umma, based on the precedents of the Prophet. They were called **Sunnis,** which derived from *Sunna.* When a situation arose for which the Qur'an offered no solution, Sunni scholars searched for a precedent in the Sunna, which gained an authority comparable to the Qur'an itself.

What basically distinguished Sunni and Shi'ite Muslims was the Shi'ite doctrine of the *imamate.* According to the Sunnis, the caliph, the elected successor of the Prophet, possessed political and military leadership but not Muhammad's religious authority. In contrast, according to the

Woven Silk Fragment This tenth-century piece from Khurasan, in northern Iran, shows elephants used as pack animals and an elegant Kufic border inscription reading "Glory and prosperity to Qa'id Abu-l-Mansur Bakht-tegin, may Allah perpetuate his happiness," which identifies the original owner. *(Louvre © Photo R.M.N./Art Resource, NY)*

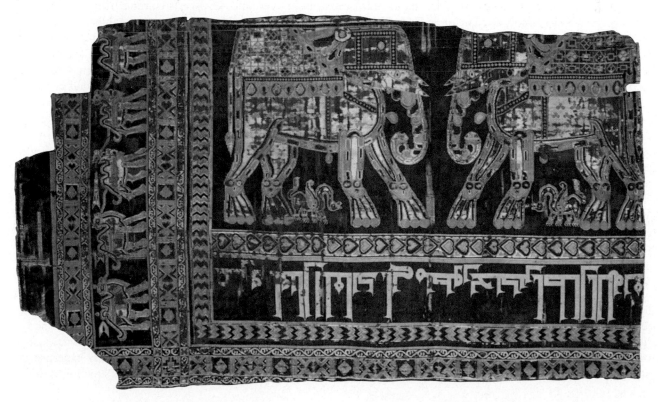

Shi'ites, the imam (leader) is directly descended from the Prophet and is the sinless, divinely inspired political leader and religious guide of the community. Put another way, both Sunnis and Shi'ites maintain that authority within Islam lies first in the Qur'an and then in the Sunna. Who interprets these sources? Shi'ites claim that the imam does, for he is invested with divine grace and insight. Sunnis insist that interpretation comes from the consensus of the **ulama,** a group of religious scholars.

The Umayyad caliphs were Sunnis, and throughout the Umayyad period the Shi'ites constituted a major source of discontent. Shi'ite rebellions expressed religious opposition in political terms. The Shi'ites condemned the Umayyads as worldly and sensual rulers, in contrast to the pious and true "successors" of Muhammad.

The Abbasid clan, which based its claim to the caliphate on the descent of Abbas, Muhammad's uncle, exploited the situation. The Abbasids agitated the Shi'ites, encouraged dissension among tribal factions, and contrasted Abbasid piety with the pleasure-loving style of the Umayyads.

The Abbasid Caliphate

In 747 Abu' al-Abbas led a rebellion against the Umayyads, and in 750 he won general recognition as caliph. Damascus had served as the headquarters of Umayyad rule over the eastern Mediterranean countries and the Hijaz, the region of Mecca and Medina in Arabia. Abu' al-Abbas's successor, al-Mansur (r. 754–775), founded the city of Baghdad and made it his capital. Thus the geographical center of the caliphate shifted eastward to former Sasanid territories: southern Iraq, parts of Persia (modern Iran), and Khurasan. The first three Abbasid caliphs crushed their opponents, eliminated their Shi'ite supporters, and created a new ruling elite drawn from newly converted Persian families that had traditionally served the ruler. The Abbasid revolution established a basis for rule and citizenship more cosmopolitan and Islamic than the narrow, elitist, and Arab basis that had characterized Umayyad government. The Abbasids worked to identify their rule with Islam. They patronized the ulama, built mosques, and supported the development of Islamic scholarship. Moreover, under the Umayyads the Muslim state had been a federation of regional and tribal armies; during the Abbasid caliphate, provincial governors gradually won semi-independent power. Although at first Muslims represented only a small minority of the conquered peoples, Abbasid rule provided the religious-political milieu in which Islam gained, over time, the allegiance of the vast majority of the populations from Spain to Afghanistan.

The Abbasids also borrowed heavily from Persian culture. Following Persian tradition, the Abbasid caliphs claimed to rule by divine right, as reflected in the change of their title from "successor of the Prophet" to "deputy of God." A magnificent palace with hundreds of attendants and elaborate court ceremonial deliberately isolated the caliph from the people he ruled. Subjects had to bow before the caliph, kissing the ground, a symbol of his absolute power.[17]

Baghdad came to represent the political ideals of the new dynasty. Located on both banks of the Tigris River and linked by canals to rich agricultural lands, the city had easy access to a plentiful food supply. It also had strong commercial potential, attracting business people who could be taxed for governmental revenues. Baghdad was designed to reflect the splendor and distance of the caliph: the walled palace, the army barracks, and the state bureaucracy staffed largely by Persians sat on the west bank of the Tigris; outside the walls were the markets, bazaars, mosques, and residences of the ordinary people.

Under the third caliph, Harun al-Rashid (r. 786–809), Baghdad emerged as a flourishing commercial, artistic, and scientific center—the greatest city in Islam and one of the most cosmopolitan cities in the world. Its population of about one million people—an astoundingly large size in preindustrial times—represented a huge demand for goods and services. Baghdad served as an entrepôt for textiles, slaves, and foodstuffs coming from Oman, East Africa, and India. Harun al-Rashid established a library, the Bayt al-Hikma (House of Wisdom), that translated Greek medical and philosophical texts. The scholar Hunayn ib Ishaq al-Ibadi (808–873) translated Galen's medical works into Arabic and made Baghdad a center for the study and practice of medicine. Likewise, under the caliph al-Mamun (r. 813–833), impetus was given to the study of astronomy, and through a program of astronomical observations, Muslim astronomers sought to correct and complement Ptolemaic astronomy. Above all, studies in Qur'anic textual analysis, history, poetry, law, and philosophy—all in Arabic—reflected the development of a distinctly Islamic literary and scientific culture.

The Abbasids made one other significant innovation. The caliph al-Mu'taşim (r. 833–842) recruited a retinue of several thousand Turkish soldiers. They were bought as slaves, converted to Islam, and often freed for military service. Islamicists call them "slave soldiers" because they were or had been slaves. Why this change? Scholars have speculated that the use of slave soldiers was a response to a manpower shortage; that as heavy cavalry with expertise as horse archers, the Turks had military skills superior to those of the Arabs and other peoples; and that al-Mu'taşim felt he could trust the Turks more than the Arabs, Persians, Khurasans, and other recruits. In any case, slave soldiers—later Slavs, Indians, and sub-Saharan blacks—were a standard feature of Muslim armies in the Middle East down to the twentieth century.[18]

Administration of Islamic Territories

The Islamic conquests brought into being a new imperial system that dominated southwestern Asia and North Africa. The Muslims adopted the patterns of administration used by the Byzantines in Egypt and Syria and by the Sasanids in Persia. Arab **emirs,** or governors, were appointed and given overall responsibility for good order, maintenance of the armed forces, and tax collecting. Below them, experienced native officials—Greeks, Syrians, Copts (Egyptian Christians)—remained in office. Thus there was continuity with previous administrations.

The Umayyad caliphate witnessed the further development of the imperial administration. At the head stood the caliph, who led the holy war against unbelievers. Theoretically, he had the ultimate responsibility for the interpretation of the sacred law. In practice, the ulama interpreted the law as revealed in the Qur'an and in the Sunna. In the course of time, the ulama's interpretations constituted a rich body of law, the **shari'a,** which covered social, criminal, political, commercial, and ritualistic matters. The ulama enjoyed great prestige in the Muslim community and was consulted by the caliph on difficult legal and spiritual matters. The **qadis,** or judges, who were well versed in the sacred law, carried out the judicial functions of the state. Nevertheless, Muslim law prescribed that all people have access to the caliph, and he set aside special times for hearing petitions and for the direct redress of grievances.

The central administrative organ was the diwan, which collected the taxes that paid soldiers' salaries (see page 247) and financed charitable and public works that the caliph undertook, such as aid to the poor (as the Qur'an prescribed) and the construction of mosques, irrigation works, and public baths.

As Arab conquests extended into Spain, Central Asia, and Afghanistan, lines of communication had to be kept open. Emirs and other officials, remote from the capital at Damascus and later Baghdad, might revolt. Thus a relay network known as the *barid* was established to convey letters and intelligence reports between the capital and the various outposts. The barid employed a special technical vocabulary, as similar networks used by the Byzantine and Sasanid empires had done.

The early Abbasid period witnessed considerable economic expansion and population growth, so the work of government became more complicated. New and specialized departments emerged, each with a hierarchy of officials. The most important new official was the **vizier,** a position that the Abbasids adopted from the Persians. The vizier was the caliph's chief assistant, advising the caliph on matters of general policy, supervising the bureaucratic administration, and, under the caliph, overseeing the army, the provincial governors, and relations with foreign governments. As the caliphs withdrew from leading Friday prayers and other routine functions, the viziers gradually assumed power. But the authority and power of the vizier usually depended on the caliph's personality and direct involvement in state affairs. Many viziers used their offices for personal gain and wealth. Although some careers ended with the vizier's execution, there were always candidates seeking the job.

In theory, the caliph and his central administration governed the whole empire. In practice, the many parts of the empire enjoyed considerable local independence; and as long as public order was maintained and taxes were forwarded to the diwan, the central government rarely interfered. In theory, Muslim towns did not possess the chartered self-governing status of the towns and cities of medieval Europe (see pages 385–386). In practice, although a capable governor kept a careful eye on municipal activities, wealthy merchants and property owners had broad local autonomy.

DECENTRALIZATION

The Umayyad state comprised virtually all Islamic provinces and territories. Under the Abbasids, decentralization began nearly from the start of the dynasty. In 755 an Umayyad prince who had escaped death at the hands of the triumphant Abbasids and fled to Spain set up an independent regime at Córdoba (see Map 9.1). In 800 the emir in Tunisia in North Africa set himself up as an independent ruler and refused to place the caliph's name on the local coinage. In 820 Tahir, the son of a slave, was rewarded with the governorship of Khurasan because he had supported the caliphate. Once there, Tahir ruled independently of Baghdad, not even mentioning the caliph's name in the traditional Friday prayers in recognition of caliphal authority.

Likewise, in 969 the Fatimids, a Shi'ite dynasty who claimed descent from Muhammad's daughter Fatima, conquered the Abbasid province of Egypt. The Fatimids founded the city of Cairo as their capital. Later the

Ayyubid Dynasty replaced the Fatimids, and in 1250 the Mamluks replaced the Ayyubids and ruled Egypt until the Ottoman conquest in 1517.

This sort of decentralization occurred all over the Muslim world. The enormous distance separating many provinces from the imperial capital enabled the provinces to throw off the caliph's jurisdiction. Particularism and ethnic or tribal tendencies, combined with strength and fierce ambition, led to the creation of local dynasties. Incompetent caliphs at Baghdad were unable to enforce their authority over distant and strong local rulers. This pattern led to the decline of the Abbasids and invasion by foreign powers.

Decline of the Abbasids

In the later ninth century, rebellions shook Arabia, Syria, and Persia, and a slave revolt devastated Iraq (see page 257). These disorders hurt agricultural productivity and in turn cut tax receipts. Having severely taxed the urban mercantile groups, the caliphate had already alienated the commercial classes. Disorder and disintegration threatened the Muslim state.

First, the inordinately large military salaries paid to Turkish troops severely strained the financial resources of the caliphate. Then, the luxury and extravagance of the caliphal court imposed another heavy burden. In the caliph's palace complexes, maintained by staffs numbering in the tens of thousands, an important visitor would be conducted through elaborate rituals and confronted with indications of the caliph's majesty and power: rank upon rank of lavishly appointed guards, pages, servants, slaves, and other retainers; lush parks full of exotic wild beasts; fantastic arrays of gold and silver objects, ornamented furniture, precious carpets and tapestries, pools of mercury, and ingenious mechanical devices. The most famous of the mechanical devices was a gold and silver tree with leaves that rustled, branches that swayed, and mechanical birds that sang as the breezes blew.[19]

Some caliphs in the early tenth century worked to halt the process of decay. But in 945 the Ayyubids, a Shi'ite clan originating in Daylam, the mountainous region on the southern shores of the Caspian Sea, overran Iraq and occupied Baghdad. The caliph, al-Mu'taşim, was forced to recognize the Ayyubid leader as *amir al-umara* (commander-in-chief) and to allow the celebration of Shi'ite festivals—though the caliph and most of the people were Sunnis. A year later, the caliph was accused of plotting against his new masters, snatched from his throne, dragged through the streets, and blinded. Blinding was a practice that the Ayyubids adopted from the Byzantines as a way of rendering a ruler incapable of carrying out his duties. This incident marks the practical collapse of the Abbasid caliphate. Abbasid caliphs, however, remained as puppets of successive Ayyubid leaders and symbols of Muslim unity until the Mongols killed the last Abbasid in 1258.

The Assault of the Turks and Mongols

In the mid-tenth century, the Seljuk Turks began to besiege the Islamic world. Originating in Turkestan in Central Asia and displaying great physical endurance and mobility, the Turks surged westward. They accepted Sunni Islam near Bukhara (then a great Persian commercial and intellectual center), swarmed over the rest of Persia, and pushed through Iraq and Syria. Baghdad fell to them on December 18, 1055, and the caliph became a puppet of the Turkish *sultan*—literally, "he with authority." The sultans replaced the Ayyubids as masters of the Abbasid caliphate. The Turks did not acquire all of the former Abbasid state. To the west, the Shi'ite Fatimids had conquered present-day central Algeria, Sicily, and, in 969, Egypt.

In the early thirteenth century appeared the Mongols, a nomadic people from the vast plains of Central Asia (see pages 319–328). In 1206 their leader, Chinggis Khan (1162–1227), having welded Mongol and related Turkish tribes into a strong confederation, began to sweep westward, leaving a trail of blood and destruction. The Mongols used terror as a weapon, and out of fear the rich commercial centers of Central Asia—Khwarazm, Bukhara (whose mosques were turned into stables), Herat, Samarkand, and Baikal (whose people were all slaughtered or enslaved)—fell before them. When Chinggis Khan died, his empire stretched from northern China and Korea to the Caspian Sea and from the Danube River to the Arctic. Throughout the 1200s, the Mongols extended their conquests to include Russia, China, and the Abbasid Empire.

Chinggis Khan's grandson Hulagu (1217–1265) led the attack on the Abbasids. His armies sacked and burned Baghdad and killed the last Abbasid caliph in 1258. Two years later, they took Damascus, and only a major defeat at Ayn Jalut in Syria saved Egypt and the Muslim lands in North Africa and perhaps Spain.

Hulagu tried to eradicate Muslim culture, but his descendant Ghazan embraced Islam in 1295 and worked for the revival of Muslim culture. As the Turks had done earlier, the Mongols, once converted, injected new vigor into the faith and spirit of Islam. In the Middle East, the Mongols governed through Persian viziers and native financial officials.

Jonah and the Whale   When the Mongol ruler Ghazan asked his chief minister, the remarkable Persian polymath Rashid al-Din—a Jew by birth who converted to Islam, a physician by training —to write a history of the Mongols in Persia, he responded with the *Collection of Histories,* which treats China, India, the Jews, Muhammad and the caliphs, pre- and post-Islamic Persia, even the Franks (Europeans). To explain the section on the Jews, a Chinese artist inserted this illustration of the Old Testament prophet Jonah; the story represents divine mercy for those who reform. The Chinese artist had never seen a whale, but he possessed imagination and mastery of movement. The artist testifies to the considerable Chinese migration to Persia in the early fourteenth century. *(Courtesy of Edinburgh University Library, Or Ms 20, fol 23N)*

THE LIFE OF THE PEOPLE

When the Prophet appeared, Arab society consisted of independent Bedouin tribal groups loosely held together by loyalty to a strong leader and by the belief that all members of a tribe were descended from a common ancestor. Heads of families elected the *sheik,* or tribal chief. He was usually chosen from among elite warrior families whose members had a strong sense of their superiority. Birth determined aristocracy.

According to the Qur'an, however, birth counted for nothing; zeal for Islam was the only criterion for honor: "O ye folk, verily we have created you male and female. . . . Verily the most honourable of you in the sight of God is the most pious of you."[20] The idea of social equality founded on piety was a basic Muslim doctrine.

When Muhammad defined social equality, he was thinking about equality among Muslims alone. But even among Muslims, a sense of pride in ancestry could not be destroyed by a stroke of the pen. Claims of birth remained strong among the first Muslims, and after Islam spread outside of Arabia, full-blooded Arab tribesmen regarded themselves as superior to foreign converts.

The Classes of Society

In the Umayyad period, Muslim society consisted of several classes. At the top were the caliph's household and the ruling Arab Muslims. Descended from Bedouin tribespeople and composed of warriors, veterans, governing officials, and town settlers, this class constituted the ruling elite. Because birth continued to determine membership, it was more a caste than a class. It was also a relatively small group, greatly outnumbered by Muslim villagers and country people.

Converts constituted the second class in Islamic society. Converts to Islam had to attach themselves to one of the Arab tribes as clients. For economic, social, and cultural reasons, they greatly resented having to do this. They believed they represented a culture superior to the culture of the Arab tribespeople. From the Muslim converts eventually came the members of the commercial and learned professions—merchants, traders, teachers, doctors, artists, and interpreters of the shari'a. Second-class citizenship led some Muslim converts to adopt Shi'ism (see page 249) and other unorthodox doctrines inimical to the state. Over the centuries, Berber, Copt, Persian, Aramaean, and other converts to Islam intermarried with their Muslim conquerors. Gradually, assimilation united peoples of various ethnic and "national" backgrounds. However, in the words of one scholar, "an

Arabian remained a native of the peninsula, but an Arab became one who professed Islam and spoke Arabic, regardless of national origin."[21]

Dhimmis, or "protected peoples"—Jews, Christians, and Zoroastrians—formed the third class. They were allowed to practice their religions, maintain their houses of worship, and conduct their business affairs, as long as they gave unequivocal recognition to Muslim political supremacy and paid a small tax. Here is a formula drawn up in the ninth century as a pact between Muslims and their nonbelieving subjects:

I accord to you and to the Christians of the city of so-and-so that which is accorded to the dhimmis . . . safe-conduct . . . namely:

You will be subject to the authority of Islam and to no contrary authority. You will not refuse to carry out any obligation which we think fit to impose upon you by virtue of this authority.

Lustre Dish: Prince Khusraw Discovers Shirin Bathing Major Persian pottery centers at Ravy and Kashan produced ceramic masterpieces, often in styles influenced by Chinese artists or by imported Chinese porcelains. The subjects are derived from Persian literature. *(Courtesy of the Freer Gallery of Art, Smithsonian Institution, Washington, D.C., 41.11)*

If any one of you speaks improperly of Muhammed, may God bless and save him, the Book of God, or of His religion, he forfeits the protection [dhimma] of God, of the Commander of the Faithful, and of all the Muslims; his property and his life are at the disposal of the Commander of the Faithful. . . .

If any one of them commits fornication with a Muslim woman or goes through a form of marriage with her or robs a Muslim on the highway or subverts a Muslim from his religion or aids those who made war against the Muslims by fighting with them or by showing them the weak points of the Muslims, or by harboring their spies, he has contravened his pact . . . and his life and his property are at the disposal of the Muslims. . . .

You may not display crosses in Muslim cities, nor proclaim polytheism, nor build churches or meeting places for your prayers . . . nor proclaim your polytheistic beliefs on the subject of Jesus [beliefs relating to the Trinity]. . . .

Every adult male of sound mind among you shall have to pay a poll tax [jizya] of one dinar, in good coin, at the beginning of each year.[22]

Restrictions placed on Christians and Jews were not severe, and both groups seem to have thrived under Muslim rule. Rare outbursts of violence against Christians and Jews occurred only when Muslims felt that the dhimmis had stepped out of line and broken the agreement. The social position of the "protected peoples" deteriorated during the Crusades (see pages 375–376) and the Mongol invasions, when there was a general rise of religious loyalties. At those times, Muslims suspected the dhimmis, often rightly, of collaborating with the enemies of Islam.

What was the fate of Jews living under Islam? How does their experience compare with that of Jews living in Christian Europe? Recent scholarship shows that in Europe, Jews were first marginalized in the Christian social order, then completely expelled from it (see pages 374–376). In Islam, though marginalized, Jews participated fully in commercial and professional activities, some attaining an economic equality with their Muslim counterparts. Why? The 17th Sura (chapter) of the Qur'an, titled Bani Isra'il, "The Children of Israel," accords to the Jews a special respect because they were "the people of the Book." Scriptural admonitions of the Qur'an carried over into social and political legislation, and "the relative stability over time of the basic law regarding their (Jews') legal status assured them a considerable degree of continuity."[23] In contrast, Western Christian legislation about the Jews fluctuated, making their legal position more ambiguous, tenuous, and insecure. Also, Islamic culture was an urban and commercial culture that gave the merchant considerable respect; medieval Christian culture was basically rural and agricultural; it did not revere the business person.

By the beginning of the tenth century, Islamic society had undergone significant change. The courtier al-Fadl b. Yahya, writing in 903, divided humankind into four classes:

Firstly, rulers elevated to office by their deserts; secondly, viziers, distinguished by their wisdom and understanding; thirdly, the upper classes, elevated by their wealth; and fourthly, the middle classes to which belong men marked by their culture. The remainder are filthy refuse, a torrent of scum, base cattle, none of whom thinks of anything but his food and sleep.[24]

The last category hardly reflects compassion for the poor and unfortunate. However, it is clear that birth as a sign of social distinction had yielded to wealth and talent.

Slavery

At the bottom of the social scale were slaves. Slavery had long existed in the ancient Middle East, and Islam accepted it as a natural institution. The Qur'anic acceptance of slavery parallels that of the Old and New Testaments. But the Qur'an prescribes a just and humane treatment of slaves. A master is not to treat his slaves contemptuously. He should feed and clothe his slaves adequately; give them moderate, not excessive, work; and not punish them severely. The Qur'an also explicitly encourages the freeing of slaves and urges owners whose slaves ask for their freedom to give them the opportunity to buy it.[25]

Muslim expansion ensured a steady flow of slaves. Prisoners of war or people captured in raids or purchased in markets, slaves constituted very large numbers in the Islamic world. (See the feature "Listening to the Past: A Treatise on Buying Slaves" on pages 276–277.) The great Muslim commander Musa ibn Nusayr, himself the son of a Christian enslaved in Iraq, is reputed to have taken 300,000 prisoners of war in his North African campaigns (708–818) and 30,000 virgins from the Visigothic nobility of Spain. (These numbers are surely greatly inflated, as most medieval numbers are.) Every soldier, from general to private, had a share of slaves from captured prisoners. Tradition holds that one of the Prophet's ten closest companions, 'Abd al Rahman bin 'Awf, freed 30,000 slaves at his death in 652.

How were slaves employed? A great household required slaves for many purposes. Women worked as cooks, cleaners, laundresses, and nursemaids. A few performed as

Slave Market at Zabid, Yemen During the thirteenth century, this market offered slaves of many races—women and children for domestic purposes and for harems, boys to be trained for military and administrative service. Manumission (encouraged by the Qur'an) and the promotion of some slaves to high positions worked against the growth of class consciousness. (*Bibliothèque nationale de France*)

singers, musicians, dancers, and reciters of poetry. Many women also served as concubines, and Muslim society did not consider their sexual services degrading. Not only rulers but high officials and rich merchants owned many concubines. Down the economic ladder, artisans and tradesmen often had a few concubines who assumed domestic tasks as well as sexual ones.

According to tradition, the seclusion of women in the harem protected their virtue (see page 261), and when men had the means the harem was secured by eunuch guards. The use of eunuch guards seems to have been a practice Muslims adopted from the Byzantines and Persians. Early Muslim law forbade castration, so in the early Islamic period Muslims secured European eunuchs from the slave markets at Prague (in the modern Czech Republic) and Verdun in northeastern France; Central Asian eunuchs from Kharazon in the Caspian Sea region; and African eunuchs from Bornu (in modern Nigeria). After the seventeenth century, Baghirmi, a region southeast of Lake Chad in Africa, produced eunuchs for the Islamic world. Because of the insatiable demand for eunuch guards, the cost of eunuchs was very high, perhaps seven times that of uncastrated male slaves.

Muslims also employed eunuchs as secretaries, tutors, and commercial agents, possibly because unlike men with ordinary desires, eunuchs were said to be more tractable and dependable. In the tenth century, the caliph of Baghdad had seven thousand black eunuchs and four thousand white ones in his palace.

Besides administrative, business, or domestic services, male slaves, eunuchs or not, were also set to work as longshoremen on the docks, as oarsmen on ships, in construction crews, in factories, and in gold and silver mines. The existence of large numbers of male slaves led to another aspect of Islamic culture: the strict seclusion of upper-class women, the financial inability of young Muslims to marry or buy concubines, and the glorification of aggressively virile and macho attitudes in a military society led to homosexual activity. According to one authority, "sex between men entered pervasively into the ethic of the upper classes. . . . The Muslim stereotype of such sexual relations answered the idea of the sex act as an act of domination."[26]

Male slaves also fought as soldiers. Any free person could buy a slave, but only a ruler could own military slaves. In the ninth century, the rulers of Tunisia formed a special corps of black military slaves, and at the end of that century the Tulunid rulers of Egypt built an army of 24,000 white and 45,000 black slaves. The Fatimid rulers of Egypt (969–1171) raised large black battalions, and a Persian visitor to Cairo between 1046 and 1049 estimated an army of 100,000 slaves, of whom 30,000 were black soldiers. Likewise, the trans-Saharan slave trade (see page 288) afforded the Almoravid rulers of Morocco and parts of Spain the opportunity to use black soldiers until they were defeated by insurgent Al-mohad forces also using black slave soldiers.

Slavery in the Islamic world differed in at least two fundamental ways from the slavery later practiced in South and North America. First, Muslims did not identify slavery with blackness as Europeans did in the Americas. The general and widespread use of Caucasian slaves in Islamic societies made that connection impossible. Second, slavery in the Islamic world was not the virtual equivalent of commercial plantation agriculture as practiced in the southern United States, the Caribbean, and Brazil in the eighteenth and nineteenth centuries. True, in the tenth century, large numbers of black slaves worked on the date plantations in northeastern Arabia. But massive revolts of black slaves from East Africa called Zanj, provoked by mercilessly harsh labor conditions in the salt flats and on the sugar and cotton plantations of southwestern Persia, erupted in 869. Gathering momentum, the Zanj captured the rich cities of Ahwaz, Basra, and Wasit and threatened Baghdad. Only the strenuous efforts of the commander of the caliph's armies, which were composed of Turkish slaves and included naval as well as land forces, halted and gradually crushed the Zanj in 883. The long and destructive Zanj revolt ended the Muslim experiment of plantation agriculture.[27]

Race

From ancient times to very recently, most peoples used the term *race* to designate an ethnic or a national group defined by language, culture, or religion, such as "the Irish race," "the Jewish race," or "the Japanese race." Since about 1950, however, the American usage of the word to denote major divisions among peoples according to perceived physical differences—Asian, black, white—has spread to other countries. Physical traits, rather than linguistic, historical, or cultural features, now seem to determine "race." While ancient and medieval peoples often looked on outsiders with hostility and prejudice, that prejudice existed because the foreigners spoke a different language, practiced a different religion, and had different dietary, marriage, or social customs. Thus the ancient Greeks considered outsiders "barbarians," Jews considered Gentiles "heathens," and Romans had contempt for all non-Romans.

The rise and spread of Islam changed this attitude. By conquest and conversion, and by a single religious culture, Islam attempted to create a universal civilization, incorporating very different peoples such as Chinese, East Indians, sub-Saharan blacks, and white Europeans, all bound by one religious-political text, the Qur'an. The Qur'an stresses that there are no superior and inferior races; it shows no color prejudice, emphasizes that piety is more important than race, and condemns those who claim social distinction on the basis of birth. It is indifferent to what we label racial differences. Scholars have taken the Qur'an at face value. Thus a distinguished British historian, Arnold Toynbee, wrote:

The Arabs and all other white Muslims have always been free of colour-prejudice vis-à-vis the non-white races; and at the present day, Muslims still make the dichotomy of the human family which Western Christians used to make in the Middle Ages. They (Muslims) divide mankind into Believers and Unbelievers who are all potentially Believers. . . . This liberality is more remarkable to White Muslims than it was in White Western Christianity in our Middle Ages.[28]

Views of authorities like Toynbee, which rested entirely on the study of the Qur'an, have shaped interpretations of race in the Muslim world. But the Qur'an, like the Judeo-Christian Scriptures, sets forth religious ideals, not actual social practice. Literary and social evidence suggests that scholars' assumptions rest more on myth and imagination than on the historical facts.

The very first story of the folklore classic *The Thousand and One Nights* relates the tale of King Shahzaman, who returns home unexpectedly to find his wife asleep in the arms of a black male slave. Enraged, Shahzaman kills them both with his sword. He then visits his brother, Shahriyar, ruler of a neighboring kingdom. Sitting at a palace window overlooking a garden, Shahzaman sees

a door open in the palace through which came twenty slave girls and twenty Negroes. In their midst was his brother's queen, a woman of surpassing beauty.... The king's wife called out: "O Messood" and there promptly came to her a black slave who mounted her after smothering her with embraces and kisses. So also did the Negroes with the slave girls.

When Shahriyar heard of this, he imposed the same death penalty as his brother had. This story poses problems: Did these kings react as any man would on discovering his wife having sex with another man? Or were the kings especially resentful of the blacks' supposed sexual prowess?

Another tale in the *Nights* describes a black slave who led a life of exemplary piety and virtue. As his reward, he turned white at the moment of his death. Isn't this tale suggestive of relative Muslim attitudes toward the races? All the slaves, black and white, in *The Thousand and One Nights* worked as household servants, porters, nannies for children, or attendants at the public baths.[29]

In the centuries of the classical Islamic period, a significant difference existed between white and black slaves. Islamic law declared that the offspring of a free male and a slave woman were free, because lineage was in the paternal line. Many Muslims took slave women as concubines, and a few black women gained wealth and influence as concubines and court musicians. Almost no black male slaves did so. In the tenth century, the Nubian slave Abu'l-Misk Kafur (from a region of modern northern Sudan) became regent of Egypt, which contemporary Muslim writers found extraordinary. He seems to have been the exception that proved the rule. The millions of other black slaves never rose above menial positions. The obvious explanation is racial discrimination.

Enlightenment philosophers in the eighteenth century and nineteenth-century abolitionists developed the notion that complete social harmony existed in Islamic society—that it was free of color prejudice. This was a myth, an ideological stick used by the opponents of slavery in the Western Hemisphere, and later of apartheid in South Africa, to flail the defenders of slavery and the advocates of the separation of the races. The evidence shows that the toleration of blacks varied considerably in time and place; suspicion, hostility, and discrimination were often the norm.[30] Even so, many caliphs were the sons of Turkish, Greek, Slavic, or black slave women.

An Interracial Couple Scolded Black people appear in many Islamic paintings but rarely in an erotic situation. Here a Mughal painting (1629) illustrates the story by the Persian painter Sadi of a black man and an Indian girl chastised for flirting. She seems to be sitting on his lap, and he seems to protest the old man's correction. In a multiracial society, such relationships were virtually inevitable. *(British Library)*

Women in Classical Islamic Society

Arab tribal law gave women virtually no legal status. At birth girls could be buried alive by their fathers. They were sold into marriage by their guardians for a price. Their husbands could terminate the union at will. And women had virtually no property or succession rights. The Qur'an sought to improve the social position of women.

The hadith—records of what Muhammad said and did, and what believers in the first two centuries after his death believed he said and did (see page 241)—also provide information about his wives. (Scholars dispute the number of those wives, though most hadith traditions put the number at fourteen, nine of whom were alive when he died. The Qur'an limits the number of wives for Muslims to four, but classical interpreters held that the Prophet had the right to unrestricted polygamy, a prerogative God's sunna gave to all prophets as his spokesmen on earth.) Some hadith portray the Prophet's wives as subject to common human frailties, such as jealousy; other hadith report miraculous events in their lives. Most hadith describe the wives as "mothers of the believers"— models of piety and righteousness, whose every act illustrates their commitment to promoting God's order on earth by personal example.

Muhammad's wives also became examplars of juridic norms. They and other prominent women sometimes exercised political influence in the succession struggles that followed Muhammad's death. For example, Aisha, daughter of Abu Bakr (the first caliph) and probably Muhammad's favorite wife, played a "leading role" in rallying support for the movement opposing Ali, who succeeded Uthman in 656 (see page 248). Likewise, Umm Salama, member of a wealthy and prominent clan in Mecca, at first supported Ali, then switched sides and supported the Umayyads. Although the hadith usually depict women in terms of moral virtue, domesticity, and saintly ideals, the hadith also show some prominent women in "public" and political roles.[31]

The Qur'an, like the religious writings of all traditions, represents moral precept rather than social practice, and the texts are open to different interpretations. Yet modern scholars tend to agree that the Islamic sacred book intended women as the spiritual and sexual equals of men and gave women considerable economic rights. In the early Umayyad period, moreover, women played an active role in the religious, economic, and political life of the community. They owned property. They had freedom of movement and traveled widely. Women participated with men in the public religious rituals and observances. But this Islamic ideal of women and men of equal value to the community did not last.[32] As Islamic society changed, the precepts of the Qur'an were interpreted to meet different circumstances.

In the later Umayyad period, the status of women declined. The rapid conquest of vast territories led to the influx of large numbers of slave women. As wealth replaced birth as the criterion of social status, scholars speculate, men more and more viewed women as possessions, as a form of wealth. The increasingly inferior status of women is revealed in three ways: in the relationship of women to their husbands, in the practice of veiling women, and in the seclusion of women in harems (see page 261).

On the rights and duties of a husband to his wife, the Qur'an states that "men are in charge of women because Allah hath made the one to excel the other, and because they (men) spend of their property (for the support of women). So good women are obedient, guarding in secret that which Allah hath guarded."[33] A tenth-century interpreter, Abu Ja'far Muhammad ibn-Jarir al-Tabari, commented on that passage in this way:

Men are in charge of their women with respect to disciplining (or chastising) them, and to providing them with restrictive guidance concerning their duties toward God and themselves (i.e., the men), by virtue of that by which God has given excellence (or preference) to the men over their wives: i.e., the payment of their dowers to them, spending of their wealth on them, and providing for them in full.[34]

A thirteenth-century commentator on the same Qur'anic passage goes into more detail and argues that women are incapable of and unfit for any public duties, such as participating in religious rites, giving evidence in the law courts, or being involved in any public political decisions.[35] Muslim society fully accepted this view, and later interpreters further categorized the ways in which men were superior to women.

The Sunni aphorism "There shall be no monkery Islam" captures the importance of marriage in Muslim culture and the Muslim belief that a sexually frustrated person is dangerous to the community. Islam vehemently discourages sexual abstinence. Islam expects that every man and woman, unless physically incapable or financially unable, will marry: marriage is a safeguard of chastity, essential to the stability both of the family and of society. Marriage in Muslim society is a sacred contract between two families.

As in medieval Europe and in Ming China, marriage in Muslim society was considered too important an undertaking to be left to the romantic emotions of the young. Families or guardians, not the prospective bride and groom, identified suitable partners and finalized the contract. The official wedding ceremony consisted of an offer and its acceptance by representatives of the bride's and groom's parents at a meeting before witnesses. A wedding banquet at which men and women feasted separately followed; the quality of the celebration, of the gifts, and of the food depended on the relative wealth of the two families. Because it was absolutely essential that the bride be a virgin, marriages were arranged shortly after the onset of the girl's menarche at age twelve or thirteen. Husbands were perhaps ten to fifteen years older. Youthful marriages ensured a long period of fertility.

A wife's responsibilities depended on the financial status of her husband. A farmer's wife helped in the fields, ground the corn, carried water, prepared food, and did the myriad tasks necessary in rural life. Shopkeepers' wives in the cities sometimes helped in business. In an upper-class household, the lady supervised servants, looked after all domestic arrangements, and did whatever was needed for her husband's comfort.

In every case, children were the wife's special domain. A mother exercised authority over her children and enjoyed their respect. A Muslim tradition asserts that "Paradise is at the mother's feet." Thus, as in Chinese culture, the prestige of the young wife depended on the production of children—especially sons—as rapidly as possible. A wife's failure to have children was one of the main reasons for a man to take a second wife or to divorce his wife entirely.

Like the Jewish tradition, Muslim law permits divorce, but the Qur'an seeks to preserve the union and to protect a possible child's paternity. The law prescribes that if a man intends to divorce his wife, he should avoid hasty action and not have intercourse with her for three months; hopefully, they will reconcile. If the woman becomes pregnant during that period, the father can be identified:

Women who are divorced have to wait for three monthly periods (before remarriage), and if they believe in God and the Last Day, they must not hide unlawfully what God has formed within their wombs. Their (ex-)husbands would do well to take them back in that period, if they wish to be reconciled. Women also have recognized rights as men have, though men are over them in rank.[36]

Some interpreters of the Islamic traditions on divorce show a marked similarity to the Christian attitude. For example, some Pharisees asked Jesus whether it was permissible for a man to divorce his wife. When the Pharisees quoted the Mosaic Law as allowing divorce, Jesus discussed the Mosaic Law as a concession to human weakness, arguing that what God has joined together no one should separate. In other words, Jesus held that divorce is wrong, whatever the law does to regulate it (Mark 10:2–9). Likewise, the commentator Ibn Urnan reported the Prophet as saying, "The lawful thing which God hates most is divorce."[37]

Interpretations of the Qur'an's statements on polygamy give an example of the declining status of women in Muslim society. The Qur'an permits a man to have four wives, provided "that all are treated justly. . . . Marry of the women who seem good to you, two or three or four; and if ye fear that you cannot do justice (to so many) then one (only) or the captives that your right hand possess."[38] Muslim jurists interpreted the statement as having legal force. The Prophet's emphasis on justice to the several wives, however, was understood as a mere recommendation.[39] Although the Qur'an allows polygamy, only very wealthy men could afford several wives. The vast majority of Muslim males were monogamous because women could not earn money and men had difficulty enough supporting one wife.

In contrast to the Christian view of sexual activity as something inherently shameful and even within marriage only a cure for concupiscence, Islam maintains a healthy acceptance of sexual pleasure for both males and females. Islam holds that sexual satisfaction for both partners in marriage is necessary to prevent extramarital activity. Men, however, are entitled to as many as four legal partners. Women have to be content with one. Because satisfaction of the sexual impulse for males allows polygamy,

one can speculate that fear of its inverse—one woman with four husbands—might explain the assumption of women's insatiability, which is at the core of the Muslim concept of female sexuality. Since Islam assumes that a sexually frustrated individual is a very problematic believer and a troublesome citizen, . . . the distrust of women is even greater.[40]

Modern sociologists contend that polygamy affects individuals' sense of identity. It supports men's self-images as primarily sexual beings. And, by emphasizing wives' inability to satisfy their husbands, it undermines women's confidence in their sexuality. The function of polygamy as a device to humiliate women is evident in an aphorism from Moroccan folklore: "Debase a woman by bringing in (the house) another one."[41]

In many present-day Muslim cultures, few issues are more sensitive than those of the veiling and the seclusion of women. These practices have their roots in pre-Islamic times, and they took firm hold in classical Islamic society. The head veil seems to have been the mark of freeborn urban women; wearing the veil distinguished free women from slave women. Country and desert women did not wear veils because they interfered with work. Probably of Byzantine or Persian origin, the veil indicated respectability and modesty. As the Arab conquerors subjugated various peoples, they adopted some of the vanquished peoples' customs, one of which was veiling. The Qur'an contains no specific rule about the veil, but its few vague references have been interpreted as sanctioning the practice. Gradually, all parts of a woman's body were considered *pudendal* (shameful because they are capable of arousing sexual desire) and were not allowed to be seen in public.

Even more restrictive of the freedom of women than veiling was the practice of *purdah,* literally seclusion behind a screen or curtain—the **harem** system. The English word *harem* comes from the Arabic *haram,* meaning "forbidden" or "sacrosanct," which the women's quarters of a house or palace were considered to be. The practice of secluding women in a harem also derives from Arabic contacts with other Eastern cultures. Scholars do not know precisely when the harem system began, but within "one-and-a-half centuries after the death of the Prophet, the (harem) system was fully established. . . . Amongst the richer classes, the women were shut off from the rest of the household."[42] The harem became another symbol of male prestige and prosperity, as well as a way to distinguish upper-class women from peasants.

Trade and Commerce

Islam had a highly positive disposition toward profit-making enterprises. In the period from 1000 to 1500, there was less ideological resistance to the striving for profit in trade and commerce in the Muslim world than there was in the Christian West. Christianity tended to condemn the acquisition of wealth beyond one's basic needs. "For Islam, the stress is laid rather upon the good use to be made of one's possessions, the merit that lies in expending them intelligently and distributing them with generosity—an attitude more favourable to economic expansion than that of the Christian theologians."[43]

Since Muslim theology and law were fully compatible with profitable economic activity, trade and commerce played a prominent role in the Islamic world. Muhammad had earned his living in business as a representative of the city of Mecca, which carried on a brisk trade from southern Palestine to southwestern Arabia. Although Bedouin nomads were among the first converts to Islam, Islam arose in a mercantile, not an agricultural, setting. The merchant had a respectable place in Muslim society. According to the sayings of the Prophet:

The honest, truthful Muslim merchant will stand with the martyrs on the Day of Judgment.

I commend the merchants to you, for they are the couriers of the horizons and God's trusted servants on earth.[44]

In contrast to the social values of the medieval West and of Confucian China, Muslims tended to look with disdain on agricultural labor and to hold trade in esteem. The Qur'an, moreover, has no prohibition against trade with Christians or other unbelievers.

Western scholars have tended to focus attention on the Mediterranean Sea as the source of Islamic mercantile influence on Europe in the Middle Ages. From the broad perspective of Muslim commerce, however, the Mediterranean held a position much subordinate to other waterways: the Black Sea; the Caspian Sea and the Volga River, which gave access deep into Russia; the Aral Sea, from which caravans departed for China; the Gulf of Aden; and the Arabian Sea and the Indian Ocean, which linked the Arabian gulf region with eastern Africa, the Indian subcontinent, and eventually Indonesia and the Philippines. These served as the main commercial seaways of the Islamic world (see Map 9.2).

Cairo was the major Mediterranean entrepôt for intercontinental trade. An Egyptian official, the *wakil-al-tryjar,* served as the legal representative of foreign merchants from Central Asia, Persia, Iraq, northern Europe (especially Venice), the Byzantine Empire, and Spain. They or their agents sailed up the Nile to the Aswan region, traveled east from Aswan by caravan to the Red Sea, and sailed down the Red Sea to Aden, whence they crossed the Indian Ocean to India. They exchanged textiles, glass, gold, silver, and copper for Asian spices, dyes, and drugs and for Chinese silks and porcelains. Muslim and Jewish merchants dominated the trade with India; both spoke and wrote Arabic. Their commercial practices included the *sakk,* an Arabic word that is the root of the English *check,* an order to a banker to pay money held on account to a third party; the practice can be traced to Roman Palestine. Muslims originated other business devices, such as the bill of exchange, a written order from one person to another to pay a specified sum of money to a designated person or party; and the idea of the joint stock company, an arrangement that lets a group of people invest in a venture and share its profits (and losses) in proportion to the amount each has invested.

Between 1250 and 1500, Islamic trade changed markedly. In maritime technology, the adoption from the Chinese of the magnetic compass, an instrument for determining directions at sea by means of a magnetic needle turning on a pivot, allowed greater reconnaissance of

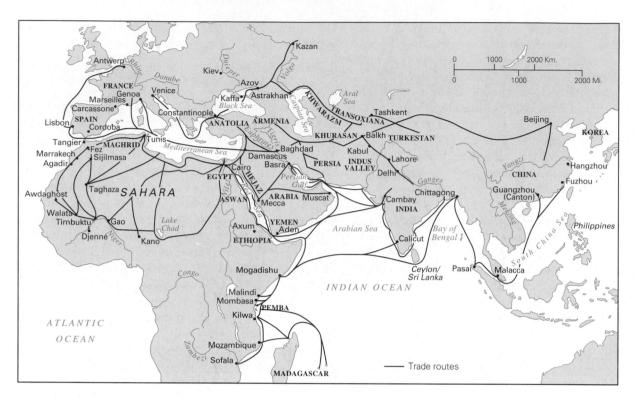

MAP 9.2 Major Trade Routes of the Thirteenth and Fourteenth Centuries   Muslim merchants carried on extensive trade in Southeast Asia, Central Asia, southern Europe, Africa, and the Indian Ocean long before the arrival (in the last area) of Europeans.

the Arabian Sea and the Indian Ocean. The construction of larger ships led to a shift in long-distance cargoes from luxury goods such as pepper, spices, and drugs to bulk goods such as sugar, rice, and timber. Venetian galleys sailing the Mediterranean came to carry up to 250 tons of cargo, but the *dhows* plying the Indian Ocean were built to carry even more, up to 400 tons. The teak forests of western India supplied the wood for Arab ships.

Commercial routes also shifted. The Mongol invasions, culminating in the capture of Baghdad and the fall of the Abbasid caliphate (see page 252), led to the decline of Iraq and the rise of Egypt as the center of Muslim trade. In the fourteenth century, Persian and Arab seamen sailed down the east coast of Africa and established trading towns between Somalia and Sofala (see page 298). These thirty to fifty urban centers—each merchant controlled, fortified, and independent—linked Zimbabwe in southern Africa (see page 300) with the Indian Ocean trade and the Middle Eastern trade. The overland route, through Persia and Central Asia, to China and the Persian Gulf route both declined in importance.[45]

A private ninth-century list mentions a great variety of commodities transported into and through the Islamic world by land and by sea:

Imported from India: tigers, leopards, elephants, leopard skins, red rubies, white sandalwood, ebony, and coconuts

From China: aromatics, silk, porcelain, paper, ink, peacocks, fiery horses, saddles, felts, cinnamon

From the Byzantines: silver and gold vessels, embroidered cloths, fiery horses, slave girls, rare articles in red copper, strong locks, lyres, water engineers, specialists in plowing and cultivation, marble workers, and eunuchs

From Arabia: Arab horses, ostriches, thoroughbred she-camels, and tanned hides

From Barbary and Maghrib (the Arabic name for northwest Africa, an area that included Morocco, Algeria, and Tunisia): leopards, acacia, felts, and black falcons

From Egypt: ambling donkeys, fine cloths, papyrus, balsam oil, and, from its mines, high-quality topaz

THE LIFE OF THE PEOPLE

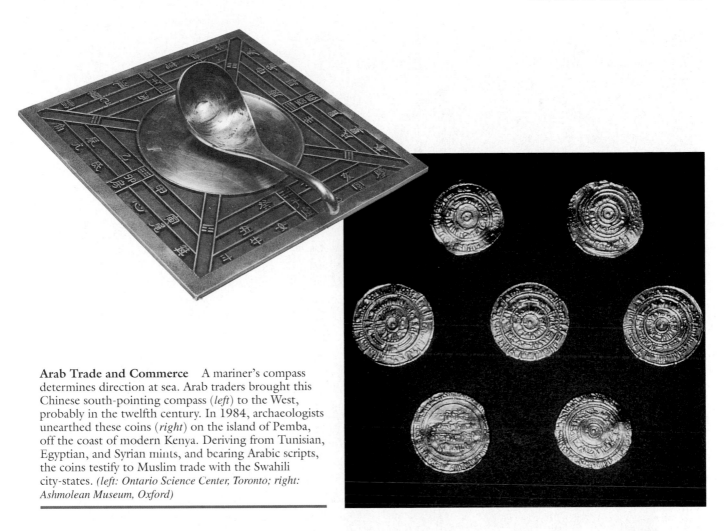

Arab Trade and Commerce   A mariner's compass determines direction at sea. Arab traders brought this Chinese south-pointing compass (*left*) to the West, probably in the twelfth century. In 1984, archaeologists unearthed these coins (*right*) on the island of Pemba, off the coast of modern Kenya. Deriving from Tunisian, Egyptian, and Syrian mints, and bearing Arabic scripts, the coins testify to Muslim trade with the Swahili city-states. *(left: Ontario Science Center, Toronto; right: Ashmolean Museum, Oxford)*

From the Khazars (a people living on the northern shore of the Black Sea): slaves, slave women, armor, helmets, and hoods of mail

From Samarkand: paper

From Ahwaz (a city in southwestern Persia): sugar, silk brocades, castanet players and dancing girls, kinds of dates, grape molasses, and candy.[46]

Camels made long-distance land transportation possible. Stubborn and vicious, camels nevertheless proved more efficient for desert transportation than horses or oxen. The use of the camel to carry heavy and bulky freight facilitated the development of world commerce.

Vigorous long-distance trade had significant consequences. Commodities produced in one part of the world became available in many other places, providing a uniformity of consumer goods among diverse peoples living over a vast area. Trade promoted technological advances in navigation, shipbuilding, and cartography. All this trade obviously generated very great wealth.

Did Muslim economic activity amount to a kind of capitalism? If by capitalism is meant private (not state) ownership of the means of production, the production of goods for market sale, profit as the main motive for economic activity, competition, a money economy, and the lending of money at interest, then, unquestionably, the medieval Muslim economy had capitalistic features. Students of Muslim economic life have not made a systematic and thorough investigation of Muslims' industries, businesses, and seaports, but the impressionistic evidence is overwhelming: "Not only did the Muslim world know a capitalist sector, but this sector was apparently the most extensive in history before the establishment of the world market created by the Western European bourgeoisie, and this did not outstrip it in importance until the sixteenth century."[47]

Design for a Water Clock, Egypt From a book describing the construction of various mechanical devices, this clock from the Mamluk period (1354) was to be run by water and operated by a system of reservoirs, pulleys, and floats. Below the arcade with signs of the zodiac (*top*) stand twelve doorways. A figure emerges from one of these doorways on every daylight hour. During the night, one of the circles in the lower arch lights up on every hour. *(Museum of Fine Arts, Boston. Francis Bartlett Donation of 1912 and Picture Fund 14.533)*

Urban Centers

Long-distance trade provided the wealth that made possible a gracious and sophisticated culture in the cities of the Muslim world. (See the feature "Individuals in Society: Abu 'Abdallah Ibn Battuta.") Although cities and mercantile centers dotted the entire Islamic world, the cities of Baghdad and Córdoba at their peak in the tenth century stand out as the finest examples of cosmopolitan Muslim civilization. On Baghdad's streets thronged a kaleidoscope of races, creeds, costumes, and cultures, an almost infinite variety of peoples: returning travelers, administrative officials, slaves, visitors, merchants from Asia, Africa, and Europe. Shops and marketplaces offered the rich and extravagant a dazzling and exotic array of goods from all over the world.

The caliph Harun al-Rashid (r. 786–809) presided over a glamorous court. He invited writers, dancers, musicians, poets, and artists to live in Baghdad, and he is reputed to have rewarded one singer with a hundred thousand silver pieces for a single song. This brilliant era provided the background for the tales that appear in *The Thousand and One Nights* (see page 257).

The central plot of the fictional tales involves the efforts of Scheherazade to keep her husband, Schariar, legendary king of Samarkand, from killing her. She entertains him

INDIVIDUALS IN SOCIETY

ABU 'ABDALLAH IBN BATTUTA

In 1354 the sultan of Morocco appointed a scribe to write an account of the travels of Ibn Battuta (1304–1368), who between 1325 and 1354 had traveled through most of the Islamic world. The two men collaborated. The result was a *Rihla*, or travel book, written in Arabic for educated people and later hailed as the richest eyewitness account of fourteenth-century Islamic culture. It has often been compared to the Venetian Marco Polo's *Travels* (see page 330).

Ibn Battuta was born in Tangiers to a family of legal scholars. As a youth, he studied Muslim legal sciences, gained fluency in Arabic, and acquired the qualities considered essential for a civilized Muslim gentleman: courtesy, manners, the social polish that eases relations among people.

At age twenty-one, he left Tangiers to make the *hajii* (pilgrimage) to Mecca. He crossed North Africa and visited Alexandria, Cairo, Damascus, and Medina. Reaching Mecca in October 1326, he immediately praised God for his safe journey, kissed the Holy Stone at the Ka'ba, and recited the ritual prayers. There he decided to see more of the world.

In the next four years, he traveled to Iraq and to Basra and Baghdad in Persia, then returned to Mecca before sailing down the coast of Africa as far as modern Tanzania. On the return voyage, he visited Oman and the Persian Gulf region, then traveled by land across central Arabia to Mecca. Strengthened by his stay in the holy city, he decided to go to India by way of Egypt, Syria, and Anatolia; across the Black Sea to the plains of western Central Asia, detouring to see Constantinople; back to the Asian steppe; east to Khurasan and Afghanistan; and down to Delhi in northern India.

For eight years, Ibn Battuta served as a *qadi*, or judge, in the service of the sultan of Delhi. In 1341 the sultan chose him to lead a diplomatic mission to China; the expedition was shipwrecked off the southeastern coast of India. Ibn Battuta used the disaster to travel through southern India, Ceylon (Sri Lanka), and the Maldive Islands. Thence he went on his own to China, stopping in Bengal and Sumatra before reaching the southern coast of China. Returning to Mecca in 1346, he set off for home, getting to Fez in Morocco in 1349. After a brief trip across the Strait of Gibraltar to Granada, he undertook his last journey, by camel caravan across the Sahara to Mali in the West African

Sudan (see page 292), returning home in 1354. Scholars estimate that he had traveled about seventy-five thousand miles. He retired to a provincial Moroccan town, where he held a judicial post until he died.

Ibn Battuta had a driving intellectual curiosity to see and understand the world. At every stop, he sought out the learned jurists and pious men at the

A traveler, perhaps Ibn Battuta, as depicted on a 1375 European map.
(Bibliothèque nationale de France)

mosques and madrasas. He marveled at the Lighthouse of Alexandria, eighteen hundred years old in his day; at the vast harbor at Kaffa (modern Feodosiya), in southern Ukraine on the Black Sea, whose two hundred Genoese ships were loaded with silks and slaves for the markets at Venice, Cairo, and Damascus; and at the elephants in the sultan's procession in Delhi, which carried machines that tossed gold and silver coins to the crowds.

He must have had an iron constitution. Besides walking long distances on his land trips, he endured fevers, dysentery, malaria, the scorching heat of the Sahara, and the freezing cold of the steppe. His thirst for adventure was stronger than his fear of nomadic warriors and bandits on land and the dangers of storms and pirates at sea.

QUESTIONS FOR ANALYSIS

1. Trace the routes of Ibn Battuta's travels on a map.
2. How did a common Muslim culture facilitate his travels?

Source: R. E. Dunn, *The Adventures of Ibn Battuta: A Muslim Traveler of the Fourteenth Century* (Berkeley: University of California Press, 1986).

with one tale a night for 1,001 nights. The best-known tales are "Aladdin and His Lamp," "Sinbad the Sailor," and "Ali Baba and the Forty Thieves." Also known as *The Arabian Nights,* this book offers a sumptuous collection of caliphs, viziers, and genies, varieties of sexual experiences, and fabulous happenings. *The Arabian Nights,* though folklore, has provided many of the images that Europeans have used since the eighteenth century to describe the Islamic world.

Córdoba in southern Spain competed with Baghdad for the cultural leadership of the Islamic world. In the tenth century, no city in Asia or Europe could equal dazzling Córdoba. Its streets were well paved and lighted, and the city had an abundant supply of fresh water. With a population of about 1 million, Córdoba contained 1,600 mosques, 900 public baths, 213,177 houses for ordinary people, and 60,000 mansions for generals, officials, and the wealthy. In its 80,455 shops, 13,000 weavers produced silks, woolens, and brocades that were internationally famous. The English language has memorialized the city's leather with the word *cordovan.* Córdoba utilized the Syrian process of manufacturing crystal. It was a great educational center with 27 free schools and a library containing 400,000 volumes. (By contrast, the great Benedictine abbey of Saint-Gall in Switzerland had about 600 books. The use of paper—whose manufacture the Muslims had learned from the Chinese—instead of vellum, gave rise to this great disparity.) Through Iran and Córdoba, the Indian game of chess entered western Europe. Córdoba's scholars made contributions in chemistry, medicine and surgery, music, philosophy, and mathematics. Its fame was so great it is no wonder that the contemporary Saxon nun Hrosthwita of Gandersheim (d. 1000) described the city as the "ornament of the world."[48]

Education and Intellectual Life

Urban and sophisticated Muslim culture possessed a strong educational foundation. Recent scholarly research provides exciting information about medieval Muslim education. Muslim culture placed extraordinary emphasis on knowledge, especially religious knowledge; indeed, knowledge and learning were esteemed above every other human activity. Knowledge provided the guidelines by which men and women should live. What kinds of educational institutions existed in the Muslim world? What was the method of instruction? What social or practical purposes did Muslim education serve?

Islam is a religion of the law, and the institution for instruction in Muslim jurisprudence was the **madrasa,** the school for the study of Muslim law and religious science. The Arabic noun *madrasa* derives from a verb meaning "to study." The first madrasas were probably established in Khurasan in northeastern Persia. By 1193 thirty madrasas existed in Damascus; between 1200 and 1250, sixty more were established there. Aleppo, Jerusalem, Alexandria, and above all Cairo also witnessed the foundation of madrasas.

Schools were urban phenomena. Wealthy merchants endowed these schools, providing salaries for the teachers, stipends for students, and living accommodations for both. The *sheik,* or teacher, served as a guide to the correct path of living. All Islamic higher education rested on a close relationship between teacher and students, so in selecting a teacher, the student (or his father) considered the character and intellectual reputation of the sheik, not that of any institution. Students built their subsequent careers on the reputation of their teachers.

Learning depended heavily on memorization. In primary school, which was often attached to the institution of higher learning, a boy began his education by memorizing the entire Qur'an. Normally, he achieved this feat by the time he was seven or eight! In adolescence a student learned by heart an introductory work in one of the branches of knowledge, such as jurisprudence or grammar. Later he analyzed the texts in detail. Because the hadith laid great stress on memory, students learned the entire texts through memory and willpower. Memorizing four hundred to five hundred lines a day was considered outstanding. Every class day, the sheik examined the student on the previous day's learning and determined whether the student fully understood what he had memorized. Students of course learned to write, for they had to write down the teacher's commentary on a particular text. But the overwhelming emphasis was on the oral transmission of knowledge.

Because Islamic education focused on particular books or texts, when the student had mastered that text to his teacher's satisfaction, the teacher issued the student an *ijaza,* or license, certifying that he had studied a book or collection of traditions with his teacher. The ijaza allowed the student to transmit on the authority of his teacher a text to the next generation. The ijaza legalized the transmission of sacred knowledge.[49]

Apart from the fundamental goal of preparing men to live wisely and in accordance with God's law, Muslim higher education aimed at preparing men to perform religious and legal functions in the umma, or community: as Qur'an- or hadith-readers; as preachers in the mosques; as professors, educators, copyists; and especially as judges. Judges issued *fatwas,* or legal opinions, in the public

Mechanical Hand Washer   Building on the work of the Greek engineer and inventor Archimedes (see page 137), the Arab scientist ibn al-Razzaz al-Raziri (ca 1200) designed practical devices to serve general social needs and illustrated them in a mechanical engineering handbook. In this diagram, a device in the form of a servant pours water with his right hand and offers a towel with his left. The device resembles a modern faucet that releases water when hands are held under it. *(Courtesy of the Freer Gallery of Art, Smithsonian Institution, Washington, D.C. Purchase, F1930.75a)*

courts; their training was in the Qur'an, hadith, or some text forming part of the shari'a. Islam did not know the division between religious and secular knowledge characteristic of the modern Western world.

What about women—what educational opportunities were available to them? Although tradition holds that Muhammad said, "The seeking of knowledge is a duty of every Muslim," Islamic culture was ambivalent on the issue of female education. Because of the basic Islamic principle, "Men are the guardians of women, because God has set the one over the other," the law excluded women from participation in the legal, religious, or civic occupations for which the madrasa prepared young men. Moreover, educational theorists insisted that men should study in a sexually isolated environment because feminine allure would distract male students. Rich evidence shows that no woman studied or held a professorship in the schools of Cairo, for example. Nevertheless, many young women received substantial educations from their parents or family members; the initiative invariably rested with their fathers or older brothers. The daughter of Ali ibn Muhammad al-Diruti al Mahalli, for example, memorized the Qur'an, learned to write, and received instruction in several sacred works. One biographical dictionary containing the lives of 1,075 women reveals that 411 had memorized the Qur'an, studied with a particular teacher, and received the ijaza. After marriage, responsibility for a woman's education belonged to her husband.[50]

How does Islamic higher education compare with that available in medieval Europe (see pages 389–390) or Ming

China? There are some striking similarities and some major differences. In the Christian West and in China, primary and higher education was institutional. The church operated schools and universities in Europe. Local villages or towns ran schools in China. In contrast, in the Islamic world the transmission of knowledge depended overwhelmingly on the personal relationship of teacher and student: though dispensed through the madrasa, education was not institutional. In Europe, the reward for satisfactory completion of a course of study was a degree granted by the university. In Muslim culture, it was not the school but the individual teacher who granted the ijaza. In China, the imperial civil service examination tested candidates' knowledge and rewarded achievement with appointments in the state bureaucracy.

In all three cultures, education rested heavily on the study of basic religious, legal, or philosophical texts: the Old and New Testaments or the Justinian *Code* in Europe; the ethical writings of Confucian philosophy in China; the Qur'an, hadith, and legal texts deriving from these in the Muslim world. Also in all three cultures, memorization played a large role in the acquisition and transmission of information. In the European university, however, the professor lectured on biblical text or passages of the *Code,* and in the Muslim madrasa the sheik commented on a section of the Qur'an or hadith. Both professors and sheiks sometimes disagreed fiercely about the correct interpretations of a particular text, forcing students to question, to think critically, and to choose between divergent opinions. Such does not appear to be the case in Ming China; there critical thinking and individual imagination were discouraged.

Finally, educated people in each culture shared the same broad literary and religious or ethical culture, giving that culture cohesion and stability. Just as a man who took a degree at Cambridge University in England shared the Latin language and general philosophical outlook of someone with a degree from Montpellier in France or Naples in Italy, so a Muslim gentleman from Cairo spoke and read the same Arabic and knew the same hadith as a man from Baghdad or Samarkand. Such education as women received in Christian Europe, the Islamic world, or Ming China began and usually ended in the home and with the family.

In the Muslim world, the spread of the Arabic language, not only among the educated classes but also among all people, was the decisive element in the creation of a common means of communication and a universal culture. Recent scholarship demonstrates that after the establishment of the Islamic empire, the major influence in the cultural transformation of the Byzantine–Sasanid–North African and the Central Asian worlds was language. The Arabic language proved more important than religion in this regard. Whereas conversion to Islam was gradual, linguistic conversion went much faster. Arabic became the official language of the state and its bureaucracies in former Byzantine and Sasanid territories. Muslim conquerors forbade Persian-speaking people to use their native language. Islamic rulers required tribute from monotheistic peoples—the Persians and Greeks—but they did not force them to change their religions. Instead, conquered peoples were compelled to submit to a linguistic conversion—to adopt the Arabic language.[51] In time Arabic produced a cohesive and "international" culture over a large part of the Eurasian world.

The cosmopolitan nature of the Muslim world gave rise to a period of intellectual vitality. In spite of schism, warfare, and dynastic conflicts, the sacred Arabic language and dedication to scholarship and learning combined Semitic, Hellenic, and Persian knowledge. "A scholar might publish in Samarkand the definitive work on arithmetic used in the religious schools of Cairo. Or, in a dialogue with colleagues in Baghdad and Hamadan, he could claim to have recovered the unalloyed teachings of Aristotle in the libraries of Fez and Cordoba."[52] Modern scholars consider Muslim creativity and vitality from about 900 to 1300 one of the most brilliant periods in the world's history.

The Persian scholar al-Khwarizmi (d. ca 850) harmonized Greek and Indian findings to produce astronomical tables that formed the basis for later Eastern and Western research. Al-Khwarizmi also studied mathematics, and his textbook on algebra (from the Arabic *al-Jabr*) was the first work in which the word *algebra* is used to mean the "transposing of negative terms in an equation to the opposite side."

Muslim medical knowledge far surpassed that of the West. The Baghdad physician al-Razi (865–925) produced an encyclopedic treatise on medicine that was translated into Latin and circulated widely in the West. Al-Razi was the first physician to make the clinical distinction between measles and smallpox. The great surgeon of Córdoba, al-Zahrawi (d. 1013), produced an important work in which he discussed the cauterization of wounds (searing with a branding iron) and the crushing of stones in the bladder. In Ibn Sina of Bukhara (980–1037), known in the West as Avicenna, Muslim science reached its peak. His *al-Qanun* codified all Greco-Arabic medical thought, described the contagious nature of tuberculosis and the spreading of diseases, and listed 760 pharmaceutical drugs. Muslim scholars also wrote works on geography and jurisprudence.

Likewise, in philosophy the Muslims made significant contributions. Although the majority of the ulama considered philosophy incompatible with jurisprudence and theology, a minority of them obviously did not. Al-Kindi (d. ca 870) was the first Muslim thinker to try to harmonize Greek philosophy and the religious precepts of the Qur'an. He sought to integrate Islamic concepts of human beings and their relations to God and the universe with the principles of ethical and social conduct discussed by Plato and Aristotle.

Inspired by Plato's *Republic* and Aristotle's *Politics,* the distinguished philosopher al-Farabi (d. 950) wrote a political treatise describing an ideal city whose ruler is morally and intellectually perfect and who has as his goal the citizens' complete happiness. Avicenna maintained

that the truths found by human reason cannot conflict with the truths of revelation as given in the Qur'an. Ibn Rushid, or Averroës (1126–1198), of Córdoba, a judge in Seville and later royal court physician, paraphrased and commented on the works of Aristotle. He insisted on the right to subject all knowledge, except the dogmas of faith, to the test of reason and on the essential harmony between religion and philosophy.

At the start of the fourteenth century, Islamic learning as revealed in astronomy, mathematics, medicine, architecture, and philosophical investigation was highly advanced, perhaps the most creative in the world. In the development and transmission of ancient Egyptian, Persian, and Greek wisdom, Muslims played a vital role. They also incorporated into their studies

Pharmacist Preparing Drugs The translation of Greek scientific treatises into Arabic, combined with considerable botanical experimentation, gave Muslims virtually unrivaled medical knowledge. Treatment for many ailments was by prescription drugs. In this thirteenth-century illustration, a pharmacist prepares a drug in a cauldron over a brazier. It has been said that the pharmacy as an institution is an Islamic invention. *(The Metropolitan Museum of Art, Bequest of Cora Timkin Burnett Collection of Persian Miniatures and Other Persian Art Objects, Bequest of Cora Timken Burnett, 1957 [57.51.21]. Photograph © 1991 The Metropolitan Museum of Art)*

new information from China and India. And they not only preserved and transmitted ancient wisdom "in the medieval Middle East," but they also "developed an approach rarely used by the ancients—experiment. Through this and other means, they brought major advances in virtually all the sciences."[53]

Sufism

Like the world's other major religions—Buddhism, Hinduism, Judaism, and Christianity—Islam also developed a mystical tradition. It arose as a popular movement in the ninth and tenth centuries as a reaction to what some especially devout individuals perceived as the materialism of the Umayyad regime. These people were called *Sufis,* an Arabic term deriving from *suf* (wool), a reference to the woolen garments worn by early Muslim ascetics. Sufis wanted a personal union with God—divine love and knowledge through intuition rather than through rational deduction and study of the shari'a. They followed an ascetic routine (denial of physical desires to gain a spiritual goal), dedicating themselves to fasting, prayer, meditation on the Qur'an, and the avoidance of sin. These practices are summarized in the word *zuhd,* meaning "renunciation."

The woman mystic Rabia (d. 801) epitomized this combination of renunciation and devotionalism. An attractive woman who refused marriage so that nothing would distract her from a total commitment to God, Rabia attracted followers, whom she served as a spiritual guide. Her poem in the form of prayer captures her deep devotion: "O my lord, if I worship thee from fear of hell, and if I worship thee in hope of paradise, exclude me thence, but if I worship thee for thine own sake, then withhold not from me thine eternal beauty."

In the twelfth century, groups of Sufis gathered around sheiks (teachers), and the term *tariqa,* which originally meant "spiritual path," came to designate the sheiks' ritual system and the fraternity or brotherhood of a particular community or order. A member of a Sufi order was called a *dervish.* The ritual of Sufi brotherhoods directed the dervish to a hypnotic or ecstatic trance, either through the constant repetition of certain prayers or through physical exertions such as whirling or dancing (hence the English phrase "whirling dervish" for one who dances with abandonment). Some Sufis acquired reputations as charismatic holy men to whom ordinary Muslims came seeking spiritual consolation, healing, charity, or political mediation between tribal and factional rivals.

Probably the most famous medieval Sufi was the Spanish mystic-philosopher Ibn al-'Arabi (1165–1240). Born in Valencia and educated in Seville, then a leading center of Islamic culture, Ibn al-'Arabi traveled widely in Spain, North Africa, and Arabia seeking masters of Sufism. He visited Mecca, where he received a "divine commandment" to begin his major work, *The Meccan Revelation,* which evolved into a personal encyclopedia of 560 chapters. At Mecca the wisdom of a beautiful young girl inspired him to write a collection of love poems, *The Interpreter of Desires,* for which he composed a mystical commentary. In 1223, after visits to Egypt, Anatolia, Baghdad, and Aleppo, Ibn al-'Arabi concluded his pilgrimage through the Islamic world at Damascus, where he produced *The Bezels [Edges] of Wisdom,* considered one of the greatest works of Sufism.

The Muslim View of the West

What did early Muslims think of Jesus? Of Europeans? Jesus is mentioned in ninety-three verses of the Qur'an, which affirms that he was born of Mary the Virgin. He is described as a righteous prophet who performed miracles and continued the work of Abraham and Moses, and he was a sign of the coming Judgment Day. But Muslims held that Jesus was only an apostle, not God, and those (that is, Christians) who called Jesus divine committed blasphemy, showing contempt for God. Muslims esteemed the Judeo-Christian Scriptures as part of God's revelation, although they believed that Christian communities had corrupted the Scriptures and that the Qur'an superseded them. The Christian doctrine of the Trinity—that there is one God in three persons, Father, Son, and Holy Spirit—posed a powerful obstacle to Muslim-Christian understanding because of Islam's total and uncompromising monotheism.[54]

Europeans and Muslims of the Middle East were geographical neighbors. The two peoples shared a common cultural heritage from the Judeo-Christian past. But a thick psychological iron curtain restricted contact between them. The Muslim assault on Christian Europe in the eighth and ninth centuries—villages were burned, monasteries sacked, and Christians sold into slavery (see page 370)—left a legacy of bitter hostility. Europeans' fierce intolerance also helped buttress the barrier between the two peoples. Christians felt threatened by a faith that acknowledged God as creator of the universe but denied the doctrine of the Trinity; that accepted Christ as a prophet but denied his divinity; that believed in the Judgment Day but seemed to describe Heaven in sensuous terms. Popes preached against the Muslims;

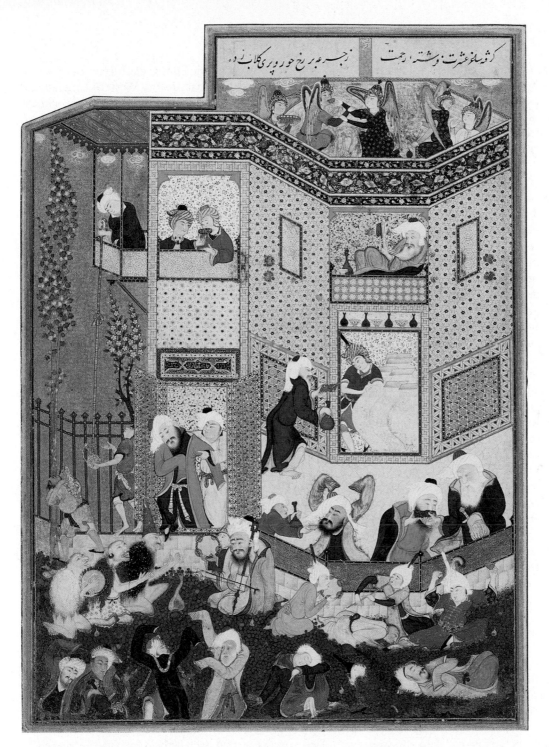

Sufi Collective Ritual   Collective or group rituals, in which Sufis tried through ecstatic experiences to come closer to God, have always fascinated outsiders, including non-Sufi Muslims. Here the sixteenth-century Persian painter Sultan Muhammad illustrates the writing of the fourteenth-century lyric poet Hafiz. Just as Hafiz's poetry moved back and forth between profane and mystical themes, so it is difficult to determine whether the ecstasy achieved here is alcoholic or spiritual. Many figures seem to enjoy wine. Notice the various musical instruments and the delicate floral patterns so characteristic of Persian art. *(Courtesy of the Arthur M. Sackler Museum, Harvard University Art Museums. Promised gift of Mr. and Mrs. Stuart Cary Welch, Jr. Partially owned by the Metropolitan Museum of Art and the Arthur M. Sackler Museum, Harvard University, 1988. In honor of the students of Harvard University and Radcliffe College. Photo by Rick Stafford. © President and Fellows of Harvard College)*

theologians penned tracts against them; and church councils condemned them. Europeans' perception of Islam as a menace helped inspire the Crusades of the eleventh through thirteenth centuries (see pages 374–376). The knightly class believed that it had a sacred obligation to fight the Muslims. As a popular song during the Second Crusade put it: "God has brought before you his suit against the Turks and Saracens [Crusaders' hostile term for Muslims], who have done him great despite [injury]. They have seized his fiefs, where God was first served [that is, the holy places in Palestine] and recognized as Lord."[55]

During the Crusades, Europeans imposed Christianity on any lands they conquered from Islam, and at times they compelled Muslims to choose among conversion, exile, and death. By the thirteenth century, Western literature, such as the Florentine poet Dante's *Divine Comedy,* portrayed the Muslims as the most dreadful of Europe's enemies, guilty of every kind of crime.

Muslims had a strong aversion to travel in Europe. They were quite willing to trade with Europeans, but they rejected European culture. Medieval Europe had no resident Muslim communities where a traveler could find the mosques, food, or other things needed for the Muslim way of life. Muslims generally had a horror of going among those they perceived as infidels, and often when compelled to make diplomatic or business contacts, they preferred to send Jewish or Christian intermediaries, the dhimmis. Commercially, from the Muslim perspective, Europe had very little to offer, apart from fine English woolens, which Muslims admired, and the slaves from southern Russia and central and southeastern Europe.

Did Western culture have any impact on Islam? Muslims considered Christianity to be a flawed religion superseded by Islam. "For the Muslim, Christ was a precursor, for the Christian Muhammad was an impostor. For the Muslim, Christianity was an early, incomplete, and obsolete form of the true religion."[56] Religion dominated the Islamic perception of Europe. Muslims understood Europe not as Western, European, or white but as Christian. And the fact that European culture was Christian immediately discredited it in Muslim eyes. Christians were presumed to be hostile to Islam and were thought to be culturally inferior. Thus Muslims had no interest in them.

An enormous quantity of Muslim historical writing survives from the period between about 800 and 1600. Although the material reflects some knowledge of European geography, it shows an almost total lack of interest among Muslim scholars in European languages, life, and culture. Before the nineteenth century, not a single grammar book or dictionary of any Western language existed in the Muslim world. By contrast, Western scholarship on the Middle East steadily advanced. By the early seventeenth century, a curious European student could find an extensive literature on the history, religion, and culture of the Muslim peoples. In 1633 a professorship in Arabic studies was founded at Cambridge University in England.[57]

As in language and literature, so in science, engineering, and medicine: the medieval West had no influence on the Muslim world. Muslims had only contempt for Western science. Western art, however, attracted and influenced Muslim artists. At least from the time of the visit of the Venetian artist Gentile Bellini to the court of Sultan Mehmet II in Istanbul (1479–1481), Turkish, Persian, and Indian artists seemed fascinated by Western techniques, materials, and subject matter, and Muslim artists imitated them.

Muslims also showed interest in European knowledge of the art of warfare. During the Crusades, the Muslims adopted Frankish weapons and methods of fortification. Islam, however, distinguished between Byzantium, which was held in fair regard as a realm of culture, and "the land of the Franks," or western Europe, which was perceived as backward and barbaric, and Europeans as "ignorant infidels."[58]

SUMMARY

Islam represents a powerful phenomenon in world history. Its universal monotheistic creed helps to explain its initial attractiveness to Bedouin tribes. Driven by the religious zeal of the jihad, Muslims carried their faith from the Arabian peninsula through the Middle East to North Africa, Spain, and southern France in the west and to the borders of China and northern India in the east—within the short span of one hundred years. Economic need, the political weaknesses of their enemies, strong military organization, and the practice of establishing army cities in newly conquered territories account for their expansion.

Two successive dynasties—the Umayyad, centered at Damascus in Syria, and the Abbasid, located at Baghdad in Iraq—governed the Islamic state. A large imperial bureaucracy headed by a vizier supervised the administration of the state. All government agencies evolved from the diwan. As provincial governors acquired independent power, which the caliphs could not check, centralized authority within the Islamic state disintegrated.

Commerce and trade also spread the faith of Muhammad. Although its first adherents were nomads, Islam developed and flourished in a mercantile milieu. By land and sea, Muslim merchants transported a rich variety of goods across Asia, the Middle East, Africa, and western Europe. Muslim business procedures and terminology greatly influenced the West.

On the basis of the wealth that trade generated, a gracious, sophisticated, and cosmopolitan culture developed with centers at Baghdad and Córdoba. In the tenth and eleventh centuries, the Islamic world witnessed enormous intellectual vitality and creativity. Muslim scholars produced important work in many disciplines, especially mathematics, medicine, and philosophy. Muslim civilization in the Middle Ages was far in advance of that of Christian Europe, and Muslims, with some justification, looked on Europeans as ignorant barbarians.

KEY TERMS

Ka'ba	Sunnis
Qur'an	ulama
caliph	emirs
hadith	shari'a
umma	qadis
Five Pillars of Islam	vizier
jihad	dhimmis
diwan	harem
imam	madrasa
Shi'ites	

NOTES

1. F. M. Donner, *The Early Islamic Conquests* (Princeton, N.J.: Princeton University Press, 1981), pp. 14–37.

2. See A. Rippin, *Muslims: Their Religious Beliefs and Practices.* Vol. 1: *The Formative Period* (New York: Routledge, 1990), pp. 30–40.

3. Quoted in F. E. Peters, *A Reader on Classical Islam* (Princeton, N.J.: Princeton University Press, 1994), p. 47.

4. J. L. Esposito, *Islam: The Straight Path* (New York: Oxford University Press, 1988), pp. 6–17; the quotation is on p. 15.

5. Donner, *The Early Islamic Conquests,* pp. 57–60.

6. Quoted in J. O'Faolain and L. Martines, eds., *Not in God's Image: Women in History from the Greeks to the Victorians* (New York: Harper & Row, 1973), pp. 108–115.

7. See F. M. Donner, "Muhammad and the Caliphate," in *The Oxford History of Islam,* ed. J. L. Esposito (New York: Oxford University Press, 1999), pp. 3–13.

8. Quoted in Peters, *A Reader on Classical Islam,* pp. 154–155; the quotations are on p. 155.

9. See P. Crone, "The Early Islamic World," in *War and Society in the Ancient and Medieval Worlds: Asia, the Mediterranean, Europe, and Meso-America,* ed. K. Raaflaub and N. Rosenstein (Cambridge, Mass.: Harvard University Press, 1999), p. 312.

10. Ibid., pp. 312–313.

11. Quoted in Donner, *The Early Islamic Conquests,* p. 217.

12. Donner, *The Early Islamic Conquests,* pp. 92–101.

13. R. G. Hoyland, ed., *Seeing Islam as Others Saw It: A Survey and Evaluation of Christian, Jewish and Zoroastrian Writings on Early Islam* (Princeton, N.J.: Darwin Press, 1997), pp. 524–525.

14. G. E. von Grunebaum, *Medieval Islam: A Study in Cultural Orientation* (Chicago: University of Chicago Press, 1954), pp. 142–150.

15. Crone, "The Early Islamic World," p. 324.

16. Ibid., p. 325.

17. Esposito, *Islam,* pp. 57–58; A. Hourani, *A History of the Arab Peoples* (Cambridge, Mass.: Harvard University Press, 1991), p. 36.

18. Crone, "The Early Islamic World," pp. 319, 321.

19. L. I. Conrad, "Caliphate," in *Dictionary of the Middle Ages,* vol. 3, ed. J. R. Strayer (New York: Scribner's, 1983), p. 49.

20. Quoted in R. Levy, *The Social Structure of Islam,* 2d ed. (Cambridge: Cambridge University Press, 1957), p. 56.

21. P. K. Hitti, *The Near East in History* (Princeton, N.J.: Van Nostrand, 1961), p. 229.

22. B. Lewis, ed. and trans., *Islam: From the Prophet Muhammad to the Capture of Constantinople.* Vol. 2: *Religion and Society* (New York: Harper & Row, 1975), pp. 219–221.

23. M. R. Cohen, *Under Crescent and Cross: The Jews in the Middle Ages* (Princeton, N.J.: Princeton University Press, 1994), Chap. 4; the quotation is on p. 74.

24. Quoted in Levy, *The Social Structure of Islam,* p. 67.

25. R. Segal, *Islam's Black Slaves* (New York: Farrar, Straus and Giroux, 2001), p. 35; see also Esposito, *Islam,* p. 45.

26. M. G. S. Hodgson, quoted in Segal, *Islam's Black Slaves,* pp. 41–42.

27. Segal, *Islam's Black Slaves,* p. 44.

28. Quoted in B. Lewis, *Race and Slavery in the Middle East* (New York: Oxford University Press, 1990), p. 19.

29. Ibid., p. 20. This section leans on Lewis's book on race.

30. Ibid., pp. 54–71.

31. See B. F. Stowasser, *Women in the Qur'an, Tradition, and Interpretation* (New York: Oxford University Press, 1994), pp. 94–118.

32. N. Coulson and D. Hinchcliffe, "Women and Law Reform in Contemporary Islam," in *Women in the Muslim World,* ed. L. Beck and N. Keddie (Cambridge, Mass.: Harvard University Press, 1982), p. 37.

33. Quoted in B. F. Stowasser, "The Status of Women in Early Islam," in *Muslim Women,* ed. F. Hussain (New York: St. Martin's Press, 1984), p. 25.

34. Quoted ibid., pp. 25–26.

35. Ibid., p. 26.

36. Peters, *A Reader on Classical Islam,* pp. 249–250; the quotation is on p. 250.

37. Ibid.

38. Ibid., p. 16.

39. G. Nashat, "Women in Pre-Revolutionary Iran: A Historical Overview," in *Women and Revolution in Iran,* ed. G. Nashat (Boulder, Colo.: Westview Press, 1983), pp. 47–48.

40. F. Mernissi, *Beyond the Veil: Male-Female Dynamics in Modern Muslim Society* (New York: Schenkman, 1975), p. 16.

41. Ibid.

42. Quoted in D. J. Gerner, "Roles in Transition: The Evolving Position of Women in Arab Islamic Countries," in *Muslim Women,* ed. F. Hussain (New York: St. Martin's Press, 1984), p. 73.

43. Quoted in Cohen, *Under Crescent and Cross,* p. 90.

44. Quoted in Lewis, *Religion and Society,* p. 126.

45. S. D. Curtin, *Cross-Cultural Trade in World History* (Cambridge: Cambridge University Press, 1986), pp. 113–115.

46. Adapted from Lewis, *Religion and Society,* pp. 154–157.

47. M. Rodinson, *Islam and Capitalism,* trans. Brian Pearce (Austin: University of Texas Press, 1981), p. 56.

48. R. Hillenbrand, "Cordoba," in *Dictionary of the Middle Ages,* vol. 3, ed. J. R. Strayer (New York: Scribner's, 1983), pp. 597–601.

49. I have leaned heavily here on the important study of J. Berkey, *The Transmission of Knowledge in Medieval Cairo: A Social History of Islamic Education* (Princeton, N.J.: Princeton University Press, 1992), pp. 22–43.

50. Ibid., pp. 161–181; the quotation is on p. 161.

51. A. Dallal, "Science, Medicine, and Technology: The Making of a Scientific Culture," in *The Oxford History of Islam,* ed. J. L. Esposito (New York: Oxford University Press, 1999), pp. 158–159.

52. P. Brown, "Understanding Islam," *New York Review of Books,* February 22, 1979, pp. 30–33.

53. B. Lewis, *What Went Wrong? Western Impact and Middle Eastern Response* (New York: Oxford University Press, 2002), pp. 78–79.

54. See J. I. Smith, "Islam and Christianity: Historical, Cultural and Religious Interaction from the Seventh to the Fifteenth Centuries," in *The Oxford History of Islam,* ed. J. L. Esposito (New York: Oxford University Press, 1999), pp. 317–321.

55. Quoted in R. W. Southern, *The Making of the Middle Ages* (New Haven, Conn.: Yale University Press, 1961), p. 55.

56. B. Lewis, *The Muslim Discovery of Europe* (New York: W. W. Norton, 1982), p. 297.

57. Ibid., pp. 296–297.

58. Ibid., p. 222.

▌SUGGESTED READING

The titles by Peters and Cohen cited in the Notes are especially useful: Peters for its rich collection of documents on many facets of the culture of classical Islam, Cohen for the study of Jews and Christians living in Muslim societies. C. Lindholm, *The Anthropology of Islam* (1995), argues that Islam is the most egalitarian of the Middle Eastern religions. Perhaps the best introduction to Shi'ism is Y. Richard, *Shi'ite Islam* (1994). For the social, commercial, and political significance of the obligatory Muslim pilgrimage to Mecca, see F. E. Peters, *The Hajj: The Muslim Pilgrimage to Mecca and the Holy Places* (1994). For general surveys, the curious student may consult A. Hourani, *A History of the Arab Peoples* (1991), a readable and important synthesis, and S. Fisher and W. Ochsenwald, *The Middle East: A History* (1990), which has helpful bibliographical material. "Peoples of the Book: Muslim and Jewish Thought," in M. L. Colish's splendid synthesis *Medieval Foundations of the Western Intellectual Tradition, 400–1400* (1997), treats many aspects of the intellectual history discussed in this chapter. For the Prophet, see W. M. Watt, *Muhammad at Mecca* (1953) and *Muhammad at Medina* (1956), and M. Rodinson, *Mohammed,* trans. A. Carter (1971). M. G. S. Hodgson, *The Venture of Islam.* Vol. 1: *The Classical Age of Islam* (1964), is comprehensive but for the specialist. K. Cragg and R. M. G. Speight, eds., *Islam from Within: Anthology of a Religion* (1980), offers a fine collection of primary materials on the beginnings of Islam. For the cultural impact of Islam, G. E. von Grunebaum, *Classical Islam: A History 600–1258,* trans. K. Watson (1970), remains valuable. B. Lewis, *A Middle East Mosaic: Fragments of Life, Letters, and History* (2000), is a rich source for many aspects of Islamic life, culture, and prejudices.

The best starting point for the study of Muslim expansion is P. Crone, "The Early Islamic World," in *War and Society in the Ancient and Medieval Worlds,* ed. K. Raaflaub and N. Rosenstein (1999); the thesis here should be compared with that of F. M. Donner, *The Early Islamic Conquests* (1981). For the ways in which the Arabs came to terms with non-Muslim peoples of their conquered territories, see the studies in C. E. Bosworth, *The Arabs, Byzantium, and Iran* (1996). For the early evolution of Muslim religious beliefs and practices, see the title by Rippin cited in the Notes. For law and religious authority, in addition to the title by Berkey cited in the Notes, see N. J. Coulson, *A History of Islamic Law* (1964); J. N. D. Anderson, *Islamic Law in the Modern World* (1959); R. P. Mottahedeh, *Loyalty and Leadership in Early Islamic Society* (1986); and S. D. Gottein, *Studies in Islamic History and Institutions* (1966).

For Muslim trade and commerce, see the excellent study by O. R. Constable, *Trade and Traders in Muslim Spain: The Commercial Realignment of the Iberian Peninsula, 900–1500* (1994). The older study by A. L. Udovich, *Partnership and Profit in Medieval Islam* (1970), is still helpful but should be compared with the work by Rodinson cited in the Notes. For agricultural practices, see A. M. Watson, *Agricultural Innovation in the Early Islamic World* (1983), and the fascinating material in T. F. Glick, *Islamic and Christian Spain in the Early Middle Ages* (1979). For slavery in the Arab world, see B. Lewis, *Race and Slavery in the Middle East* (1990), which demythologizes the Western view of the Middle East as free of racial prejudice, and G. Murray, *Slavery in the Arab World* (1989), which explains the persistence of slavery in Muslim societies in sexual, not economic, terms. W. M. Watson, *Islam and the Integration of Society* (1961), provides an important sociological interpretation of factors that led to the unity of very diverse peoples.

In the avalanche of material on women and gender in Islamic societies, J. Tucker, *Gender and Islamic History* (1993), which offers a broad sketch and an excellent introduction to the many problems in the study of gender, is especially recommended. B. F. Stowasser, *Women in the Qur'an: Traditions and Interpretation* (1994), gives a fine analysis of the

Qur'an's statement on women. The following studies contain fascinating and important discussions: L. Ahmed, *Women and Gender in Islam: Historical Roots of a Modern Debate* (1992); D. Kandiyoti, "Islam and Patriarchy: A Comparative Perspective," in *Women in Middle Eastern History,* ed. B. Baron and N. Keddie (1991); J. F. Tucker, "The Arab Family in History: 'Otherness' and the Study of the Family," in *Arab Women: Old Boundaries, New Frontiers,* ed. J. F. Tucker (1993), which, although focusing on the period since 1800, will interest students of any period; N. Hijab, *Woman-power* (1988); and G. Nashat, "Women in the Middle East, 8000 B.C.–A.D. 1800," in *Restoring Women to History* (1988).

For Islamic art, see the stunning achievement of S. S. Blair and J. M. Bloom, *The Art and Architecture of Islam, 1250–1800* (1994), which authoritatively treats the trends in Islamic art and discusses virtually all the masterpieces in Islamic lands. The older studies by O. Grabar, *The Formation of Islamic Art* (1987), and D. Talbot Rice, *Islamic Art,* rev. ed. (1985), provide valuable material.

On the Mongols, see P. Ratchnevsky, *Genghis Khan* (1993), which is based on Chinese, Mongol, and Persian sources, as well as European ones, to give a balanced account of the great world conqueror; M. Rossabi, *Khubilai Khan: His Life and Times* (1988); and D. Morgan, *The Mongols* (1986), an especially readable study. R. E. Dunn, *The Adventures of Ibn Battuta: A Muslim Traveler of the Fourteenth Century* (1987), gives a fascinating account of Asian and African societies by a Muslim world traveler.

LISTENING TO THE PAST

A TREATISE ON BUYING SLAVES

Ibn Butlan (d. 1066) was a Christian who practiced medicine in Baghdad. He wrote an important scientific treatise on the importance of good hygiene and diet, but his most popular work was his "Treatise on Buying Slaves, A Consumer's Guide," a section of which is reprinted here.

The Turkish women combine beauty and whiteness and grace. Their faces tend to look sullen, but their eyes, though small, are sweet. They have a smooth brownness and their stature is between medium and short. There are very few tall ones among them. The beautiful ones are extremely beautiful and the ugly ones exceptional. They are treasure houses for children, gold mines for generation. It very rarely happens that their children are ugly or badly formed. They are clean and refined. . . . Bad breath is hardly ever found among them, nor any with large buttocks, but they have some nasty characteristics and are of little loyalty.

The women of Daylam [in northern Iran] are both outwardly and inherently beautiful, but they have the worst characters of all and the coarsest natures. They can endure hardship . . . in every respect.

The women of the Alans [a people of the northern Caucasus] are reddish-white and well-fleshed. The cold humor predominates in their temperaments. They are better suited for service than for pleasure since they have good characters in that they are trustworthy and honest and are both reliant and compliant. Also, they are far from licentious.

The Greek women are blond, with straight hair and blue eyes. As slaves they are obedient, adaptable, serviceable, well meaning, loyal, trustworthy and reliable. They are good as trea-

surers because they are meticulous and not very generous. Sometimes they are skilled in some fine handicraft.

The Armenians would be beautiful were it not for their peculiarly ugly feet, though they are well built, energetic and strong. Chastity is rare or absent among them and thievery widespread. Avarice is very rare among them, but they are coarse in nature and speech. Cleanliness is not in their language. They are slaves for hard work and service. . . . This race is untrustworthy even when they are contented, not to speak of when they are angry. Their women are useless for pleasure. In fine, the Armenians are the worst of the whites as the Zanj are the worst of the blacks. And how much do they resemble one another in the strength of their bodies, their great wickedness, and their coarse natures!

QUESTIONS FOR ANALYSIS

1. How valid are broad generalizations about ethnic and racial characteristics?

2. How do assumptions about race, ethnic origins, and social status influence perceptions of beauty?

3. According to this guide, what physical and character traits were most desirable in female slaves? What is meant by the phrase "gold mines for generation"?

Source: Excerpts from *The Travels of Ibn Battuta,* vols I, II, and III, trans. H. A. R. Gibb (London: The Hakluyt Society, 1958). Reprinted in Bernard Lewis, *A Middle East Mosaic: Fragments of Life, Letters, and History* (New York: Random House, 2000), pp. 187–188. Used by permission of David Higham Associates.

Female slaves of many ethnic and racial backgrounds in the Aurat Bazaar, Istanbul, 1838. *(From Bernard Lewis,* What Went Wrong. *© 2002 by Bernard Lewis. Used by permission of Oxford University Press.)*

Bronze striated head (marked with stripes, grooves, or ridges in parallel lines) showing an Oni of Ife, thirteenth to fourteenth century. (© *Jerry Thompson*)

10 AFRICAN SOCIETIES AND KINGDOMS, ca 400–1450

Between about 400 and 1500, Africa witnessed the development of some centralized, bureaucratized, and socially stratified civilizations alongside a spectrum of communities with a more attenuated form of social organization that functioned at the level of lineage or descent groups. Until fairly recently, ethnocentrism, Eurocentrism, and white racism have limited what Asians, Europeans, and Americans have known about Africa. The more that historians, sociologists, and anthropologists have learned about early African civilizations, the more they have come to appreciate the richness, diversity, and dynamism of those cultures.

- What patterns of social and political organization prevailed among the peoples of Africa?
- What types of agriculture and commerce did Africans engage in?
- What values do Africans' art, architecture, and religions express?

In a discussion of the major civilizations of Africa before 1500, these are the questions this chapter explores.

THE LAND AND PEOPLES OF AFRICA

Africa is immense. The world's second largest continent (after Asia), it is three times as big as Europe and covers 20 percent of the earth's land surface. The coastal regions of Africa have most felt the impact of other cultures, and African peoples in turn have influenced European, Middle Eastern, and Asian societies. African peoples have never been isolated from other peoples. Five climatic zones roughly divide the continent (see Map 10.1). Fertile land with unpredictable rainfall borders parts of the Mediterranean coast in the north and the southwestern coast of the Cape of Good Hope in the south. Inland from these areas lies dry steppe country with little plant life. The southern fringe of this area is called the Sahel. The steppe gradually gives way to Africa's great deserts: the Sahara in the north and the Namib and Kalahari in the south. The vast Sahara—3.5 million square miles—takes its name from the Arabic word for "tan," the color of the desert. (Folk etymology ascribes the word *Sahara* to an ancient Arabic word that sounds like a parched man's gasp

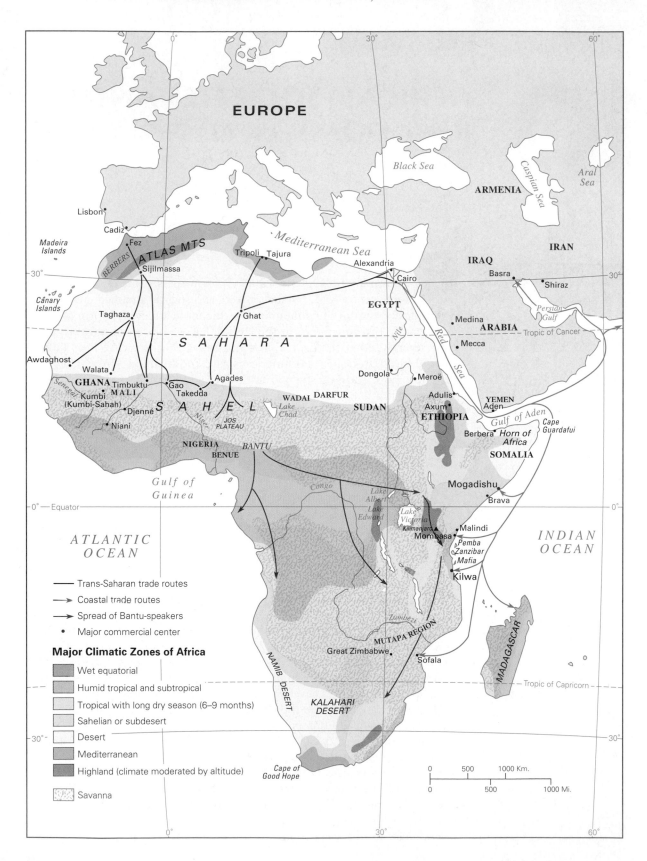

EUROPE

Black Sea

Caspian Sea

Aral Sea

ARMENIA

Mediterranean Sea

IRAN

Lisbon

Cadiz

Madeira Islands

Fez

ATLAS MTS

BERBERS

Sijilmassa

Tripoli   Tajura

Alexandria

IRAQ

Basra

Cairo

Shiraz

Canary Islands

Taghaza

Ghat

EGYPT

Persian Gulf

S A H A R A

Medina   ARABIA

Nile

Red Sea

Tropic of Cancer

Mecca

Awdaghost

Walata

GHANA   Timbuktu

Kumbi   MALI   Gao

(Kumbi-Sahah)   Takedda

Djenné

Senegal

Agades

Dongola   Meroë

Niger

WADAI   DARFUR

Lake Chad

SUDAN

Adulis

Axum

ETHIOPIA

YEMEN

Aden

Gulf of Aden

Cape Guardafui

Niani

JOS PLATEAU

SAHEL

Berbera   *Horn of Africa*

NIGERIA

BENUE

BANTU

SOMALIA

Gulf of Guinea

Congo

Lake Albert

Lake Edward

Lake Victoria

Kilimanjaro▲

Mogadishu

Brava

0° — Equator

ATLANTIC OCEAN

Malindi

Mombasa

Pemba

Zanzibar

Mafia

INDIAN OCEAN

Kilwa

— Trans-Saharan trade routes

→ Coastal trade routes

→ Spread of Bantu-speakers

• Major commercial center

Zambezi

MUTAPA REGION

Major Climatic Zones of Africa

Great Zimbabwe

Sofala

MADAGASCAR

Tropic of Capricorn

Wet equatorial

Humid tropical and subtropical

Tropical with long dry season (6–9 months)

Sahelian or subdesert

Desert

Mediterranean

Highland (climate moderated by altitude)

Savanna

NAMIB DESERT

KALAHARI DESERT

Cape of Good Hope

0   500   1000 Km.

0   500   1000 Mi.

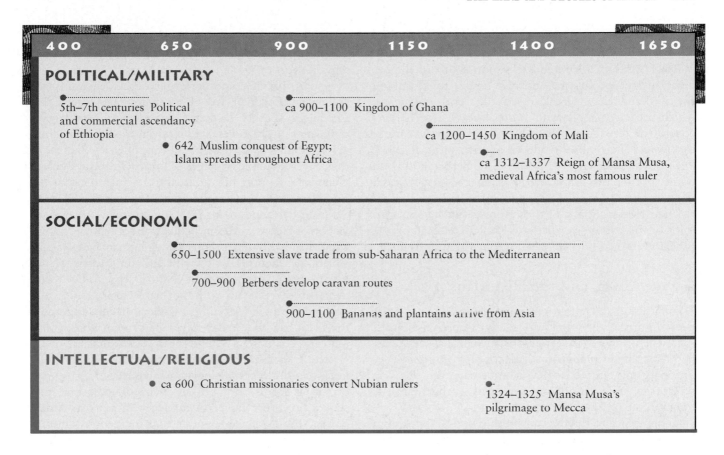

| | 400 | 650 | 900 | 1150 | 1400 | 1650 |

POLITICAL/MILITARY

- 5th–7th centuries Political and commercial ascendancy of Ethiopia
- 642 Muslim conquest of Egypt; Islam spreads throughout Africa
- ca 900–1100 Kingdom of Ghana
- ca 1200–1450 Kingdom of Mali
- ca 1312–1337 Reign of Mansa Musa, medieval Africa's most famous ruler

SOCIAL/ECONOMIC

- 650–1500 Extensive slave trade from sub-Saharan Africa to the Mediterranean
- 700–900 Berbers develop caravan routes
- 900–1100 Bananas and plantains arrive from Asia

INTELLECTUAL/RELIGIOUS

- ca 600 Christian missionaries convert Nubian rulers
- 1324–1325 Mansa Musa's pilgrimage to Mecca

for water.) The Savanna—flat grassland—extends in a swath across the widest part of the continent, as well as across parts of south-central Africa and along the eastern coast. One of the richest habitats in the world and accounting for perhaps 55 percent of the African continent, the Savanna has always invited migration and cultural contacts. Thus it is the most important region of West Africa historically. Dense, humid, tropical rain forests stretch along coastal West Africa and on both sides of the equator in central Africa until they are stopped by volcanic mountains two-thirds of the way across the continent.

The climate in most of Africa is tropical. Subtropical climates are limited to the northern and southern coasts and to regions of high elevation. Rainfall is seasonal in most parts of the continent and is very sparse in desert and semidesert areas.

MAP 10.1 Africa Before 1500   For centuries trade linked West Africa with Mediterranean and Asian societies. Note the various climatic zones, the trans-Saharan trade routes, and the trade routes along the coast of East Africa.

Geography and climate have shaped the economic development of the peoples of Africa just as they have shaped the lives of people everywhere else. In the eastern African plains, the earliest humans hunted wild animals. The drier steppe regions favored the development of herding. Wetter Savanna regions, like the Nile Valley, encouraged the rise of grain-based agriculture. The tropical forests favored hunting and gathering and, later, root-based agriculture. Regions around rivers and lakes supported economies based on fishing.

The peoples of Africa are as diverse as the topography of the continent. In North Africa, contacts with Asian and European civilizations date back to the ancient Phoenicians, Greeks, and Romans. The native Berbers, who lived along the Mediterranean, intermingled with many different peoples—with Muslim Arabs, who first conquered the region of North Africa in the seventh and eighth centuries C.E.; with Spanish Muslims and Jews, many of whom settled in North Africa after their expulsion from Spain in 1492 (see pages 466–467); and with sub-Saharan blacks.[1] The peoples living along the east, or Swahili, coast developed a maritime civilization and had rich commercial contacts with southern Arabia, the Persian Gulf, India, China, and the Malay Archipelago.

Black Africans inhabited the region south of the Sahara, an area of savanna and rain forest. In describing them, the ancient Greeks used the term *Ethiopians,* which means "people with burnt faces." The Berbers coined the term *Akal-n-Iquinawen,* which survives today as *Guinea.* The Arabs introduced another term, *Bilad al-Sudan,* which survives as *Sudan.* The Berber and Arab words both mean "land of the blacks." Short-statured peoples sometimes called Pygmies inhabited the equatorial rain forests. South of those forests, in the southern third of the continent, lived the Khoisan, a small people of yellow-brown skin color who primarily were hunters.

Egypt, Africa, and the Historians

Popular usage of the term *race* (see page 257) has often been imprecise and inaccurate. Anthropologists insist that when applied to geographical, national, religious, linguistic, or cultural groups, the concept of race is inappropriate and refuted by the scientific data. But the issue of race has posed significant problems for historians, as the example of Egypt shows.

Geographically, Egypt is obviously a part of the African continent. But from the days of the ancient Greek historian Herodotus of Halicarnassus, who visited Egypt (see page 16), down to the present, scholars have vigorously, even violently, debated whether racially and culturally Egypt is part of the Mediterranean world or part of the African world. The notion of race poses an important but very complicated problem for students of all civilizations. Unfortunately, the application of general characteristics and patterns of behavior to peoples based on perceptions of physical differences is one of the legacies of imperialism and colonialism. Were Egyptians of the first century B.C.E. black people who made enormous contributions to the Western world in architecture (the pyramids), mathematics, philosophy (the ideas of Socrates), science, and religion (the idea of divine kingship)? A Senegalese scholar, Cheikh Anta Diop, argues that much Western historical writing since the eighteenth century has been a "European racist plot" to destroy the evidence that the people of the pharaohs belonged to the Negro world. Diop and his followers in Africa and the United States have amassed architectural and linguistic evidence, as well as a small mountain of quotations from Greek and Roman writers and from the Bible, to insist that the ancient Egyptians belonged to the black race. Diop claims to have examined the skin of ancient Egyptian mummies and says that on the basis of "infallible scientific techniques . . . the epidermis of those mummies was pigmented in the same way as that of all other (sub-Saharan) African negroes."[2]

Against this view, another group of scholars holds that the ancient Egyptians were Caucasians. They believe that Phoenician, Berber, Libyan, Hebrew, and Greek peoples populated Egypt and created its civilization. These scholars claim that Diop has badly misunderstood the evidence. For example, whereas Diop relies on the Book of Genesis to support his thesis, those who argue that the Egyptians were Caucasians point out that the Hebrew Scriptures are not an anthropological treatise but a collection of Hebrew, Mesopotamian, and Egyptian legends concerned with the origins of all human peoples—by which the Hebrew writers meant ethnic groups, not racial ones in the twentieth-century sense. They point out that the pharaohs of the first century B.C.E. descended from the Macedonian generals whom Alexander the Great had placed over Egypt. They were white. A few scholars presenting a "white thesis" assert that Egypt exercised a "civilizing mission" in sub-Saharan Africa. Genetic theories, perhaps inevitably, have been challenged on many fronts, notably an archaeological one that proves no direct Egyptian influence in tropical Africa. Rather, the evidence suggests that indigenous cultures south of the Sahara developed independently, without any Egyptian influence. Both the "black thesis" and the "white thesis" are extremist.

A third proposition, perhaps the most plausible, holds that ancient Egypt, at the crossroads of three continents, was a melting pot of different cultures and peoples. To attribute Egyptian civilization to any one group is blatant racism. The great achievements of Egyptian culture resulted from the contributions of many diverse peoples. Moderate scholars believe that there were black Africans in ancient Egypt, primarily in Upper Egypt (south of what is now Cairo), but that other racial groups constituted the majority of the population.[3] On this complex issue, the jury is still out.

In the seventh and early eighth centuries, the Arabs conquered all of North Africa, taking control of Egypt between 639 and 642 (see page 244); ever since Egypt has been an integral part of the Muslim world. Egypt's strategic location and commercial importance made it a logical target for Crusaders in the Middle Ages. In 1250 the Mamluks, a military warrior caste that originated in Anatolia, took over Egypt. With their slave soldiers, the Mamluks ruled until they were overthrown by the Ottoman Turks in 1517. The Mamluk tradition of cavalry soldiers fighting with swords and shields proved no match for Turkish artillery.

Early African Societies

Africa was one of the sites where agriculture began. Archaeological investigations suggest that knowledge of cultivation moved west from ancient Judaea (southern Palestine) and arrived in the Nile Delta in Egypt about the fifth millennium before Christ. Settled agriculture then traveled down the Nile Valley and moved west across the southern edge of the Sahara to the central and western Sudan. By the first century B.C.E., settled agriculture existed in West Africa. From there it spread to the equatorial forests. African farmers learned to domesticate plants, including millet, sorghum, and yams. Cereal-growing people probably taught forest people to plant regular fields. Gradually African farmers also learned to clear land by burning. They evolved a sedentary way of life: living in villages, clearing fields, relying on root crops, and fishing.

Between 1500 and 1000 B.C.E., settled agriculture also spread southward from Ethiopia along the Rift Val-

ley of present-day Kenya and Tanzania. Archaeological evidence reveals that the peoples of this region grew cereals, raised cattle, and used tools made of wood and stone. Cattle raising spread more quickly than did planting. Early African peoples prized cattle highly. Many trading agreements, marriage alliances, political compacts, and treaties were negotiated in terms of cattle.

Cereals such as millet and sorghum are indigenous to Africa. Scholars speculate that traders brought bananas, taros (a type of yam), sugar cane, and coconut palms to Africa from Southeast Asia. Because tropical forest conditions were ideal for banana trees, their cultivation spread rapidly; they were easier to raise than cereal grains. Donkeys, pigs, chickens, geese, and ducks were also domesticated.

The evolution to a settled life had profound effects. In contrast to nomadic conditions, settled societies made shared or common needs more apparent, and those needs strengthened ties among extended families. Population also increased:

Tassili Rock Painting This scene of cattle grazing near the group of huts (represented on the left by stylized white ovals) reflects the domestication of animals and the development of settled pastoral agriculture. Women and children seem to perform most of the domestic chores. Tassili is a mountainous region in the Sahara. *(Henri Lhote, Montrichard, France)*

Nok Woman   Hundreds of terra-cotta sculptures such as the head of this woman survive from the Nok culture, which originated in the central plateau of northern Nigeria in the first millennium B.C.E. *(National Museum, Lagos, Nigeria/Werner Forman Archive/Art Resource, NY)*

The change from a hunter-gatherer economy to a settled farming economy affected population numbers. . . . What remains uncertain is whether in the agricultural economy there were more people, better fed, or more people, less well fed. . . . In precolonial Africa agricultural and pastoral populations may not have increased steadily over time, but fluctuated cyclically, growing and declining, though overall slowly growing.[4]

Scholars dispute the route by which ironworking spread to sub-Saharan Africa. Some believe that the Phoenicians brought the technique for smelting iron to northwestern Africa and that from the north it spread southward. Others insist that it spread from the Meroe region on the Nile westward. Most of West Africa had acquired knowledge of ironworking by 250 B.C.E., and archaeologists believe that Meroe achieved pre-eminence as an iron-smelting center only in the first century B.C.E. Thus a stronger case can probably be made for the Phoenicians. The great trans-Saharan trade routes may have carried ironworking south from the Mediterranean coast. In any

case, ancient iron tools found at the village of Nok on the Jos Plateau in present-day Nigeria seem to prove a knowledge of ironworking in West Africa. The Nok culture, which enjoys enduring fame for its fine terra-cotta (baked clay) sculptures, flourished from about 800 B.C.E. to 200 C.E.

Bantu Migrations

The spread of ironworking seems to be linked to the migrations of the **Bantu** people. Today the overwhelming majority of the 70 million people living south of the Congo River speak a Bantu language. Because very few Muslims or Europeans penetrated beyond the east coast, very few written sources for the early history of the region survive. Lacking written sources, modern scholars have tried to reconstruct the history of the Bantu-speakers on the basis of linguistics, oral traditions (rarely reliable beyond three hundred years back), and archaeology. The word *Bantu* is a linguistic classification, and on the basis of linguistics (the study of the nature, structure, and modification of human speech), students have been able to explain the migratory patterns of African peoples east and south of the equatorial forest. There are hundreds of Bantu languages, including Zulu, Sotho, and Xhosa, which are part of the southern African linguistic and cultural nexus. Swahili is spoken in eastern, and to a limited extent central, Africa.

Bantu-speaking peoples originated in the Benue region, the borderlands of modern Cameroon and Nigeria. In the second millennium B.C.E. they began to spread south and east into the forest zone of equatorial Africa. From there, groups moved onto the Savanna along the lower Congo River. Since they had words for fishing, fishhooks, fish traps, dugout canoes, paddles, yams, and goats, linguists assume that they were fishermen and that they cultivated roots. Because initially they lacked words for grains and cattle herding, they probably were not involved in those activities.

During the next fifteen hundred years, Bantu-speakers migrated throughout the Savanna, adopted mixed agriculture, and learned ironworking. Mixed agriculture (cultivating cereals and raising livestock) and ironworking were practiced in western East Africa (the region of modern Burundi) in the first century before Christ. In the first millennium C.E., Bantu-speakers migrated into eastern and southern Africa. They did not displace earlier peoples, but assimilated with them. The earlier inhabitants gradually adopted a form of Bantu speech.

The settled cultivation of cereals and the keeping of livestock, together with intermarriage with indigenous peoples, apparently led over a long time to considerable population increases and the need to migrate further. The so-called Bantu migrations should not be seen as a single movement of cultivating, ironworking, Bantu-speaking black people sweeping across Africa from west to east and displacing all peoples in their path. Rather, those migrations were "a series of interrelated diffusions and syntheses, as small groups of Bantu-speakers interacted with preexisting peoples and new technical developments to produce a range of distinct cultural syntheses across the southern half of Africa."[5]

Thus Bantu expansion and the settlement of the lands of eastern and southern Africa provides the dominant theme during the first millennium and a half C.E. Enormous differences in the quality of the environment conditioned settlement. Some regions were well watered; others were very arid. This situation resulted in very uneven population distribution. The largest concentration of people seems to have been in the region bounded on the west by the Congo River and on the north, south, and east by Lakes Edward, Victoria, and Kilimanjaro, comprising parts of modern Uganda, Rwanda, and Tanzania. There the agricultural system rested on the cultivation of sorghum and yams. Between 900 and 1100, bananas and plantains (a starchy form of the banana) arrived from Asia. Because little effort was needed for their cultivation and the yield was much higher than for yams, bananas soon became the staple crop. The Bantu population greatly expanded, and Bantu villages multiplied, leading to further migration southward and eastward.[6] By the eighth century, Bantu-speaking people had reached the region of present-day Zimbabwe. By the fifteenth century, they had reached the southeastern coast of Africa.

Kingdoms of the Western Sudan, ca 1000 B.C.E.–200 C.E.

The region bounded on the north by the Sahara, on the south by the Gulf of Guinea, on the west by the Atlantic Ocean, and on the east by the mountains of Ethiopia is known as the **Sudan.** In the Savanna of the western Sudan—where the Bantu migrations originated—a series of dynamic kingdoms emerged in the millennium before European intrusion.

Between 1000 B.C.E. and 200 C.E., the peoples of the western Sudan made the momentous shift from nomadic hunting to settled agriculture. The rich Savanna proved ideally suited to the production of cereals, especially rice, millet, and sorghum, and people situated near the Senegal River and Lake Chad supplemented their diet with

fish. Food supply tends to affect population, and the peoples of the region—known as the Mande-speakers and the Chadic-speakers, or Sao—increased dramatically in number. By 400 C.E. the entire Savanna, particularly the areas around Lake Chad, the Niger River bend, and present-day central Nigeria (see Map 10.1), had a large population.

Families and clans affiliated by blood kinship lived together in villages or small city-states. The basic social unit was the extended family. A chief, in consultation with a council of elders, governed a village. Some villages seem to have formed kingdoms. Village chiefs were responsible to regional heads, who answered to provincial governors, who in turn were responsible to a king. The chiefs and their families formed an aristocracy.

Kingship in the Sudan may have emerged from the priesthood, whose members were believed to make rain and to have contact with spirit powers. African kings always had religious sanction or support for their authority and were often considered divine. In this respect, early African kingship bears a strong resemblance to Germanic kingship of the same period: the authority of the king rested in part on the ruler's ability to negotiate with outside powers, such as the gods.

African religions were animistic and polytheistic. Most people believed that a supreme being had created the universe and was the source of all life. The supreme being breathed spirit into all living things, and the *anima,* or spirit, residing in such things as trees, water, and earth had to be appeased. In the cycle of the agricultural year, for example, all the spirits had to be propitiated from the time of clearing the land through sowing the seed to the final harvest. Because special ceremonies were necessary to satisfy the spirits, special priests with the knowledge and power to communicate with them through sacred rituals were needed. Thus the heads of families and villages were likely to be priests. The head of each family was responsible for maintaining the family ritual cults—ceremonies honoring the dead and living members of the family.[7]

In sum, the most prominent feature of early African society was a strong sense of community, based on the blood relationship and on religion. (See the feature "Individuals in Society: An Unknown Artist of Djenné.") Extended families made up the villages that collectively formed small kingdoms. What spurred the expansion of these small kingdoms into formidable powers controlling sizable territory was the development of long-distance trade. And what made long-distance or trans-Saharan trade possible was the camel.

The Trans-Saharan Trade

The expression "trans-Saharan trade" refers to the north-south trade across the Sahara (see Map 10.1). The camel had an impact on this trade comparable to the impact of the horse on European agriculture (see pages 393–394). Although scholars dispute exactly when the camel was introduced from Central Asia—first into North Africa, then into the Sahara and the Sudan—they agree that it was before 200 C.E. Camels can carry about five hundred pounds as far as twenty-five miles a day and can go for days without drinking, living on the water stored in their stomachs. Sometimes stupid and vicious, camels had to be loaded on a daily, sometimes twice-daily, basis. And much of the cargo for a long trip was provisions for the journey itself. Nevertheless, camels proved more efficient for desert transportation than horses or oxen, and the use of this beast to carry heavy and bulky freight not only brought economic and social change to Africa but also affected the development of world commerce.

Sometime in the fifth century, the North African **Berbers** fashioned a saddle for use on the camel. This saddle had no direct effect on commercial operations, for a merchant usually walked and guided the camel on foot. But the saddle gave the Berbers and later the Arabian inhabitants of the region maneuverability on the animal and thus a powerful political and military advantage: they came to dominate the desert and to create lucrative routes across it. The Berbers determined who could enter the desert, and they extracted large sums of protection money from merchant caravans in exchange for a safe trip.

Between 700 and 900 C.E., the Berbers developed a network of caravan routes between the Mediterranean coast and the Sudan (see Map 10.1). The Morocco-Niger route ran from Fez to Sijilmassa on the edge of the desert and then south by way of Taghaza and Walata and back to Fez. Another route originated at Sijilmassa and extended due south to Timbuktu with a stop at Taghaza. A third route ran south from Tripoli to Lake Chad. A fourth ran from Egypt to Gao by way of the Saharan oases of Ghat and Agades and then on to Takedda.

The long expedition across the Sahara testifies to the spirit of the traders and to their passion for wealth. Because of the blistering sun and daytime temperatures of 110 degrees, the caravan drivers preferred to travel at night, when the temperature might drop to the low 20s. Ibn Battuta, an Arab traveler who made the journey in the fourteenth century when trans-Saharan traffic was at its height, wrote an account of the experience (see page 265).

Nomadic raiders, the Tuareg Berbers, posed a serious threat. The Tuaregs lived in the desert uplands and preyed on the caravans as a way of life. Thus merchants made safe-conduct agreements with them and selected guides from among them. Caravans of twelve thousand camels were reported in the fourteenth century. Large numbers of merchants crossed the desert together to discourage attack. Blinding sandstorms often isolated part of a line of camels and on at least one occasion buried alive some camels and drivers. Water was the biggest problem. The Tuaregs sometimes poisoned wells to wipe out caravans and steal their goods. To satisfy normal thirst and to compensate for constant sweating, a gallon of water a day per person was required. Desperate thirst sometimes forced the traders to kill camels and drink the foul, brackish water in their stomachs. It took Ibn Battuta twenty-five days to travel from Sijilmassa to the oasis of Taghaza and another sixty-five days to travel from Taghaza to the important market town of Walata.

The Arab-Berber merchants from North Africa who controlled the caravan trade carried manufactured goods—silk and cotton cloth, beads, mirrors—as well as dates and salt (essential in tropical climates to replace the loss from perspiration) from the Saharan oases and mines to the Sudan. These products were exchanged for the much-coveted commodities of the West African savanna—gold, ivory, gum, kola nuts (eaten as a stimulant), and captive slaves.

The steady growth of trans-Saharan trade had three important effects on West African society. The trade stimulated gold mining and the search for slaves. Parts of modern-day Senegal, Nigeria, and Ghana contained rich veins of gold. Both sexes shared in mining it. Men sank the shafts and hacked out gold-bearing rocks and crushed them, separating the gold from the soil. Women washed the gold in gourds. Alluvial gold (mixed with soil, sand, or gravel) was separated from the soil by panning. Scholars estimate that by the eleventh century nine tons were exported to Europe annually—a prodigious amount for the time, since even with modern machinery and sophisticated techniques, the total gold exports from the same region in 1937 amounted to only twenty-one tons. A large percentage of this metal went to Egypt. From there it was transported down the Red Sea and eventually to India (see Map 10.3 on page 296) to pay for the spices and silks demanded by Mediterranean commerce. West African gold proved "absolutely vital for the monetization of the medieval Mediterranean economy and for the maintenance of its balance of payments with South Asia."[8] African gold linked the entire world, exclusive of the Western Hemisphere.

Slaves were West Africa's second most valuable export (after gold). African slaves, like their early European and

INDIVIDUALS IN SOCIETY

AN UNKNOWN ARTIST OF DJENNÉ

Kneeling figure with entwined serpents (18¾ inches high), from Mali, eleventh to fourteenth century.
(Maurice D. Galleher, Ada Turnbull Hertle, Laura T. Magnuson funds, 1983.917. Photograph © 1988, The Art Institute of Chicago)

In the thirteenth century, the market in slaves, gold, and salt at Djenné on the Niger River delta attracted Berber, Muslim, and black traders and brought the region considerable economic prosperity. After accepting Islam, the ruler built a mosque said to be more imposing than the Ka'ba at Mecca (see page 240). A cultural center, Djenné supported mosques and madrasas, scholars and artists.

About 1975, when severe drought caused the Niger's water level to drop, archaeologists discovered a fragment of terra-cotta sculpture (right). Terra cotta is a hard, waterproof, usually brownish orange ceramic clay that is shaped, fired over low heat, and left unglazed. This 18¾-inch figure, composed of geometric shapes (cylinders and cones), is kneeling. It has long graceful arms, each bearing ten bracelets, and elongated fingers. Two serpents coil around the arms. One serpent's head lies like a pendant on the figure's chest, below which is a triangular navel, in keeping with the overall geometric approach to depicting human anatomy characteristic of delta artists. The head is missing, and time has eroded the original shape of the legs. The figure rests on a terra-cotta base.

Who was the artist who made the kneeling figure? What was its purpose? What significance do the coiled snakes have? As in the court cultures of Mughal India and Renaissance Italy (see page 454), artists in many African societies produced works on the specific commissions of princes, merchants, or rulers. Artists did not work to convey their own personal messages. When a work was completed, the patron's name, not the artist's, was associated with it. The bracelets on this figure's arms suggest gold, indicating that the model was very rich. The figure is either a portrait of a royal person or a representation of a protective family spirit.

Serpent cults played an important role in the cultural myths and legends of early West African peoples, just as they did among the Aztec of Central America (see page 427). Serpents were thought to possess supernatural powers, with which kings wanted to be associated. Serpents also were thought to embody the spirits and qualities of ancestors. In Djenné, West Africa, the snake cult lent a special mystique to the ruler. Coiling around his arms, the snake gave him strength in battle, an important trait since the first duty of any king was to protect his people. The serpent's head lying on his chest implies that the wisdom and experience of his ancestors were close to his heart.

Why would a ruler who had accepted Islam retain such a powerful pagan symbol? For practical political reasons. While many royal courts adopted the faith of Muhammad, it did not make deep inroads among ordinary people. A wise ruler might no doubt feel he must continue his people's traditions if he wanted to keep their loyalty. Perhaps like some early Roman and Germanic chieftains who accepted Christianity, the king shown here was quite willing to accept divine assistance from wherever it came; he "put his money on both horses."

Like most African tribal artifacts, the kneeling figure had a particular ritual or ceremonial purpose. As an individual (not a group) image, it was believed to embody the spirits of the dead and perpetuate the essence of the tribe's ancestry. Although we can tell more about the patron of this work of art than about the artist who made it, the artist has provided us with some valuable information about his society.

QUESTIONS FOR ANALYSIS

1. How would you describe the kneeling terra-cotta figure?
2. What does it tell us about Djenné, one early West African society?

Source: The Art Institute of Chicago: The Essential Guide (1933). The authors especially wish to thank curator Amy M. Mooney.

TABLE 10.1   ESTIMATED MAGNITUDE OF TRANS-SAHARAN SLAVE TRADE, 650–1500

YEARS	ANNUAL AVERAGE OF SLAVES TRADED	TOTAL
650–800	1,000	150,000
800–900	3,000	300,000
900–1100	8,700	1,740,000
1100–1400	5,500	1,650,000
1400–1500	4,300	430,000

Source: From R. A. Austen, "The Trans-Saharan Slave Trade: A Tentative Census," in The Uncommon Market: Essays in the Economic History of the Atlantic Slave Trade, ed. H. A. Gemery and J. S. Hogendorn (New York: Academic Press, 1979). Used with permission.

date the growth of African cities from around the beginning of the ninth century. Families that had profited from trade tended to congregate in the border zones between the Savanna and the Sahara. They acted as middlemen between the miners to the south and Muslim merchants from the north. By the early thirteenth century, these families had become powerful black merchant dynasties. Muslim traders from the Mediterranean settled permanently in the trading depots, from which they organized the trans-Saharan caravans. The concentration of people stimulated agriculture and the craft industries. Gradually cities of sizable population emerged. Djenné, Gao, and Timbuktu, which enjoyed commanding positions on the Niger River bend, became centers of the export-import trade. Sijilmassa grew into a thriving market center. Kumbi, with between fifteen thousand and twenty thousand inhabitants, was probably the largest city in the western Sudan in the twelfth century. (By European standards, Kumbi was a metropolis; London and Paris achieved its size only in the late thirteenth century.) Between 1100 and 1400, these cities played a dynamic role in the commercial life of West Africa and Europe and became centers of intellectual creativity.

Perhaps the most influential consequence of the trans-Saharan trade was the introduction of Islam to West African society. After the Muslim conquest of Egypt in 642 (see page 244), Islam spread southward from Egypt up the Nile Valley and west to Darfur and Wadai. This Muslim penetration came not by military force but, as in the trans-Saharan trade routes in West Africa, by gradual commercial passage. Muslim expansion from the Arabian peninsula across the Red Sea to the Horn of Africa, then southward along the coast of East Africa represents a third direction of Islam's growth in Africa. From ports on the Red Sea and the Gulf of Aden, maritime trade carried the Prophet's teachings to East Africa and the Indian Ocean. Muslims founded the port city of **Mogadishu,** today the capital of Somalia, between the eighth and tenth centuries. In the twelfth century, Mogadishu developed into a Muslim sultanate, a monarchy that employed a slave military corps against foreign and domestic enemies. Archaeological evidence, confirmed by Arabic sources, reveals a rapid Islamic expansion along Africa's east coast in the thirteenth century. Many settlers came from Yemen in the southern Arabian peninsula, and one family set up the Abul-Mawahib dynasty in Kilwa.[11] When Ibn Battuta visited Kilwa in 1331, he discovered a center for the discovery of Islamic law.

By the tenth century, Muslim Berbers controlled the north-south trade routes to the Savanna. By the eleventh century, African rulers of Gao and Timbuktu had accepted

Asian counterparts, seem to have been peoples captured in war. In the Muslim cities of North Africa, southern Europe, and southwestern Asia, the demand for household slaves was high among the elite. Slaves were also needed to work the gold and salt mines. Recent research suggests, moreover, that large numbers of black slaves were recruited through the trans-Saharan trade for Muslim military service. High death rates from disease, manumission, and the assimilation of some blacks into Muslim society meant that the demand for slaves remained high for centuries. Table 10.1 shows one scholar's tentative conclusions, based on many kinds of evidence, about the scope of the trans-Saharan slave trade. The total number of blacks enslaved over an 850-year period may be tentatively estimated at over 4 million.[9]

Slavery in Muslim societies, as in European and Asian countries before the fifteenth century, was not based on skin color. Muslims also enslaved Caucasians who had been purchased, seized in war, or kidnapped from Europe. The households of wealthy Muslims in Córdoba, Alexandria, or Tunis often included slaves of a number of races, all of whom had been completely cut off from their cultural roots. Likewise, West African kings who sold blacks to traders from the north also bought a few white slaves—Slavic, British, and Turkish—for their domestic needs. Race had little to do with the phenomenon of slavery.[10]

The trans-Saharan trade also stimulated the development of vigorous urban centers in West Africa. Scholars

Islam. The king of Ghana was also influenced by Islam. Muslims quickly became integral to West African government and society.

Conversion to Islam introduced West Africans to a rich and sophisticated culture. By the late eleventh century, Muslims were guiding the ruler of Ghana in the operation of his administrative machinery. The king of Ghana adopted the Muslim diwan, the agency for keeping financial records (see page 251). Because efficient government depends on the preservation of records, the arrival of Islam in West Africa marked the advent of written documents there. Arab Muslims also taught the rulers of Ghana how to manufacture bricks, and royal palaces and mosques began to be built of brick. African rulers corresponded with Muslim architects, theologians, and other intellectuals, who advised them on statecraft and religion. Islam accelerated the development of the African empires of the ninth through fifteenth centuries.

AFRICAN KINGDOMS AND EMPIRES (CA 800–1450)

All African societies shared one basic feature: a close relationship between political and social organization. Ethnic or blood ties bound clan members together. What scholars call **stateless societies** were culturally homogeneous ethnic societies. The smallest ones numbered fewer than a hundred people and were nomadic hunting groups. Larger stateless societies of perhaps several thousand people lived a settled and often agricultural or herding life.

The period from about 800 to 1450 witnessed the flowering of several powerful African states. In the western Sudan, the large empires of Ghana and Mali developed, complete with large royal bureaucracies. On the east coast emerged powerful city-states based on sophisticated mercantile activities and, like Sudan, very much influenced by Islam. In Ethiopia, in central East Africa, kings relied on the Christian faith of their people to strengthen political authority. In South Africa, the empire of Great Zimbabwe, built on the gold trade with the east coast, flourished.

The Kingdom of Ghana (ca 900–1100)

So remarkable was the kingdom of **Ghana** during the age of Africa's great empires that writers throughout the medieval world, such as the fourteenth-century Muslim historian Ibn Khaldun, praised it as a model for other rulers. Medieval Ghana also holds a central place in the historical consciousness of the modern state of Ghana. Since this former British colony attained independence in 1957, its political leaders have hailed the medieval period as a glorious heritage. The name of the modern republic of Ghana—which in fact lies far from the site of the old kingdom—was selected to signify the rebirth of an age of gold in black Africa.

The nucleus of the territory that became the kingdom of Ghana was inhabited by Soninke people who called their ruler **ghana,** or war chief. By the late eighth century, Muslim traders and other foreigners applied the word to the region where the Soninke lived, the black kingdom south of the Sahara. The Soninke themselves called their land "Aoukar" or "Awkar," by which they meant the region north of the Senegal and Niger Rivers. Only the southern part of Aoukar received enough rainfall to be agriculturally productive, and it was in this area that the civilization of Ghana developed. Skillful farming and an efficient system of irrigation led to the production of abundant crops, which eventually supported a population of as many as 200,000.

The Soninke name for their king—war chief—aptly describes the king's major preoccupation in the tenth century. In 992 Ghana captured the Berber town of Awdaghost, strategically situated on the trans-Saharan trade route (see Map 10.1). Thereafter Ghana controlled the southern portion of a major caravan route. Before the year 1000, the rulers of Ghana had extended their influence almost to the Atlantic coast and had captured a number of small kingdoms in the south and east. By the beginning of the eleventh century, the king exercised sway over a territory approximately the size of Texas. No other power in the West African region could successfully challenge him.

Throughout this vast West African area, all authority sprang from the king. Religious ceremonies and court rituals emphasized the king's sacredness and were intended to strengthen his authority. The king's position was hereditary in the matrilineal line—that is, the heir of the ruling king was one of the king's sister's sons (presumably the eldest or fittest for battle). According to the eleventh-century Spanish Muslim geographer al-Bakri (1040?–1094), "This is their custom . . . the kingdom is inherited only by the son of the king's sister. He the king has no doubt that his successor is a son of his sister, while he is not certain that his son is in fact his own."[12]

A council of ministers assisted the king in the work of government, and from the ninth century on, most of these ministers were Muslims. Detailed evidence about the early Ghanaian bureaucracy has not survived, but scholars suspect that separate agencies were responsible for taxation, royal property, foreigners, forests, and the

The Great Friday Mosque, Djenné   The mosque at Djenné was built in the form of a parallelogram. Inside, nine long rows of adobe columns run along a north-south axis and support a flat roof of palm logs. A pointed arch links each column to the next in its row, forming nine east-west archways facing the *mihrab,* the niche indicating the direction of Mecca and from which the *imam* (prayer leader) speaks. This mosque (rebuilt in 1907 on a thirteenth-century model) testifies to the considerable wealth, geometrical knowledge, and manpower of the region. *(Copyright Carollee Pelos. From* Spectacular Vernacular: The Adobe Tradition, *Chapter 11, "Histories of the Great Mosques of Djenné" [New York: Aperture, 1996])*

army. The royal administration was well served by Muslim ideas, skills, and especially literacy. The king and his people, however, clung to their ancestral religion, and the basic cultural institutions of Ghana remained tribal.

The king of Ghana held his court in **Kumbi.** Al-Bakri provides a valuable picture of the city in the eleventh century:

The city of Ghana consists of two towns lying on a plain, one of which is inhabited by Muslims and is large, possessing twelve mosques—one of which is a congregational mosque for Friday prayer; each has its imam, its muezzin and paid reciters of the Quran. The town possesses a large number of jurisconsults and learned men.[13]

Either for their own protection or to preserve their special identity, the Muslims lived separate from the African artisans and tradespeople. The Muslim community in Ghana must have been large and prosperous to have supported twelve mosques. The *imam* was the religious leader who

conducted the ritual worship, especially the main prayer service on Fridays. The *muezzin* led the prayer responses after the imam; he needed a strong voice so that those at a distance and the women in the harems, or enclosures, could hear. Muslim religious leaders exercised civil authority over their coreligionists. Their presence and that of other learned Muslims also suggests vigorous intellectual activity.

Al-Bakri describes the town where the king lived and the royal court:

The town inhabited by the king is six miles from the Muslim one and is called Al Ghana. . . . The residence of the king consists of a palace and a number of dome-shaped dwellings, all of them surrounded by a strong enclosure, like a city wall. In the town . . . is a mosque, where Muslims who come on diplomatic missions to the king pray. The town where the king lives is surrounded by domed huts, woods, and copses where priest-magicians live; in these woods also are the religious idols and tombs of the kings. Special guards protect this area and prevent anyone from entering it so that no foreigners know what is inside. Here also are the king's prisons, and if anyone is imprisoned there, nothing more is heard of him.[14]

The king adorns himself, as do the women here, with necklaces and bracelets; on their heads they wear caps decorated with gold, sewn on material of fine cotton stuffing. When he holds court in order to hear the people's complaints and to do justice, he sits in a pavilion around which stand ten horses wearing golden trappings; behind him ten pages stand, holding shields and swords decorated with gold; at his right are the sons of the chiefs of the country, splendidly dressed and with their hair sprinkled with gold. The governor of the city sits on the ground in front of the king with other officials likewise sitting around him. Excellently pedigreed dogs guard the door of the pavilion. . . . The noise of a sort-of drum, called a daba, and made from a long hollow log, announces the start of the royal audience. When the king's coreligionists appear before him, they fall on their knees and toss dust on their heads—this is their way of greeting their sovereign. Muslims show respect by clapping their hands.[15]

What sort of juridical system did Ghana have? How was the guilt or innocence of an accused person determined? Justice derived from the king, who heard cases at court or on his travels throughout his kingdom. As al-Bakri recounts:

When a man is accused of denying a debt or of having shed blood or some other crime, a headman (village chief) takes a thin piece of wood, which is sour and bitter to taste, and pours upon it some water which he then gives to the defendant to drink. If the man vomits, his innocence is recognized and he is congratulated. If he does not vomit and the drink remains in his stomach, the accusation is accepted as justified.[16]

This appeal to the supernatural for judgment was very similar to the justice by ordeal that prevailed among the Germanic peoples of western Europe at the same time. Complicated cases in Ghana seem to have been appealed to the king, who often relied on the advice of Muslim legal experts.

The king's elaborate court, the administrative machinery he built, and the extensive territories he governed were all expensive. The king of Ghana needed a lot of money, and he apparently had four main sources of support. The royal estates—some hereditary, others conquered in war—produced annual revenue, mostly in the form of foodstuffs for the royal household. The king also received tribute annually from subordinate chieftains

(lack of evidence prevents an estimate of the value of this tax). Customs duties on goods entering and leaving the country generated revenues. Salt was the largest import. Berber merchants paid a tax to the king on the cloth, metalwork, weapons, and other goods that they brought into the country from North Africa; in return these traders received royal protection from bandits. African traders bringing gold into Ghana from the south also paid the customs duty.

Finally, the royal treasury held a monopoly on the export of gold. The gold industry was undoubtedly the king's largest source of income. It was on gold that the fame of medieval Ghana rested. The ninth-century geographer al-Ya-qubi wrote, "Its king is mighty, and in his lands are gold mines. Under his authority are various other kingdoms—and in all this region there is gold."[17]

The governing aristocracy—the king, his court, and Muslim administrators—occupied the highest rung on the Ghanaian social ladder. On the next rung stood the merchant class. Considerably below the merchants stood the farmers, cattle breeders, supervisors of the gold mines, and skilled craftsmen and weavers—what today might be called the middle class. Some merchants and miners must have enjoyed great wealth, but, as in all aristocratic societies, money alone did not suffice. High status was based on blood and royal service. At the bottom of the social ladder were slaves, who worked in households, on farms, and in the mines. As in Asian and European societies of the time, slaves accounted for only a small percentage of the population.

Apart from these social classes stood the army. According to al-Bakri, "the king of Ghana can put 200,000 warriors in the field, more than 40,000 being armed with bow and arrow."[18] Like most medieval estimates, this is probably a gross exaggeration. Even a modern industrialized state with sophisticated means of transportation, communication, and supply lines would have enormous difficulty mobilizing so many men for battle. The king of Ghana, however, was not called "war chief" for nothing. He maintained at his palace a crack standing force of a thousand men, comparable to the Roman Praetorian Guard. These thoroughly disciplined, well-armed, totally loyal troops protected the king and the royal court. They lived in special compounds, enjoyed the favor of the king, and sometimes acted as his personal ambassadors to subordinate rulers. In wartime, this regular army was augmented by levies of soldiers from conquered peoples and by the use of slaves and free reserves. The force that the king could field was sizable, if not as huge as al-Bakri estimated.

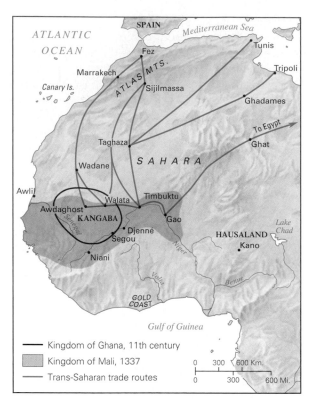

MAP 10.2 The Kingdom of Mali   The economic strength of the kingdom of Mali rested heavily on the trans-Saharan trade.

The Kingdom of Mali (ca 1200–1450)

During the century after the collapse of Kumbi, a cloud of obscurity hung over the western Sudan. The kingdom of Ghana split into several small kingdoms that feuded among themselves. One people, the Mandinke, lived in the kingdom of Kangaba on the upper Niger River. The Mandinke had long been part of the Ghanaian empire, and the Mandinke and Soninke belonged to the same language group. Kangaba formed the core of the new empire of Mali. Building on Ghanaian foundations, Mali developed into a better-organized and more powerful state than Ghana.

The kingdom of Mali (see Map 10.2) owed its greatness to two fundamental assets. First, its strong agricultural and commercial base provided for a large population and enormous wealth. Second, Mali had two rulers, Sundiata and Mansa Musa, who combined military success with exceptionally creative personalities. (See the feature "Listening to the Past: The Epic of Old Mali" on pages 304–305.)

The earliest surviving evidence about the Mandinke, dating from the early eleventh century, indicates that they were extremely successful at agriculture. Consistently large harvests throughout the twelfth and thirteenth centuries meant a plentiful supply of food, which encouraged steady population growth. The geographical location of Kangaba also placed the Mandinke in an ideal position in West African trade. Earlier, during the period of Ghanaian hegemony, the Mandinke had acted as middlemen in the gold and salt traffic flowing north and south. In the thirteenth century, Mandinke traders formed companies, traveled widely, and gradually became a major force in the entire West African trade.

Sundiata (r. ca 1230–1255) set up his capital at Niani, transforming the city into an important financial and trading center. He then embarked on a policy of imperial expansion. Through a series of military victories, Sundiata and his successors absorbed into Mali other territories of the former kingdom of Ghana and established hegemony over the trading cities of Gao, Djenné, and Walata.

These expansionist policies were continued in the fourteenth century by Sundiata's descendant Mansa Musa (r. ca 1312–1337), early Africa's most famous ruler. In the language of the Mandinke, *mansa* means "emperor." Mansa Musa fought many campaigns and checked every attempt at rebellion. Ultimately his influence extended northward to several Berber cities in the Sahara, eastward to Timbuktu and Gao, and westward as far as the Atlantic Ocean. Throughout his territories, he maintained strict royal control over the rich trans-Saharan trade. Thus this empire, roughly twice the size of the Ghanaian kingdom and containing perhaps 8 million people, brought Mansa Musa fabulous wealth.

Mansa Musa built on the foundations of his predecessors. The stratified aristocratic structure of Malian society perpetuated the pattern set in Ghana, as did the system of provincial administration and annual tribute. The emperor took responsibility for the territories that formed the heart of the empire and appointed governors to rule the outlying provinces or dependent kingdoms. But Mansa Musa made a significant innovation: in a practice strikingly similar to a system used in both China and France at that time, he appointed members of the royal family as provincial governors. He could count on their loyalty, and they received valuable experience in the work of government.

In another aspect of administration, Mansa Musa also differed from his predecessors. He became a devout Muslim. Although most of the Mandinke clung to their ancestral animism, Islamic practices and influences in Mali multiplied.

The most celebrated event of Mansa Musa's reign was his pilgrimage to Mecca in 1324–1325, during which he paid a state visit to the sultan of Egypt. Mansa Musa's entrance into Cairo was magnificent. Preceded by five hundred slaves, each carrying a six-pound staff of gold, he followed with a huge host of retainers, including one hundred elephants each bearing one hundred pounds of gold. The emperor lavished his wealth on the citizens of the Egyptian capital. Writing twelve years later, al-Omari, one of the sultan's officials, recounts:

This man Mansa Musa spread upon Cairo the flood of his generosity: there was no person, officer of the court, or holder of any office of the Sultanate who did not receive a sum of gold from him. The people of Cairo earned incalculable sums from him, whether by buying and selling or by gifts. So much gold was current in Cairo that it ruined the value of money.[19]

Mansa Musa's gold brought about terrible inflation throughout Egypt. For the first time, the Mediterranean world gained concrete knowledge of the wealth and power of the black kingdom of Mali, and it began to be known as one of the great empires of the world. Mali retained this international reputation into the fifteenth century.

Musa's pilgrimage also had significant consequences within Mali. He gained some understanding of the Mediterranean countries and opened diplomatic relations with the Muslim rulers of Morocco and Egypt. His zeal for the Muslim faith and Islamic culture increased. Musa brought back from Arabia the distinguished architect al-Saheli, whom he commissioned to build new mosques at Timbuktu and other cities. These mosques served as centers for the conversion of Africans. Musa employed Muslim engineers to build in brick. He also encouraged Malian merchants and traders to wear the distinctive flowing robes and turbans of Muslim males.

Timbuktu began as a campsite for desert nomads. Under Mansa Musa, it grew into a thriving entrepôt, attracting merchants and traders from North Africa and all parts of the Mediterranean world. These people brought with them cosmopolitan attitudes and ideas. In the fifteenth century, Timbuktu developed into a great center for scholarship and learning. Architects, astronomers, poets, lawyers, mathematicians, and theologians flocked there. One hundred fifty schools were devoted to the study of the Qur'an. The school of Islamic law enjoyed a distinction in Africa comparable to the prestige of the school at Cairo (see page 266). A vigorous trade in books flourished in Timbuktu. Leo Africanus, a sixteenth-century Muslim traveler and writer who later converted to Christianity, recounts that around 1500 Timbuktu had a

Dogon Couple   This seated couple, made of wood and metal, tells us a great deal about the culture of the people who lived in the Dogon region at the bend of the Niger River in West Africa, in what is now Mali. The man's right arm circles the woman's shoulder and rests on her breast; his left hand points toward his genitals. He carries a quiver on his back; she bears an infant on hers. The mutually dependent figures indicate that the man is progenitor, protector, and provider; the woman is childbearer and nurturer. Dogon society was strongly patrilineal and famous for its artwork. This piece was done between the sixteenth and twentieth centuries. *(The Metropolitan Museum of Art, Gift of Lester Wunderman, 1977 [1977.394.15]. Photograph © 1993 The Metropolitan Museum of Art)*

great store of doctors, judges, priests, and other learned men that are bountifully maintained at the king's cost and charges. And hitherto are brought diverse manuscripts or written books out of Barbarie the north African states, from Egypt to the Atlantic Ocean which are sold for more money than any other merchandise.

It is easy to understand why the university at Timbuktu was called by a contemporary writer "the Queen of the Sudan." Timbuktu's tradition and reputation for African scholarship lasted until the eighteenth century.

Moreover, in the fourteenth and fifteenth centuries, many Muslim intellectuals and Arab traders married native African women. These unions brought into being a group of racially mixed people. The necessity of living together harmoniously, the traditional awareness of diverse cultures, and the cosmopolitan atmosphere of Timbuktu all contributed to a rare degree of racial toleration and understanding. After visiting the court of Mansa Musa's successor in 1352–1353, Ibn Battuta observed that

the Negroes possess some admirable qualities. They are seldom unjust, and have a greater abhorrence of injustice than any other people. Their sultan shows no mercy to anyone who is guilty of the least act of it. There is complete security in their country. Neither traveler nor inhabitant in it has anything to fear from robbers. . . . They do not confiscate the property of any white man who dies in their country, even if it be uncounted wealth. On the contrary, they give it into the charge of some trustworthy person among the whites, until the rightful heir takes possession of it.[20]

Ethiopia: The Christian Kingdom of Axum

Egyptian culture exerted a profound influence on the sub-Saharan kingdom of Nubia in northeastern Africa (see Map 10.3). Nubia's capital was at Meroe; thus the country is often referred to as the Nubian kingdom of Meroe. As part of the Roman Empire, Egypt was naturally subject to Hellenistic and Roman cultural forces, and it became an early center of Christianity. Nubia, however, was never part of the Roman Empire; its people clung to ancient Egyptian religious ideas. Christian missionaries went to the Upper Nile region and succeeded in converting the Nubian rulers around 600 C.E. By that time, there were three separate Nubian states, of which the kingdom of Nobatia, centered at Dongola, was the strongest. The Christian rulers of Nobatia had close ties with **Ethiopia.**

According to Ethiopian oral tradition, the queen of Sheba visited the Hebrew king Solomon (r. 961–922 B.C.E.) in Jerusalem to acquire some of his wisdom. They slept together, and the queen conceived a son. When the boy reached maturity, he returned to Israel, received Solomon's blessing, and was crowned king of Ethiopia as Menelik I. Except for a period in the twelfth and thirteenth centuries, all rulers of Ethiopia supposedly descended from Menelik. Because of the vast treasure of

gold, spices, and precious stones that the queen of Sheba took to Solomon's court (1 Kings 10, 2 Chronicles 9), modern scholars believe that she actually headed a trade mission. Although these scholars also identify the land of Sheba with modern Yemen, artists usually portray the queen as a black woman. The legend suggests ancient contacts between Ethiopia and western Asia.

Tradition ascribes to Frumentius (ca 300–380 C.E.), a Syrian Christian trader, the introduction of Christianity into Ethiopia. Kidnapped en route from India to Tyre (now a town in southern Lebanon), Frumentius was taken to **Axum** and appointed tutor to the future king, Ezana. Later, Frumentius went to Alexandria in Egypt, where he was consecrated the first bishop of Axum. Thus Christianity came to Ethiopia from Egypt in the Monophysite form. Shortly after members of the royal court accepted Christianity, it became the Ethiopian state religion. The future of Ethiopia was to be inextricably tied up with Christianity, a unique situation in black Africa.

Ethiopia's acceptance of Christianity led to the production of ecclesiastical documents and royal chronicles, making Ethiopia the first black African society that can be studied from written records. The Scriptures were translated into Ge'ez, the language of Axum; pagan temples were dedicated to Christian saints; and, as in early medieval Ireland (see page 218) and in the Orthodox church of the Byzantine world, the monasteries were the main cultural institutions of the Christian faith in Ethiopia. From the monasteries, monks went out to preach and convert the people, who resorted to the monasteries in times of need. As the Ethiopian state expanded, vibrant monasteries made daughter foundations, as in medieval Europe (see pages 372–374).

Monastic records provide fascinating information about early Ethiopian society. Settlements were made on the warm and moist plateau lands, not in the arid lowlands or the river valleys. Farmers used a scratch plow (unique in sub-Saharan Africa) to cultivate wheat and barley and to rotate those cereals. Plentiful rainfall seems to have helped produce abundant crops, which in turn led to population growth. In contrast to most of sub-Saharan Africa, both sexes probably married young. Because of ecclesiastical opposition to polygyny, monogamy was the norm, except for kings and the very rich. The abundance of land meant that young couples could establish independent households, and widely scattered farms, with the parish church as the central social unit, seem to have been the usual pattern of existence.

Above the broad class of peasant farmers stood warrior-nobles. Their wealth and status derived from their fighting skills, which kings rewarded with grants of estates and

Aerial View of Church of Saint George, Lalibela   The cross is the basic Christian symbol. When the capital of Ethiopia was moved south from Axum to Lalibela, this church was carved out of volcanic rock and dedicated to the third-century Palestinian martyr Saint George, who had a large cult in Ethiopia. Concentric Greek crosses, formed of four equal arms and symbolizing the universal Christian church, composed the roof. *(Kal Muller/Woodfin Camp & Associates)*

with the right to collect tribute from the peasants. To acquire lands and to hold warriors' loyalty, Ethiopian kings had to pursue a policy of constant territorial expansion. Nobles maintained order in their regions, supplied kings with fighting men, and displayed their superior status by the size of their households and their generosity to the poor.

The Solomonid kings of Ethiopia (so called because of their theoretical descent from King Solomon and the queen of Sheba) exerted their authority by constant travel to oversee and overawe their peoples and to extend their kingdoms. Until the fifteenth century, they had no truly permanent capital, but ruled from itinerant military

camps. Amda Siyon (r. 1314–1344), who defeated the Muslims at Ifat and spread his kingdom to the south and west, proved to be Ethiopia's greatest ruler.[21]

From the fifth through seventh centuries, Axum was an important and cosmopolitan center, whose mercantile activities played a part in international commerce. Its military and political power was the dominant influence in East Africa. The expansion of Islam in the eighth century reduced Axum's trading contacts with the Byzantine Empire and ended its control of the Red Sea trade routes.

Ethiopia's high mountains encouraged an inward concentration of attention and hindered access from the outside. Twelfth-century Crusaders returning from the

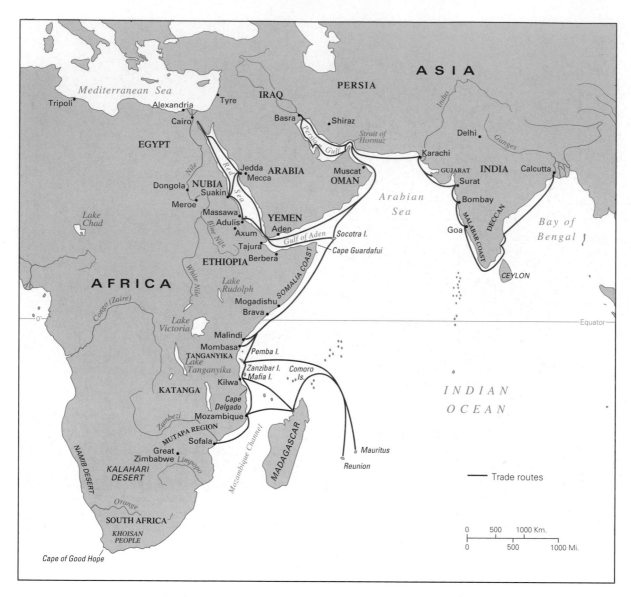

MAP 10.3 Trade Routes Between East Africa and India The Indian Ocean, controlled by the Muslim merchant fleet until the arrival of the Portuguese in the late fifteenth century, was of far greater importance to world trade than the Mediterranean. Gold from Great Zimbabwe passed through the cities on the East African coast before shipment north to the Middle East and east to India and China.

Middle East told of a powerful Christian ruler, Prester John, whose lands lay behind Muslim lines and who was eager to help restore the Holy Land to Christian control. Europeans identified that kingdom with Ethiopia. In the later thirteenth century, the dynasty of the Solomonid kings witnessed a literary and artistic renaissance particularly notable for works of hagiography (biographies of saints), biblical exegesis, and manuscript illumination. The most striking feature of Ethiopian society in the period from 500 to 1500 was the close relationship between the church and the state. Christianity inspired a fierce devotion and tended to equate doctrinal heresy with political rebellion, thus reinforcing central monarchical power.

Emperor Yekuno Amlak   The Ethiopian emperor's claim of possessing Solomon's blood won him considerable popular support in his war against the decaying Zagwe dynasty, which he overthrew in 1270. Here he receives Muslim ambassadors while slaves attend him. *(British Library)*

The East African City-States

In the first century C.E., a merchant seaman from Alexandria in Egypt sailed down the Red Sea and out into the Indian Ocean. Along the coasts of East Africa and India, he found seaports. He took careful notes on all he observed, and the result, *Periplus of the Erythraean Sea* (as the Greeks called the Indian Ocean), is the earliest surviving literary evidence of the city-states of the East African coast. Although primarily preoccupied with geography and navigation, the *Periplus* includes accounts of the local peoples and their commercial activities. Even in the days of the Roman emperors, the *Periplus* testifies, the East African coast had strong commercial links with India and the Mediterranean.

Greco-Roman ships traveled from Adulis on the Red Sea around the tip of the Gulf of Aden and down the African coast that the Greeks called "Azania," in modern-day Kenya and Tanzania (see Map 10.3). These ships carried manufactured goods—cotton cloth, copper and brass, iron tools, and gold and silver plate. At the African coastal emporiums, Mediterranean merchants exchanged these goods for cinnamon, myrrh and frankincense, captive slaves, and animal byproducts such as ivory, rhinoceros horns, and tortoise shells. Somewhere around Cape Guardafui on the Horn of Africa, the ships caught the monsoon winds eastward to India, where ivory was in great demand.

An omission in the *Periplus* has created a debate over the racial characteristics of the native peoples in East Africa and the dates of Bantu migrations into the area. The author, writing in the first century, did not describe the natives; apparently he did not find their skin color striking enough to comment on. Yet in the fifth century, there are references to these peoples as "Ethiopians." Could this mean that migrating black Bantu-speakers reached the east coast between the first and fifth centuries? Possibly. The distinguished archaeologist Neville Chittick, however, thinks not: "The writer of the *Periplus* made few comments on the physical nature of the inhabitants of the countries which he described . . . therefore nothing can be based on the mere omission of any mention of skin color."[22]

In the first few centuries of the Christian era, many merchants and seamen from the Mediterranean settled in East African coastal towns. Succeeding centuries saw the arrival of more traders. The great emigration from Arabia after the death of Muhammad accelerated Muslim penetration of the area, which the Arabs called the *Zanj,* "land of the blacks." Arabic Muslims established along the coast small trading colonies whose local peoples were ruled by kings and practiced various animistic religions.

Eventually—whether through Muslim political hegemony or gradual assimilation—the coastal peoples slowly converted to Islam. Indigenous African religions, however, remained strong in the interior of the continent.

Beginning in the late twelfth century, fresh waves of Arabs and of Persians from Shiraz poured down the coast, first settling at Mogadishu, then pressing southward to Kilwa (see Map 10.3). Everywhere they landed, they introduced Islamic culture to the indigenous population. Similarly, from the earliest Christian centuries through the Middle Ages, Indonesians crossed the Indian Ocean and settled on the African coast and on the large island of Madagascar, or Malagasy, an Indonesian name. All these immigrants intermarried with Africans, and the resulting society combined Asian, African, and especially Islamic traits. The East African coastal culture was called **Swahili,** after a Bantu language whose vocabulary and poetic forms exhibit a strong Arabic influence. The thirteenth-century Muslim mosque at Mogadishu and the fiercely Muslim populations of Mombasa and Kilwa in the fourteenth century attest to strong Muslim influence.

By the late thirteenth century, **Kilwa** had become the most powerful city on the coast, exercising political hegemony as far north as Pemba and as far south as Sofala (see Map 10.3). In the fourteenth and fifteenth centuries, the coastal cities were great commercial empires comparable to Venice and Genoa (see page 387). Like those Italian city-states, Kilwa, Mombasa, and Mafia were situated on offshore islands. The tidal currents that isolated them from the mainland also protected them from landside attack.

Much current knowledge about life in the East African trading societies rests on the account of Ibn Battuta. When he arrived at Kilwa, he found, in the words of a modern historian,

the city large and elegant, its buildings, as was typical along the coast, constructed of stone and coral rag [roofing slate].

Great Mosque at Kilwa   Built between the thirteenth and fifteenth centuries to serve the Muslim commercial aristocracy of Kilwa on the Indian Ocean, the mosque attests to the wealth and power of the East African city-states. *(Marc & Evelyn Bernheim/Woodfin Camp & Associates)*

Houses were generally single storied, consisting of a number of small rooms separated by thick walls supporting heavy stone roofing slabs laid across mangrove poles. Some of the more formidable structures contained second and third stories, and many were embellished with cut stone decorative borders framing the entranceways. Tapestries and ornamental niches covered the walls and the floors were carpeted. Of course, such appointments were only for the wealthy; the poorer classes occupied the timeless mud and straw huts of Africa, their robes a simple loincloth, their dinner a millet porridge.[23]

On the mainland were fields and orchards of rice, millet, oranges, mangoes, and bananas, and pastures and yards for cattle, sheep, and poultry. Yields were apparently high; Ibn Battuta noted that the rich enjoyed three enormous meals a day and were very fat.

From among the rich mercantile families that controlled the coastal cities arose a ruler who by the fourteenth century had taken the Arabic title *sheik*. The sheik governed both the island city and the nearby mainland. Farther inland, tribal chiefs ruled with the advice of councils of elders.

The Portuguese, approaching the East African coastal cities in the late fifteenth century, were astounded at their enormous wealth and prosperity. This wealth rested on monopolistic control of all trade in the area. Some coastal cities manufactured goods for export: Mogadishu produced cloth for the Egyptian market; Mombasa and Malindi processed iron tools; and Sofala made cottons for the interior trade. The bulk of the cities' exports, however, consisted of animal products—leopard skins, tortoise shell, ambergris, ivory—and gold. The gold originated in the Mutapa region south of the Zambezi River, where the Bantu mined it. As in tenth-century Ghana, gold was a royal monopoly in the fourteenth-century coastal city-states. The Mutapa kings received it as annual tribute, prohibited outsiders from entering the mines or participating in the trade, and controlled shipments down the Zambezi to the coastal markets. The prosperity of Kilwa rested on its traffic in gold.

African goods satisfied the widespread aristocratic demand for luxury goods. In Arabia, leopard skins were made into saddles, shells were made into combs, and ambergris was used in the manufacture of perfumes. Because the tusks of African elephants were larger and more durable than the tusks of Indian elephants, African ivory was in great demand in India for sword and dagger handles, carved decorative objects, and the ceremonial bangles used in Hindu marriage rituals. In China, the wealthy valued African ivory for use in the construction of sedan chairs.

Copper Coin from Mogadishu, Twelfth Century   Islamic proscriptions against representation of the human form, combined with a deep veneration for writing, prevented the use of rulers' portraits on coinage, as the Romans, Byzantines, and Sasanids had. Instead, Islamic coins since the Umayyad period were decorated exclusively with writing. Sultan Haran ibn Sulayman of Kilwa on the east African coast minted this coin, a symbol of the region's Muslim culture and of its rich maritime trade. *(Courtesy of the Trustees of the British Museum)*

In exchange for these natural products, the Swahili cities bought pottery, glassware and beads, and many varieties of cloth. Swahili kings imposed enormous duties on imports, perhaps more than 80 percent of the value of the goods themselves. Even so, traders who came to Africa made fabulous profits.

Slaves were another export from the East African coast. Reports of slave trading began with the *Periplus*. The trade accelerated with the establishment of Muslim settlements in the eighth century and continued down to the arrival of the Portuguese in the late fifteenth century. In fact, the East African coastal trade in slaves persisted at least to the beginning of the twentieth century.

As in West Africa, traders obtained slaves primarily through raids and kidnapping. As early as the tenth century, Arabs from Oman enticed hungry children with dates. When the children accepted the sweet fruits, they were abducted and enslaved. Profit was the traders' motive.

The Arabs called the northern Somalia coast *Ras Assir* (Cape of Slaves). From there, Arab traders transported slaves northward up the Red Sea to the markets of Arabia, Persia, and Iraq. Muslim dealers also shipped blacks from the region of Zanzibar across the Indian Ocean to markets in India. Rulers of the Deccan Plateau in central India used large numbers of black slave soldiers in their military campaigns. Slaves also worked on the docks and *dhows* (typical Arab lateen-rigged ships) in the Muslim-controlled Indian Ocean and as domestic servants and concubines throughout South and East Asia.

As early as the tenth century, sources mention persons with "lacquer-black bodies" in the possession of wealthy families in Song China.[24] In 1178 a Chinese official noted in a memorial to the emperor that Arab traders were shipping thousands of blacks from East Africa to the Chinese port of Guangzhou (Canton) by way of the Malay Archipelago. The Chinese employed these slaves as household servants, as musicians, and, because East Africans were often expert swimmers, as divers to caulk the leaky seams of ships below the water line.

By the thirteenth century, Africans living in many parts of South and East Asia had made significant economic and cultural contributions to their societies. Neither Asian nor Western scholars have adequately explored this subject. It appears, however, that in Indian, Chinese, and East African markets, slaves were never as valuable a commodity as ivory. Thus the volume of the Eastern slave trade did not approach that of the trans-Saharan trade.[25]

South Africa

South Africa, the region bordered on the northwest by tropical grasslands and on the northeast by the Zambezi River (see Map 10.3), enjoys a mild and temperate climate. Desert conditions prevail along the Atlantic coast, which gets less than five inches of annual rainfall. Eastward, rainfall increases, though some areas receive less than twenty inches a year. Although the Limpopo Valley in the east is very dry, temperate grasslands characterize the highlands to the north and northwest (the region of the modern Orange Free State, the Transvaal, and Zimbabwe). Considerable variations in climate occur throughout much of South Africa from year to year.

Located at the southern extremity of the Afro-Eurasian landmass, South Africa has a history that is very different from the histories of West Africa, the Nile Valley, and the east coast. Over the centuries, North and West Africa felt the influences of Phoenician, Greek, Roman, and Muslim cultures; the Nile Valley experienced the impact of major Egyptian, Assyrian, Persian, and Muslim civilizations; and the coast of East Africa had important contacts across the Indian Ocean with southern and eastern Asia and across the Red Sea with Arabia and Persia. South Africa, however, remained far removed from the outside world until the arrival of the Portuguese in the late fifteenth century—with one important exception. Bantu-speaking people reached South Africa in the eighth century. They brought with them skills in ironworking and mixed farming (settled crop production plus cattle and sheep raising) and an immunity to the kinds of diseases that later decimated the Amerindians of South America (see pages 525–527).

The earliest residents of South Africa were hunters and gatherers. In the first millennium after the birth of Christ, new farming techniques from the north arrived. A lack of water and timber (which were needed to produce the charcoal used in iron smelting) slowed the spread of iron technology and tools and thus of crop production in western South Africa. These advances, however, reached the western coastal region by 1500. By that date, Khoisan-speakers were farming in the arid western regions. To the east, descendants of Bantu immigrants grew sorghum, raised sheep and cattle, and fought with iron-headed spears. They practiced polygamy and traced their descent in the male line.

In 1871 a German explorer discovered the ruined city of **Great Zimbabwe** southeast of what is now Nyanda in Zimbabwe. Archaeologists consider Great Zimbabwe the most powerful monument in Africa south of the Nile Valley and the Ethiopian highlands. The ruins consist of two vast complexes of dry-stone buildings, a fortress, and an elliptically shaped enclosure commonly called the Temple. Stone carvings, gold and copper ornaments, and Asian ceramics once decorated the buildings. The ruins extend over sixty acres and are encircled by a massive wall. The entire city was built from local granite between the eleventh and fifteenth centuries without any outside influence.

These ruins tell a remarkable story. Great Zimbabwe was the political and religious capital of a vast empire. During the first millennium C.E., settled crop cultivation, cattle raising, and work in metal led to a steady buildup in population in the Zambezi-Limpopo region. The area also contained a rich gold-bearing belt. Gold ore lay near the surface; alluvial gold lay in the Zambezi River tributaries. In the tenth century, the inhabitants collected the alluvial gold by panning and washing; after the year 1000, the gold was worked in open mines with iron picks. Traders shipped the gold eastward to Sofala (see Map 10.3). The wealth and power of Great Zimbabwe rested on this gold trade.[26]

Great Zimbabwe declined in the fifteenth century, perhaps because the area had become agriculturally exhausted and could no longer support the large popula-

Ruins of Great Zimbabwe Considered the most impressive monument in the African interior south of the Ethiopian highlands, these ruins of Great Zimbabwe consist of two complexes of dry-stone buildings, some surrounded by a massive serpentine wall thirty-two feet high and seventeen feet thick at its maximum. Great Zimbabwe was the center of a state whose wealth rested on gold. Towers were probably used for defensive purposes. *(Robert Aberman/Barbara Heller/Werner Forman Archive/Art Resource, NY)*

Bird at Top of Monolith, 14½ inches, Great Zimbabwe, ca 1200–1400 C.E. The walls and buildings at Great Zimbabwe seem intended to reflect the wealth and power of the ruler. Among the archaeological finds there are monoliths crowned by soapstone birds; this one also appears to have an alligator-like creature on the side of the monolith. Scholars debate the significance of these birds: were they symbols of royal power? eagles? messengers from the spiritual world to the terrestrial? And what does the alligator mean? *(Courtesy of the National Archives of Zimbabwe)*

tion. Some people migrated northward and settled in the valley of the Mazoe River, a tributary of the Zambezi. This region also contained gold, and there the settlers built a new empire in the tradition of Great Zimbabwe. Rulers of this empire were called "Mwene Mutapa," and their power too was based on the gold trade carried on by means of the Zambezi River and Indian Ocean ports. It was this gold that the Portuguese sought when they arrived on the East African coast in the late fifteenth century.

SUMMARY

In the fifteenth century, the African continent contained a number of very different societies and civilizations and many diverse ethnic groups. All of North Africa, from Morocco in the west to Egypt in the east, was part of the Muslim world. In West Africa, Mali continued the brisk trade in salt, gold, and slaves that had originated many centuries earlier. Islam, which had spread to sub-Saharan Africa through the caravan trade, had a tremendous influence on the peoples of the western Sudan, their governmental bureaucracies, and their vibrant urban centers. The kings of Ethiopia ruled a uniquely Christian kingdom, partly by right of their Solomonic blood, frequently by force of arms. The impact of the Islamic faith was also felt in East Africa, whose bustling port cities were in touch with the cultures of the Indian Ocean and the Mediterranean Sea. While the city-states of the eastern coast—Kilwa, Mombasa, and Mogadishu—conducted complicated mercantile activities with foreign societies, the mountain-protected kingdom of Ethiopia increasingly led an isolated, inward-looking existence. In South Africa, the vast empire of Great Zimbabwe was yielding to yet another kingdom whose power was based on precious gold.

The student beginning the study of African history should bear in mind the enormous diversity of African peoples and cultures, a diversity both within and across regions. It is, therefore, difficult and often dangerous to make broad generalizations about African life. Statements such as "African culture is . . . " or "African peoples are . . . " are virtually meaningless. African peoples are not now and never have been homogeneous. This rich diversity helps explain why the study of African history is so exciting and challenging.

KEY TERMS

Bantu	Kumbi
Sudan	Timbuktu
Berbers	Ethiopia
Mogadishu	Axum
stateless societies	Swahili
Ghana	Kilwa
ghana	Great Zimbabwe

NOTES

1. J. Hiernaux, *The People of Africa* (New York: Scribner's, 1975), pp. 46–48.

2. C. A. Diop, "The African Origins of Western Civilization," and R. Mauny, "A Review of Diop," in *Problems in African History: The Precolonial Centuries,* ed. R. O. Collins et al. (New York: Markus Weiner Publishing, 1994), pp. 32–40, 41–49; the quotations are on p. 42.
3. Mauny, "A Review of Diop." For contrasting views of Afrocentrism in American higher education, see T. Martin, *The Jewish Onslaught: Despatches from the Wellesley Battlefront* (Dover, Mass.: The Majority Press, 1993), and M. Lefkowitz, *Not out of Africa: How Afrocentrism Became an Excuse to Teach Myth as History* (New York: Basic Books, 1996).
4. "African Historical Demography," in *Proceedings of a Seminar Held in the Centre of African Studies,* University of Edinburgh, April 29–30, 1977, p. 3.
5. T. Spear, "Bantu Migrations," in *Problems in African History: The Precolonial Centuries,* ed. R. O. Collins et al. (New York: Markus Weiner Publishing, 1994), p. 98.
6. J. Iliffe, *Africans: The History of a Continent* (Cambridge: Cambridge University Press, 1995), pp. 105–111; J. L. Newman, *The Peopling of Africa: A Geographic Interpretation* (New Haven, Conn.: Yale University Press, 1995), pp. 140–147.
7. J. S. Trimingham, *Islam in West Africa* (Oxford: Oxford University Press, 1959), pp. 6–9.
8. R. A. Austen, *Africa in Economic History* (London: James Currey/Heinemann, 1987), p. 36.
9. R. A. Austen, "The Trans-Saharan Slave Trade: A Tentative Census," in *The Uncommon Market: Essays in the Economic History of the Atlantic Slave Trade,* ed. H. A. Gemery and J. S. Hogendorn (New York: Academic Press, 1979), pp. 1–71, esp. p. 66.
10. R. N. July, *Precolonial Africa: An Economic and Social History* (New York: Scribner's, 1975), pp. 124–129.
11. See N. Levtzion, "Islam in Africa to 1800: Merchants, Chiefs, and Saints," in *The Oxford History of Islam,* ed. J. L. Esposito (New York: Oxford University Press, 1999), pp. 502–504.
12. Quoted in J. O. Hunwick, "Islam in West Africa, A.D. 1000–1800," in *A Thousand Years of West African History,* ed. J. F. Ade Ajayi and I. Espie (New York: Humanities Press, 1972), pp. 244–245.
13. Quoted in A. A. Boahen, "Kingdoms of West Africa, c. A.D. 500–1600," in *The Horizon History of Africa* (New York: American Heritage, 1971), p. 183.
14. Al-Bakri, *Kitab al-mughrib fdhikr bilad Ifriqiya wa'l-Maghrib (Description de l'Afrique Septentrionale),* trans. De Shane (Paris: Adrien-Maisonneuve, 1965), pp. 328–329.
15. Quoted in R. Oliver and C. Oliver, eds., *Africa in the Days of Exploration* (Englewood Cliffs, N.J.: Prentice-Hall, 1965), p. 10.
16. Quoted in Boahen, "Kingdoms of West Africa, c. A.D. 500–1600," p. 184.
17. Quoted in E. J. Murphy, *History of African Civilization* (New York: Delta, 1972), p. 109.
18. Quoted ibid., p. 111.
19. Quoted ibid., p. 120.
20. Quoted in Oliver and Oliver, *Africa in the Days of Exploration,* p. 18.
21. Iliffe, *Africans,* pp. 57–61.
22. H. N. Chittick, "The Peopling of the East African Coast," in *East Africa and the Orient: Cultural Syntheses in Pre-Colonial Times,* ed. H. N. Chittick and R. I. Rotberg (New York: Africana Publishing, 1975), p. 19.
23. July, *Precolonial Africa,* p. 209.
24. Austen, "The Trans-Saharan Slave Trade," p. 65; J. H. Harris, *The African Presence in Asia* (Evanston, Ill.: Northwestern University

Press, 1971), pp. 3–6, 27–30; and P. Wheatley, "Analecta Sino-Africana Recensa," in Chittick and Rotberg, *East Africa and the Orient,* p. 109.

25. I. Hrbek, ed., *General History of Africa.* Vol. 3: *Africa from the Seventh to the Eleventh Century* (Berkeley: University of California Press; New York: UNESCO, 1991), pp. 294–295, 346–347.

26. P. Curtin et al., *African History,* rev. ed. (New York: Longman, 1984), pp. 284–287.

SUGGESTED READING

Perhaps the best starting point for the study of early African history is J. Iliffe, *Africans: The History of a Continent* (1995), which has colonization and population as its main themes; although the peoples of Africa are studied with rare sensitivity, the style is not always clear. J. L. Newman, *The Peopling of Africa: A Geographic Interpretation* (1995), uses many types of evidence to explore population distribution and technological change down to the beginning of European colonization in the late nineteenth century. M. A. Ogutu and S. S. Kenyanchui, *An Introduction to African History* (1991), offers a useful sketch from a strongly Afrocentric point of view. J. Reader, *Africa: A Biography of a Continent* (1997), is a well-researched, exciting, and popular account with considerable material on Africa before 1450. The titles by Austen, Chittick, Curtin et al., Hiernaux, Hrbek, and Wheatley listed in the Notes represent some of the most reliable scholarship on early African history, and they are especially recommended. Most contain useful bibliographies. The enterprising student should also see B. Davidson, *African Civilization Revisited* (1991), a useful collection of primary documents with material on all parts of Africa; R. O. Collins, ed., *Problems in African History: The Precolonial Centuries* (1993), another collection of sources;

and V. B. Khapoya, *The African Experience* (1994), and R. Oliver, *The African Experience* (1991), both of which offer broad interpretations.

For specific topics in early African history, see, in addition to the topics in the Notes, J. Suret-Canale, "The Traditional Societies in Tropical Africa and the Concept of the 'Asiatic Production,'" in J. Suret-Canale, *Essays on African History* (1988), which explores a Marxist understanding of precolonial African societies. For the east coast, see J. de Vere Allen, *Swahili Origins* (1993), a study of the problem of Swahili identity; R. Oliver and G. Mathews, eds., *History of East Africa* (1963), perhaps still the standard general work on this part of the continent; and G. S. P. Freeman-Grenville, *The East African Coast: Select Documents from the First to the Earlier Nineteenth Century* (1962), which has valuable material from Arabic, Chinese, and Portuguese perspectives. The works of J. S. Trimingham, *A History of Islam in West Africa* (1970) and *Islam in East Africa* (1974), remain standard studies on the important issue of Islam. J. Kritzeck and W. H. Lewis, eds., *Islam in Africa* (1969), and M. Lombard, *The Golden Age of Islam* (1975), are also helpful. For the importance of the camel to African trade, R. W. Bulliet, *The Camel and the Wheel* (1975), is basic. For southern Africa, see Chapter 1 of L. Thompson, *A History of South Africa,* rev. ed. (1995).

Students interested in the art of early Africa will find the following titles provocative and attractively produced: K. Ezra, *Royal Art of Benin* (1992); E. Eyo and F. Willett, *Treasures of Ancient Nigeria* (1980); and P. Ben-Amos, *The Art of Benin* (1980), which describes the political, social, and religious significance of Benin art through beautiful illustrations. C. Beckwith and A. Fisher, *African Art: People and Ancient Culture of Ethiopia and the Horn of Africa* (1990), is a splendidly illustrated appreciation of Ethiopian art and culture.

THE EPIC OF OLD MALI

Just as the Greek epic poems the Iliad *and the* Odyssey *serve as essential sources for the early history of ancient Greece, so the testimony of African griots (storytellers) provides information about early West African societies. There were three classes of griots. Musician-entertainers in the service of nobles formed the lowest group. In the middle group were griots who acted as praise-singers of kings and as their advisers. "Traditionalists" who were attached to a royal household and whose function was to recite from memory in sung poems the royal family's historic traditions and to stress the family's rights and precedence constituted the highest-ranking griots. The Mandinke griot Djeli Mamadou Kouyate was a member of this third group. This selection is from the beginning of his account of old Mali, which is an important source for the early history of the kingdom of Mali.*

I am a griot. It is I, Djeli Mamadou Kouyate, son of Bintou Kouyate and Djeli Kediane Kouyate, master in the art of eloquence. Since time immemorial the Kouyates have been in the service of the Keita princes of Mali; we are vessels of speech, we are the repositories which harbor secrets many centuries old. The art of eloquence has no secrets for us; without us the names of kings would vanish into oblivion, we are the memory of mankind; by the spoken word we bring to life the deeds and exploits of kings for younger generations. . . . I know the list of all the sovereigns who succeeded to the throne of Mali. . . . I teach kings the history of their ancestors so that the lives of the ancients might serve them as an example, for the world is old, but the future springs from the past. . . . Listen to my word, you who want to know; by my mouth you will learn the history of Mali. . . . Listen to the story of the Buffalo. I am going to tell you of Maghan Sundiata, of Mari-Djata, of Sogolon Djata, of Nare Maghan Djata: the man of many names against whom sorcery could avail nothing. . . . Listen then, sons of Mali, children of the black people, listen to my word, for I am going to tell you of Sundiata, the father of the Bright Country, of the savanna land, the ancestor of those who draw the bow, the master of a hundred vanished kings.

QUESTIONS FOR ANALYSIS

1. How did Djeli Mamadou Kouyate secure his position as a griot?

2. What did Kouyate understand his social function to be?

3. According to Kouyate, what purpose does history serve among the Mali? Does this purpose resemble that among any other people you have studied, such as the Christians, Muslims, or Chinese?

4. Consider the value of oral history for the modern historian.

Source: B. Davidson, *African Civilization Revisited* (Trenton, N.J.: Africa World Press, 1991), p. 90.

A griot retells the history of his people. *(Bibliothèque nationale de France)*

Mongol army attacking a walled city, from a Persian manuscript. Note the use of catapults on both sides. (*Staatsbibliothek zu Berlin/Bildarchiv Preussischer Kulturbesitz. Foto: Ruth Schacht, 1979*)

11 SOUTHERN AND CENTRAL ASIA TO THE RISE OF THE MONGOLS, CA 300–1400

The large chunks of Asia treated in this chapter underwent profound changes during the eleven centuries examined here. In the Indian subcontinent regional cultures flourished and the area had its first encounter with Islam. Southeast Asia developed several distinct cultures, most of them borrowing ideas and techniques from India. The Central Asian grasslands gave birth to nomadic confederations capable of dominating major states—first the Turks, then later, even more spectacularly, the Mongols.

Ancient India was covered in Chapter 3, but this is the first chapter to treat Southeast Asia or to look at Central Asia on its own terms rather than as a problem for nearby agricultural societies.

- What impact did India's political division have on its cultural and economic development?
- How did trade contribute to the development of states in Southeast Asia?
- What gave the nomadic pastoralists military advantages over the settled civilizations?
- How was the world changed by the Mongol unification of much of Eurasia?

This chapter will explore these questions.

INDIA, 300–1400

Chapter 3 traced the early development of Indian civilization, including the emergence of the principal religious traditions of Hinduism, Buddhism, and Jainism; the impact of the Persian and Greek invasions; and the Mauryan dynasty, with its great pro-Buddhist king, Ashoka. As discussed at the end of that chapter, after the Mauryan dynasty broke apart in 184 B.C.E., India was politically divided into small kingdoms for several centuries. Northwest India fell to the Shakas, a nomadic group from the Central Asian grasslands.

The Gupta Empire (ca 320–480)

In the early fourth century a state emerged in the Ganges plain that was able to bring large parts of north India under its control. The rulers of this Indian empire, the Guptas, consciously modeled their rule after that of the Mauryan Empire, and the founder took the name of the founder of that dynasty, Chandragupta. Although the Guptas never controlled as much territory as the Mauryans had, they united north India and received tribute from states in Nepal and the Indus Valley, thus giving large parts of India a period of peace and political unity.

The real creator of the Gupta Empire was Chandragupta's son Samudragupta (r. ca 335–375). Samudragupta once issued gold coins with the legend, "After conquering the earth the Great King of Kings with the strength of an invincible hero is going to conquer the heavens."[1] By means of military conquest and shrewd alliances, Samudragupta brought much of India, from the Himalayas in the north to the Vindhya Mountains in the south, under his government.

Under Samudragupta's son Chandragupta II (r. ca 375–415), the glory of the Guptas reached its highest point. Perhaps Chandragupta's most significant exploit was the overthrow of the Shakas in west India. As a result, the busy trade between west India and the Middle East and China came under the protection of the Guptas. Indian agricultural cash crops, especially sugar, cotton, pepper, and cinnamon, were in great demand elsewhere.

The great crisis of the Gupta Empire was the invasion of the Huns. The migration of these nomads from Central Asia shook much of Eurasia. Around 450 a group of them known as the White Huns thundered into India. Mustering his full might, the ruler Skandagupta (r. ca 455–467) threw back the invaders. Although the Huns failed to uproot the Gupta Empire, they dealt the dynasty a fatal blow.

The Guptas' administrative system was not as centralized as the Mauryans'. In the central regions they drew their revenue from a tax on agriculture of one-quarter of the harvest and maintained monopolies on key products such as metals and salt (reminiscent of Chinese practice). They also exacted labor service for the construction and upkeep of roads, wells, and irrigation systems. More distant areas were assigned to governors allowed considerable leeway, and governorships often became hereditary. Areas still farther away were encouraged to become vassal states, able to participate in the splendor of the capital and royal court in subordinate roles and to engage in profitable trade, but not required to turn over much in the way of revenue.

The Gupta kings were patrons of the arts. During their ascendancy, Sanskrit masterpieces were preserved, and traditional epic poems and verses on mythological themes were reworked and polished. Poets composed epics for the courts of the Gupta kings, and other writers experimented with prose romances and popular tales.

The Gupta period also saw the rise of Indian drama. India's greatest poet, Kalidasa (ca 380–450), like Shakespeare, wrote poems as well as plays in verse. His most highly esteemed play, *Shakuntala,* concerns a daughter of a hermit who enthralls a king out hunting. The king sets up house with her, then returns to his court and owing to a curse forgets her. Only much later does he acknowledge their child as his true heir. Equally loved is Kalidasa's one-hundred-verse poem "The Cloud Messenger," about a demigod who asks a passing cloud to carry a message to his wife, from whom he has long been separated. At one point he instructs the cloud to tell her:

I see your body in the sinuous creeper, your gaze in the
    startled eyes of deer,
your cheek in the moon, your hair in the plumage of
    peacocks,
and in the tiny ripples of the river I see your sidelong
    glances,
but alas, my dearest, nowhere do I see your whole
    likeness.[2]

In mathematics, too, the Gupta period could boast of impressive intellectual achievements. The so-called Arabic numerals were actually of Indian origin. Indian mathematicians developed place-value notation that was far more efficient than the numerical systems of the Egyptians, Greeks, and Romans. It was a base ten system, with separate columns for ones, tens, and hundreds, as well as a zero sign to indicate the absence of units in a given column. This system greatly facilitated calculation and spread to the rest of Eurasia by the seventh century.

The Gupta rulers were Hindus but tolerated all faiths. Buddhist pilgrims from other areas of Asia reported that Buddhist monasteries with hundreds or even thousands of monks and nuns flourished in the cities. The Chinese Buddhist pilgrim Faxian, during his six years in Gupta India, found the Buddhist monasteries flourishing but also noted the popularity of the many gods of Hinduism. He described India as a peaceful land, where people could move about freely without needing passports and where the upper castes were vegetarians. He was the first to make explicit reference to "untouchables," remarking that they hovered around the margins of Indian society, carrying gongs to warn upper-caste people of their polluting presence.

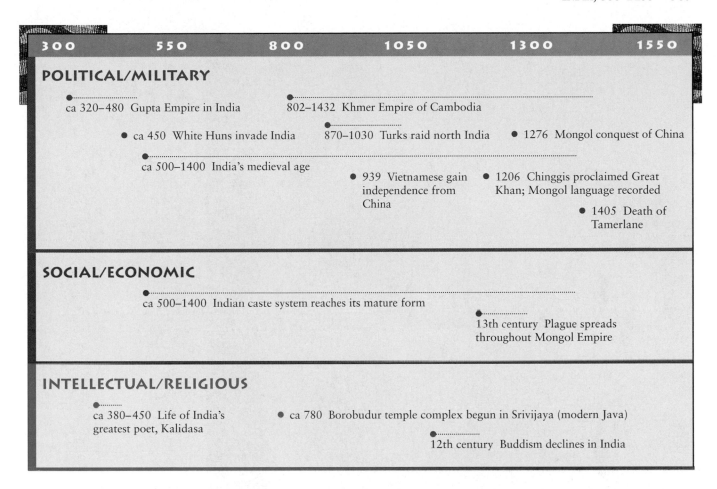

300	550	800	1050	1300	1550

POLITICAL/MILITARY

ca 320–480 Gupta Empire in India

802–1432 Khmer Empire of Cambodia

ca 450 White Huns invade India

870–1030 Turks raid north India

1276 Mongol conquest of China

ca 500–1400 India's medieval age

939 Vietnamese gain independence from China

1206 Chinggis proclaimed Great Khan; Mongol language recorded

1405 Death of Tamerlane

SOCIAL/ECONOMIC

ca 500–1400 Indian caste system reaches its mature form

13th century Plague spreads throughout Mongol Empire

INTELLECTUAL/RELIGIOUS

ca 380–450 Life of India's greatest poet, Kalidasa

ca 780 Borobudur temple complex begun in Srivijaya (modern Java)

12th century Buddism declines in India

India's Medieval Age (ca 500–1400) and the First Encounter with Islam

After the decline of the Gupta Empire, India once again broke into separate kingdoms that were frequently at war with each other. Most of the dynasties were short-lived, but a balance of power was maintained between the four major regions of India, with none gaining enough of an advantage to conquer the others. Particularly notable are the Cholas, who dominated the southern tip of the peninsula, Sri Lanka, and much of the eastern Indian Ocean to the twelfth century (see Map 11.1).

Political division fostered the development of regional cultures. Literature came to be written in regional languages, among them Marathi, Bengali, and Assamese. Commerce continued as before, and the coasts of India remained important in the sea trade of the Indian Ocean.

The first encounters with Islam occurred in this period. In 711, after pirates had plundered a richly laden Arab ship near the mouth of the Indus, the Ummayad governor of Iraq sent a force with six thousand horses and six thousand camels to seize the Sind area. The western part of India remained a part of the caliphate for centuries, but Islam did not spread much beyond this foothold. During the ninth and tenth centuries tribes of Turkish-speaking herdsmen and warriors from Central Asia moved into the region of today's northeastern Iran and western Afghanistan, then known as Khurasan. Converts to Islam, they first served as military forces for the caliphate in Baghdad, but as its authority weakened (see page 252), they made themselves rulers of an effectively independent Khurasan and frequently sent raiding parties into north India. Beginning in 997, Mahmud of Ghazni (r. 997–1030) led seventeen annual forays into India from his base in modern Afghanistan. His goal was plunder to finance his wars against other Muslim rulers in Central Asia. Toward this end, he systematically looted Indian palaces and temples, viewing religious statues as infidels' idols. His court chronicler, undoubtedly exaggerating, reported that in 1025 the Hindu inhabitants of one town on his route calmly watched as his troops reached the walls of their temple to Shiva, confident that

Mriga Jataka The fifth-century Buddhist caves at Ajanta contain the most important wall paintings from the Gupta period. This painting is an illustration of one of the 547 Jatakas (legends of the Buddha's life), and shows a royal servant with a dog on a leash. *(Satish Pavashav/Dinodia Picture Agency)*

Shiva would protect his worshipers. The Turkish soldiers, undeterred, seized more than 2 million dinars' worth of gold and jewels and killed fifty thousand Hindus. Eventually even the Arab conquerors of the Sind fell to the Turks. By 1030 the Indus Valley, the Punjab, and the rest of northwest India were in the grip of the Turks.

The new rulers encouraged the spread of Islam, but the Indian caste system made it difficult to convert higher-caste Indians. Al-Biruni (d. 1048), a Persian scholar who spent much of his later life at the court of Mahmud and learned Sanskrit, gave some thought to the obstacles to Hindu-Muslim communication. The most basic barrier, he wrote, was language, but the religious gulf was also fundamental:

They totally differ from us in religion, as we believe in nothing in which they believe, and vice versa. On the whole, there is very little disputing about theological topics among them; at the utmost they fight with words, but they will never stake their soul or body or property on religious controversy. . . .

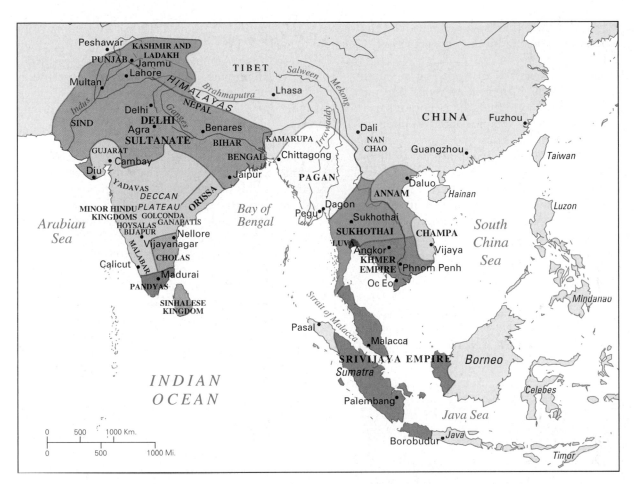

MAP 11.1 South and Southeast Asia in the Thirteenth Century   The extensive coastlines of South and Southeast Asia and the predictable monsoon winds aided seafaring in this region. Note the Strait of Malacca, through which most east-west sea trade passed.

They call foreigners impure and forbid having any connection with them, be it by intermarriage or any kind of relationship, or by sitting, eating, and drinking with them, because thereby, they think, they would be polluted.[3]

After the initial period of raids and destruction of temples, the Muslim Turks came to an accommodation with the Hindus, who were classed as a **protected people,** like the Christians and Jews, and allowed to follow their religion. They had to pay a special tax but did not have to perform military service. Local chiefs and rajas were often allowed to remain in control of their domains as long as they paid tribute. Most Indians looked on the Muslim conquerors as a new ruling caste, capable of governing and taxing them but otherwise peripheral to their lives. The myriad castes largely governed themselves, isolating

the newcomers. Nevertheless, over the course of several centuries Islam gained a strong hold on north India, especially in the Indus Valley (modern Pakistan) and in Bengal at the mouth of the Ganges River (modern Bangladesh). Moreover, the sultanate seems to have had a positive effect on the economy. Much of the wealth confiscated from temples was put to more productive use, and India's first truly large cities emerged. The Turks also were eager to employ skilled workers, giving new opportunities to low-caste manual and artisan labor.

The Muslim rulers were much more hostile to Buddhism than to Hinduism, seeing Buddhism as a competitive proselytizing religion. In 1193 a Turkish raiding party destroyed the great Buddhist university at Nalanda in Bihar. Buddhist monks were killed or forced to flee to Buddhist centers in Southeast Asia, Nepal, and Tibet.

Buddhism, which had thrived for so long in peaceful and friendly competition with Hinduism, was forced out of its native land.

Hinduism, however, remained as strong as ever. South India was largely unaffected by these invasions, and traditional Hindu culture flourished there under native kings ruling small kingdoms. Temple-centered Hinduism flourished, as did devotional cults and mystical movements. This was a great age of religious art and architecture in India. Extraordinary temples, covered with elaborate bas-relief, were built in many areas. Sexual passion and the union of men and women were frequently depicted, symbolically representing passion for and union with the temple god.

Mahmud and his successors had their capital in Afghanistan. After them a new line of Turkish rulers arose there,

Hindu Temple   Medieval Hindu temples were frequently decorated with scenes of sexual passion. Here Vishnu caresses Lakshami at the Parshvinath Temple. *(Richard Ashworth/Robert Harding Picture Library)*

led by Muhammad of Ghur (d. 1206). Muhammad captured Delhi and extended his control nearly throughout north India. Like Mahmud, Muhammad and his generals considered Hindu and Buddhist religious statues nothing more than idols; Muslim troops destroyed them in vast numbers. Buddhist centers of worship and learning especially suffered. When Muhammad of Ghur fell to an assassin in 1206, one of his generals, the former slave Qutb-ud-din, seized the reins of power and established a government at Delhi, separate from the government in Afghanistan. This sultanate of Delhi lasted for three centuries, even though dynasties changed several times. (See the feature "Listening to the Past: To Commemorate Building a Well" on pages 334–335.)

The North African Muslim world traveler Ibn Battuta (1304–1368) (see page 265), who journeyed through Africa and Asia from 1325 to 1354, served for several years as a judge at the court of one of the Delhi sultans. He praised the sultan for his insistence on the observance of ritual prayers and many acts of generosity to those in need, but he also considered the sultan overly violent. Here is just one of many examples he offered of how quick the sultan was to execute:

During the years of the famine, the Sultan had given orders to dig wells outside the capital, and have grain crops sown in those parts. He provided the cultivators with the seed, as well as with all that was necessary for cultivation in the way of money and supplies, and required them to cultivate these crops for the [royal] grain-store. When the jurist 'Afif al-Din heard of this, he said, "This crop will not produce what is hoped for." Some informer told the Sultan what he had said, so the Sultan jailed him, and said to him, "What reason have you to meddle with the government's business?" Some time later he released him, and as 'Afif al-Din went to his house he was met on the way by two friends of his, also jurists, who said to him, "Praise be to God for your release," to which our jurist replied, "Praise be to God who has delivered us from the evildoers." They then separated, but they had not reached their houses before this was reported to the Sultan, and he commanded all three to be fetched and brought before him. "Take out this fellow," he said, referring to 'Afif al-Din, "and cut off his head baldrickwise," that is, the head is cut off along with an arm and part of the chest, "and behead the other two." They said to him, "He deserves punishment, to be sure, for what he said, but in our case for what crime are you killing us?" He replied, "You heard what he said and did not disavow it, so you as good as agreed with it." So they were all put to death, God Most High have mercy on them.[4]

A major accomplishment of the Delhi sultanate was holding off the Mongols. Chinggis Khan and his troops entered the Indus Valley in 1221 in pursuit of the shah of Khurasan. The sultan wisely kept out of the way, and when Chinggis left some troops in the area, the sultan made no attempt to challenge them. Two generations later, in 1299, a Mongol khan launched a campaign into India with 200,000 men, but the sultan of the time was able to defeat them. Two years later the Mongols returned and camped at Delhi for two months, but they eventually left without taking the sultan's fort. Another Mongol raid in 1306–1307 also was successfully repulsed.

Although the Turks by this time were highly cosmopolitan, they had retained their martial skills and understanding of steppe warfare. They were expert horsemen, and horses thrived in northwest India. The south and east of India, like the south of China, were less hospitable to raising horses and generally had to import them. In India's case, though, the climate of the south and east was well suited to elephants, which had been used as weapons of war in India since early times. Rulers in the northwest imported elephants from more tropical regions. The Delhi sultanate is said to have had as many as one thousand war elephants at its height. After one of his victories, the sultan arranged for his court to watch as thousands of Mongol prisoners were trampled to death by elephants.

During the fourteenth century, however, the Delhi sultanate was in decline and proved unable to ward off the armies of Tamerlane (see page 328), who took Delhi in 1398. Tamerlane's chronicler reported that when the troops drew up for battle outside Delhi, the sultanate had 10,000 horsemen, 20,000 foot soldiers, and 120 war elephants, with archers riding in the structures on the elephants' backs. Although Tamerlane's men were alarmed at the sight of the elephants, he dug trenches to trap them and also shot at their drivers. The sultan fled, leaving the city to surrender. Tamerlane took as booty all of the elephants, loading them with treasures seized from the city. Ruy Gonzalez de Clavijo, an ambassador from the king of Castile who arrived in Samarkand in 1403, was greatly impressed by these well-trained elephants. "When all the elephants together charged abreast, it seemed as though the solid earth itself shook at their onrush," he observed, noting that he thought each elephant was worth a thousand foot soldiers in battle.[5]

Daily Life in Medieval India

For the overwhelming majority of people in medieval India, it did not matter much how large a territory was controlled by their king. Local institutions played a much larger role in their lives than the state. Guilds oversaw conditions of work and trade; local councils handled law and order at the town or village level; religious sects gave members a sense of belonging and identity, as did local castes.

Like peasant societies elsewhere, including China, Japan, and Southeast Asia, in India agricultural life ordinarily meant village life. The average farmer worked a small plot of land outside the village, aided by the efforts of the extended family. All the family members pooled their resources—human, animal, and material—under the direction of the head of the family. Joint struggles strengthened family solidarity.

The agricultural year began with spring plowing. The ancient plow, drawn by two oxen wearing yokes and collars, had an iron-tipped share and a handle with which the farmer guided it. Rice, the most important and popular grain, was sown at the beginning of the long rainy season. Beans, lentils, and peas were the farmer's friends, for they grew during the cold season and were harvested in the spring when fresh food was scarce. Cereal crops such as wheat, barley, and millet, grown twice a year, provided carbohydrates and other nutrients. Sugar cane was another important crop. Some families cultivated vegetables, spices, and flowers in their gardens. Village orchards kept people supplied with fruit, and the inhabitants of well-situated villages could eat their fill of fresh and dried fruit and sell the surplus at a nearby town.

Indian farmers raised livestock. Most highly valued were cattle. They were used for plowing and esteemed for their milk, hides, and horns, but Hindus did not slaughter them for meat. Like the Islamic and Jewish prohibition on the consumption of pork, the eating of beef was forbidden among Hindus.

Farmers fortunate enough to raise surpluses found ready markets in towns and cities. There they came into contact with merchants and traders, some of whom dealt in local commodities and others in East-West trade. Like their Roman counterparts, Indian merchants enjoyed a respectable place in society. There were huge profits to be made in foreign commerce. Daring Indian sailors founded new trading centers along the coasts of Southeast Asia and in the process spread Indian culture. Other Indian merchants specialized in the caravan trade that linked China, Iran, India, and the West.

Local craftsmen and tradesmen lived and worked in specific parts of a town or village. They were frequently organized into guilds, corresponding mostly with castes, with guild heads and guild rules. The textile industries were particularly well developed. Silk (which had entered India from China), muslin, calico, linen, wool, and cotton were produced in large quantities and traded throughout India. The cutting and polishing of precious stones was an industry associated more with foreign trade.

In the cities shops were open to the street; families lived on the floors above. The busiest tradesmen dealt in milk and cheese, oil, spices, and perfumes. Equally prominent but disreputable were tavern keepers. Indian taverns were haunts of criminals and con artists, and in the worst of them fighting was as common as drinking. In addition to these tradesmen and merchants, a host of peddlers shuffled through towns and villages selling everything from needles to freshly cut flowers.

Leatherworkers were economically important but were considered outcastes, as Indian religious and social customs condemned those who made a living handling the skins of dead animals. Masons, carpenters, and brickmakers were more highly respected. As in all agricultural societies, blacksmiths were essential, though of low caste.

Villages were often walled, as in north China and the Middle East, and the typical village was divided into quarters by two main streets that intersected at the center of the village. The streets were unpaved, and the rainy season turned them into a muddy soup. Cattle and sheep roamed as freely as people. Some families kept pets, such as cats or parrots. Half-wild mongooses served as effective protection against snakes. The pond outside the village served as its main source of water and also as a spawning ground for fish, birds, and mosquitoes. Women drawing water frequently encountered water buffalo wallowing in the shallows. After the farmers returned from the fields in the evening, the village gates were closed until morning.

In this period the caste system reached its mature form. Within the broad division into the four *varna* (strata) of Brahman, Kshatriya, Vaishya, and Shudra, the population was subdivided into numerous castes, or **jati.** Each caste had a proper occupation. In addition, its members married only within the caste and ate only with other members. Members of high-status castes feared pollution from contact with lower-caste individuals and had to undertake rituals of purification to remove the taint. Eventually Indian society comprised perhaps as many as three thousand castes. Each caste had its own governing body, which enforced the rules of the caste. Those incapable of living up to the rules were expelled, becoming outcastes. These unfortunates lived hard lives, performing tasks that others considered unclean or lowly.

The life of the well-to-do is described in the *Kamasutra* (Book on the Art of Love). Comfortable surroundings provided a place for men to enjoy poetry, painting, and music in the company of like-minded friends. Well-trained courtesans added to the pleasures of the wealthy, but it was also acceptable for a man to have several wives. Those who did were advised not to let one speak ill of the other and to try to keep each of them happy by taking them to gardens, giving them presents, telling them secrets, and loving them well.

For all members of Indian society, regardless of caste, marriage and the family were the focus of life. As in China, the joint family was under the authority of the eldest male, who might take several wives. The family affirmed its solidarity by the religious ritual of honoring its dead ancestors—a ritual that linked the living and the dead, much like ancestor worship in China. People commonly lived in extended families: grandparents, uncles and aunts, cousins, and nieces and nephews all lived together in the same house or compound.

Children were viewed as a great source of happiness. The poet Kalidasa depicts children as the greatest joy of their father's life:

With their teeth half-shown in causeless laughter,
and their efforts at talking so sweetly uncertain,
when children ask to sit on his lap
a man is blessed, even by the dirt on their bodies.[6]

Children in poor households worked as soon as they were able. Children in wealthier households faced the age-old irritations of reading, writing, and arithmetic. Less attention was paid to daughters, though in the most prosperous families they were often literate.

Boys of the three upper varnas underwent a religious initiation, the sacred thread investiture, symbolizing a second birth. Ideally, they then entered into a period of religious training at the hands of *gurus,* Brahman teachers with whom the boys boarded. In reality, relatively few went through this expensive education. Having completed their education, young men were ready to lead adult lives, the first and foremost step in which was marriage.

Women's situations seem to have deteriorated since the Vedic age. They could no longer own or inherit property and were barred from participating in many rituals. Because girls who had lost their virginity could seldom hope to find good husbands, and thus would become financial burdens and social disgraces to their families, daughters were customarily married before their first menstrual periods, with consummation delayed until the girl reached puberty.

As in China, in India women ideally spent their entire lives, from childhood to old age, under the authority of men. Indian law was blunt: "A woman is not independent, the males are her masters. . . . Their fathers protect them in childhood, their husbands protect them in youth, and their sons protect them in age; a woman is never fit for independence."[7]

Two Indian Women
Indian women not only applied cosmetics but also adorned themselves with a wide variety of jewelry. The scene here was engraved on the ivory top of a chest or stool. *(National Museum of Afghanistan, Kabul. Drawing by Frances Mortimer Price)*

Women of high rank rarely left the house, and then only with a chaperone. Wives' bonds with their husbands were so strong that it was felt a wife should have no life apart from her husband. Widows were expected to lead the hard life of the ascetic, sleeping on the ground; eating only one simple meal a day, without meat, wine, salt, or honey; wearing plain undyed clothes without jewelry; and shaving their heads. A widow was viewed as inauspicious to everyone but her children, and she did not attend family festivals. Among high-caste Hindus, a widow would be praised for throwing herself on her husband's funeral pyre. Buddhist sects objected to this practice, called **sati,** but some writers declared that by self-immolation a widow could expunge both her own and her husband's sins, so that both would enjoy eternal bliss in Heaven.

Within the home the position of a wife often depended chiefly on her own intelligence and strength of character. Wives were traditionally supposed to be humble, cheerful, and diligent even toward worthless husbands. As in other patriarchal societies, however, occasionally a woman ruled the roost. An Indian verse paints a vivid picture of what a henpecked husband could expect:

But when she has him in her clutches
it's all housework and errands!

"Fetch a knife to cut this gourd!"
"Get me some fresh fruit!"
"We want wood to boil the greens,
and for a fire in the evening!"
"Now paint my feet!"
"Come and massage my back!"
So . . . resist the wiles of women,
avoid their friendship and company.
The little pleasure you get from them
will only lead you into trouble.[8]

The most eagerly desired event was the birth of a child. Before consummating their marriage, newlyweds repeated traditional prayers for the wife to become pregnant immediately. While pregnant, the wife was nearly suffocated with affection and attention and rigorously circumscribed by religious ritual. At labor and birth, while the women of the household prepared for the birth, the husband performed rituals intended to guarantee an easy delivery and a healthy child. After the birth the parents performed rituals intended to bring the baby happiness, prosperity, and desirable intellectual, physical, and moral qualities. Infants were pampered until they reached the age of schooling and preparation for the adult world.

For women who did not want to accept the strictures of married life, the main way out was to join a Buddhist or Jain religious community.

SOUTHEAST ASIA, TO 1400

Much as Roman culture spread to Europe and Chinese culture spread to Korea, Japan, and Vietnam, in the first millennium C.E. Indian learning, technology, and material culture spread to Southeast Asia, both mainland and insular.

Southeast Asia is a tropical region that is more like India than China, with temperatures hovering around 80°F and rain falling dependably throughout the year. The topography of mainland Southeast Asia is marked by several mountain ranges that extend from south China to the Bay of Bengal or the South China Sea (see Map 11.1). Between these north-south ranges are the valleys of the major rivers—the Irrawaddy and the Salween in Burma, the Chao Phraya in Thailand, and the Red and Mekong in Vietnam. It was easy for people to migrate south along these rivers but harder for them to cross the heavily forested mountains, which divided the region into areas that had limited contact with each other. The indigenous population was originally mostly Malay, but migrations over the centuries brought many other peoples, including speakers of Austro-Asiatic, Austronesian, and Sino-Tibetan-Burmese languages, some of whom moved on to the islands of the Pacific.

The northern part of modern Vietnam was under Chinese political control off and on from the second century B.C.E. to the tenth century C.E. (see pages 200–201), but for the rest of Southeast Asia, Indian influence was of much greater significance. The first state to appear in Southeast Asia, called **Funan** by Chinese visitors, had its capital in southern Vietnam. In the first to sixth centuries C.E. Funan extended its control over much of Indochina and the Malay Peninsula, so that it could dominate trade at the key point of the Isthmus of Kra. Merchants from northwest India would offload their goods and carry them across the narrow strip of land. The ports of Funan offered food and lodging to the merchants as they waited for the winds to shift to continue their voyages. Brahman priests and Buddhist monks from India settled along with the traders, serving the Indian population and attracting local converts. Rulers often invited Indian priests and monks to serve under them, using them as foreign experts knowledgeable about law, government, architecture, and other fields.

Sixth-century Chinese sources report that the Funan king lived in a multistory palace and the common people lived in houses built on piles with roofs of bamboo leaves. The king rode about on an elephant, but a more important means of transportation was narrow boats measuring up to ninety feet long. The people enjoyed both cockfighting and pig fighting. Instead of drawing water from wells, as the Chinese did, they made pools, from which dozens of nearby families would draw water. When in mourning, people would shave their hair and beards. They worshiped a variety of deities represented by bronze statues, some with multiple arms and heads.

After the decline of Funan, maritime trade continued to grow, and petty kingdoms appeared in many places. Indian traders frequently established small settlements, generally located on the coast and stretching from modern Thailand in the west to the Mekong Delta of modern Vietnam. Contact with the local populations led to intermarriage and the creation of hybrid cultures. Local rulers often adopted Indian customs and values, embraced Hinduism and Buddhism, and learned **Sanskrit,** India's classical literary language. Sanskrit gave different peoples a common mode of written expression, much as Chinese did in East Asia and Latin did in Europe.

Outside the courts of the rulers, native societies maintained their own cultural identities even when they assimilated various Indian customs. For instance, the Javanese took up the *Ramayana,* the Indian epic poem describing the deeds of the Vedic heroes, but they added to it native Javanese legends, thus creating a work that did not belong solely to either culture.

When the Indians entered mainland Southeast Asia, they encountered both long-settled peoples and migrants moving southward from the frontiers of China. As in other such extensive migrations, the newcomers fought one another as often as they fought the native populations. In 939 the Vietnamese finally became independent of China and extended their power southward along the coast of present-day Vietnam. The Thais had long lived in what is today southwest China and north Burma. In the eighth century the Thai tribes united in a confederacy and even expanded northward against Tang China. Like China, however, the Thai confederacy fell to the Mongols in 1253. Still farther west another tribal people, the Burmese, migrated to the area of modern Burma in the eighth century. They also established a state, which they ruled from their capital, Pagan, and came into contact with India and Sri Lanka.

The most important mainland state was the Khmer Empire of Cambodia, which controlled the heart of the

Angkor Wat   The Khmer rulers built both Buddhist and Hindu temples, the most elaborate of which is the twelfth-century Angkor Wat, dedicated to the Hindu god Shiva and decorated with bas-relief carvings of Indian legends and Khmer history. *(Robert Harding Picture Library)*

region. The Khmers were indigenous to the area. Their empire, founded in 802, eventually extended south to the sea and the northeast Malay Peninsula. Indian influence was pervasive; the impressive temple complex at Angkor Wat was dedicated to the Hindu god Vishnu. Social organization, however, was not modeled on the Indian caste system but on indigenous traditions. A large part of the population was of servile status, many descended from non-Khmer mountain tribes defeated by the Khmers. Generally successful in a long series of wars with the Vietnamese, the Khmers reached the peak of their power in 1219 and then declined.

Far different from these land-based states was the maritime empire of **Srivijaya,** which from the sixth century on held the important Strait of Malacca, through which most of the sea traffic between China and India passed. Based on the island of Sumatra, the Srivijayan navy ruled the waters around Sumatra, Borneo, and Java, and the empire came to control the southern part of the Malay Peninsula as well. This state, held together as much by alliances as direct rule, was in many ways like the Gupta state in India, securing its prominence and binding its vassals/allies through its splendor and promise of riches through trade.

Much as the Korean and Japanese rulers adapted Chinese models, the Srivijayan rulers drew on Indian traditions to justify their rule and organize their state. The Sanskrit writing system was used for government documents, and Indians were often employed as priests, scribes, and administrators. Sanskrit also broke down the barriers raised by the many different native languages of the region. Indian mythology took hold, as did Indian architecture and sculpture. Kings and their courts, the first to embrace Indian culture, consciously spread it to their subjects. The Chinese Buddhist monk Yixing (d. 727) stopped at Srivijaya for six months in 671 on his way to India to study Sanskrit grammar and for four years on his return journey. He found there a thousand monks, some of whom helped him translate Sanskrit texts.

Borobudur, the most magnificent Buddhist temple complex, was begun around 780. This stone monument depicts the ten tiers of Buddhist cosmology. When pilgrims made the three-mile-long winding ascent, they passed numerous sculpted reliefs depicting the journey from ignorance to enlightenment.

After several centuries of prosperity, Srivijaya suffered a stunning blow in 1025. The Chola state in south India launched a large naval raid and captured the Srivijaya king and capital. Unable to hold their gains, the Indians retreated, but the Srivijaya Empire never regained its vigor. By the mid-thirteenth century the arrival of Chinese traders had further weakened the empire, and eventually it fell to local rivals.

Buddhism became progressively more dominant in Southeast Asia after 800. Mahayana Buddhism became important in Srivijaya, but Theravada Buddhism, closer to the original Buddhism of early India, became the dominant form in mainland Southeast Asia. Buddhist missionaries from India and Sri Lanka played a prominent role in these developments. Local converts continued the process by making pilgrimages to India and Sri Lanka to worship and to observe Indian life for themselves.

The Spread of Indian Culture in Comparative Perspective

The social, cultural, and political systems developed in India, China, and Rome all had enormous impact on neighboring peoples whose cultures were originally not as advanced. Some of the mechanisms for cultural spread were similar in all three cases, but differences were important as well.

In the case of Rome and both Han and Tang China, strong states came to rule directly outlying regions, bringing their civilizations with them. India's states, even its largest empires, such as the Mauryan and Gupta, did not have comparable centralized bureaucracies administered by professional officeholders. Outlying areas tended to be in the hands of local lords who had consented to recognize the overlordship of the stronger state, and most of the time India was politically divided.

The expansion of Indian culture into Southeast Asia thus came not from conquest and extending direct political control, but from the extension of trading networks, with missionaries following along. This made it closer to the way Japan adopted features of Chinese culture, often through the intermediary of Korea. In both cases, the cultural exchange was largely voluntary, as the Japanese or Southeast Asians sought to adopt more up-to-date technologies (such as writing) or were persuaded of the truth of religious ideas they learned from foreigners.

CENTRAL ASIA, TO 1400

One experience Rome, India, China, and the Middle East all shared was conflict with **nomads** who came from the very broad region referred to as Central Asia. This broad region was dominated by the arid **grasslands** (called the steppe) that stretched from Hungary, through southern Russia and across Central Asia (today's Tajikistan, Turkmenistan, Kazakhstan, Kyrgyzstan, and Uzbekistan), to Mongolia and parts of north China. The grasslands are easily crossed by horses but not suited to crop agriculture. They can support only a thin population of nomadic herders.

This common ecology also led to common forms of social and political organization based on families, clans, tribes, and sometimes tribal confederations. In their search for water and good pastures, nomadic groups often came into conflict with other nomadic groups pursuing the same resources, which the two would then fight over, as there was normally no higher political authority able to settle differences of this sort. Groups on the losing end, especially if they were small, faced the threat of extermination or slavery, which prompted them to make alliances with other groups or move far away. Thus, over the centuries, the ethnic groups living in particular sections of the grasslands would change. Groups on the winning end of intertribal conflicts could exact tribute from those they defeated, sometimes so much that they could devote themselves entirely to war, leaving to their slaves and vassals the work of tending herds.

To get the products of the agricultural societies nearby, especially grain, woven textiles, iron, tea, and wood, nomadic herders would trade their own products, such as horses and furs. When trade was difficult, they would turn to raiding to seize what they needed. Much of the time nomadic herders raided other nomads, but relatively nearby agricultural settlements also were often targets. The nomads' skill as horsemen and archers made it difficult for farmers or townsmen to oppose them. It was largely to defend against the raids of the Xiongnu nomads, for example, that the Chinese built the Great Wall.

Political organization among nomadic herders was generally very simple. Clans had chiefs, as did tribes (which were coalitions of clans, often related to each other). Leadership within a group was based on military prowess and often settled by fighting. Occasionally a charismatic leader would emerge who was able to extend alliances to form confederations of tribes. From the point of view of the settled societies, which have left most of the records about these nomadic groups, large confederations were much more of a threat, since they could plan coordinated attacks on cities and towns. Large confederations rarely lasted more than a century or so, however, and when they broke up, tribes again spent much of their time fighting with each other, relieving some of the pressure on their settled neighbors.

The three most wide-ranging and successful confederations were those of the Xiongnu/Huns, who emerged in the third century B.C.E. in the area near China; the Turks, who had their origins in the same area in the fourth and fifth centuries C.E.; and the Mongols, who did not become important until the late twelfth century. In all three cases, the entire grasslands area was eventually swept up in the movement of peoples and armies.

The might of the Xiongnu caused rival groups to move west, resulting in the arrival of the Shakas and Kushans in Afghanistan and north India and later the Huns in Europe. The Turks, after their heyday as a power in the east in the seventh century, broke up into several rival groups, some of whom moved west. From the mid-eighth to the mid-tenth century Turks were living on the borders of Abbasid Persia. By the mid- to late tenth century many were serving in the Abbasid armies. By the eleventh century they had gained the upper hand, and in 1055 the Abbasid caliph recognized the Turk Tughril Beg as the sultan (see page 252). From there Turkish power was extended into Syria, Palestine, and other parts of the realm. (Asia Minor is now called Turkey because Turks migrated there by the thousands over several centuries.) Another Turkish confederation had established itself in Afghanistan and extended its control into north India. Thus by the twelfth century separate groups of Turks controlled much of Central Asia and the adjoining lands from Syria to north India and into Chinese Turkestan, then occupied by Uighur Turks. There was, however, no single political unit uniting all of these Turkish forces. Such a unified empire was put together briefly by the next major power on the grasslands, the Mongols.

In Mongolia in the twelfth century ambitious Mongols did not aspire to match the Turks or other groups that had migrated west, but the groups that had stayed in the east had mastered ways to extract resources from China, the largest and richest country in the region. In the tenth and eleventh centuries the Khitans had accomplished this; in the twelfth century the Jurchens had overthrown the Khitans and extended their reach even deeper into China. The Khitans and Jurchens formed hybrid nomadic-urban states, with northern sections where tribesmen continued to live in the traditional way, and southern sections politically controlled by the non-Chinese

rulers but settled largely by Chinese (in much the same fashion as the Turks in north India). The Khitans and Jurchens had scripts created to record their languages and adopted many Chinese governing practices. They built cities in pastoral areas as centers of consumption and trade. In both cases, their elite became culturally dual, adept in Chinese ways as well as their own traditions.

The Mongols lived north of these hybrid nomadic-settled societies and maintained their traditional ways. Chinese, Persian, and European observers have all left descriptions of the daily life of the Mongols, which they found strikingly different from their own. The daily life of the peasants of China, India, Vietnam, and Japan had much more in common with each other than with the Mongol pastoralists. Before considering the military conquests of the Mongols, it is useful to look more closely at their way of life.

Daily Life of the Mongols

Before their great conquests the Mongols did not have cities, towns, or villages. Rather, they moved with their animals between winter and summer pastures. They had to keep their belongings to a minimum because they had to be able to pack up and move everything they owned when it was time to move.

Because they needed to be able to move their settlements, the Mongols lived in portable tents called **yurts** rather than in houses. The yurts, about twelve to fifteen feet in diameter, were constructed of light wooden frames covered by layers of wool felt, greased to make them waterproof. The yurts were always round, since this shape held up better against the strong winds that blew across the treeless grasslands. The yurts could be dismantled and loaded onto pack animals or carts in a short time. The floor of the yurt would be covered with dried grass or straw, then felt, skins, or rugs. In the center would be the hearth, directly under the smoke hole. Usually the yurt was set up with the entrance facing south. The master's bed would be on the north. Goat horns would be attached to the frame of the yurt and used as hooks to hang joints of meat, cooking utensils, bows, quivers of arrows, and the like. A group of families traveling together would set up their yurts in a circle open to the south and draw up their wagons in a circle around the yurts for protection.

For food the Mongols ate mostly animal products. The most common meat was mutton, supplemented with wild game. The Mongols milked sheep, goats, cows, and horses and made cheese and fermented alcoholic drinks from the milk. When grain or vegetables could be obtained through trade with agricultural regions, they were added to the diet. Wood was scarce, so the common fuel for the cook fires was dried animal dung or grasses. Without granaries to store food for years of famine, the Mongols' survival was endangered whenever weather or diseases of their animals threatened their food supply.

Because of the intense cold of the grasslands in the winter, the Mongols made much use of furs and skins for clothing. Both men and women usually wore silk trousers and tunics (the silk obtained from China). Over this they wore robes of fur, for the very coldest times in two layers—an inner layer with the hair on the inside and an outer layer with the hair on the outside. Hats were of felt or fur, boots of felt or leather. Women's clothing differed from men's in that it had more pleats and tucks to make it more formfitting. Men wore leather belts to which their bows and quivers could be attached. Women of high rank wore elaborate headdresses decorated with feathers.

Mongol women had to work very hard and had to be able to care for the animals when the men were away hunting or fighting. They normally drove the carts and set up and dismantled the yurts. They were also the ones who milked the sheep, goats, and cows and made the butter and cheese. In addition, they made the felt, prepared the skins, and sewed the clothes. Because water was scarce, clothes were not washed with water, nor were dishes. Women, like men, had to be expert riders, and many also learned to shoot. Women participated actively in family decisions, especially as wives and mothers. In *The Secret History of the Mongols*, a work written in Mongolian in the mid-thirteenth century, Chinggis Khan's mother and wife frequently make impassioned speeches on the importance of family loyalty.

Mongol men kept as busy as the women. They made carts and wagons and the frames for the yurts. They also made harnesses for the horses and oxen, leather saddles, and the equipment needed for hunting and war, such as bows and arrows. Men also had charge of the horses, and they milked the mares. Young horses were allowed to run wild until it was time to break them in. Catching them took great skill in the use of a long springy pole with a noose at the end. One specialist among the nomads was

Mongol Yurt   A Chinese artist has captured the essential features of a Mongol yurt to illustrate the story of a Chinese woman who married a nomad. *(The Metropolitan Museum of Art, Gift of The Dillon Fund, 1973 [1973.120.3]. Photograph © 1994 The Metropolitan Museum of Art)*

the blacksmith, who made stirrups, knives, and other metal tools.

Kinship underlay most social relationships. Normally each family occupied a yurt, and groups of families camping together were usually related along the male line (brothers, uncles and nephews, and so on). More distant patrilineal relatives were recognized as members of the same clan and could call on each other for aid. People from the same clan could not marry each other, so clans had to cooperate to provide brides. When a woman's husband died, she would be inherited by another male in the family, such as her husband's brother or his son by another woman. Tribes were groups of clans, often distantly related. Both clans and tribes had recognized chiefs who would make decisions on where to graze and when to retaliate against another tribe that had stolen animals or people. Women were sometimes abducted for brides. When tribes stole men from each other, they normally made them into slaves, and slaves were forced to do much of the heavy work. They would not necessarily remain slaves their entire lives, however, as their original tribes might be able to recapture them or make exchanges for them, or their masters might free them.

Even though population was sparse in the regions where the Mongols lived, conflict over resources was endemic, and each camp had to be on the alert for attacks. Defending against attacks and retaliating against raids was as much a part of the Mongols' daily life as caring for their herds and trading with nearby settlements.

Mongol children learned to ride at a young age, first riding on goats. The horses they later rode were short and stocky, almost like ponies, but nimble and able to endure long journeys and bitter cold. Even in the winter they survived by grazing, foraging beneath the snow. The prime weapon boys had to learn to use was the compound bow, which had a pull of about 160 pounds and a range of more than 200 yards. Other commonly used weapons were small battle-axes and lances fitted with hooks to pull enemies off their saddles.

From their teenage years Mongol men participated in battles, and among the Mongols courage in battle was essential to male self-esteem. Hunting was a common form of military training. Each year there would be one big hunt when mounted hunters would form a vast ring perhaps ten or more miles in circumference, then gradually shrink it down, trapping all the animals before killing them. On military campaigns a Mongol soldier had to be able to ride for days without stopping to cook food; he had to carry a supply of dried milk curd and cured meat, which could be supplemented by blood let from the neck of his horse. When time permitted, the soldiers would pause to hunt, adding to their food dogs, wolves, foxes, mice, and rats.

A common specialist among the Mongols was the shaman, a religious expert able to communicate with the gods. The high god of the Mongols was Heaven, but they recognized many other gods as well. Some groups of Mongols, especially those closer to settled communities, converted to Buddhism, Nestorian Christianity, or Manichaeism.

Chinggis Khan and the Creation of the Mongol Empire

In the mid-twelfth century, the Mongols were just one of many peoples in the eastern grasslands, neither particularly numerous nor especially advanced. Why did the Mongols suddenly emerge on the historical stage? One explanation is ecological. A drop in the mean annual temperature created a subsistence crisis. As pastures shrank, the Mongols and other nomads had to get more of their food from the agricultural world.

But the Mongols ended up getting much more than just enough to eat. A second reason for their sudden rise has to do with the appearance of a single individual, the brilliant but utterly ruthless Temujin (r. ca 1162–1227), later called Chinggis.

Chinggis's early career was recorded in *The Secret History of the Mongols*, written within a few decades of his death in 1227. In Chinggis's youth the Mongol tribes were in competition with the Tartar tribes, a situation encouraged by the strongest power in the region, the Jurchens. Chinggis's father had built up a modest following and had arranged for his future marriage to the daughter of a more powerful Mongol leader. When Chinggis's father was poisoned by a rival, his followers, not ready to follow a boy of twelve, drifted away, leaving Chinggis and his mother and brothers in a vulnerable position. In 1182 Chinggis was captured and carried in a cage to a rival's camp. After a daring midnight escape, he led his followers to join a stronger chieftain whom his father had once aided. With the chieftain's help, Chinggis began avenging the insults he had received.

As Chinggis subdued the Tartars, Kereyids, Naimans, Merkids, and other Mongol and Turkish tribes, he built up an army of loyal followers. He mastered the art of winning allies through displays of personal courage in battle and generosity to his followers. He also was willing to turn against former allies who proved troublesome. To those who opposed him, he could be merciless. He once asserted that nothing gave more pleasure than massacring one's enemies, seizing their horses and cattle, and

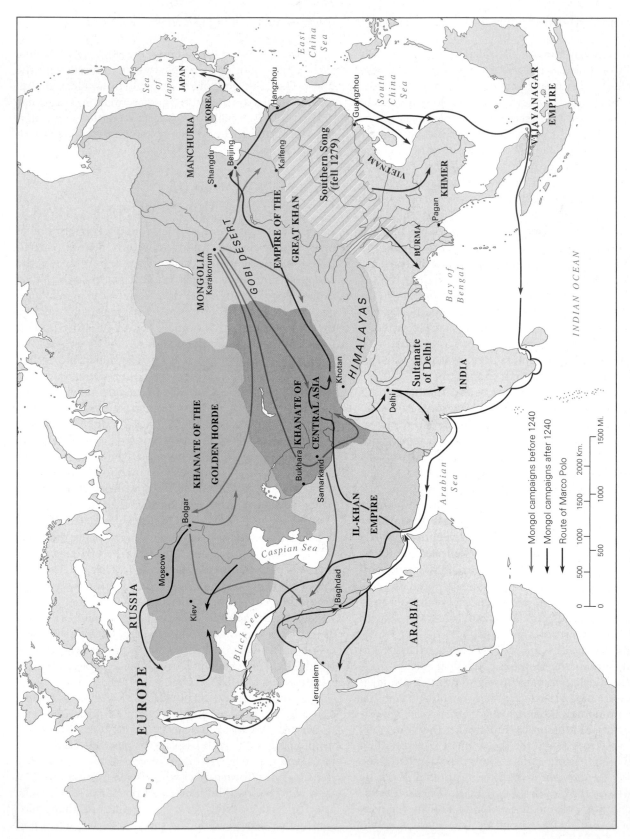

MAP 11.2 The Mongol Empire The creation of the vast Mongol Empire facilitated communication across Eurasia and led to both the spread of deadly plagues and the transfer of technical and scientific knowledge. After the death of Chinggis in 1227, the empire was divided into four khanates, ruled by different lines of his successors. In the 1270s, the Mongols conquered southern China, but most of their subsequent campaigns did not lead to further territorial gains.

ravishing their women. Sometimes Chinggis would kill all the men in a defeated tribe to prevent any later vendettas. At other times he would take them on as soldiers in his own armies. Courage impressed him. One of his leading generals, Jebe, first attracted his attention when he held his ground against overwhelming opposition and shot Chinggis's horse out from under him.

In 1206, at a great gathering of tribal leaders, Chinggis was proclaimed the **Great Khan.** He decreed that Mongol, until then an unwritten language, be written down in a script used by the Uighur Turks. With this script a record was made of the Mongol laws and customs, ranging from the rules for the annual hunt to punishments of death for robbery and adultery. Another measure adopted at this assembly was a postal relay system to send messages rapidly by mounted courier.

With the tribes of Mongolia united, the energies previously devoted to infighting and vendettas were redirected to exacting tribute from the settled populations nearby, starting with the Jurchen (Jin) state that extended into north China (see Map 11.2). In this Chinggis was following the precedent of the Jurchens, who had defeated the Khitans to get access to China's wealth a century earlier.

After Chinggis subjugated a city, he would send envoys to cities farther out to demand submission and threaten destruction. Those who opened their city gates and submitted without fighting could become allies and retain local power, but those who resisted faced the prospect of mass slaughter. He despised city dwellers and would sometimes use them as living shields in the next battle. After the Mongol armies swept across north China in 1212–1213, ninety-odd cities lay in rubble. Beijing, captured in 1215, burned for more than a month. Not surprisingly many governors of cities and rulers of small states hastened to offer submission.

Chinggis preferred conquest to administration and did not stay in north China to set up an administrative structure like that used by earlier nomadic conquerors. He left that to subordinates and turned his attention westward, to Central Asia and Persia, then in the hands of the Turks. In 1218 Chinggis proposed to the Khwarazm shah of Persia that he accept Mongol overlordship and establish trade relations. The shah, to show his determination to resist, ordered the envoy and the merchants who had accompanied him killed. The next year Chinggis led an army of 100,000 soldiers west to retaliate. Mongol forces not only destroyed the shah's army but also pursued the shah to an island in the Caspian Sea, where he died. To complete the conquest, Chinggis sacked one Persian city after another, demolishing buildings and massacring hundreds of thousands of people. The irrigation systems that were needed for agriculture in this dry region were destroyed as well.

On his return from Central Asia in 1226, Chinggis turned his attention to the Tanguts, who ruled the Xia state in northwest China. They had earlier declined to join forces with the Mongols and now suffered the consequences. The following years, during the siege of their capital, Chinggis died of illness. Before he died, he instructed his sons not to fall out among themselves but instead to divide the spoils.

Chinggis's Successors

Although Mongol tribal leaders traditionally had had to win their positions, after Chinggis died the empire was divided into four **khanates,** with one of the lines of his descendants taking charge of each one. Chinggis's third son, Ogodei, became Great Khan, and he directed the next round of invasions.

In 1237 representatives of all four lines led 150,000 Mongol, Turkish, and Persian troops into Europe. During the next five years they gained control of Moscow and Kievan Russia and looted cities in Poland and Hungary. They were poised to attack deeper into Europe when they learned of the death of Ogodei in 1241. To participate in the election of a new khan, the army returned to the Mongols' new capital city, Karakorum.

Once Ogodei's son was certified as his successor, the Mongols turned their attention to Persia and the Middle East. In 1256 a Mongol army took northwest Iran, then pushed on to the Abbasid capital of Baghdad. When it fell in 1258, the last Abbasid caliph was murdered, and the population was put to the sword. The Mongol onslaught was successfully resisted, however, by both the Delhi sultanate (see page 313) and the Mamluk rulers in Egypt (see page 282).

Under Chinggis's grandson Khubilai (r. 1260–1294) the Mongols completed their conquest of Korea and China. Mongol troops poured across the Yalu River in 1231, but Korea did not fully surrender until 1258. By then the Mongols were ready to concentrate on China. South China had never been captured by non-Chinese, in large part because horses were of no strategic advantage in a land of rivers and canals. Perhaps because they were entering a very different type of terrain, the Mongols proceeded deliberately. First they surrounded the Song empire by taking its westernmost province in 1252, destroying the Nanzhao kingdom in modern Yunnan in 1254, and then continuing south and taking Annam (northern Vietnam) in 1257. A surrendered

MONGOL CONQUESTS

1206	Chinggis made Great Khan
1215	Fall of Beijing (Jurchens)
1220	Fall of Bukhara and Samarkand in Central Asia
1227	Death of Chinggis
1237–1241	Raids into eastern Europe
1257	Conquest of Annam (northern Vietnam)
1258	Conquest of Abassid capital of Baghdad Conquest of Korea
1260	Accession of Khubilai
1274	First attempt at invading Japan
1276	Surrender of Song Dynasty (China)
1281	Second attempt at invading Japan
1293	Expedition to Java
mid-14th century	Decline of Mongol power; ouster or absorption

Song commander advised them to build a navy to attack the great Song cities located on rivers. During the five-year siege of a central Chinese river port, both sides used thousands of boats and tens of thousands of troops. The Mongols employed experts in naval and siege warfare from all over their empire—Chinese, Korean, Jurchen, Uighur, and Persian. Catapults designed by Muslim engineers launched a barrage of rocks weighing up to a hundred pounds each. During their advance toward the Chinese capital of Hangzhou, the Mongols ordered the total slaughter of the people of the major city of Changzhou, and in 1276 the Chinese empress dowager surrendered in hopes of sparing the people of the capital a similar fate.

Having overrun China and Korea, Khubilai turned his eyes toward Japan. In 1274 a force of 30,000 soldiers and support personnel sailed from Korea to Japan. In 1281 a combined Mongol and Chinese fleet of about 150,000 made a second attempt to conquer Japan. On both occasions the Mongols managed to land but were beaten back by Japanese samurai armies. The decisive factor was two fierce storms that destroyed the Mongol fleets. The Italian traveler Marco Polo (see page 330) recounted what he heard about one invasion force:

It happened, after some time, that a north wind began to blow with great force, and the ships of the Tartars, which lay near the shore of the island, were driven foul of each other. . . . The gale, however, increased to so violent a degree that a number of vessels foundered. The people belonging to them, by floating upon the pieces of the wreck, saved themselves upon an island lying about four miles from the coast of Zipangu [Japan].[9]

The Japanese claimed that they had been saved by the *kamikaze,* the "divine wind" (which later lent its name to the thousands of Japanese aviators who crashed their airplanes into American warships during World War II).

A decade later, in 1293, Khubilai tried sending a fleet to the islands of Southeast Asia, including Java, but it met with no more success than the fleets sent to Japan.

Why were the Mongols so successful against so many different types of enemies? Even though their population was tiny compared to that of the large agricultural

Gold-decorated Saddle   The Mongols, like earlier nomads, prized fine metalwork. The gold panels that decorate this saddle were found in the tomb of a Mongol girl of about eighteen. The central motif of the front arch is a reclining deer; surrounding it are peonies. *(Collection of Inner Mongolia Museum, Huhehaote)*

societies they conquered, their tactics, their weapons, and their organization all gave them advantages. Like other nomads before them, they were superb horsemen and excellent archers. Their horses were extremely nimble, able to change direction quickly, thus allowing the Mongols to maneuver easily and ride through infantry forces armed with swords, lances, and javelins. Usually the only armies that could stand up well against the Mongols were other nomadic ones.

Marco Polo left a vivid description of the Mongol soldiers' endurance and military skill:

They are brave in battle, almost to desperation, setting little value upon their lives, and exposing themselves without hesitation to all manner of danger. Their disposition is cruel. They are capable of supporting every kind of privation, and when there is a necessity for it, can live for a month on the milk of their mares, and upon such wild animals as they may chance to catch. The men are habituated to remain on horseback during two days and two nights, without dismounting, sleeping in that situation whilst their horses graze. No people on earth can surpass them in fortitude under difficulties, nor show greater patience under wants of every kind.[10]

The Mongols were also open to new military technologies and did not insist on fighting in their traditional ways. To attack walled cities, they learned how to use catapults and other engines of war. At first they employed Chinese catapults, but when they later learned that those used by the Turks in Afghanistan were half again as powerful, they quickly adopted the better model. The Mongols also used exploding arrows and gunpowder projectiles developed by the Chinese.

Because of his early experiences with intertribal feuding, Chinggis mistrusted traditional Mongol tribal loyalties, and as he fashioned a new army, he gave it a new, nontribal structure. Chinggis also created an elite bodyguard of ten thousand sons and brothers of commanders, which served directly under him. Chinggis allowed commanders to pass their posts to their sons, but he could remove them at will. Marco Polo explained the decimal hierarchy of his armies this way:

When one of the great Tartar chiefs proceeds on an expedition, he puts himself at the head of an army of a hundred thousand horse, and organizes them in the following manner. He appoints an officer to the command of every ten men, and others to command a hundred, a thousand, and ten thousand men, respectively. Thus ten of the officers commanding ten men take their orders from him who commands a hundred; of these, each ten, from him who commands a thousand; and each ten of these latter, from him who commands ten thousand. By this arrangement each officer has only to attend to the management of ten men or ten bodies of men.[11]

The Mongols also made good use of intelligence and tried to exploit internal divisions in the countries they attacked. Thus, when attacking the Jurchens in north China, they appealed to the Khitans, who had been defeated by the Jurchens a century earlier, to join them. In Syria they exploited the resentment of Christians against their Muslim rulers.

The Mongols as Rulers

The success of the Mongols in ruling vast territories was due in large part to their willingness to incorporate other ethnic groups into their armies and governments. Whatever their nationality, those who served the Mongols loyally were rewarded and given important posts. (See the feature "Individuals in Society: Mukhali.") Uighurs, Tibetans, Persians, Chinese, and Russians came to hold powerful positions in the Mongol government. Chinese helped breach the walls of Baghdad in the 1250s, and Muslims operated the catapults that helped reduce Chinese cities in the 1270s.

Since, in Mongol eyes, the purpose of fighting was to gain riches, they regularly would loot the settlements they conquered, taking whatever they wanted, including the residents. Land would be granted to military commanders, nobles, and army units, to be governed and exploited as the recipients wished. Those who had worked on the land would be given to them as serfs. The Mongols built a capital city in modern Mongolia, called Karakorum, and to bring it up to the level of the cities they conquered, they transported skilled workers from those cities. For instance, after Bukhara and Samarkand were captured in 1219–1220, some thirty thousand artisans were seized and transported to Mongolia. Sometimes these slaves gradually improved their status. A French goldsmith working in Budapest named Guillaume Boucher was captured by the Mongols in 1242 and taken to Karakorum, where he lived for at least the next fifteen years. He gradually won favor and was put in charge of fifty workers to make gold and silver vessels for the Mongol court.

The traditional nomad disdain for farmers led some commanders to suggest turning north China into a gi-

gantic pasture after it was conquered. In time, though, the Mongols came to realize that simply appropriating the wealth and human resources of the settled lands was not as good as extracting regular revenue from them. A Sinified Khitan who had been working for the Jurchens in China explained to the Mongols that collecting taxes from farmers would be highly profitable: they could extract a revenue of 500,000 ounces of silver, 80,000 bolts of silk, and more than 20,000 tons of grain from the region by taxing it. The Mongols gave this a try, but soon political rivals convinced the khan that he would gain even more by letting Central Asian Muslim merchants bid against each other for licenses to collect taxes any way they could, a system called **tax-farming.** Ordinary Chinese found this method of tax collecting much more oppressive than traditional Chinese methods, since there was little to keep the tax collectors from seizing everything they could.

By the second half of the thirteenth century there was no longer a genuine pan-Asian Mongol Empire. Much of Asia was in the hands of Mongol successor states, but these were generally hostile to each other. Khubilai was often at war with the khanate of Central Asia, then held by his cousin Khaidu, and he had little contact with the khanate of the Golden Horde in south Russia. The Mongols adapted their methods of government to the existing traditions of each place they ruled, and the regions now went their separate ways.

In China the Mongols resisted assimilation and purposely avoided many Chinese social and political practices. The rulers conducted their business in the Mongol language and spent their summers in Mongolia. Khubilai discouraged Mongols from marrying Chinese and took only Mongol women into the palace. Some Mongol princes preferred to live in yurts erected on the palace grounds rather than in the grand palaces constructed at Beijing. Chinese were treated as legally inferior not only to the Mongols but also to all other non-Chinese.

In Central Asia, Persia, and Russia the Mongols tended to merge with the Turkish nomads already there and like them converted to Islam. Russia in the thirteenth century was not a strongly centralized state, and the Mongols were satisfied to see Russian princes and lords continue to rule their territories as long as they turned over adequate tribute (which, of course, added to the burden on peasants). The city of Moscow became the center of Mongol tribute collection and grew in importance at the expense of Kiev. In the Middle East the Mongol Il-khans were more active as rulers, again continuing the traditions of the caliphate. In Mongolia itself Mongol traditions were maintained, though more and more of the

MUKHALI

The Mongol conquests were carried out in large part by those who had been vanquished by Chinggis. If members of defeated tribes proved their loyalty to Chinggis, they could rise to the highest ranks in his organization.

Mukhali was born in 1170 into the "White" clan of the Jalair tribe, hereditary serfs of the Jurkins, a Mongol tribe. When the Jurkins were defeated by Chinggis in 1197, Mukhali's father gave him and his brother to Chinggis as personal hereditary slaves.

Within a couple of years Mukhali was leading campaigns. In the final battle against the Kereyids, Mukhali led his picked troops into the camp of Chinggis's former patron, the Ong Khan. At the assembly of 1206, when Chinggis was made Great Khan, Mukhali was appointed myriarch of the left wing of the newly reorganized army and granted immunity for up to nine breaches of the law. The first thousand-man corps under his command was made up of his own Jalair tribesmen, who were given to him as his personal property.

In his capacity as commander in chief of the left wing, Mukhali played a leading role in the 1211 campaigns against the Jurchens. He was as ruthless as Chinggis. In 1213, when Chinggis was attacking north China, Mukhali seized the town of Mizhou and ordered all the inhabitants massacred. Perhaps not surprisingly, several Chinese generals serving the Jurchens soon defected to him. In his campaigns in Liaodong in 1214, Mukhali had under his campaign a newly formed Khitan-Chinese army and a special corps of twelve thousand Chinese auxiliary troops.

In 1217 Mukhali was back in Chinggis's camp in Mongolia, where he was given new honors, including the hereditary title of prince, a golden seal, and a white standard with nine tails and a black crescent in the middle. In addition, he was appointed commander in chief of operations in north China. Of the sixty-two thousand troops under his command, about twenty-three thousand were Mongols or Onguts, the rest Chinese and Khitan auxiliaries.

Mukhali spent the next six years of his life campaigning in north China. He regularly reappointed defeated generals and officials and listened to their advice. An envoy from the Chinese who met him in 1221–1222 described him as very tall with curly whiskers and a dark complexion. He was also

Mongol soldiers, as depicted in a Persian history of the Mongols.
(Bibliothèque nationale de France)

reported to have had four Mongol and four Jurchen secondary wives.

The Secret History of the Mongols, a work written in Mongolian in the mid-thirteenth century, portrays Mukhali as one of Chinggis's closest followers, one of the few men able to exert any real influence on him. For instance, when Chinggis was getting ready to begin his campaign against the shah of Khwarazm in Central Asia, one of his wives urged him first to name his heir. When Chinggis asked his first son, Jochi, what he thought of the idea, before he could speak the second son, Chagadai, called Jochi a bastard son of a Merkid, and the two brothers were soon wrestling. At this tense moment it was Mukhali who pulled the brothers apart.

A soldier to the end, Mukhali was still leading troops into battle at age fifty-three, when he died in north China in 1223.

QUESTIONS FOR ANALYSIS

1. What does Mukhali's life indicate about the nature of slavery in Mongol society?
2. Why would Mukhali have incorporated defeated Jurchens and Chinese into his armies?

Puppet Show The performing arts, including both opera and puppet shows, flourished in Chinese cities during Mongol occupation. In this fourteenth-century anonymous painting, men, women, and children are watching a puppet show. Among the most popular types of stories for the theater were farces, love stories, moral tales, and war stories. *(Zhu Yu [Junbi], Chinese, 1293–1365, Street Scenes in Times of Peace. Handscroll, ink and colors on paper, 26 × 790 cm. Kate S. Buckingham Fund, 1952.8 [detail]. Photograph © 1988, The Art Institute of Chicago)*

Mongols converted to Lamaist Buddhism (the form of Buddhism common in Tibet).

Mongol control in each of the khanates lasted about a century. In the mid-fourteenth century the Mongol dynasty in China deteriorated into civil war, and in the 1360s the Mongols withdrew back to Mongolia. There was a similar loss of Mongol power in Persia and Central Asia. Only on the south Russian steppe was the Golden Horde able to maintain its hold for another century. As Mongol rule in Central Asia declined, a new conqueror emerged, known as Tamerlane (Timur the Lame). Not a nomad but a highly civilized Turkish noble, Tamerlane in the 1360s struck out from his base in Samarkand into Persia, north India, southern Russia, and beyond. His armies used the terror tactics that the Mongols had perfected, massacring the citizens of cities that resisted. With his death in 1405, however, Tamerlane's empire fell apart.

EAST-WEST COMMUNICATION DURING THE MONGOL ERA

The Mongols did more to encourage the movement of people and goods across Eurasia than any earlier political entity. They had never looked down on merchants, the way the elites of many traditional states did, and they welcomed the arrival of merchants from distant lands. Even when different groups of Mongols were fighting among themselves, they usually allowed caravans to pass unharassed.

The Mongol practice of transporting skilled people from the lands they conquered also brought people into contact with each other in new ways. Besides those forced to move, the Mongols recruited administrators from all over. Chinese, Persians, and Arabs served the Mongols, and the Mongols often sent them far from home. Especially prominent were the Uighur Turks of Chinese Central Asia, whose familiarity with Chinese civilization and fluency in Turkish were extremely valuable in facilitating communication. Literate Uighurs provided many of the clerks and administrators running the Mongol administration.

One of the most interesting of those who served the Mongols was Rashid al-Din (ca 1247–1318). A Jew from Persia and the son of an apothecary, Rashid al-Din converted to Islam at the age of thirty and entered the service of the Mongol khan of Persia as a physician. He rose in government service, traveling widely, and eventually became prime minister. Rashid al-Din became friends with the ambassador from China, and together they arranged for translations of Chinese works on medicine, agronomy, and statecraft. He had ideas on economic management that he communicated to Mongol officials in Central Asia and China. Aware of the great differences between cultures, he believed that the Mongols should try to rule in accord with the moral principles of the majority in each land. On that basis he convinced the Mongol khan of Persia to convert to Islam. Rashid al-Din undertook to explain the great variety of cultures by writing a history of the world that was much more comprehensive than any previously written. The parts on Europe were based on information he obtained from European

Depictions of Europeans   The Mongol Empire, by facilitating travel across Asia, increased knowledge of faraway lands. Rashid al-Din's *History of the World* included a history of the Franks, illustrated here with images of Western popes (*left*) conferring with Byzantine emperors (*right*). (*Topkapi Saray Museum, Ms.H.1653, fol 303*)

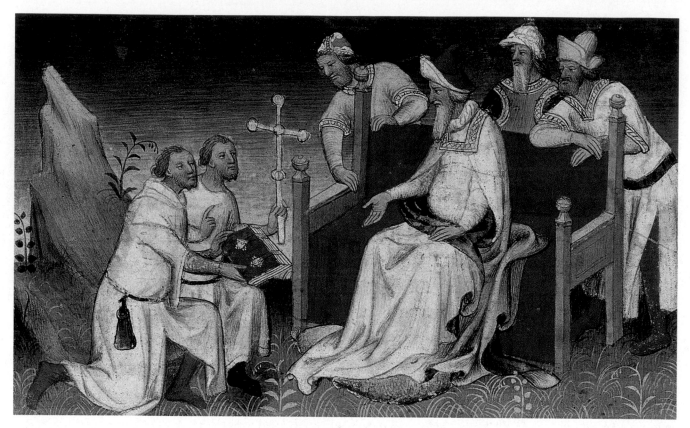

Marco Polo Meeting Khubilai Khan Illustrated European versions of Marco Polo's book show that it was just as difficult for Europeans to imagine what Mongols looked like as it was for Persians to imagine Europeans. *(Bibliothèque nationale de France)*

monks. The sections on China seem to be based on Chinese informants and perhaps Chinese Buddhist narratives. This book was often richly illustrated, with depictions of Europeans based on European paintings and depictions of Chinese based on Chinese paintings, leading to the spread of artistic styles as well.

The Mongols were remarkably open to religious experts from all the lands they encountered. Khubilai, for instance, welcomed Buddhist, Daoist, Islamic, and Christian clergymen to his court and gave tax exemptions to clerics of all religions. More Europeans made their way as far as Mongolia and China in the Mongol period than ever before. Popes and kings sent envoys to the Mongol court in the hope of enlisting the Mongols on their side in their long-standing conflict with Muslim forces over the Holy Land. These and other European visitors were especially interested in finding Christians who had been cut off from the West by the spread of Islam, and in fact there were considerable numbers of

Nestorian Christians in Central Asia. Those who left written records of their trips often mention meeting other Europeans in China or Mongolia. There were enough Europeans in Beijing to build a cathedral and appoint a bishop.

The most famous European visitor to the Mongol lands was Marco Polo. The Western world learned of the wealth and sophistication of China when Marco Polo returned from a long sojourn in Asia to dictate his famous *Travels*. Marco Polo described his warm reception by Khubilai and all the lands under the khan's control. He was enormously impressed with the Mongol ruler and awed by the wealth and splendor of Chinese cities. There have always been skeptics who do not believe Marco Polo's tale, and even today some scholars think that he may have learned about China from Persian merchants he met in the Middle East. But most of what he wrote about China tallies well with Chinese sources. The great popularity of his book in Europe contributed enormously to familiarizing Europeans with the notion of Asia as a land of riches.

The more rapid transfer of people and goods across Central Asia spread more than ideas and inventions. It also spread diseases, the most deadly of which was the plague known in Europe as the Black Death. Europe had not had an outbreak of the plague since about 700 and the Middle East since 1200. There was a pocket of active plague in the southwestern mountains of modern Yunnan province in China, the area that had been the independent Nanzhao kingdom of Thai peoples and relatively isolated until the Mongols invaded it in the mid-thirteenth century. Once the Mongols established a garrison there, flea-invested rats carrying plague were transported to central China, then northwest China, and from there to Central Asia and beyond. When caravans carrying goods stopped at oasis towns, the rats and fleas would move from the heavily loaded camels and carts, soon infecting local rats, dogs, and people. Between the oases, desert rodents were infected, and they also passed the disease to dogs and people. By the time the Mongols were assaulting the city of Kaffa in the Crimea in 1346, they themselves were infected by the plague and had to withdraw. But the disease did not retreat and was carried throughout the Mediterranean by the rats on ships. The Black Death of Europe thus was initiated through breaching of the isolation of a remote region in southwest China. The confusion of the mid-fourteenth century that led to the loss of Mongol power in China, Iran, and Central Asia probably owes something to the effect of the spread of the plague and other diseases.

Traditionally, the historians of each of the countries conquered by the Mongols portrayed them as a scourge. Russian historians, for instance, saw this as a period of bondage that set Russia back and cut it off from western Europe. Today it is more common to celebrate the genius of the Mongol military machine and treat the spread of ideas and inventions as an obvious good, probably because we see global communication as a good in our own world. There is no reason to assume, however, that every person or every society benefited equally from the improved communications and the new political institutions of the Mongol era. Merchants involved in long-distance trade prospered, but those enslaved and transported hundreds or thousands of miles from home would not have seen themselves as the beneficiaries of opportunities to encounter cultures different from their own, but rather as the most pitiable of victims.

The places that were ruled by Mongol government for a century or more—China, Central Asia, Persia, and Russia—do not seem to have advanced at a more rapid rate during that century than they did in earlier centuries, either economically or culturally. Indeed, judged by the record of earlier centuries, the Mongol period was generally one of setbacks. By Chinese standards Mongol imposition of hereditary status distinctions was a step backward from a much more mobile and open society, and placing Persians, Arabs, or Tibetans over Chinese did not arouse interest in foreign cultures. Much more in the way of foreign music and foreign styles in clothing, art, and furnishings was integrated into Chinese civilization in Tang times than in Mongol times.

In terms of the spread of technological and scientific ideas, Europe seems to have been by far the main beneficiary of increased communication, largely because in 1200 it lagged farther behind than the other areas. Chinese inventions such as printing, gunpowder, and the compass spread westward. Persian expertise in astronomy and mathematics also spread. In terms of the spread of religions, Islam probably gained the most. It spread into Chinese Central Asia, which had previously been Buddhist, and into Anatolia as Turks pushed out by the Mongols moved west, putting pressure on the Byzantine Empire.

Perhaps because it was not invaded itself, Europe also seems to have been energized by the Mongol-imposed peace in ways that the other major civilizations were not. The goods from China and elsewhere in the East brought by merchants like Marco Polo to Europe whetted the appetites of Europeans for increased contacts with the East, and the demand for Asian goods eventually culminated in the great age of European exploration and expansion. By comparison, in areas the Mongols had directly attacked, protecting their own civilization became a higher priority than drawing from the outside to enrich or enlarge it.

SUMMARY

The Gupta period is often called India's classical age, but in less than two centuries India reverted to its more typical pattern of regional states. Over the next several centuries Arab and Turkish armies brought Islam to India. Although Buddhism declined, Hinduism continued to flourish. In these developments lay the origins of the modern nations of India, Pakistan, and Bangladesh. Throughout the medieval period India continued to be the center of a very active seaborne trade, and this trade helped carry Indian ideas and practices to Southeast Asia. Local rulers used experts from India to establish strong states.

The nomadic pastoral societies of Central Asia differed in fundamental ways from the settled agricultural societies that lay to their south. Their mastery of the horse and mounted warfare gave them a military advantage that they repeatedly used to overawe or conquer their neighbors. This was carried to the farthest extreme by Chinggis Khan, who through his charismatic leadership and military genius was able to conquer an enormous empire in the early thirteenth century. For a century Mongol hegemony fostered unprecedented East-West trade and contact. More Europeans made their way east than ever before, and Chinese inventions such as printing and the compass made their way west. The Mongols did not try to change the cultures of the countries they conquered, but they still had an enormous impact on them.

KEY TERMS

protected people	nomads
jati	grasslands
sati	yurts
Funan	Great Khan
Sanskrit	khanates
Srivijaya	tax-farming

NOTES

1. Hermann Kulke and Dietmar Rothermund, *A History of India* (London: Routledge, 1990), pp. 86–87.
2. Quoted in A. L. Basham, *The Wonder That Was India,* 2d ed. (New York: Grove Press, 1959), p. 420.
3. Edward C. Sachau, *Alberuni's India,* vol. 1 (London: Kegan Paul, 1910), pp. 19–20, slightly modified.
4. H. A. R. Gibb, *The Travels of Ibn Battuta* (Cambridge: Cambridge University Press for the Hukluyt Society, 1971), pp. 700–701.
5. Guy le Strang, trans., *Clavijo, Embassy to Tamerlane, 1403–1406* (London: Routledge, 1928), pp. 265–266.
6. Quoted in Basham, *The Wonder That Was India,* p. 161.
7. G. Buhler, trans., *The Sacred Laws of the Aryas.* Part 2: *Vasishtha and Baudhayana* (Oxford: Clarendon Press, 1882), p. 31.
8. Quoted in Basham, *The Wonder That Was India,* pp. 459–460.
9. *The Travels of Marco Polo, the Venetian,* ed. Manuel Komroff (New York: Boni and Liveright, 1926), p. 265.
10. Ibid., p. 93.
11. Ibid., pp. 93–94.

SUGGESTED READING

For Indian history, see the general histories listed in the Suggested Reading for Chapter 3, to which should be added S. A. A. Rizvi, *The Wonder That Was India.* Vol. 2: *1200–1700* (1987). An extensive survey of the Islamic invasions of India is provided in J. F. Richards, "The Islamic Frontier in the East: Expansion into South Asia," *South Asia* 4 (1974):90–109, in which Richards makes the point that many Indian princes put up stiff resistance to the invaders. R. Eaton, *The Rise of Islam and the Bengal Frontier* (1993), offers a major reinterpretation of the spread of Islam. A good treatment of early Islam in India is K. A. Nizami, *Some Aspects of Religion and Politics in India During the Thirteenth Century* (reprint 1970). In *Islam in the Indian Subcontinent* (1980), A. Schimmel surveys many aspects of Islam, including architecture, life, art, and traditions. K. N. Chaudhuri, *Asia Before Europe* (1990), discusses the economy and civilization of cultures within the basin of the Indian Ocean. Two works concentrate on the sultanate of Delhi: M. Habib and K. A. Nizami, eds., *Comprehensive History of India.* Vol. 5: *Delhi Sultanate* (1970); and P. Hardy, "The Growth of Authority over a Conquered Political Elite: The Early Delhi Sultanate as a Possible Case Study," in J. F. Richards, ed., *Kingship and Authority in South Asia* (1998). The *Kamasutra* is now available in a modern translation by M. Vatsyayana and W. Doniger (2002).

General histories of Southeast Asia include D. G. E. Hall, *A History of South-East Asia* (1966); J. F. Cady, *Southeast Asia: Its Historical Development* (1964); and D. R. SarDesai, *Southeast Asia: Past and Present* (1989). More specifically on the early stages of Southeast Asian history are G. Coedes, *The Making of Southeast Asia* (1966); O. W. Wolters, *Early Indonesian Commerce: A Study of the Origins of Sri Vijaya* (1967); and L. Shaffer, *Maritime Southeast Asia to 1500* (1996). The connections between India and early Southeast Asia are treated in two books by H. G. Q. Wales: *The Indianization of China and of South-East Asia* (1967) and *The Making of Greater India,* 3d ed. (1974).

For the early history of Central Asia, see P. B. Golden, *An Introduction to the History of the Turkic Peoples* (1992), which covers the spread of the Turks through Central Asia and the Middle East. D. Simon, ed., *The Cambridge History of Early Inner Asia* (1990), is an ambitious collection that ranges in time from prehistory to the early thirteenth century and in space from the Near East to India and China. S. A. M. Adshead, *Central Asia in World History* (1993), places Central Asia in a larger historical context. A. Kessler, *Empires Beyond the Great Wall: The Heritage of Genghis Khan* (1993), is a well-illustrated volume on the steppe societies from the Xiongnu to the Mongols. T. Barfield, *The Perilous Frontier: Nomadic Empires and China* (1989), offers an explanation of the recurrent confederations of nomadic tribes near China in terms of the benefits they could derive when China had a strong state. The Khitan state is the subject of the large and fully documented study by K. Wittfogel and C. Feng, *History of Chinese Society: Liao (907–1125)* (1946). On the Jurchens, see J. Tao, *The Jurchen in Twelfth-Century China: A Study of Sinicization* (1976). On these states as well as the Mongols, see H. Franke and D. Twitchett, ed., *The Cambridge History of China,* vol. 6 (1994).

E. D. Phillips, *The Mongols* (1969), covers both their history and their way of life. For the founding of the Mongol Empire, see H. D. Martin, *The Rise of Chinghis Khan and His Conquest of North China* (1950), or P. Ratchnevsky, *Genghis Khan: His Life and Legacy* (1992). Overviews of the Mongol conquests include J. J. Saunders, *The History of the Mongol Conquests* (2001), and T. Allsen, *Culture and Conquest in Mongol Eurasia* (2001). P. Kahn, *The Secret History of the Mongols: The Origin of Chinghis Khan* (1984), is a readable version of and the best source for Mongol social practices and values. M. Rossabi provides a lively account of the life of one of the most important Yuan rulers in *Khubilai Khan: His Life and Times* (1988).

For Marco Polo, see L. Olschki, *Marco Polo's Asia* (1960); F. Wood, *Did Marco Polo Go to China?* (1995), which assembles the evidence against believing that Marco Polo saw everything he said he did; and J. Larner, *Marco Polo and the Discovery of the World* (1999), which takes the opposite stance. On Ibn Battuta, see R. E. Dunn, *The Adventures of Ibn Battuta, A Muslim Traveler of the 14th Century* (1986). On other East-West travelers during the period of Mongol domination, see I. de Rachewiltz, *Papal Envoys to the Great Khans* (1971). On the links between the Mongol conquest and the spread of bubonic plague, see W. McNeill, *Plagues and Peoples* (1976). Juivaini's Persian account of the Mongols has been translated by J. A. Boyle, *The History of the World Conquerer* (1958). J. L. Abu-Lughod, *Before European Hegemony: The World System A.D. 1250–1350* (1989), examines the period of Mongol domination from a global perspective.

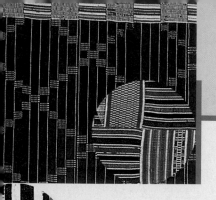

TO COMMEMORATE BUILDING A WELL

uch of what we know of medieval India comes from inscriptions carved in stone. Inscribed stones record the genealogies and victories of kings, the establishment of temples, and the construction of bridges, wells, and charitable works. The inscription translated in part below, written in Sanskrit, is dated 1276. It was found twelve miles southwest of modern Delhi.

Before commending the donor of the well, the author of this inscription praises the god Shiva and the rulers of the region. A list of earlier rulers comes next, followed by lengthy praise for the military accomplishments of the current sultan, and even for the charms of courtesans, who "proudly dressed in many coloured raiments moved about without fear, filling the air with the tinkle of their bracelets, produced by the wanton movements of their hands." Next comes praise for the sultan's capital city:

The metropolis of the lord of many hundreds of cities, the charming great city called Delhi, flourishes like a crescent-headed arrow on the side of his enemies. Like the earth, it is the storehouse of innumerable jewels; like the sky, a source of delight; like the nether regions, the abode of many Daityas; like Maya herself, the most bewitching.

In that city of Delhi, renowned under the name Yoganipura, there was a householder who was the wealthy abode of innumerable good qualities, devoid of blemishes, wise, noble-minded, given to meritorious acts, named Uddhara.

Where the clear Candrabhaga joined the beautiful Vitasta, the Vipasa and Satadru; opposite is situated the Indus (Sindhu), the good friend with its tributaries, without high waves. Honey is useless, sugar cane juice is useless, so is the nectar

in Heaven. If one drinks the nectar of the Indus, even his nectar of knowledge becomes insipid. In this northernly region, in which the earth is washed by the divine nectar of Sindhu, which removes all kinds of distress, there is Uccapuri, which laughs at the city of gods that is situated on the banks of the heavenly Ganga.

In that city lived his father Haripala, whose father was Yasoraja. His father was Dallahara, whose father was Kipu. This is his genealogy on the father's side. Uddhara's mother was Candi, the daughter of Prthu, whose father was Hasiscandra; his father was Utshahana, the son of Sahadeva, who was the son of Tola. Tola's father was Vyagharahara, who was the son of Singha and grandson of Gaura. In the work entitled *Vamsavali,* the two genealogies have been given in detail; here in this record, the names have been taken to the extent desired to recall them to memory.

He had three wives, embodiments, as it were, of will, wisdom, and energy. The eldest wife, Jajala, was accompanied by Rajasri and Katandevi. Her son was named Hariraja, pure in body, speech, and mind, renowned, the abode of the sixty-four arts, apparently like Vishnu, the sole protector of the universe. His two younger brothers, named Sthiraraja and Jaitra, shine forth along with a sister, Virada. The second wife also had at first a daughter, the liberal-minded Dhanavati. After her, Ratandevi had two sons, Gunaraja and Bhupati. There was also a son, Haradeva, known as Natha, and also another girl. She had also another son, Uttamaraja, and a daughter named Sadali. Thus, we have here the root, stem, branches, fruits, and flowers of this Wishing Tree.

Numerous and extensive free inns were established in different places by this performer of

The text, in the Nagari script of Sanskrit, was engraved on a slab of black stone 1 foot, 3 inches, by 3 feet, 11 inches. (From Pushpa Prasad, *Sanskrit Inscriptions of Delhi Sultanate, 1191–1526* [Delhi: Oxford University Press, 1990])

sacrifice. But here, this wise one, with a view to relieving the exhaustion of tired travelers, had a well excavated. To the east of the village Palamba and to the west of Kusumbhapura, he made a well which quenches thirst and removes fatigue.

May this well, like a lovely woman with rotund, heaving breasts, gorgeous with undulating necklaces, be the assuager of the thirst of many a lovesick swain and perfumed with the mass of petals from the flowery trees. This well, being very clear, laughs at the minds of good people taking it as turbid. Like the supreme knowledge of philosophers, it shines, causing restfulness to the self.

May this devout and noble Lord Uddhara, whose pleasure rests in the final salvation in Heaven, who is a devotee of Siva, accompanied by sons, wives, friends, and dependents, have the good fortune to enjoy all the worldly pleasures.

This praiseworthy eulogy has been composed by Pandit Yogisvara of eternal fame, to record the construction of this well of Uddhara, the sole receptacle of all blessings.

QUESTIONS FOR ANALYSIS

1. Why would an inscription for a well praise the ruler before the actual donor?

2. What can you infer about Uddhara's social status?

3. What sorts of imagery does the author use? Why compare a well to a woman?

Source: Adapted from Pushpa Prasad, ed., *Sanskrit Inscriptions of Delhi Sultanate, 1191–1526*, pp. 12–15. Copyright © 1990. Reproduced by permission of Oxford University Press India, New Delhi.

The scholar depicted in this small painting (a little under a foot square) appreciates books, paintings, music, and warmed wine. He is seated in front of a freestanding painted screen on which is hung a portrait of himself. His servant boy pours wine for him as he looks up from his book. Other books and scrolls are laid on a nearby table, along with the lute scholars had been playing since the time of Confucius. *(National Palace Museum, Taipei, Taiwan, Republic of China)*

CHAPTER

12

EAST ASIA, CA 800–1400

CHAPTER OUTLINE

- China (800–ca 1400)

- Korea (780–1392)

- Japan in the Heian and Kamakura Eras (794–1333)

During the six centuries between 800 and 1400, East Asia was the most advanced region of the world. At least that is what the Venetian Marco Polo thought when he got there in the late thirteenth century after traveling through much of Asia. For several centuries the Chinese economy had grown spectacularly, and in fields as diverse as rice cultivation, the production of iron and steel, and the printing of books, China's methods of production were highly advanced. Its system of government was also advanced for its time. In the Song period the principle that the government should be in the hands of highly educated scholar-officials, selected through the competitive written civil service examinations, became well established.

During the previous millennium basic elements of Chinese culture had spread beyond China's borders, creating a large cultural sphere centered on the use of Chinese as the language of civilization. Beginning around 800, however, in East Asia the pendulum shifted toward cultural differentiation, as Japan and Korea developed in distinctive ways. This process is particularly evident in Japan, which by 1200 had developed into a feudal society dominated by samurai quite unlike China's literati elite. Yet none of these countries was ever cut off from the others. China and Korea both had to deal with the same menacing neighbors to the north, the Khitans, the Jurchens, and finally the Mongols. Even Japan had to mobilize its resources to fend off two Mongol attacks.

- What allowed China to take the lead economically and intellectually in this period?
- How did the competition between civilian control and military control fare in each of these countries?
- In what ways did changes beyond their borders shape the developments in these countries?
- How could China, Korea, and Japan have all drawn on both Confucian and Buddhist teachings and yet ended up with elites as distinct as the Chinese scholar-official, the Korean aristocrat, and the Japanese samurai?

This chapter will explore these questions.

CHINA (800–CA 1400)

Chinese historians traditionally viewed dynasties as following a typical cycle. Founders were vigorous men able to recruit able followers to serve as officials and generals. Externally they would extend China's borders; internally they would bring peace. They would collect low but fairly assessed taxes. Over time, however, emperors born in the palace would be used to luxury and lack the founder's strength and wisdom. Entrenched interests would find ways to avoid taxes, forcing the government to impose heavier taxes on the poor. Impoverished peasants would flee, the morale of those in the government and armies would decline, and the dynasty would find itself able neither to maintain internal peace nor to defend its borders.

Viewed in terms of this theory of the dynastic cycle, by 800 the Tang Dynasty was in decline. It had ruled China for nearly two centuries, but its high point was in the past. A massive rebellion had wracked it in the mid-eighth century, and the Uighur Turks and Tibetans were menacing its borders. Many of the centralizing features of the government had been abandoned, with power falling more and more to regional military governors.

Chinese political theorists always made the assumption that a strong, centralized government was better than a weak one or political division, but if anything the late Tang period seems to have been both intellectually and economically more vibrant than the early Tang. Less control from the central government seems to have stimulated trade and economic growth. And among educated men, analyzing the problems the country faced was one of the first stages in a major revitalization of Confucianism. For several centuries Buddhism seemed more vital than Confucianism. Beginning in the late Tang period Confucian teachers began claiming that the teachings of the Confucian sages contained all the wisdom one needed and a true Confucian would reject Buddhist teachings.

Nevertheless, the increasing power of non-Chinese peoples in the north did pose long-term problems for the Chinese. When in the tenth century China broke up into separate contending states, several in the north had non-Chinese rulers. Two of these states eventually proved to be long-lasting: the Song, which came to control almost all of China proper south of the Great Wall, and the Liao, whose ruling house was Khitan and who held the territory of modern Beijing and areas north (see Map 12.1). Although the Song Dynasty had a much larger population, the Liao was militarily the stronger of the two.

The Song Dynasty (960–1279)

The founder of the Song Dynasty, Taizu (r. 960–976), was a general whose troops elevated him to emperor when the previous ruler was succeeded by a young child. Taizu worked to make sure that such an act could not happen in the future by placing the armies under central government control. He retired or rotated his own generals and assigned civil officials to supervise them. In time civil bureaucrats came to dominate every aspect of Song government and society. The civil service examination system was greatly expanded to provide the dynasty with a constant flow of men trained in the Confucian classics.

Curbing the generals ended warlordism but did not solve the military problem of defending against the Khitans to the north. After several attempts to push them back beyond the Great Wall, the Song concluded a peace treaty with them. The Song agreed to make huge annual payments of gold and silk to the Khitans, in a sense paying them not to invade. Even so, the Song rulers had to maintain a standing army of more than a million men. By the middle of the eleventh century military expenses consumed half the government's revenues. China produced swords, armor, and arrowheads in huge quantities but had difficulty maintaining enough horses and well-trained horsemen. Even though China was the economic powerhouse of the region, with by far the largest population, in this period when the horse was a major weapon of war, it was not easy to convert wealth to military advantage.

In the early twelfth century the military situation rapidly worsened when the Khitan state was destroyed by another tribal confederation, led by the Jurchens. Although the Song allied with the Jurchens, the Jurchens quickly realized how easy it would be to defeat the Song. When they marched into the Song capital in 1126, they captured the emperor and took him and his entire court hostage. Song forces rallied around a prince, who reestablished a Song court in the south at Hangzhou (see Map 12.2). This Southern Song Dynasty controlled only about two-thirds of the former Song territories, but the social, cultural, and intellectual life there remained vibrant until the Song fell to the Mongols in 1279.

The Scholar-Officials and Neo-Confucianism

The Song period saw the full flowering of one of the most distinctive features of Chinese civilization, the scholar-official class certified through highly competitive civil service examinations. This elite was both broader and better

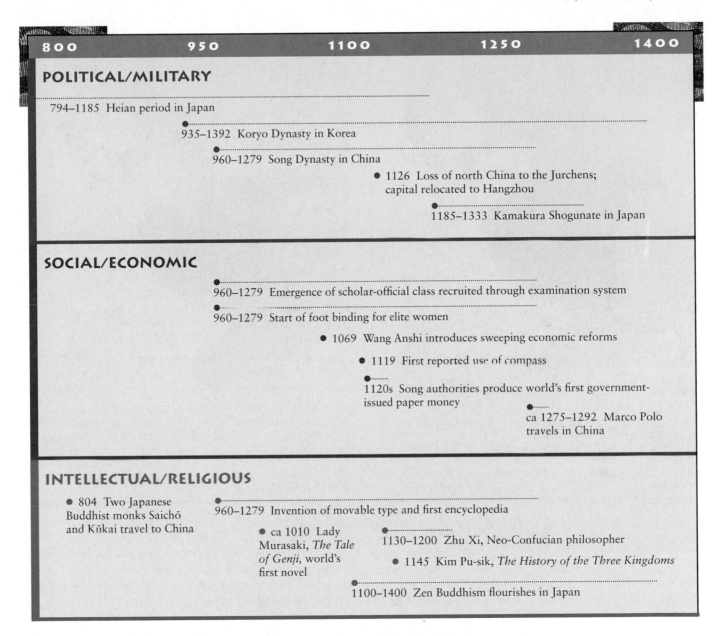

800	950	1100	1250	1400

POLITICAL/MILITARY

794–1185 Heian period in Japan

935–1392 Koryo Dynasty in Korea

960–1279 Song Dynasty in China

1126 Loss of north China to the Jurchens; capital relocated to Hangzhou

1185–1333 Kamakura Shogunate in Japan

SOCIAL/ECONOMIC

960–1279 Emergence of scholar-official class recruited through examination system

960–1279 Start of foot binding for elite women

1069 Wang Anshi introduces sweeping economic reforms

1119 First reported use of compass

1120s Song authorities produce world's first government-issued paper money

ca 1275–1292 Marco Polo travels in China

INTELLECTUAL/RELIGIOUS

804 Two Japanese Buddhist monks Saichō and Kūkai travel to China

960–1279 Invention of movable type and first encyclopedia

ca 1010 Lady Murasaki, *The Tale of Genji*, world's first novel

1130–1200 Zhu Xi, Neo-Confucian philosopher

1145 Kim Pu-sik, *The History of the Three Kingdoms*

1100–1400 Zen Buddhism flourishes in Japan

educated than the elites of earlier periods in Chinese history. Once the **examination system** was fully developed, aristocratic habits and prejudices largely disappeared.

The invention of printing should be given some credit for this development. Tang craftsmen developed the art of carving words and pictures into wooden blocks, inking them, and then pressing paper onto the blocks. Each block consisted of an entire page of text and illustrations. Such whole-page blocks were used for printing as early as the middle of the ninth century, and in the eleventh century **movable type** (one piece of type for each character) was in-

vented. Movable type was never widely used in China because whole-block printing was more efficient, but when movable type reached Europe in the fifteenth century, it revolutionized the communication of ideas. In China as in Europe, the introduction of printing dramatically lowered the price of books, thus aiding the spread of literacy.

Among the upper class the availability of cheaper books enabled scholars to amass their own libraries. Song publishers printed the classics of Chinese literature in huge editions to satisfy scholarly appetites. Works on philosophy, science, and medicine also were avidly consumed, as

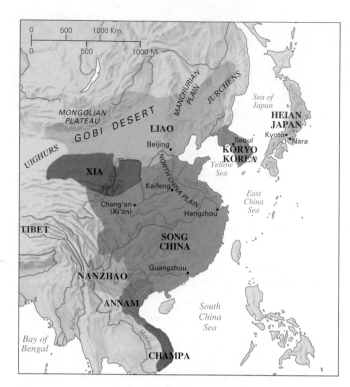

MAP 12.1 East Asia in 1000 The Song Empire did not extend as far as its predecessor, the Tang, and faced powerful rivals to the north—the Liao Dynasty of the Khitans and the Xia Dynasty of the Tanguts. Korea under the Koryo Dynasty maintained regular contact with Song China, but Japan, by the late Heian period, was no longer deeply involved with the mainland.

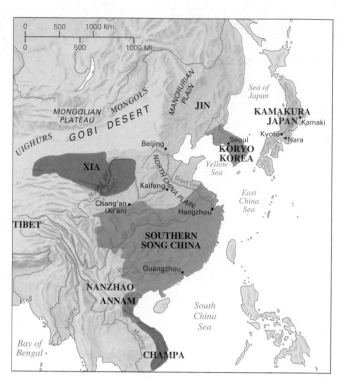

MAP 12.2 East Asia in 1200 By 1200 military families dominated both Korea and Japan, but their borders were little changed. On the mainland, the Liao Dynasty had been overthrown by the Jurchens' Jin Dynasty, which also seized the northern third of the Song Empire. Because the Song relocated its capital to Hangzhou in the south, this period is called the Southern Song period.

were Buddhist texts. Han and Tang poetry and historical works became the models for Song writers. One popular literary innovation was the encyclopedia, which first appeared in the Song period, at least five centuries before publication of a European encyclopedia.

Not only did the examination system annually recruit four to five times the number of scholars it had in Tang times, but it also came to carry such prestige that the number of scholars entering each competition escalated rapidly, from fewer than 30,000 early in the eleventh century, to nearly 80,000 by the end of that century, to about 400,000 by the dynasty's end. To prepare for the examinations, men had to memorize the classics in order to be able to recognize even the most obscure passages. They also had to master specific forms of composition, including poetic genres. Candidates were usually asked to discuss policy issues, but the examinations tested general education more than knowledge of government laws and regulations. Those who became officials this way had

usually tried the exams several times and were on average a little over thirty years of age when they succeeded. The great majority of those who devoted years to preparing for the exams, however, never became officials.

The life of the educated man involved more than study for the civil service examinations. Many took to refined pursuits such as collecting antiques or old books and practicing the arts—especially poetry writing, calligraphy, and painting. For many individuals these interests overshadowed any philosophical, political, or economic concerns; others found in them occasional outlets for creative activity and aesthetic pleasure. In the Song period the engagement of the elite with the arts led to extraordinary achievement in calligraphy and painting, especially landscape painting. But even more people were involved as connoisseurs. A large share of the informal social life of upper-class men was centered on these refined pastimes, as they gathered to compose or criticize poetry, to view each other's treasures, and to patronize young talents.

This new scholar-official elite produced some extraordinary men, able to hold high court offices while pursuing diverse intellectual interests. Ouyang Xiu spared time in his busy official career to write love songs, histories viewed as models of prose style, and the first analytical catalogue of rubbings of ancient stone and bronze inscriptions. Sima Guang, besides serving as prime minister, wrote a narrative history of China from the Warring States Period (403–221 B.C.E.) to the founding of the Song Dynasty. Su Shi wrote more than twenty-seven hundred poems and eight hundred letters while active in opposition politics. He was also an esteemed painter and calligrapher and theorist of the arts. Su Song, another high official, constructed an eighty-foot-tall mechanical clock. He adapted the water-powered clock invented in the Tang period by adding a chain-driven mechanism. The clock told not only the time of day but also the day of the month, the phase of the moon, and the position of certain stars and planets in the sky. At the top was a mechanically rotated armillary sphere. (See also the feature "Individuals in Society: Shen Gua.")

These highly educated men accepted the Confucian responsibility to aid the ruler in the governing of the country. In this period, however, this commitment tended to embroil them in unpleasant factional politics. The main dispute originated in the need to raise revenues to support the army. In 1069 the young Song emperor Shenzong (r. 1067–1085) appointed Wang Anshi as his chief counselor. Wang proposed a series of sweeping reforms. Realizing that government income was ultimately linked to the prosperity of the individual peasant taxpayer, he instituted measures he thought would help them, such as low-cost loans and replacing labor service with a tax. To raise revenues, he also expanded state monopolies on tea, salt, and wine. Many well-respected scholars and officials, led by the statesman-historian Sima Guang, thought that Wang's policies would do more harm than good and resisted enforcing them. Wang, with the emperor's support, responded by transferring them out of the capital, in effect banishing them. When the emperor died, his mother took over as regent for his son and brought back the opponents, who were quick to retaliate against the reformers. When she died, the young emperor reversed her decisions, and there was another round of demotions and banishments.

Politics was not the only issue scholars in this period debated. During the eleventh century many Confucian teachers gathered around them students preparing to take the civil service examinations. The most inspiring of these teachers urged their disciples to set their sights on the higher goals of attaining the wisdom of the sages.

Landscape Painting Centuries before Western artists began to see natural scenery as anything more than background, Chinese artists had made landscape painting into a great art. Mountains had long been sacred places, and artists of the tenth and eleventh centuries developed ways to convey their majesty and associations with immortality. In this painting by Fan Kuan (active ca 990–1020), a towering central peak dwarfs the mule train in the foreground. Like many other Chinese paintings, this one was done with ink on silk, using very little color. The scroll could be hung on a wall or rolled up for storage. *(National Palace Museum, Taipei, Taiwan, Republic of China)*

Chinese Paper Money   Chinese paper currency indicated the unit of currency and the date and place of issue. The Mongols continued the use of paper money, and this note dates from the Mongol period. (© *Cultural Relics Data Center of China*)

The Medieval Chinese Economic Revolution (800–1100)

In 742 China's population was still approximately 50 million, very close to what it had been in 2 C.E. Over the next three centuries, with the expansion of rice cultivation in central and south China, the country's food supply steadily increased, and so did its population, which reached 100 million by 1100. China was certainly the largest country in the world at the time; its population probably exceeded that of all of Europe (as it has ever since).

Agricultural prosperity and denser settlement patterns aided commercialization of the economy. Peasants in Song China did not aim at self-sufficiency. They had found that producing for the market made possible a better life. Peasants in more densely populated regions with numerous markets sold their surpluses and bought charcoal, tea, oil, and wine. In many places, farmers specialized in commercial crops, such as sugar, oranges, cotton, silk, and tea. (See the feature "Global Trade: Tea" on pages 344–345.) The need to transport the products of interregional trade stimulated the inland and coastal shipping industries, providing employment for shipbuilders and sailors and business opportunities for enterprising families with enough capital to purchase a boat. Marco Polo, the Venetian merchant who wrote of his visit to China in the late thirteenth century, was astounded at the boat traffic on the Yangzi River. He claimed to have seen no less than fifteen thousand vessels at one city on the river, "and yet there are other towns where the number is still greater."[1]

As marketing increased, demand for money grew enormously, leading eventually to the creation of the world's first **paper money.** The late Tang government had abandoned the use of bolts of silk as supplementary currency, which increased the demand for copper coins. By 1085 the output of coins had increased tenfold to more than 6 billion coins a year. To avoid the weight and bulk of coins for large transactions, local merchants in late Tang times started trading receipts from deposit shops where they had left money or goods. The early Song authorities awarded a small set of shops a monopoly on the issuing of these certificates of deposit, and in the 1120s the government took over the system, producing the world's first government-issued paper money. Marco Polo wrote one of the earliest descriptions of how Chinese paper money was issued:

The coinage of this paper money is authenticated with as much form and ceremony as if it were actually of pure gold or silver; for to each note a number of officers, specially

Metaphysical theories about the workings of the cosmos in terms of *li* (principle) and *qi* (vital energy) were developed in response to the challenge of the sophisticated metaphysics of Buddhism.

Neo-Confucianism, as this movement is generally termed, was more fully developed in the twelfth century by the immensely learned Zhu Xi. Besides serving in office, he wrote, compiled, or edited almost a hundred books, corresponded with dozens of other scholars, and still regularly taught groups of disciples, many of whom stayed with him for years at a time. Although he was treated as a political threat during his lifetime, within decades of his death his writings came to be considered orthodox, and in subsequent centuries candidates for the examinations had to be familiar with his commentaries on the classics.

INDIVIDUALS IN SOCIETY

SHEN GUA

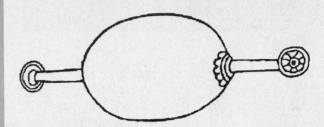

Among the advances of the Song period was the development of gunpowder. An eleventh-century manual on military technology illustrated this "thunderbolt ball," filled with gunpowder and iron scraps and hurled at the enemy with a catapult.
(Zeng Gongliang and Ding Du, Wujing zongyao [Zhongguo bingshu jicheng, 1988 ed.], 12:59 [p. 640])

In the eleventh century it was not rare for Chinese men of letters to have broad interests, but few could compare to Shen Gua (1031–1095), a man who tried his hand at everything from mathematics, geography, economics, engineering, medicine, divination, and archaeology to military strategy and diplomacy.

In his youth Shen Gua traveled widely with his father, who served as a provincial official. His own career as an official, which started when he was only twenty, also took him to many places, adding to his knowledge of geography. He received a post in the capital in 1066, just before Wang Anshi's rise to power, and he generally sided with Wang in the political disputes of the day. He eventually held high astronomical, ritual, and financial posts, but he also became involved in waterworks and the construction of defense walls. He was sent as an envoy to the Khitans in 1075 to try to settle a boundary dispute. When a military campaign that he advised failed in 1082, he was demoted and later retired to write.

It is from his book of notes that we know the breadth of his interests. In one note Shen describes how, on assignment to inspect the frontier, he made a relief map of wood and glue-soaked sawdust to show the mountains, roads, rivers, and passes. The emperor was so impressed when he saw it that he ordered all the border prefectures to make relief maps. Elsewhere Shen describes the use of petroleum and explains how to make movable type from clay. Shen Gua often applied a mathematical approach to issues that his contemporaries did not think of in those terms. He once computed the total number of possible situations on a go board, and another time he calculated the longest possible military campaign given the limits of human carriers who had to carry their own food as well as food for the soldiers.

Shen Gua is especially known for what might be called scientific explanations. In one place, he explains the deflection of the compass from due south. In another note he identifies petrified bamboo and from its existence argues that the region where it was found must have been much warmer and more humid in ancient times. He argued against the theory that tides are caused by the rising and setting of the sun, demonstrating that they correlate rather with the cycles of the moon. He proposed switching from a lunar calendar to a solar one of 365 days, saying that even though his contemporaries would reject his idea,

"surely in the future some will use my theory." To convince his readers that the sun and the moon were spherical, not flat, he suggested that they cover a ball with fine powder on one side and then look at it obliquely. The powder was the part of the moon illuminated by the sun, and as one looks at it obliquely, the white part would be crescent shaped, like a waxing moon. He did not, however, realize that the sun and moon had entirely different orbits and explained why they did not collide by positing that they were both composed of *qi* (vital energy) and had form but not substance.

Shen Gua also wrote on medicine and criticized his contemporaries for paying more attention to old treatises than to clinical experience. Yet he also was sometimes stronger on theory than on observation. In one note he argues that longevity pills could be made from cinnabar. He reasoned that if cinnabar could be transformed in one direction, it ought to be susceptible to transformation in the opposite direction as well. Therefore, since melted cinnabar causes death, solid cinnabar should prevent death.

QUESTIONS FOR ANALYSIS

1. Do you think Shen Gua's wide travels added to his curiosity about the material world?
2. In what ways could Shen Gua have used his scientific interests in his work as an official?
3. How does Shen Gua's understanding of the natural world compare to that of the early Greeks?

GLOBAL TRADE

TEA

Tea is made from the young leaves and leaf buds of *Camellia sinensis,* a plant native to the hills of southwest China. As an item of trade, tea has a very long history. Already by Han times (206 B.C.E.–220 C.E.), tea was being grown and drunk in southwest China, and for several centuries thereafter it was looked on as a local product of the region with useful pharmacologic properties, such as countering the effects of wine. By Tang times (608–907) it was being widely cultivated in the Yangzi River valley and was a major item of interregional trade. Tea was common enough in Tang life that poets often mentioned it in their poems. In the eighth century Lu Yu wrote an entire treatise on the wonders of tea.

During the Tang Dynasty tea was a major commercial crop, especially in the southeast. The most intensive time for tea production was the harvest season, since young leaves were of much more value than mature ones. Women, mobilized for about a month each year, would come out to help pick the tea. Not only were tea merchants among the wealthiest merchants, but from the late eighth century on, taxes on tea became a major item of government revenue.

Tea circulated in several forms, loose and compressed (brick), powder and leaf. The cost of tea varied both by

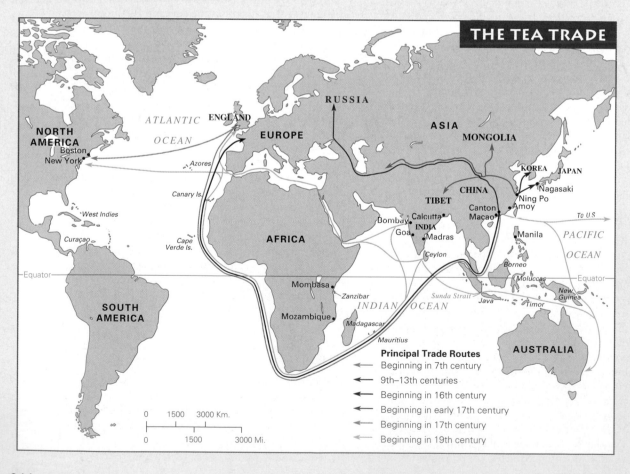

THE TEA TRADE

Principal Trade Routes

← Beginning in 7th century
← 9th–13th centuries
← Beginning in 16th century
← Beginning in early 17th century
← Beginning in 17th century
← Beginning in 19th century

Tea-leaf jar, fourteenth century, south China. This 42-centimeter-tall jar was imported to Japan, where it was treasured as an art object and used by tea masters. In the sixteenth century it came into the possession of the first Tokugawa shogun, Ieyasu.
(The Tokugawa Reimeikai Foundation)

form and by region of origin. In Song times (960–1279), the cheapest tea could cost as little as 18 cash per catty, the most expensive 275. In Kaifeng in the 1070s the most popular type of tea was loose tea powdered at water mills. The tea exported from Sichuan to Tibet, however, was formed into solid bricks.

The Song Dynasty established a government monopoly on tea. Only those who purchased government licenses could legally trade in tea. The dynasty also used its control of tea to ensure a supply of horses, needed for military purposes. The government could do this because the countries on its borders that produced the best horses—Tibet, Central Asia, Mongolia, and so on—were not suitable for cultivating tea. Thus the Song government insisted on horses for tea.

Tea reached Korea and Japan as a part of Buddhist culture. Buddhist monks drank it to help them stay awake during long hours of recitation or meditation. The priest Saichō, patriarch of Tendai Buddhism, visited China in 804–805 and reportedly brought back tea seeds. Tea drinking did not become widespread in Japan, however, until the twelfth century, when Zen monasteries popularized its use. By the fourteenth century tea imported from China was still prized, but the Japanese had already begun to appreciate the distinctive flavors of teas from different regions of Japan.

With the development of the tea ceremony, tea drinking became an art in Japan, with much attention to the selection and handling of tea utensils. In both Japan and Korea, offerings of tea became a regular part of offerings to ancestors.

Tea did not become important in Europe until the seventeenth century. Tea first reached Russia in 1618, when a Chinese embassy presented some to the tsar. Under agreements between the Chinese and Russian governments, camel trains would arrive in China laden with furs and return carrying tea, taking about a year for the return trip. By 1700 Russia was receiving more than 600 camel loads of tea annually. By 1800 it was receiving more than 6,000 loads, amounting to more than 3.5 million pounds. Tea reached western Europe in the sixteenth century, both via Arabs and via Jesuit priests traveling on Portuguese ships.

In Britain, where tea drinking would become a national institution, tea was first drunk in coffeehouses. Samuel Pepys recorded in his famous diary having his first cup of tea in 1660. By the end of the seventeenth century tea made up more than 90 percent of China's exports to England. In the eighteenth century, tea drinking spread to homes and tea gardens. Queen Anne (r. 1702–1714) was credited with starting the custom of drinking tea instead of ale for breakfast. In the nineteenth century afternoon tea became a central feature of British social life.

Already by the end of the eighteenth century Britain imported so much tea from China that it worried about the outflow of silver to pay for it. Efforts to balance trade with China involved promoting the sale of Indian opium to China and efforts to grow tea in British colonies. Using tea seeds collected in China and a tea plant indigenous to India's Assam province, tea was eventually grown successfully in both India and Sri Lanka. By the end of the nineteenth century huge tea plantations had been established in India, and India surpassed China as an exporter of tea.

The spread of the popularity of drinking tea also stimulated the desire for fine cups to drink it from. Importation of Chinese ceramics, therefore, often accompanied adoption of its tea customs.

appointed, not only subscribe their names, but affix their signets also; and when this has been regularly done by the whole of them, the principal officer . . . having dipped into vermilion the royal seal committed to his custody, stamps with it the piece of paper, so that the form of the seal tinged with the vermilion remains impressed upon it.[2]

To this day U.S. paper money carries the signatures of federal officials, the seals of the Federal Reserve Bank, and the Great Seal of the United States; only the vermilion is absent.

With the intensification of trade, merchants became progressively more specialized and organized. They set up partnerships and joint stock companies, with a separation of owners (shareholders) and managers. In the large cities merchants were organized into guilds according to the type of product sold, and they arranged sales from wholesalers to shopowners and periodically set prices. When the government wanted to requisition supplies or assess taxes, they dealt with the guild heads.

Foreign trade also flourished in the Song period. The government sent missions to Southeast Asian countries to encourage their traders to come to China. Chinese merchants sailing Chinese ships began to displace Indian and Arab merchants in the South Seas. Ship design was improved in several ways. Watertight bulkheads improved buoyancy and protected cargo. Stern-mounted rudders improved steering. Some of these ships were powered by both oars and sails and large enough to hold several hundred men.

Also important to oceangoing travel was the perfection of the **compass.** The way a magnetic needle would point north had been known for some time, but in Song times it was reduced in size and attached to a fixed stem (rather than floating in water). In some cases it was put in a small protective case with a glass top, making it suitable for sea travel. The first reports of a compass used in this way date to 1119.

The Song also witnessed many advances in industrial techniques. Traditional industries such as silk, lacquer, porcelain, and paper reached very high levels of technical perfection. Papermaking flourished with the demand for paper for books, documents, money, and wrapping paper. Heavy industry, especially iron, also grew astoundingly.

City Life In Song times many cities in China grew to 50,000 or more people, and the capital, Kaifeng, reached over a million. The bustle of a commercial city is shown here in a detail from a seventeen-foot-long handscroll painted in the twelfth century. This scene shows draymen and porters, peddlers and shopkeepers, monks and scholars, a storyteller, a fortuneteller, a scribe, a woman in a sedan chair. *(The Palace Museum, Beijing)*

With advances in metallurgy, iron production reached around 125,000 tons per year in 1078, a sixfold increase over the output in 800. At first charcoal was used in the production process, leading to deforestation of parts of north China. By the end of the eleventh century, however, bituminous coke had largely taken the place of charcoal. Much of this iron was put to military purposes. Mass-production methods were used to make iron armor in small, medium, and large sizes. High-quality steel for swords was made through high-temperature metallurgy. Huge bellows, often driven by water wheels, were used to superheat the molten ore. The needs of the army also brought Chinese engineers to experiment with the use of gunpowder. In the wars against the Jurchens, those defending a besieged city used gunpowder to propel projectiles at the enemy.

The quickening of the economy fueled the growth of cities. Dozens of cities had 50,000 or more residents, and quite a few had more than 100,000. Both the capitals are estimated to have had in the vicinity of a million residents. Marco Polo described Hangzhou as the finest and most splendid city in the world. He reported that it had ten marketplaces, each half a mile long, where forty thousand to fifty thousand people would go to shop on any given day. There were also bathhouses; permanent shops selling things such as spices, drugs, and pearls; and innumerable courtesans—"adorned in much finery, highly perfumed, occupying well-furnished houses, and attended by many female domestics"—who were able to intoxicate the visitor with their "wanton arts."[3]

The medieval economic revolution shifted the economic center of China south to the Yangzi River drainage area. This area had many advantages over the north China plain. Rice, which grew in the south, provides more calories per unit of land, and therefore allows denser settlements. The milder temperatures often allowed two crops to be grown on the same plot of land, a summer and a winter crop. The abundance of rivers and streams facilitated shipping, which reduced the cost of transportation and thus made regional specialization economically more feasible. In the first half of the Song Dynasty, the capital was still in the north, but on the Grand Canal, which linked it to the rich south.

The economic revolution of Song times cannot be attributed to intellectual change, as Confucian scholars did not reinterpret the classics to defend the morality of commerce. But neither did scholar-officials take a unified stand against economic development. As officials they had to work to produce revenue to cover government expenses such as defense, and this was much easier to do when commerce was thriving.

Transplanting Rice   To get the maximum yield per plot and to make it possible to grow two crops in the same field, Chinese farmers grew rice seedlings in a seed bed and then, when a field was free, transplanted the seedlings into the flooded field. Because the Song government wanted to promote up-to-date agricultural technology, in the twelfth century it commissioned a set of twelve illustrations of the steps to be followed. This painting comes from a later version of those illustrations. *(Courtesy of the Freer Gallery of Art, Smithsonian Institution, Washington, D.C. [54.21])*

Ordinary people benefited from the Song economic revolution in many ways. There were more opportunities for the sons of farmers to leave agriculture and find work in cities. Those who stayed in agriculture had a better chance to improve their situations by taking up sideline production of wine, charcoal, paper, or textiles. Energetic farmers who grew cash crops such as sugar, tea, mulberry leaves (for silk), and cotton (recently introduced from India) could grow rich. Greater interregional trade led to the availability of more goods at the rural markets held every five to ten days.

Of course not everyone grew rich. Poor farmers who fell into debt had to sell their land, and if they still owed money, they could be forced to sell their daughters as maids, concubines, or prostitutes. The prosperity of the cities created a huge demand for women to serve the rich in these ways, and Song sources mention that criminals would kidnap girls and women to sell in distant cities at huge profits.

推輪生大軴	輕
軸何太勤末	帛
坯擊兼絲綺	益

Draw Loom Weaving was women's work, even when it required large and complex draw looms, needed to make multicolor brocades. This illustration of a woman at a draw loom, with a child perched above to handle the different yarns, is from a set of pictures of the stages in textile production issued by the Song government to encourage the use of up-to-date techniques. *(Courtesy of the Freer Gallery of Art, Smithsonian Institution, Washington, D.C. [54.20])*

Women's Lives

With the spread of printing, more books and more types of books survive from the Song period than from earlier periods, letting us catch more glimpses of women's lives. Song stories, documents, and legal cases show us widows who ran inns, maids sent out by their mistresses to do errands, midwives who delivered babies, pious women who spent their days chanting sutras, nuns who called on such women to explain Buddhist doctrine, girls who learned to read with their brothers, farmers' daughters who made money by weaving mats, childless widows who accused their nephews of depriving them of their property, wives who were jealous of the concubines their husbands brought home, and women with large dowries who used part of them to help their husbands' sisters marry well.

Families who could afford it tried to keep their wives and daughters at home, where there was plenty for them to do. Not only was there the work of tending children and preparing meals, but spinning, weaving, and sewing also were considered women's work and took a great deal of time. Families that raised silkworms also needed women to do much of the work of coddling the worms and getting them to spin their cocoons. Within the home women generally had considerable say and took an active interest in issues such as the selection of marriage partners for their children.

Women tended to marry between the ages of sixteen and twenty. The husbands were, on average, a couple of years older than they were. The marriage would have been arranged by their parents, who would have either called on a professional matchmaker (usually an older woman) or turned to a friend or relative for suggestions. Before the wedding took place, written agreements would be exchanged, which would list the prospective bride's and groom's birth dates, parents, and grandparents; the gifts that would be exchanged; and the dowry the bride would bring. The idea was to match families of approximately equal status, but a young man who had just passed the civil service exams would be considered a good prospect even if his family had little wealth or rank.

A few days before the wedding the bride's family would send to the groom's family her dowry, which at a minimum would contain boxes full of clothes and bedding but in better-off families also would include items of substantial value, such as gold jewelry or deeds to land. On the day of the wedding the groom and some of his friends and relatives would go to the bride's home to get her. She would be elaborately dressed and would tearfully bid farewell to everyone in her family. She would be carried to her new home in a fancy sedan chair to the sound of music, alerting everyone on the street that a wedding was taking place. Meanwhile the groom's family's friends and relatives would have gathered at his home, and when the bridal party arrived, they would be there to greet them. The bride would have to kneel and bow to her new parents-in-law and later also to the tablets representing the family's ancestors. Other ceremonies symbolized her new tie to her husband, whom she was meeting for the first time. A classical ritual still practiced was for the new couple to drink wine from the same cup. A ritual that had become popular in Song times was to attach a string to both of them, literally tying them together. Later they would be shown to their new bedroom, where the bride's dowry had already been placed, and people would toss beans or rice on the bed, symbolizing the desired fertility. After teasing them, the guests would finally leave them alone and go out to the courtyard for a wedding feast.

The young bride's first priority was to try to win over her mother-in-law, since everyone knew that mothers-in-law were hard to please. One way to do this was to quickly bear a son for the family. Within the patrilineal system, a woman fully secured her position in the family by becoming the mother of one of the men. Every community had older women skilled in midwifery who could be called to help when she went into labor. If the family was well-to-do, they might also arrange for a wet nurse to help her take care of the newborn, though some Song scholars disapproved of depriving another child for the sake of one's own child.

Women frequently had four, five, or six children, but likely one or more would die in infancy or early childhood. If a son reached adulthood and married before the woman herself was widowed, she would be considered fortunate, for she would have always had an adult man who could take care of business for her—first her husband, then her grown son. But in the days when infectious diseases took many people in their twenties and thirties, it was not uncommon for a woman to be widowed while in her twenties, when her children were still very young. If her husband had brothers and they had not yet divided their households, she would simply stay with them, assuming they were not so poor that they could not afford a few more mouths to feed. Otherwise, she could try to return to her natal family, to her brothers if her parents were no longer living. Taking another husband was also a possibility, though it was considered an inferior alternative from a moral point of view.

A woman with a healthy and prosperous husband faced another challenge in middle age: her husband could bring home a **concubine** (more than one if he could afford it). Moralists insisted that it was wrong for a wife to be jealous of her husband's concubines, but many could not get used to their husbands paying so much attention to another woman. Wives outranked concubines and could give them orders in the house, but a concubine had her own ways of getting back, especially if she was twenty and the wife was forty and no longer very attractive. The children born to a concubine were considered just as much children of the family as the wife's children, and if the wife had had only daughters and the concubine had a son, the wife would find herself in her old age dependent on the concubine's son.

As a woman's children grew up, she would start thinking of suitable marriage partners. Many women liked the idea of bringing another woman from their natal family—perhaps a brother's daughter—to be a daughter-in-law. But there were those who thought such marriages just resulted in relatives falling out with each other.

Women whose sons and daughters were all married could take it easy. They had daughters-in-law to do the cooking and cleaning. They could enjoy their grandchildren and help with their education. Many found more time for religious devotions at this stage of their lives. Their sons, still living with them, were often devoted to them and did their best to make their late years comfortable.

Neo-Confucianism is sometimes blamed for a decline in the status of women in Song times, largely because one of the best known of the Neo-Confucian teachers, Cheng Yi, once told a follower that it would be better for a widow to die of starvation than to lose her virtue by remarrying. In later centuries this saying was often quoted to justify pressuring widows, even very young ones, to stay with their husbands' families and not remarry. In Song times, however, widows frequently remarried.

It is true that **foot binding** began during the Song Dynasty, but it was not recommended by Neo-Confucian teachers; rather it was associated with the pleasure quarters and with women's efforts to beautify themselves. Mothers bound the feet of girls aged five to eight with long strips of cloth to keep them from growing and to bend the four smaller toes under to make the foot narrow and arched. The hope was that the girl would be judged more beautiful. Foot binding spread gradually during Song times but was probably still largely an elite practice. In later centuries it became extremely common in north and central China, eventually spreading to all classes. Women with bound feet were less mobile than women with natural feet, but only those who could afford servants bound their feet so tightly that walking was difficult.

KOREA (780–1392)

As discussed in Chapter 7, during the Silla period Korea was strongly tied to Tang China and avidly copied China's model. This changed along with so much else in North Asia during the centuries between 800 and 1400. In this period Korea lived more in the shadows of the powerful nomad states of the Khitans, Jurchens, and Mongols than of the Chinese.

The Silla Dynasty began to decline after the king was killed in a revolt in 780. For the next 155 years the kings were selected from several collateral lines, and the majority of them met violent deaths. Rebellions and coups d'état followed one after the other, as different groups of nobles placed their candidates on the throne and killed as many of their opponents as they could. As conditions deteriorated, serfs absconded in large numbers, and independent merchants and seamen of humble origins came to dominate the three-way trade between China, Korea, and Japan.

The dynasty that emerged from this confusion was called Koryo (935–1392). (The English word *Korea* derives from the name of this dynasty.) During this time Korea developed more independently of the China model than it had in Silla times, just as contemporary Japan was doing (see the next section). This was not because the Chinese model was rejected—indeed the Koryo capital was laid out on the Chinese model, and the government was closely patterned on the Tang system. Measures such as these did nothing to alter the fundamentally aristocratic structure of Korean society.

The founder of the dynasty, Wang Kon, was a man of relatively obscure maritime background, but he needed the support of the old aristocracy to maintain his control. His successors introduced civil service examinations on the Chinese model, as well as examinations for Buddhist clergy, but since the aristocrats were the best educated and government schools admitted only sons of aristocrats, this system served primarily to solidify their control. Politics was largely the competition among aristocratic clans for influence at court and marriage of their daughters to the royal princes. Like the Heian aristocrats in Japan, the Koryo aristocrats wanted to stay in the capital and only reluctantly accepted posts in the provinces.

At the other end of the social scale, the serf/slave stratum seems to have increased in size. This lowborn stratum included not only privately held slaves but also large numbers of government slaves, as well as government workers in mines, porcelain factories, and other government industries. Sometimes entire villages or groups of villages were considered lowborn. There were occasional slave revolts, and some manumitted slaves did rise in status, but prejudice against anyone with slave ancestors was so strong that the law provided that "only if there is no evidence of lowborn status for eight generations in one's official household registration may one receive a position in the government."[4] In China and Japan, by contrast, slavery was a much more minor element in the social landscape.

The commercial economy declined in Korea during this period, showing that it was not closely linked to China's economy, then booming. Except for the capital, there were no cities of commercial importance, and in the countryside the use of money decreased. One industry that did flourish was ceramics. Connoisseurs have long appreciated the elegance of the pale green Koryo celadon pottery, decorated with designs executed in inlaid white or gray clay.

Buddhism remained strong throughout Korea, and monasteries became major centers of art and learning. As in Song China and Kamakura Japan, Chan (Zen) and Tiantai (Tendai) were the leading Buddhist teachings. The founder of the Koryo Dynasty attributed the dynasty's success to the Buddha's protection, and he and his successors were ardent patrons of the church. The entire Buddhist canon was printed in the eleventh century and again in the thirteenth. (The 81,258 individual woodblocks used to print it still survive in a monastery in southern Korea.) As in medieval Europe, aristocrats who entered the church occupied the major abbacies. Monasteries played the same roles as they did in China and Japan, such as engaging in money lending and charitable works. Like Japan (but not China), some monasteries accumulated military power.

The most important literary work of the Koryo period is *The History of the Three Kingdoms,* compiled in 1145 in Chinese by Kim Pu-sik. Modeled on Chinese histories, it is the best source of information on early Korean history.

The Koryo Dynasty was preserved in name long after the ruling family had lost most of its power. In 1170 the palace guards massacred the civil officials at court and placed a new king on the throne. The coup leaders scrapped the privileges that had kept the aristocrats in power and appointed themselves to the top posts. After incessant infighting among the generals and a series of coups, in 1196 the general Ch'oe Ch'ung-hon took control. Ch'oe had a private army of about three thousand warrior-retainers and an even larger number of slaves. The domination of Korea by the Ch'oe family was much like the contemporary situation in Japan, where warrior bands were seizing power. Moreover, because the Ch'oe were content to dominate the government while leaving the Koryo king on the throne, they had much in common with the Japanese shoguns, who followed a similar strategy.

Although Korea adopted many ideas from China, it could not so easily adopt the Chinese assumption that it was the largest, most powerful, and most advanced society in the world. Korea, from early times, recognized China as in many ways senior to it, but when strong states emerged to its north in Manchuria, Korea was ready to accommodate them as well. Koryo's first neighbor to the north was the Khitan state of Liao, which in 1010 invaded and sacked the capital. Koryo acceded to vassal status, but Liao invaded again in 1018. This time Koryo was able to repel the Khitans. Afterward a defensive wall was built across the Korean peninsula south of the Yalu River. When the Jurchens supplanted the Khitans, Koryo agreed to send them tribute as well. As mentioned in Chapter 11, Korea was conquered by the Mongols and the figurehead Koryo kings were moved to Beijing, where they married Mongol princesses, their descendants becoming more Mongol than Korean. This was a time of hardship for the Korean people. In the year 1254 alone, the Mongols enslaved 200,000 Koreans and took them away. Ordinary people in Korea suffered grievously when their land was used as a launching pad for the huge Mongol invasions of Japan, as nine hundred ships and the provisions for the soldiers on them had to be procured from the Korean countryside. In this period Korea also suffered from frequent attacks by Japanese pirates, somewhat like the depredations of the Norsemen in Europe a little earlier (see page 370). The Mongol overlords did little to provide protection, and the harried coastal people had little choice but to retreat inland. Korean scholars, familiar with the Neo-Confucian learning of Song and Yuan China, began demanding major reforms such as reallocation of land.

When Mongol rule in China fell apart in the mid-fourteenth century, it declined in Korea as well. Chinese rebels opposing the Mongols entered Korea and even briefly captured the capital in 1361. When the Ming Dynasty was established in 1368, the Koryo court was unsure how to respond. In 1388 a general, Yi Song-gye, was sent to oppose a Ming army at the northwest frontier. When he saw the strength of the Ming, he concluded that making an alliance was more sensible than fighting and led his troops back to the capital, where in 1392 he usurped the throne, founding the Yi Dynasty.

Celadon Vase   Korea is justly famous for the quality of its ceramics, especially its celadons (ceramics with a grayish blue-green glaze). This early-twelfth-century ewer, probably used for warmed wine, is shaped to resemble a bamboo shoot. *(Courtesy of the Trustees of the Victoria & Albert Museum/Photographer: Ian Thomas)*

JAPAN IN THE HEIAN AND KAMAKURA ERAS (794–1333)

As discussed in Chapter 7, during the seventh and eighth centuries the Japanese ruling house pursued a vigorous policy of adopting useful ideas, techniques, and policies from the more advanced civilization of China. The rulers built a splendid capital along Chinese lines in Nara and fostered the growth of Buddhism.

The Heian Period (794–1185)

After less than a century Nara was abandoned and the Japanese imperial court moved the capital to Heian (modern Kyoto). This new capital was, like Nara, modeled on the Tang capital of Chang'an (although neither of the Japanese capitals had walls, a major feature of Chinese cities), and for the first century at Heian the government continued to follow Chinese models. With the decline of the Tang Dynasty in the late ninth century, the Japanese stopped sending embassies to China

JAPAN, CA 800–1400

794–1185	Heian era and aristocratic court culture
804–806	Saichō and Kūkai go to China and return with new Buddhist teachings
894	Last official embassy to China
995–1027	Fujiwara Michinaga is dominant
ca 1010	Lady Murasaki writes *The Tale of Genji*
1185–1333	Kamakura Shogunate and Japanese feudalism
12th–13th centuries	Eisai and Dogen introduce Zen from China

and rejected dependence on Chinese models. Japan's intellectual and cultural childhood had come to an end, and it was ready to go its own way.

Only the first two Heian emperors were activists. Thereafter political management was taken over by a series of regents from the Fujiwara family, who supplied most of the empresses in this period. The emperors continued to be honored, even venerated, because of their presumed divine descent, but it was the Fujiwaras who ruled. Fujiwara dominance represented the privatization of political power and a reversion to clan politics within an ostensibly bureaucratic system of rule. The bureaucracy built on the Chinese model was not abolished, but it became merely ceremonial. Japanese government took a very different course than that in China, where political contenders sought the throne and successful contenders deposed the old emperor and founded new dynasties. In Japan, for the next thousand years, political contenders sought to manipulate the emperor but not to supplant him.

The Fujiwaras reached the apogee of their glory under Fujiwara Michinaga (966–1027), who dominated the court for more than thirty years. He was the father of four empresses, the uncle of two emperors, and the grandfather of three emperors. He acquired great landholdings and built fine palaces for himself and his family. After ensuring that his sons could continue to rule, he retired to a Buddhist monastery, all the while continuing to exercise most of the control himself. Like many aristocrats of the period, he was learned in music, poetry, Chinese literature and history, and Buddhism.

By the end of the eleventh century several emperors who did not have Fujiwara mothers found a device to counter Fujiwara control: they abdicated but continued to exercise power by controlling their young sons on the throne. This system of rule has been called **cloistered government,** because the retired emperors took Buddhist orders. Thus for a time the imperial house was a contender for political power along with other aristocratic groups.

The rise of a warrior elite finally brought an end to the domination of the Fujiwaras and other Heian aristocratic families. In 1156 civil war broke out, fed by declining central power, feuds among the great families, and the ambitions of local lords. The two most powerful contenders in the struggle were the Taira and Minamoto clans, who quickly outstripped both the emperor and the Fujiwaras. Both clans relied on **samurai,** skilled warriors who were rapidly becoming a new social class. By 1192 the Minamoto clan had vanquished all opposition, and their leader, Yoritomo (1147–1199), became **shogun,** or general-in-chief. With him began the Kamakura Shogunate, which lasted until 1333. This period is often referred to as Japan's feudal period because it was dominated by a military class tied to their superiors by bonds of loyalty and supported by landed estates rather than salaries.

The Samurai

The emergence of the samurai was made possible by the development of private landed estates. The equal-field system of allotting land in standard amounts to all adult males, copied from Tang China, began breaking down in the eighth century (much as it did in China) because the government failed to keep accurate records and reallocate land. Those who brought new land into cultivation could hold it as private land, as could monasteries, the imperial

Samurai Armor   A member of the Taira clan once wore this twelfth-century set of armor. Armor had to serve the practical purpose of defense, but as in medieval Europe and medieval Islam, it was often embellished, turning armor into works of art. *(Courtesy of Suzanne Perrin)*

family, and certain high-ranking officials. By the ninth century local lords began escaping imperial taxes and control by formally giving (commending) their land to these tax-exempt entities. The local lord then received his land back as a tenant and paid his protector a small rent. The monastery or privileged individual received a steady income from the land, and the local lord was thereafter free of imperial taxes and control. By the end of the thirteenth century most land seems to have been taken off the tax rolls in this way. Each plot of land could thus have several people with rights to shares of its produce, ranging from the cultivator, to a local lord, to an estate manager working for him, to a regional strongman, to a noble or temple in the capital. Unlike peasants in medieval Europe,

where similar practices of commendation occurred, the cultivators in Japan never became serfs.

In spite of his legal status as a tenant, the local lord continued to exercise actual authority over the land—all the more so, in fact, since imperial officials could no longer touch him. To keep order local lords organized private armies of samurai. A samurai and his lord had a double bond: in return for the samurai's loyalty and service, the lord granted him land or income. Each samurai entered into his lord's service in a formal ceremony that included a religious element. The samurai had their own military and social code of conduct, later called **Bushido,** or "Way of the Warrior." Loyalty to the lord came before anything else. In addition, samurai were expected to respect the gods, keep honorable company, be fair and even generous to others, and be sympathetic to the weak and helpless. Honor was so important that a samurai would commit the act of ritual suicide by disemboweling himself rather than face dishonor.

The symbols of the samurai were their swords, with which they were expected to be expert, and the cherry blossom, which falls with the spring wind, signifying the way in which samurai willingly gave their lives for their lords. Like knights in Europe, samurai went into battle in armor and often on horseback. Like the ancient Spartans, samurai were expected to make do with little and like it. Physical hardship became routine, and soft living was despised as weak and unworthy. The life of the samurai was a far cry from the sensitive, poetry-writing aristocrat so admired in Heian court society.

The Kamakura Shogunate (1185–1333)

The Kamakura Shogunate derives its name from Kamakura, a city near modern Tokyo that was the seat of the Minamoto clan. Yoritomo's victory meant that the emperor was once again an ornament, honored but powerless. It was the military commander, or shogun, who actually ruled.

Yoritomo's rule was an extension of the way in which he ran his own estate. Having established his government at Kamakura, Yoritomo created three bodies, staffed by his retainers, to handle political and legal matters. His administrative board drafted government policy; another board regulated lords and samurai; and a board of inquiry served as the court of the land.

For administration at the local level, Yoritomo created two groups of officials: military land stewards and military governors. To cope with the emergence of hard-to-tax estates, **military land stewards** were put in charge of seeing to the estates' proper operation and maintaining law and order in return for a share of the produce. **Military governors** oversaw the military and police protection of the provinces. They supervised the conduct of the land stewards in peacetime and commanded the provincial samurai in war.

The process of reducing power holders to figureheads went one step further in 1219 when the Hojo family, powerful vassals of the shogun, reduced the shogun to a figurehead. Until 1333 the Hojo family held the reins of power by serving as regents, and the shogun joined the emperor as a political ornament.

The Mongols' massive seaborne invasion (see page 324) rudely interrupted Japan's self-imposed isolation in the thirteenth century. Although the Hojo regents rebuffed the Mongols, they were unable to reward their vassals in the traditional way because little booty was found among the wreckage of the Mongol fleets. Discontent grew among the samurai, and by the fourteenth century the entire political system was breaking down. Both the imperial and the shogunate families were fighting among themselves. Many samurai were becoming impoverished as land grants were divided. Poverty created a pool of warriors ready for plunder, and the samurai shifted their loyalty to local officials who could offer them adequate maintenance.

The factional disputes among Japan's leading families remained explosive until 1331, when the emperor Go-Daigo tried to recapture real power. His attempt sparked an uprising by the great families, local lords, samurai, and even Buddhist monasteries, which commanded the allegiance of thousands of samurai. Go-Daigo destroyed the Kamakura Shogunate in 1333 but soon lost the loyalty of his followers. By 1338 one of his most important military supporters, Ashikaga Takauji, had turned on him and established the Ashikaga Shogunate, which lasted until 1573. Takauji's victory was also a victory for the samurai, who took over civil authority throughout Japan.

Culture During the Heian and Kamakura Periods

The brilliant aristocratic culture of the Heian period was strongly focused on the capital. It was there that nobles, palace ladies, and imperial family members lived a highly refined and leisured life. Their society was one in which niceties of birth, rank, and breeding counted for everything. From their diaries we know of the pains aristocratic women took in selecting the color combinations of the twelve layers of kimonos they wore. Even among men, knowing how to dress tastefully was more important than skill with a horse or sword. The elegance of one's calligraphy and the allusions in one's poems were matters of intense concern to both men and women at court. Courtiers did not like to leave the capital, and some shuddered at the sight of ordinary working people. The court lady Sei Shonagon recorded in her *Pillow Book* encountering a group of commoners on a pilgrimage: "They looked like so many basket-worms as they crowded together in their hideous clothes, leaving hardly an inch of space between themselves and me. I really felt like pushing them all over sideways."[5] (See the feature "Listening to the Past: The Pillow Book of Sei Shonagon" on pages 358–359.)

In this period a new script was developed for writing Japanese phonetically. Each symbol, based on a simplified Chinese character, represented one of the syllables used in Japanese (such as *ka, ha,* and *ta*). Although "serious" essays, histories, and government documents continued to be written in Chinese, less formal works such as poetry and memoirs were written in Japanese. Mastering the new writing system took much less time than mastering writing in Chinese and aided the spread of literacy, especially among women.

The literary masterpiece of this period is ***The Tale of Genji,*** written in Japanese by Lady Murasaki in about 1010. This long work, the first novel ever written in any language, depicts court life, with close attention to dialogue and personality. The world it depicts is one where taste mattered above all, and people spent time assessing the color combinations of the robes the women wore and the choice of stationery a man or woman selected to write a note. Murasaki also wrote a diary that is similarly revealing of aristocratic culture. In one passage she tells of an occasion when word got out that she had read the Chinese classics:

Worried what people would think if they heard such rumors, I pretended to be unable to read even the inscriptions on the screens. Then Her Majesty asked me to read to her here and there from the collected works of [the Tang Chinese poet] Bo Juyi, and, because she evinced a desire to know much more about such things, we carefully chose a time when other women would not be present and, amateur that I was, I read with her the two books of Bo Juyi's New Ballads *in secret; we started the summer before last.*[6]

Apparently even in Heian Japan, the great age of women writers, a woman was wise to hide her erudition.

During the Kamakura period the tradition of long narrative works was continued with the war tale. *The Tale of the Heike,* written by a courtier in the early thirteenth century, tells the story of the fall of the Taira family and the rise of the Minamoto clan. The tale reached a large audience because blind minstrels would chant sections of the tale to the accompaniment of the lute for popular audiences. The story is suffused with the Buddhist idea of the transience of life and the illusory nature of glory. Yet it also celebrates strength, courage, loyalty, and pride. The Minamoto warriors from the east are portrayed as the toughest. In one scene one of them dismissed his own prowess with the bow, claiming that other warriors from his region could pierce three sets of armor with their arrows. He then bragged about the martial spirit of warriors from the east:

Genji   In *The Tale of Genji* the prince was depicted as artistic and sensitive. Here, in a detail from a twelfth-century handscroll illustrating the great novel, Genji is depicted cradling the child born of his wife's liaison with another man. *(The Tokugawa Art Museum, Nagoya)*

They are bold horsemen who never fall, nor do they let their horses stumble on the roughest road. When they fight they do not care if even their parents or children are killed; they ride over their bodies and continue the battle.

The warriors of the western provinces are quite different. If their parents are killed they retire from the battle and perform Buddhist rites to console the souls of the dead. Only after the mourning is over will they fight again. If their children are slain, their grief is so deep that they cease fighting altogether. When their rations are given out, they plant rice in the fields and go out to fight only after reaping it. They dislike the heat of summer. They grumble at the severe cold of winter. This is not the way of the soldiers of the eastern provinces.[7]

Both within aristocratic circles and outside them Buddhism remained very strong throughout this period. A mission sent to China in 804 included two monks in search of new texts. Saichō spent time at Mount Tiantai and brought back Tendai (Chinese Tiantai) teachings. Tendai's basic message is that all living beings share the Buddha nature and can be brought to salvation. In addition, the Buddhas and bodhisattvas are always at work helping people to achieve salvation. Tendai practices include strict monastic discipline, prayer, textual study, and meditation. Once back in Japan, Saichō established a monastery on Mount Hiei, outside Kyoto, which grew to be one of the most important monasteries in Japan. By the twelfth century this monastery and its many branch temples had vast lands and a powerful army of monk-soldiers to protect its interests. Whenever the monastery felt that its interests were at risk, it sent the monk-soldiers into the capital to carry its sacred symbols in an attempt to intimidate the civil authorities.

Kūkai, the other monk on the 804 mission to China, came back with texts from another school of Bud-dhism—Shingon, or **Esoteric Buddhism.** Esoteric Buddhism is based on the idea that teachings containing the secrets of enlightenment have been secretly transmitted from the Buddha. An adept can gain access to these mysteries through initiation into the mandalas (cosmic diagrams), mudras (gestures), and mantras (verbal formulas). The popularity of Esoteric Buddhism proved a great stimulus to art. On his return to Japan, Kūkai attracted many followers and was allowed to establish a monastery at Mount Koya, south of Osaka.

Only later, during the Kamakura period, did Buddhism begin a vigorous proselytizing phase. Honen propagated the Pure Land teaching (see pages 197–198), preaching

Zen Rock Garden   Rock gardens, such as this one at Ryoanji in Kyoto, capture the austere aesthetic of Zen Buddhism. *(Photo courtesy of the International Society for Educational Information)*

that paradise could be reached through simple faith in the Buddha and repeating the name of the Buddha Amitabha. Neither philosophical understanding of Buddhist scriptures nor devotion to rituals was necessary. Nichiren, a fiery and intolerant preacher, proclaimed that to be saved people had only to invoke sincerely the Lotus Sutra. These lay versions of Buddhism found a receptive audience among ordinary people in the countryside.

It was also during the Kamakura period that Zen (Chan) came to flourish in Japan. As mentioned in Chapter 7, Zen teachings originated in Tang China. Rejecting the authority of the sutras, Zen teachers claimed the superiority of mind-to-mind transmission of Buddhist truth and monastic discipline. When Japanese monks went to China in the twelfth century looking for ways to revitalize Japanese Buddhism, they were impressed by the rigorous monastic life of the Chan/Zen monasteries. Eisai introduced Rinzai Zen, which held that enlightenment could be achieved suddenly through insight into one's own true nature, and he practiced rigorous meditation. This teaching found eager patrons among the samurai, who were attracted to its discipline. Soto Zen teachings, introduced a century later from China by Dogen, focused specifically on seated meditation, which Dogen believed held the secret of enlightenment. After Dogen's death, Soto Zen incorporated elements of Esoteric Buddhism and popular practices such as prayers for material benefit, which gave it wide popular appeal.

Buddhist sentiments pervade much of Japanese literature from this period. For instance, Kamo no Chōmei (1153–1216) wrote a memoir describing the world he knew before and after becoming a monk and settling into a ten-foot-square hut. He stressed the disasters he had personally witnessed, such as a tornado and an earthquake, a fire that had destroyed huge sections of the city, and a two-year famine that resulted in tens of thousands of bodies abandoned in the city. Social circumstances also made life difficult to endure:

The poor man who is the neighbor of a wealthy family is always ashamed of his wretched appearance, and makes his entrances and exits in bursts of flattery. And when he sees how envious his wife and children and his servants are, or hears how the rich family despises him, his mind is incessantly torn by an agitation that leaves not a moment's peace. If a man's house stands in a crowded place and a fire breaks out in the neighborhood, he cannot escape the danger. If it stands in a remote situation, he must put up with the nuisance of going back and forth to the city, and there is always a danger of robbers.[8]

In the Ashikaga period Zen temples served as literary salons where monks, nobles, and warriors could mingle. An aesthetic style marked by restraint came to supplant the aristocratic style of the Heian period. The rock gardens of the major Zen temples of Heian offer an example of this aesthetic, as do some of the minimalist ink paintings of the period.

SUMMARY

In the period from 800 to 1400, China was probably the most advanced society in the world, with a booming economy, a highly developed material culture, and a sophisticated form of government that recruited officials on the basis of their education rather than their birth or military prowess. Philosophy and the arts all flourished. The other principal countries of East Asia, particularly Korea and Japan, were developing in other directions in this period. In both Korea and Japan, after a period in which court aristocrats were dominant both politically and culturally, generals and military interests gained dominance. In the case of Japan, this proved to be a long-term development, and the samurai developed a very distinct ethos. All three countries were affected by the rise of the Mongols. Neither China nor Korea was able to repel the Mongols, though they spent decades trying. Japan marshaled its resources to repulse two seaborne attempts at invasion.

KEY TERMS

examination system
movable type
Neo-Confucianism
paper money
compass
concubine
foot binding
cloistered government
samurai
shogun
Bushido
military land stewards
military governors
The Tale of Genji
Esoteric Buddhism

NOTES

1. *The Travels of Marco Polo, the Venetian,* ed. Manuel Komroff (New York: Boni and Liveright, 1926), p. 227.
2. Ibid., p. 159.
3. Ibid., p. 235.

(continued on page 360)

LISTENING TO THE PAST

THE PILLOW BOOK OF SEI SHONAGON

*Beginning in the late tenth century, Japan
produced a series of great women writers. At the time
women were much freer than men to write in
vernacular Japanese, giving them a large advantage.
Lady Murasaki, author of the novel* The Tale of
Genji, *is the most famous of the women writers of the
period, but her contemporary Sei Shonagon is
equally noteworthy. Sei Shonagon served as a lady in
waiting to Empress Sadako during the last decade of
the tenth century (990–1000). Her only known work
is* The Pillow Book, *a collection of notes, character
sketches, anecdotes, descriptions of nature, and
eccentric lists such as boring things, awkward things,
hateful things, and things that have lost their power.*

*The Pillow Book portrays the lovemaking/
marriage system among the aristocracy more or less
as it is depicted in* The Tale of Genji. *Marriages
were arranged for family interests, and men could
have more than one wife. Wives and their children
commonly stayed in their own homes, where their
husbands and fathers would visit them. But once a
man had an heir by his wife, there was nothing to
prevent him from establishing relations with other
women. Some relationships were long-term, but many
were brief, and men often had several lovers at the
same time. Some women became known for their
amorous conquests, others as abandoned women
whose husbands ignored them. The following
passage from* The Pillow Book *looks on this
lovemaking system with amused detachment.*

It is so stiflingly hot in the Seventh Month that
even at night one keeps all the doors and lattices
open. At such times it is delightful to wake up
when the moon is shining and to look outside. I
enjoy it even when there is no moon. But to wake
up at dawn and see a pale sliver of a moon in the
sky—well, I need hardly say how perfect that is.

I like to see a bright new straw mat that has just
been spread out on a well-polished floor. The best
place for one's three-foot curtain of state is in the
front of the room near the veranda. It is pointless
to put it in the rear of the room, as it is most
unlikely that anyone will peer in from that
direction.

It is dawn and a woman is lying in bed after her
lover has taken his leave. She is covered up to her
head with a light mauve robe that has a lining of
dark violet; the colour of both the outside and the
lining is fresh and glossy. The woman, who
appears to be asleep, wears an unlined orange
robe and a dark crimson skirt of stiff silk whose
cords hang loosely by her side, as if they have
been left untied. Her thick tresses tumble over
each other in cascades, and one can imagine how
long her hair must be when it falls freely down
her back.

Nearby another woman's lover is making his
way home in the misty dawn. He is wearing loose
violet trousers, an orange hunting costume, so
lightly coloured that one can hardly tell whether it
has been dyed or not, a white robe of still silk, and
a scarlet robe of glossy, beaten silk. His clothes,
which are damp from the mist, hang loosely about
him. From the dishevelment of his side locks one
can tell how negligently he must have tucked his
hair into the black lacquered head-dress when he
got up. He wants to return and write his next-
morning letter before the dew on the morning
glories has had time to vanish; but the path seems
endless, and to divert himself he hums "the
sprouts in the flax fields."

As he walks along, he passes a house with an
open lattice. He is on his way to report for official
duty, but cannot help stopping to lift up the blind
and peep into the room. It amuses him to think
that a man has probably been spending the night
here and has only recently got up to leave, just as

During the Heian period, noblewomen were fashion-conscious. Wearing numerous layers of clothing gave women the opportunity to choose different designs and colors for their robes. The layers also kept them warm in drafty homes. *(The Museum Yamato Bunkakan)*

happened to himself. Perhaps that man too had felt the charm of the dew.

Looking around the room, he notices near the woman's pillow an open fan with a magnolia frame and purple paper; and at the foot of her curtain of state he sees some narrow strips of Michinoku paper and also some other paper of a faded colour, either orange-red or maple.

The woman senses that someone is watching her and, looking up from under her bedclothes, sees a gentleman leaning against the wall by the threshold, a smile on his face. She can tell at once that he is the sort of man with whom she need feel no reserve. All the same, she does not want to enter into any familiar relations with him, and she is annoyed that he should have seen her asleep.

"Well, well, Madam," says the man, leaning forward so that the upper part of his body comes behind her curtains, "what a long nap you're having after your morning adieu! You really are a lie-abed!"

"You call me that, Sir," she replied, "only because you're annoyed at having had to get up before the dew had time to settle."

Their conversation may be commonplace, yet I find there is something delightful about the scene.

Now the gentleman leans further forward and, using his own fan, tries to get hold of the fan by the woman's pillow. Fearing his closeness, she moves further back into her curtain enclosure, her heart pounding. The gentleman picks up the magnolia fan and, while examining it, says in a slightly bitter tone, "How standoffish you are!"

But now it is growing light, there is a sound of people's voices, and it looks as if the sun will soon be up. Only a short while ago this same man was hurrying home to write his next-morning letter before the mists had time to clear. Alas, how easily his intentions have been forgotten!

While all this is afoot, the woman's original lover has been busy with his own next-morning letter, and now, quite unexpectedly, the messenger arrives at her house. The letter is attached to a spray of bush-clover, still damp with dew, and the paper gives off a delicious aroma of incense. Because of the new visitor, however, the woman's servants cannot deliver it to her.

Finally it becomes unseemly for the gentleman to stay any longer. As he goes, he is amused to think that a similar scene may be taking place in the house he left earlier that morning.

QUESTIONS FOR ANALYSIS

1. What sorts of images does Sei Shonagon evoke to convey an impression of a scene?

2. What can you learn from this passage about the material culture of Japan in this period?

3. Why do you think Sei Shonagon was highly esteemed as a writer?

Source: Ivan Morris, trans., *The Pillow Book of Sei Shonagon* (New York: Penguin Books, 1970), pp. 60–62. Copyright © 1990 Columbia University Press. Reprinted with permission of Columbia University Press and Oxford University Press.

4. Peter H. Lee, ed., *Sourcebook of Korean Civilization* (New York: Columbia University Press, 1993), p. 327.

5. Ivan Morris, trans., *The Pillow Book of Sei Shonagon* (New York: Penguin Books, 1970), p. 258.

6. Quoted in M. Collcott, M. Jansen, and I. Kumakura, *Cultural Atlas of Japan* (New York: Facts on File, 1988), p. 82, slightly modified.

7. Ibid., p. 101.

8. Donald Keene, ed., *Anthology of Japanese Literature* (New York: Grove Press, 1960), p. 205.

SUGGESTED READING

General histories of China are listed in Chapter 4. Probably the best general introduction to the Song period is J. Gernet, *Daily Life in China on the Eve of the Mongol Invasion, 1250–76* (1962). The flourishing economy of the Song is analyzed in Y. Shiba, *Commerce and Society in Sung China* (1970). Song foreign relations are covered in the symposium volume edited by M. Rossabi, *China Among Equals: The Middle Kingdom and Its Neighbors* (1983). On Song government, see J. Chaffee's study of the examination system, *The Thorny Gates of Learning in Sung China: A Social History of Examinations* (1985); J. Liu on Wang Anshi, *Reform in Sung China: Wang An-Shih (1021–1086) and His New Policies* (1957); and B. McKnight, *Law and Order in Sung China* (1992).

On Neo-Confucianism and the scholar-official elite, see A. C. Graham, *Two Chinese Philosophers: Ch'eng Ming-tao and Ch'eng Yi-ch'uan* (1958); P. Bol, *"This Culture of Ours": Intellectual Transitions in T'ang and Sung China* (1992); and R. Hymes, *Statesmen and Gentlemen: The Elite of Fu-chou, Chiang-hsi, in Northern and Southern Sung* (1986). On popular religion, see V. Hansen, *Changing the Gods in Medieval*

China, 1127–1276 (1990); E. Davis, *Society and the Supernatural in Song China* (2001); and R. Hymes, *Way and Byway: Taoism, Local Religion, and Models of Divinity in Sung and Modern China* (2002). For a study of women's lives, see P. Ebrey, *The Inner Quarters: Marriage and the Lives of Chinese Women in the Sung Period* (1993).

General histories of Korea and Japan are listed in Chapter 7. R. Lancaster et al., *Buddhism in Koryo: A Royal Religion* (2002), deals with an important issue in Korean history. I. Morris, *The World of the Shining Prince: Court Life in Ancient Japan* (1964), provides an engaging portrait of Heian culture. Lady Murasaki's *The Tale of Genji* has been translated by E. G. Seidensticker (1976); I. Morris has translated *The Pillow Book of Sei Shonagon,* 2 vols. (1967).

Japanese feudalism, like its medieval European counterpart, continues to inspire discussion and disagreement. Some provocative works include P. Duus, *Feudalism in Japan,* 2d ed. (1976); E. O. Reischauer, "Japanese Feudalism," in R. Coulborn, ed., *Feudalism in History* (1956), pp. 26–48; and T. Keirstead, *The Geography of Power in Medieval Japan* (1992), which attempts to determine the cultural framework of the feudal land system. For military affairs, see W. W. Farris, *Heavenly Warriors* (1992), which argues against Western analogies in explaining the dominance of the samurai, and K. F. Friday, *Hired Swords* (1992), which treats the evolution of state military development in connection with the emergence of the samurai. P. Varley, *Warriors of Japan* (1994), draws on war tales to examine samurai culture. A good sense of the world-view of the samurai also can be found by reading literary works of the period in translation, such as *The Tale of the Heike,* trans. H. Kitagawa and B. Tsuchida (1976), and *Yoshitsune,* trans. H. McCullough (1971). On Zen Buddhism in the medieval era, see M. Collcutt, *Five Mountains, the Rinzai Zen Monastic Institution in Medieval Japan* (1981), and H. Dumoulin, *A History of Zen Buddhism* (1963).

Allegorical harvesting scenes from a German manuscript, *Speculum Virginum*, ca 1190.
(Rheinisches Landesmuseum, Bonn)

13 EUROPE IN THE MIDDLE AGES

Historians commonly divide long eras into shorter time periods, according to the features they believe characteristic of those periods. Historians do this as a tool or hypothesis for dealing with vast amounts of material. The Italian Renaissance humanist Francesco Petrarch (1304–1374) coined the term *Middle Ages* to describe the period in European history from about 500 to 1350. Petrarch believed that his own age was a golden age marked by an intellectual and cultural brilliance that recaptured the cultural splendor of ancient Roman civilization. Between the Roman world and the Renaissance, Petrarch believed, there were "the Middle Ages," a time of gothic barbarism and intellectual stagnation (see page 452).

Scholars have adopted Petrarch's terminology and time divisions when studying the postclassical European world before about 1350. But Petrarch had it wrong about barbarism and stagnation. When urban life declined and Roman political institutions decayed in western Europe, Europeans developed new political and economic devices to serve their social needs. Between about 1050 and 1350, Europeans displayed enormous intellectual energy and creative vitality. That later period witnessed the beginnings of ideas and institutions that not only shaped the Western world but subsequently influenced societies around the world.

During the millennium from about 500 to 1500, Europe was not isolated from contacts with other peoples. A small volume of trade trickled across Central Asia to Europe on routes commonly called the Silk Road. In the early eighth century, Muslim forces from North Africa conquered Spain. Later, the Arabs overran Sicily and penetrated southern Italy. They attacked Naples and, in 839, pillaged Ancona in central Italy. In subsequent centuries, Islamic learning profoundly affected European culture in areas such as architecture, medicine, philosophy, and poetry. In the late eighth century, pagan Northmen, or Vikings, from Scandinavia made deep incursions into Europe, from Iceland and Ireland to Russia. The Vikings also influenced Europeans' political, economic, and social institutions. After 1095, Europeans' own imperialistic expansion in the Middle East during the crusading movement, the first large-scale colonizing action beyond the geographical boundaries of the European continent, helped shape the identity of the West. The evidence of medieval art suggests that in the twelfth and thirteenth centuries a few sub-Saharan African people lived in western Europe, although this subject remains to be adequately explored. The period we call the European Middle Ages witnessed many such intercontinental links.

- How did Charlemagne acquire and govern his empire? What Merovingian institutions did he utilize? What is meant by the term *Carolingian Renaissance?*

- In the period from about 900 to 1350, was feudalism—as a method of government, a social "system," and a cultural force—possible without manorialism?

- How did the Christian church and civil governments influence one another during the Middle Ages?

- How did medieval rulers work to solve their problems of government, thereby laying the foundations of modern states?

- How did medieval towns originate, and how do they reveal the beginnings of radical change in European society?

- What were the salient marks of creativity in the central Middle Ages?

- What factors precipitated crises in the later Middle Ages, and how were these crises interrelated?

- In the period from about 800 to 1350, how did Islam and Christian Europe affect each other militarily? What cultural influences did Islam exert on Europe, including artistic, philosophical, and literary elements?

These are among the questions this chapter will explore.

THE FRANKISH KINGDOM

The Frankish kingdom that had emerged under Clovis (see page 223) by the early sixth century included most of what is now France and a large section of southwestern Germany. Clovis's baptism into Orthodox Christianity won him church support against other Germanic tribes. Although his family, the Merovingians, continued to lead France for two centuries after his death, they were troubled years. Then a new dynasty—the Carolingians—moved to the throne.

Clovis's descendant Charles Martel defeated Muslim invaders in 732 at the Battle of Tours in central France.[1] Muslims and Christians have interpreted the battle differently. Muslims considered it a minor skirmish and attributed the Frankish victory to Muslim difficulties in maintaining supply lines over long distances and to ethnic conflicts and unrest in Islamic Spain. Christians considered the Frankish victory one of the great battles of

history because it halted Muslim expansion in Europe. A century later, in 843, Charles Martel's three great-great-grandsons, after a bitter war, concluded the Treaty of Verdun, which divided the European continent among them. Civil disorder and foreign invasion then wracked Europe for about the next 150 years.

Between 732 and 843, a distinctly European society emerged. A new kind of social and political organization, later called feudalism, appeared. And for the first time since the collapse of the Roman Empire, most of western Europe was united under one government, which reached its peak under Charles Martel's grandson, Charlemagne. Christian missionary activity among the Germanic peoples continued, and strong ties were forged with the Roman papacy. A revival of study and learning—the Carolingian Renaissance—occurred during the reign of Charlemagne.

The Merovingians and the Rise of the Carolingians

When Clovis died, following Frankish custom, he divided his kingdom among his four sons. For the next two centuries, the land was often wracked by civil war. These wars had several causes. Lacking a clear principle of succession, any male of Merovingian blood could claim the throne, and within the family there were always many possibilities. In addition, members of the royal family and their followers hoped to win land, booty, and plunder. So brutal were these wars that historians used the term *Dark Ages* to apply to the entire Merovingian period. Yet recent research has presented a more complex picture, suggesting that the wars did not fundamentally threaten the kingdom and even served as "a unifying part of the structure of the Frankish state."[2]

Merovingian kings based their administration on the *civitas,* the city and the surrounding territory over which a *count* presided. The count raised troops, collected royal revenues, and provided justice on the basis of local, not royal, law. At the king's court—that is, wherever he was present—an official called the *mayor of the palace* supervised legal, financial, and household officials; the mayor of the palace also governed in the king's absence. That position, combined with advantageous marriages, a well-earned reputation for military strength, and the help of the church, paved the way for the rise to power of one family, the Carolingians.[3]

In the eighth century, Irish, Frankish, and Anglo-Saxon missionaries were active throughout the Frankish kingdom. The Englishman Boniface (680–754) is the most famous of these, and his achievements were remarkable. He helped shape the structure of the Frankish church, held

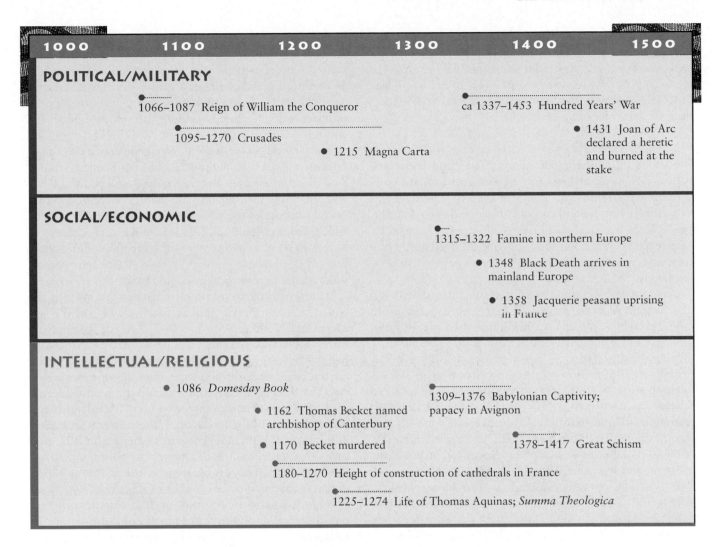

| 1000 | 1100 | 1200 | 1300 | 1400 | 1500 |

POLITICAL/MILITARY

1066–1087 Reign of William the Conqueror

ca 1337–1453 Hundred Years' War

1095–1270 Crusades

1215 Magna Carta

1431 Joan of Arc declared a heretic and burned at the stake

SOCIAL/ECONOMIC

1315–1322 Famine in northern Europe

1348 Black Death arrives in mainland Europe

1358 Jacquerie peasant uprising in France

INTELLECTUAL/RELIGIOUS

1086 *Domesday Book*

1162 Thomas Becket named archbishop of Canterbury

1309–1376 Babylonian Captivity; papacy in Avignon

1170 Becket murdered

1378–1417 Great Schism

1180–1270 Height of construction of cathedrals in France

1225–1274 Life of Thomas Aquinas; *Summa Theologica*

councils to reform it, and tried to establish *The Rule of Saint Benedict* in all the monasteries he founded. The Carolingian mayors Charles Martel (r. 714–741) and Pippin III (r. 751–768) backed these efforts, as missionaries also preached obedience to secular authority. Their support of the church had dividends for the family.

Charles Martel had exercised the power of the king of the Franks. His son Pippin III aspired to the title as well. Pippin did not want to murder the ineffectual Merovingian king, but he wanted the kingship. He consulted Pope Zacharias, who condoned the removal of the king and Pippin's assumption of the throne.

When Pippin died, his son Charles the Great (r. 768–814), generally known as Charlemagne, succeeded him. In the autumn of the year 800, Charlemagne visited Rome, where on Christmas Day Pope Leo III crowned him Holy Roman emperor. The event had momentous consequences. In taking as his motto *Renovatio romani imperi* (Revival of the Roman Empire), Charlemagne was deliberately perpetuating old Roman imperial ideas, while identifying with the new Rome of the Christian church.[4] Charlemagne and his government represented a fusion of Frankish practices and Christian ideals, the two basic elements of medieval European society.

The Empire of Charlemagne

Charlemagne built on the military and diplomatic foundations of his ancestors. Einhard, his secretary and biographer, wrote a lengthy idealization of the warrior-ruler. It has serious flaws but is the earliest medieval biography of a layman, and historians consider it generally accurate:

Charles was large and strong, and of lofty stature, though not disproportionately tall . . . the upper part of his head was round, his eyes very large and animated, nose a little long, hair fair, and face laughing and merry. Thus his appearance was always stately and dignified . . . although his neck was thick and somewhat short, and his belly rather prominent; but the symmetry of the rest of his body concealed these defects. His health was excellent, except during the four years preceding his death.[5]

Though crude and brutal, Charlemagne was a man of enormous intelligence. He appreciated good literature, such as Saint Augustine's *City of God,* and Einhard considered him an unusually effective speaker. Charlemagne had four legal wives and six concubines and even after the age of sixty-five continued to sire children. Three of his sons reached adulthood, but only one outlived him. Four surviving grandsons, however, ensured perpetuation of the family.[6]

Charlemagne's most striking characteristic was his phenomenal energy, which helps to explain his great military achievements. Continuing the expansionist policies of his ancestors, Charlemagne fought more than fifty campaigns. His only defeat came when he tried to occupy Basque territory in northwestern Spain. When his long siege of Saragossa proved unsuccessful and the Saxons on his northeastern borders rebelled, Charlemagne decided to withdraw. At Roncesvalles in 778, the Basques annihilated his rear guard, which was under the command of Count Roland. The expedition inspired the great medieval epic *The Song of Roland,* written around 1100, which portrays Roland as the ideal chivalric knight and Charlemagne as exercising a sacred kind of kingship. Although many of the epic's details differ from the historical evidence, *The Song of Roland* is important because it reveals the popular image of Charlemagne in later centuries.

By around 805, the Frankish kingdom included all of continental Europe except Spain, Scandinavia, southern Italy, and the Slavic fringes of the East (see Map 13.1). The Muslims in northeastern Spain were checked by the establishment of strongly fortified areas known both as *marches* and as *marks.* Not since the third century C.E. had any ruler controlled so much of the Western world.

Charlemagne ruled a vast rural world dotted with isolated estates and characterized by constant petty violence. His empire was not a state as people today understand that term; it was a collection of peoples and semibarbaric tribes. Apart from a small class of warrior-aristocrats and clergy, almost everyone engaged in agriculture. Trade and commerce played only a small part in the economy. Cities served as the headquarters of bishops and as ecclesiastical centers.

By constant travel, personal appearances, and the sheer force of his personality, Charlemagne sought to awe conquered peoples with his fierce presence and terrible justice. By confiscating the estates of great territorial magnates, he acquired lands and goods with which to gain the support of lesser lords, further expanding the territory under his control.

The political power of the Carolingians rested on the cooperation of the dominant social class, the Frankish aristocracy. The Carolingians themselves had emerged from this aristocracy, and their military and political success depended on the support of the nobility. The lands and booty with which Charles Martel and Charlemagne rewarded their followers in these noble families enabled the nobles to improve their economic position. In short, Carolingian success was a matter of reciprocal help and reward.[7]

For administrative purposes, Charlemagne divided his entire kingdom into counties, based closely on the old Merovingian civitas (see page 364). Each of the approximately six hundred counties was governed by a count, who had full military and judicial power and held his office for life but could be removed by the emperor for misconduct. As a link between local authorities and the central government, Charlemagne appointed officials called *missi dominici,* "agents of the lord king." The empire was divided into visitorial districts. Each year, beginning in 802, two missi, usually a count and a bishop or abbot, visited assigned districts. They checked up on the counts and their districts' judicial, financial, and clerical activities.

A modern state has institutions of government such as a civil service and courts of law. These did not exist in Charlemagne's empire. Instead, dependent relationships cemented by oaths promising faith and loyalty held society together. Nevertheless, although the empire lacked viable institutions, Carolingian abbots and bishops who served as Charlemagne's advisers worked out what was for their time a sophisticated political ideology.

In letters and treatises, churchmen set before their ruler high standards of behavior and of government. They wrote that although a ruler holds power from God, the ruler is obliged to respect the law just as all subjects of the empire were required to obey the ruler. The abbots and bishops envisioned a unified Christian society presided over by a king who was responsible for maintaining peace, law, and order and dispensing justice, without which, they pointed out, neither the ruler nor the kingdom had any justification. These views derived largely from Saint Augustine's theories of kingship. Inevitably, they could not be realized in an illiterate, preindustrial society. But they were the seeds from which medieval and even modern ideas of government were to develop.

MAP 13.1 The Carolingian World The extent of Charlemagne's nominal jurisdiction was extraordinary. It was not equaled until the nineteenth century.

The Carolingian Intellectual Revival

It is ironic that Charlemagne's most enduring legacy was the stimulus he gave to scholarship and learning. Barely literate, preoccupied with the control of vast territories, much more a warrior than a thinker, Charlemagne nevertheless set in motion a cultural revival that had widespread and long-lasting consequences.

The revival of learning associated with Charlemagne and his court at Aachen drew its greatest inspiration from seventh- and eighth-century intellectual developments in the Anglo-Saxon kingdom of Northumbria, situated at the northernmost tip of the old Roman world (see Map 13.1). Northumbrian monasteries produced scores of religious books, commentaries on the Scriptures, illuminated manuscripts, law codes, and collections of letters and sermons.

The finest representative of Northumbrian and indeed all Anglo-Saxon scholarship is the Venerable Bede (ca 673–735). The author of learned commentaries on the Scriptures, Bede also produced the *Ecclesiastical History of the English Nation,* our chief source of information about early Britain. He discussed the validity of his evidence, compared various sources, and exercised a rare critical judgment. For these reasons, he has been called "the first scientific intellect among the Germanic peoples of Europe."[8]

At his court at Aachen, Charlemagne assembled learned men from all over Europe. The most important scholar and the leader of the palace school was the Northumbrian Alcuin (ca 735–804). From 781 until his death, Alcuin was the emperor's chief adviser on religious and educational matters. He prepared some of the emperor's official documents and wrote many moral *exempla,* or "models," which set high standards for royal behavior and constitute a treatise on kingship. Alcuin's letters to Charlemagne set forth political theories on the authority, power, and responsibilities of a Christian ruler.

Scholars at Charlemagne's court copied books and manuscripts and built up libraries. They used the beautifully clear handwriting now known as Carolingian minuscule, from which modern Roman type is derived. This script is called "minuscule" because it has lowercase as well as capital letters; the script that the Romans used had only capitals. Because lowercase letters are smaller than capitals, scribes using Carolingian minuscule could put more words on each sheet of vellum and could increase the number of texts they copied.

Scholars established schools all across Europe, attaching them to monasteries and cathedrals. They placed great emphasis on the education of priests, trying to make all priests at least able to read, write, and do simple arithmetic. The greatest contribution of the scholars at Aachen was not so much the originality of their ideas as their hard work of salvaging and preserving the thought and writings of the ancients. The Carolingian Renaissance was a rebirth of interest in, study of, and preservation of the language, ideas, and achievements of classical Greece and Rome.

Once basic literacy was established, monastic and other scholars went on to more difficult work. By the middle of the ninth century, there was a great outpouring of more sophisticated books. Ecclesiastical writers, imbued with the legal ideas of ancient Rome and the theocratic ideals of Saint Augustine, instructed the semibarbaric rulers of the West. And it is no accident that medical study in the West began, at Salerno in southern Italy, in the late ninth century, *after* the Carolingian Ren-

aissance. By the tenth century, the patterns of thought and lifestyles of educated western Europeans were those of Rome and Latin Christianity. Even the violence and destruction of the great invasions of the late ninth and tenth centuries could not destroy the strong foundations laid by Alcuin and his colleagues.

Aristocratic Resurgence

Charlemagne left his vast empire to his sole surviving son, Louis the Pious (r. 814–840). Initially, the new king proved as tough as his father, banishing from his court real and supposed conspirators, crushing rebellions, and punishing his enemies. In 821, though, Louis seems to have undergone a change and began to pardon some rebels and allow exiles to return. The emperor underestimated the magnates; they stirred jealousy among his sons and plotted to augment their own wealth and power.

Between 817 and his death, Louis made several divisions of the empire. Dissatisfied with their portions and hoping to win the imperial title, his three sons—Lothar, Louis the German, and Charles the Bald—fought bitterly among themselves. Finally, in the Treaty of Verdun of 843, they agreed to divide the empire.

In the past, historians accounted for the collapse of the Carolingian Empire by stressing the fratricidal wars among Charlemagne's three grandsons. Recent work, however, emphasizes the conspiracies and revolts of the magnates. Charlemagne had tried to prevent the office of count from becoming hereditary in one family, but that is precisely what happened in the ninth century. In addition, some nobles acquired several counties. As they gained power, they could effectively block the king's authority in their lands. The administrative system built by Pippin III and Charlemagne survived, but imperial control weakened. The local magnates held the power.[9]

FEUDALISM AND MANORIALISM

Feudalism, long used to describe medieval society, was a term invented in the seventeenth century and popularized in the eighteenth by political philosophers who disparaged it as a symbol of entrenched aristocratic privilege. Scholars have struggled to work out a definition of feudalism that can apply to the entire Middle Ages (ca 500–1500), but they have not succeeded.

Two main explanations for the rise of feudalism have emerged. According to the older explanation, the eighth-century Carolingian kings and magnates needed armed retainers who could fight on horseback. Around this time, a new Chinese technology, the stirrup, arrived in Europe and was adopted by riders, who could use it to gain leverage and thus use the force of the galloping horse to impale an enemy with a spear. It took time and money to equip and train these riders, so the king and magnates bound their retainers by oaths of loyalty. The second approach dismisses the stirrup, pointing out that most warfare was conducted by infantry. In this view, feudal relationships arose as kings and magnates purchased the support and loyalty of followers with lands or estates confiscated from the church.

Whatever the exact causes, the weakening of central power within the Carolingian Empire led to an increase in the power of local authorities, the counts. They governed virtually independent territories in which weak and distant kings could not interfere. "Political power had become a private, heritable property for great counts and lords."[10] This was feudalism as a form of government.

Feudalism concerned the rights, powers, and lifestyles of the military elite. *Manorialism* involved the services of the peasant class. The two were linked. The economic power of the warrior class rested on landed estates, which were worked by peasants. Peasants needed protection, and lords demanded something in return for that protection. Free farmers surrendered themselves and their land to the lord's jurisdiction. The land was given back to them to farm, but they were tied to the land by various payments and services. Those obligations varied from place to place, but certain practices became common everywhere. The peasant had to give the lord a percentage of the annual harvest, pay a fine to marry someone from outside the lord's estate, and pay a fine—usually the best sheep or cow owned—to inherit property. Most significant, the peasant lost his freedom and became a *serf,* part of the lord's permanent labor force, bound to the land and unable to leave it without the lord's permission. With large tracts of land and a small pool of labor, the most profitable form of capital was not land but laborers.

The transition from freedom to serfdom was slow, depending on the degree of political order in a given region. By the year 800, though, perhaps 60 percent of the population of western Europe had been reduced to serfdom. While there were many economic levels within this serf class, from the highly prosperous to the desperately poor, all had lost their freedom.

Homage and Fealty Although the rite of entering a feudal relationship varied widely across Europe and sometimes was entirely verbal, we have a few illustrations of it. Here the vassal kneels before the lord, places his clasped hands between those of the lord, and declares, "I become your man." Sometimes the lord handed over a clump of earth, representing the fief, and the ceremony concluded with a kiss, symbolizing peace between them. *(Osterreichische Nationalbibliothek)*

CRISIS AND RECOVERY

After the Treaty of Verdun and the division of Charlemagne's empire among his grandsons, continental Europe presented an easy target for foreign invaders. All three kingdoms were torn by domestic dissension and disorder. No European political power was strong enough to put up effective resistance to external attacks.

Assaults on Western Europe

From the moors of Scotland to the mountains of Sicily, there arose in the ninth century the Christian prayer, "Save us, O God, from the violence of the Northmen." The Northmen, also known as Normans or Vikings, were pagan Germanic peoples from Norway, Sweden, and Denmark who had remained beyond the sway of the Christianizing and civilizing influences of the Carolingian Empire. Some scholars believe that the name *Viking* derives from the Old Norse word *vik,* meaning "creek." A Viking, then, was a pirate who waited in a creek or bay to attack passing vessels.

Viking assaults began around 787, and by the mid-tenth century the Vikings had brought large sections of continental Europe and Britain under their sway. In the east, they pierced the rivers of Russia as far as the Black Sea. In the west, they sailed as far as Iceland, Greenland, and even the coast of North America, perhaps as far south as Long Island Sound, New York.

The Vikings were superb seamen with advanced methods of boatbuilding. Propelled either by oars or by sails, deckless, and about sixty-five feet long, a Viking ship could carry between forty and sixty men—quite enough to harass an isolated monastery or village. Against these ships navigated by thoroughly experienced and utterly fearless sailors, the Carolingian Empire, with no navy, was helpless. The Vikings moved swiftly, attacked, and escaped to return again.

Scholars disagree about the reasons for Viking attacks and migrations. Some maintain that overpopulation forced the Vikings to emigrate. Others argue that climatic conditions and crop failures forced migration. Still others insist that the Vikings were looking for trade and new commercial contacts, along with targets for plunder. At first they attacked and sailed off laden with booty. Later, on returning, they settled down and colonized the areas they had conquered. Between 876 and 954, Viking control extended from Dublin across the Irish Sea to Britain, then across northern Britain and the North Sea to the Vikings' Scandinavian homelands. These invaders also overran a large part of northwestern France and called the territory Norsemanland, from which the word *Normandy* derives.

Scarcely had the savagery of the Viking assaults begun to subside when Europe was hit from the east and south. Beginning about 890, Magyar tribes crossed the Danube and pushed steadily westward. (People thought of them as returning Huns, so the Magyars came to be known as Hungarians.) They subdued northern Italy, compelled Bavaria and Saxony to pay tribute, and penetrated even into the Rhineland and Burgundy. These roving bandits attacked isolated villages and monasteries, taking prisoners and selling them in the Eastern slave markets. The Magyars were not colonizers; their sole object was booty and plunder.

From the south, the Muslims also began new encroachments, concentrating on the two southern peninsulas, Italy and Spain. Seventh- and early-eighth-century Islamic movements had been for conquest and colonization, but the goal of ninth- and tenth-century incursions was plunder. In Italy the Muslims drove northward and sacked Rome in 846. Most of Spain had remained under their domination since the eighth century. Expert seamen, they sailed around the Iberian Peninsula and braved the dangerous shoals and winds of the Atlantic coast. They also attacked Mediterranean settlements along the coast of Provence. But Muslim attacks on the European continent in the ninth and tenth centuries were less destructive than the assaults of the more primitive Vikings and Magyars.

What was the effect of these invasions on the structure of European society? Viking, Magyar, and Muslim attacks accelerated the development of feudalism. Lords capable of rallying fighting men, supporting them, and putting up resistance to the invaders did so. They also assumed political power in their territories. Weak and defenseless people sought the protection of local strongmen. Free peasants sank to the level of serfs. Consequently, European society became further fragmented. Public power became increasingly decentralized.

The ninth-century invaders left significant traces of their own cultures. The Muslims made an important contribution to European agriculture, primarily through their influence in Spain. The Vikings, too, made positive contributions to the areas they settled. They carried everywhere their unrivaled knowledge of shipbuilding and seamanship. The northeastern and central parts of England where the Vikings settled became known as the Danelaw because Danish law and customs, not English, prevailed there. York in northern England, once a Roman army camp and then an Anglo-Saxon town, became a thriving center of Viking trade with Scandinavia. At

Dublin on the east coast of Ireland, Viking ironworkers, steelworkers, and combmakers established a center for trade with the Hebrides, Iceland, and Norway. The Irish cities of Limerick, Cork, Wexford, and Waterford trace their origins to Viking trading centers.

The Restoration of Order

The eleventh century witnessed the beginnings of political stability in western Europe. Foreign invasions gradually declined, and domestic disorder subsided. This development gave people security in their persons and property. Political order and security provided the foundation for economic recovery and contributed to a slow increase in population.

In the tenth century, Charlemagne's descendants continued to hold the royal title in the West Frankish kingdom, but they exercised no effective control over the magnates. Throughout what is now France, regional differences abounded. Northern French society, for example, had strong feudal elements, but in the south vassalage was almost unknown. Southern territories used Roman law, but the northern counties and duchies relied on unwritten customary law that was not codified until the thirteenth century.

Normandy gradually emerged as the strongest territory with the greatest level of peace. In 911, the West Frankish ruler Charles the Simple, unable to oust the Vikings, officially recognized their leader, Rollo, and later invested him with lands. The Vikings were baptized and pledged their support to Charles. Viking raids ended, and the late tenth and early eleventh centuries saw the assimilation of Norman and French.

After the death of the last Carolingian ruler in 987, an assembly of nobles elected Hugh Capet, the head of a powerful clan of the West Frankish kingdom, as king. The history of France as a separate kingdom begins with this event. The first Capetian kings were weak compared to the duke of Normandy, but by hanging on to what they had, they laid the foundation for later political stability.

In Anglo-Saxon England, recovery followed a different pattern. The Vikings had made a concerted effort to conquer and rule the whole island, and perhaps no part of Europe suffered more. The victory of the remarkable Alfred, king of the West Saxons, over Guthrun the Dane at Edington in 878 inaugurated a great political revival. Alfred and his immediate successors built a system of local defenses and slowly extended royal rule beyond Wessex (the area controlled by the West Saxons) to other Anglo-Saxon peoples until one law—royal law—replaced local custom. Alfred and his successors also laid the foundations for a system of local government responsible directly to the king. Under the pressure of the Vikings, the seven kingdoms of England were gradually united under one ruler.

In the east, the German king Otto I (r. 936–973) inflicted a crushing defeat on the Magyars in 955 at Lechfeld, halting their westward expansion, ending the threat to Germany, and making himself a hero to the Germans. Otto's victory revived the German monarchy. To symbolize his intention to continue the tradition of Charlemagne, Otto selected Aachen as the site of his coronation.

The basis of Otto's power was an alliance with and control of the church. Otto asserted the right to control church appointments. Bishops and abbots had to perform feudal homage for the lands that accompanied the church office. This practice, later called **lay investiture,** led to a grave crisis in the eleventh century (see pages 372–373) Otto's coronation by the pope in 962 revived the imperial dignity and laid the foundation for the Holy Roman Empire. He also filled a power vacuum in northern Italy and brought peace and stability to the region. Here, too, were the seeds of future conflict.

Plague, climatic changes, and invasions had drastically reduced the population in northern Italy, though the cities there survived. By the ninth century, some cities, especially Venice, showed economic recovery. Through privileged access to Byzantine markets, Venice imported silk, textiles, cosmetics, and Crimean slaves, which it sold to Padua and other cities. Its commerce stimulated the growth of Lombard cities such as Milan and Cremona, which, along with Sicily, fed Venice in exchange for luxury goods. The rising economic importance of Venice, Genoa, Pisa, and other Italian cities became a central factor in the struggle between the pope and the Holy Roman emperor.

REVIVAL AND REFORM IN THE CHRISTIAN CHURCH

The eleventh century witnessed the beginnings of a remarkable religious revival. Monasteries, always the leaders in ecclesiastical reform, remodeled themselves under the leadership of the Burgundian abbey of Cluny. Subsequently, new religious orders, such as the Cistercians, were founded and became a broad spiritual movement.

The papacy itself, after a century of corruption and decadence, was cleaned up. The popes worked to clarify church doctrine and codify church law. They and their officials sought to communicate with all the clergy and peoples of Europe through a clearly defined, obedient hierarchy of bishops. Pope Gregory VII's strong assertion of papal power led to profound changes and serious conflict with secular authorities. The revival of the church manifested itself in the crusading movement.

Monastic Revival

The Viking, Magyar, and Muslim invaders attacked and ransacked many monasteries across Europe. Some religious communities fled and dispersed. In the period of political disorder that followed the disintegration of the Carolingian Empire, many religious houses fell under the control and domination of local feudal lords. Powerful laymen appointed themselves as abbots but kept their wives or mistresses. They took for themselves the lands and goods of monasteries, spending monastic revenues and selling monastic offices. The level of spiritual observance and intellectual activity declined.

In 909 William the Pious, duke of Aquitaine, established the abbey of Cluny near Macon in Burgundy. In his charter of endowment, Duke William declared that Cluny was to enjoy complete independence from all feudal (or secular) and episcopal lordship. The new monastery was to be subordinate only to the authority of Saints Peter and Paul as represented by the pope.

This monastery and its foundation charter came to exert vast religious influence. The first two abbots of Cluny set very high standards of religious behavior and stressed strict observance of *The Rule of Saint Benedict.* Cluny gradually came to stand for clerical celibacy and the suppression of *simony* (the sale of church offices). In the eleventh century, a series of highly able abbots ruled Cluny for a long time. These abbots paid careful attention to sound economic management. In a disorderly world, Cluny represented religious and political stability. Laypersons placed lands under Cluny's custody and monastic houses under its jurisdiction for reform. Benefactors wanted to be associated with Cluniac piety. Moreover, properties and monasteries under Cluny's jurisdiction enjoyed special protection, at least theoretically, from violence. In this way, hundreds of monasteries, primarily in France and Spain, came under Cluny's authority.

Deeply impressed laypeople showered gifts on monasteries with good reputations. Jewelry, rich vestments, elaborately carved sacred vessels, and lands and properties poured into some houses. But with this wealth came lay influence. And as the monasteries became richer, the lifestyle of the monks grew increasingly luxurious. Monastic observance and spiritual fervor declined. Soon fresh demands for reform were heard. The result was the founding of new religious orders in the late eleventh and early twelfth centuries.

The best representative of the new reforming spirit was the Cistercian order. The Cistercians combined a very simple liturgical life, a radical rejection of the traditional feudal sources of income (such as the possession of mills and serfs), and many innovative economic practices. The Cistercians' dynamic growth and rapid expansion had a profound impact on European society.

Reform of the Papacy

In the tenth century, the papacy provided little leadership to the Christian peoples of western Europe. Factions in Rome sought to control the papacy for their own material gain. Popes were appointed to advance the political ambitions of their families—the great aristocratic families of Rome—and not because of special spiritual qualifications.

Serious efforts at reform began under Pope Leo IX (r. 1049–1054). He traveled widely, holding councils that issued decrees against violence, simony, and clerical marriage. Although celibacy had been an obligation for ordination since the fourth century, in the tenth and eleventh centuries probably a majority of European priests were married or living with a woman.

A church council produced another reform—removing the influence of Roman aristocratic factions in papal elections. Since the eighth century, the priests of the major churches around Rome had constituted a special group, called a "college," that advised the pope. They were called "cardinals," from the Latin *cardo,* or "hinge." They were the hinges on which the church turned. The Lateran Synod of 1059 decreed that these cardinals had the sole authority and power to elect the pope and that they would govern the church when the office was vacant. By 1073 the reform movement was well advanced. That year, Cardinal Hildebrand was elected as Pope Gregory VII, and reform took on a political character.

Cardinal Hildebrand believed that the pope, as the successor of Saint Peter, was the vicar of God on earth and that papal orders were the orders of God. Once Hildebrand became pope, he and his assistants began to insist on the "freedom of the church." By this they meant the freedom of churchmen to obey canon law and their freedom from control and interference by laypeople.

"Freedom of the church" pointed to the end of lay investiture, the selection and appointment of church officials by lay authorities. When bishops or abbots received the symbols of their office from lay officials, those officials seemed to be distributing spiritual authority. Papal opposition to this practice was not new in the eleventh century, but Gregory's attempt to end lay investiture was a radical departure. Feudal monarchs depended on the literacy and administrative skills of church officials to operate their governments. Gregory's new stand seemed to spell disaster for royal administration and provoked a crisis.

In February 1075, Pope Gregory held a council that published a decree against lay investiture. According to this ruling, clerics who accepted investiture from laymen were to be deposed, and laymen who invested clerics were to be *excommunicated*—cut off from the sacraments and the Christian community. Henry IV of the Holy Roman Empire, William the Conqueror of England, and Philip I of France, however, all immediately protested.

The strongest reaction came from Henry IV. In two basic ways, the relationship of the emperor to the papacy differed from that of other monarchs: the pope crowned the emperor, and both emperor and pope claimed northern Italy. Of course, beneath the question of lay investiture, a more fundamental issue was at stake. Gregory's decree raised the question of the proper rule of the monarch in a Christian society. Did a king have ultimate jurisdiction over all his subjects, including the clergy? For centuries, the answer had been yes.

In January 1076, the German bishops who had been invested by Henry withdrew their allegiance from the pope. Gregory excommunicated them and suspended Henry from the kingship—delighting German nobles, who now did not need to obey the king's commands. By Christmas, ironically, the clergy supported the emperor, while the great nobles favored the pope.

In January 1077, Henry arrived at the pope's residence in Canossa in northern Italy and, according to legend, stood outside in the snow for three days seeking forgiveness. As a priest, Gregory was obliged to grant absolution and readmit the emperor into the Christian community. Although the emperor, the most powerful ruler in Europe, bowed before the pope, Henry actually won a victory—albeit a temporary one. He regained the kingship and authority over his subjects, but for the next two hundred years, rulers in Germany and elsewhere were reluctant to challenge the pope.

The lay investiture issue itself remained unresolved until 1122, when a compromise was forged. Bishops were to be chosen by the clergy in the presence of the emperor or his delegate. The papacy technically won, as the ruler could no longer invest. But lay rulers retained an effective veto power, since they could be present at the election.

The Countess Matilda A staunch supporter of the reforming ideals of the papacy, the Countess Matilda of Tuscany (ca 1046–1115) arranged the dramatic meeting of the pope and emperor at her castle at Canossa near Reggio Emilia in the Apennines. The arrangement of the figures—with Henry IV kneeling, Gregory lecturing, and Matilda persuading—suggests contemporary understanding of the scene where Henry received absolution. Matilda's vast estates in northern Italy and her political contacts in Rome made her a powerful figure in the late eleventh century *(Biblioteca Apostolica Vaticana)*

The long controversy had tremendous social and political consequences in Germany. From 1075 to 1125, civil war raged in the land, and the emperors—preoccupied with their struggle with the pope—could do little to stop it. The nobles gained power, subordinating knights and reducing free men and serfs to servile status. When the investiture issue was finally settled in 1122, the nobility held the balance of power in Germany.

Eleventh- and twelfth-century popes pressed reform. They expanded the papal chancery (writing office) and the papal chapel, which, with the college of cardinals, constituted the Roman curia, or papal court. The curia formulated laws for all of Christendom. Papal legates published those laws at councils, or assemblies of clergy and people. The papal curia, with its administrative, financial, and legal bureaucracies, became the first well-organized institution of monarchical authority in medieval Europe.

THE CRUSADES

Crusades in the late eleventh and early twelfth centuries were holy wars sponsored by the papacy for the recovery of the Holy Land from the Muslims. They grew out of the long conflict between Christians and Muslims in Spain (see page 377). Although people of all ages and classes participated in the Crusades, so many knights did so that crusading became a distinctive feature of the upper-class lifestyle. In an aristocratic, military society, men coveted reputations as Crusaders; the Christian knight who had been to the Holy Land enjoyed great prestige. The Crusades manifested the religious and chivalric ideals—as well as the tremendous vitality—of medieval society.

Background of the Crusades

The Roman papacy supported the holy war in Spain and by the late eleventh century had strong reasons for wanting to launch an expedition against Muslims in the East as well. The papacy had been involved in the bitter struggle over investiture with the German emperors. If the pope could muster a large army against the enemies of Christianity, his claim to be leader of Christian society in the West would be strengthened. Moreover, in 1054 a serious theological disagreement had split the Greek church of Byzantium and the Roman church of the West. The pope believed that a crusade would lead to strong Roman influence in Greek territories and eventually the reunion of the two churches.

In 1071 at Manzikert in eastern Anatolia, Turkish soldiers defeated a Greek army and occupied much of Asia Minor. The emperor at Constantinople appealed to the West for support. Shortly afterward, the city of Jerusalem, the scene of Christ's preaching and burial, fell to the Turks. Pilgrimages to holy places in the Middle East became very dangerous, and the papacy claimed to be outraged that the holy city was in the hands of unbelievers. Since the Muslims had held Palestine since the eighth century, the papacy actually feared that the Seljuk Turks would be less accommodating to Christian pilgrims than the previous Muslim rulers had been.

In 1095 Pope Urban II journeyed to Clermont in France and on November 27 called for a great Christian holy war against the infidels. Urban's appeal at Clermont represents his policy of *rapprochement,* or reconciliation, with Byzantium, with church union his ultimate goal. (Mutual ill will, quarrels, and the plundering of Byzantine property by undisciplined westerners were to frustrate this hope.) He urged Christian knights who had been fighting one another to direct their energies against the true enemies of God, the Muslims. Urban proclaimed an *indulgence,* or remission of the temporal penalties imposed by the church for sin, to those who would fight for and regain Jerusalem.

Encouraged by popular preachers such as Peter the Hermit, great lords from northern France and thousands of people of all classes joined the crusade. Although most of the Crusaders were French, pilgrims from many regions streamed southward from the Rhineland, through Germany and the Balkans. Of all of the developments of the central Middle Ages, none better reveals Europeans' religious and emotional fervor and the influence of the reformed papacy than the extraordinary outpouring of support for the First Crusade. (See the feature "Listening to the Past: An Arab View of the Crusades" on pages 414–415.)

Motives and Course of the Crusades

The Crusades also brought to the surface latent Christian prejudice against the Jews. Between the sixth and tenth centuries, descendants of **Sephardic** (from the modern Hebrew word *Separaddi,* meaning Spanish or Portuguese) **Jews** had settled along the trade routes of western Europe; in the eleventh century, they played a major role in the international trade between the Muslim Middle East and the West. Jews also lent money to peasants, townspeople, and nobles. When the First Crusade was launched, many poor knights had to borrow from Jews to equip themselves for the expedition. Debt bred resentment.

The experience of the Rhineland Jews illustrates how the Crusades, launched against Muslims in the Middle East, often affected minorities within Europe. Beginning in the late tenth century Jews had trickled into the city of Speyer—partly through Jewish perception of opportunity and partly because of the direct invitation of the bishop of Speyer. The bishop's charter meant that Jews could openly practice their religion, could not be assaulted, and could buy and sell goods.

But Christians resented Jews as newcomers, outsiders, and aliens; for enjoying the special protection of the bishop; and for providing economic competition. Anti-Semitic ideology had received enormous impetus from the virulent anti-Semitic writings of Christian apologists in the first six centuries C.E. Jews, they argued, were *deicides* (Christ-killers). By the eleventh century, anti-Semitism was an old and deeply rooted element in Western society.

Late in April 1096, a large band of Crusaders approached Speyer and randomly murdered eleven Jews. The bishop took the entire Jewish community into his castle, arrested some of the burghers, and cut off their hands. News of these events raced up the Rhine to Worms, creating confusion in the Jewish community. Some took refuge with Christian friends; others sought the bishop's protection. A combination of Crusaders and burghers killed a large number of Jews, looted and burned synagogues and desecrated the Torah (see page 39) and other books. Proceeding on to the old and prosperous city of Mainz, Crusaders continued attacking Jews. Facing overwhelming odds, eleven hundred Jews killed their families and themselves. The Jews were never passive; everywhere they put up resistance. If the Crusades had begun as opposition to Islam, after 1096 that hostility extended to those Christians saw as enemies of society—lepers, Jews, and homosexuals (see pages 383–384).

The First Crusade was successful, mostly because of the dynamic enthusiasm of the participants. The Crusaders had little more than religious zeal. They knew little of the geography or climate of the Middle East. Although there were several counts with military experience, the Crusaders could never agree on a leader, and the entire expedition was marked by disputes among the great lords. Lines of supply were never set up. Starvation and disease wracked the army, and the Turks slaughtered hundreds of noncombatants. Nevertheless, convinced that "God wills it," the war cry of the Crusaders, the army pressed on and in 1099 captured Jerusalem. Although the Crusaders fought bravely, Arab disunity was a chief reason for their victory. At Jerusalem, Edessa, Tripoli, and Antioch, Crusader kingdoms were founded on the Western feudal model (see Map 13.2).

Between 1096 and 1270, the crusading ideal was expressed in eight papally approved expeditions to the East. Despite the success of the First Crusade, none of the later ones accomplished very much. During the Fourth Crusade (1202–1204), careless preparation and inadequate financing had disastrous consequences for Latin-Byzantine relations. In April 1204, the Crusaders and Venetians stormed Constantinople; sacked the city, destroying its magnificent library; and grabbed thousands of relics, which were later sold in Europe. The Byzantine Empire, as a political unit, never recovered from this destruction.

MAP 13.2 The Routes of the Crusades The Crusades led to a major cultural encounter between Muslim and Christian values. What significant intellectual and economic effects resulted?

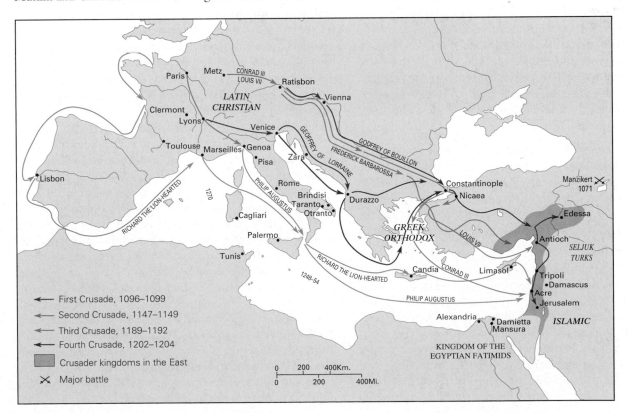

The empire splintered into three parts and soon consisted of little more than the city of Constantinople. Moreover, the assault of one Christian people on another—when one of the goals of the crusade was reunion of the Greek and Latin churches—made the split between the churches permanent.

In the entire crusading movement, fewer women than men participated directly, since the Crusades were primarily military expeditions. Eleanor of Aquitaine (1122?–1204) accompanied her husband, King Louis VII, on the Second Crusade (1147–1149), and the thirteenth-century English chronicler Matthew Paris says that large numbers of women went on the Seventh Crusade (1248–1254) so that they could obtain the crusading indulgence. Women who stayed home assumed their husbands' responsibilities in the management of estates, the dispensation of justice to vassals and serfs, and the protection of property from attack. The many women who operated inns and shops in the towns through which crusading armies passed profited from the rental of lodgings and the sale of foodstuffs, clothing, arms, and fodder for animals. For prostitutes, also, crusading armies offered business opportunities.

Cultural Consequences

The Crusades introduced some Europeans to Eastern luxury goods, but their immediate cultural impact on the West remains debatable. By the late eleventh century, strong economic and intellectual ties with the East had already been made. The Crusades testify to the religious enthusiasm of the central Middle Ages, but Steven Runciman, a distinguished scholar of the Crusades, concludes in his three-volume history:

In the long sequence of interaction and fusion between orient and occident out of which our civilization has grown, the Crusades were a tragic and destructive episode. . . . High ideals were besmirched by cruelty and greed, enterprise and endurance by a blind and narrow self-righteousness; and the Holy War itself was nothing more than a long act of intolerance in the name of God.[11]

Along the Syrian and Palestinian coasts, the Crusaders set up a string of feudal states that managed to survive for about two centuries before the Muslims reconquered them. The Crusaders left two more permanent legacies in the Middle East that continue to affect us today. First, the long struggle between Islam and Christendom, and the example of persecution set by Christian kings and prelates, left an inheritance of deep bitterness; relations between Muslims and their Christian and Jewish subjects

worsened. Second, European merchants, primarily Italians, had established communities in the Crusader states. After those kingdoms collapsed, Muslim rulers still encouraged trade with European businessmen. Commerce with the West benefited both Muslims and Europeans, and it continued to flourish.[12]

The European Crusades represent the first great colonizing movement beyond the geographical boundaries of the European continent. The ideal of a sacred mission to conquer or convert Muslim peoples entered Europeans' consciousness and became a continuing goal. When, in 1492, Christopher Columbus sailed west hoping to reach India, he used the language of the Crusades in his diaries, which show that he was preoccupied with the conquest of Jerusalem (see Chapter 6). Columbus wanted to establish a Christian base in India from which a new crusade could be launched against Islam.

But most medieval and early modern Europeans knew very little about Islam or its adherents. As the crusading goal of conquest and conversion persisted through the centuries, Europeans adopted a strategy that served as a central feature of Western thought and warfare: the dehumanization of the enemy. They described Muslims as "filth." In turn, Muslims called Europeans "infidels" (unbelievers) and considered them "barbarians" because of the unsophisticated level of European medical, philosophical, and mathematical knowledge in comparison to that of the Islamic world. Whereas Europeans perceived the Crusades as sacred religious movements, Muslims saw them as expansionist and imperialistic. Even today, some Muslims see the conflict between Arab and Jew as just another manifestation of the medieval Crusades. Some Arab historians interpret the Jews and the state of Israel as new Crusaders or as tools of Western imperialism.

For Jewish-Christian relations, the Crusades proved to be a disaster. After the experience of the Rhineland Jews during the First Crusade (see page 374), any burst of Christian zeal or enthusiasm evoked in European Jews suspicion, unease, and fear. From 1095 on, most Christians did not regard Jews (or Muslims) as normal human beings, viewing them instead as inhuman monsters. According to one scholar, "Every time a crusade was summoned against the Muslims there was a new outbreak of anti-Semitism in Europe which became an indelible European habit." The "Christian" enthusiasm associated with the Protestant Reformation of the early sixteenth century, the Counter-Reformation of the late sixteenth century, and the Thirty Years' War of the seventeenth century aroused new waves of anti-Semitism. This anti-Semitism eventually found its most frightful and appalling expression in the Nazism of the twentieth century.[13]

Although the legal position of Jews in European society deteriorated after the First Crusade, and despite the pervasive anti-Semitism of the time, Jewish culture flourished. In the period from about 1000 to 1400, Jews worked as tradesmen, craftsmen, moneychangers, and long-distance business people. They established schools for education in the Torah (the body of Hebraic religious law) and the Talmud (rabbinic commentary on the Torah) and produced beautifully illuminated manuscripts. Scholars enjoyed great respect in Jewish communities, and Christian and Muslim nobles sought Jewish physicians. Although both Jewish and Christian law banned Jews from the emerging universities (see pages 389–390), Jews flocked to university towns. In spite of harassment and humiliation—at Pisa on the Feast of Saint Catherine (November 25) students seized the stoutest Jew they could find, put him on scales, and fined the Jewish community his weight in sweets—Jews became students and professors. In 1300 Jacob ben Machir was even appointed dean of the medical school at Montpellier. Andalusian Spain, the safest place for Jews in the Latin West until the fifteenth century, witnessed a "golden age" of Jewish culture in science, music, medicine, philosophy, and especially Hebrew poetry.

THE EXPANSION OF LATIN CHRISTENDOM

The period after the millennial year 1000 witnessed great migrations and cross-regional contacts. The movement of peoples and ideas from western France, the heartland of Christendom, and from western Germany into frontier regions—Ireland, Scandinavia, the Baltic lands, eastern Europe, and Spain—had, by about 1300, profound cultural consequences for those fringe territories. Wars of expansion, the establishment of new Christian bishoprics, and the vast migration of colonists, together with the papal emphasis on a unified Christian world, brought about the gradual Europeanization of the frontier.

Northern and Eastern Europe

Beginning in 1177, Norman knights from England began to seize land and build themselves estates in Ireland. Ireland had been technically Christian since the days of Saint Patrick (see page 213), but the coming of the Normans transformed the Irish church from a monastic structure to an episcopal one. The Normans also brought the fief and feudal cavalry to Ireland, as they did to Scotland beginning about the same time.

Latin Christian influences entered Scandinavia and the Baltic lands primarily through the creation of dioceses. This took place in Denmark in the tenth and eleventh centuries, and the institutional church spread rather quickly due to the support offered by the strong throne. Dioceses were established in Norway and Sweden in the eleventh century, and in 1164 Uppsala, long the center of the pagan cults of Odin and Thor, became a Catholic archdiocese.

Otto I (see page 371) planted a string of dioceses along his northern and eastern frontiers, hoping to pacify the newly conquered Slavs in eastern Europe. Frequent Slavic revolts illustrate the people's resentment of German lords and clerics and indicate that the church did not easily penetrate the region. In 1157, though, Albert the Bear (d. 1170) began a ruthless program to pacify the region. He built several castles, which he filled with knights recruited from the Rhineland and used as bases to crush any revolt.

The church also moved into central Europe, first in Bohemia in the tenth century and from there into Poland and Hungary in the eleventh century. In the twelfth and thirteenth centuries, thousands of settlers poured into eastern Europe. They settled in Silesia, Mecklenburg, Bohemia, Poland, Hungary, and Transylvania. New immigrants were German in descent, name, language, and law. Hundreds of small market towns populated by these newcomers supplied the needs of the rural countryside. Larger towns such as Cracow and Riga engaged in long-distance trade and gradually grew into large urban centers.[14]

Spain

About 950 Caliph Abd al-Rahman III (912–961) of the Umayyad Dynasty of Córdoba ruled most of the Iberian Peninsula, from Gibraltar in the south to the Ebro River in the north (see Map 13.3). Christian Spain consisted of the small kingdoms of Castile, León, Catalonia, Aragon, Navarre, and Portugal. When civil wars erupted among Rahman's descendants, though, Muslim lands were split among several small kingdoms, and the Christian reconquest was made easier.

Fourteenth-century clerics used the term **reconquista** (reconquest) to describe what they called a sacred and patriotic crusade to wrest Spain from "alien" Muslim hands. This religious myth became part of Spanish national psychology. The reconquest took several centuries, however. In 1085 Alfonso VI of Castile and León captured Toledo and invited French knights to settle the central plateau of Spain. In 1233 James the Conqueror of Aragon took Valencia, and in 1236 Ferdinand of Castile and León captured the Muslim intellectual and

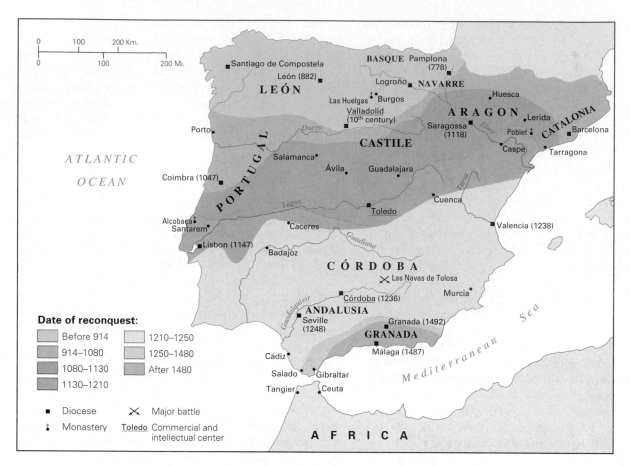

MAP 13.3 The Reconquista   The Christian conquest of Muslim Spain was followed by ecclesiastical reorganization, with the establishment of dioceses, monasteries, and the Latin liturgy, which gradually tied the peninsula to the heartland of Christian Europe and to the Roman papacy. *(Source: Adapted from David Nicholas,* The Evolution of the Medieval World. *© Longman Group UK Limited 1993. Reprinted by permission of Pearson Education Limited.)*

industrial center of Córdoba. When Seville fell to Ferdinand's forces in 1248, Christians held all of the peninsula save for the small state of Granada.

As the Christians advanced, they changed the face of Spanish cities, transforming mosques into cathedrals and, in the process, destroying Muslim art—just as the Muslims, in the eighth century, had destroyed the pagan temples they found. The reconquista also meant the establishment of the Roman institutional church throughout Spain. There were fifty-one bishoprics in the region by 1300. Spanish rulers also established several Cistercian monasteries, which exercised a broad cultural, military, political, and economic influence as well as a religious one.

Behind the advancing Christian armies came settlers. Most settlers came from within the peninsula, as the Christian kings recruited immigrants from Catalonia, Castile, and León. Many of these immigrants settled in the cities that were depopulated with the expulsion of Muslims. Muslim Spain had had more cities than any other country in Europe, and foreign business people flocked to these urban areas as well.[15]

Toward a Christian Society

By about 1300, these frontier areas of northern and eastern Europe and Spain shared a broad cultural uniformity with the core regions of western Christendom: France, Germany, England, and Italy. The papal reform movement of the eleventh century had increased the prestige of the papacy and loyalty to it. Loyalty meant, on the

Almohad Banner   At Las Navas de Tolosa in 1212, King Alfonso VIII of Castile won a decisive victory over the Almohads, a puritanical Muslim sect from North Africa that had ruled most of Spain in the twelfth century. The Spanish victory marked the beginning of Muslim decline. *(Institut Amatller d'Art Hispanic)*

local level, following the Roman liturgy, which led to a broad uniformity of religious practice across Europe.

During the reign of Pope Innocent III (1198–1216), papal directives and legates flowed to all parts of Europe, and twelve hundred prelates obediently left their homes from across Europe to come to Rome for the Fourth Lateran Council in 1215. The papacy was recognized as the nerve center of a homogeneous Christian society. Europeans identified themselves as Christians and even described themselves as belonging to "the Christian race." As in the Islamic world, religion had replaced tribal, political, and ethnic structures as the essence of culture.[16]

MEDIEVAL ORIGINS OF THE MODERN WESTERN STATE

Rome's great legacy to Western civilization had been the concepts of the state and the law. But for almost five hundred years after the disintegration of the Roman Empire in the West, the state as a reality did not exist. Political authority was completely decentralized. Power was spread among many feudal lords, who gave their localities such protection and security as their strength allowed and whose laws affected a relative few. In the mid-eleventh century, many overlapping layers of authority—earls, counts, barons, knights—existed between a king and the ordinary people.

In these circumstances, medieval rulers had common goals. To increase public order, they wanted to establish an effective means of communication with all peoples. They also wanted more revenue and efficient bureaucracies. The solutions they found to these problems laid the foundations for modern national states.

The modern state is an organized territory with definite geographical boundaries that are recognized by other states. It has a body of law and institutions of government. If the state claims to govern according to law, it is guided in its actions by the law. The modern national state counts on the loyalty of its citizens, or at least of a majority of them. In return, it provides order so that citizens can go about their daily work and other activities. It protects its citizens in their persons and property. The state tries to prevent violence and to apprehend and punish those who commit it. It supplies a currency or medium of exchange that permits financial and commercial transactions. The state conducts relations with foreign governments. In order to accomplish even these minimal functions, the state must have officials, bureaucracies, laws, courts of law, soldiers, information, and money. States with these attributes are relatively recent developments.

Unification and Communication

Political developments in England, France, and Germany provide good examples of the beginnings of the national state in the central Middle Ages. Under the pressure of the Viking invasions of the ninth and tenth centuries, the seven kingdoms of Anglo-Saxon England united under one king. At the same time, for reasons historians still

The Bayeux Tapestry Measuring 231 feet by 19½ inches, the Bayeux Tapestry gives a narrative description of the events surrounding the Norman Conquest of England. The tapestry provides an important historical source for the clothing, armor, and lifestyles of the Norman and Anglo-Saxon warrior class. (*Tapisserie de Bayeux et avec autorisation spéciale de la Ville de Bayeux*)

cannot fully explain, England was divided into local *shires,* or counties, each under the jurisdiction of a sheriff appointed by the king. The kingdom of England, therefore, had a political head start on the rest of Europe.

When Edward the Confessor (r. 1042–1066) died, his cousin Duke William of Normandy claimed the English throne and won it by defeating his Anglo-Saxon rival at the Battle of Hastings. As William the Conqueror (r. 1066–1087) subdued the rest of the country, he distributed land to his Norman followers and required all feudal lords to swear an oath of allegiance to him as king. He retained the Anglo-Saxon institution of sheriff but replaced Anglo-Saxons with Normans in this office. The sheriff had the responsibility of catching criminals, collecting taxes, and raising soldiers for the king when ordered.

In 1085 William decided to conduct a systematic survey of the entire country to determine how much wealth there was in his new kingdom and who had it. Groups of royal officials or judges were sent to every part of England. A priest and six local people swore an oath to answer truthfully. Because they swore (Latin, *juror*), they were called *jurors,* and from this small body of local people, the jury system in English-speaking countries gradually evolved. The records collected from the entire country, called **Domesday Book,** provided William and his descendants vital information for governing the country.

In 1128 William's granddaughter Matilda married Geoffrey of Anjou. Their son, who became Henry II of England, inherited the French provinces of Normandy, Anjou, and Touraine in northwestern France. When Henry married the great heiress Eleanor of Aquitaine in 1152, he claimed lordship over Aquitaine, Poitou, and Gascony in southwestern France as well. The histories of England and France were thus closely intertwined in the central Middle Ages.

In the early twelfth century, France consisted of a number of virtually independent provinces, each governed by its local ruler. Unlike the king of England, the king of France had jurisdiction over a very small area. Chroniclers called King Louis VI (r. 1108–1137) *roi de Saint-Denis,* king of Saint-Denis, because the territory he controlled was limited to Paris and the Saint-Denis area surrounding the city. This region, the Île-de-France or royal domain, became the nucleus of the French state. The clear goal of the medieval French king was to increase the royal domain and extend his authority.

The work of unifying France began under Louis VI's grandson Philip II (r. 1180–1223), called "Augustus" because he vastly enlarged the territory of the kingdom. By the end of his reign, Philip was effectively master of northern France. His descendants acquired important holdings in southern France, and by 1300 most of the provinces of modern France had been added to the royal domain through diplomacy, marriage, war, and inheritance. The king of France was stronger than any group of nobles who might try to challenge his authority.

Philip Augustus also devised a method of governing the provinces and building communication between the central government in Paris and local communities. He let each province retain its own institutions and laws, but he dispatched royal agents to each province with the authority to act for the king. These agents were appointed by, paid by, and responsible to the king. This policy reflected the fundamental principle of French administration: royal interests superseded local interests. At the same time, the French system was characterized by a high degree of centralization from Paris and a great variety of customs, laws, and provincial institutions at the local level. The system occasionally fell into disrepair, but it lasted until the Revolution of 1789.

The political problems of Germany differed from those of France and England. The eleventh-century investiture controversy between the German emperor and the Roman papacy left Germany shattered and divided (see pages 372–373). In the twelfth and thirteenth centuries, Germany was split into hundreds of independent provinces, principalities, bishoprics, duchies, and free cities.

There were several barriers to the development of a strong central government. Unlike the French kings, the German rulers lacked a strong royal domain to use as a source of revenue and a base from which to expand royal power. No accepted principle of succession to the throne existed; as a result, the death of the Holy Roman emperor was often followed by civil war and anarchy. Moreover, German rulers were continually attracted south by the wealth of the northern Italian cities or by dreams of restoring the imperial glory of Charlemagne. Time after time, the German kings got involved in Italian affairs, and in turn the papacy, fearful of a strong German power in northern Italy, interfered in German affairs. Consequently, in contrast to France and England, the German Empire witnessed little royal centralization.

Instead, Germany evolved in the direction of *territorial lordships*. From about 1050 to 1400, and down to 1871, German history is regional history. The great duchies—Saxony, Swabia, Bavaria, and Thuringia—emerged as defensive units against Magyar and Slavic invaders, while the great archbishoprics—Salzburg, Mainz, Trier, and Cologne—were established as missionary centers for Scandinavia and eastern Europe. Under Otto I and his successors, a sort of confederacy (a weak union of strong principalities) developed in which the emperor shared power with princes, dukes, counts, archbishops, and bishops. Regionally based authority became the German pattern.[17]

Frederick Barbarossa (r. 1152–1190) of the house of Hohenstaufen tried valiantly to unify the empire. Just as the French rulers branched out from the Île-de-France, Frederick tried to do so from his family duchy of Swabia in southwestern Germany. Outside Swabia, Frederick tried to make feudalism work as a system of government. He made alliances with the great lay princes, who acknowledged that their lands were fiefs of the emperor in return for Frederick's recognition of their military and

The Chancellery at Palermo
Reflecting the fact that Vandals, Ostrogoths, Greeks, Muslims, and Normans had left their imprint on Sicily, the imperial court bureaucracy kept official records in Greek, Arabic, and Latin, as this manuscript illustration shows. (*Burgerbibliothek Bern*)

political jurisdiction over those lands. He even compelled the great churchmen to become his vassals, so that when they died, he could control their estates.

Unfortunately, Frederick did not concentrate his efforts and resources in one area. He, too, became embroiled in the affairs of Italy, hoping to cash in on the wealth Italian cities had gained through trade. He led six expeditions into Italy, but his brutal methods provoked revolts, and the cities, allied with the papacy, defeated him in 1176. Frederick was forced to recognize the autonomy of the cities. Meanwhile, back in Germany, Frederick's absence allowed the princes and magnates to consolidate their power.

Law and Justice

Throughout Europe in the twelfth and thirteenth centuries, the law was a hodgepodge of Germanic customs, feudal rights, and provincial practices. Kings wanted to blend these elements into a uniform system of rules acceptable and applicable to all their peoples. In France and England, kings successfully contributed to the development of national states through the administration of their laws.

The French king Louis IX (r. 1226–1270) was famous in his time for his concern for justice. Each French province, even after being made part of the kingdom of France, retained its unique laws and procedures, but Louis IX created a royal judicial system. He established the Parlement of Paris, a kind of supreme court that welcomed appeals from local administrators and from the courts of feudal lords throughout France.

Louis was also the first French monarch to publish laws for the entire kingdom. The Parlement of Paris registered (or announced) these laws, which forbade private warfare, judicial duels, gambling, blaspheming, and prostitution. Louis sought to identify justice with the kingship, and gradually royal justice touched all parts of the kingdom.

Under Henry II (r. 1154–1189), England developed and extended a **common law**—a law common to and accepted by the entire country. No other country in medieval Europe did so. Each year Henry sent out *circuit judges* (royal officials who traveled in a given circuit or district) to hear civil and criminal cases. Wherever the king's judges sat, there sat the king's court. Slowly, the king's court gained jurisdiction over all property disputes and criminal actions.

Proving guilt or innocence in criminal cases could pose a problem. Where there was no specific accuser, the court sought witnesses, then looked for written evi-

dence. If the judges found neither and the suspect had a bad reputation in the community, the person went to trial by ordeal. He or she was bound hand and foot and dropped into a lake or river. Because water was supposed to be a pure substance, it would reject anything foul or unclean. Thus the innocent person would sink and the guilty person float. Because God determined guilt or innocence, a priest had to be present to bless the water. Henry disliked the system because the clergy controlled the procedure and because many suspicious people seemed to beat the system and escape punishment, but he had no alternative. Then in 1215 the church's Fourth Lateran Council forbade priests' participation in such trials, effectively ending them. Royal justice was desacralized.[18] In the course of the thirteenth century, the king's judges adopted the practice of calling on twelve people to decide the accused's guilt or innocence. Trial by jury was only gradually accepted; medieval people had more confidence in the judgment of God than in that of ordinary people.

One aspect of Henry's judicial reform failed, doomed by the dispute between secular and religious authority. In the 1160s, many literate people accused of crimes claimed "benefit of clergy." Although they were not clerics and had no intention of being ordained, the claim gave them the right to be tried in church courts, which meted out punishments far milder than those handed down in secular courts. In 1164 Henry insisted that everyone in the kingdom, including clerics, be subject to the royal courts. Thomas Becket, Henry's friend and former chief adviser and now archbishop of Canterbury, vigorously protested. Their quarrel dragged on for years until, in 1170, a raging Henry wished aloud that Becket were destroyed. Four knights obliged, killing him.

Becket's murder—in his own cathedral during the Christmas season—turned public opinion across Europe against the king. He was forced to abandon his attempts to bring clerics under the authority of the royal courts. Meanwhile, miracles were recorded at Becket's tomb, and Canterbury Cathedral became a major pilgrimage and tourist site.

Henry's son John (r. 1199–1216) also met with disappointment. He lost the French province of Normandy to Philip Augustus in 1204 and spent the rest of his reign trying to win it back. Saddled with heavy debt from his father and brother Richard (r. 1189–1199), John alienated his barons by squeezing as much money as possible from them. Still in need of funds, he infuriated town dwellers by extorting money from them and threatening to revoke the towns' charters of self-government. Then he rejected the pope's choice as archbishop of Canterbury, angering the church.

When John's military campaign failed in 1214, it was clear that the French lands that had once belonged to the English king were lost for good. His ineptitude as a soldier in a culture that idealized military glory turned the people against him. The barons revolted and in 1215 forced him to attach his seal to Magna Carta—the "Great Charter," which became the cornerstone of English justice and law. Magna Carta signifies the principle that the king and the government shall be under the law and that everyone, including the king, must obey the law. Some clauses contain the germ of the ideas of due process of law and the right to a fair and speedy trial. Every English king in the Middle Ages reissued Magna Carta as evidence of his promise to observe the law.

In the later Middle Ages, English common law developed features that differed strikingly from the system of Roman law operative in continental Europe. Common law relied on precedents: a decision in an important case served as an authority for deciding similar cases. By contrast, continental judges, trained in Roman law, used the fixed legal maxims of the sixth-century text known as the Justinian *Code* to decide their cases. Thus the common-law system evolved and reflected the changing experience of the people, while the Roman-law tradition tended toward an absolutist approach. In countries influenced by common law, such as Canada and the United States, the court is open to the public; in countries with Roman-law traditions, such as France and the Latin American nations, courts need not be public. Under common law, people accused in criminal cases have a right to see the evidence against them; under the other system, they do not.

The extension of law and justice led to a phenomenal amount of legal codification all over Europe. Legal texts and encyclopedias exalted royal authority, consolidated royal power, and emphasized political and social uniformity. The pressure for social conformity in turn contributed to a rising hostility toward minorities, Jews, and homosexuals.

By the late eleventh century, many towns in western Europe had small Jewish populations. The laws of most countries forbade Jews to own land, though they could hold land pledged to them for debts. By the twelfth century, many Jews were usurers: they lent to consumers, but primarily to new business enterprises. Like other business people, the Jews preferred to live near their work; they also settled close to their synagogues or schools. Thus originated the Jews' street or quarter or ghetto. Such neighborhoods gradually became legally defined sections where Jews were required to live.

Jews had been generally tolerated and had become important parts of the urban economies through trade and finance. Some Jews had risen to positions of power and prominence. Through the twelfth century, for example, Jews managed the papal household. The later twelfth and entire thirteenth centuries, however, witnessed increasingly ugly anti-Semitism. Why? Present scholarship does not provide completely satisfactory answers, but we have some clues. Shifting agricultural and economic patterns aggravated social tensions. The indebtedness of peasants and nobles to Jews in an increasingly cash-based economy; the xenophobia that accompanied and followed the Crusades; Christian merchants' and financiers' resentment of Jewish business competition; the spread of vicious accusations of ritual murders or sacrileges against Christian property and persons; royal and papal legislation aimed at social conformity—these factors all contributed to rising anti-Semitism. Philip Augustus of France used hostility toward Jews as an excuse to imprison them and then to demand heavy ransom for their release. The Fourth Lateran Council of 1215 forbade Jews to hold public office and restricted their financial activities. In 1290 Edward I of England capitalized on mercantile and other resentment of Jews to expel them from the country in return for a large financial grant. In 1302 Philip IV of France followed suit and confiscated their property. Fear, ignorance, greed, stupidity, and the pressure for social conformity all played a part in anti-Semitism of the central Middle Ages.

Early Christians displayed no special prejudice against homosexuals. Some of the church fathers, such as Saint John Chrysostom (347–407), preached against them, but a general indifference toward homosexual activity prevailed throughout the early Middle Ages. In the early twelfth century, a large body of homosexual literature circulated.

Beginning in the late twelfth century, however, a profound change occurred in public attitudes toward homosexual behavior. Scholars have only begun to investigate why this occurred, and the root cause of intolerance rarely yields to easy analysis. In the thirteenth century, a fear of foreigners, especially Muslims, became associated with the crusading movement. Heretics were the most despised minority in an age that stressed religious and social uniformity. The notion spread that both Muslims and heretics, the great foreign and domestic menaces to the security of Christian Europe, were inclined toward homosexual relations. In addition, the systematization of law and the rising strength of the state made any religious or sexual distinctiveness increasingly unacceptable. Whatever the precise cause, "between 1250 and 1300 homosexual

The Jews Demonized   The Fourth Lateran Council of 1215 required that Jews wear distinctive clothing—special caps and the Star of David—so that they could be distinguished from Christians. In this caricature from an English treasury record for 1233, Isaac of Norwich (*top center*), reputedly the richest Jew in England, wears a crown implying his enormous influence and power. The figure at left (holding scales) suggests the Jewish occupation of money lending. At right Satan leads Jews to Hell. (*Crown copyright material in the Public Record Office is reproduced by permission of the Controller of the Britannic Majesty's Stationery Office [E 3721]*)

activity passed from being completely legal in most of Europe to incurring the death penalty in all but a few legal compilations."[19] Spain, France, England, Norway, and several Italian city-states adopted laws condemning homosexual acts. Most of these laws remained on statute books until the twentieth century. Anti-Semitism and hostility toward homosexuals were at odds with the general creativity and vitality of the period.

ECONOMIC REVIVAL

A salient manifestation of Europe's recovery after the tenth-century disorders and of the vitality of the central Middle Ages was the rise of towns and the growth of a new business and commercial class. These developments laid the foundations for Europe's transformation, centuries later, from a rural agricultural society into an industrial urban society—a change with global implications.

Why and how did these developments occur when they did? Part of the answer has already been given. Without increased agricultural output, there would not have been an adequate food supply for new town dwellers. Without a rise in population, there would have been no one to people the towns. Without a minimum of peace and political stability, merchants could not have transported and sold goods.

The Rise of Towns

Early medieval society was traditional, agricultural, and rural. The emergence of a new class that was none of these constituted a social revolution. The new class—artisans and merchants—came from the peasantry. They were landless younger sons of large families, driven away by land shortages. Or they were forced by war and famine to seek new possibilities. Or they were unusually enterprising and adventurous, curious and willing to take a chance.

Some medieval towns that had become flourishing centers of trade by the mid-twelfth century had originally been Roman army camps, or perhaps forts erected during the ninth-century Viking invasions. York in northern England, Bordeaux in west-central France, and Cologne in west-central Germany are good examples of ancient towns that underwent revitalization in the eleventh century. Great cathedrals and monasteries, which represented a demand for goods and services, also attracted concentrations of people. The restoration of order and political stability promoted rebirth and new development. Medieval towns had a few characteristics in common. Walls enclosed the town. (The terms *burgher* and *bourgeois* derive from the Old English and Old German words *burg, burgh, borg,* and *borough* for "a walled or fortified place.") The town had a marketplace. It often had a mint for the coining of money and a court to settle disputes.

In each town, many people inhabited a small, cramped area. As population increased, towns rebuilt their walls, expanding the living space to accommodate growing numbers. Through an archaeological investigation of the amount of land gradually enclosed by walls, historians have gained a rough estimate of medieval town populations. For example, the walled area of the German city of Cologne equaled 100 hectares in the tenth century (1 hectare = 2.471 acres), about 185 hectares in 1106, about 320 in 1180, and 397 in the fourteenth century. In 1180 Cologne's population was at least 32,000; in the mid-fourteenth century, perhaps 40,000.[20]

The aristocratic nobility glanced down with contempt and derision at the moneygrubbing townspeople but were not above borrowing from them. The rural peasantry peered up with suspicion and fear at the town dwellers. Some farmers fled to the towns seeking wealth and freedom. But most farmers wondered what the point of making money was. They believed that only land had real permanence. Nor did the new commercial class make much sense initially to churchmen. The immediate goal of the middle class was obviously not salvation. It would be a long while before churchmen developed a theological justification for the new class.

Town Liberties and Town Life

The history of towns in the eleventh through thirteenth centuries consists largely of merchants' efforts to acquire liberties. In the Middle Ages, *liberties* meant special privileges. For the town dweller, liberties included the privilege of living and trading on the lord's land. The most important privilege a medieval townsperson could gain was personal freedom. It gradually developed that an individual who lived in a town for a year and a day, and was accepted by the townspeople, was free of servile obligations and servile status. More than anything else, perhaps, the personal freedom that came with residence in a town contributed to the emancipation of the serfs in the central Middle Ages. Liberty meant citizenship, and, unlike foreigners and outsiders of any kind, a full citizen of a town did not have to pay taxes and tolls in the market. Obviously, this exemption increased profits.

In the twelfth and thirteenth centuries, towns fought for, and slowly gained, legal and political rights. Gradually, towns across Europe acquired the right to hold municipal courts that alone could judge members of the town. In effect, this right gave them judicial independence.[21]

In the acquisition of full rights of self-government, the **merchant guilds** played a large role. Medieval people were long accustomed to communal enterprises. In the late tenth and early eleventh centuries, those who were engaged in foreign trade joined together in merchant guilds; united enterprise provided them greater security and less risk of losses than did individual action. At about the same time, the artisans and craftsmen of particular trades formed their own guilds. These were the butchers, bakers, and candlestick makers. Members of the *craft guilds* determined the quality, quantity, and price of the goods produced and the number of apprentices and journeymen affiliated with the guild.

Research indicates that, by the fifteenth century, women composed the majority of the adult urban population. Many women were heads of households.[22] They engaged in every kind of urban commercial activity, both as helpmates to their husbands and independently. In many manufacturing trades women predominated, and in some places women were a large percentage of the labor force. In fourteenth-century Frankfurt, for example, about 33 percent of the crafts and trades were entirely female, about 40 percent wholly male, and the remaining crafts roughly divided between the sexes. Craft guilds provided greater opportunity for women than did merchant guilds. Most members of the Paris silk and woolen trades were women, and some achieved the mastership. Widows frequently followed their late husbands' professions.

Recent research demonstrates that women with ready access to cash—such as female innkeepers, alewives, and women in trade—"extended credit on purchases, gave cash advances to good customers or accepted articles on pawn . . . and many widows supplemented their earnings from their late husbands' businesses or homesteads by putting out cash at interest." Likewise, Christian noblewomen, nuns, and Jewish businesswomen participated in moneylending. Wherever Jews lived, Jewish women were active moneylenders.[23]

By the late eleventh century, especially in the towns of the Low Countries and northern Italy, the leaders of the merchant guilds were quite rich and powerful. They constituted an oligarchy in their towns, controlling economic life and bargaining with kings and lords for political independence. Full rights of self-government included the right to hold a town court, the right to select the mayor and other municipal officials, and the right to tax and collect taxes.

A charter that King Henry II of England granted to the merchants of Lincoln around 1157 nicely illustrates the town's rights. The passages quoted clearly suggest that the merchant guild had been the governing body in the city for almost a century and that anyone who lived in Lincoln for a year and a day was considered free:

Henry, by the grace of God, etc. . . . Know that I have granted to my citizens of Lincoln all their liberties and customs and laws which they had in the time of Edward [King Edward the Confessor] and William and Henry, kings of England. And I have granted them their gild-merchant, comprising men of the city and other merchants of the shire, as well and freely as they had it in the time of our aforesaid predecessors. . . . I also confirm to them that if anyone has lived in Lincoln for a year and a day without dispute from any claimant, and has paid the customs [tax levied by the king] . . . then let the defendant remain in peace in my city of Lincoln as my citizen, without [having to defend his] right.[24]

Kings and lords discovered that towns attracted increasing numbers of people—people whom the lords could tax. Moreover, when burghers bargained for a town's political independence, they offered sizable amounts of ready cash. Consequently, feudal lords ultimately agreed to self-government.

Medieval cities served, above all else, as markets. In some respects the entire city was a marketplace. The place where a product was made and sold was also typically the merchant's residence. Usually the ground floor was the scene of production. A window or door opened from the main workroom directly onto the street, and passersby could look in and see the goods being produced. The merchant's family lived above the business on the second or third floor. As the business and the family expanded, the merchant built additional stories on top of the house.

Because space within the town walls was limited, expansion occurred upward. Second and third stories were built jutting out over the ground floor and thus over the street. Since the streets were narrow to begin with, houses lacked fresh air and light. Initially, houses were made of wood and thatched with straw. Fire was a constant danger and spread rapidly. Municipal governments consequently urged construction in stone or brick.

Most medieval cities developed haphazardly. There was little town planning. Air and water pollution presented serious problems. Many families raised pigs for household consumption in sties next to their houses. Horses and oxen, the chief means of transportation and power, dropped tons of dung on the streets every year. It was universal practice in the early towns to dump household waste, both animal and human, into the road in front of

Spanish Apothecary   Town life meant variety—of peoples and products. Within the town walls, a Spanish pharmacist, seated outside his shop, describes the merits of his goods to a crowd of Christians and Muslims. *(From the* Cantigas *of Alfonso X, ca 1283. El Escorial/Laurie Platt Winfrey, Inc.)*

one's house. The stench must have been abominable. Lack of space, air pollution, and sanitation problems bedeviled urban people in medieval times, as they do today. Still, people wanted to get into medieval cities because they represented opportunities for economic advancement, social mobility, and improvement in legal status.

The Revival of Long-Distance Trade

The eleventh century witnessed a remarkable revival of trade, as artisans and craftsmen manufactured goods for local and foreign consumption (see Map 13.4). Most trade centered in towns and was controlled by professional traders. The transportation of goods involved serious risks. Shipwrecks were common. Pirates infested the sea-lanes, and robbers and thieves roamed virtually all of the land routes. Since the risks were so great, merchants preferred to share them. A group of people would thus pool some of their capital to finance an expedition to a distant place. When the ship or caravan returned and the goods brought back were sold, the investors would share the profits. If disaster struck the caravan, an investor's loss was limited to the amount of that individual's investment.

The Italian cities, especially Venice, led the West in trade in general and completely dominated the Asian market. Ships carried salt from the Venetian lagoon; pepper and other spices from North Africa; and slaves, silks, and purple textiles from the East to northern and western Europe. Lombard and Tuscan merchants exchanged those goods at the town markets and regional fairs of France, Flanders, and England. (Fairs were periodic gatherings that attracted buyers, sellers, and goods from all over Europe.) Flanders controlled the cloth industry: the towns of Bruges, Ghent, and Ypres built up a vast industry in the manufacture of cloth. Italian merchants exchanged their products for Flemish tapestries, fine broadcloth, and other textiles.

Two circumstances help to explain the lead Venice and the Flemish towns gained in long-distance trade. Both enjoyed a high degree of peace and political stability, but geographical factors were equally, if not more, important (see Map 13.4). Venice was ideally located at the northwestern end of the Adriatic Sea, with easy access to the transalpine land routes as well as the Adriatic and Mediterranean sea-lanes. The markets of North Africa, Byzantium, and Russia and the great fairs of Ghent in Flanders and Champagne in France provided commercial opportunities that Venice quickly seized. The geographical situation of Flanders also offered unusual possibilities. Just across the Channel from England, Flanders had easy access to English wool. Indeed, Flanders and England developed a very close economic relationship.

Wool was the cornerstone of the English medieval economy. Scholars have estimated that, by the end of the twelfth century, roughly 6 million sheep grazed on the English moors and downs.[25] Population growth in the twelfth century and the success of the Flemish and Italian textile industries created foreign demand for English wool. The production of English wool stimulated Flemish manufacturing, and the expansion of the Flemish cloth industry in turn spurred the production of English wool. The availability of raw wool also encouraged the development of domestic cloth manufacture within England. The port cities of London, Hull, Boston, and Bristol thrived on the wool trade. In the thirteenth century, commercial families in these towns grew fabulously rich.

The Commercial Revolution

A steadily expanding volume of international trade from the late eleventh through the thirteenth century was a sign of the great economic surge, but it was not the only one. In cities all across Europe, trading and transportation firms opened branch offices. Credit was widely extended, considerably facilitating exchange. Merchants devised the letter of credit, which made unnecessary the slow and dangerous shipment of coin for payment.

A new capitalistic spirit developed. Professional merchants were always on the lookout for new markets and opportunities. They invested surplus capital in new enterprises. They became involved in a wide variety of operations. The typical prosperous merchant in the later thirteenth century might well have been involved in buying and selling, shipping, lending some capital at interest, and other types of banking. Medieval merchants were fiercely competitive. Some scholars consider capitalism a modern phenomenon, beginning in the fifteenth or sixteenth century. But in their use of capital to make more money, in their speculative pursuits and willingness to gamble, in their competitive spirit, and in the variety of their interests and operations, medieval businessmen displayed the traits of capitalists.

The ventures of the German Hanseatic League illustrate these impulses. The **Hanseatic League** was a mercantile association of towns formed to achieve mutual security and exclusive trading rights. During the thirteenth century, perhaps two hundred cities from Holland to Poland joined the league, but Lübeck always remained the dominant member. From the thirteenth to the sixteenth century, the Hanseatic League controlled trade over a Novgorod-Reval-Lübeck-Hamburg-Bruges-London axis—that is, the trade

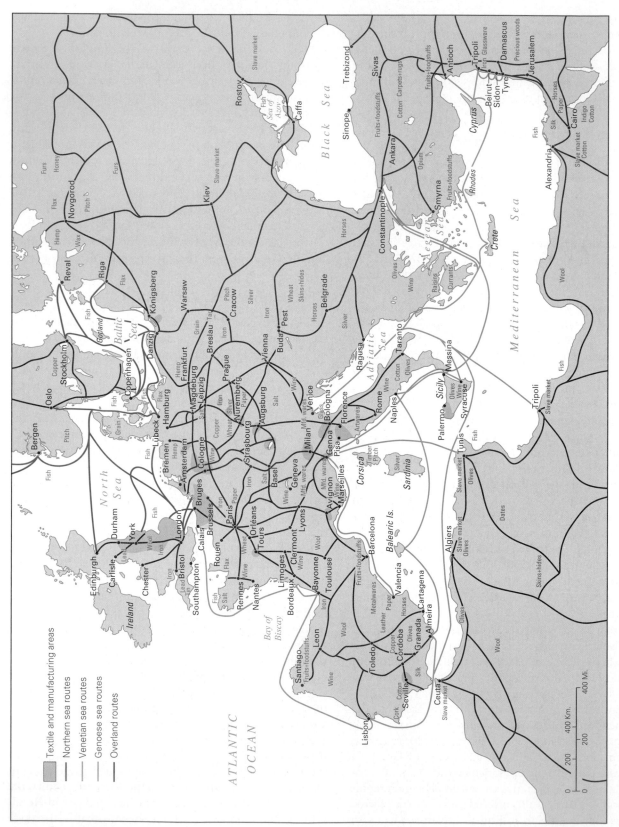

MAP 13.4 Trade and Manufacturing in Medieval Europe Note the number of cities and the sources of silver, iron, copper, lead, paper, wool, carpets and rugs, and slaves.

Textile and manufacturing areas
Northern sea routes
Venetian sea routes
Genoese sea routes
Overland routes

of northern Europe (see Map 13.4). In the fourteenth century, Hanseatic merchants branched out into southern Germany and Italy by land and into French, Spanish, and Portuguese ports by sea.

The ships of league cities carried furs, wax, copper, fish, grain, timber, and wine. These goods were exchanged for finished products, mainly cloth and salt, from western cities. At cities such as Bruges and London, Hanseatic merchants secured special trading concessions exempting them from all tolls and allowing them to trade at local fairs. Hanseatic merchants established foreign trading centers called "factories." (The term *factory* was used in the seventeenth and eighteenth centuries to mean business offices and places in Asia and Africa where goods were stored and slaves held before being shipped to Europe or the Americas; see page 288.) The most famous factory was the London Steelyard, a walled community with warehouses, offices, a church, and residential quarters for company representatives.[26]

By the late thirteenth century, Hanseatic merchants had developed an important business tool, the business register. Merchants publicly recorded their debts and contracts and received a league guarantee for them. This device proved a decisive factor in the later development of credit and commerce in northern Europe. These activities required capital, risk taking, and aggressive pursuit of opportunities—the essential ingredients of capitalism. They also yielded fat profits.

These developments added up to what one modern scholar has called "a commercial revolution, . . . probably the greatest turning point in the history of our civilization."[27] The commercial revolution created a great deal of new wealth. Wealth meant a higher standard of living. The new availability of something as simple as spices, for example, allowed for variety in food. Dietary habits gradually changed. Tastes became more sophisticated. Contact with Eastern civilizations introduced Europeans to eating utensils, and table manners improved. Nobles learned to eat with forks and knives instead of tearing the meat from a roast with their fingers. They began to use napkins instead of wiping their greasy fingers on the dogs lying under the table.

The existence of wealth did not escape the attention of kings and other rulers. Wealth could be taxed, and through taxation kings could create strong and centralized states. In the years to come, alliances with the middle classes were to enable kings to defeat feudal powers and aristocratic interests and to build the states that came to be called "modern."

The commercial revolution also provided the opportunity for thousands of serfs to improve their social position.

The slow but steady transformation of European society from almost completely rural and isolated to a relatively more sophisticated one constituted the greatest effect of the commercial revolution that began in the eleventh century. The commercial changes of the eleventh through thirteenth centuries laid the economic foundations for the later development of urban life and culture.

UNIVERSITIES, GOTHIC ART, AND POETRY

Just as the first strong secular states emerged in the thirteenth century, so did the first universities. This was no coincidence. The new bureaucratic states and the church needed educated administrators, and universities were a response to this need.

Since the time of the Carolingian Empire, monasteries and cathedral schools had offered the only formal instruction available. Monasteries were located in rural environments and geared to religious concerns. They wished to maintain an atmosphere of seclusion and silence and were unwilling to accept large numbers of noisy lay students. In contrast, schools attached to cathedrals and run by the bishop and his clergy were frequently situated in bustling cities, and in the eleventh century in Bologna and other Italian cities wealthy businessmen established municipal schools. Inhabited by people of many backgrounds and "nationalities," cities stimulated the growth and exchange of ideas. In the course of the twelfth century, cathedral schools in France and municipal schools in Italy developed into universities.

The growth of the University of Bologna coincided with a revival of interest in Roman law. The study of Roman law as embodied in Justinian's *Code* had never completely died out in the West, but this sudden burst of interest seems to have been inspired by Irnerius (d. 1125), a great teacher at Bologna. Irnerius not only explained the Roman law of Justinian's *Code* but applied it to difficult practical situations.

At Salerno, interest in medicine had persisted for centuries. Greek and Muslim physicians there had studied the use of herbs as cures and experimented with surgery. The twelfth century ushered in a new interest in Greek medical texts and in the work of Arab and Greek doctors. Students of medicine poured into Salerno and soon attracted royal attention. In 1140, when King Roger II (r. 1130–1154) of Sicily took the practice of medicine under royal control, his ordinance stated: "Who, from now on, wishes to practice medicine, has to present himself before our officials and examiners, in order to pass their judgment. . . . In this way we are taking care that our subjects are not endangered by the inexperience of the physicians."[28]

In the first decades of the twelfth century, students converged on Paris. They crowded into the cathedral school of Notre Dame and spilled over into the area later called the Latin Quarter—whose name probably reflects the Italian origin of many of the students. The cathedral school's international reputation had already drawn to Paris scholars from all over Europe. One of the most famous of them was Peter Abélard (1079–1142).

Fascinated by logic, which he believed could be used to solve most problems, Abélard used a method of systematic doubting in his writing and teaching. As he put it, "By doubting we come to questioning, and by questioning we perceive the truth." Other scholars merely asserted theological principles; Abélard discussed and analyzed them.

The influx of students eager for learning and the presence of dedicated and imaginative teachers created the atmosphere in which universities grew. In northern Europe—at Paris and later at Oxford and Cambridge in England—associations or guilds of professors organized universities. They established the curriculum, set the length of time for study, and determined the form and content of examinations. University faculties grouped themselves according to academic disciplines, or schools—law, medicine, arts, and theology. The professors, known as schoolmen or **Scholastics,** developed a method of thinking, reasoning, and writing in which questions were raised and authorities cited on both sides of a question. The goal of the Scholastic method was to arrive at definitive answers and to provide a rational explanation for what was believed on faith.

The Scholastic approach rested on the recovery of classical philosophical texts and on ancient Greek and Arabic texts that had entered Europe in the early twelfth century. Thirteenth-century philosophers relied on Latin translations of these texts, especially translations of Aristotle. The Scholastics reinterpreted Aristotelian texts in a Christian sense.

Thirteenth-century Scholastics devoted an enormous amount of time to collecting and organizing knowledge on all topics. These collections were published as *summa,* or reference books. There were summa on law, philosophy, vegetation, animal life, and theology. Saint Thomas Aquinas (1225–1274), a professor at Paris, produced the most famous collection, the *Summa Theologica,* which deals with a vast number of theological questions.

Aquinas drew an important distinction between faith and reason. He maintained that, although reason can demonstrate many basic Christian principles such as the existence of God, other fundamental teachings such as the Trinity and original sin cannot be proved by logic. That reason cannot establish them does not, however, mean they are contrary to reason. Rather, people understand such doctrines through revelation embodied in Scripture. Scripture cannot contradict reason, nor reason Scripture:

The light of faith that is freely infused into us does not destroy the light of natural knowledge [reason] implanted in us naturally. . . . Indeed, were that the case, one or the other would have to be false, and, since both are given to us by God, God would have to be the author of untruth, which is impossible.[29]

Thomas Aquinas and all medieval intellectuals held that the end of both faith and reason was the knowledge of, and union with, God. His work later became the fundamental text of Roman Catholic doctrine.

At all universities, the standard method of teaching was the *lecture*—that is, a reading. The professor read a passage from the Bible, Justinian's *Code,* or one of Aristotle's treatises. He then explained and interpreted the passage; his interpretation was called a *gloss.* Students wrote down everything. Because books had to be copied by hand, they were extremely expensive, and few students could afford them. Examinations were given after three, four, or five years of study, when the student applied for a degree. The professors determined the amount of material students had to know for each degree, and students frequently insisted that the professors specify precisely what that material was. Examinations were oral and very difficult. If the candidate passed, he was awarded the first, or bachelor's, degree. Further study, about as long, arduous, and expensive as it is today, enabled the graduate to try for the master's and doctor's degrees. Degrees were technically licenses to teach. Most students, however, did not become teachers. They staffed the expanding royal and papal administrations.

From Romanesque Gloom to "Uninterrupted Light"

Between 1180 and 1270 in France alone, eighty cathedrals, about five hundred abbey churches, and tens of thousands of parish churches were constructed. All these churches displayed a new architectual style. Fifteenth-century critics called the new style **Gothic** because they mistakenly believed the fifth-century Goths had invented it. It actually developed partly in reaction to the earlier Romanesque style, which resembled ancient Roman architecture. Cathedrals, abbeys, and village churches testify to the deep religious faith and piety of medieval people.

The inspiration for the Gothic style originated in the brain of Suger, abbot of Saint-Denis, who had decided to

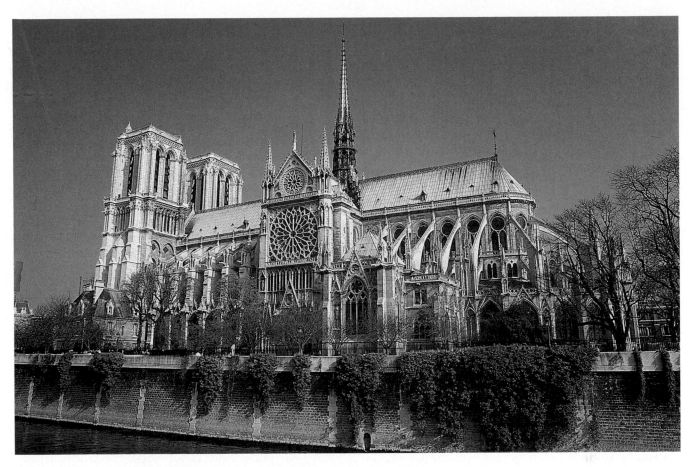

Notre Dame Cathedral, Paris (begun 1163), View from the South   This view offers a fine example of the twin towers (*left*), the spire, the great rose window over the south portal, and the flying buttresses that support the walls and the vaults. Like hundreds of other churches in medieval Europe, it was dedicated to the Virgin. With a nave rising 226 feet, Notre Dame was the tallest building in Europe. *(David R. Frazier/Photo Researchers)*

reconstruct the old Carolingian church at his monastery. The basic features of Gothic architecture—the pointed arch, the ribbed vault, and the flying buttress—allowed unprecedented interior lightness. From Muslim Spain, Islamic methods of ribbed vaulting seem to have heavily influenced the building of Gothic churches. Although architectural historians cannot absolutely prove the connection, "it does not seem pure accident that . . . the first systematic experiments in rib-vaulting started within ten years (1085) of the capture of Toledo," which "contained the finest examples of Islamic rib-vaults."[30] Since the ceiling of a Gothic church weighed less than that of a Romanesque church, the walls could be thinner. Stained-glass windows were cut into the stone, so that the interior, Suger exulted, "would shine with the wonderful and uninterrupted light of most sacred windows, pervading the interior beauty."[31]

The construction of a Gothic cathedral represented a gigantic investment of time, money, and corporate effort. The bishop and the clergy of the cathedral made the decision to build, but they depended on the support of all social classes. Bishops raised revenue from kings, the nobility, the clergy, and those with the greatest amount of ready cash—the commercial classes.

Cathedrals served secular as well as religious purposes. The sanctuary containing the altar and the bishop's chair belonged to the clergy, but the rest of the church belonged to the people. In addition to marriages, baptisms, and funerals, there were scores of feast days on which the entire town gathered in the cathedral for festivities. Local guilds met in the cathedrals to arrange business deals and to plan recreational events and the support of disabled members. Magistrates and municipal officials held political meetings there. Pilgrims slept there, lovers courted there, and traveling actors staged plays there. First and foremost, however, the cathedral was intended to teach the people the doctrines of Christian faith through visual images. Architecture became the servant of theology.

As Gothic churches became more skeletal and had more windows, stained glass replaced manuscript illumination as the leading kind of painting. Thousands of scenes in the cathedral celebrate nature, country life, and the activities of ordinary people.

Troubadour Poetry

The word *troubadour* comes from the Provençal word *trobar,* which in turn derives from the Arabic *taraba,* meaning "to sing" or "to sing poetry." A troubadour was a poet of Provence who wrote lyric verse in his or her native language and sang it at one of the noble courts. Troubadour songs had a variety of themes. Men sang about "courtly love," the pure love a knight felt for his lady, whom he sought to win by military prowess and patience; about the love a knight felt for the wife of his feudal lord; or about carnal desires seeking satisfaction. Some poems exalted the married state, and others idealized adulterous relationships; some were earthy and bawdy, and others advised young girls to remain chaste in preparation for marriage. The married Countess Beatrice of Dia (1150–1200?) expresses the hurt she felt after being jilted by a young knight:

Lovely lover, gracious, kind,
When will I overcome your fight?
O if I could lie with you one night!
Feel those loving lips on mine!
　Listen, one thing sets me afire:
Here in my husband's place I want you,
If you'll just keep your promise true:
　Give me everything I desire.[32]

Troubadours certainly felt Hispano-Arabic influences. In the eleventh century, Christians of southern France were in intimate contact with the Arabized world of Andalusia, where reverence for the lady in a "courtly" tradition had long existed. Troubadour poetry represents another facet of the strong Muslim influence on European culture and life.[33]

The songs of the troubadours were widely imitated in Italy, England, and Germany, and they spurred the development of vernacular languages. Most of the troubadours came from and wrote for the aristocratic classes, and their poetry suggests the interests and values of noble culture in the central Middle Ages.

LIFE IN CHRISTIAN EUROPE IN THE CENTRAL MIDDLE AGES

In the late ninth century, medieval intellectuals described Christian society as composed of those who pray (the monks), those who fight (the nobles), and those who work (the peasants). According to this image of social structure, function determined social classification.[34] Reality, however, was somewhat different. The division of society into fighters, monks, and peasants presents too static a view of a world in which there was considerable social mobility. Moreover, such a social scheme does not take into consideration townspeople and the emerging commercial classes. That omission, however, is easy to understand. Traders and other city dwellers were not typical members of medieval society. Medieval people were usually contemptuous (at least officially) of profitmaking activities, and even after the appearance of urban commercial groups, the ideological view of medieval Christian society remained the one formulated in the ninth century: the three-part division among peasants, nobles, and monks.

Those Who Work

According to one modern scholar, "Peasants are rural dwellers who possess (if they do not own) the means of agricultural production."[35] Some peasants worked continuously on the land. Others supplemented their ordinary work as brewers, carpenters, tailors, or housemaids with wage labor in the field. In either case, all peasants supported lords, clergy, townspeople, and themselves. The men and women who worked the land in the twelfth and thirteenth centuries made up the overwhelming majority of the population, probably more than 90 percent. Yet it is difficult to form a coherent picture of them. First, the medieval records that serve as our sources were written by and for the aristocratic classes; they do not give the peasants' perspective. Second, peasants' conditions varied widely across Europe: geography, climate, and individual initiative determined the quality of life in any particular area.[36] Third, although we tend to lump all people who worked the land into one category, the peasantry, there were in fact many kinds of peasants, from complete slaves to very rich farmers. The status of rural workers fluctuated widely, and the period from about 1050 to 1300 saw considerable social mobility.

Slaves were found in western Europe in the central Middle Ages, but in steadily declining numbers. That the word *slave* derives from *Slav* attests to the widespread trade in men and women from the Slavic areas. Legal language differed considerably from place to place, and the distinction between slave and serf was not always clear. Both lacked freedom—the power to do as one wished—and both were subject to the arbitrary will of one person, the lord. A serf, however, could not be bought and sold like an animal or an inanimate object, as a slave could.

The serf was required to perform labor services on the lord's land. The number of workdays varied, but it was usually three days a week except in the planting or harvest seasons, when it increased. Serfs frequently had to pay arbitrary levies, as for marriage or inheritance. The precise amounts of tax paid to the lord depended on local custom and tradition. A free person had to do none of these things. For his or her landholding, rent had to be paid to the lord, and that was often the sole obligation. A free person could move and live as he or she wished.

Serfs were tied to the land, and serfdom was a hereditary condition. A person born a serf was likely to die a serf, though many did secure their freedom. About 1187 Glanvill, an official of King Henry II and an expert on English law, described how **villeins** (literally, "inhabitants of small villages")—as English serfs were called—could be made free:

No person of villein status can seek his freedom with his own money, . . . because all the chattels of a villein are deemed to be the property of his lord. If, however, a third party provides the money and buys the villein in order to free him, then he can maintain himself for ever in a state of freedom as against his lord who sold him. . . . If any villein stays peaceably for a year and a day in a privileged town and is admitted as a citizen into their commune, that is to say, their gild, he is thereby freed from villeinage.[37]

Thus, with the advent of a money economy, serfs could save money and, through a third-person intermediary, buy their freedom. (See the feature "Individuals in Society: Jean Mouflet of Sens.")

The economic revival that began in the eleventh century (see pages 384–387) advanced the cause of individual liberty. Hundreds of new towns arose in Ireland, in eastern Europe, and in reconquest Spain; their settlers often came from long distances. The thirteenth century witnessed enormous immigration to many parts of Europe that previously had been sparsely settled. Immigration and colonization provided the opportunity for freedom and social mobility.[38]

Another opportunity for increased personal freedom, or at least for a reduction in traditional manorial obligations and dues, was provided by the reclamation of waste- and forestland in the eleventh and twelfth centuries. Marshes and fens were drained and slowly made

The Three Classes Medieval people believed that their society was divided among clerics, warriors, and workers, here represented by a monk, a knight, and a peasant. The new commercial class had no recognized place in the agrarian military world. *(The British Library)*

arable. This type of agricultural advancement frequently improved the peasants' social and legal condition.

In the central Middle Ages, most European peasants, free and unfree, lived on a **manor,** the estate of a lord. The manor was the basic unit of medieval rural organization and the center of rural life. The arable land of the manor was divided into two sections. The *demesne,* or home farm, was cultivated by the peasants for the lord. The other, usually larger section was held by the peasantry. All the arable land, both the lord's and the peasants', was divided into strips, and the strips belonging to any given individual were scattered throughout the manor. All peasants cooperated in the cultivation of the land, working it as a group. All shared in any disaster as well as in any large harvest.

The fundamental objective of all medieval agriculture was the production of an adequate food supply. Using the method that historians have called the *open-field system,* peasants divided the arable land of a manor into two or three fields without hedges or fences to mark the individual holdings of the lord, serfs, and freemen. Beginning in the eleventh century in parts of France, England, and Germany, peasants divided all the arable land into three large fields. In any one year, two of the fields were cultivated and one lay fallow. One part of the land was sown with winter cereals such as rye and wheat, the other with spring crops such as peas, beans, and barley. Each year the crop was rotated. Local needs, the fertility of the soil, and dietary customs determined what was planted and the method of crop rotation.

The plow and the harrow (a cultivating instrument with heavy teeth that breaks up and smoothes the soil) were increasingly drawn by horses. The development of the padded horse collar, resting on the horse's shoulders and attached to the load by shafts, led to an agricultural revolution. The horse collar let the animal put its entire weight into the task of pulling. In the twelfth century, the use of horses, rather than oxen, spread because horses' greater strength brought greater efficiency to farming. Horses, however, were an enormous investment, perhaps comparable to a modern tractor. They had to be shod (another indication of increased iron production), and the oats they ate were costly.

The thirteenth century witnessed a tremendous spurt in the use of horses to haul carts to market. Farmers increasingly relied on horses to pull wagons because they could travel much faster than oxen. Consequently, goods reached market faster, and the number of markets within an area to which the peasant had access increased. The opportunities and temptations for consumer spending on nonagricultural goods multiplied.[39]

Agricultural yields varied widely from place to place and from year to year. By twentieth-century standards, they were very low. Inadequate soil preparation, poor seed selection, lack of manure—all made low yields virtually inevitable. And, like farmers of all times and places, medieval peasants were at the mercy of the weather. Yet there was striking improvement over time. Researchers have tentatively concluded that between the ninth and early thirteenth centuries, yields of cereals approximately doubled, and on the best-managed estates farmers harvested five bushels of grain for every bushel of seed planted.

For most people in medieval Europe, life meant country life. A person's horizons were not likely to extend beyond the manor on which he or she was born. Most people rarely traveled more than twenty-five miles beyond their villages. Their world was small, narrow, and provincial: limited by the boundaries of the province.

Scholars have recently spent much energy investigating the structure of medieval peasant households. Because little concrete evidence survives, conclusions are very tentative. It appears, however, that a peasant household consisted of a simple nuclear family: a married couple alone, a couple of children, or a widow or widower with children. Peasant households were *not* extended families containing grandparents or married sons and daughters and their children. Before the first appearance of the Black Death (see pages 399–401), perhaps 94 percent of peasant farmers married, and both bride and groom were in their early twenties. The typical household numbered about five people—the parents and three children.[40]

Women played a significant role in the agricultural life of medieval Europe. Women worked with men in wheat and grain cultivation, in the vineyards, and in the harvest and preparation of crops needed by the textile industry— flax and plants used for dyeing cloth, such as madder (which produces shades of red) and woad (which yields blue dye). Especially at harvest time, women shared with their fathers and husbands the backbreaking labor in the fields, work that was especially difficult for them because of weaker muscular development and frequent pregnancies. Lords of great estates commonly hired female day laborers to shear sheep, pick hops (used in the manufacture of beer and ale), tend gardens, and do household chores such as cleaning, laundry, and baking. Servant girls in the country considered their hired status as temporary, until they married. Thrifty farm wives contributed to the family income by selling for cash the produce of their gardens or kitchens: butter, cheese, eggs, fruit, soap, mustard, cucumbers. In a year of crisis, careful management was often all that separated a household from starvation. And starvation was a very real danger to the peasantry down to the eighteenth century.

Women managed the house. The size and quality of peasants' houses varied according to their relative prosperity and usually depended on the amount of land held. The poorest peasants lived in windowless cottages built of wood and clay or wattle and thatched with straw. These cottages consisted of one large room that served as the kitchen and living quarters for all. The house had an earthen floor and a fireplace. The lack of windows meant that the room was very sooty. A trestle table, several stools, one or two beds, and a chest for storing clothes constituted the furniture. A shed attached to the house provided storage for tools and shelter for animals. Prosperous peasants added rooms and furniture as they could be afforded, and some wealthy peasants in the early fourteenth century had two-story houses with separate bedrooms for parents and children.

Women dominated in the production of ale for the community market. They had to know how to mix the correct proportions of barley, water, yeast, and hops in twelve-gallon vats of hot liquid. Brewing was hard and

INDIVIDUALS IN SOCIETY

JEAN MOUFLET OF SENS

Throughout most of Western history, the vast majority of people left little behind that identifies them as individuals. Baptismal, marriage, and death records; wills; grants for memorial masses; and, after the eighteenth century, brief census information collected by governments—these forms of evidence provide exciting information about groups of people but little about individuals. Before the nineteenth century, most people were illiterate; the relative few who could write, such as business people, used such literary skills as they had in matters connected with their work. The historian, therefore, has great difficulty reconstructing the life of an "ordinary" person. An exception occurs when a person committed a crime in a society that kept judicial records or when he or she made a legal agreement that was preserved. Such is the case of Jean Mouflet of Sens.*

We know little about him except what is revealed in a document granting what was probably the central desire of his life—his personal freedom. His ancestors had been serfs on the lands of the abbey of Saint-Pierre-le-Vif in the Sénonais region of France. There a serf was subject to legal disabilities that debased his dignity and implied inferior status. Work required on the lord's land bred resentment, because work was simultaneously needed on the rustic's own land. At death a peasant gave the lord a token, or not so token, gift—his best beast. Marriage presented another disability, first because one partner had to change dwelling and to do so had to gain the lord's permission; second because it raised the question of children: whose dependents did they become? Special "gifts" to the lord "encouraged" him to resolve these issues. Again, an unfree person, even if he or she possessed the expected dowry, could not become a monk or nun or enter holy orders without the lord's permission, because the lord stood to lose labor services. Finally, residence in a town for a year and a day did not always ensure freedom; years after the person settled there, the lord could claim him or her as a dependent.

In 1249 Jean Mouflet made an agreement with the abbot: in return for an annual payment, the monastery would recognize Jean as a "citizen of Sens." With a stroke of his quill, the abbot manumitted Jean and his heirs, ending centuries of servile obligations.

The agreement describes Jean as a leather merchant. Other evidence reveals that he had a large leather shop in the leather goods section of town† that he leased for the very high rent of fifty shillings a year. If not "rich," Jean was certainly well-to-do. Circumstantial evidence suggests that Jean's father had originally left the land to become a leatherworker and taught his son the trade. The agreement was witnessed by Jean's wife, Douce, daughter of a wealthy and prominent citizen of Sens, Félis Charpentier. To have been a suitable candidate for Douce, Jean would have to have been extremely industrious, very lucky, and accepted as a "rising young man" by the grudging burghers of the town. Such a giant step upward in one generation seems unlikely.

In addition to viticulture (the cultivation of grapes), the Sénonais was well suited for cereal production and for animal grazing. Jean undoubtedly bought hides from local herders and manufactured boots and shoes; saddles, bridles, and reins for horses; and belts and purses. He may also have made wine-skins for local vintners or for those of Champagne. It is also fair to assume that the wealthy cathedral clergy, the townspeople, and, if his goods were of sufficiently high quality, the merchants of the nearby fairs of Champagne were his customers.

By private agreements with lords, servile peasants gained the most basic of human rights—freedom.

The customary form of manumission, not the manner in which Jean Mouflet gained his freedom. (British Library)

QUESTIONS FOR ANALYSIS

1. What is human freedom?
2. How did trade and commerce contribute to the development of individual liberty?

*This essay rests on the fine study of W. C. Jordan, *From Servitude to Freedom: Manumission in the Sénonais in the Thirteenth Century* (Philadelphia: University of Pennsylvania Press, 1986).
†As in all medieval towns, merchants in particular trades—butchers, bakers, leatherworkers—had shops in one area. Sens is still a major French leather-tanning center.

Saint Maurice   The cult of Saint Maurice (d. 287), a soldier executed by the Romans for refusing to renounce his Christian faith, presents a paradox. Although no solid evidence for him has survived, his cult spread widely in the Carolingian period. Later, he was held up as a model knight and declared a patron of the Holy Roman Empire and protector of the imperial (German) army in wars against the pagan Slavs. His image was used on coins, and his cult was promoted by the archbishops of Magdeburg. Always, until 1240, he was portrayed as a white man. Then, from 1240 to the sixteenth century, he was represented as a black man, as in this sandstone statue from Magdeburg Cathedral (ca 1240–1250). Who commissioned this statue? Who carved it? What black man served as the model? Only further research can answer these questions, as well as the question of his race. *(Image of the Black Project, Harvard University/Hickey-Robertson, Houston)*

dangerous work. Records of the English coroners' courts reveal that 5 percent of women who died lost their lives in brewing accidents, falling into the vats of boiling liquid.[41] Ale was the universal drink of the common people in northern Europe. By modern American standards, the rate of consumption was heroic. Each monk of Abingdon Abbey in twelfth-century England was allotted three gallons a day, and a man working in the fields for ten hours probably drank much more.[42]

The mainstay of the diet for peasants everywhere—and for all other classes—was bread. It was a hard, black substance made of barley, millet, and oats, rarely of expensive wheat flour. The housewife usually baked the household supply once a week. If sheep, cows, or goats were raised, she also made cheese.

The diet of those living in an area with access to a river, lake, or stream was supplemented with fish, which could be preserved by salting. In many places, severe laws against hunting and trapping in the forests restricted deer and other game to the king and nobility. These laws were flagrantly violated, however, and stolen rabbits often found their way to the peasants' tables.

Except for the rare chicken or illegally caught wild game, meat appeared on the table only on the great feast days of the Christian year: Christmas, Easter, and Pentecost. Then the meat was likely to be pork from the pig slaughtered in the fall and salted for the rest of the year. Some scholars believe that by the mid-thirteenth century, there was a great increase in the consumption of meat generally. If so, this improvement in diet is further evidence of an improved standard of living.

Those Who Fight

The nobility, though a small fraction of the total population, strongly influenced all aspects of medieval culture—political, economic, religious, educational, and artistic. For that reason, European society in the twelfth and thirteenth centuries may be termed aristocratic.

Members of the nobility enjoyed a special legal status. A nobleman was free personally and in his possessions. He was limited only by his military obligation to king, duke, or prince. As the result of his liberty, he had certain rights and responsibilities. He raised troops and commanded them in the field. He held courts that dispensed a sort of justice. Sometimes he coined money for use within his territories. As lord of the people who settled on his lands, he made political decisions affecting them, resolved disputes among them, and protected them in time of attack. The liberty and privileges of the noble were inheritable, perpetuated by blood and not by wealth alone.

The nobleman was a professional fighter. His social function, as churchmen described it, was to protect the weak, the poor, and the churches by arms. He possessed a horse and a sword. These, and the leisure time in which to learn how to use them in combat, were the visible signs of his nobility. He was encouraged to display chivalric virtues—courtesy, loyalty to his commander, and generosity.

The responsibilities of a noble in the central Middle Ages depended on the size and extent of his estates, the number of his dependents, and his position in his territory relative to others of his class and to the king. As a vassal a noble was required to fight for his lord or for the king when called on to do so. By the mid-twelfth century, this service was limited in most parts of western Europe to forty days a year. The noble was obliged to attend his lord's court on important occasions when the lord wanted to put on great displays, such as at Easter, Pentecost, and Christmas. When the lord knighted his eldest son or married off his eldest daughter, he called his vassals to his court. They were expected to attend and to present a contribution known as a "gracious aid."

Until the late thirteenth century, when royal authority intervened, a noble in France or England had great power over the knights and peasants on his estates. He maintained order among them and dispensed justice to them. The quality of life on the manor and its productivity were related in no small way to the temperament and decency of the lord—and his lady.

Women played a large and important role in the functioning of the estate. They were responsible for the practical management of the household's "inner economy"—cooking, brewing, spinning, weaving, caring for yard animals. The lifestyle of the medieval warrior-nobles required constant travel, both for purposes of war and for the supervision of distant properties. When the lord was away for long periods—on crusade, for instance, the lord could be gone from two to five years, if he returned at all—his wife often became the sole manager of the family properties. Between 1060 and 1080, the lady Hersendis was the sole manager of her family's properties in northern France while her husband was on crusade in the Holy Land.

Medieval warfare was largely a matter of brief skirmishes, and few men were killed in any single encounter. But altogether the number slain ran high, and there were many widows. Aristocratic widows frequently controlled family properties and fortunes and exercised great authority. Although the evidence is scattered and sketchy, there are indications that women performed many of the functions of men. In Spain, France, and Germany they bought, sold, and otherwise transferred property.

Those Who Pray

Monasticism represented some of the finest aspirations of medieval civilization. The monasteries were devoted to prayer, and their standards of Christian behavior influenced the entire church. The monasteries produced the educated elite that was continually drawn into the administrative service of kings and great lords. Monks kept alive the remains of classical culture and experimented with new styles of architecture and art. They introduced new techniques of estate management and land reclamation. Although relatively few in number in the central Middle Ages, the monks played a significant role in medieval society.

Toward the end of his *Ecclesiastical History of England and Normandy,* when he was well into his sixties, Orderic Vitalis (ca 1075–ca 1140), a monk of the Norman abbey of Saint Evroul, interrupted his narrative to explain movingly how he happened to become a monk:

And so, O glorious God, you didst inspire my father Odeleric to renounce me utterly and . . . weeping, he gave me, a weeping child, into the care of the monk Reginald, and sent me away into exile for love of thee, and never saw me again. . . . [H]e promised me for his part that if I became a monk I should taste of the joys of Heaven. . . . And so, a boy of ten, I crossed the English channel and came into Normandy as an exile, unknown to all, knowing no one.[43]

Orderic was the third son of a knight who held lands in western England. Concern for the provision of his two older sons probably led the knight to give his youngest boy to the monastery.

Medieval monasteries were religious institutions whose organization and structure fulfilled the social needs of the feudal nobility. The monasteries provided noble children with both an honorable and aristocratic life and opportunities for ecclesiastical careers.[44] As medieval society changed economically, and as European society ever so slowly developed middle-class traits, the monasteries almost inevitably drew their manpower, when they were able, from the middle classes. Until that time, they were preserves of the aristocratic nobility.

Through the Middle Ages, social class also defined the kinds of religious life open to women. Kings and nobles usually established convents for their daughters, sisters, aunts, or aging mothers. Entrance was restricted to women of the founder's class. Since a wellborn lady could not honorably be apprenticed to a tradesperson or do any kind of manual labor, the sole alternative to life at home was the religious life.

Although the level of intellectual life in the women's houses varied widely, the career of Hildegard of Bingen suggests the activities of some nuns in the central Middle Ages. The tenth child of a lesser noble family, Hildegard (1098–1179) was given when eight years old as an oblate to an abbey in the Rhineland, where she learned Latin and received a good education. In 1147 Hildegard founded the convent of Rupertsberg near Bingen. There she produced a body of writings including the *Scivias* (Know the Ways), a record of her mystical visions that incorporates vast theological learning; the *Physica* (On the Physical Elements), a classification of the natural elements, such as plants, animals, metals, and the movements of the heavenly bodies; a mystery play; and a medical work that led a distinguished twentieth-century historian of science to describe Hildegard as "one of the most original writers of the Latin West in the twelfth century."[45] An exceptionally gifted person, Hildegard represents the Benedictine ideal of great learning combined with a devoted monastic life. Like intellectual monks, however, intellectual nuns were not typical of the era.

In medieval Europe, the monasteries of men greatly outnumbered those of women. The pattern of life within individual monasteries varied widely from house to house and from region to region. One central activity, however—the work of God—was performed everywhere. Daily life centered on the liturgy.

Seven times a day and once during the night, the monks went to choir to chant the psalms and other prayers prescribed by Saint Benedict. Prayers were offered for peace, rain, good harvests, the civil authorities, the monks' families, and their benefactors. Monastic patrons in turn lavished gifts on the monasteries, which often became very wealthy. Through their prayers, the monks performed a valuable service for the rest of society.

Monks and nuns engaged in virtually every aspect of medieval European economic life. Taking advantage of local opportunities, they worked in agriculture, of course, and in sheep farming (for wool production), in viticulture (the cultivation of grapes for wine production), in beekeeping (for the production of honey, the universal sweetener), in coal and iron mining, in horse breeding, and even in banking, where, as one reliable scholar puts it, "it was clerics and ecclesiastical institutions (monasteries and nunneries) that constituted the main providers of credit."[46] Profits from these enterprises supported a variety of social services. Schools for the education of the young; homes for orphaned children, unwed mothers, and the elderly; hospitals for the sick; and inns for travelers were often associated with monasteries and nunneries. In an age when there was no conception of social welfare or public responsibility for the poor, the sick, and the unfortunate, monasteries fulfilled important social needs.

CRISES OF THE LATER MIDDLE AGES

In the later years of the thirteenth century, Europeans seemed to run out of steam. The crusading movement gradually fizzled out. Few new cathedrals were constructed, and if a cathedral had not been completed by 1300, the chances were high that it never would be. The strong rulers of England and France, building on the foundations of their predecessors, increased their authority and gained the loyalty of all their subjects. The vigor of those kings, however, did not pass to their immediate descendants. Meanwhile, the church, which for two centuries had guided Christian society, began to face grave difficulties. A violent dispute between the papacy and the kings of England and France badly damaged the prestige of the pope. But religious struggle was only one of the crises that would face European society in the fourteenth century.

A Challenge to Religious Authority

In 1294 King Edward I of England and Philip the Fair of France declared war on each other. To finance this war, both kings laid taxes on the clergy. Kings had been taxing the church for decades. Pope Boniface VIII (r. 1294–1303), arguing from precedent, insisted that kings gain papal consent for taxation of the clergy and forbade churchmen to pay the taxes. Edward and Philip refused to accept this decree. Edward immediately denied the clergy the protection of the law, an action that meant its members could be attacked with impunity. Philip halted the shipment of all ecclesiastical revenue to Rome. Boniface had to back down.

Philip the Fair and his ministers continued their attack on all powers in France outside royal authority. Philip arrested a French bishop. When Boniface protested, Philip replied with the trumped-up charge that the pope was a heretic. The papacy and the French monarchy waged a bitter war of propaganda. Finally, in 1302, in a letter titled *Unam Sanctam* (because its opening sentence spoke of one holy Catholic church), Boniface insisted that all Christians, including kings, are subject to the pope. Philip's university-trained advisers, with an argument drawn from Roman law, maintained that the king of France was completely sovereign in his kingdom and responsible to God alone. French mercenary troops went to Italy and arrested the aged pope. Although Boniface was soon freed, he died shortly afterward.

The Great Famine and the Black Death

Economic difficulties originating in the later thirteenth century were fully manifest by the start of the fourteenth. In the first decade, the countries of northern Europe experienced considerable price inflation. The costs of grain, livestock, and dairy products rose sharply. Severe weather, which historical geographers label the Little Ice Age, made a serious situation frightful. An unusual number of storms brought torrential rains, ruining the wheat, oat, and hay crops on which people and animals almost everywhere depended. Population had steadily increased in the twelfth and thirteenth centuries. The amount of food yielded, however, did not match the level of population growth. Bad weather had disastrous results. Poor harvests—one in four was likely to be poor—led to scarcity and starva-

tion. Almost all of northern Europe suffered a terrible famine in the years 1315 to 1317. Then in 1318 disease hit cattle and sheep, drastically reducing the herds and flocks. Another bad harvest in 1321 brought famine, starvation, and death. Famine had dire social consequences: rustics were forced to sell or mortgage their lands for money to buy food; the number of vagabonds, or homeless people, greatly increased, as did petty crime; and the dispossessed and starving focused their bitterness on land speculators and Jews. An undernourished population was ripe for the Grim Reaper, who appeared in 1348 in the form of the **Black Death** (see Map 13.5).[47]

In October 1347, Genoese ships traveling from the Crimea in southern Russia brought the bubonic plague to Messina, from which it spread across Sicily and up into Italy. By late spring of 1348, southern Germany was attacked.

MAP 13.5 The Course of the Black Death in Fourteenth-Century Europe   Note the routes that the bubonic plague took across Europe. How do you account for the fact that several regions were spared the "dreadful death"?

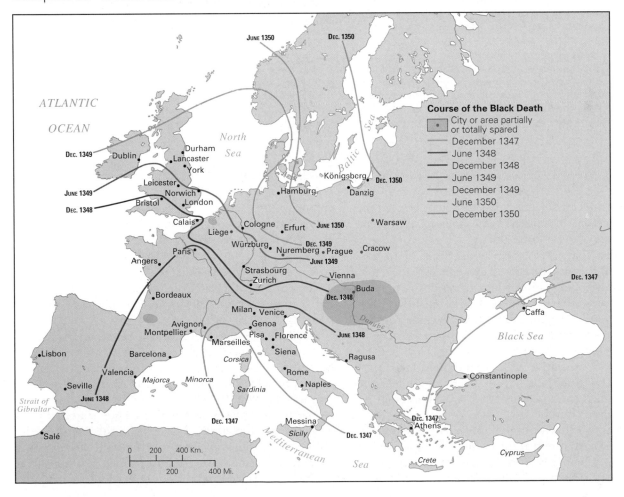

Procession of Saint Gregory   According to the *Golden Legend,* a thirteenth-century collection of saints' lives, the bubonic plague ravaged Rome when Gregory I was elected pope (r. 590–604). He immediately ordered special prayers and processions around the city. Here, as people circle the walls, new victims fall (*center*). The architecture, the cardinals, and the friars all indicate that this painting dates from the fourteenth, not the sixth, century. *(Musée Condé, Chantilly/Art Resource, NY)*

Frightened French authorities chased a galley bearing the disease from the port of Marseilles, but not before plague had infected the city. In June 1348 two ships entered the Bristol Channel and introduced it into England. All Europe felt the scourge of this horrible disease.

The bacillus that causes the plague, *Pasteurella pestis,* likes to live in the bloodstream of an animal or, ideally, in the stomach of a flea. The flea in turn resides in the hair of a rodent, often the hardy, nimble, and vagabond black rat. In the fourteenth century, the host black rat traveled by ship, where it could feast for months on a cargo of grain or live snugly among bales of cloth. Fleas bearing the bacillus also had no trouble nesting in saddlebags.[48] Comfortable, well-fed, and having greatly multiplied, the black rats ended their ocean voyage and descended on the great cities of Europe.

The plague took two forms—bubonic and pneumonic. The rat was the transmitter of the bubonic form of the disease. The pneumonic form was communicated directly from one person to another.

Urban conditions were ideal for the spread of disease. Narrow streets filled with mud, refuse, and human excrement were as much cesspools as thoroughfares. Dead animals and sore-covered beggars greeted the traveler. Houses whose upper stories projected over the lower ones eliminated light and air. And extreme overcrowding was commonplace. When all members of an aristocratic family lived and slept in one room, it should not be surprising that six or eight persons in a middle-class or poor household slept in one bed.

Standards of personal hygiene remained frightfully low. Fleas and body lice were universal afflictions: one more bite did not cause much alarm. But if that nibble came from a bacillus-bearing flea, an entire household or area was doomed.

The symptoms of the bubonic plague started with a growth the size of a nut or an apple in the armpit, in the groin, or on the neck. This was the boil, or *buba,* that gave the disease its name and caused agonizing pain. If the buba was lanced and the pus thoroughly drained, the victim had a chance of recovery. The secondary stage was the appearance of black spots or blotches caused by bleeding under the skin. Finally, the victim began to cough violently and spit blood. This stage, indicating the presence of thousands of bacilli in the bloodstream, signaled the end, and death followed in two or three days. Rather than evoking compassion for the victim, a French scientist has written, everything about the bubonic plague provoked horror and disgust: "All the matter which exuded from their bodies let off an unbearable stench; sweat, excrement, spittle, breath, so fetid as to be overpowering; urine turbid, thick, black or red."[49]

Physicians could sometimes ease the pain but had no cure. Most people—lay, scholarly, and medical—believed that the Black Death was caused by some "vicious property in the air" that carried the disease from place to place. When ignorance was joined to fear and ancient bigotry, savage cruelty sometimes resulted. Many people believed that the Jews had poisoned the wells of Christian communities and thereby infected the drinking water. This charge led to the murder of thousands of Jews across Europe. According to one chronicler, sixteen thousand were killed at the imperial city of Strasbourg alone in 1349. That this figure is probably a typically medieval numerical exaggeration does not lessen the horror of the massacre.

The Italian writer Giovanni Boccaccio (1313–1375), describing the course of the disease in Florence in the preface to his book of tales, *The Decameron,* pinpointed the cause of the spread:

Moreover, the virulence of the pest was the greater by reason that intercourse was apt to convey it from the sick to the whole, just as fire devours things dry or greasy when they are brought close to it. Nay, the evil went yet further, for not merely by speech or association with the sick was the malady communicated to the healthy with consequent peril of common death, but any that touched the clothes of the sick or aught else that had been touched or used by them, seemed thereby to contract the disease.[50]

Because population figures for the period before the arrival of the plague do not exist for most countries and cities, only educated guesses can be made about mortality rates. Of a total English population of perhaps 4.2 million, probably 1.4 million died of the Black Death in its several visits.[51] Densely populated Italian cities endured incredible losses. Florence lost between one-half and two-thirds of its 1347 population of 85,000 when the plague visited in 1348. The disease recurred intermittently in the 1360s and 1370s and reappeared many times down to 1700. Population losses in Bohemia and Poland seem to have been much less. Historians of medicine have postulated that people with blood type O are immune to the bubonic disease; since this blood type predominated in Hungary, that region would have been slightly affected. No estimates of population losses have ever been attempted for Russia and the Balkans.

The traditional thesis of a rat-based bubonic plague has recently been strongly challenged. Using comparative evidence from later visits from the plague in medieval Europe (after 1347–1348), from early modern Europe, from India and China in the late nineteenth century, and from Manchuria in the early twentieth century, one scholar has reached interesting conclusions. He argues that later European visits of the plague were not the same disease as that of 1347 and that, while humans possess no natural immunity to the rat-based disease, the steady decline in the mortality rate in later medieval plagues indicates that humans adapted to it. This historian also claims that later visits of the plague did not provoke the same social, psychological, and political reactions as the initial attack had.[52] A consensus awaits.

Economic historians and demographers sharply dispute the impact of the plague on the economy in the late fourteenth century. The traditional view that the plague had a disastrous effect has been greatly modified. In England it appears that by about 1375, most landlords enjoyed revenues near those of the pre-plague years. By the early fifteenth century, seigneurial prosperity reached a medieval peak. Why? The answer appears to lie in the fact that England and many parts of Europe suffered from overpopulation in the early fourteenth century. Population losses caused by the Black Death "led to increased productivity by restoring a more efficient balance between labour, land, and capital."[53] Population decline meant a sharp increase in per capita wealth. Increased demand for labor meant greater mobility among peasant and working classes. Wages rose, providing better distribution of income. The shortage of labor and steady requests for higher wages put landlords on the defensive. Some places, such as Florence, experienced economic prosperity as a long-term consequence of the plague.

Even more significant than the social effects were the psychological consequences. The knowledge that the disease meant almost certain death provoked the most profound pessimism. It is not surprising that some sought release in orgies and gross sensuality, while others turned to the severest forms of asceticism and frenzied religious fervor. Groups of *flagellants,* men and women who whipped and scourged themselves as penance for their and society's sins, believed that the Black Death was God's punishment for humanity's wickedness.

The Hundred Years' War (ca 1337–1453)

The centuries-old struggle between the English and French monarchies, the Hundred Years' War, fought intermittently from 1337 to 1453, represents a serious political crisis. Its causes were both distant and immediate. The English claimed Aquitaine as an ancient feudal inheritance. In 1329 England's King Edward III (r. 1327–1377) paid homage to Philip VI (r. 1328–1350) for Aquitaine. French policy, however, was strongly expansionist, and in 1337 Philip, determined to exercise full jurisdiction there, confiscated the duchy. This action was the immediate cause of the war. Edward III maintained that the only way he could exercise his rightful sovereignty over Aquitaine was by assuming the title of king of France.[54] As the grandson and eldest surviving male descendant of Philip the Fair, he believed he could rightfully make this claim.

For centuries, economic factors involving the wool trade and the control of Flemish towns had served as justifications for war between France and England. The wool trade between England and Flanders was the cornerstone of both countries' economies; they were closely interdependent. Flanders was a fief of the French crown, and the Flemish aristocracy was highly sympathetic to the monarchy in Paris. But the wealth of Flemish merchants and cloth manufacturers depended on English wool, and Flemish burghers strongly supported the claims of Edward III.

The Hundred Years' War was popular because it presented unusual opportunities for wealth and advancement. Poor knights and knights who were unemployed were promised regular wages. Great nobles expected to be rewarded with estates. Royal exhortations to the troops before battles repeatedly stressed that, if victorious, the men might keep whatever they seized. The French chronicler Jean Froissart wrote that, at the time of Edward III's military expedition of 1359 to France, men of all ranks flocked to the English king's banner. Some came to acquire honor, but many came in order "to loot and pillage the fair and plenteous land of France."[55]

The period of the Hundred Years' War witnessed the final flowering of the aristocratic code of medieval chivalry. War was considered an ennobling experience: there was something elevating, manly, fine, and beautiful about it.

The chivalric code applied only to the aristocratic military elite. English knights fought French ones as social equals fighting according to a mutually accepted code of behavior. The infantry troops were looked on as inferior beings. When a peasant force at Longueil destroyed a contingent of English knights, their comrades mourned them because "it was too much that so many good fighters had been killed by mere peasants."[56]

The war, fought almost entirely in France and the Low Countries (see Map 13.6), consisted mainly of a series of random sieges and cavalry raids. During the war's early stages, England was highly successful. At Crécy in northern France in 1346, English longbowmen scored a great victory over French knights and crossbowmen. Although the fire of the longbow was not very accurate, it allowed for rapid reloading, and English archers could send off three arrows to the French crossbowmen's one. The result was a blinding shower of arrows that unhorsed the French knights and caused mass confusion. The firing of cannon—probably the first use of artillery in the West—created further panic. Thereupon the English horsemen charged and butchered the French.

Ten years later, Edward the Black Prince, using the same tactics as at Crécy, smashed the French at Poitiers, captured the French king, and held him for ransom. Again, at Agincourt near Arras in 1415, the chivalric English soldier-king Henry V (r. 1413–1422) gained the field over vastly superior numbers. By 1419 the English had advanced to the walls of Paris. But the French cause was not lost. Though England scored the initial victories, France won the war.

The ultimate French success rests heavily on the actions of an obscure French peasant girl, Joan of Arc, whose vision and work revived French fortunes and led to victory. Born in 1412 to well-to-do peasants in the village of Domrémy in Champagne, Joan of Arc grew up in a pious household. During adolescence she began to hear voices, which she later said belonged to Saint Michael, Saint Catherine, and Saint Margaret. In 1428 these voices told her that the dauphin (the uncrowned King Charles VII) had to be crowned and the English expelled from France. Joan went to the French court, persuaded the king to reject the rumor that he was illegitimate, and secured his support for her relief of the besieged city of Orléans (see Map 13.6).

Joan arrived before Orléans on April 28, 1429. Seventeen years old, she knew little of warfare and believed that if she could keep the French troops from swearing and frequenting brothels, victory would be theirs. On May 8 the English, weakened by disease and lack of supplies, withdrew from Orléans. Ten days later, Charles VII was crowned king at Reims. These two events marked the turning point in the war.

In 1430 England's allies, the Burgundians, captured Joan and sold her to the English. When the English handed her over to the ecclesiastical authorities for trial, the French court did not intervene. The English wanted Joan eliminated for obvious political reasons, but sorcery (witchcraft) was the charge at her trial. Witch persecution

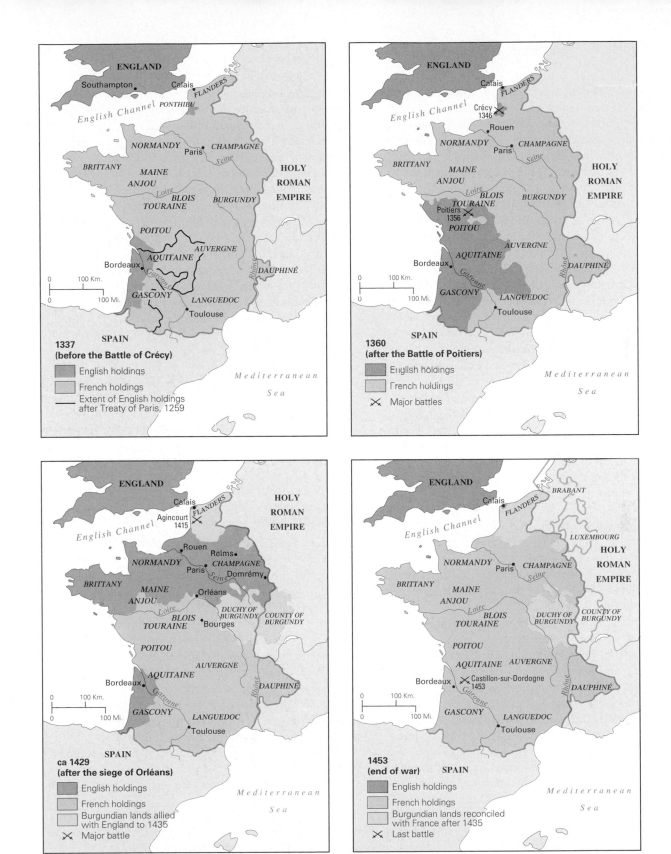

MAP 13.6 English Holdings in France During the Hundred Years' War The year 1429 marked the greatest extent of English holdings in France. Why is it unlikely that England could have held these territories permanently?

was increasing in the fifteenth century, and Joan's wearing of men's clothes appeared not only aberrant but indicative of contact with the Devil. In 1431 the court condemned her as a heretic. Her claim of direct inspiration from God, thereby denying the authority of church officials, constituted heresy. She was burned at the stake in the marketplace at Rouen. A new trial in 1456 rehabilitated her name. In 1920 she was canonized, and today she is revered as the second patron saint of France.

The relief of Orléans stimulated French pride and rallied French resources. As the war dragged on, loss of life mounted, and money appeared to be flowing into a bottomless pit, demands for an end increased in England. The clergy and intellectuals pressed for peace. Parliamentary opposition to additional war grants stiffened. Slowly the French reconquered Normandy and finally ejected the English from Aquitaine. At the war's end in 1453, only the town of Calais remained in English hands (see Map 13.6).

For both France and England, the war proved a disaster. In France the English had slaughtered thousands of soldiers and civilians. In the years after the Black Death, this additional killing meant a grave loss of population. Destruction of hundreds of thousands of acres of rich farmland left the rural economy of many parts of France a shambles. The war had disrupted trade and the great fairs, resulting in the drastic reduction of French participation in international commerce. Defeat in battle and heavy taxation contributed to widespread dissatisfaction and aggravated peasant grievances.

The long war had a profound impact on the political and cultural lives of the two countries. Most notably, it stimulated the development of the English Parliament. Between 1250 and 1450, representative assemblies from several classes of society flourished in many European countries. In the English Parliament, French Estates, German diets, and Spanish cortes, deliberative practices developed that laid the foundations for the representative institutions of modern liberal-democratic nations. Representative assemblies declined in most countries after the fifteenth century, but the English Parliament endured. Edward III's constant need for money to pay for the war compelled him to summon not only the great barons and bishops but knights of the shires and burgesses from the towns as well. Between the outbreak of the war in 1337 and the king's death in 1377, parliamentary assemblies met twenty-seven times. Parliament met in thirty-seven of the fifty years of Edward's reign.[57]

In England theoretical consent to taxation and legislation was given in one assembly for the entire country. France had no such single assembly; instead, there were many regional or provincial assemblies. Why did a national representative assembly fail to develop in France? The initiative for convening assemblies rested with the king, who needed revenue almost as much as the English ruler.

No one in France wanted a national assembly. Linguistic, geographical, economic, legal, and political differences were very strong. People tended to think of themselves as Breton, Norman, Burgundian, or whatever, rather than French. Through much of the fourteenth and early fifteenth centuries, weak monarchs lacked the power to call a national assembly. Provincial assemblies, highly jealous of their independence, did not want a national assembly. The costs of sending delegates to it would be high, and the result was likely to be increased taxation.

In both countries, however, the war did promote *nationalism*—the feeling of unity and identity that binds together a people who speak the same language, have a common ancestry and customs, and live in the same area. In the fourteenth century, nationalism largely took the form of hostility toward foreigners. Both Philip VI and Edward III drummed up support for the war by portraying the enemy as an alien, evil people. Perhaps no one expressed this national consciousness better than Joan of Arc, when she exulted that the enemy had been "driven out of *France*."

Religious Crisis

In times of crisis or disaster, people of all faiths have sought the consolation of religion. In the fourteenth century, however, Christian church leaders offered little solace. In fact, those leaders of the church added to the sorrow and misery of the times.

From 1309 to 1376, the popes lived in the city of Avignon in southeastern France. In order to control the church and its policies, Philip the Fair of France pressured Pope Clement V to settle in Avignon. Critically ill with cancer, Clement lacked the will to resist Philip. This period in church history is often called the **Babylonian Captivity** (referring to the seventy years the ancient Hebrews were held captive in Mesopotamian Babylon).

The Avignon papacy reformed its financial administration and centralized its government. But the seven popes at Avignon concentrated on bureaucratic matters to the exclusion of spiritual objectives. In 1377 Pope Gregory XI (r. 1370–1378) brought the papal court back to Rome. At Gregory's death, Roman citizens demanded an Italian pope who would remain in Rome.

Urban VI (r. 1378–1389), Gregory's successor, had excellent intentions for church reform. He wanted to abolish simony, pluralism (holding several church offices at the same time), absenteeism, clerical extravagance, and ostentation, but he went about the work of reform in a tactless, arrogant, and bullheaded manner. Urban's quick temper and irrational behavior have led scholars to question his sanity. His actions brought disaster.

The cardinals slipped away from Rome, met at Anagni, and declared Urban's election invalid because it had come about under threats from the Roman mob. The cardinals elected Cardinal Robert of Geneva, the cousin of King Charles V of France, as pope. Cardinal Robert took the name Clement VII (r. 1378–1394) and set himself up at Avignon in opposition to the legally elected Urban. So began the **Great Schism,** which divided Western Christendom until 1417.

The powers of Europe aligned themselves with Urban or Clement along strictly political lines. France recognized the Frenchman, Clement; England, France's historic enemy, recognized Urban. The scandal provoked horror and vigorous cries for reform. The common people—hardpressed by inflation, wars, and plague—were thoroughly confused about which pope was legitimate. The schism weakened the religious faith of many Christians and gave rise to instability and religious excesses. At a time when ordinary Christians needed the consolation of religion and confidence in religious leaders, church officials were fighting among themselves for power.

The English reformer John Wyclif (1329–1384) wrote that papal claims of temporal power had no foundation in the Scriptures and that the church should be stripped of its property. He argued that the Scriptures alone should be the standard of Christian belief and practice and not pious practices such as pilgrimages and the veneration of the saints. Sincere Christians, said Wyclif, should read the Scriptures for themselves. These views had broad social and economic significance. Wyclif's idea that every Christian free of sin possessed lordship was seized by the peasants during a revolt in 1381 and used to justify their goals.

Although Wyclif's ideas were vigorously condemned by ecclesiastical authorities, they were widely disseminated by humble clerics and enjoyed great popularity in the early fifteenth century. The teachings of Wyclif's followers, called Lollards, allowed women to preach and to consecrate the Eucharist. Women, some well educated, played a significant role in the movement. After Anne, sister of Wenceslaus, king of Germany and Bohemia, married Richard II of England, members of Queen Anne's household carried Lollard principles back to Bohemia, where they were read by Jan Hus, rector of the University of Prague.

In response to continued calls throughout Europe for a council, the two colleges of cardinals—one at Rome,

the other at Avignon—summoned a council at Pisa in 1409. This gathering deposed both popes and selected another, but neither the Avignon pope nor the Roman pope would resign, and the appalling result was the creation of a threefold schism.

Finally, because of the pressure of the German emperor Sigismund, a great council met at Constance (1414–1418). It had three objectives: to end the schism, to reform the church "in head and members" (from top to bottom), and to wipe out heresy. The council condemned Jan Hus as a Wycliffite, and he was burned at the stake. The council eventually deposed the three schismatic popes and elected a new leader, the Roman cardinal Colonna, who took the name Martin V (1417–1431).

Martin proceeded to dissolve the council. Nothing was done about reform. The schism was over, and though councils subsequently met at Basel and at Ferrara-Florence, in 1450 the papacy held a jubilee, celebrating its triumph over the conciliar movement. In the later fifteenth century, the papacy concentrated on Italian problems to the exclusion of universal Christian interests. The schism and the conciliar movement, however, had exposed the crying need for ecclesiastical reform, thus laying the foundations for the great reform efforts of the sixteenth century.

Peasant Revolts

Early in the thirteenth century, the French preacher Jacques de Vitry asked rhetorically, "How many serfs have killed their lords or burnt their castles?"[58] In the fourteenth and fifteenth centuries, social and economic conditions caused a great increase in peasant uprisings.

In 1358, when French taxation for the Hundred Years' War fell heavily on the poor, the frustrations of the French peasantry exploded in a massive uprising called the **Jacquerie,** after a supposedly happy agricultural laborer, Jacques Bonhomme (Good Fellow). Two years earlier, the English had captured the French king John and many nobles and held them for ransom. The peasants resented paying for their lords' release. Recently hit by plague, experiencing famine in some areas, and harassed by "fur-collar criminals," peasants erupted in anger and frustration in Picardy, Champagne, and the area around Paris. Crowds swept through the countryside, slashing the throats of nobles, burning their castles, raping their wives and daughters, and killing or maiming their horses and cattle. Artisans, small merchants, and parish priests joined the peasants. Urban and rural groups committed terrible destruction, and for several weeks the nobles were on the defensive. Then the upper class united to repress the revolt with merciless ferocity. Thousands of the "Jacques," innocent as well as guilty, were cut down.

The Peasants' Revolt in England in 1381, involving perhaps a hundred thousand people, was probably the largest single uprising of the entire Middle Ages. The causes of the rebellion were complex and varied from place to place. In general, though, the thirteenth century had witnessed the steady commutation of labor services for cash rents, and the Black Death had drastically cut the labor supply. As a result, peasants demanded higher wages and fewer manorial obligations. Thirty years earlier, the parliamentary Statute of Laborers of 1351 had declared:

Whereas to curb the malice of servants who after the pestilence were idle and unwilling to serve without securing excessive wages, it was recently ordained . . . that such servants, both men and women, shall be bound to serve in return for salaries and wages that were customary . . . five or six years earlier.[59]

This attempt by landlords to freeze wages and social mobility could not be enforced. As a matter of fact, the condition of the English peasantry steadily improved in the course of the fourteenth century. Why then was the outburst in 1381 so serious? It was provoked by a crisis of rising expectations.

The relative prosperity of the laboring classes led to demands that the upper classes were unwilling to grant. Unable to climb higher, the peasants found release for their economic frustrations in revolt. But economic grievances combined with other factors. The south of England, where the revolt broke out, had been subjected to frequent and destructive French raids. The English government did little to protect the south, and villages grew increasingly scared and insecure. Moreover, decades of aristocratic violence, much of it perpetrated against the weak peasantry, had bred hostility and bitterness. In France frustration over the lack of permanent victory increased. In England the social and religious agitation of the popular preacher John Ball fanned the embers of discontent. Sayings such as Ball's famous couplet "When Adam delved and Eve span; Who was then the gentleman?" reflect real revolutionary sentiment.

The straw that broke the camel's back in England was the reimposition of a head tax on all adult males. Beginning with assaults on the tax collectors, the uprising in England followed much the same course as had the Jacquerie in France. Castles and manors were sacked; manorial records were destroyed. Many nobles, including the archbishop of Canterbury, who had ordered the collection of the tax, were murdered. Urban discontent merged with rural violence. Apprentices and journeymen, frustrated because the highest positions in the guilds were closed to them, rioted.

The boy-king Richard II (r. 1377–1399) met the leaders of the revolt, agreed to charters ensuring the peasants' freedom, tricked them with false promises, and then proceeded to crush the uprising with terrible ferocity. Although the nobility tried to restore ancient duties of serfdom, virtually a century of freedom had elapsed, and the

Prostitute Invites a Traveling Merchant   Poverty and male violence drove women into prostitution, which, though denounced by moralists, was accepted as a normal part of the medieval social fabric. In the cities and larger towns where prostitution flourished, public officials passed laws requiring prostitutes to wear a special mark on their clothing, regulated hours of business, forbade women to drag men into their houses, and denied business to women with the "burning sickness," gonorrhea. *(Bodleian Library, University of Oxford, MS. Bodl. 264, fol. 245V)*

commutation of manorial services continued. Rural serf-dom had disappeared in England by 1550.

Conditions in England and France were not unique. In Florence in 1378, the *ciompi,* or poor propertyless workers, revolted. Serious social trouble occurred in Lübeck, Brunswick, and other German cities. In Spain in 1391, massive uprisings in Seville and Barcelona took the form of vicious attacks on Jewish communities. Rebellions and up-risings everywhere reveal deep peasant and working-class frustration and the general socioeconomic crisis of the time.

RACE AND ETHNICITY ON THE FRONTIERS

In the twelfth and thirteenth centuries, many people mi-grated from one part of Europe to another: the English into Scotland and Ireland; Germans, French, and Flem-ings into Poland, Bohemia, and Hungary; the French into Spain. In the fourteenth century, many Germans moved into eastern Europe, fleeing the Black Death. The colonization of frontier regions meant that peoples of different ethnic or racial backgrounds lived side by side. Race relations became a basic factor in the lives of those living in frontier areas.

Racial categories rest on socially constructed beliefs and customs, not on any biological or anthropological classifi-cation. When late medieval chroniclers used the language of race—words such as *gens* (race or clan) and *natio* (species, stock, or kind)—they meant cultural differences. Medieval scholars held that peoples differed according to descent, language, customs, and laws. Descent or blood, basic to the color racism of the United States, played an insignificant part in medieval ideas about race and ethnic-ity. Rather, the chief marks of an ethnic group were lan-guage (which could be learned), customs (for example, dietary practices, dance, marriage and death rituals, cloth-ing, and hairstyles, all of which could be adopted), and laws (which could be changed or modified). What role did race and ethnicity play in relations between native peoples and settlers in the later Middle Ages?

In the early periods of conquest and colonization, and in all frontier regions, a legal dualism existed: native peoples remained subject to their traditional laws; new-comers brought and were subject to the laws of the countries from which they came. On the Prussian and Polish frontier, for example, the law was that "men who come there . . . should be judged on account of any crime or contract engaged in there according to Polish custom if they are Poles and according to German custom if they are Germans."[60] The same dualism operated in Spain

Spanish Bullfight   Muslims introduced bullfighting to Spain in the eleventh century. The sport takes place in a large out-door arena, the object being for the bullfighter or matador (*torero*) to kill a wild bull (*toro*) with a sword. Here unsport-ing spectators goad the bull with whips. *(From the* Cantigas *of Alfonso X, ca 1283. El Escorial/Laurie Platt Winfrey, Inc.)*

with respect to Muslims and Christians. Subject peoples experienced some disabilities, but the broad trend was toward a legal pluralism.

The great exception to this pattern was Ireland, where the English practiced an extreme form of racial discrimi-nation toward the native Irish. The English distinguished between the free and the unfree, and the entire Irish pop-ulation, simply by the fact of Irish birth, was unfree. A le-gal structure modeled on that of England, with county courts, itinerant justices, and the common law (see pages 382–383), was set up. But the Irish had no access to the common-law courts. In civil (property) disputes, an En-glish defendant need not respond to his Irish plaintiff; no Irish person could make a will; and an Irish widow could not claim her dower rights (enjoyment of part of the es-tate during her lifetime). In criminal procedures, the murder of an Irishman was not considered a felony. An English defendant in the criminal matter would claim "that he is not held to answer . . . since he [the plaintiff] is Irish and not of free blood."[61] This emphasis on blood descent naturally provoked bitterness, but only in the Tudor period (see Chapter 15) was the English common law opened to the subject Irish population.

English View of the Irish   Depicting a subject or colonial people as barbaric and uncivilized has long been a way of denigrating and dehumanizing the enemy. In this thirteenth-century miniature, a king (in a bath) and his courtiers devour horse-flesh with their hands, without plates or eating utensils. The viewer is supposed to think that this is how Irish kingship was conferred. *(Bodleian Library, University of Oxford, MS. Laud. Misc. 720f. 226R)*

The later Middle Ages witnessed a movement away from legal pluralism or dualism and toward a legal homogeneity and an emphasis on blood descent. Competition for ecclesiastical offices and the cultural divisions between town and country people became arenas for ethnic tension and racial conflict. Since bishoprics and abbacies carried religious authority, spiritual charisma, and often rights of appointment to subordinate positions, they were natural objects of ambition. When prelates of a language or "nationality" different from that of the local people gained church positions, the latter felt a loss of influence. Bishops were supposed to be pastors. Their pastoral work involved preaching, teaching, and comforting, duties that could be performed effectively only when the bishop (or priest) could communicate with the people. Ideally in a pluralistic society, he should be bilingual; often he was not.

In the late thirteenth century, as waves of Germans migrated into Danzig on the Baltic, into Silesia, and into the Polish countryside and towns, they encountered Jakub Swinka, archbishop of Gniezno (1283–1314), whose jurisdiction included these areas of settlement. The bishop hated Germans and referred to them as "dog heads." His German contemporary, Bishop John of Cracow, detested the Poles, wanted to expel all Polish people, and refused to appoint Poles to any church office. In Ireland, English colonists and the native Irish competed for ecclesiastical offices until 1217, when the English government in London decreed:

Since the election of Irishmen in our land of Ireland has often disturbed the peace of that land, we command you . . . that henceforth you allow no Irishman to be elected . . . or preferred in any cathedral . . . (and) you should seek by all means to procure election and promotion to vacant bishoprics of . . . honest Englishmen.[62]

Although criticized by the pope and not totally enforceable, this law remained in effect in many dioceses for centuries.

Likewise, the arrival of Cistercians and mendicants (Franciscans and Dominicans) from France and Germany in Baltic and Slavic lands provoked racial and "national" hostilities. In the fourteenth and fifteenth centuries, in contrast to earlier centuries, racial or ethnic prejudices became conspicuous. Slavic prelates and princes saw the German mendicants as "instruments of cultural colonization," and Slavs were strongly discouraged from becoming members. In 1333, when John of Drazic, bishop of Prague, founded a friary at Roudnice (Raudnitz), he specified that "we shall admit no one to this convent or monastery of any nation except a Bohemian [Czech], born of two Czech-speaking parents."[63]

Everywhere in Europe, towns recruited people from the countryside (see pages 384–387). In frontier regions, townspeople were usually long-distance immigrants and, in eastern Europe, Ireland, and Scotland, ethnically different from the surrounding rural population. In eastern

Europe, German was the language of the towns; in Ireland, French, the tongue of noble Norman or English settlers, predominated. In fourteenth-century Prague, between 63 percent and 80 percent of new burgesses bore identifiable German names, as did almost all city council members. Towns in eastern Europe "had the character of German islands in Slav, Baltic, Estonian, or Magyar seas."[64] Although native peoples commonly held humbler positions, both immigrant and native townspeople prospered during the expanding economy of the thirteenth century. When economic recession hit during the fourteenth century, ethnic tensions multiplied.

Just as the social and legal status of the Jews in western Europe worsened in the wake of the great famine and the Black Death (see pages 399–401), on the frontiers of Latin Europe discrimination, ghettoization, and racism—now based on blood descent—characterized the attitudes of colonists toward native peoples. But the latter also could express racial savagery. Regulations drawn up by various guilds were explicitly racist, with protectionist bars for some groups and exclusionist laws for others. One set of laws applicable to parts of eastern Europe required that applicants for guild membership be of German descent and sometimes prove it. Cobblers in fourteenth-century Beeskow, a town close to the large Slavic population of Lausitz in Silesia, required that "an apprentice who comes to learn his craft should be brought before the master and guild members. . . . We forbid the sons of barbers, linen workers, shepherds, Slavs."[65]

Intermarriage was forbidden in many places, such as Riga on the Baltic (now the capital of Latvia), where legislation for the bakers guild stipulated that "whoever wishes to have the privilege of membership in our company shall not take as a wife any woman who is ill-famed . . . or non-German; if he does marry such a woman, he must leave the company and office." The most extensive attempt to prevent intermarriage and protect racial purity is embodied in Ireland's Statute of Kilkenny (1366), which stated that

there were to be no marriages between those of immigrant and native stock; that the English inhabitants of Ireland must employ the English language and bear English names; that they must ride in the English way (i.e., with saddles) and have English apparel; that no Irishmen were to be granted ecclesiastical benefices or admitted to monasteries in the English parts of Ireland; and that the Irish game of hurling and the maintenance of Irish minstrels were forbidden to English settlers.[66]

Rulers of the Christian kingdoms of Spain drew up comparable legislation discriminating against the Mudéjars.

All these laws had an economic basis: to protect the financial interests of the privileged German, English, or Spanish colonial minorities. The laws also reflect a racism that not only pervaded the lives of frontier peoples at the end of the Middle Ages but also sowed the seeds of difficulties still unresolved in the twenty-first century.

SUMMARY

The culture that emerged in Europe between 732 and 843 has justifiably been called the "first" European civilization. That civilization was Christian, feudal, and infused with Latin ideas and models. Almost all people were baptized Christians. Latin was the common language—written as well as spoken—of educated people everywhere. This culture resulted from the mutual cooperation of civil and ecclesiastical authorities. Kings and church leaders supported each other's goals and utilized each other's prestige and power. Kings encouraged preaching and publicized church doctrines, such as the stress on monogamous marriage. In return, church officials urged obedience to royal authority. The support that Charlemagne gave to education and learning, the intellectual movement known as the Carolingian Renaissance, proved his most enduring legacy.

The enormous size of Charlemagne's empire, the domestic squabbles among his descendants, the resurgence of aristocratic power, and the invasions of the Vikings, Magyars, and Muslims—these factors all contributed to the empire's disintegration. As the empire broke down, a new form of decentralized government, later known as feudalism, emerged. In a feudal society, public and political power was held by a small group of military leaders. No civil or religious authority could maintain a stable government over a very wide area. Local strongmen provided what little security existed. Commerce and long-distance trade were drastically reduced. Because of their agricultural and commercial impact, the Viking and Muslim invaders were the most dynamic and creative forces of the period.

In the eleventh century, rulers and local authorities gradually imposed some degree of order within their territories. Peace and domestic security contributed to a rise in population, bringing larger crops for the peasants and improving trading conditions for the townspeople. The church overthrew the domination of lay influences, and the spread of the Cluniac and Cistercian orders marked the ascendancy of monasticism. The Gregorian reform movement, with its stress on the "freedom of the church," led to a grave conflict with kings over lay investiture. The papacy achieved a technical success on the religious issue, but in Germany the greatly increased power of the nobility, at the expense of the emperor, represents the significant social consequence. Having put its own house in order, the Roman papacy in the twelfth and thirteenth centuries built the first strong government bureaucracy. In the central Middle Ages, the church exercised general leadership of European society. The Crusades exhibit that leadership, though their consequences for Byzantine-Western and for Christian-Muslim relations proved disastrous.

Through the instruments of justice and finance, the kings of England and France attacked feudal rights and provincial practices, built centralized bureaucracies, and gradually came in contact with all their subjects. In so doing, these rulers laid the foundations for modern national states. The German emperors shared power with territorial lordships. Medieval cities recruited people from the countryside and brought into being a new social class: the middle class. Cities provided economic opportunity, which, together with the revival of long-distance trade and a new capitalistic spirit, led to greater wealth, a higher standard of living, and upward social mobility.

In the twelfth and thirteenth centuries, universities—institutions of higher learning unique to the West—emerged from cathedral and municipal schools and provided trained officials for the new government bureaucracies. The soaring Gothic cathedrals that medieval towns erected demonstrated civic pride, deep religious faith, and economic vitality.

The performance of agricultural services and the payment of rents preoccupied peasants throughout the Middle Ages. Though peasants led hard lives, the reclamation of waste- and forestlands, migration to frontier territory, or flight to a town offered a means of social mobility. The Christian faith, though perhaps not understood on an intellectual level, provided emotional and spiritual solace. Aristocratic values and attitudes shaded all aspects of medieval culture. Trained for war, nobles often devoted considerable time to fighting, yet a noble might shoulder heavy judicial, political, and economic responsibilities, depending on the size of his estates. In their prayers, monks and nuns battled for the Lord. In their chants and rich ceremonials, in their architecture and literary productions, and in the examples of many monks' lives, the monasteries inspired Christian peoples. As the crucibles of sacred art, the monasteries became the cultural centers of Christian Europe.

Late medieval preachers likened the crises of their times to the Four Horsemen of the Apocalypse in the Book of Revelation, who brought famine, war, disease, and death. The crises of the fourteenth and fifteenth centuries were acids that burned deeply into the fabric of traditional medieval European society. Bad weather—beyond human control—brought poor harvests, which contributed to the international economic depression. Disease fostered widespread depression and dissatisfaction. Population losses caused by the Black Death and the Hundred Years' War encouraged the working classes to try to profit from the labor shortage by selling their services for a higher price. When peasant frustrations exploded in uprisings, the frightened nobility and upper middle class joined to crush the revolts. But events had heightened social consciousness among the poor.

The migration of peoples from the European heartland to the frontier regions of Iberia, Ireland, the Baltic, and eastern Europe led to ethnic friction between native peoples and new settlers. Economic difficulties heightened ethnic consciousness and spawned a vicious racism.

Religion held society together. European culture was a Christian culture. But the Great Schism weakened the prestige of the church and people's faith in papal authority. The conciliar movement, by denying the church's universal sovereignty, strengthened the claims of secular governments to jurisdiction over all their peoples. The later Middle Ages witnessed a steady shift of loyalty away from the church and toward the emerging national states.

KEY TERMS

lay investiture	Scholastics
Crusades	Gothic
Sephardic Jews	villeins
reconquista	manor
Domesday Book	Black Death
common law	Babylonian Captivity
merchant guilds	Great Schism
Hanseatic League	Jacquerie

NOTES

1. The sources, both Muslim and Christian, dispute the date (732 or 733) and the place (Poitiers or Tours) of this battle. I. Wood, *The Merovingian Kingdoms, 450–751* (New York: Longman, 1994), pp. 283–286, offers a careful analysis of all the evidence.
2. Ibid., p. 101.
3. Ibid., pp. 60–66; and E. James, *The Franks* (New York: Basil Blackwell, 1988), pp. 191–194.
4. See P. Geary, "Carolingians and the Carolingian Empire," in *Dictionary of the Middle Ages*, vol. 3, ed. J. R. Strayer (New York: Charles Scribner's Sons, 1983), p. 110.

5. Einhard, *The Life of Charlemagne,* with a foreword by S. Painter (Ann Arbor: University of Michigan Press, 1960), pp. 50–51.

6. P. Stafford, *Queens, Concubines, and Dowagers: The King's Wife in the Early Middle Ages* (Athens: University of Georgia Press, 1983), pp. 60–62.

7. See R. McKitterick, *The Frankish Kingdoms and the Early Carolingians, 751–987* (New York: Longman, 1983), pp. 30–37.

8. R. W. Southern, *Medieval Humanism and Other Studies* (Oxford: Basil Blackwell, 1970), p. 3.

9. McKitterick, *The Frankish Kingdoms,* pp. 134–136, 169.

10. On the thorny issue of feudalism, see S. Reynolds, *Fiefs and Vassals: The Medieval Evidence Reconsidered* (Oxford: Clarendon Press, 1996), pp. 2–3; E. A. R. Brown, "The Tyranny of a Construct: Feudalism and Historians of Medieval Europe," *American Historical Review* 79 (1974): 1060–1088; and J. R. Strayer, "The Two Levels of Feudalism," in *Medieval Statecraft and the Perspectives of History* (Princeton, N.J.: Princeton University Press, 1971), pp. 63–71; the quotation is on page 71.

11. S. Runciman, *A History of the Crusades.* Vol. 3: *The Kingdom of Acre* (Cambridge: Cambridge University Press, 1955), p. 480.

12. See B. Lewis, *The Muslim Discovery of Europe* (New York: W. W. Norton, 1982), pp. 23–25.

13. K. Armstrong, *Holy War: The Crusades and Their Impact on Today's World* (New York: Doubleday, 1991), pp. 373–375.

14. R. Bartlett, *The Making of Europe: Conquest, Colonization and Cultural Change, 950–1350* (Princeton, N.J.: Princeton University Press, 1993), pp. 8, 24, 34–35.

15. Ibid., pp. 11–15.

16. Ibid., pp. 250–255.

17. B. Arnold, *Princes and Territories in Medieval Germany* (New York: Cambridge University Press, 1991), pp. 65–72.

18. R. Bartlett, *Trial by Fire and Water: The Medieval Judicial Ordeal* (Oxford: Clarendon Press, 1986), pp. 25–27, Chap. 3.

19. J. Boswell, *Christianity, Social Tolerance, and Homosexuality: Gay People in Western Europe from the Beginning of the Christian Era to the Fourteenth Century* (Chicago: University of Chicago Press, 1980), pp. 270–293; the quotation is from page 293. For alternative interpretations, see K. Thomas, "Rescuing Homosexual History," *New York Review of Books,* December 4, 1980, pp. 26ff.; and J. DuQ. Adams, *Speculum* 56 (April 1981): 350ff. For the French monarchy's persecution of the Jews, see J. W. Baldwin, *The Government of Philip Augustus: Foundations of French Royal Power in the Middle Ages* (Berkeley: University of California Press, 1986), pp. 51–52, and W. C. Jordan, *The French Monarchy and the Jews* (Philadelphia: University of Pennsylvania Press, 1989).

20. J. C. Russell, *Medieval Regions and Their Cities* (Bloomington: University of Indiana Press, 1972), p. 91.

21. H. Pirenne, *Economic and Social History of Medieval Europe* (New York: Harcourt, Brace, 1956), p. 53.

22. See D. Herlihy, *Medieval and Renaissance Pistoia: The Social History of an Italian Town, 1200–1430* (New Haven, Conn.: Yale University Press, 1967), p. 257.

23. W. C. Jordan, *Women and Credit in Pre-Industrial and Developing Societies* (Philadelphia: University of Pennsylvania Press, 1993), pp. 20 et seq.

24. D. C. Douglas and G. W. Greenaway, eds., *English Historical Documents,* vol. 2 (London: Eyre and Spottiswode, 1961), pp. 969–970.

25. M. M. Postan, *The Medieval Economy and Society: An Economic History of Britain in the Middle Ages* (Baltimore: Penguin Books, 1975), pp. 213–214.

26. See P. Dollinger, *The German Hansa,* trans. and ed. D. S. Ault and S. H. Steinberg (Stanford, Calif.: Stanford University Press, 1970).

27. R. S. Lopez, "The Trade of Medieval Europe: The South," in *The Cambridge Economic History of Europe,* vol. 2, ed. M. M. Postan and E. E. Rich (Cambridge: Cambridge University Press, 1952), p. 289.

28. Quoted in H. E. Sigerist, *Civilization and Disease* (Chicago: University of Chicago Press, 1943), p. 102.

29. Quoted in J. H. Mundy, *Europe in the High Middle Ages, 1150–1309* (New York: Basic Books, 1973), pp. 474–475.

30. J. Bony, *French Gothic Architecture of the Twelfth and Thirteenth Centuries* (Berkeley: University of California Press, 1983), p. 13.

31. E. Panofsky, trans. and ed., *Abbot Suger on the Abbey Church of St.-Denis and Its Art Treasures* (Princeton, N.J.: Princeton University Press, 1946), p. 101.

32. Quoted in J. J. Wilhelm, ed., *Lyrics of the Middle Ages: An Anthology* (New York: Garland Publishers, 1993), pp. 94–95.

33. I have leaned on the very persuasive interpretation of M. R. Mcnocal, *The Arabic Role in Medieval Literary History* (Philadelphia: University of Pennsylvania Press, 1990), pp. ix–xv, 27–33.

34. G. Duby, *The Chivalrous Society,* trans. C. Postan (Berkeley: University of California Press, 1977), pp. 90–93.

35. B. A. Hanawalt, *The Ties That Bound: Peasant Families in Medieval England* (New York: Oxford University Press, 1986), p. 5.

36. E. Power, "Peasant Life and Rural Conditions," in J. R. Tanner et al., *The Cambridge Medieval History,* vol. 7 (Cambridge: Cambridge University Press, 1958), p. 716.

37. Glanvill, "De Legibus Angliae," bk. 5, chap. 5, in *Social Life in Britain from the Conquest to the Reformation,* ed. G. G. Coulton (London: Cambridge University Press, 1956), pp. 338–339.

38. See R. Bartlett, "Colonial Towns and Colonial Traders," in *The Making of Europe: Conquest, Colonization and Cultural Change, 950–1350* (Princeton, N.J.: Princeton University Press, 1993), pp. 167–196.

39. See John L. Langdon, *Horses, Oxen, and Technological Innovation: The Use of Draught Animals in English Farming, 1066–1500* (New York: Cambridge University Press, 1986), esp. pp. 254–270.

40. See Hanawalt, *The Ties That Bound,* pp. 90–100.

41. Ibid., p. 149.

42. On this quantity and medieval measurements, see D. Knowles, "The Measures of Monastic Beverages," in *The Monastic Order in England* (Cambridge: Cambridge University Press, 1962), p. 717.

43. M. Chibnall, ed. and trans., *The Ecclesiastical History of Orderic Vitalis* (Oxford: Oxford University Press, 1972), 2.xiii.

44. R. W. Southern, *Western Society and the Church in the Middle Ages* (Baltimore: Penguin Books, 1970), pp. 224–230, esp. p. 228.

45. See M. W. Labarge, *A Small Sound of the Trumpet: Women in Medieval Life* (Boston: Beacon Press, 1986), pp. 104–105.

46. Jordan, *Women and Credit in Pre-Industrial and Developing Societies,* p. 61.

47. See W. C. Jordan, *The Great Famine: Northern Europe in the Early Fourteenth Century* (Princeton, N.J.: Princeton University Press, 1996), pp. 97–102.

48. W. H. McNeill, *Plagues and Peoples* (New York: Doubleday, 1976), pp. 151–168.

49. Quoted in P. Ziegler, *The Black Death* (Harmondsworth, Eng.: Pelican Books, 1969), p. 20.

50. J. M. Rigg, trans., *The Decameron of Giovanni Boccaccio* (London: J. M. Dent & Sons, 1903), p. 6.

51. Ziegler, *The Black Death,* pp. 232–239.

52. J. Hatcher, *Plague, Population and the English Economy, 1348–1530* (London: Macmillan Education, 1986), p. 33.

53. See S. K. Cohn, Jr., "The Black Death: End of the Paradigm," *American Historical Review,* 107 (June 2002): 703–738.

54. See G. P. Cuttino, "Historical Revision: The Causes of the Hundred Years' War," *Speculum* 31 (July 1956): 463–472.

55. J. Barnie, *War in Medieval English Society: Social Values and the Hundred Years' War* (Ithaca, N.Y.: Cornell University Press, 1974), p. 34.

56. Ibid., pp. 72–73.

57. See G. O. Sayles, *The King's Parliament of England* (New York: W. W. Norton, 1974), app., pp. 137–141.

58. Quoted in M. Bloch, *French Rural History,* trans. J. Sondeimer (Berkeley: University of California Press, 1966), p. 169.

59. C. Stephenson and G. F. Marcham, eds., *Sources of English Constitutional History,* rev. ed. (New York: Harper & Row, 1972), p. 225.

60. Quoted in Bartlett, *The Making of Europe,* p. 205.

61. Quoted ibid., p. 215.

62. Quoted ibid., p. 224.

63. Quoted ibid., p. 228.

64. Ibid., p. 233.

65. Ibid., p. 238.

66. Quoted ibid., p. 239.

▌SUGGESTED READING

For further exploration of the social, religious, political, and economic issues raised in this chapter, the curious student should begin with the titles by Arnold, Baldwin, Bartlett, Boswell, Dollinger, Herlihy, Jordan, McKitterick, Reynolds, Strayer, and Wood listed in the Notes. R. McKitterick, *The Carolingians and the Written Word* (1989), and P. Riche, *Education and Culture in the Barbarian West,* trans. J. Contreni (1976), should prove useful for study of the Carolingian Renaissance.

I. S. Robinson, *The Papacy, 1073–1198: Continuity and Innovation* (1990), treats the changing role of the papacy and the development of papal government, as does C. Morris, *The Papal Monarchy: The Western Church, 1050–1250* (1989).

The following studies provide exciting and highly readable general accounts of the Crusades: J. Riley-Smith, *What Were the Crusades?* (1977), and R. C. Finucane, *Soldiers of the Faith: Crusaders and Muslims at War* (1983). There are excellent articles on many facets of the Crusades in J. R. Strayer, ed., *Dictionary of the Middle Ages,* vol. 4 (1984). For the Fourth Crusade, see the excellent study of D. E. Queller, *The Fourth Crusade: The Capture of Constantinople* (1977), which gives an important revisionist interpretation. B. Lewis, *The Muslim Discovery of Europe* (1982), gives the Muslim view of the Crusades.

G. O. Sayles, *The Medieval Foundations of England* (1961), traces political and social conditions to the end of the twelfth century. For the Becket controversy, see F. Barlow, *Thomas Becket* (1986). J. C. Holt, *Magna Carta* (1969), remains the best modern treatment of the document.

For Spain, R. Fletcher, *The Quest for El Cid* (1990), provides an excellent introduction to Spanish social and political conditions through a study of Rodrigo Dias, the eleventh-century soldier of fortune who became the Spanish national hero. Fletcher's *Moorish Spain* (1992) provides a highly readable sketch of the history of Islamic Spain from the eighth to the seventeenth century. For the developing social and economic importance of the Flemish towns, see D. Nicholas, *Medieval Flanders* (1992).

For France, E. Hallam, *The Capetian Kings of France, 987–1328* (1980), is a readable introduction. Advanced students of medieval French administrative history should see J. Baldwin, *The Government of Philip Augustus: Foundations of French Royal Power in the Middle Ages* (1986), and J. R. Strayer, *The Reign of Philip the Fair* (1980). On Germany, see H. Furhman, *Germany in the High Middle Ages,* trans. T. Reuther (1986), and M. Pacaut, *Frederick Barbarossa,* trans. A. J. Pomerans (1980), perhaps the best one-volume treatment of that important ruler.

For the economic revival of Europe, see P. Spufford, *Money and Its Use in Medieval Europe* (Cambridge: Cambridge University Press, 1988), an exciting and valuable study of how money changed not only commerce but also society. T. H. Lloyd, *England and the German Hanse, 1157–1611: A Study in Their Trade and Commercial Diplomacy* (1992), is essential for northern European commercial development.

For women, see C. Klapisch-Zuber, ed., *A History of Women.* Vol. 2: *Silences of the Middle Ages* (1992), which contains useful essays on many aspects of women's lives and status; and S. Shahar, *The Fourth Estate: Women in the Middle Ages* (1983), a provocative work. J. M. Bennett, *Women in the Medieval English Countryside: Gender and Household in Brigstock Before the Plague* (1987), is a fascinating case study.

Those interested in the origins of medieval towns and cities will learn how historians use the evidence of coins, archaeology, tax records, geography, and laws in J. F. Benton, ed., *Town Origins: The Evidence of Medieval England* (1968). S. Reynolds, *An Introduction to the History of English Medieval Towns* (1982), explores the social structure, political organization, and economic livelihood of English towns. R. H. Hilton, *English and French Towns in Feudal Society* (1992), is an exciting comparative study.

For the new currents of thought in the central Middle Ages, see M. T. Clanchy, *Abelard: A Medieval Life* (1997), which incorporates recent international research. For the development of literacy among laypeople and the formation of a literate mentality, the advanced student should see M. T. Clanchy, *From Memory to Written Record: England, 1066–1307,* 2d ed. (1992). Written by outstanding scholars in a variety of fields, R. L. Benson and G. Constable with C. D. Lanham, eds., *Renaissance and Renewal in the Twelfth Century* (1982), contains an invaluable collection of articles.

On the medieval universities, H. De Ridder-Symoens, ed., *A History of the University in Europe.* Vol. 1: *Universities in the Middle Ages* (1991), offers good interpretations by leading scholars. For the beginnings of Scholasticism and humanism, see the essential R. W. Southern, *Scholastic Humanism and the Unification of Western Europe,* vol. 1 (1994).

F. and J. Gies, *Cathedral, Forge, and Waterwheel* (1993), provides an illustrated survey of medieval technological achievements. The following studies are valuable for the evolution and development of the Gothic style: J. Harvey, *The Master Builders* (1971); J. Bony, *French Gothic Architecture of the Twelfth and Thirteenth Centuries* (1983). C. A. Bruzelius, *The Thirteenth-Century Church at St. Denis* (1985), traces later reconstruction of the church. J. Gimpel, *The Medieval Machine: The Industrial Revolution of the Middle Ages* (1977), discusses the mechanical and scientific problems involved in early industrialization.

On troubadour poetry, see, in addition to the title by Wilhelm cited in the Notes, M. Bogin, *The Women Troubadours* (1980).

The conflict between Pope Boniface VIII and the kings of France and England is well treated in J. R. Strayer, *The Reign of Philip the Fair* (1980), and M. Prestwich, *Edward I* (1988), both sound and important biographies.

For a broad treatment of frontier regions, see R. Bartlett, *The Making of Europe: Conquest, Colonization and Cultural Change, 950–1350* (1993).

The student interested in aspects of medieval slavery, serfdom, or the peasantry should see P. Bonnassie, *From Slavery to Feudalism* (1991); P. Freedman, *The Origins of Peasant Servitude in Medieval Catalonia* (1991); and the highly important work of W. C. Jordan, *From Servitude to Freedom: Manumission in the Sénonais in the Thirteenth Century* (1986).

For the origins and status of the nobility in the central Middle Ages, students are strongly urged to see the study by Duby cited in the Notes. Social mobility among both aristocracy and peasantry is discussed in T. Evergates, *Feudal Society in the Bailliage of Troyes Under the Counts of Champagne, 1152–1284* (1976).

On the monks, see the titles listed in the Suggested Reading for Chapter 8. B. D. Hill's articles "Benedictines" and "Cistercian Order," in J. R. Strayer, ed., *Dictionary of the Middle Ages,* vols. 2 and 3 (1982 and 1983), are broad surveys of the premier monastic orders with useful bibliographies. B. Harvey, *Living and Dying in England: The Monastic Experience, 1100–1540* (1993), has valuable material on monastic diet, clothing, routine, sickness, and death. L. J. Lekai, *The Cistercians: Ideals and Reality* (1977), synthesizes research on the white monks and carries their story down to the twentieth century. Both W. Braunfels, *Monasteries of Western Europe: The Architecture of the Orders* (1972), and C. Brooke, *The Monastic World* (1974), have splendid illustrations and good bibliographies. The best study of medieval English Cistercian architecture is P. Fergusson, *Architecture of Solitude: Cistercian Abbeys in Twelfth Century England* (1984).

For women and children, see B. Hanawalt, *Growing Up in Medieval London: The Experience of Childhood in History* (1993), which has exciting material on class and gender, apprenticeship, and the culture of matrimony; and C. Brooke, *The Medieval Idea of Marriage* (1991), which answers his question, "What is marriage and what sets it apart from other human relationships?" J. M. Bennett, *Women in the Medieval English Countryside* (1987), is an important and pioneering study of women in rural, preindustrial society.

For further treatment of nuns, see J. K. McNamara, *Sisters in Arms* (1996), a broad survey tracing the lives of religious women, from the mothers of the Egyptian desert to the twentieth century; B. Newman, *Sister of Wisdom: St. Hildegard's Theology of the Feminine* (1987), a learned and lucidly written study; S. Elkins, *Holy Women in Twelfth-Century England* (1985); and C. Bynum, *Jesus as Mother: Studies in the Spirituality of the High Middle Ages* (1984), which contains valuable articles on facets of women's religious history and an excellent contrast of the differing spirituality of monks and nuns.

The best starting point for study of the great epidemic that swept the European continent is D. Herlihy, *The Black Death and the Transformation of the West* (1997), a fine treatment of the causes and cultural consequences of the disease. For the social implications of the Black Death, see L. Poos, *A Rural Society After the Black Death: Essex, 1350–1525* (1991); G. Huppert, *After the Black Death: A Social History of Early Modern Europe* (1986); and W. H. McNeill, *Plagues and Peoples* (1976). For the economic effects of the plague, see J. Hatcher, *Plague, Population, and the English Economy, ca. 1300–1450* (1977). The older study of P. Ziegler, *The Black Death* (1969), remains important.

For the background and early part of the long military conflicts of the fourteenth and fifteenth centuries, see the provocative M. M. Vale, *The Origins of the Hundred Years War: The Angevin Legacy, 1250–1340* (1996). See also C. Allmand, *The Hundred Years War: England and France at War, ca 1300–1450* (1988). The broad survey of J. Keegan, *A History of Warfare* (1993), contains a useful summary of significant changes in military technology during the war. J. Keegan, *The Face of Battle* (1977), Chap. 2: "Agincourt," describes what war meant to the ordinary soldier. For strategy, tactics, armaments, and costumes of war, see H. W. Koch, *Medieval Warfare* (1978), a beautifully illustrated book.

T. F. Glick, *From Muslim Fortress to Christian Castle: Social and Cultural Change in Medieval Spain* (1995), explores the reorganization of Spanish society after the reconquest, bringing considerable cultural change. P. C. Maddern, *Violence and Social Order: East Anglia, 1422–1442* (1991), deals with social disorder in eastern England. I. M. W. Harvey, *Jack Cade's Rebellion of 1450* (1991), is an important work in local history. Students are especially encouraged to consult the brilliant work of E. L. Ladurie, *The Peasants of Languedoc,* trans. J. Day (1976). J. C. Holt, *Robin Hood* (1982), is a soundly researched and highly readable study of the famous outlaw.

D. Herlihy, *Women, Family and Society in Medieval Europe: Historical Essays, 1978–1991* (1995), contains several valuable articles dealing with the later Middle Ages, while the exciting study by B. Gottlieb, *The Family in the Western World from the Black Death to the Industrial Age* (1993), explores the family's political, emotional, and cultural roles. For prostitution, see L. L. Otis, *Prostitution in Medieval Society: The History of an Urban Institution in Languedoc* (1987), and J. Rossiaud, *Medieval Prostitution* (1995), a very good treatment of prostitution's social and cultural significance.

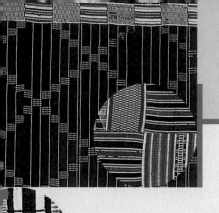

LISTENING TO THE PAST

AN ARAB VIEW OF THE CRUSADES

The Crusades helped shape the understanding *that Arabs and Europeans had of each other and all subsequent relations between the Christian West and the Arab world. To medieval Christians, the Crusades were papally approved military expeditions for the recovery of holy places in Palestine; to the Arabs, these campaigns were "Frankish wars" or "Frankish invasions" for the acquisition of territory.*

Early in the thirteenth century, Ibn Al-Athir (1160–1223), a native of Mosul, an important economic and cultural center in northern Mesopotamia (modern Iraq), wrote a history of the First Crusade. He relied on Arab sources for the events he described. Here is his account of the Crusaders' capture of Antioch.

The power of the Franks first became apparent when in the year 478/1085–86* they invaded the territories of Islam and took Toledo and other parts of Andalusia [in Spain]. Then in 484/1091 they attacked and conquered the island of Sicily and turned their attention to the African coast. Certain of their conquests there were won back again but they had other successes, as you will see.

In 490/1097 the Franks attacked Syria. This is how it all began: Baldwin, their King, a kinsman of Roger the Frank who had conquered Sicily, assembled a great army and sent word to Roger saying: "I have assembled a great army and now I am on my way to you, to use your bases for my conquest of the African coast. Thus you and I shall become neighbors."

Roger called together his companions and consulted them about these proposals. "This will

be a fine thing for them and for us!" they declared, "for by this means these lands will be converted to the Faith!" At this Roger raised one leg and farted loudly, and swore that it was of more use than their advice. "Why?" "Because if this army comes here it will need quantities of provisions and fleets of ships to transport it to Africa, as well as reinforcements from my own troops. Then, if the Franks succeed in conquering this territory they will take it over and will need provisioning from Sicily. This will cost me my annual profit from the harvest. If they fail they will return here and be an embarrassment to me here in my own domain." . . .

He summoned Baldwin's messenger and said to him: "If you have decided to make war on the Muslims your best course will be to free Jerusalem from their rule and thereby win great honor. I am bound by certain promises and treaties of allegiance with the ruler of Africa." So the Franks made ready to set out to attack Syria.

Another story is that the Fatimids of Egypt were afraid when they saw the Seljuqids extending their empire through Syria as far as Gaza, until they reached the Egyptian border and Atsiz invaded Egypt itself. They therefore sent to invite the Franks to invade Syria and so protect Egypt from the Muslims.[†] But God knows best.

When the Franks decided to attack Syria they marched east to Constantinople, so that they could cross the straits and advance into Muslim territory by the easier, land route. When they reached Constantinople, the Emperor of the East refused them permission to pass through his domains. He said: "Unless you first promise me Antioch, I shall not allow you to cross into the

*Muslims traditionally date events from Muhammad's hegira, or emigration, to Medina, which occurred in 622 according to the Christian calendar.

†Although Muslims, Fatimids were related doctrinally to the Shi'ites, but the dominant Sunni Muslims considered the Fatimids heretics.

Muslim empire." His real intention was to incite them to attack the Muslims, for he was convinced that the Turks, whose invincible control over Asia Minor he had observed, would exterminate every one of them. They accepted his conditions and in 490/1097 they crossed the Bosphorus at Constantinople. . . . They . . . reached Antioch, which they besieged.

When Yaghi Siyan, the ruler of Antioch, heard of their approach, he was not sure how the Christian people of the city would react, so he made the Muslims go outside the city on their own to dig trenches, and the next day sent the Christians out alone to continue the task. When they were ready to return home at the end of the day he refused to allow them. "Antioch is yours," he said, "but you will have to leave it to me until I see what happens between us and the Franks." "Who will protect our children and our wives?" they said. "I shall look after them for you." So they resigned themselves to their fate, and lived in the Frankish camp for nine months, while the city was under siege.

Yaghi Siyan showed unparalleled courage and wisdom, strength and judgment. If all the Franks who died had survived they would have overrun all the lands of Islam. He protected the families of the Christians in Antioch and would not allow a hair of their heads to be touched.

After the siege had been going on for a long time the Franks made a deal with . . . a cuirass-maker called Ruzbih whom they bribed with a fortune in money and lands. He worked in the tower that stood over the riverbed, where the river flowed out of the city into the valley. The Franks sealed their pact with the cuirass-maker, God damn him! and made their way to the water-gate. They opened it and entered the city. Another gang of them climbed the tower with their ropes. At dawn, when more than 500 of them were in the city and the defenders were worn out after the night watch, they sounded their trumpets. . . . Panic seized Yaghi Siyan and he opened the city gates and fled in terror, with an escort of thirty pages. His army commander arrived, but when he discovered on enquiry that Yaghi Siyan had fled, he made his escape by another gate. This was of great help to the Franks,

Miniature showing heavily armored knights fighting Muslims. *(Bibliothèque nationale de France)*

for if he had stood firm for an hour, they would have been wiped out. They entered the city by the gates and sacked it, slaughtering all the Muslims they found there. This happened in jumada I (491/April/May 1098). . . .

It was the discord between the Muslim princes . . . that enabled the Franks to overrun the country.

QUESTIONS FOR ANALYSIS

1. From the Arab perspective, when did the crusade begin?

2. How did Ibn Al-Athir explain the Crusaders' expedition to Syria?

3. Why did Antioch fall to the Crusaders?

4. The use of dialogue in historical narrative is a very old device dating from the Greek historian Thucydides (fifth century B.C.E.). Assess the value of Ibn Al-Athir's dialogues for the modern historian.

Sources: P. J. Geary, ed., *Readings in Medieval History* (Peterborough, Ontario: Broadview Press, 1991), pp. 443–444; E. J. Costello, trans., *Arab Historians of the Crusades* (Berkeley and Los Angeles: University of California Press, 1969).

Gold mask assemblage, at least thirteen hundred years old. Excavated from an ancient Peruvian tomb in the town of Sipán. *(© Walter Alva. Photo provided by the Department of Anthropology, UCLA)*

CHAPTER

14

CIVILIZATIONS OF THE AMERICAS, CA 400–1500

CHAPTER OUTLINE

- The Geography and Peoples of the Americas

- Mesoamerican Civilizations from the Olmecs to the Toltecs

- Aztec Society: Religion and War

- The Incas of Peru

- North America and the Mound Builders

Between approximately 300 B.C.E. and 1500 C.E., sophisticated civilizations developed in the Western Hemisphere. But unlike most other societies in the world, which felt the influences of other cultures—sub-Saharan Africa, for example, experienced the impact of Muslims, Asians, and Europeans—American societies grew in almost total isolation from other peoples. Then, in 1501–1502, the Florentine explorer Amerigo Vespucci (1451–1512) sailed down the eastern coast of South America to Brazil. Convinced that he had found a new world, Vespucci published an account of his voyage. Shortly thereafter the German geographer Martin Waldseemüller proposed that this new world be called "America" to preserve Vespucci's memory. Initially applied only to South America, by the end of the sixteenth century the term *America* was used for both continents in the Western Hemisphere.

Our use of the word **Indian** for the indigenous peoples of the Americas stems from early European explorers' geographical misconceptions of where they were—they believed they were near the East Indies (see page 510). South America contained a great diversity of peoples, cultures, and linguistic groups. Modern scholars estimate that around 1500 there were 350 tribal groups, 15 distinct cultural centers, and 150 linguistic stocks. Historians and anthropologists have tended to focus attention on the Maya, Incas, and Aztecs, but the inhabitants of those three empires represent a minority of the total indigenous population; they lived in geographical regions that covered a small percentage of Mesoamerica and South America. Other native peoples included the Aymaras, Caribs, Chibchas, Chichimecas, Ge, Guaranis, Mapuches, Otonis, Pueblos, Quibayas, Tupis, and Zapotecs (see Map 14.1). In North America, aboriginal peoples represent comparable diversity. These peoples shared no unified sense of themselves as "Indians." None of their languages had the word *Indian.* Nor was there any tendency among these peoples to unite in a common resistance to the foreign invaders.[1] Rather, when confronting Europeans, each group or polity sought the most advantageous situation for itself alone. Of course, the idea of "discovery" meant nothing to them. Because much more is known about the Aztecs, Maya, and Incas than about other native peoples, the focus of this chapter is on them. The central feature of early American societies, however, is their great indigenous and cultural diversity.

417

- What is the geography of the Americas, and how did it shape the lives of the native peoples?
- What patterns of social and political organization did the Maya, Aztecs, and Incas display?
- What were the significant cultural achievements of the Maya, Aztecs, and Incas?
- Who were the North American mound builders, and what do the material remains of their culture tell us about them?

This chapter will consider these questions.

THE GEOGRAPHY AND PEOPLES OF THE AMERICAS

The distance from the Bering Strait, which separates Asia from North America, to the southern tip of South America is about eleven thousand miles. A mountain range extends all the way from Alaska to the tip of South America, crossing Central America from northwest to southeast and making for rugged country along virtually the entire western coast of both continents.

Scholars use the term **Mesoamerica** to designate the area of present-day Mexico and Central America. Mexico is dominated by high plateaus bounded by coastal plains. Geographers have labeled the plateau regions "cold lands," the valleys between the plateaus "temperate lands," and the Gulf and Pacific coastal regions "hot lands." The Caribbean coast of Central America—modern Belize, Guatemala, Honduras, Nicaragua, El Salvador, Costa Rica, and Panama—is characterized by thick jungle lowlands, heavy rainfall, and torrid heat; it is an area generally unhealthy for humans. Central America's western uplands, with their more temperate climate and good agricultural land, support the densest population in the region.

Like Africa, South America is a continent of extremely varied terrain (see Map 14.4). The entire western coast is edged by the Andes, the highest mountain range in the Western Hemisphere. On the east coast, another mountain range—the Brazilian Highlands—accounts for one-fourth of the area of modern-day Brazil. Three-fourths of South America—almost the entire interior of the continent—is lowland plains. The Amazon River, at 4,000 miles the second-longest river in the world, bisects the north-central part of the continent, draining 2.7 million square miles of land. Tropical lowland rain forests with dense growth and annual rainfall in excess of 80 inches extend from the Amazon and

Orinoco River basins northward all the way to southern Mexico.

Most scholars believe that people began crossing the Bering Strait from Russian Siberia between fifty thousand and twenty thousand years ago, when the strait was narrower than it is today. Skeletal finds indicate that these immigrants belonged to several ethnic groups now known collectively as American Indians, or Amerindians. Amerindians were nomadic peoples who lived by hunting small animals, fishing, and gathering wild fruits. As soon as an area had been exploited and a group had grown too large for the land to support, some families broke off from the group and moved on, usually southward. Gradually the newcomers spread throughout the Americas, losing contact with one another.

By the late fifteenth century, three kinds of Amerindian societies had emerged. First, largely nomadic groups depended on hunting, fishing, and gathering for subsistence; they had changed little from their ancestors who had crossed the Bering Strait thousands of years before. A second group of Amerindians, whom historians label sedentary or semi-sedentary, relied primarily on the domestication of plants for food; they led a settled or semi-settled farming life. A third group lived in large, sometimes densely populated settlements supported by agricultural surpluses; specialization of labor, large-scale construction projects, and different social classes characterized this group. These complex cultures existed only in Mesoamerica and western South America. In 1492 the polities of the Anáhuacs (Aztecs), Maya, and Tahuantinsuyas (Incas) were perhaps the best representatives of the third group.[2]

Amerindians in central Mexico built *chinampas*, floating gardens. They dredged soil from the bottom of a lake or pond, placed the soil on mats of woven twigs, and then planted crops in the soil. Chinampas were enormously productive, yielding up to three harvests a year. So extensive was this method of agriculture that central Mexico became known as the chinampas region. In Peru, meanwhile, people terraced the slopes of the Andes with stone retaining walls to keep the hillsides from sliding. Both chinampas and terraced slopes required the large labor force that became available with stable settlement.

Agricultural advancement had definitive social and political consequences. Careful cultivation of the land brought a reliable and steady food supply, which contributed to a relatively high fertility rate and in turn to a population boom. Because corn and potatoes require much less labor than does grain, Amerindian civilizations had a large pool of people who were not involved in agriculture and thus were available to construct religious and political buildings and serve in standing armies.[3]

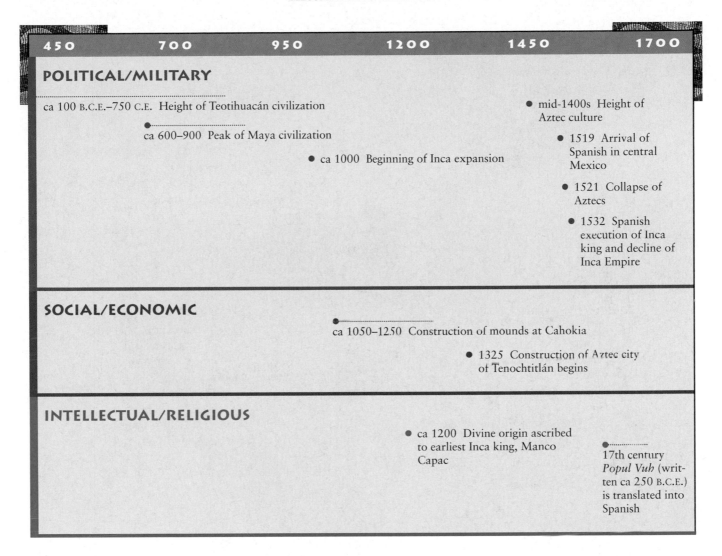

450	700	950	1200	1450	1700

POLITICAL/MILITARY

ca 100 B.C.E.–750 C.E. Height of Teotihuacán civilization

ca 600–900 Peak of Maya civilization

ca 1000 Beginning of Inca expansion

● mid-1400s Height of Aztec culture

● 1519 Arrival of Spanish in central Mexico

● 1521 Collapse of Aztecs

● 1532 Spanish execution of Inca king and decline of Inca Empire

SOCIAL/ECONOMIC

ca 1050–1250 Construction of mounds at Cahokia

● 1325 Construction of Aztec city of Tenochtitlán begins

INTELLECTUAL/RELIGIOUS

● ca 1200 Divine origin ascribed to earliest Inca king, Manco Capac

17th century *Popul Vuh* (written ca 250 B.C.E.) is translated into Spanish

MESOAMERICAN CIVILIZATIONS FROM THE OLMECS TO THE TOLTECS

Several American civilizations arose between roughly 1500 B.C.E. and 900 C.E.: the civilizations of the Olmecs, the Maya, Teotihuacán, and the Toltecs. Scholars believe that the Olmec civilization is the oldest of the early advanced Amerindian civilizations. Olmec culture, based on agriculture, spread over regions in central Mexico that lie thousands of miles apart. The Olmec practice of building scattered ceremonial centers found its highest cultural expression in the civilization of the Maya. The Maya occupied the area of present-day Yucatán, the highland crescent of eastern Chiapas in Mexico, and much of modern Guatemala and western Honduras. In the central plateau of Mexico, an "empire" centered at Teotihuacán arose. Scholars hotly debate whether the Teotihuacán territory constituted an empire, but they agree that Teotihuacán society was heavily stratified and that it exercised military, religious, and political power over a wide area. The Toltecs, whose culture adopted many features of the Teotihuacán and Olmec civilizations, were the last advanced Amerindian civilization before the rise of the Aztecs.

The Olmecs

The word **Olmec** comes from an Aztec term for the peoples living in southern Veracruz and western Tabasco, Mexico, between about 1500 and 300 B.C.E. They did not call themselves Olmecs or consider themselves a unified group, but their culture penetrated and influenced

MAP 14.1 The Peoples of South America   The major indigenous peoples of South America represented a great variety of languages and cultures. *(Source: Adapted from* The Times Atlas of World History, *3d ed. © Times Books. Reproduced by permission of HarperCollins Publishers Ltd.)*

all parts of Mesoamerica. All later Mesoamerican cultures derived from the Olmecs. Modern knowledge of the Olmecs rests entirely on archaeological evidence—pyramids, jade objects, axes, figurines, and stone monuments.

The Olmecs cultivated maize, squash, beans, and other plants and supplemented that diet with wild game and fish. Originally they lived in egalitarian societies that had no distinctions based on status or wealth. After 1500 B.C.E., more complex, hierarchical societies evolved. Anthropologists call these societies chieftains. Most peoples continued to live in small hamlets, villages, and towns along the rivers of the region, while the leaders of the societies resided in the large cities today known as San Lorenzo, La Venta, Tres Zapotes, and Laguna de los Cerros. These cities contained palaces (large private houses) for the elite, large plazas, temples (ritual centers), ball courts, water reservoirs, and carved stone drains for the disposal of wastes. The Olmecs developed a sophisticated system of symbols, as shown in their art; this system clearly influenced the Maya (see page 423). They invented monumental stone sculptures, a characteristic of every subsequent Mesoamerican civilization. In starting a tradition of ruler portraits in stone, the Olmecs also laid the foundations for a practice adopted by the Maya and other peoples. They had sacred ceremonial sites where they sometimes practiced human sacrifice. They erected special courts on which men played a game with a hard rubber ball that was both religious ritual and sport. Finally, the Olmecs engaged in long-distance trade, exchanging rubber, cacao (from which chocolate is made), pottery, figurines, jaguar pelts, and the services of painters and sculptors for obsidian (a hard, black volcanic glass from which paddle-shaped weapons were made), basalt, iron ore, shells, and various perishable goods. Commercial networks extended as far away as central and western Mexico and the Pacific coast.[4]

Around 900 B.C.E. San Lorenzo, the center of early Olmec culture, was destroyed, probably by migrating peoples from the north, and power passed to La Venta in Tabasco. Archaeological excavation at La Venta has uncovered a huge volcano-shaped pyramid. Standing 110 feet high at an inaccessible site on an island in the Tonala River, the so-called Great Pyramid was the center of the Olmec religion. The upward thrust of this monument, like that of the cathedrals of medieval Europe, may have represented the human effort to get closer to the gods. Built of huge stone slabs, the Great Pyramid required, scholars estimated, some 800,000 man-hours of labor. It testifies to the region's bumper harvests, which were able to support a labor force large enough to build such a monument. Around 300 B.C.E. La Venta fell, and Tres

Zapotes, 100 miles to the northwest, became the leading Olmec site.

Olmec ceremonialism, magnificent sculpture, skillful stonework, social organization, and writing were important cultural advances that paved the way for the developments of the Classic period (300–900 C.E.), the golden age of Mesoamerican civilization. Just as the ancient Sumerians laid the foundations for later Mesopotamian cultures (see Chapter 1), so the Olmecs heavily influenced subsequent Mesoamerican societies.

The Maya of Central America

In the Classic period, the Maya attained a level of intellectual and artistic achievement equaled by no other Amerindian people and by few peoples anywhere. The Maya developed a sophisticated system of writing, perhaps derived partly from the Olmecs. They invented a calendar more accurate than the European Gregorian calendar. And they made advances in mathematics that Europeans did not match for several centuries.

Who were the Maya, and where did they come from? What was the basis of their culture? What is the significance of their intellectual and artistic achievement? The word *Maya* seems to derive from *Zamna,* the name of a Maya god. Linguistic evidence leads scholars to believe that the first Maya were a small North American Indian group that emigrated from southern Oregon and northern California to the western highlands of Guatemala. Between the third and second millennia B.C.E., various groups, including the Cholans and Tzeltalans, broke away from the parent group and moved north and east into the Yucatán peninsula. The Cholan-speaking Maya, who occupied the area during the time of great cultural achievement, apparently created the culture.

Maya culture rested on agriculture. The staple crop in Mesoamerica was maize (corn). In 1972 a geographer and an aerial photographer studying the Campeche region of the Yucatán peninsula (see Map 14.2) proved that the Maya practiced intensive agriculture in raised, narrow, rectangular plots that they built above the low-lying, seasonally flooded land bordering rivers. Because of poor soil caused by heavy tropical rainfall and the fierce sun, farmers may also have relied on *milpa* for growing maize. Using this method, farmers cut down the trees in a patch of forest and set the wood and brush afire. They then used a stick to poke holes through the ash and planted maize seeds in the holes. A milpa (the word refers to both the area and the method) produced for only two years, after which it had to lie fallow for between four and seven years. Throughout the Yucatán

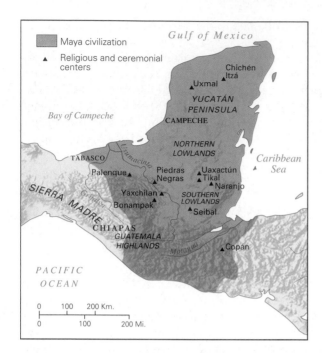

MAP 14.2 The Maya World, 300–900 C.E. Archaeologists have discovered the ruins of dozens of Maya city-states. Only the largest of them are shown here. Called the "Greeks of the New World," the Maya perfected the only written language in the Western Hemisphere, developed a sophisticated political system and a flourishing trade network, and created elegant art.

Palace Doorway Lintel at Yaxchilan, Mexico Lady Xoc, principal wife of King Shield-Jaguar, who holds a torch over her, pulls a thorn-lined rope through her tongue to sanctify with her blood the birth of a younger wife's child—reflecting the importance of blood sacrifice in Maya culture. The elaborate headdresses and clothes of the couple show their royal status. *(© Justin Kerr 1985)*

peninsula, the method of burning and planting in the fertile ashes, known as *swidden agriculture,* remains the typical farming practice today.

In addition to maize, the Maya grew beans, squash, chili peppers, some root crops, and fruit trees. The raised-field and milpa systems of intensive agriculture yielded food sufficient to support large population centers. The entire Maya region could have had as many as 14 million inhabitants. At Uxmal, Uaxactún, Copán, Piedras Negras, Tikal, Palenque, and Chichén Itzá (see Map 14.2), archaeologists have uncovered the palaces of nobles, elaborate pyramids where nobles were buried, engraved *steles* (stone-slab monuments), masonry temples, altars, sophisticated polychrome pottery, and courts for games played with a rubber ball. The largest site, Tikal, may have had forty thousand people. Since these centers lacked industrial activities, scholars avoid calling them cities. Rather they were religious and ceremonial centers.

Public fairs accompanying important religious festivals in population centers seem to have been the major Maya economic institutions. Jade, obsidian, beads of red spiny oyster shell, lengths of cloth, and cacao (chocolate) beans— all in high demand in the Mesoamerican world—served as the medium of exchange. The extensive trade among Maya communities, plus a common language, promoted the union of the peoples of the region and gave them a common sense of identity. Merchants trading beyond Maya regions, such as with the Zapotecs of the Valley of Oaxaca and the Teotihuacanos of the central valley of Mexico, were considered state ambassadors bearing "gifts" to royal neighbors, who reciprocated with their own "gifts." Since this long-distance trade played an important part in international relations, the merchants

After a Maya Battle   Richly dressed Maya victors lead captives from the battlefield, probably to their fate—sacrifice. (© *Justin Kerr*)

conducting it were high nobles or even members of the royal family.

Lacking iron tools until a few centuries before the Spanish conquest and beasts of burden until after the conquest, how were goods transported to distant regions? The extensive networks of rivers and swamps were the main arteries of transportation; over them large canoes carved out of hardwood trees carried cargoes of cloth and maize. Wide roads also linked Maya centers; on the roads merchants and lords were borne in litters, goods and produce on human backs. Trade produced considerable wealth that seems to have been concentrated in a noble class, for the Maya had no distinctly mercantile class. They did have a sharply defined hierarchical society. A hereditary elite owned private land, defended society, carried on commercial activities, exercised political power, and directed religious rituals. The intellectual class also belonged to the ruling nobility. The rest of the people were free workers, serfs, and slaves.

A fierce and warlike people, the Maya fought wars "for land, for slaves, to avenge insults and punish theft, and to control trade routes and the sources of various valued products, particularly salt." Long periods without rain caused crop failure, which led to famine and then war with other centers for food. Within the same communities, domestic strife between factions over the succession to the kingship, property, or perceived insults seems to have been common.[5]

Yet the Maya also cultivated the arts of peace. They developed a system of hieroglyphic writing with 850 characters and used it to record chronology, religion, and astronomy in books made of bark paper and deerskin. The recent deciphering of this writing has demonstrated that inscriptions on steles are actually historical documents recording the births, accessions, marriages, wars, and deaths of Maya kings. An understanding of the civilization's dynastic history allows scholars to interpret more accurately Maya pictorial imagery and to detect patterns in Maya art. They are finding that the imagery explicitly portrays the text in pictorial scenes and on stelar carvings.[6]

In the sixteenth century, Spanish friars taught Maya students to write their language in the Roman script so that the friars could understand Maya culture. Maya deities and sacrificial customs, however, provoked Spanish outrage. To hasten Maya conversion to Christianity, the priests tried to extirpate all native religion by destroying Maya sculpture and books. Only one Maya hieroglyphic book survived: the *Popul Vuh,* or Book of Council, which was written in European script by a young Quiché noble. Scholars call this document the Maya "Bible," meaning that like the Judeo-Christian Scriptures, the *Popul Vuh* gives the Maya view of the creation of the world, concepts of good and evil, and the entire nature and purpose of the living experience.

From careful observation of the earth's movements around the sun, the Maya invented a calendar of eighteen 20-day months and one 5-day month, for a total of 365 days. Using a system of bars (— = 5) and dots (∘ = 1), the Maya devised a form of mathematics based on the vigesimal (20) rather than the decimal (10) system. They proved themselves masters of abstract knowledge—notably in astronomy, mathematics, calendric development, and the recording of history.

Maya civilization lasted about a thousand years, reaching its peak between approximately 600 and 900 C.E., the period when the Tang Dynasty was flourishing in China,

Maya Burial Urn After tightly wrapping the bodies of royal and noble persons in cloth, the K'iché Maya people of Guatemala placed them in urns and buried them in pyramids or sacred caves. The lid represents a divine being through whose mouth gifts may have been offered the deceased. The figure on top of the lid with corncobs stands for the maize-god. The size of this object, fifty-two inches, suggests that the Maya people were very short. *(Museum of Fine Arts, Boston, Gift of Landon T. Clay [1988. 1290a–b]. © 2002 Museum of Fine Arts, Boston)*

Islam was spreading in the Middle East, and Carolingian rulers were extending their sway in Europe. Between the eighth and tenth centuries, the Maya abandoned their cultural and ceremonial centers, and Maya civilization collapsed. Archaeologists and historians attribute the decline to a combination of agricultural failures due to land exhaustion and drought; overpopulation; disease; and constant wars fought as an extension of economic and political goals. These wars brought widespread destruction, which aggravated agrarian problems. Maya royal ideology also played a role in their decline: just as in good times kings at-

tributed moral authority and prosperity to themselves, so in bad times, when military, economic, and social conditions deteriorated, they became the objects of blame.[7]

In 1527 the Spaniards faced a formidable task when they attempted to conquer the Yucatán. The Maya polity did not involve a single political entity, as that of the Aztecs and Incas did; instead the Maya had several cultural centers. The Spaniards had great trouble imposing a centralized government on a divided people using guerrilla and hit-and-run tactics. Although the Spaniards established some degree of control in 1545, only in 1697 did the last independent Maya group fall to the Europeans.

Teotihuacán and Toltec Civilizations

During the Classic period, **Teotihuacán** in central Mexico witnessed the flowering of a remarkable civilization built by a new people from regions east and south of the Valley of Mexico. The city of Teotihuacán had a population of over 200,000—larger than any European city at the time. The inhabitants were stratified into distinct social classes. The rich and powerful resided in a special precinct, in houses of palatial splendor. Ordinary working people, tradespeople, artisans, and obsidian craftsmen lived in apartment compounds, or *barrios,* on the edge of the city. Agricultural laborers lived outside the city. Teotihuacán was a great commercial center, the entrepôt for trade and culture for all of Mesoamerica. It was also the ceremonial center, a capital filled with artworks, a mecca that attracted thousands of pilgrims a year.

In the center of the city stood the Pyramids of the Sun and the Moon. The Pyramid of the Sun is built of sun-dried bricks and faced with stone. Each of its sides is seven hundred feet long and two hundred feet high. The smaller Pyramid of the Moon is similar in construction. In lesser temples, natives and outlanders worshiped the rain-god and the feathered serpent later called Quetzalcoatl. These gods were associated with the production of corn, the staple of the people's diet.

Although Teotihuacán dominated Mesoamerican civilization during the Classic period, other centers also flourished. In the isolated valley of Oaxaca at modern-day Monte Albán (see Map 14.3), for example, Zapotecan-speaking peoples established a great religious center whose temples and elaborately decorated tombs testify to the wealth of the nobility. The art—and probably the entire culture—of Monte Albán and other centers derived from Teotihuacán.

As had happened to San Lorenzo and La Venta, Teotihuacán collapsed before invaders. Around 700 B.C.E. less-developed peoples from the southwest burned Teotihuacán; Monte Albán fell shortly afterward. By 900 the golden age of Mesoamerica had ended. There followed an interregnum known as the "Time of Troubles" (ca 800–1000), characterized by disorder and extreme militarism. Whereas nature gods and their priests seem to have governed the great cities of the earlier period, militant gods and warriors dominated the petty states that now arose. Among these states, the most powerful heir to Teotihuacán was the Toltec confederation, a weak union of strong states. The **Toltecs** admired the culture of their predecessors and sought to absorb and preserve it. Through intermarriage, they assimilated with the Teotihuacán people. In fact, every new Mesoamerican confederation became the cultural successor of earlier confederations.

Under Topiltzin (r. ca 980–1000), the Toltecs extended their hegemony over most of central Mexico. Topiltzin established his capital at Tula. Its splendor and power became legendary during his reign. (See the feature "Individuals in Society: Quetzalcoatl.")

After the reign of Topiltzin, troubles beset the Toltec state. Drought led to crop failure. Northern peoples, the Chichimecas, attacked the borders in waves. Weak, incompetent rulers could not quell domestic uprisings. When the last Toltec king committed suicide in 1174, the Toltec state collapsed. In 1224 the Chichimecas captured Tula.

The last of the Chichimecas to arrive in central Mexico were the Aztecs. As before, the vanquished strongly influenced the victors: the Aztecs absorbed the cultural achievements of the Toltecs. The Aztecs—building on Olmec, Maya, Teotihuacán, and Toltec antecedents—created the last unifying civilization in Mexico before the arrival of the Europeans.

AZTEC SOCIETY: RELIGION AND WAR

Although the terms *Aztec* and *Mexica* are used interchangeably here, **Mexica** is actually the more accurate word because it is a pre-Columbian term designating the dominant ethnic people of the island capital of Tenochtitlán-Tlalelolco. **Aztec** derives from *Aztlan,* the legendary homeland of the Mexica people before their migration into the Valley of Mexico, is *not* a pre-Columbian word, and was popularized by nineteenth-century historians.[8]

The Aztecs who appeared in the Valley of Mexico spoke the same **Nahuatl** language as the Toltecs but otherwise had nothing in common with them. Poor, unwelcome, looked on as foreign barbarians, the Aztecs had to settle on a few swampy islands in Lake Texcoco. From these unpromising beginnings, they rapidly assimilated the culture of the Toltecs and in 1428 embarked on a policy of territorial expansion. By the time Cortés arrived in 1519, the Aztec confederation encompassed all of central Mexico from the Gulf of Mexico to the Pacific as far south as Guatemala (see Map 14.3). Thirty-eight subordinate provinces paid tribute to the Aztec king.

MAP 14.3 The Aztec Empire, 1519   The Aztecs controlled much of central Mexico. The Maya survived in the Yucatán peninsula and some of present-day Guatemala. Notice the number of cities.

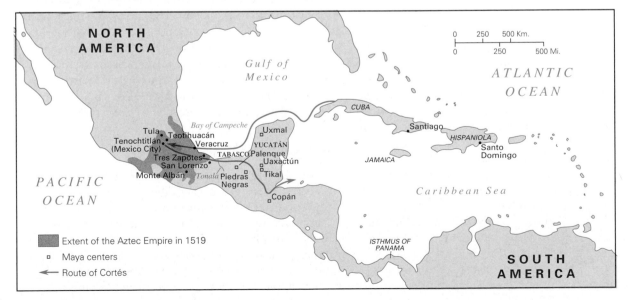

The growth of a strong mercantile class led to an influx of tropical wares and luxury goods: cotton, feathers, cocoa, skins, turquoise jewelry, and gold. The upper classes enjoyed an elegant and extravagant lifestyle; the court of Emperor Montezuma II (r. 1502–1520) was more magnificent than anything in western Europe. How, in less than two hundred years, had the Mexicans (from the Aztec word *mizquitl,* meaning "desolate land," or from *Mixitli,* the Aztec god of war) grown from an insignificant tribe of wandering nomads to a people of vast power and fabulous wealth?

The Aztecs' pictorial records attribute their success to the power of their war-god Huitzilopochtli and to their own drive and willpower. Will and determination they unquestionably had, but there is another explanation for their success: the Aztec state was geared for war.

War was inextricably woven into the fabric of Mexica society. Rather than depending on professional soldiers or foreign mercenaries, as some European princes and city-states did (see pages 544 and 550), the Aztecs relied on their own citizens, and all levels of society were involved. Kings ordered war to acquire tribute for state use and captives for religious sacrifices. Nobles fought to win greater wealth. Commoners fought as a means of social advancement: the ordinary warrior who distinguished himself in battle could earn the status of meritocratic noble (*cuahpipiltin*), a Mexica rank comparable to that of European knight. This status brought the right to own land, to be supported by the king, to share in future war booty, and to hold civic and military office.

War required considerable advance planning by the king. He ordered the calling up of men from the city wards on a rotating basis so that military service was equitably shared. Men fought as ward units bound together by neighborhood and kinship ties. The king determined the route, the number of days the army would march, and the battle plans once the target was reached. The lack of wheeled carts or wagons and of draft animals meant that all food and supplies had to be carried by porters. Scholars project that there was one porter for every two men, each porter carrying fifty pounds of maize. This meant that an "army could carry food for only eight days, giving an effective combat radius of about thirty-six miles—three days going, one day fighting, one day recuperating, and three days returning." To solve this logistical problem, an army might live on the passing countryside, and already-subject peoples would be warned about what they should be prepared to supply.[9]

Preceded by priests carrying on their backs images or statues of the gods, an army marched about twelve miles per day. Aztec messengers went ahead and warned the enemy city that attack was imminent. If it promptly surrendered, the amount of tribute would be modest. If not, battle followed shortly after the Aztec army reached its target.

The beat of the commander's drum, usually at dawn, signaled the start of battle. First, archers and slingers released a hail of arrows and stones. When soldiers—wearing armor consisting of thick sleeveless jackets of unspun cotton quilted between two layers of cloth, which an arrow could not penetrate—advanced, the real barrage began. Each man carried a shield twenty-eight inches in diameter, a spear, and a broadsword made of oak and obsidian (an extremely hard, black volcanic glass, which the Spaniards later saw could slice the head off a horse with a single blow). As opposing armies approached each other, spear throwers cast darts that, though lacking the distance of arrows, could penetrate the cotton armor of front-rank soldiers.

Then combatants switched to obsidian broadswords. Only the front ranks engaged the enemy in close combat, but with their numerical superiority the Aztecs could extend the frontline and encircle the enemy. Units were rotated in and out of battle about every fifteen minutes, bringing up fresh troops. A crippling blow to a foe's knees or to one of the muscles in the back of the thigh enabled the Aztec warrior to bring his enemy to the ground. Once the captive was subdued, men with ropes tied him up and took him to the rear of the battlefield. The goal was not to kill the enemy but to turn him into a tribute producer or to take him to Tenochtitlán as a sacrificial victim. Wounded Aztecs also were taken to the rear, where medical specialists tended them. Runners carried the news of victory or defeat to the king. (Thus an Aztec ruler did not personally command operations on the battlefield, as many European princes did.) Dead Aztecs were identified so that their families could be recompensed and their wards instructed to replace them. If the battle occurred far from home, the bodies of the dead were cremated on the battlefield. Then the army returned to the capital.[10]

Religion and Culture

In Mexica society, religion was the dynamic factor that transformed other aspects of the culture: economic security, social mobility, education, and especially war. War was an article of religious faith. The state religion of the Aztecs initially gave them powerful advantages over other groups in central Mexico; it inspired them to conquer vast territories in a remarkably short time.[11] But that religion also created economic and political stresses

INDIVIDUALS IN SOCIETY

QUETZALCOATL

Legends are popular beliefs about someone or something that are handed down from the past. They often lack a basis in historical—that is, verifiable—evidence, but they are generally believed to embody the ideals of a people or society. When legends become involved in religious faith, they acquire an established quality and become part of a people's core beliefs. Faith has been defined as "the confident assurance of what we hope for, and conviction of what we do not see" (Hebrews 11:1). How can we be confident of hopes and dreams, certain of what we do not see? Religious faith always presents a paradox, and belief systems have played a powerful part in historical events, as the Mexica god Quetzalcoatl illustrates.

Quetzalcoatl (pronounced kat-sal-koat-al), meaning "feathered serpent," was an important figure in Aztec culture. Students of the history of religions trace his origins either to an ancient deity of the Toltecs or to a historical Toltec ruler credited with the discovery of the cereal maize. He is believed to have been a great supporter of the arts, sciences, and calendar; he was also associated with peace. We do not know whether the historical ruler took his name from the god or, as a successful king, he was revered and deified. Considered the god of civilization, Quetzalcoatl represented to the Mexica the forces of good and light. He was pitted against the Toltecs' original tribal god, Tezcatlipoca, who stood for evil, darkness, and war. When the Aztecs absorbed Toltec culture, they adopted Quetzalcoatl and linked him with the worship of Huitzilopochtli, their war-god.

We may plausibly assume that the Toltec king Topiltzin (see page 425) took the name Quetzalcoatl. According to the "Song of Quetzalcoatl," a long Aztec glorification of Topiltzin,

He was very rich and had everything necessary to eat and drink, and the corn under his reign was in abundance. . . . And more than that the said Quetzalcoatl had all the wealth of the world, gold and silver and green stones, jade and other precious things. *

Whatever reality lies behind this legend, it became a cornerstone of Aztec tradition; it also played a profound role in Mexica history. Later Aztec legends describe a powerful struggle between Tezcatlipoca, who required human sacrifices, and Quetzalcoatl. Tezcatlipoca won this battle, and the priest-king Topiltzin-Quetzalcoatl was driven into exile. As he departed, he promised to return and regain his kingdom. By a remarkable coincidence, Quetzalcoatl promised to return in 1519, the year the Spanish explorer Hernando Cortés landed in Mexico. Cortés learned the legend and exploited it for his own purposes. Native and Spanish accounts tell us that Montezuma identified Cortés with the god Quetzalcoatl. Cortés took it as his right that Montezuma should house him in the imperial palace close to the shrine of the Aztec gods (and near the imperial treasury). When, on a tour of the city, Montezuma led Cortés up the many steps of the sacred temple, the emperor stopped and said to Cortés that he must be tired with all those steps. No, Cortés replied, "we" are never tired (as all mortals, but not gods, become). When Montezuma told Cortés that he would share all that he possessed with the Spaniards and that they "must truly be the men whom his ancestors had long ago prophesized, saying that they would come from the direction of the sunrise to rule over these lands," Cortés replied that "he did indeed come from the direction of the sunrise" and that he brought the message of the one true God, Jesus Christ. The conquistador knew that Montezuma would interpret his words as meaning that he was Quetzalcoatl.

Quetzalcoatl, or Precious Feather Snake. (© Musée de l'Homme)

QUESTIONS FOR ANALYSIS

1. Assess the role of Quetzalcoatl in the fall of the Aztec Empire.
2. What is reality—what we believe or what can be scientifically demonstrated?

*Quoted in I. Bernal, *Mexico Before Cortez: Art, History, and Legend,* rev. ed., trans. W. Barnstone (New York: Anchor Books, 1975), p. 68.

Sources: Bernal Díaz, *The Conquest of New Spain,* trans. J. M. Cohen (New York: Penguin Books, 1978); T. Todorov, *The Conquest of America,* trans. R. Howard (New York: Harper & Row, 1984).

The Goddess Tlazolteotl   The Aztecs believed that Tla-zolteotl (sometimes called "Mother of the Gods") consumed the sins of humankind by eating refuse. As the goddess of childbirth, Tlazolteotl was extensively worshiped. Notice the squatting position for childbirth, then common all over the world. *(Dumbarton Oaks, Pre-Columbian Collection, Washington, D.C.)*

that could not easily be resolved and that ultimately contributed heavily to the society's collapse.

Chief among the Aztecs' many gods was **Huitzil-opochtli,** who symbolized the sun blazing at high noon. The sun, the source of all life, had to be kept moving in its orbit if darkness was not to overtake the world. To keep it moving, Aztecs believed, the sun had to be fed frequently precious fluids—that is, human blood. Human sacrifice was a sacred duty, essential for the preservation and prosperity of humankind. Black-robed priests carried out the ritual:

The victim was stretched out on his back on a slightly convex stone with his arms and legs held by four priests, while a fifth ripped him open with a flint knife and tore out his heart. The

sacrifice also often took place in a manner which the Spanish described as gladiatorio: the captive was tied to a huge disk of stone . . . by a rope that left him free to move; he was armed with wooden weapons, and he had to fight several normally-armed Aztec warriors in turn. If, by an extraordinary chance, he did not succumb to their attacks, he was spared; but nearly always the "gladiator" fell, gravely wounded, and a few moments later he died on the stone, with his body opened by the black-robed, long-haired priests.[12]

Mass sacrifice was also practiced:

Mass sacrifices involving hundreds and thousands of victims could be carried out to commemorate special events. The Spanish chroniclers were told, for example, that at the dedication in 1487 of the great pyramid of Tenochtitlán, four lines of prisoners of war stretching for two miles each were sacrificed by a team of executioners who worked night and day for four days. Allotting two minutes for sacrifice, the demographer and historian Sherbourne Cook estimated that the number of victims associated with that single event was 14,100. The scale of these rituals could be dismissed as exaggerations were it not for the encounters of Spanish explorers with . . . rows of human skulls in the plazas of the Aztec cities. . . . In the plaza of Xocotlan "there were . . . more than one hundred thousand of them."[13]

The Mexica did not invent human sacrifice; it seems to have been practiced by many Mesoamerican peoples. The Maya, for example, dedicated their temples with the blood of freshly executed victims. Anthropologists have proposed several explanations—none of them completely satisfactory—for the Aztecs' practice of human sacrifice and the cannibalism that often accompanied it. Some suggest that human sacrifice served to regulate population growth. Yet ritual slaughter had been practiced by earlier peoples—the Olmecs, the Maya, the dwellers of Teotihuacán, and the Toltecs—in all likelihood before population density had reached the point of threatening the food supply. Moreover, almost all the victims were men, instead of women of childbearing age, whose deaths would have had more of an effect on population growth.

According to a second hypothesis, the ordinary people were given victims' bodies as a source of protein.[14] These people lived on a diet of corn, beans, squash, tomatoes, and peppers. Wildlife was scarce, and dog meat, chicken, turkey, and fish were virtually restricted to the upper classes. The testimony of modern nutritionists that beans supply ample protein, and the evidence that, in an area teeming with wild game, the Huron Indians of North America ritually executed captives and feasted on their stewed bodies, weaken the validity of this theory.

A third, more plausible, theory holds that ritual human sacrifice was an instrument of state terrorism—that the Aztec rulers crushed dissent with terror. The Aztecs controlled a large confederation of city-states by sacrificing prisoners seized in battle; by taking hostages from among defeated peoples as ransom against future revolt; and by demanding from subject states an annual tribute of people to be sacrificed to Huitzilopochtli. Unsuccessful generals, corrupt judges, and careless public officials, even people who accidentally entered forbidden precincts of the royal palaces, were routinely sacrificed. When the supply of such victims ran out, slaves, plebeians, and even infants suffered ritual execution. The emperor Montezuma II, who celebrated his coronation with the sacrifice of fifty-one hundred people, could be said to have ruled by sacrifice. Trumpets blasted and drums beat all day long announcing the sacrifice of yet another victim.

How can we at the start of the twenty-first century understand such a terrifying and nightmarish daily ritual? First, we have to remember that in the middle of the twentieth century, as millions of human beings were marched to their deaths, most of the world said nothing (or very little) and went about their daily tasks. Five hundred years ago, as priests performed the actual sacrifices, "the average person" watched. All persons were involved in or complicit in the sacrifices by various means: by the pleasure and satisfaction a household took when one of its warriors brought back a victim for sacrifice; by members of the *calpullis,* the basic civic or local unit, taking their turns in duties at the sacrificial temples; by these groups presenting a sacrificial victim to a temple (much as European medieval guilds donated windows to the local church or cathedral); by the care in feeding, clothing, parading to the temples, and, if necessary, drugging victims for their sacrifice; and by the popular celebrations at mass executions. The Nahuatl-speaking people accepted the ritual sacrifices because the victims, whether captives from hostile tribes or social outcasts from within, represented outsiders, foreigners, "the other."[15]

The Mexica state religion required constant warfare for two basic reasons. One was to meet the gods' needs for human sacrifice; the other was to acquire warriors for the next phase of imperial expansion. "The sacred campaigns of Huitzilopochtli were synchronized with the political and economic needs of the Mexica nation as a whole."[16] Moreover, defeated peoples had to pay tribute in foodstuffs to support rulers, nobles, warriors, and the imperial bureaucracy. The vanquished supplied laborers for agriculture, the economic basis of Mexica society. Likewise, conquered peoples had to produce workers for the construction and maintenance of the entire Aztec infrastructure—roads, dike

Aztec Standard-Bearer   The wide stairways leading from Aztec plazas to temple sanctuaries at the top held pairs of sculptures in the form of standard-bearers. This twenty-five-inch seated figure from the late fifteenth or early sixteenth century is clothed in only a loincloth and would have held a banner in its cupped right hand (now damaged). *(The Metropolitan Museum of Art, Harris Brisbane Dick Fund, 1962 [62.47]. Photograph © 1993 The Metropolitan Museum of Art)*

systems, aqueducts, causeways, and the royal palaces. Finally, merchants also benefited, for war opened new markets for traders' goods in subject territories.

When the Spaniards under Hernando Cortés (1485–1547) arrived in central Mexico in 1519, the sacred cult of Huitzilopochtli had created a combination of interrelated problems for the emperor Montezuma II. The thirty-eight provinces of the empire, never really assimilated into the Mexica state and usually governed by members of the defeated dynasty, seethed with rebellion. Population increases at the capital, Tenochtitlán, had forced the emperor to lay increasingly heavier tribute on conquered provinces, which in turn murdered the tribute collectors. Invasion and reconquest followed. "The provinces were being crushed beneath a cycle of imperial oppression: increases in tribute, revolt, reconquest, retribution, higher tribute, resentment, and repeated revolt."[17] By causing death in battle and by sacrifice of thousands of food producers, Mexica religion destroyed the very economic basis of the empire.

Faced with grave crisis, Montezuma attempted to solve the problem by freezing social positions. He purged the court of many officials, drastically modified the dress and behavior of the merchant class, and severely limited the honors given to lowborn warriors and all but the highest nobility. These reforms provoked great resentment, reduced incentive, and virtually ended social mobility. Scholars have traditionally portrayed Montezuma as weak-willed and indecisive when faced with the Spaniards. But recent research has shown that he was a very determined, even autocratic, ruler. Terrible domestic problems whose roots lay in a religious cult requiring appalling human slaughter offer the fundamental explanation for the Mexica collapse.[18]

The Life of the People

A wealth of information has survived about fifteenth- and sixteenth-century Mexico. The Aztecs wrote many books recounting their history, geography, and religious practices. They loved making speeches, which scribes copied down. The Aztecs also preserved records of their legal disputes, which alone amounted to vast files. The Spanish conquerors subsequently destroyed much of this material. But enough documents remain to construct a picture of the Mexica people at the time of the Spanish intrusion.

No sharp social distinctions existed among the Aztecs during their early migrations. All were equally poor. The head of a family was both provider and warrior, and a sort of tribal democracy prevailed in which all adult males participated in important decision making. By the early sixteenth century, however, Aztec society had changed. A stratified social structure had come into being, and the warrior aristocracy exercised great authority.

Scholars do not yet understand precisely how this change evolved. According to Aztec legend, the Mexica admired the Toltecs and chose their first king, Acamapichti, from among them. The many children he fathered with Mexica women formed the nucleus of the noble class. At

the time of the Spanish intrusion into Mexico, men who had distinguished themselves in war occupied the highest military and social positions in the state. Generals, judges, and governors of provinces were appointed by the emperor from among his servants who had earned reputations as war heroes. These great lords, or **tecuhtli,** dressed luxuriously and lived in palaces. The provincial governors exercised full political, judicial, and military authority on the emperor's behalf. In their territories they maintained order, settled disputes, and judged legal cases; oversaw the cultivation of land; and made sure that tribute—in food or gold—was paid. The governors also led troops in wartime. These functions resembled those of feudal lords in western Europe during the Middle Ages (see pages 396–397). Just as only nobles in France and England could wear fur and carry a sword, just as gold jewelry and elaborate hairstyles for women distinguished royal and noble classes in African kingdoms, so in Mexica societies only the tecuhtli could wear jewelry and embroidered cloaks.

Beneath the great nobility of soldiers and imperial officials was the class of warriors. Theoretically every freeman could be a warrior, and parents dedicated their male children to war, burying a male child's umbilical cord with some arrows and a shield on the day of his birth. In actuality the sons of nobles enjoyed advantages deriving from their fathers' position and influence in the state. At the age of six, boys entered a school that trained them for war. Future warriors were taught to fight with a *macana,* a paddle-shaped wooden club edged with bits of obsidian. Youths were also trained in the use of spears, bows and arrows, and lances fitted with obsidian points. They learned to live on little food and sleep and to accept pain without complaint. At about age eighteen, a warrior fought his first campaign. If he captured a prisoner for ritual sacrifice, he acquired the title *iyac,* or warrior. If in later campaigns he succeeded in killing or capturing four of the enemy, he became a *tequiua*—one who shared in the booty and thus was a member of the nobility. If a young man failed in several campaigns to capture the required four prisoners, he joined the **maceualtin,** the plebeian or working class.

The maceualtin were the ordinary citizens—the backbone of Aztec society and the vast majority of the population. The word *maceualti* means "worker" and implied boorish speech and vulgar behavior. Members of this class performed all sorts of agricultural, military, and domestic services and carried heavy public burdens not required of noble warriors. Government officials assigned the maceualtin work on the temples, roads, and bridges. Army officers called them up for military duty, but Mexica

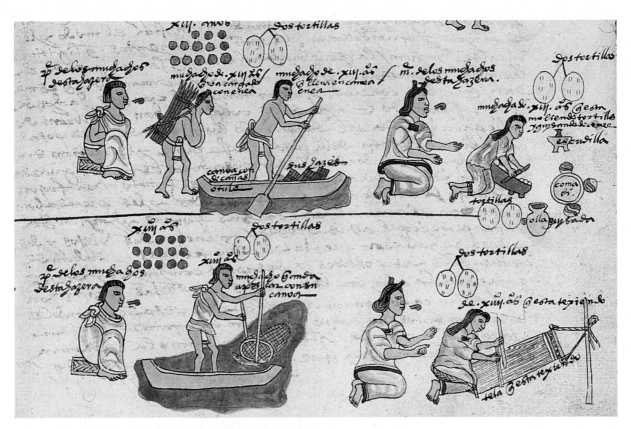

Aztec Youth   As shown in this codex, Aztec society had basic learning requirements for each age (indicated by dots) of childhood and youth. In the upper panel, boys of age thirteen gather firewood and collect reeds and herbs in a boat, while girls learn to make tortillas on a terra-cotta grill. At fourteen (*lower panel*), boys learn to fish from a boat, and girls are taught to weave. (*The Bodleian Library, University of Oxford, MS Arch. Selden. A.1, fol. 60r*)

considered this an honor and a religious rite, not a burden. Unlike nobles, priests, orphans, and slaves, maceualtin paid taxes. Maceualtin in the capital, however, possessed certain rights: they held their plots of land for life, and they received a small share of the tribute paid by the provinces to the emperor.

Beneath the maceualtin were the *tlalmaitl,* the landless workers or serfs. Some social historians speculate that this class originated during the "Time of Troubles," a period of migrations and upheavals in which weak and defenseless people placed themselves under the protection of strong warriors (see page 425). The tlalmaitl provided agricultural labor, paid rents in kind, and were bound to the soil—they could not move off the land. The tlalmaitl resembled in many ways the serfs of western Europe, but unlike serfs they performed military service when called on to do so. They enjoyed some rights as citizens and generally were accorded more respect than slaves.

Slaves were the lowest social class. Like Asian, European, and African slaves, most were prisoners captured in war or kidnapped from enemy tribes. But Aztecs who stole from a temple or private house or plotted against the emperor could also be enslaved, and people in serious debt sometimes voluntarily sold themselves into slavery. Female slaves often became their masters' concubines. Mexica slaves, however, differed fundamentally from European ones: "Tlatlocotin slaves could possess goods, save money, buy land and houses and even slaves for their own service."[19] Slaves could purchase their freedom. If a male slave married a free woman, their offspring were free, and a slave who escaped and managed to enter the emperor's palace was automatically free. Most slaves eventually gained their freedom. Mexica slavery, therefore, had some humane qualities and resembled slavery in Islamic societies (see pages 255–257).

Women of all social classes played important roles in Mexica society, but those roles were restricted entirely to the domestic sphere. As the little hands of the newborn male child were closed around a tiny bow and arrow indicating his warrior destiny, so the infant female's hands were wrapped around miniature weaving instruments and a small broom: weaving was a sacred and exclusively female art; the broom signaled a female's responsibility for the household shrines and for keeping the household swept and free of contamination. Almost all of the Mexica people married, a man at about twenty when he had secured one or two captives, a woman a couple of years earlier. As in pre-modern Asian and European societies, parents selected their children's spouses, using neighborhood women as go-betweens. Save for the few women vowed to the service of the temple, marriage and the household were a woman's fate; marriage represented social maturity for both sexes. Pregnancy became the occasion for family and neighborhood feasts, and a successful birth launched celebrations lasting from ten to twenty days.

Women took no part in public affairs—with a few notable exceptions. As the bearing of children was both a social duty and a sacred act, midwives enjoyed great respect. The number of midwives at a birth indicated rank: a noblewoman often had two or three midwives. As in the medieval European West, in a very difficult birth midwives sacrificed the life of the child for that of the mother. Mexica society also awarded high status and authority to female physicians and herbalists. They treated men as well as women, setting broken bones and prescribing herbal remedies for a variety of ailments. The sources, though limited, imply that a few women skilled at market trading achieved economic independence. The woman weaver capable of executing complicated designs also had the community's esteem. Prostitutes in the state brothels, not local Mexica but tribute girls from the provinces given to successful warriors as part of their rewards, probably did not enjoy esteem.[20]

Alongside the secular social classes stood the temple priests. Huitzilopochtli and each of the numerous lesser gods had many priests to oversee the upkeep of the temple, assist at religious ceremonies, and perform ritual sacrifices. The priests also did a brisk business in foretelling the future from signs and omens. Aztecs consulted priests on the selection of wives and husbands, on the future careers of newborn babies, and before leaving on journeys or for war. Temples possessed enormous wealth in gold and silver ceremonial vessels, statues, buildings, and land. Fifteen provincial villages had to provide food for the temple at Texcoco and wood for its eternal fires. The priests who had custody of all this property did not marry and were expected to live moral and upright lives. From the temple revenues and resources, the priests supported schools, aided the poor, and maintained hospitals. The chief priests had the ear of the emperor and often exercised great power and influence.

At the peak of the social pyramid stood the emperor. The various Aztec historians contradict one another about the origin of the imperial dynasty, but modern scholars tend to accept the verdict of one sixteenth-century authority that the "custom has always been preserved among the Mexicans (that) the sons of kings have not ruled by right of inheritance, but by election."[21] A small oligarchy of the chief priests, warriors, and state officials made the selection. If none of the sons proved satisfactory, a brother or nephew of the emperor was chosen, but election was always restricted to the royal family.

The Aztec emperor was expected to be a great warrior who had led Mexica and allied armies into battle. All his other duties pertained to the welfare of his people. It was up to the emperor to see that justice was done—he was the final court of appeal. He also held ultimate responsibility for ensuring an adequate food supply. The emperor Montezuma I (r. 1440–1467) distributed twenty thousand loads of stockpiled grain when a flood hit Tenochtitlán. The records show that the Aztec emperors took their public duties seriously.

Gender, Culture, and Power

In 1519 the council of the newly established port city of Veracruz on the Gulf of Mexico wrote to the emperor Charles V, "In addition to . . . children and men and women being killed and offered in sacrifices, we have learned and have been informed that they (the native peoples of Mexico) are doubtless all sodomites and engage in that abominable sin."[22] The sin the councilors referred to was sexual relations between males. The councilors wanted imperial and papal permission to punish "evil and rebellious natives."

What appalled the Spaniards were the **berdaches,** biological males dressed as women who performed the domestic tasks of women—cooking, cleaning, housekeeping, weaving, and embroidering. Berdaches were not trained in military skills and did not go to war. According to information an Aztec elder provided the Franciscan missionary-ethnographer Bernardino de Sahagûn, evidence that has been confirmed by many other sources, parents chose the gender roles of their male children. When a mother had produced four or five consecutive sons, the next son was dressed in women's clothes and taught to act like a woman. Customarily, men (and boys) did not do women's work. Once made a transvestite, however, a male child played the female role for the rest of his life and never again assumed the dress or conduct of a male. Tribal customs and laws throughout the Americas fully sanctioned this practice.

At about the onset of puberty, the berdache began to serve the sexual needs of the young men of the community. In the Mexica world *caciques* (chieftains or powerful lords), and in the Inca world (see pages 435–441) *oregones* (nobles), used berdaches for their personal pleasure or established them in brothels as prostitutes. In exchange for some service or price, the caciques and oregones supplied the berdaches to their friends and men of their class. The possession of large numbers of women or berdaches enhanced a lord's status and prestige. Berdaches, moreover, were stronger than women and could carry heftier burdens and perform heavier work.

In addition to the peoples of Mexico, Central America, and the Andes, evidence of berdaches survives among many indigenous peoples of North America, including the Timucua tribe of what is now northern Florida, the Mohicans of New York and Connecticut, the Tulelos of Virginia, the Sioux of the Dakotas, and the tribes of the Iroquois Confederacy of upper New York State.

How are we to interpret this phenomenon of socially institutionalized homosexuality among American indigenous peoples? The sources pose a major difficulty. Most information comes to us filtered through sixteenth- and seventeenth-century Iberian and French mentalities. That information, therefore, carries Christian moral and theological values. It also bears Spanish and French political, social, and cultural values. The conquistadors used charges of sodomy as a weapon with which to justify the forcible conquest of New World peoples. Europeans described the native peoples as "barbaric," and they came to Mexico, the Caribbean, and South America, they claimed, "to

George Catlin: Dance to the Berdache Determined to study and paint the Indians, Catlin (1796–1872) lived among the Sioux in the Dakota Territory from 1832 to 1836. His paintings not only do not romanticize the Indians but also portray them as individuals and display none of the racist contempt typical of his time. The social role of the berdache shocked him, however, as it had sixteenth-century Spaniards. Observing the dance and sexual activities, Catlin commented that the berdache "is driven to the most servile and degrading duties. . . . This is one of the most disgusting customs I have ever seen in Indian country." The warriors seem to mock the berdache; why, since they have used him sexually? *(National Museum of American Art, Washington, D.C./Art Resource, NY)*

bring civilization" and "to extirpate the evil of sodomitical behavior." Europeans knew of homosexual activity in their own societies (see pages 383–384), but they had never seen the permanent transvestism of the berdaches. Such American practices demonstrated to Europeans the peoples' "barbarism."

At the same time, the Nahuatl-speaking peoples of central and southern Mexico, the Incas of Peru, and the native Americans of North America did not have twentieth-century Western concepts of homosexuals and homosexuality. The Indians did not consider homosexual relations as sin or vice. They made no laws against it. Rather, chieftains used berdaches as instruments of pleasure and symbols of power.[23]

The Cities of the Aztecs

When the Spanish entered **Tenochtitlán** (which they called Mexico City) in November 1519, they could not believe their eyes. According to Bernal Díaz, one of Cortés's companions,

when we saw all those cities and villages built in the water, and other great towns on dry land, and that straight and level causeway leading to Mexico, we were astounded. These great towns and cues (temples) and buildings rising from the water, all made of stone, seemed like an enchanted vision. . . . Indeed, some of our soldiers asked whether it was not all a dream.[24]

Tenochtitlán The great Mexican archaeologist Ignacio Marquina designed this reconstruction of the central plaza of the Mexica city as it looked in 1519. The temple precinct, an area about five hundred square yards, contained more than eighty structures, pyramids, pools, and homes of gods and of the men and women who served them. Accustomed to the clutter and filth of Spanish cities, the elegance and cleanliness of Tenochtitlán amazed the Spaniards. *(Enrique Franco-Torrijos)*

Tenochtitlán had about 60,000 households. The upper class practiced polygamy and had many children, and many households included servants and slaves. The total population probably numbered around 250,000. At the time, no European city and few Asian ones could boast a population even half that size. The total Aztec Empire has been estimated at around 5 million inhabitants.

Originally built on salt marshes, Tenochtitlán was approached by four great highways that connected it with the mainland. Bridges stood at intervals (comparable to modern Paris). Stone and adobe walls surrounded the city itself, making it (somewhat like medieval Constantinople; see page 233) highly defensible and capable of resisting a prolonged siege. Wide, straight streets and canals crisscrossed the city. Boats and canoes plied the canals. Lining the roads and canals stood thousands of rectangular one-story houses of mortar faced with stucco. Although space was limited, many small gardens and parks were alive with the colors and scents of flowers. The Mexica loved flowers and used them in ritual ceremonies.

A large aqueduct whose sophisticated engineering astounded Cortés carried pure water from distant springs and supplied fountains in the parks. Streets and canals opened onto public squares and marketplaces. Tradespeople offered every kind of merchandise. Butchers hawked turkeys, ducks, chickens, rabbits, and deer; grocers sold kidney beans, squash, avocados, corn, and all kinds of peppers. Artisans sold intricately designed gold, silver, and feathered jewelry. Seamstresses offered sandals, loincloths and cloaks for men, and blouses and long skirts for women—the clothing customarily worn by ordinary people—and embroidered robes and cloaks for the rich. Slaves for domestic service, wood for building, herbs for seasoning and medicine, honey and sweets, knives, jars, smoking tobacco, even human excrement used to cure animal skins—all these wares made a dazzling spectacle.

At one side of the central square of Tenochtitlán stood the great temple of Huitzilopochtli. Built as a pyramid and approached by three flights of 120 steps each, the temple was about 100 feet high and dominated the city's skyline. According to Cortés, it was "so large that within the precincts, which are surrounded by a very high wall, a town of some five hundred inhabitants could easily be built. All round inside this wall there are very elegant quarters with very large rooms and corridors where their priests live."[25]

Travelers, perhaps inevitably, compare what they see abroad with what is familiar to them at home. Tenochtitlán thoroughly astounded Cortés, and in his letter to the emperor Charles V, he describes the city in comparison to his homeland: "the market square," where 60,000 people a day came to buy and sell, "was twice as big as Salamanca"; the beautifully constructed "towers," as the Spaniards called the pyramids, rose higher "than the cathedral at Seville"; Montezuma's palace was "so marvelous that it seems to me to be impossible to describe its excellence and grandeur[;] . . . in Spain there is nothing to compare with it." Accustomed to the squalor and filth of Spanish cities, the cleanliness of Tenochtitlán dumbfounded the Spaniards, as did all the evidence of its ordered and elegant planning.[26]

Describing the Aztec way of life for the emperor, Cortés concluded, "Considering that they are barbarous and so far from the knowledge of God and cut off from all civilized nations, it is truly remarkable to see what they have achieved in all things."[27] Certainly Cortés's views reflect his own culture and outlook, but it is undeniable that Mexica culture was remarkable.

THE INCAS OF PERU

In the late 1980s, archaeologists working in the river valleys on the west coast of present-day Peru uncovered stunning evidence of complex societies that flourished between five thousand and three thousand years ago—roughly the same period as the great pyramids of Egypt. In spite of the altitude and dryness of the semidesert region, scores of settlements existed (see Map 14.4). Perhaps the most spectacular was the one at Pampa de las Llamas-Moxeke in the Casma Valley. Stepped pyramids and U-shaped buildings, some more than ten stories high, dominated these settlements. Were these structures cultic temples? places for food storage? centers for such commercial activity that we can call them cities? Why did the inhabitants abandon these settlements and move into the Andean highlands? Scholars have only begun to process these vast remains, but radiocarbon dating has already demonstrated that the settlements are older than the Maya and Aztec structures.[28]

Another archaeological discovery is providing scholars with rich information about pre-Columbian society. For some time, the villagers of Sipán in northern Peru supplemented their meager incomes by plundering ancient cemeteries and pyramids. One night in 1987, while digging deep in a pyramid, they broke into one of the richest funerary chambers ever located, and they filled their sacks with ceramic, gold, and silver objects. A dispute about the distribution of the loot led one dissatisfied thief to go to the police. When archaeologists from Lima and the United States arrived, they ranked the discoveries at Sipán with those at Tutankhamen's tomb in Egypt

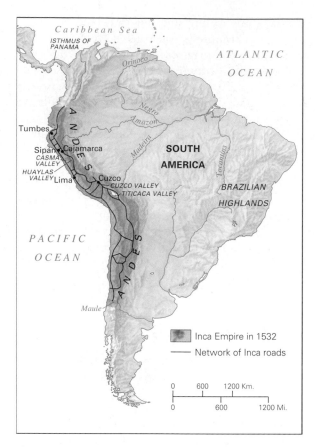

MAP 14.4 The Inca Empire, 1532 South America, which extends 4,750 miles in length and 3,300 miles from east to west at its widest point, contains every climatic zone and probably the richest variety of vegetation on earth. Roads built by the Incas linked most of the Andean region.

and the terra-cotta statues of the Qin Dynasty warriors near Xian, China.

The treasures from the royal tombs at Sipán derive from the Moche civilization, which flourished along a 250-mile stretch of Peru's northern coast between 100 and 800 C.E. Rivers that flowed out of the Andes into the valleys allowed the Moche people to develop complex irrigation systems for agricultural development. Each Moche valley contained a large ceremonial center with palaces and pyramids surrounded by settlements of up to ten thousand people. The dazzling gold and silver artifacts, elaborate headdresses, and ceramic vessels display a remarkable skill in metalwork. Much of later Inca technology seems clearly based on the work of the Moche.[29]

Like the Aztecs, the **Incas** were "a small militaristic group that came to power late, conquered surrounding groups, and established one of the most extraordinary empires in the world."[30] Gradually, Inca culture spread throughout Peru. Modern knowledge of the Incas is concentrated in the last century before Spanish intrusion (1438–1532); today's scholars know far less about earlier developments.

In the center of Peru rise the cold highlands of the Andes. Six valleys of fertile and wooded land at altitudes ranging from eight thousand to eleven thousand feet punctuate highland Peru. The largest of these valleys are the Huaylas, Cuzco, and Titicaca. It was there that Inca civilization developed and flourished.

Archaeologists still do not understand how people of the Andean region acquired a knowledge of agriculture. Around 2500 B.C.E. they were relying on fish and mussels for food. Textiles found in gravesites indicate the cultivation of cotton for ordinary clothing, ceremonial dress, and fishnets. Andean geography—with towering mountains, isolated valleys, and little arable land—posed an almost insurmountable barrier to agriculture. What land there was had to be irrigated, and human beings needed warm clothing to work in the cold climate. They also required a diet that included some meat and fat. Coca (the dried leaves of a plant native to the Andes and from which cocaine is derived), chewed in moderation as a dietary supplement, enhanced their stamina and their ability to withstand the cold.

Around 200 B.C.E. the Andean peoples displayed an enormous burst of creative energy. High-altitude valleys were connected to mountain life and vegetation to form a single interdependent agricultural system called "vertical archipelagoes," capable of supporting large communities. Such vertical archipelagoes often extended more than thirty-seven miles from top to bottom.[31] These terraces were shored up with earthen walls to retain moisture, enabling the production of bumper crops of white potatoes.

Potatoes ordinarily cannot be stored for long periods, but Andean peoples developed a product called *chuñu,* freeze-dried potatoes made by subjecting potatoes alternately to nightly frosts and daily sun. Chuñu will keep unspoiled for several years. The construction of irrigation channels also facilitated the cultivation of corn. Potatoes and corn required far less labor and time than did the cultivation of wheat in Europe or rice in China. By the fifteenth century, enough food was harvested to feed not only the farmers themselves but also massive armies and administrative bureaucracies and thousands of industrial workers.

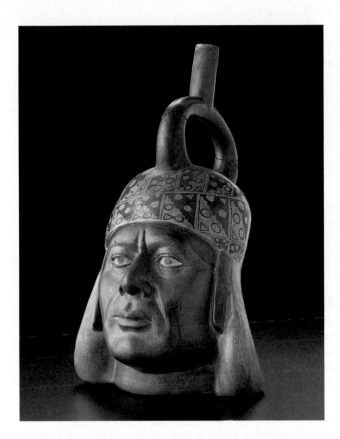

Portrait Vessel of a Ruler   Artisans of the Moche culture on the northern coast of Peru produced objects representing many aspects of their world, including this flat-bottomed stirrup-spout jar with a ruler's face. The commanding expression conveys a strong sense of power, as does the elaborate headdress with the geometric designs of Moche textiles worn only by elite persons. *(South America, Peru, North Coast, Moche Culture, Portrait Vessel of a Ruler, earthenware with pigmented clay slip, 300–700, 35.6 × 24.1, Kate S. Buckingham Endowment, 1955.2338, ¾ view. Photograph by Robert Hashimoto. Photograph © 1999, The Art Institute of Chicago)*

Colombian Lime Container   The use of coca in rituals is an ancient tradition in South America. Pieces of coca leaves were placed in the mouth with small amounts of powdered lime made from calcined seashells. The lime helped release the hallucinogens in the coca. This nine-inch gold bottle for holding lime, typical of the rich paraphernalia made in the Quimbaya region of Colombia, shows a seated nude figure with rings in the ears and beads across the forehead and at the neck, wrists, knees, and ankles. A tiny spatula would be used to secure the lime through the bottle's narrow neck. *(The Metropolitan Museum of Art, Jan Mitchell and Sons Collection, Gift of Jan Mitchell, 1991 [1991.419.22]. Photograph © 1992 The Metropolitan Museum of Art)*

Inca Imperialism

Who were the Incas? *Inca* was originally the name of the governing family of an Amerindian group that settled in the basin of Cuzco (see Map 14.4). From that family, the name was gradually extended to all peoples living in the Andes valleys. The Incas themselves used the word to identify their ruler or emperor. Here the term is used for both the ruler and the people.

As with the Aztecs, so with the Incas: religious ideology was the force that transformed the culture. Religious concepts created pressure for imperialist expansion—with fatal consequences.

The Incas believed their ruler descended from the sun-god and that the health and prosperity of the state depended on him. Dead rulers were thought to link the people to the sun-god. When the ruler died, his corpse was preserved as a mummy in elaborate clothing and housed in a sacred and magnificent chamber. The mummy was brought in procession to all important state ceremonies, his advice was sought in times of crisis, and hundreds of human beings were sacrificed to him. In ordinary times, the dead ruler was carried to visit his friends, and his heirs and relatives came to dine with him. Some scholars call this behavior the "cult of the royal mummies" because it was a kind of ancestor worship.

The mummies were also a powerful dynamic force in Inca society. According to the principle of the "split inheritance," when an Inca ruler died, the imperial office, insignia, and rights and duties of the monarchy passed to the new king. The dead ruler, however, retained full and complete ownership of all his estates and properties. His royal descendants as a group managed his lands and sources of income for him and used the revenues to care for his mummy and to maintain his cult. Thus a new ruler came to the throne land- or property-poor. In order to live in the royal style, strengthen his administration, and reward his supporters, he had to win his own possessions by means of war and imperial expansion.[32]

Around 1000 C.E. the Incas were one of many small groups fighting among themselves for land and water. As they began to conquer their neighbors, a body of religious lore came into being that ascribed divine origin to their earliest king, Manco Capac (ca 1200), and promised warriors the gods' favor and protection. Strong historical evidence, however, dates only from the reign of Pachacuti Inca (1438–1471), who launched the imperialist phase of Inca civilization. (See the feature "Listening to the Past: The Death of Inca Yupanque [Pachacuti Inca] in 1471" on pages 446–447.)

If the cult of ancestor or mummy worship satisfied some Inca social needs, in time it also created serious problems. The desire for conquest provided incentives for courageous (or ambitious) nobles: those who were victorious in battle and gained new territories for the state could expect lands, additional wives, servants, herds of llamas, gold, silver, fine clothes, and other symbols of high status. And even common soldiers who distinguished themselves in battle could be rewarded with booty and raised to noble status. The imperial interests of the emperor paralleled those of other social groups. Thus, under Pachacuti Inca and his successors, Topa Inca (r. 1471–1493) and Huayna Capac (r. 1493–1525), Inca domination was gradually extended by warfare to the frontier of present-day Ecuador and Colombia in the north and to the Maule River in present-day Chile in the south (see Map 14.4), an area of about 350,000 square miles. Eighty provinces, scores of ethnic groups, and 16 million people came under Inca control. A remarkable system of roads held the empire together.

Before Inca civilization, each group that entered the Andes valleys had its own distinct language. These languages were not written and have become extinct. Scholars will probably never understand the linguistic condition of Peru before the fifteenth century when Pachacuti made **Quechua** (pronounced "keshwa") the official language of his people and administration. Conquered peoples were forced to adopt the language, and Quechua spread the Inca way of life throughout the Andes. Though not written until the Spanish in Peru adopted it as a second official language, Quechua had replaced local languages by the seventeenth and eighteenth centuries and is still spoken by most Peruvians today.

Both the Aztecs and the Incas ruled very ethnically diverse peoples. Whereas the Aztecs tended to control their subject peoples through terror, the Incas governed by means of imperial unification. They imposed not only their language but also their entire panoply of gods. Magnificent temples scattered throughout the expanding empire housed idols of these gods. Priests led prayers and elaborate rituals, and on such occasions as a terrible natural disaster or a great military victory, they sacrificed human beings to the gods. Subject peoples were required to worship the state gods. Imperial unification was also achieved through the forced participation of local chieftains in the central bureaucracy and through a policy of colonization called **mitima.** To prevent rebellion in newly conquered territories, Pachacuti transferred all their inhabitants to other parts of the empire, replacing them with workers who had lived longer under Inca rule and whose independent spirit had been broken.[33] An excellent system of roads—averaging three feet in width, some paved and others not—facilitated the transportation of armies and the rapid communication of royal orders by runners. The roads followed straight lines wherever possible but also crossed pontoon bridges and tunneled through hills. This great feat of Inca engineering bears striking comparison with ancient Roman roads, which also linked an empire.

Rapid Inca expansion, however, produced stresses. Although the pressure for growth remained unabated, in the reign of Topa Inca open lands began to be scarce. Topa Inca's attempts to penetrate the tropical Amazon forest east of the Andes led to repeated military disasters. The Incas waged wars with highly trained armies drawn up in massed formation and fought pitched battles on level ground, often engaging in hand-to-hand combat. But in dense jungles, the troops could not maneuver or maintain order against enemies using guerrilla tactics and sniping at them with deadly blowguns. Another source of stress was revolts among subject peoples in conquered territories. It took Huayna Capac several years to put down a revolt in Ecuador. Even the system of roads and trained runners eventually caused administrative prob-

Machu Picchu   The citadel of Machu Picchu, surrounded by mountains in the clouds, clings to a spectacular crag in upland Peru. It was discovered in 1911 by the young American explorer Hiram Bingham. Its origin and the reason for its abandonment remain unknown. (*W. McIntyre/Photo Researchers, Inc.*)

lems. The average runner could cover about 50 leagues, or 175 miles, per day—a remarkable feat of physical endurance, especially at high altitude—but the larger the empire became, the greater the distances to be covered. The roundtrip from the capital at Cuzco to Quito in Ecuador, for example, took from ten to twelve days, so that an emperor might have to base urgent decisions on incomplete or out-of-date information. The empire was overextended. "In short, the cult of the royal mummies helped to drive the Inca expansion, but it also linked economic stress, administrative problems, and political instabilities in a cyclical relationship."[34]

When the Inca Huayna Capac died in 1525, his throne was bitterly contested by two of his sons, Huascar and Atauhualpa. Inca law called for a dying emperor to assign the throne to his most competent son by his principal wife, who had to be the ruler's full sister. Huascar, unlike Atauhualpa, was the result of such an incestuous union and thus had a legitimate claim to the throne. Atauhualpa, who had fought with Huayna Capac in his last campaign, tried to convince Huascar that their father had divided the kingdom and had given him (Atauhualpa) the northern part. Huascar bitterly rejected his half brother's claim.

When Huascar came to the throne, the problems facing the Inca Empire had become critical: the dead rulers controlled too much of Peru's land and resources. Huascar proposed a radical solution: "Annoyed one day with these dead (his ancestors), [he] said that he ought to order them all buried and take from them all that they had, and that there should not be dead men but living ones, because (the dead) had all that was best in the country."[35]

Although Atauhualpa had the grave liability of being born of a nonincestuous union, to the great nobility responsible for the cult of the royal mummies, Huascar's proposal represented a grave threat to the established order: Huascar intended to insult the mummies who linked the Inca people to the gods, and if his proposals were enacted, the anger of the mummies would ensure a disastrous future. (The nobility did not say the obvious—that if Huascar buried the dead and took their vast properties, the nobles would be deprived of wealth and power.) Not surprisingly, the nobles threw their support behind Atauhualpa.

In the civil war that began in 1532, Atauhualpa's veteran warriors easily defeated Huascar's green recruits. On his way to his coronation at Cuzco, Atauhualpa encountered Pizarro and 168 Spaniards who had recently entered the kingdom. The Spaniards quickly became the real victors in the Inca kingdom (see pages 516–517). The cult of the royal mummies had brought, or at least contributed heavily to, the Inca collapse.

Inca Society

The **ayllu,** or clan, served as the fundamental social unit of Inca society. All members of the ayllu owed allegiance to the **curacas,** or headman, who conducted relations with outsiders. The ayllu held specific lands, granted it by hamlet or provincial authorities on a long-term basis, and individual families tended to work the same plots for generations. Cooperation in the cultivation of the land and intermarriage among members of the ayllu wove people there into a tight web of connections.

In return for the land, all men had to perform public duties and pay tribute to the authorities. Their duties included building and maintaining palaces, temples, roads, and irrigation systems. Tribute consisted of potatoes, corn, and other vegetables paid to the hamlet head, who in turn paid them to the provincial governor. A draft rotary system called **mita** (turn) determined when men of a particular hamlet performed public works; this responsibility rotated from ward to ward (divisions of the hamlet).

As the Inca Empire expanded, this pattern of social and labor organization was imposed on other, newly conquered indigenous peoples. Regional states had a distinct

ethnic identity, and by the time of the Spanish intrusion, the Incas had well-established mechanisms for public labor drafts and tribute collection. Discontent among subject peoples, however, helps to explain the quick fragmentation of imperial authority and the relative swiftness of the Spanish conquest. After the conquest, the Spaniards adopted and utilized the indigenous organization as the basis for Spanish civil and ecclesiastical administration, just as the imperial Incas (and, in Mesoamerica, the Aztecs) had done.[36]

In the fifteenth century, Pachacuti Inca and Topa Inca superimposed imperial institutions on those of kinship. They ordered allegiance to be paid to the ruler at Cuzco rather than to the curacas. They drafted local men for distant wars and relocated the entire populations of certain regions through the mitima system. Entirely new ayllus were formed, based on residence rather than kinship.

The emperors sometimes gave newly acquired lands to victorious generals, distinguished civil servants, and favorite nobles. These lords subsequently exercised authority previously held by the native curacas. Whether long-time residents or new colonists, common people had the status of peasant farmers, which entailed heavy agricultural or other obligations. Just as in medieval Europe peasants worked several days each week on their lord's lands, so the Inca people had to work on state lands (that is, the emperor's lands) or on lands assigned to the temple. Peasants also labored on roads and bridges; terraced and irrigated new arable land; served on construction crews for royal palaces, temples, and public buildings such as fortresses; acted as runners on the post roads; and excavated in the imperial gold, silver, and copper mines. The imperial government annually determined the number of laborers needed for these various undertakings, and each district had to supply an assigned quota. The government also made an ayllu responsible for the state-owned granaries and for the production of cloth for army uniforms.

The state required everyone to marry and even decided when and sometimes whom a person should marry. Men married around the age of twenty, women a little younger. The Incas did not especially prize virginity; premarital sex was common. The marriage ceremony consisted of the joining of hands and the exchange of a pair of sandals. This ritual was followed by a large wedding feast, at which the state presented the bride and groom with two sets of clothing, one for everyday wear and one for festive occasions. If a man or woman did not find a satisfactory mate, the provincial governor selected one for him or her. Travel was forbidden, so couples necessarily came from the same region. Like most warring so-

Mochica Earring   Elites of the Moche period (ca 100 B.C.E.–500 C.E.) on the northern coast of Peru commissioned vast quantities of jewelry. This gold and turquoise earring depicts a warrior-priest wearing an owl-head necklace, holding a removable war club (right hand) and shield (left hand), and flanked by attendants. Peanuts had recently been domesticated in the area, and the peanut beading around the edge suggests the leader's power over natural fertility in an agriculturally marginal region. The reverse side is of silver. *(Photograph by Susan Einstein, courtesy of UCLA Fowler Museum of Cultural History)*

cieties with high male death rates, the Incas practiced polygamy, though the cost of supporting many wives restricted it largely to the upper classes.

The Incas relied heavily on local authorities and cultural norms for day-to-day matters. In some ways, however, the common people were denied choice and initiative and led regimented lives. The Incas did, however, take care of the poor and aged, distribute grain in times of shortage and famine, and supply assistance in natural disasters. Scholars have debated whether Inca society was socialistic, totalitarian, or a forerunner of the welfare state; it may be merely a matter of definition. Although the Inca economy was strictly regulated, there certainly was not an equal distribution of wealth. Everything above and beyond the masses' basic needs went to the emperor and the nobility.

The backbreaking labor of ordinary people in the fields and mines made possible the luxurious lifestyle of the great Inca nobility. The nobles—called *oregones*, or "big ears," by the Spanish because they pierced their ears and distended the lobes with heavy jewelry—were the ruling

Inca's kinsmen. Lesser nobles included the curacas, royal household servants, public officials, and entertainers. As the empire expanded in the fifteenth century, there arose a noble class of warriors, governors, and local officials, whose support the ruling Inca secured with gifts of land, precious metals, and llamas and alpacas (llamas were used as beasts of burden; alpacas were raised for their long fine wool). The nobility was exempt from agricultural work and from other kinds of public service.

NORTH AMERICA AND THE MOUND BUILDERS

As in South America and Mesoamerica, so in the fifteenth century North America contained hundreds of different societies. Excluding the Inuit people of the Arctic region, anthropologists classify six major cultural areas in North America: the Northwest Coast peoples living along the Pacific coast from southern Alaska to northern California; the Plains peoples inhabiting the region from north of the Canadian border south to Texas and from the Mississippi River west to the Rocky Mountains; the Plateau peoples of the area extending from above the Canadian border through the plateau and mountain region of the Rocky Mountains to the Southwest and including much of California; the Eastern Woodlands peoples inhabiting much of the eastern United States from the Atlantic Ocean to the Mississippi River and including the Great Lakes region; the Northern peoples of the area covering most of Canada; and the Southwest peoples of the region comprising all or parts of the present states of Arizona, New Mexico, Colorado, and Utah. In 1492, between 1 million and 2 million people lived on this vast continent of 9,400,000 square miles (the third largest continent, after Asia and Africa). Some peoples formed sedentary agricultural societies; others led a nomadic existence.

Whereas the agricultural regions of Mesoamerica and South America had dense populations at that time, North America was very sparsely settled, perhaps one person for every square mile. Forests and woodlands covered most of what is now the eastern United States—hence the label "Eastern Woodlands." The peoples of this area lived in villages and practiced agriculture, growing corn, pumpkins, squash, beans, sunflowers, and tobacco. They also hunted wild game and fished in the numerous streams and rivers.

Around 1300 B.C.E., some of these peoples began to build massive earthworks, mounds of earth and stone. The mounds differed in shape, size, and purpose: some

MAP 14.5 The Mound-Building Cultures   Mound-building peoples, while concentrated in the Ohio Valley, had extensive trading contacts with peoples in the Great Plains, the Northeast, the Southeast, and the Caribbean regions.

were conical, others elongated or wall-like, others pyramidical, and still others, called effigy mounds, in serpentine, bird, or animal form. The Ohio and Mississippi Valleys contain the richest concentration of mounds, but they have been found from the Great Lakes down to the Gulf of Mexico (see Map 14.5). The earliest mound, at Poverty Point, Louisiana, dates from about 1300 B.C.E. and consists of six octagonal ramparts, one within the other, that measure 6 feet high and more than 400 yards across. It seems to belong more to the Olmec culture of Veracruz (see page 419) than to North America and may have served as a defensive fortress. Another mound, near the town of Adena, Ohio, was probably built between 600 B.C.E. and 200 C.E. It is serpentine in shape, 1,254 feet long and 20 feet wide; hence it is called the Great Serpent Mound.

At Cahokia, near East St. Louis, Illinois, archaeologists have uncovered the largest mound of all. Begun about 1050 C.E. and completed about 1250 C.E., the complex at Cahokia covered 5½ square miles and was the ceremonial center for perhaps 38,000 people. A fence of wooden posts surrounded the core. More than 500 rectangular mounds or houses, inside and outside the fence, served as tombs and as the bases for temples and palaces. Within the fence, the largest mound rose in four stages to a height of 100 feet. At its top, a small conical platform supported a wooden fence and a rectangular temple. The mounds at Cahokia represent the culture of the Mississippian **mound builders.**

What do the mounds tell us about the societies of these indigenous peoples? All of our evidence derives from the mounds and their contents. The largest mounds served as burial chambers for chieftains and, in many cases, the women and retainers who were sacrificed in order to assist the chief in the afterlife. Mounds also contain valuable artifacts, such as jewelry made from copper from Michigan, mica (a mineral used in building) from the Appalachians, obsidian from the Rocky Mountains, conch shells from the Caribbean, and pipestone from Minnesota.

From these burial items, archaeologists have deduced that mound culture was hierarchial, governed by a chieftain. The chief had religious responsibilities, such as managing long-distance trade and gift-giving. As with the Chinese, the exchange of goods was not perceived as a form of commerce, but as a means of showing respect and of establishing bonds among diverse groups. Chiefs governed large towns of several thousand inhabitants. The towns served as political and ceremonial centers, and they controlled surrounding villages of a few hundred people. Burial items suggest trade over a wide area of central North America; since the indigenous peoples lacked the wheel and pack animals, such as horses, goods must have been transported by canoe or by human porters.

Pottery in the form of bowls, jars, bottles, and effigy pipes in various shapes best reveals Mississippian peoples' art. Designs showing eagles, plumed serpents, warriors decapitating victims, and ceremonially ornamented priests suggest a strong Mexican influence. The symbolism of Mississippian art deals so strongly with death that scholars speak of a "Death Cult" or a "Vulture Cult."[37]

Cahokia mound culture reached its peak before 1300 C.E. When the first white men uncovered the mounds, they had long been deserted. Why? Crop failure? overpopulation? war, as the fence around Cahokia implies? Additional research of archaeologists may answer these questions.

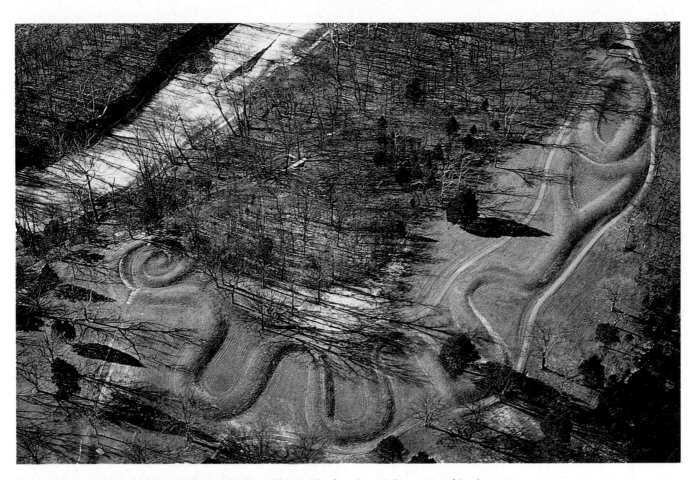

Great Serpent Mound, Adams County, Ohio   This 1,254-foot-long Adena mound in the form of a writhing snake has its "head" at the highest point, suggesting an open mouth ready to swallow a huge egg formed by a heap of stones. (*Georg Gerster/Photo Researchers, Inc.*)

Two-Faced Pipe Bowl   Also called a calumet, the peace pipe was a sacred object to Amerindians. Important in all religious, war, and peace ceremonies, pipes were made from a red stone taken from the Pipestone quarry in southwestern Minnesota. The material was also named catlinite for the Philadelphia traveler and artist George Catlin (see page 433). The bowl of this beautiful pipe contains two human faces, one facing the smoker, the other on the back of the bowl. The carver, Running Cloud, gave it to a Dr. Jarvis in payment for some medical service in the 1830s. (*United States, Plains; Sioux [Sisseton], early 19th century, catlinite or red pipestone, lead inlay, 5¼ [13.3] long. Brooklyn Museum of Art, Frank Sherman Benson Fund and the Henry L. Batterman Fund, 50.67.104*)

SUMMARY

Several strong Amerindian civilizations flourished in the Western Hemisphere in the years between 300 B.C.E. and 1500 C.E. The Maya are justly renowned for their art and their accomplishments in abstract thought, especially mathematics. The Aztecs built a unified culture based heavily on the Toltec heritage and distinguished by achievements in engineering, sculpture, and architecture. The Incas revealed a genius for organization, and their state was virtually unique in its time for assuming responsibility for all its people. In both the Mexica and the Inca societies, religious ideology shaped other facets of the culture. The Mexica cult of war and human sacrifice and the Inca cult of the royal mummies posed serious dilemmas and contributed to the weakening of those societies.

Inca culture did not die with the Spaniard Pizarro's strangulation of Atauhualpa (see page 517). In May 1536 his successor, Inca Mancu Yupanque, led a massive revolt against the Spanish and then led his people to Machu Picchu deep in the Valcahamba range of the Andes. Inca military resistance to Spanish domination continued throughout the sixteenth to eighteenth centuries. In 1780 Jose Gabriel Kunturkanki, a highly educated businessman and landowner, proclaimed himself Inca Tupac Amaru II and launched a native independence movement that the Spanish put down with the greatest difficulty.

Between about 1300 B.C.E. and 1300 C.E., in the region extending from the Great Lakes south to the Gulf of Mexico, and from the Atlantic Ocean west to the Mississippi River, people erected large earthworks reflecting complex societies. Some of these mounds served as burial tombs for their leaders; others functioned as defensive fortresses. The mound builders were not isolated. Artifacts suggest that they had cultural contacts with the Olmecs and Mexica of Mesoamerica, as well as with peoples throughout central North America.

KEY TERMS

Indian	maceualtin
Mesoamerica	berdaches
Olmec	Tenochtitlán
Teotihuacán	Incas
Toltecs	Quechua
Mexica	mitima
Aztec	ayllu
Nahuatl	curacas
Huitzilopochtli	mita
tecuhtli	mound builders

NOTES

1. See J. Lockhart and S. B. Schwartz, *Early Latin America: A History of Colonial Spanish America and Brazil* (Cambridge: Cambridge University Press, 1983), pp. 31–33; M. A. Burkholder and L. Johnson, *Colonial Latin America* (New York: Oxford University Press, 1998), pp. 1–5.
2. Lockhart and Schwartz, *Early Latin America,* pp. 33–49.
3. F. Braudel, *The Structures of Everyday Life: Civilization and Capitalism, 15th–18th Century,* vol. 1, trans. S. Reynolds (New York: Harper & Row, 1981), pp. 160–161.
4. R. A. Diehl and M. A. Coe, "Olmec Archeology," in *The Olmec World: Ritual and Rulership* (Princeton, N.J.: Princeton University Press, 1996), pp. 11–25.
5. D. Webster, *The Fall of the Ancient Maya: Solving the Mystery of the Maya Collapse* (New York: Thames & Hudson, 2002), pp. 98–99. The same scholar's article "Ancient Maya Warfare," in *War and Society in the Ancient and Medieval Worlds: Asia, the Mediterranean, and Mesoamerica,* eds. K. Raaflaub and N. Rosenstein (Cambridge, Mass.: Harvard University Press, 1999), pp. 333–360, argues that the Maya went to war frequently and that warfare was an essential ingredient of their society.
6. L. Schele and M. E. Miller, *The Blood of Kings: Dynasty and Ritual in Maya Art* (New York: Braziller, 1986), pp. 14–15, passim.
7. Webster, *The Fall of the Ancient Maya,* pp. 327–347.
8. G. W. Conrad and A. A. Demarest, *Religion and Empire: The Dynamics of Aztec and Inca Expansionism* (New York: Cambridge University Press, 1993), p. 71.
9. R. Hassig, "The Aztec World," in *War and Society in the Ancient and Medieval Worlds: Asia, the Mediterranean, and Mesoamerica,* eds. K. Raaflaub and N. Rosenstein (Cambridge, Mass.: Harvard University Press, 1999), pp. 375–377.
10. Ibid., pp. 377–378.
11. J. Soustelle, *Daily Life of the Aztecs on the Eve of the Spanish Conquest,* trans. P. O'Brian (Stanford, Calif.: Stanford University Press, 1970), p. 97.
12. M. Harris, *Cannibals and Kings* (New York: Random House, 1977), pp. 99–110; the quotation is from p. 106.
13. Ibid., pp. 109–110.
14. R. Padden, *The Hummingbird and the Hawk* (Columbus: Ohio State University Press, 1967), pp. 76–99.
15. I. Clendinnen, *Aztecs: An Interpretation* (New York: Cambridge University Press, 1992), pp. 88–115.
16. Conrad and Demarest, *Religion and Empire,* p. 49.
17. Ibid., p. 57.
18. Ibid., pp. 66–70.
19. Soustelle, *Daily Life of the Aztecs,* p. 74.
20. Clendinnen, *Aztecs,* pp. 153–173.
21. Quoted in Soustelle, *Daily Life of the Aztecs,* p. 89.
22. Quoted in R. Trexler, *Sex and Conquest: Gendered Violence, Political Order, and the European Conquest of the Americas* (Ithaca, N.Y.: Cornell University Press, 1995), p. 1. This section leans on Trexler's important and provocative study.
23. Ibid., Chaps. 1, 4, 5, and passim.
24. B. Díaz, *The Conquest of New Spain,* trans. J. M. Cohen (New York: Penguin Books, 1978), p. 214.
25. Quoted in J. H. Perry, *The Discovery of South America* (New York: Taplinger, 1979), pp. 161–163.
26. Quoted in Clendinnen, *Aztecs,* pp. 16–17.
27. Quoted in Perry, *The Discovery of South America,* p. 163.

28. William K. Stevens, "Andean Culture Found to Be as Old as the Great Pyramids," *New York Times*, October 3, 1989, p. C1.

29. John Noble Wilford, "Lost Civilization Yields Its Riches as Thieves Fall Out," *New York Times*, July 29, 1994, pp. C1, C28.

30. J. A. Mason, *The Ancient Civilizations of Peru* (New York: Penguin Books, 1978), p. 108.

31. W. Sullivan, *The Secret of the Incas: Myth, Astronomy, and the War Against Time* (New York: Crown Publishers, 1996), pp. 22–24.

32. Conrad and Demarest, *Religion and Empire*, pp. 91–94.

33. Mason, *The Ancient Civilizations of Peru*, p. 123.

34. Ibid., p. 132.

35. Ibid., p. 136.

36. Lockhart and Schwartz, *Early Latin America*, pp. 37–48.

37. See M. Stokstad, *Art History* (New York: Prentice Hall and H. N. Abrams, 1995), pp. 444, 460–462; Paul Carlson, *The Plains Indians* (College Station: Texas A&M Press, 1998), pp. 25–27.

SUGGESTED READING

The titles by Clendinnen, Diehl and Coe, Conrad and Demarest, Hassig, Lockhart and Schwartz, Schele and Miller, Sullivan, Trexler, and Webster cited in the Notes represent some of the most exciting research on pre-Columbian Mesoamerican and Andean societies. For the Maya, students should also see D. Freidel, *A Forest of Kings: The Untold Story of the Ancient Maya* (1990), a splendidly illustrated work providing expert treatment of many facets of the Maya world; R. Wright, *Time Among the Mayas* (1989), which gives a highly readable account of Maya agricultural and religious calendars; M. D. Coe, *The Maya*, 4th ed. (1987), a sound and well-illustrated survey; the same scholar's *Breaking the Maya Code* (1992); and R. J. Sharer, *Daily Life in Maya Civilization* (1996).

For the gradually expanding literature on the Aztecs, see J. Lockhart, *The Nahuas After the Conquest: A Social and Cultural History of the Indians of Central America, Sixteenth Through Eighteenth Centuries* (1992), and the same author's edition and translation of *We People Here: Nahuatl Accounts of the Conquest of Mexico* (1993). R. F. Townsend, *The Aztecs* (1992), discusses the various classes of Mexica society, as well as expansion, education, and religious ritual in a clearly illustrated study. M. León-Portilla, *The Aztec Image of Self and Society: An Introduction to Nahua Culture* (1992), is perhaps the best appreciation of Aztec religious ritual and symbolism. For warfare, R. Hassig, *Aztec Warfare: Imperial Expansion and Political Control* (1988), is probably the standard work.

J. de Batanzos, *Narrative of the Incas,* trans. and ed. R. Hamilton and D. Buchanan (1996), is an invaluable source for the Incas; it was written by a Spaniard married to an Inca princess, offers fascinating information about Inca customs, and reflects a female oral tradition. W. Sullivan, *The Secret of the Incas: Myth, Astronomy, and the War Against Time* (1996), explains the role of myth and astronomy in the rise and fall of the Inca Empire. For a fine survey of the best literature on preconquest Andean civilization, see B. Larson, "Andean Communities, Political Cultures, and Markets: The Changing Contours of a Field," in *Ethnicity, Markets, and Migration in the Andes: At the Crossroads of History and Anthropology,* ed. B. Larson and O. Harris (1995).

Students wanting to explore aspects of the entire hemisphere before the arrival of Columbus might begin with J. E. Kicza, "The People and Civilizations of the Americas Before Contact," in *Essays in Global and Comparative History,* ed. M. Adas (1998); J. E. Kicza, "Introduction," in *The Indian in Latin American History: Resistance, Resilience, and Acculturation* (1993); B. Fagan, *Kingdoms of Gold, Kingdoms of Jade* (1991), a fine work in comparative anthropology; and *America in 1492,* ed. A. M. Josephy (1992), an interesting collection of essays, many written by leading scholars. For the impact of the Spanish on Mesoamerican peoples, see I. Clendinnen, *Ambivalent Conquests: Maya and Spanish in Yucatan, 1517–1570* (1987), a profoundly sensitive, learned, and important study; R. Wright, *Stolen Continents: The Americas Through Indian Eyes Since 1492* (1992), which emphasizes the persistence and survival of native American cultures and peoples; and *In the Wake of Contact: Biological Responses to Conquest,* ed. C. S. Larsen and G. Milner (1994), a useful collection of articles dealing with many parts of the world.

The following older studies may also prove helpful for particular topics: S. Masuda, I. Shimada, and C. Morris, eds., *Andean Ecology and Civilization* (1985), and E. R. Wolfe, ed., *The Valley of Mexico: Studies in Pre-Hispanic Ecology and Society* (1976), are important for environmental research; L. Baudin, *A Socialist Empire: The Incas of Peru* (1961), gives a provocative interpretation of the Incas; V. W. Van Hagen, *Realm of the Incas* (1961), offers a popular account; F. Katz, *The Ancient American Civilisations* (1972), is a standard anthropological work that surveys all the major Mesoamerican cultures; and T. Todorov, *The Conquest of America,* trans. R. Howard (1984), is an important but difficult study of cross-cultural perceptions.

LISTENING TO THE PAST

THE DEATH OF INCA YUPANQUE (PACHACUTI INCA) IN 1471

In 1551 the Spaniard Juan de Betanzos began to write Narrative of the Incas. *Although Betanzos had only the Spanish equivalent of a grade school education when he arrived in Peru, and although he lacked dictionaries and grammar books, he had two powerful assets. First, he learned Quechua and earned a reputation for being the best interpreter and translator in postconquest Peru. Second, Betanzos had married Angelina Yupanque, an Inca princess (her Inca name was Cuxirimay Ocllo) who was the widow of Atauhualpa and who also had been Pizarro's mistress. Through her, Betanzos gained immediate and firsthand access to the Inca oral tradition. When he finished his book six years later, modern scholars believe he had produced "the most authentic chronicle that we have."*

Narrative of the Incas *provides a mine of information about Inca customs and social history. There is so much description of marriage, childbirth, weaning, coming-of-age ceremonies, and death that the work shows a strong female experience, undoubtedly the influence of Betanzos's wife. Here is his account of the death of Inca Yupanque (Pachacuti Inca) in 1471.*

Since there were instructions for the idolatries and activities that you have heard about, Inca Yupanque ordered that immediately after he died these activities and sacrifices should be done. In addition, as soon as this was done, word should be sent to all the land, and from all the provinces and towns they should bring again all that was necessary for the service of the new lord, including gold, silver, livestock, clothing, and the rest of the things needed to replenish all the storehouses that, because of his

death, had been emptied for the sacrifices and things he ordered to be done, and it should be so abundant because he realized that the state of the one who was thus Inca was growing greater.

While Inca Yupanque was talking and ordering what was to be done after he died, he raised his voice in a song that is still sung today in his memory by those of his generation. This song went as follows: "Since I bloomed like the flower of the garden, up to now I have given order and justice in this life and world as long as my strength lasted. Now I have turned into earth." Saying these words of his song, Inca Yupanque Pachacuti expired, leaving in all the land justice and order, as already stated. And his people were well supplied with idols, idolatries, and activities. After he was dead, he was taken to a town named Patallacta, where he had ordered some houses built in which his body was to be entombed. He was buried by putting his body in the earth in a large new clay urn, with him very well dressed. Inca Yupanque ordered that a golden image made to resemble him be placed on top of his tomb. And it was to be worshiped in place of him by the people who went there. Soon it was placed there. He ordered that a statue be made of his fingernails and hair that had been cut in his lifetime. It was made in that town where his body was kept. They very ceremoniously brought this statue on a litter to the city of Cuzco for the fiestas in the city. This statue was placed in the houses of Topa Inca Yupanque. When there were fiestas in the city, they brought it out for them with the rest of the statues. What is more laughable about this lord Inca Yupanque is that, when he wanted to make some idol, he entered the house of the Sun and acted as though the Sun spoke to him, and he himself answered the Sun to make his people believe that the Sun ordered him to make those idols and *guacas** and so that they would worship them as such.

When the statue was in the city, Topa Inca Yupanque ordered those of his own lineage to bring this statue out for the feasts that were held in Cuzco. When they brought it out like this, they sang about the things that the Inca did in his life, both in the wars and in his city. Thus they served and revered him, changing its garments as he used to do, and serving it as he was served when he was alive. All of which was done thus.

This statue, along with the gold image that was on top of his tomb, was taken by Manco Inca from the city when he revolted. On the advice that Doña Angelina Yupanque gave to the Marquis Don Francisco Pizarro, he got it and the rest of the wealth with it. Only the body is in Patallacta at this time, and judging by it, in his lifetime he seems to have been a tall man. They say that he died at the age of one hundred twenty years. After his father's death, Topa Inca Yupanque ordered that none of the descendants of his father, Inca Yupanque, were to settle the area beyond the rivers of Cuzco. From that time until today the descendants of Inca Yupanque were called *Capacaillo Ynga Yupangue haguaynin,* which means "lineage of kings," "descendants and grandchildren of Inca Yupanque." These are the most highly regarded of all the lineages of Cuzco. These are the ones who were ordered to wear two feathers on their heads.

As time passed, this generation of *orejones* [*oregones*]† multiplied. There were and are today many who became heads of families and renowned as firstborn. Because they married women who were not of their lineage, they took a variety of family names. Seeing this, those of Inca Yupanque ordered that those who had mixed with other people's blood should take new family names and extra names so that those of his lineage could clearly be called *Capacaillo* and descendants of Inca Yupanque. When the Spaniards came, all of this diminished, to the point where they all say they are from that lineage.

* Any object, place, or person worshiped as a deity.
† Nobles.

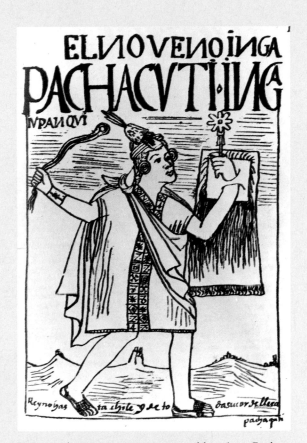

Revered as a great conqueror and lawgiver, Pachacuti Inca here wears the sacred fringed headband symbolizing his royal authority, and the large earrings of the *oregones,* the nobility. *(Pachacuti Inca, from* Nueva Coronica & Buen Gobierno, *by Guaman Poma de Ayala. Courtesy, Institut d'Ethnologie, Paris. © Musée de l'Homme)*

QUESTIONS FOR ANALYSIS

1. How does this account of the Inca's death and burial relate to the "cult of the royal mummies" described on page 438?

2. Does Juan de Betanzos show any sign of disapproval, contempt, or "cultural limitation" for Inca funeral practices?

Source: Narrative of the Incas by Juan de Betanzos, trans. and ed. Roland Hamilton and Dana Buchanan from the Palma de Mallorca manuscript (Austin: University of Texas Press, 1996), pp. 138–139. Copyright © 1996. Used by permission of the University of Texas Press.

INDEX

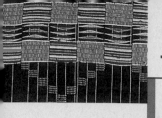

	AFRICA AND THE MIDDLE EAST	THE AMERICAS
10,000 B.C.E.	New Stone Age culture, ca 10,000–3500	Migration into Americas begins, ca 20,000
5000 B.C.E.	Farming begins in Tigris-Euphrates and Nile River Valleys, ca 6000 First writing in Sumeria; city-states emerge, ca 3500 Unification of Egypt, 3100–2660	Maize domesticated in Mexico, ca 5000
2500 B.C.E.	Egypt's Old Kingdom, 2660–2180 Akkadian empire, ca 2331–2200 Egypt's Middle Kingdom, 2080–1640 Hyksos "invade" Egypt, 1640–1570 Hammurabi, 1792–1750 Hebrew monotheism, ca 1700	First pottery in Americas, Ecuador, ca 3000 First metalworking in Peru, ca 2000
1500 B.C.E.	Egypt's New Kingdom; Egyptian empire, ca 1570–1075 Hittite Empire, ca 1475–1200 Akhenaten institutes worship of Aton, ca 1360 Moses leads Hebrews out of Egypt, ca 1300–1200 Political fragmentation of Egypt; rise of small kingdoms, ca 1100–700 United Hebrew kingdom, 1020–922	Olmec civilization, Mexico, ca 1500 B.C.E.–300 C.E.
1000 B.C.E.	Ironworking spreads throughout Africa, ca 1000 B.C.E.–300 C.E. Assyrian Empire, 900–612 Zoroaster, ca 600 Babylonian captivity of Hebrews, 586–539 Cyrus the Great founds Persian Empire, 550 Persians conquer Egypt, 525 Darius and Xerxes complete Persian conquest of Middle East, 521–464	Chavin civilization in Andes, ca 1000–200 B.C.E. Olmec center at San Lorenzo destroyed, ca 900; power passes to La Venta
500 B.C.E.		
400 B.C.E.	Alexander the Great extends empire, 334–331 Death of Alexander (323): Ptolemy conquers Egypt, Seleucus rules Asia	

EAST ASIA	INDIA AND SOUTHEAST ASIA	EUROPE
Farming begins in Yellow River Valley, ca 4000	Indus River Valley civilization, ca 2800–1800; capitals at Mohenjo-daro and Harappa	
Horse domesticated in China, ca 2500		Greek Bronze Age, 2000–1100 Arrival of Greeks in peninsular Greece Height of Minoan culture, 1700–1450
Shang Dynasty, first writing in China, ca 1500–ca 1050	Aryans arrive in India; Early Vedic Age, ca 1500–1000 Vedas, oldest Hindu sacred texts	Mycenaeans conquer Minoan Crete, ca 1450 Mycenaean Age, 1450–1200 Trojan War, ca 1180 Greek Dark Age, ca 1100–800
Zhou Dynasty, promulgation of the Mandate of Heaven, ca 1027–256 Confucius, 551–479 First written reference to iron, ca 521	Later Vedic Age, solidification of caste system, ca 1000–500 Upanishads; foundation of Hinduism, 700–500 Persians conquer parts of India, 513 Maharira, founder of Jainism, 540–486 Siddhartha Gautama (Buddha), 528–461	Greek Lyric Age; rise of Sparta and Athens, 800–500 Origin of Greek polis, ca 700 Roman Republic founded, 509
		Persian Wars, 499–479 Athenian Empire; flowering of art and philosophy, 5th century Peloponnesian War, 431–404
Warring States Period in China, 403–221 Zhuangzi and development of Daoism, 369–268	Alexander invades India, 327–326 Chandragupta founds Mauryan Dynasty, 322–ca 185	Plato, 426–347 Roman expansion, 390–146 Conquests of Alexander the Great, 334–323

	AFRICA AND THE MIDDLE EAST	THE AMERICAS
300 B.C.E.	Arsaces of Parthia begins conquest of Persia, ca 250–137 Scipio Africanus defeats Hannibal at Zama, 202	Fall of La Venta, 300; Tres Zapotes becomes leading Olmec site
200 B.C.E.		Andean peoples intensify agriculture, ca 200
100 B.C.E.	Meroë becomes iron-smelting center, 1st century B.C.E. Dead Sea Scrolls Pompey conquers Syria and Palestine, 63	
100 C.E.	Jesus Christ, ca 4 B.C.E.–30 C.E. Bantu migrations begin Jews revolt; Romans destroy temple in Jerusalem: end of Hebrew state, 70	Moche civilization flourishes in Peru, ca 100–800
200 C.E.	Camel first used for trans-Saharan transport, ca 200 Expansion of Bantu-speaking peoples, ca 200–900 Axum (Ethiopia) controls Red Sea trade, ca 250	
300 C.E.	Axum accepts Christianity, ca 4th century	Maya civilization in Central America, ca 300–1500 Classic period of Teotihuacán civilization in Mexico, ca 300–900
500 C.E.	Political and commercial ascendancy of Axum, ca 6th–7th centuries Muhammad, 570–632; the *hijra,* 622 African Mediterranean slave trade, ca 600–1900 Umayyad Dynasty, 661–750; continued expansion of Islam	Mayan civilization reaches peak, ca 600–900 Tiahuanaco civilization in South America, ca 600–1000
700 C.E.	Berbers control trans-Saharan trade, ca 700–900 Abbasid Dynasty, 750–1258; Islamic capital moved to Baghdad Decline of Ethiopia, ca 9th century Golden age of Muslim learning, ca 900–1100 Kingdom of Ghana, ca 900–1300	Teotihuacán, Monte Alban destroyed, ca 700 "Time of Troubles" in Mesoamerica, 800–1000 Toltec hegemony, ca 980–1000

EAST ASIA	INDIA AND SOUTHEAST ASIA	EUROPE
Development of Legalism, ca 250–208 Qin Dynasty unifies China; Great Wall begun, Confucian literature destroyed, 221–210 Han Dynasty, 206 B.C.E.–220 C.E.	Ashoka, 269–232	Punic Wars, destruction of Carthage, 264–146
	Greeks invade India, ca 183–145 Mithridates creates Parthian empire, ca 171–131	Late Roman Republic, 133–27
China expands, ca 111 Silk Road opens to Parthia, Rome; Buddhism enters China, ca 104 First (Chinese) written reference to Japan, 45 C.E.	First Chinese ambassadors to India and Parthia, ca 140 Bhagavad Gita, ca 100 B.C.E.–100 C.E. Shakas and Kushans invade eastern Parthia and India, 1st century C.E.	Julius Caesar killed, 44 Octavian seizes power, rules imperial Rome as Augustus, 27 B.C.E.–14 C.E.
Chinese invent paper, 105 Emperor Wu, 140–186	Kushan rule in northwestern India, 2d–3d century Roman attacks on Parthian empire, 115–211	Roman Empire at greatest extent, 117 Breakdown of pax Romana, ca 180–284
Creation of Yamato state in Japan, ca 3d century Buddhism gains popularity in China and Japan, ca 220–590 Fall of Han Dynasty, 220; Period of Division, 220–589	Fall of the Parthian empire, rise of the Sassanids, ca 225	Reforms by Diocletian, 284–305
Three Kingdoms Period in Korea, 313–668 China divides into northern, southern regimes, 316	Chandragupta I founds Gupta Dynasty in India, ca 320–480 Gupta expansion, trade with Middle East and China, ca 400 Huns invade India, ca 450	Constantine, 306–337; Edict of Milan, 313; founding of Constantinople, 324; Council of Nicaea, 325 Theodosius recognizes Christianity as official state religion, 380 Germanic raids on western Europe, 400s Clovis rules Gauls, 481–511
Sui Dynasty restores order in China, 581–618 Shotoku's "Constitution" in Japan, 604 Tang Dynasty, 618–907; cultural flowering Taika Reforms in Japan, 646 Korea unified, 668	Sanskrit drama, ca 600–1000	Saint Benedict publishes his *Rule*, 529 Code of Justinian, 529 Synod of Whitby, 664
Nara era, creation of Japan's first capital, 710–794 Heian era in Japan, 794–1185; literary flowering Era of the Five Dynasties in China, 907–960 Song Dynasty, 960–1279	Islam reaches India, 713 Khmer Empire (Kampuchea) founded, 802	Charles Martel defeats Muslims at Tours, 732 Charlemagne rules, 768–814 Viking, Magyar invasions, 845–900 Treaty of Verdun divides Carolingian Empire, 843 Cluny monastery founded, 909

	AFRICA AND THE MIDDLE EAST	THE AMERICAS
1000	Seljuk Turks take Baghdad, 1055 Islam penetrates sub-Saharan Africa, ca 11th century Great Zimbabwe built, flourishes, ca 1100–1400 Kingdom of Benin, ca 1100–1897	Inca civilization in South America, ca 1000–1500 Toltec state collapses, 1174
1200	Kingdom of Mali, ca 1200–1450 Mongol invasion of Middle East, ca 1220 Mongols conquer Baghdad, 1258; fall of Abbasid Dynasty	Manco Capac, first Inca king, ca 1200
1300	Rise of Yoruba states, West Africa, ca 1300 Height of Swahili (East African) city-states, ca 1300–1500 Mansa Musa rules Mali, 1312–1337 Ottomans invade Europe, 1356	Aztecs arrive in Valley of Mexica, found Tenochtitlán (Mexico City), ca 1325
1400	Arrival of Portuguese in Benin, ca 1440 Songhay Empire, ca 1450–1591 Atlantic slave trade, ca 1450–1850 Ottoman Empire, 1453–1918 Da Gama reaches East Africa, 1498	Height of Inca Empire, 1438–1493 Reign of Montezuma I, 1440–1468; height of Aztec culture Columbus reaches Americas, 1492
1500	Portugal dominates East Africa, ca 1500–1650 Safavid Empire in Persia, 1501–1722; height of power under Shah Abbas, 1587–1629 Peak of Ottoman power under Suleiman, 1520–1566 Height of Kanem-Bornu, 1571–1603 Battle of Lepanto, 1571, signals Ottoman naval weakness in the eastern Mediterranean	Mesoamerican and South American holocaust, ca 1500–1600 First African slaves brought to Americas, ca 1510 Cortés arrives in Mexico, 1519; Aztec Empire falls, 1521 Pizarro reaches Peru, conquers Incas, 1531
1600	Dutch West India Co. supplants Portuguese in West Africa, ca 1630 Dutch settle Cape Town, 1651	British settle Jamestown, 1607 Champlain founds Quebec, 1608 Dutch found New Amsterdam, 1624 Black slave labor allows vast increase in sugar production in the Caribbean; of sugarcane, cotton, and coffee in Brazil; and of rice in the North American Carolinas and tobacco in Virginia

EAST ASIA	INDIA AND SOUTHEAST ASIA	EUROPE
China divided into Song, Jin empires, 1127 Kamakura Shogunate, 1185–1333	Vietnam gains independence from China, ca 1000 Construction of Angkor Wat, ca 1100–1150 Muslim conquerors end Buddhism in India, 1192	Yaroslav the Wise, 1019–1054; peak of Kievan Russia Latin, Greek churches split, 1054 Norman Conquest of England, 1066 Investiture struggle, 1073–1122 Crusades, 1096–1270 Growth of trade and towns, ca 1100–1400 Barbarossa invades Italy, 1154–1158
Mongol conquest of China begins, 1215 Yuan (Mongol) Dynasty, 1271–1368 Unsuccessful Mongol invasions of Japan, 1274, 1281 Marco Polo arrives at Kublai Khan's court, ca 1275	Peak of Khmer Empire in Southeast Asia, ca 1200 Turkish sultanate at Delhi, 1206–1526	Magna Carta, 1215 Aquinas, *Summa Theologica,* 1253 Nevsky recognizes Mongol overlordship of Moscow, 1252
Ashikaga Shogunate, 1336–1408 Hung Wu defeats Mongols, 1368; founds Ming Dynasty, 1368–1644	Tamerlame conquers the Punjab, 1398	Babylonian Captivity of papacy, 1307–1377 Tver revolt in Russia, 1327–1328 Hundred Years' War, 1337–1453 Bubonic plague, 1347–1700 Beginnings of representative government, ca 1350–1500
Ming policy encourages foreign trade, ca 15th century Ming maritime expeditions to India, Middle East, Africa, 1405–1433	Sultan Mehmed II, 1451–1481 Da Gama reaches India, 1498	Italian Renaissance, ca 1400–1530 Voyagers of discovery, ca 1450–1600 Ottomans capture Constantinople, 1453; end of Byzantine Empire War of the Roses in England, 1453–1471 Unification of Spain completed, 1492
Portuguese trade monopoly in East Asia, ca 16th century Christian missionaries active in China and Japan, ca 1550–1650 Unification of Japan, 1568–1600	Babur defeats Delhi sultanate, 1526–1527; founds Mughal Empire Akbar expands Mughal Empire, 1556–1605 Spanish conquer the Philippines, 1571	Luther's Ninety-five Theses, 1517 Charles V elected Holy Roman emperor, 1519 English Reformation begins, 1532 Council of Trent, 1545–1563 Dutch declare independence, 1581 Spanish Armada, 1588
Tokugawa Shogunate, 1600–1867 Japan expels all Europeans, 1637 Manchus establish Qing Dynasty, 1644–1911 Height of Qing Dynasty under K'ang-hsi, 1662–1722	Height of Mughal Empire under Shah Jahan, 1628–1658 British found Calcutta, 1690	Romanov Dynasty in Russia, 1613–1917 Thirty Years' War, 1618–1648 English Civil War, 1642–1649 Louis XIV, king of France, 1643–1715 Growth of absolutism in central and eastern Europe, ca 1680–1790 The Enlightenment, ca 1680–1800 Ottomans besiege Vienna, 1683 Revocation of Edict of Nantes, 1685 Glorious Revolution in England, 1688

	AFRICA AND THE MIDDLE EAST	THE AMERICAS
1700	Rise of Ashanti Empire, ca 1700 Decline of Safavid Empire under Nadir Shah, 1737–1747	Silver production quadruples in Mexico and Peru, ca 1700–1800 Spain's defeat in War of the Spanish Succession results in colonial dependence on Spanish goods, 1700s
1750	Selim III introduces administrative and military reforms, 1761–1808 British seize Cape Town, 1795 Napoleon's campaign in Egypt, 1798	"French and Indian Wars," 1756–1763 Quebec Act, 1774 American Revolution, 1775–1783 Comunero revolution, New Granada, 1781
1800	Muhammad Ali founds dynasty in Egypt, 1805–1848 Slavery abolished in British Empire, 1807 Peak year of African transatlantic slave trade, 1820	Latin American wars of independence, 1806–1825 Brazil wins independence, 1822 Monroe Doctrine, 1823 Political instability in most Latin American countries, 1825–1870 U.S.-Mexican War, 1846–1848
1850	Crimean War, 1853–1856 Suez Canal opens, 1869 European "scramble for Africa," 1880–1900 Battle of Omdurman, 1898 Boer War, 1899–1902	American Civil War, 1861–1865 British North America Act, 1867, for Canada Diaz controls Mexico, 1876–1911 United States practices "dollar diplomacy" in Latin America, 1890–1920s Spanish-American War, 1898
1900	Union of South Africa formed, 1910 French annex Morocco, 1912 Ottoman Empire dissolved, 1919; Kemal's nationalist struggle in Turkey	Massive immigration from Europe and Asia to the Americas, 1880–1914 Mexican Revolution, 1910 Panama Canal opens, 1914 Mexico adopts constitution, 1917
1920	Cultural nationalism in Africa, 1920s Turkish Republic recognized, 1923 Reza Shah leads Iran, 1925–1941	U.S. "consumer revolution," 1920s Stock market crash in United States; Great Depression begins, 1929
1930	African farmers organize first "cocoa holdups," 1930–1931 Iraq gains independence, 1932	Revolutions in six South American countries, 1930 New Deal begins in United States, 1933
1940	Arabs and Jews at war in Palestine; Israel created, 1948 Apartheid system in South Africa, 1948–1991	Surprise attack by Japan on Pearl Harbor, 1941 United Nations established, 1945 Perón rules Argentina, 1946–1953

EAST ASIA	INDIA AND SOUTHEAST ASIA	EUROPE
Height of Edo urban culture in Japan, ca 1700 Height of Qing Dynasty under Emperor Ch'ien-lung, 1736–1799	Decline of Mughal Empire, ca 1700–1800 Persian invaders loot Delhi, 1739 French and British fight for control of India, 1740–1763	War of Spanish Succession, 1701–1713 Treaty of Utrecht, 1713 Cabinet system develops in England, 1714–1742
Maximum extent of Qing Empire, 1759	Treaty of Paris gives French colonies in India to Britain, 1763 Cook in Australia, 1768–1771; first British convict-settlers arrive in Australia, 1788 East India Act, 1784	Watt produces first steam engine, 1769 Outbreak of French Revolution, 1789 National Convention declares France a republic, 1792
Anglo-Chinese Opium War, 1839–1842 Treaty of Nanjing, 1842: Manchus surrender Hong Kong to British	British found Singapore, 1819 Java War, 1825–1830 British defeat last independent native state in India, 1848	Napoleonic Empire, 1804–1814 Congress of Vienna, 1814–1815 European economic penetration of non-Western countries, ca 1816–1880 Greece wins independence, 1830 Revolution of 1848
Taiping Rebellion, 1850–1864 Perry's arrival opens Japan to United States and Europe, 1853 Meiji Restoration in Japan, 1867 Adoption of constitution in Japan, 1890 Sino-Japanese War, 1894–1895 "Hundred Days of Reform" in China, 1898	Great Rebellion in India, 1857–1858 French seize Saigon, 1859 Indian National Congress formed, 1885 French acquire Indochina, 1893 United States gains Philippines, 1898	Second Empire and Third Republic in France, 1852–1914 Unification of Italy, 1859–1870 Bismarck controls Germany, 1862–1890 Franco-Prussian War, 1870–1871; foundation of the German Empire Second Reform Bill, Great Britain, 1867 Second Socialist International, 1889–1914
Boxer Rebellion in China, 1900–1903 Russo-Japanese War, 1904–1905 Chinese revolution; fall of Qing Dynasty, 1911 Chinese Republic, 1912–1949	Commonwealth of Australia, 1900 Muslim League formed, 1906 First calls for Indian independence, 1907 Amritsar massacre in India, 1919 Intensification of Indian nationalism, 1919–1947	Revolution in Russia; Tsar Nicholas II issues October Manifesto, 1905 Triple Entente (Britain, Russia, France), 1914–1918 World War I, 1914–1918 Treaty of Versailles, 1919
Kita Ikki advocates ultranationalism in Japan, 1923 Jiang Jieshi unites China, 1928	Gandhi launches nonviolent resistance campaign, 1920	Mussolini seizes power in Italy, 1922 Stalin takes power in U.S.S.R., 1927 Depths of Great Depression, 1929–1933
Japan invades China, 1931 Mao Zedong's Long March, 1934 Sino-Japanese War, 1937–1945	Gandhi's Salt March, 1930 Japan conquers Southeast Asia, 1939–1942	Hitler gains power, 1933 Civil War in Spain, 1936–1939 World War II, 1939–1945
United States drops atomic bombs on Hiroshima and Nagasaki, 1945 Chinese civil war, 1945–1949; Communists win	Philippines gain independence, 1946 India (Hindu) and Pakistan (Muslim) gain independence, 1947	Marshall Plan, 1947 NATO formed, 1949 Soviet Union and Red China sign 30-year alliance, 1949

	AFRICA AND THE MIDDLE EAST	THE AMERICAS
1950	Egypt declared a republic; Nasser named premier, 1954 Morocco, Tunisia, Sudan, and Ghana gain independence, 1956–1957 French-British Suez invasion, 1956	Castro takes power in Cuba, 1959
1960	Mali, Nigeria, and the Congo gain independence, 1960 Biafra declares independence from Nigeria, 1967 Arab-Israeli Six-Day War, 1967	Cuban missile crisis, 1962 Military dictatorship in Brazil, 1964–1985 United States escalates war in Vietnam, 1964
1970	"Yom Kippur War," 1973 Islamic revolution in Iran, 1979 Camp David Accords, 1979	Military coup in Chile, 1973 U.S. Watergate scandal, 1974 Revolutions in Nicaragua and El Salvador, 1979
1980	Iran-Iraq War, 1980–1988 Reforms in South Africa, 1989 to present	U.S. military buildup, 1980–1988 Argentina restores civilian rule, 1983
1990	Growth of Islamic fundamentalism, 1990 to present Iraq driven from Kuwait by United States and allies, 1991 Israel and Palestinians sign peace agreement, 1993 Nelson Mandela elected president of South Africa, 1994	Canada, Mexico, and United States form free-trade area (NAFTA), 1994 Haiti establishes democratic government, 1994 Permanent extension of Treaty on the Non-Proliferation of Nuclear Weapons, 1995
2000	End of Taliban regime in Afghanistan, 2001	Terrorist attack on United States, September 11, 2001

EAST ASIA	INDIA AND SOUTHEAST ASIA	EUROPE
Korean War, 1950–1953 Japan begins long period of rapid economic growth, 1950 Mao Zedong announces Great Leap Forward, 1958	Vietnamese nationalists defeat French; Vietnam divided, 1954 Islamic Republic of Pakistan declared, 1956	Death of Stalin, 1953 Warsaw Pact, 1955 Revolution in Hungary, 1956 Common Market formed, 1957
Sino-Soviet split becomes apparent, 1960 Great Proletarian Cultural Revolution in China, 1965–1969	Indira Gandhi prime minister of India, 1966–1977, 1980–1984	Student revolution in France, 1968 Soviet invasion of Czechoslovakia, 1968
China pursues modernization, 1976 to present	India-Pakistan war, 1971 Communist victory in Vietnam War, 1975 Chinese invade Vietnam, 1979	Brandt's Ostpolitik, 1969–1973 Soviet invasion of Afghanistan, 1979
Japanese foreign investment surge, 1980–1992 China crushes democracy movement, 1989	Sikh nationalism in India, 1984 to present Corazón Aquino takes power in Philippines, 1986	Soviet reform under Gorbachev, 1985–1991 Communism falls in eastern Europe, 1989–1990
Birthrates keep falling Economic growth and political repression in China, 1990 to present Hong Kong returns to Chinese rule, 1997	Vietnam embraces foreign investment, 1990 to present U.S. military bases closed in Philippines, 1991	Maastricht treaty proposes monetary union, 1990 Conservative economic policies, 1990s End of Soviet Union, 1991 Civil war in Bosnia, 1991–1995 Creation of European Union, 1993
		Euro note enters circulation, 2002

TEXT CREDITS